FIGHTING WORDS

FIGHTING WORDS
The Origins of Religious Violence

HECTOR AVALOS

Prometheus Books
59 John Glenn Drive
Amherst, New York 14228-2197

Published 2005 by Prometheus Books

Inquiries should be addressed to
Prometheus Books
59 John Glenn Drive
Amherst, New York 14228–2197
VOICE: 716–691–0133, ext. 207
FAX: 716–564–2711
WWW.PROMETHEUSBOOKS.COM

09 08 07 06 05   5 4 3 2 1

Library of Congress Cataloging-in-Publication Data

Avalos, Hector.
    Fighting words : the origins of religious violence / Hector Avalos
      p. cm.
    Includes bibliographical references and index.
    ISBN 1–59102–284–3 (alk. paper)
    1. Violence—Religious aspects. I. Title.

BL65.V55A93 2005
201'.7—dc22

                                                2004029984

Printed in the United States of America on acid-free paper

CONTENTS

ABBREVIATIONS

BASOR	*Bulletin of the American Schools of Oriental Research*
CBQ	*Catholic Biblical Quarterly*
DtrH	The Deuteronomistic History
JAAR	*Journal of the American Academy of Religion*
JAOS	*Journal of the American Oriental Society*
JBL	*Journal of Biblical Literature*
JRAS	*Journal of the Royal Asiatic Society*
JSOT	*Journal for the Study of the Old Testament*
LCL	Loeb Classical Library
NRSV	New Revised Standard Version
NT	New Testament
OT	Old Testament
SBL	Society of Biblical Literature

ACKNOWLEDGMENTS

All authors are debtors, and I am no exception. My first debt is to my wife, Cynthia Avalos, who had to suffer endless discussions of my ideas. She dealt magnificently with the primal screams that only frozen computers and burned-out monitors can generate. She also helped to proofread some of the manuscript.

Christopher Tweedt and Alexis Smith, my research assistants, helped to gather materials and/or proofread portions of the manuscript.

Dr. Stephen K. Batalden, professor in the Department of History and in the Russian and East European Studies Center at Arizona State University, provided some useful bibliography for my chapter on Stalinism. The following also read my manuscript, and made some useful comments even if they do not agree with everything I have written: Dr. Carole Fontaine; John Taylor, Professor of Hebrew Bible/Old Testament at Andover Newtown Theological School (Newton, Massachusetts); Dr. Anthony Pinn; Agnes Cullen Arnold, Professor of Humanities and Professor of Religious Studies at Rice University (Houston, Texas); and Dr. Robert Price of the Institute for Higher Critical Studies, Drew University (Madison, New Jersey).

My thanks to Steven Mitchell and Paul Kurtz who were welcoming and encouraging when I mentioned this project to them in May of 2003. Gratitude is due to the staff at Prometheus Books who assisted in the production of this tome.

As usual, I must thank Rusty, our all-knowing pet squirrel, who furnished entertainment for the sometimes word-weary author.

I, hereby, absolve them all for any transgressions.

A Note to Readers

U nless noted otherwise, all biblical quotations are from the New Revised Standard Version (National Council of Churches of Christ in the United States of America; Nashville: Thomas Nelson, 1989) as represented in the MacBible 3.0 program (Grand Rapids, MI: Zondervan, 1993).

All quotations of the Qur'an, unless otherwise noted, are from A. Yusuf Ali, *The Holy Qur'an: Text, Translation, and Commentary* (Brentwood, MD: Amana, 1983).

Foreign languages are notoriously difficult to transliterate. We have used approximations, except where noted or where an argument hinges on precise diacritics. We have used brackets to enclose words, especially in titles of articles and books, whose transliteration deviates from what is actually printed in the original publication.

INTRODUCTION

This is not simply another book about religion and violence.

It is a book presenting a new theory for religious violence. The idea for the book was born long before the now well-known events of September 11, 2001. Religious violence has preoccupied me ever since I began to ask myself how I could hold sacred the Bible, a book filled with so much violence. I then expanded the question to how anyone today can deem sacred those books that endorse any level of violence. By early 2001 I had already published an article comparing violence in the Bible and the Bhagavad Gita.[1]

Some of my thinking was influenced by a book by Regina Schwartz, *The Curse of Cain: The Violent Legacy of Monotheism* (1997).[2] The author argued therein that monotheism was inherently violent. Since monotheism advocates only one legitimate deity, then the worship of anything else is a violation of boundaries. The addition of a group of outsiders then becomes the prime ingredient for violence. The life of outsiders may be devalued, so killing them can be justified. But more intriguing was the author's allusion to the scarce resources created by monotheism. For example, belief in one god as the exclusive possession of one people may mean that outsiders are denied access to the benefits or rights provided by that one god. Such benefits could be land or national identity.

I wondered if similar mechanisms were at work not just in monotheism, but in religion as a whole. I asked myself whether religion is inherently violent. If not, what are the mechanisms by which religion sometimes becomes violent? Are those factors the same as the ones that cause other types of violence? Is there something special about religion that makes it prone to violence? Or are we misperceiving religion by focusing too much on its violent side?

The questions seemed particularly important because there is a definite stream of popular opinion and scholarship that denies that religion is the cause of some specific conflicts or of violence in general. Shortly after the attack of September 11, Andrew Sullivan noted in a *New York Times Magazine* article that "there has been a general reluctance to call it a religious war."[3] Similarly, there have been efforts to deny that the Nazi Holocaust had any religious roots, some preferring to place responsibility on evolutionary theory or atheism. Alan Jacobs has even argued that "the whole notion of religion as a cause of violence is . . . a function of the desire to believe that religion is eliminable."[4]

Along the way, I concluded that while it does not always cause violence, religion is inherently prone to violence.[5] In fact, even so-called pacifistic religions often approve of violence in subtle ways. I saw that "peace" itself was simply the name for the set of conditions favorable to a proponent group rather than some absolute rejection of violence. Other times, "peace" was simply an intermediary state in which pacifism was maintained for political and self-interest rather than for any systematic opposition to all violence.

But more important, I came to wonder *how* and *why* religions can be prone to violence. After much thought and comparison of many religions, I formulated what will be the main elements of my thesis, which I can summarize succinctly as follows:

1) Most violence is due to scarce resources, real or perceived. Whenever people perceive that there is not enough of something they value, conflict may ensue to maintain or acquire that resource. This can range from love in a family to oil on a global scale.
2) When religion causes violence, it often does so because it has *created new scarce resources*.

As I compared religious violence with secular violence, I also realized that there was a fundamental distinction between the two. Unlike many nonreligious sources of conflict, religious conflict relies solely on resources whose scarcity is wholly manufactured by, or reliant on, unverifiable premises. When the truth or falsity of opposing propositions cannot be verified, then violence becomes a common resort in adjudicating disputes. That is the differentia that makes religious violence even more tragic than nonreligious violence.

DEFINITIONS

Any claim that religion is inherently prone to violence must begin with definitions. The first pertains to religion, which is defined here as a mode of life and thought that presupposes the existence of, and relationship with, unverifiable forces and/or beings. As such, our definition is squarely and unapologetically within the empirico-rationalist tradition.

All definitions of violence are value laden insofar as we choose the type of suffering and violence we value.[6] Our definition is somatocentric insofar as it values the physical human body and regards any sort of "soul" or "spirit" as nonexistent. As we will see, religions often espouse a pneumatocentric justification for violence, in which the values of the entities called the "soul" or "spirit" are paramount to those of the body. Accordingly, *we define violence as the act of modifying and/or inflicting pain upon the human body in order to express or impose power differentials.*[7]

By this definition, pain or bodily modification can be inflicted upon a person by others or it can be self-inflicted, as in the case of self-flagellation and martyrdom. There are degrees of violence, so that a haircut or a tattoo, both bodily modifications, are not always regarded as very violent. At the same time, our definition allows for the fact that depilation and tattooing can be painful forms of torture.[8] Likewise, circumcision could be subsumed under violence in that it modifies a body for the purpose of expressing power differentials. Circumcision also imposes a power differential upon a child, as it is not the result of a mutual decision between parent and child. Killing, of course, is regarded as the ultimate imposition of a power differential on the body.

Since we regard mental processes as part of the body, then psychological and mental violence is included in our somatocentric approach. Psychological torture, for example, involves physiological changes in the body, and pain is ultimately how we experience certain neurochemical events. As long as an action relating to the expression of power modifies or inflicts pain upon a physical body, it is defined as violent, whether such injury is justified or not.

It is important to note that war is one of many forms of violence. The focus on "war," if defined as an armed conflict between collective entities, results in the thesis that religion and specific religions are not violent because they do not often engage in war.[9] This has been a particularly recurrent problem in evaluating early Christianity, as often being against military service is equated with being nonviolent. And there is evidence that even in self-described "pacifist" groups the incidence of domestic and sexual violence reported can be just as high as among the general population.[10] Ours is a more holistic approach because we realize that much religious violence does not come in the form of the large and organized effort we may associate with war. Examples of religious violence range from circumcision to killing gays and lesbians.

We recognize, but do not treat, "verbal" violence here except when it is a clear precursor to actual physical violence. Violence does include the destruction of property when that is an instrument to cause harm to the livelihood or sociopsychological welfare of any individual or community.[11] One such example is Kristallnacht (1938), when German Jews were terrorized by the destruction of their property even, if outright killing of Jews was not yet at its height in Nazi Germany.

Under our concept of violence, we can also distinguish between justified and unjustified violence. Violence in self-defense or the defense of the physical well-being of others is acceptable. The surgical modification of the body for the purposes of saving a life or empowering an individual, especially if the individual chose to be so modified, is justified violence. We hold any violence that is not based on verifiable causes and phenomena to be senseless and unethical. We will outline this argument at greater length in chapter 15. Beating a child or stoning a woman to death is not acceptable violence, regardless of the reason. We certainly do not advocate that physical injury or killing someone's body is ever justified to serve some greater spiritual good.

CAUSALITY AND HISTORICAL EXPLANATION

Since at least the time of David Hume (1711–1776), the notion of causality has undergone severe scrutiny. David Hume proposed that spatial and temporal contiguity did not constitute logical proof of causation.[12] What we call a "cause" is actually better described as a correlation that occurs in time and space between two or more events. At most, we could speak of correlations, wherein we observe that one event regularly followed temporally upon another.

Within history, the notion of cause has produced a crisis that is still underway. What would it mean to claim, for example, that Ronald Reagan's policies "caused" the fall of communism? Unlike many correlations found in nature, historical events are not usually repeatable under exactly the same circumstances. Even if there were correlations, these cannot always be seen as a "cause" any more than the correlation of a rooster crowing before sunrise means that the rooster's crow caused the sun to rise.

Within the study of war, the crisis of determining causality can be seen in the mammoth project known as the Correlates of War (COW), which seeks to find what factors can be correlated with wars. Frank Whelon Wayman and J. David Singer, one of the founders of the COW Project, are reticent to speak of causes. They see the COW Project as "searching for variables that are positively correlated with the onset of war, and ascertaining whether the association seems causal."[13] Nonetheless, Wayman and Singer propose at least three requirements for establishing causality, which can be summarized as follows:[14]

1. A postulated cause has to precede the effect in time (or at least occur simultaneously with it rather than come after it).
2. The cause and effect have to covary as demonstrated by a statistical correlation.
3. Other explanations of the cause and effect relationship have to be eliminated.[14]

So what does it mean to say that religion "causes" violence or "can cause" violence? Here we opt for a definition of "cause" that can demonstrate a logical sequence as well as a spatiotemporal one. We may say that *religion causes violence if and when the perpetration of violence is a logical consequence of beliefs in unverifiable forces and/or beings.* The expression "logical consequence" can be represented in a more formal manner: *Religious Belief X, therefore Act of Violence Y.*[15] Accordingly, attribution of religious causation requires demonstration that an act of violence had a necessary precedent in a religious belief. Without that causational belief, the specific act of violence would not have taken place.

For example, suppose person A truly believes that God has commanded him to kill homosexuals, and this person then kills a homosexual. In this case, we can say that belief X (God has commanded person A to kill homosexuals) caused the killing of the homosexual. In such a case, we may say that the religious belief was necessary, if not sufficient, to perpetrate this act of violence. In the clearest cases, the perpetrators may themselves cite such beliefs.

Most acts of religious violence are not so transparent. This has led scholars to posit political and economic factors as the main causes of many common conflicts. And indeed political and economic factors can also lead to violence. However, the notion of causation would be no less severe for positing economic and political factors, and, in fact, they may be even more elusive as causes. Disentangling the religious from other causes forms a main challenge for our thesis.

It is, indeed, also useful to make the distinction between necessary and sufficient causes. Some violence would not occur if certain religious beliefs did not exist. For example, the idea that homosexuality is evil may be necessary, but not sufficient, to explain a particular act of antigay violence. Our study will include acts of violence for which religion forms a necessary and/or sufficient basis for the violence.

Accordingly, the reader must realize that *our thesis does not claim that religion is the cause of all violence*. We certainly recognize that poverty, politics, nationalism, and even neuropsychological factors may generate violence. Nor do we necessarily claim that most violence is religious, as statistical verification is very difficult, especially for ancient history. We also recognize that within religions there may be a plurality of positions on violence, though we shall show that some descriptions of religions as peaceful rely on faulty data or lack of acquaintance with primary sources.

Our thesis proposes that when religion causes violence, it usually does so because it has created a scarce resource. The creation of scarce resources may occur when the adherents of a religion claim that the benefits of that religion are not or cannot be equally distributed to all human beings. Accordingly, we must also extend our argument to include scarcity in the chain of causation. We acknowledge that religion can also cause violence through means other than the creation of scarce resources, and we will outline some of those as we examine specific cases of religious violence.

A resource is any entity that persons utilize in the enterprise of living. Not all resources are of equal value, of course. One can live without a Rolex watch. We focus on those resources that are of high value, or at least of a value high enough to fight for. A resource may be described as scarce when it meets one or more of the following requirements: (1) It is not immediately available, and (2) accessing it, maintaining it, or acquiring it requires the expense of a significant amount of social or physical capital and labor. A scarce resource X created by religion may cause violence when at least one of two or more persons or groups (1) *desires to acquire or maintain X*, and (2) *believes violence is an allowable and proper method to acquire and/or maintain X*.

Demonstration of our thesis consists of at least two main types of evidence. The first centers on the words of perpetrators of violence themselves. Too often in debates about religion and conflict, the attribution of motives is based on secondary sources or faulty deductions. The COW Project, for example, usually does not focus on statements made by perpetrators of violence. One example of a clear attribution of violence to religious reasons can be seen in the following Hadith reported by Al-Bukhari, perhaps the most authoritative collector of traditions about Muhammad. Al-Bukhari tells us:

> The prophet said, "Allah . . . assigns for a person who participates in (holy battles) in Allah's Cause and nothing causes him to do so except belief in Allah and in His Messenger, that he will be recompensed by Allah with a reward, or booty (if he survives) or will be admitted to Paradise (if he is killed in the battle as a martyr)."[16]

Here is a clear attribution of the reason for violence from a Muslim himself. This sort of self-attribution by practitioners of a religion certainly would count as strong evidence that violence was the result of religious beliefs.

A second type of demonstration involves logical deductions, which allow us to make clear cases of a belief leading to an action much as described above. Again, we pursue examples in which we can reduce the act of violence to the following rationale: *Religious Belief X, therefore Act of Violence Y.* If we return to our example of violence against homosexuals, we can infer a religious reason when a person who commits an act of violence against a homosexual has only previously expressed religious reasons for hating homosexuals. In such a case, we need not necessarily hear him utter religious reasons at the time he commits an act of violence, nor do we need to hear him threaten an act of violence to make a reasonable inference that religion was probably the likely "cause."

We are also fortunate to have at least a bit of empirical survey data that allows us to correlate religiosity with certain beliefs about the value of Jerusalem and other sacred spaces that are important in our argumentation. One such example is the survey conducted by Jerome M. Segal, Shlomit Levy, Nadar Izzat Sa'id, and Elihu Katz.[17] We will also discuss studies on the correlation between religious belief and militarism undertaken by sociologists of religion.[18]

Likewise, we concentrate on cases in which economics and politics can be shown to derive from religious factors rather than the reverse. In sum, we will count our thesis successful by providing examples of violence that would probably not have occurred if a religious belief were not involved or where we can show that religious motives are expressly used to incite or maintain violence.

VIOLENCE AND ACADEMIC RELIGIOUS STUDIES

Our main claim here is that academic biblical scholars and scholars of religion, more often than not, maintain the value of religious texts that promote or endorse violence. This maintenance is accomplished by hermeneutic strategies that sanitize the violence, claim to espouse multivocality in readings, or claim aesthetic value to texts even if historical aspects of the texts are minimized. In this regard, we are influenced by theories that see the academic study of literature itself as a locus and instrument of power.[19]

Most of us are influenced by our training and life experience in formulating any theory. In the interest of openness and self-analysis, I provide a brief narrative about some of the recurrent issues that I see among academics who attempt to address the problem of violence in religion. Briefly, these issues are: (1) the perceived public mission of religious studies; (2) the presence of cryptoessentialism in religious studies; and (3) the place of empirico-rationalism and naturalism in religious studies.

The first problem revolves around the perceived mission of religious studies, particularly in secular institutions of higher learning. Noam Chomsky argued cogently during the Vietnam War that "it is the responsibility of intellectuals to speak truth and to expose lies."[20]

However, since public universities are funded by taxpayers, the mission of religious studies is perceived to mean that scholars must be sympathetic or neutral toward religion. Religions must be understood but not criticized. Any research indicating that religion is injurious or that particular religions are injurious can bring a response that universities, as publicly funded institutions, cannot seek to undermine the faith of constituents.

Otherwise, the notion of academic responsibility has not been consistent from field to field. Professors in the sciences, for example, routinely are expected to help solve problems in society, whether these be finding a new medication for cancer or learning how to suppress odor produced by swine containment facilities. This is particularly the case in so-called land grant universities, which are expected to be involved directly in the betterment of the society around them. In the case of science, academics are encouraged to identify a "problem" and then help to solve it.

From time to time, there have been efforts to engage in what is called "activist" scholarship, or "praxis." This sometimes means that advocates of some sort of liberation theology see their obligation, as scholars, as putting their beliefs into practice. We have seen this with all sorts of liberation theology movements in Latin America and in the United States. In South Africa there were some vocal theoreticians of this approach when apartheid ruled. For example, Gregory Baum says, "religious studies, and the human sciences in general, should not only aim at understanding reality, but also at transforming it."[21]

In truth, neutrality does not and cannot exist in the academic study of religion, even if it can be minimized in the teaching about religion in a pluralistic society. The nonneutrality of academic attitudes toward religion can be traced to at least Thomas Jefferson's vision of the first public university in the United States, the University of Virginia. Outlining a radical departure from earlier American colleges, Thomas Jefferson decided that theology would not be taught in his university. In a letter dated November 22, 1822, Jefferson told his friend Thomas Cooper, "In our university . . . there is no Professorship of Divinity. A handle has been made of this, to disseminate an idea that this is an institution, not merely of no religion, but against all religion."[22]

Jefferson actually would permit sects to fund their own professorships and be housed near enough so that students could go listen to their lectures. However, Jefferson insisted that these professorships should "maintain their independence of us and of each other."[23] His agenda in having these sectarian professorships interact with students at the University of Virginia was, in part, "to neutralize their prejudices, and make the general religion a religion of peace, reason, and morality."[24]

And, indeed, despite the complaints of creationists, science departments have very little problem teaching evolution as a fact. Evolution certainly undermines Christian literalistic understandings of Genesis, but those understandings are either held not to be suitable understandings of Christianity, or they have so little power that they can be ignored. Nor do universities have a problem teaching a heliocentric vision of the universe even if a few constituents still think it undermines their religious belief. Truth here is held to be so obvious that a religious understanding may be excluded as legitimate. Here the results of empirico-rationalist science are held to take precedence over offending religious beliefs.

By the end of the nineteenth century, bitter battles were fought over the advent of higher criticism, which undermined belief in the historicity of many parts of the Bible.[25] Among the first portions of the Bible to be submitted to close scrutiny was the Pentateuch. The main issues revolved around the Mosaic authorship of the Pentateuch. Eventually, most critical scholars rejected the idea that one person had written the whole Pentateuch. The other issue revolved around the historicity of the stories in Genesis, especially the creation stories. Eventually, geology and astronomy led scholars away from literal interpretations of Genesis, and those stories were reclassified as "myth."

The New Testament also came under fire. The publication of H. S. Reimarus's fragments in 1768 is usually taken as a benchmark date for research that systematically questioned the historicity of Jesus.[26] Reimarus argued that Jesus was a failed revolutionary whose disciples refused to admit his death. Thus, a story developed that Jesus would resurrect and return triumphantly to set up his kingdom.

Likewise, battles with the so-called fundamentalists were waged in the late nineteenth and early twentieth centuries, with a clear secularizing trend that undermined the religious views of many in the United States. George M. Marsden, writing from a Protestant perspective, wrote *The Soul of the American University: From Protestant Establishment to Established Nonbelief* (1994),[27] which charted some of the secularizing trends. Likewise, James Tunstead Burtchaell, writing from a Catholic perspective, documented in detail how many religious colleges had been secularized.[28] Both Marsden and Burtchaell wrote these works as lamentations rather than as celebrations.

Other scholars see more desectarianization (i.e., less emphasis being "Baptist" or "Lutheran") than secularization.[29]

Supreme Court decisions, particularly in the 1960s, made it clear that the academic study of religion in public institutions should be descriptive, and not prescriptive.[30] The Supreme Court also indicated that academic study ought not be hostile to religion. Accordingly, new curricula were devised to teach religion as "literature."[31] Questions that criticized religion in general or particular religions were shunned. These Supreme Court decisions also saw a new effort to shift biblical studies away from historical criticism, especially in high school curricula, to literary aesthetics, as another way to preserve the value of the text.

So, despite the claims to neutrality, there have always been efforts that undermined some religious beliefs. And what is the difference today? The difference resides simply in which religious beliefs are favored by academics at any given moment. Currently, literalistic beliefs about Genesis 1 are not favored by academics, and so they are systematically undermined. The Supreme Court has often cooperated in undermining the teaching of "scientific" creationism in schools, as in the case of *Edwards v. Aguillard* (1987), even though its principles may play a role in the religious belief of millions of Americans.

Donald Wiebe, in a penetrating analysis of the politics of religious studies, notes that modern departments of religious studies and the entire field of academic religious studies are still dominated by what we may denominate as "religionists."[32] Many are self-described Christians who may no longer advocate a hierarchical and institutional Christianity. Instead they may favor a more eclectic form of "spirituality," or "religious praxis" tailored to elite individualistic lifestyles. However, this religious orientation still retains the idea, no less verifiable than those of the institutional theologies, that religion is essentially good or should not be discarded altogether.

At the same time, Wiebe has critiqued scholarly activism on behalf of religionist causes.[33] However, here I must qualify Wiebe's criticism. All scholars are political if "political" is understood to mean that they are either supporting power structures or fighting against them. Even passivity is a political stance. In this regard, secular humanist scholars will strive to assert their "right" to advocate for what their conclusions lead them to believe. If any scholars come to believe, on the basis of their academic research, that religion or specific religious traditions are harmful to humanity, then it follows that it is their obligation to counteract those beliefs. Of course, this means a nonviolent and dialogic approach, given the current pluralistic politics.

This bring us to the problem of "crypto-essentialism," which refers to the use of essentialism while at the same time proclaiming not to do so. One common example of this is found in works where undesirable elements in some religious traditions are characterized as "deviations." Often, the word "fundamentalist" is used to devalue those traditions. We shall examine some very specific cases in which scholars attack Western essentialism in order to defend the view that Islam is "essentially" peaceful, and that those committing violence in the name of Islam are not legitimate practitioners of Islam.

The third problem in studying violence in academia is that the field of religious studies is still undergoing an epistemological identity crisis. We see this crisis discussed in books as well as in sometimes heated exchanges in the *Journal of the American Academy of Religion,* among other periodicals.[34] Among the main issues is whether the proper approach to the study of religion will entail empirico-rationalism, naturalism, or some species of epistemology that acknowledges the existence of the supernatural.[35] John Milbank, among others, sees all the social sciences themselves as a form of secular countertheology.[36]

Combined with these issues is the fact that many empirico-rationalists no longer wish to be called empirico-rationalists or positivists, but claim that they are practicing something else. By empirico-rationalism, I refer to the epistemology that affirms that only what can be verified by the five senses and/or logic deserves the term "knowledge," while all else is "belief." "Belief" is reasonable only if based on verifiable evidence and inferences. Any belief not based on verifiable evidence or logic is deemed irrelevant or meaningless. By "naturalism," I refer to the idea that natural phenomena are the only things known to exist and that religion is a natural phenomenon.[37]

Usually, avowed empirico-rationalists would say that historical conclusions fall under the category of reasonable belief, which is any belief that, while not directly verified, is based on verifiable phenomena. Unreasonable beliefs are those that neither can be verified nor are based on verifiable phenomena, and this would include God or any other supernatural entity. Thus, all religion has a natural basis, and is not some sort of reflection of the transcendent.

The view of empirico-rationalism as some sort of Western hegemony or Eurocentric invention has led to challenging the very notion of whether there is such a thing as religion at all.[38] And even if there is such a thing as religion, some would hold that outsiders can never really understand any particular religion.[39] An alternate version of anti-empirico-rationalism argues that religion is a sui generis phenomenon that cannot be reduced to any other aspect of human behavior. Such a position has been seen as simply another apologetic attempt to retain the value of religion.[40]

In reality, empirico-rationalism continues to be the premise for most of the work I see in the academy. What is different is to whom and upon whom empirico-rationalism is applied. Some self-described liberal Christian scholars, for example, may be willing to admit that the world was not created in six days, as the fundamentalists believe. In this case, they have accepted the conclusion on nothing more than empirico-rationalist grounds, whether they admit it or not. On the other hand, they may hold to the existence of a "transcendent being" for no more verifiable reasons than the fundamentalist holds to creation in six days.

And if empirico-rationalism or naturalism is held to be the proper approach to truth, then it becomes feasible to argue that the best way to deal with religious violence is to undermine religion itself. Just as we undermined the religious belief that Genesis 1 is historically true, we can undermine the belief that any religion has received instructions from a deity. Although not as frank as my proposal, the proposal of John J. Collins, who served as president of the Society of Biblical Literature in 2002, urges a more activist stance when he concludes: "Perhaps the most constructive thing a biblical critic can do toward lessening the contribution of the Bible to violence in the world, is to show that certitude is an illusion."[41]

Those academicians who believe that religion is some sort of sui generis phenomenon or some manifestation of actual transcendent forces that may be harnessed for good may, of course, have cause to argue that academia should strive to understand religion so that we may harvest its essentially good fruits. Such academics likewise should be allowed to voice such opinions in a pluralistic society.

This argument between the naturalists and the supernaturalists will not be settled here. And given this political impasse, the best we can do for now is to be frank and up-front in summarizing my own presuppositions. I am a secular humanist. To the extent that I have a worldview, that consists of (1) an empirico-rationalist approach to the definition of religion;[42] (2) a paradigm that is value laden and somatocentric when it evaluates human thought and action; (3) an activist orientation that not only allows, but obligates, a critique of religion and/or of specific religious traditions.

To the extent that I hold certain views on what is "good" or "bad," then my approach is value laden, just as is the approach of anyone else. My observations, therefore, will be accepted by those who share my values. However, my moral judgments are also grounded in facts and reason insofar as I can demonstrate logical and structural parallels between actions and ideologies. For example, whether I regard genocide as evil or not, I can demonstrate that event X constitutes a case of genocide once I have defined genocide adequately. Semantic logic is feasible regardless of value judgments.[43]

As an academic scholar of religion, it is my responsibility to analyze how religion may contribute to the detriment or well-being of humanity based on verifiable facts and reason.[44] For the same reason, in order to make any progress in ameliorating the problem of violence, one has to confront violence in each religion in a frank manner. I believe I do it evenhandedly. As a secular humanist, I do not favor one religion over another, as I hold all of them to be equally based on unverifiable grounds. We argue for example, that Judaism, Christianity, and Islam are all heavily dependent on violent premises. They all regard their scriptures as sacred despite the violence endorsed therein.

And rather than pretend I am not hegemonic, I hold that (1) all world-views, even those that claim pluralism, are hegemonic—for example, even pluralistic worldviews inevitably seek power over nonpluralistic worldviews; and (2) a pluralistic religious hegemony is a politically expedient means to persuade people to adopt a secular humanist hegemony, which I believe holds the best prospect for a nonviolent global society. Phrased more frankly, religious pluralism is good so long as it tolerates and serves the goals of secular humanism.

AN ETHICAL CRITIQUE OF RELIGIOUS VIOLENCE

Although we focus on how scarce resources cause religious violence, an over-arching theme of our thesis is that the lack of verifiability in religious belief differentiates ethically the violence attributed to religion from the violence attributed to nonreligious factors. This distinction will then lead to our main argument, which is that religious violence is always ethically reprehensible, while the same cannot be said of nonreligious violence, even if we grant that nonreligious factors can also create a great deal of violence by making certain resources scarce. We argue that the quality of the scarcity created by religion is fundamentally different.

Our argument will be framed in the form known as a fortiori argument, and *kol wahoma* in rabbinic argumentation:[45] Briefly, such an argument attempts to show that if the truth for one claim is judged to be evident, then another claim ought to be held even more evidently true. As it pertains to our argument about religious violence as compared to secular violence, an a fortiori argument would be as follows: *If any acts of violence caused by actual scarcities are judged as immoral, then acts of violence caused by resources that are not actually scarce should be judged as even more immoral.* We further develop the argument that *any act of violence predicated on the acquisition or loss of a non-existent entity is always immoral and needless because bodily well-being or life is being traded for a nonexistent gain.*

SCOPE AND ORGANIZATION

We need not study every religion in the world to establish our thesis. While most religions may be prone to violence, not all religions have an equal impact on the quality or quantity of violence that we see in the world. Religions shared by only a few tribespeople are prone to violence as well, but their scale makes them relatively insignificant on the world stage. We will concentrate on a few of the major, so-called world religions, because they have produced the largest scale of violence, and present the most pressing problems today. We also concentrate on religions that have scriptures, as that contributes to the quality and quantity of violence that can arise out of those religions.

On the most general level, our book is divided into four parts. Part 1 summarizes past explanations for violence. The aim is to place our thesis within the context of those explanations, as well as to explain why most previous explanations have not been successful in identifying the most basic mechanisms of religious violence. Part 2 introduces the theoretical underpinnings of scarce resource theory, on which our own theory is based. We discuss how religion creates scarce resources, and then focus on the following: (1) access to the divine will, particularly through inscripturation; (2) sacred space; (3) group privileging; and (4) salvation.

Part 2 also contains the main feature of our book insofar as it illustrates how our thesis applies in detail to Judaism, Christianity, and Islam. These traditions, combined, reportedly have more than 3 billion adherents.[46] Judaism, Christianity, and Islam may indeed be viewed as sects of one older religious complex sometimes called the "Abrahamic" religion(s), because they all believe Abraham is an early and crucial worshipper of the god of those three religions. Abraham is believed to be a monotheist, even if the portrayal of his god among these three religions is not very consistent.

The initial chapter on each religious tradition is subdivided by the scarce resources that we think are the most important in explaining violent mechanisms. Again, these are (1) access to the divine will, particularly through inscripturation; (2) sacred space; (3) group privileging; and (4) salvation. Discussion of each scarce resource in each religion will be followed by illustrative conflicts that can be tied to that scarce resource within the religion itself. Illustrated conflicts will be relatively balanced between ancient and modern periods to show the continuity and pervasiveness of the religious mechanisms for violence. Each tradition is accompanied by a chapter that explains how academic scholars have defended violence in that tradition.

Part 3 examines alleged instances of secular violence. This is important because many scholars assume that secular violence is largely responsible for what appears to be religious violence. We show the religious origins of major instances of violence (e.g., the Nazi Holocaust, Saint Bartholomew's Day Massacre), which have been attributed to secular and political forces. The fourth and final part synthesizes the thesis by showing how secular violence differs from religious violence. In addition, part 4 offers practical solutions and applications (e.g., foreign policy) for our theory.

All scholarship is affected to some degree by training and experience. In the interest of methodological frankness, the most relevant formal training I have received is in anthropology and in biblical and ancient Near Eastern Studies. I am very centered on philology and text in order to make my arguments. I provide quoted portions of texts in the primary languages when editions in the primary languages are available to me or when the arguments hinge on more precise linguistics. I take the challenge of *ad fontes* seriously.

Relative to perhaps many other scholars, I tend to reproduce longer quotes and allow, as much as possible, the texts to speak for themselves in the same way that an ethnographer may allow informants to speak for themselves. I fall somewhere in between Lydia Cabrera's superb ethnographic work on the Yoruba of Cuba and the ruminations on minutiae found in the Talmud.[47] As we shall see, part of the recurrent problem one finds in all fields is that primary sources are frequently not consulted, especially when dealing with claims in fields outside of our own.

SUMMARY

Embarking on a new explanation for a common phenomenon is a humbling task that requires a high degree of self-confidence. It is humbling because one encounters a mass of data and literature that one will never master. On the other hand, the very notion that one can develop any new explanation reflects the confidence that one can successfully tackle a problem whose solution has eluded so many others before. But that is what the challenge of scholarship is partly about—challenging past explanations, and waiting for one's peers to scrutinize, confirm, and/or dismantle a new one. I will count myself successful if I have prompted scholars to think in new ways about religious violence.

NOTES

1. Hector Avalos, "Violence in the Bible and the *Bhagavad Gita*," *Journal of Vaishnava Studies* 9, no. 2 (2001): 67–83.

2. Regina Schwartz, *The Curse of Cain: The Violent Legacy of Monotheism* (Chicago: University of Chicago Press, 1997).

3. Andrew Sullivan, "This *Is* a Religious War," *New York Times Magazine*, October 7, 2001, p. 47.

4. Kenneth R. Chase and Alan Jacobs, eds., *Must Christianity Be Violent? Reflections on History, Practice and Theology* (Grand Rapids, MI: Brazos, 2003), p. 231.

5. For recent similar observations, see James K. Wellman Jr. and Kyoto Tokuno, "Is Religious Violence Inevitable?" *Journal for the Scientific Study of Religion* 43, no. 3 (2004): 291–96.

6. For the political implications of defining violence, see also Stephen J. Casey, "Defining Violence," *Thought: A Review of Culture and Idea* 56, no. 220 (1981): 5–16.

7. There is now a vast literature on the social role of the body and embodiment. Among some of these studies are Chris Shilling, *The Body and Social Theory*, 2nd ed. (London: Sage, 2003); Barbara Maria Stafford, *Body Criticism: Imaging the Unseen in Enlightenment Art and Medicine* (Cambridge, MA: MIT Press, 1997); Simon J. Williams and Gillian Bendelow, *The Lived Body: Sociological Themes, Embodied Issues* (New York: Routledge, 1998); Jon L. Berquist, *Controlling Corporeality: The Body and the Household in Ancient Israel* (New Brunswick, NJ: Rutgers University Press, 2002); Dale B. Martin, *The Corinthian Body* (New Haven, CT: Yale University Press, 1995); Howard Eilberg-Schwartz, *People of the Body: Jews and Judaism from an Embodied Perspective* (Albany: State University of New York Press, 1992); and Benedict Ashley, *Theologies of the Body: Humanist and Christian* (Braintree, MA: Pope John XXIII Medical-Moral Research and Education Center, 1985).

8. For some examples, see Frances E. Mascia-Lees and Patricia Sharpe, eds., *Tattoo, Torture, Mutilation, and Adornment: The Denaturalization of the Body in Culture and Text* (Albany: State University of New York Press, 1992); and Alfred Gell, *Wrapping in Images: Tattooing in Polynesia* (Oxford: Clarendon, 1993).

9. For a recent entry into the "religion and war" theme, see Gabriel Palmer-Fernandez, *Encyclopedia of Religion and War* (New York: Routledge, 2004). This reference is uneven in the quality and selection of entries, and its introduction does not outline clear categories of theories on war and violence.

10. See Mary Anne Hildebrand, "Domestic Violence: A Challenge to Mennonite Faith and Peace Theology," *Conrad Grebel Review* (Winter 1992): 73–80.

11. Compare our definition to that of Albert Bandura, *Aggression: A Social Learning Analysis* (Englewood Cliffs, NJ: Prentice-Hall, 1973), p. 5: "Aggression is defined as behavior that results in personal injury and in destruction of property." Also the definition of Robert McAfee Brown (*Religion and Violence: A Primer for White Americans* [Stanford, CA: Stanford Alumni Association, 1973], p. 7): "The basic overall definition of violence would then become violations of personhood." Violations, therefore, need not be physical and one of the most important violations consists of "injustice."

12. David Hume, *Enquiries concerning Human Understanding*, ed. P. H. Nidditch (Oxford: Clarendon, 1975), pp. 24–79. For recent discussions of Hume, see Claudia M. Schmidt, *David Hume: Reason in History* (University Park: Pennsylvania State University Press, 2003). Colin Howson, *Hume's Problem: Induction and the Justification of Belief* (New York: Oxford University Press, 2000); and for a broader study of causality, see Stephen Kern, *A Cultural History of Causality: Science, Murder Novels, and Systems of Thought* (Princeton, NJ: Princeton University Press, 2004).

13. Frank Whelon Wayman and J. David Singer, "Evolution and Directions for Improvement in the Correlates of War Project Methodologies," in *Measuring the Correlates of War*, ed. J. David Singer and Paul F. Diehl (Ann Arbor: University of Michigan Press, 1990), p. 254.

14. Ibid., p. 247.

15. For further comments on establishing religious causality, see J. Milton Yinger, *The Scientific Study of Religion* (New York: Macmillan, 1971), pp. 93–98.

16. Al-Bukhari, 36/Book of Belief, 26/Darussalam edition, 1:73. Unless noted otherwise, all of our citations of Al-Bukhari are from the Arabic-English edition of *Shahih Al-Bukhari*, trans. Muhammad Muhsin Khan, 9 vols. (Riyadh, Saudi Arabia: Darussalam Publishers and Distributors, 1997). Having struggled through the Hadith, I will attempt to make citations more easily accessible by citing Al-Bukhari by three alternative formats, each divided by a slash, and as follows: the Hadith number/the name of the book within Al-Bukhari's collection cited by chapter/the Darussalam edition volume and page number

17. Jerome M. Segal, Shlomit Levy, Nadar Izzat Sa'id, and Elihu Katz, *Negotiating Jerusalem* (Albany: State University of New York Press, 2000).

18. Some of these earlier studies are summarized in Michael Argyle and Benjamin Beit-Hallahmi, *The Social Psychology of Religion* (London: Routledge, 1975), pp. 107–108.

19. A principal theoretician here is John Guillory, *Cultural Capital: The Problem of Literary Canon Formation* (Chicago: University of Chicago Press, 1993).

20. Noam Chomsky, "The Responsibility of Intellectuals," in *The Chomsky Reader*, ed. James Peck (New York: Pantheon Books, 1987), p. 60.

21. Gregory Baum, "Religious Studies and Theology," *Journal of Theology for Southern Africa* 70 (1990): 4–5.

22. Thomas Jefferson, *Writings*, ed. M. D. Peterson (Washington, DC: Library of America, 1984), p. 1465.

23. Ibid.

24. Ibid.

25. For some general histories of these conflicts, see John Rogerson, *Old Testament Criticism in the Nineteenth Century: England and Germany* (Philadelphia: Fortress, 1985); Hans Graf Reventlow, *The Authority of the Bible and the Rise of the Modern World*, trans. John Bowden (Philadelphia: Fortress, 1985); and Jerry Wayne Brown, *The Rise of Biblical Criticism in America, 1800–1870* (Middletown, CT: Wesleyan University Press, 1969).

26. See John P. Meier, *A Marginal Jew: Rethinking the Historical Jesus*, vol. 1, *The Roots of the Problem and the Person* (New York: Doubleday, 1991), p. 25. For a translation of Reimarus, see Charles Talbert, ed., *Reimarus: Fragments* (Philadelphia: Fortress, 1971).

27. George Marsden, *The Soul of the American University: From Protestant Establishment to Established Nonbelief* (New York: Oxford University Press, 1994).

28. James Tunstead Burtchaell, *The Dying of the Light: The Disengagement of Colleges and Universities from Their Christian Churches* (Grand Rapids, MI: Eerdmans, 1998).

29. For example, Donald Wiebe, *The Politics of Religious Studies* (New York: St. Martin's, 1999), p. 114n5.

30. There is a vast literature now on the Supreme Court and religion, but the following are ones I have found useful: Stephen H. Webb, "The Supreme Court and the Pedagogy of Religious Studies: Constitutional Parameters for the Teaching of Religion in the Public Schools," *JAAR* 70, no. 1 (2002): 135–57; Robert Alley, ed., *The Constitution and Religion: Leading Supreme Court Cases on Church and State* (Amherst, NY: Prometheus Books, 1999); and James W. Fraser, *Between Church and State: Religion and Public Education in a Multicultural America* (New York: St. Martin's, 1999).

31. For a pioneering example, see James S. Ackerman with Jane Stouder Hawley, *On Teaching the Old Testament as Literature: A Guide to Selected Biblical Narratives for Secondary Schools* (Bloomington: Indiana University Press, 1967).

32. Wiebe, *The Politics of Religious Studies.*

33. Ibid., 129–35.

34. Examples include the exchanges between Paul J. Griffiths, ("Some Confusions about Critical Intelligence: A Response to Russell T. McCutcheon") and Russell T. McCutcheon ("Talking Past Each Other—Public Intellectuals Revisited: A Rejoinder to Paul J. Griffiths and June O'Connor"), *JAAR* 66, no. 4 (1998): 893–95, 911–15; and David R. Griffin, *Religion and Scientific Naturalism: Overcoming the Conflicts* (Albany: State University of New York Press, 2000).

35. See Robert Segal, *Explaining and Interpreting Religion: Essays on the Issue,* Toronto Studies in Religion 16 (Toronto, ON: Centre for Religious Studies, 1992); J. Samuel Preus, *Explaining Religion: Criticism and Theory from Bodin to Freud* (New Haven, CT: Yale University Press, 1987); William P. Alston, *Perceiving God: The Epistemology of Religious Experience* (Ithaca, NY: Cornell University Press, 1991); and Michael C. Banner, *The Justification of Science and the Rationality of Religious Belief* (Oxford: Clarendon, 1990).

36. John Milbank, *Theology and Social Theory: Beyond Secular Reason* (Oxford: Blackwell, 1990). For recent discussions of Milbank, see John Bowlin, "Parts, Wholes, and Opposites: John Milbank as *Geisterhistoriker*," *Journal of Religious Ethics* 32, no. 2 (2004): 257–69; and Gordon E. Michaelson Jr., "Re-reading the Post-Kantian Tradition with Milbank," *Journal of Religious Ethics* 32, no. 2 (2004): 357–83.

37. For a discussion of naturalism from a nonnaturalist perspective, see William Lane Craig and J. P. Moreland, *Naturalism: A Critical Analysis* (London: Routledge, 2000). See also David Ray Griffin, "Religious Experience, Naturalism, and the Social Scientific Study of Religion," *JAAR* 68, no. 1 (2000): 99–125.

38. See, for example, Tim Fitzgerald, "Religious Studies as Cultural Studies: A Philosophical and Anthropological Critique of the Concept of Religion," *Diskus* 31 (1995): 35–47. Fitzgerald believes seeing religion as a "culture" is more definitionally sound, but he fails to see that "culture" itself may be a construct that presents no less problems than "religion." The problem in defining "culture" was seen at least sixty years ago, on which see Alfred L. Kroeber and Clyde Kluckhohn, *Culture: A Critical Review of Concepts and Definitions* (Cambridge, MA: Peabody Museum, 1952).

39. See, for example, Sarah Caldwell and Brian K. Smith, "Introduction: Who Speaks for Hinduism?" *JAAR* 68, no. 4 (2000): 705–11, and other essays in the same issue. See further, Ursula King, "Is There a Future for Religious Studies as We Know It? Some Postmodern, Feminist, and Spiritual Challenges," *JAAR* 70, no. 2 (2002): 365–88.

40. A main exponent of such an idea is Rudolf Otto, *The Idea of the Holy*, trans. John W. Harvey, 2nd ed. (London: Oxford University Press, 1950). For a critique of Otto's position, see Gregory Alles, "Toward a Genealogy of the Holy: Rudolf Otto and the Apologetics of Religion," *JAAR* 69, no. 2 (2001): 232–341.

41. John J. Collins, "The Zeal of Phinehas: The Bible and the Legitimation of Violence," *JBL* 122, no. 1 (2003): 21.

42. For a recent discussion of naturalism, see the special issue of *Philo* 3, no. 2 (Fall–Winter 2000), edited by Keith Parsons.

43. For a general discussion of semantic logic, especially in biblical studies, see Arthur Gibson, *Biblical Semantic Logic* (New York: St. Martin's, 1981); James Barr, *The Semantics of Biblical Language* (London: SCM Press, 1983).

44. For a discussion of the responsibility within religious studies, see Russell T. McCutcheon, *Critics Not Caretakers: Redescribing the Public Study of Religion* (Albany: State University of New York Press, 2001), especially pp. 155–77.

45. See Moses Mielziner, *Introduction to the Talmud*, 5th ed. (New York: Bloch, 1968), p. 251.

46. Count based on *The World Almanac and Book of Facts* (New York: World Almanac Books, 2002), p. 684.

47. Lydia Cabrera, *El Monte* (Miami: Coleccion de Chicherekú, 1971).

PART 1

PAST EXPLANATIONS OF VIOLENCE

To understand the novelty and explanatory power of our thesis, one must compare it to what has preceded it. Part 1 provides an overview of ancient and modern theories of violence in order to show that, while scarcities have figured prominently in many systematic theories of violence, few, if any of these theories, recognize the extent to which religion itself can generate scarce resources. We also show that theories of violence by academic scholars of religion are still dominated by religionist and essentialist paradigms that see "true" religion as peaceful, and deviant forms of religion as violent.

CHAPTER 1

PREMODERN THEORIES OF VIOLENCE

I n order to understand how our thesis fits within the framework of past explanations for religious violence, it is useful to provide a substantive review of some of the major previous theories of religion and violence. In truth, theories about violence can be traced all the way back to at least biblical times. In the relevant chapters, we will explain how representatives and scholars of specific religious traditions have explained violence in those traditions. This is not meant to be a review of Christian or religious attitudes toward war or military service. Instead, we attempt to explore the extent to which a sample of ancient and modern authors ascribed violence to religious beliefs.

ANCIENT HISTORY TO LATE ANTIQUITY

It is difficult to find any ancient writer who attributes violence to religion. As opposed to many modern writers who can separate religious activities from secular ones, very few ancient writers considered religion as a separable category of human experience. At the beginning of the *Iliad*, the Greek poet Homer asks who brought Agamemnon and Achilles into the contention that set the scene for the momentous siege of Troy.[1] Homer says it was Apollo who brought them together to fight (*machesthai*). Yet Homer is not really blaming the belief in gods for this battle. Rather, Homer himself seems to believe that the gods themselves can cause people to fight.[2]

The influence of Plato (427–347 BCE), founder of the Athenian Academy, cannot be overestimated in Western cultures. And it is in his *Phaedo* that we find one of the most persistent explanations for war. Plato locates the cause of war in the body, as is clear in the following passage: "The body and its desires are the only cause of wars and factions and battles; for all wars arise for the sake of gaining money, and we are compelled to gain money for the sake of the body."[3] This idea that desires of the body are the key to explaining violence finds echoes in the modern theories of René Girard, among others. Plato's focus on the body and on real world entities (e.g., money) obscured the fact that belief in nonexisting entities could also cause violence.

Lucretius (ca. 96–55 BCE), the Epicurean philosopher of the first century BCE, does not appeal to a monocausal explanation as clearly as Plato. In general, Lucretius eschewed supernatural explanations for common phenomena. In his *De Rerum Natura* (*On the Nature of Things*), Lucretius writes that the desire for anything beyond the bare necessities of food and shelter bore potential for conflict. For Lucretius, the cause of great wars lies in the useless pursuits of human beings who do not know the limits of possessions (*non cognovit quae sit habendi finis*).[4]

Philo (ca. 13 BCE–50 CE), the first-century-CE Jewish philosopher famous for his allegorical interpretation of the Bible, shows a clear Platonic influence when he remarks that the wars of the Greeks and barbarians are "all from one source, desire, be it for money or glory or pleasure."[5] As did Plato, Philo specifically uses "desire" (ἐπιθυμία) in his explanation, as well as a specific reference to "money."

The theme of desire as the cause of war has echoes in the Bible. In the book of James, one finds the question of causality expressed frankly:

> Those conflicts and disputes among you, where do they come from? Do they not come from your cravings that are at war within you?
>
> You want something and do not have it; so you commit murder. And you covet something and cannot obtain it; so you engage in disputes and conflicts. You do not have, because you do not ask.
>
> You ask and do not receive, because you ask wrongly, in order to spend what you get on your pleasures. (James 4:1–3)

Note here that, as did Philo, James identifies conflicts or wars (πόλεμοι) as originating from pleasures (ἐκ τῶν ἡδονῶν). James 4:2 also uses the verbal form (ἐπιθυμεῖτε = "you want") of the same lexeme used by Plato and Philo. In short, during the ancient period there was a long and persistent tradition that located war and conflict in bodily desires, even if sometimes those desires were viewed as completely inane or foolish.[6]

An adaptation of Homer's idea that gods could cause human beings to fight may be detected in Origen (ca. 185–254), the influential Christian apologist and textual critic. Origen wanted to convince Roman society that

Christians were not a social burden or a threat. He had no developed explanation for violence, but he seems to have espoused the notion that demons are responsible for wars. But demons directly causing wars is not the same as the idea that belief in demons or religion per se causes war.[7] In part, Origen may have also been transmitting New Testament ideas about a cosmic war between demons and human beings found particularly in Ephesians 6.

Augustine (354–430), the premier theologian of Christianity in late antiquity, provides hints that the opponents of Christianity blamed wars on the espousal of Christianity. Augustine complains that in his era almost any war results in an attack on Christianity. He quotes opponents as saying that "if it [Christianity] did not exist and the divinities were worshipped with the ancient rites . . . the war would be over much sooner."[8] Such an anti-Christian rationale, however, was not based on the idea that religion or Christianity per se could cause war. Rather, Augustine understood the anti-Christian complaint to be premised on the idea that the Roman gods were much more efficient and helpful in war.

MEDIEVAL PERIOD

Scholarship has often framed the medieval period as embodying a struggle between temporal and ecclesial institutions. To some extent this is too simple, and there has been a spate of revisionist histories that question everything from the nature of feudalism to the extent of ecclesial control.[9] Norman Cantor, in fact, argues that the concept of the Middle Ages is actually an invention of modern scholarship.[10] Nonetheless, some of the major works of the period are concerned with the allocation of power to the church and to kings when it comes to using violence. We will treat some of these works in upcoming chapters, but we treat the following as a sample of discussions about the causes of violence.

Undoubtedly, the greatest theologian of the medieval period was Saint Thomas Aquinas (1227–1274), whose influence is still felt today. He is best known for the systematic exposition of Christian doctrines embodied in his *Summa Theologica*, and it is in that book that we find his principal comments on war.[11] As outlined in his *Summa*, Aquinas was somewhat dependent upon Augustine for his theory of a just war.[12] For Aquinas a just war is determined, first and foremost, by a higher authority. Thus, war on behalf of the church was allowable. However, fighting by clerics is not allowed by Aquinas.

Aquinas does not present a broad theory to explain violence on both individual or larger scales. Aquinas addresses the causes of violence somewhat obliquely when he discusses "strife," which corresponds more to interpersonal violence. For Aquinas, interpersonal violence, as opposed to wars between larger political entities, is always sinful. The location of interpersonal violence is placed in anger on the basis of Proverbs 15:18, among other sources. For Aquinas, preferential treatment may incite someone to anger, which then causes violence. Otherwise, Aquinas has no consistent explanation for why people may become angry.

During the medieval period a principal counterpoint to Aquinas's vision of the church was provided by Marsilius of Padua (ca. 1290–1343), an advocate of imperial secular power. In his *Defender of the Peace*, Marsilius posits that "tranquility" was the principal goal of royal power.[13] His first line of support were biblical passages where peace was encouraged or commanded (e.g., Mark 9:50, Luke 2:14, John 20:19).[14] Following Aristotle, Marsilius recognizes that conflict may have many causes. However, Marsilius focuses on a single cause, namely the church's claim to "a plenitude of power," which supersedes that of temporal rulers.[15]

For Marsilius, the church should concern itself solely with otherworldly salvation, and therefore cannot have authority or wage war by its own initiative. Rather, power rests with the people, the secular sovereign being their true representative. Thus, "power" or the "plenitude of power" can be interpreted to be a scarce resource over which the church and temporal powers compete. Not surprisingly, Pope John XXII condemned Marsilius in 1327 because of these teachings.

At times, Marsilius could be mistaken for a modern secular humanist in his view of religion. Although he says that any religion with teachings outside of the biblical canon is false, he can also conceive that religious beliefs can be deliberately manufactured to manipulate behavior. A most telling passage is as follows:

> For although some of the philosophers who founded such laws or religions did not accept or believe in human resurrection and that life which is called eternal, they nevertheless feigned and persuaded others that it exists and in it pleasures and pains are in accordance with the qualities of human deeds in this mortal life, in order that they might thereby induce men reverence and fear of God, and a desire to flee the vices and to cultivate the virtues.[16]

Marsilius, indeed, could conceive that religion could create artificial rewards, but he saw those only as inducements to good behavior.

Despite their philosophical differences, neither Aquinas nor Marsilius saw religion itself as a general cause of violence, though both certainly would believe that specific religious reasons (e.g., heresy) could be a cause for violence. While Marsilius comes closest to seeing that religion can create artificial resources, he stops short of seeing that these "rewards" can be scarce resources that can cause violence.

RENAISSANCE

Ever since Jacob Burckhardt published his provocative treatise *The Civiliza-tion of the Renaissance in Italy* (1860), which has been hailed as the initiator of Renaissance studies, there have been attempts to deny that such a period actually exists.[17] Charles Homer Haskins, the Harvard medievalist, coun-tered that if there had been a Renaissance, then it began in the twelfth cen-tury, and hence the name of his response to Burckhardt, *The Renaissance of the Twelfth Century*.[18] Others, such as Elizabeth L. Eisenstein, would rather focus on inventions (e.g., printing) than on a new philosophical orientation as the main impulse for what is called the Renaissance.[19]

In any case, to the extent that we can speak of the Renaissance, we see it as a phase of elitist views of civilization marked by the advent of a new medium and economic revolution. During this period, we can cite at least four devel-opments that had a tremendous impact on the world: (1) the dissemination of information through printing; (2) the challenge of authority as the means to truth, particularly in the work of Martin Luther; (3) the encounter of Europe with the Americas; and (4) a renewed concern with Muslim encounters.

The Renaissance period was also marked by a great deal of strife and vio-lence. It is in this light that Niccolo Macchiavelli (1469–1527), the Italian statesman and diplomat, comes on the scene to provide advice on how to deal with violence. This advice is embodied in his classic work *The Prince*, written in 1513, but not published until 1532.[20] While some writers (e.g., Jean-Jacques Rousseau) saw *The Prince* as a satirical work, scholars who have exam-ined Machiavelli's private correspondence have maintained that it was serious.[21]

The Prince is famous for introducing power politics and political realism, wherein the purpose of government is to maintain power. In the case of Machiavelli, he advises that if one had to choose between being feared and being loved, it is "much more safe to be feared than to be loved."[22] Hypocrisy is a legitimate instrument to maintain power.[23] Human beings are, by nature, bad and so need incentives (rewards or punishments) to behave in the manner that a leader wishes.[24]

The Prince is notable for its sparse references to religion. Machiavelli seems to see the nominal heads of religious institutions to be no less possessed by the greed for power than secular princes. He sees Pope Julius II (1443–1513) as a good example that a rash and violent image is better than a cautionary image.[25] A prince should "appear merciful, faithful, humane, upright, and religious."[26] And although Machiavelli recommends that the prince actually have those qualities, these appearances should not overrule the need to maintain power at their expense. Power is power, and rulers, religious and secular, want it. Machiavelli sees himself as reporting what works best.

Hugo Grotius (1583–1645), renowned as the father of international law, was very concerned with the place of religion in violence. Born in Delft (Netherlands), Grotius was a child genius who had already edited an encyclopedia by the age of fifteen. He served in various diplomatic posts, and was a particular favorite of Louis XIII of France. Grotius's influence is due, among other reasons, to his comprehensive scope and crisp writing style.

His main thoughts on war and conflict are embodied in his 1625 compendium *The Law of War and Peace*.[27] Grotius begins his discourse by modifying the definition ("contending by force") of war given earlier by Cicero. Instead Grotius proposes to define it as "the state of those contending by force."[28] In other words, Grotius was more comprehensive in alluding to a more general "state" rather than restricting it to just an actual battle. A nonpacifist, Grotius wrote his treatise in order to show that war was a legitimate instrument of national policy in cases of "defense, recovery of property, and punishment."[29] Grotius approximates our notion of the role of scarce resources in conflict when he says that the aim of war is the "preservation of life and limb, and the keeping or acquiring of things useful to life."[30]

Despite his claim to use natural law, Grotius has difficulties explaining instances of genocide in the Hebrew Bible. He argues, on the one hand, that such genocides do not become permissible merely because of their existence in the Bible. On the other hand, they should not be considered cases of homicide "for these are the works of God, whose right over men is greater than that of men over brutes."[31] Grotius appeals to Psalm 137:9 to support his conclusion that it has been customary to kill civilians, including women and children.[32] He is frank in arguing that violence and terror are the proper tools of war.[33]

Another political theorist is also a primary figure in the explanation of violence. Thomas Hobbes (1588–1679), the famed English political theorist, whose classic work *Leviathan* (1651) still echoes in the works of modern political realists and spreads to other areas of social philosophy. Hobbes was an advocate of the English monarchy, and he devalued the authority of the pope. He became quite popular in the aftermath of the restoration of the monarchy under Charles II (1660–1685). However, his ideas proved to be quite inflammatory, and he was later reviled both at home and abroad.

Hobbes believed that most, if not all, religion was based on defective arguments. He singled out four as the root causes of religion, which we can summarize as follows: (1) relying on so-called spirits; (2) ignorance of causes; (3) worshipping what one fears; and (4) confusing coincidence with genuine divine prophecy.[34] Thus, relative to Grotius, Hobbes did not use scripture much to support his theories. Human beings, Hobbes postulated, were inherently violent.

It is in chapter 13 of *Leviathan* that Hobbes addresses the root causes of violence most specifically. He says, "In the nature of man, we find three prin-cipall causes of quarrell. First, Competition; Secondly, Diffidence; Thirdly, Glory."[35] Competition is the easiest to understand in Hobbes's thought, as it is similar to conceptions we advocate. He explains that "if any two men desire the same thing, which nevertheless they cannot both enjoy, they become enemies."[36] Hobbes's "Glory" is similar to what we may understand today as the search for fame or high status.

Diffidence is a more subtle phenomenon for Hobbes and best corre-sponds to our term "insecurity." When human beings feel insecure, they tend to attack because they fear survival is at stake. On the other hand, fear can make human beings look for peace. If human beings feel that their survival depends on avoiding conflict, then peace will ensue. And since human beings are always after selfish interests, the way to establish peace is to provide a sort of dictatorship, whose authority is unquestioned. This would provide unity and, therefore, peace.

THE ENLIGHTENMENT

To the extent that a true period called "the Enlightenment" actually exists, we may say that it was the period wherein the elite of Western civilization established, as a formidable proposition, the idea that reason and experience are the best judges of truth. This has become the basis of the scientific method that still dominates much of Western society. During the Enlighten-ment, many of the most influential philosophers began to de-emphasize revealed truth.

In the political sphere, the Enlightenment saw the promotion of a sepa-ration of politics and religion, with an increasing sense that religion, if main-tained at all, should be a private matter. While we cannot discuss every philosopher of the Enlightenment, here we select a few that represent the continuities and contrasts with our thesis concerning the role of religion in violence.

In his famous work *The Social Contract* (1762), Jean-Jacques Rousseau (1712–1778) provides a substantial discussion of the effect of religion and Christianity on conflict. Rousseau, once a convert to Catholicism, eventually became quite anticlerical. *The Social Contract* begins by noting that natural man was peaceful. War, Rousseau argues, "can only arise from property rela-tions,"[37] and so belongs to a later stage of human development. "Uncivilized" human beings did not fight because they owned no property.

Rousseau also believed that the first civilized governments were theo-cratic. However, in contrast to Regina Schwartz, Rousseau thought that it was polytheism, not monotheism, that resulted in the divisions that led to conflict. Indeed, Rousseau lauds Muhammad for successfully uniting religion with politics.[38] Rousseau knew that his thesis of the advantage of a unitary religion was vulnerable to simple observations from history. For example, he was presented with the question of why there were no "wars of religion" under paganism, when each nation had a wide array of cults and gods.

His answer is that "each state, having its own faith as well as its own government did not distinguish between Gods and its laws. Political war was just as much theological war; the provinces of the Gods were determined, so to speak, by the frontiers of nations."[39] Since each nation was content to have its own religion, religious wars between nations were unnecessary. The fact that people were forced to change their religion upon conquest was because of the fact that "to change faith was part of the law of conquest."[40] In other words, the desire for conquest was not "caused" by religion, but rather religious violence followed upon conquest.

But Rousseau encountered another problem in that the Romans often allowed conquered people to keep their religion. If, as Rousseau argued, it was necessary to have one state religion to have peace, then how was Rome able to survive as long as it did? His riposte, as paradoxical as it sounds, was that polytheism itself could form a single state religion. The Romans simply came to regard the conquered gods as paying homage to the Roman gods, and thus became part of the Roman pantheon. Other times, the Romans would identify a god worshipped by a conquered people with a Roman god (e.g., the Greek Zeus becomes identified with the Roman Jupiter).

When it came to explaining the role of Christianity in conflict, Rousseau encountered similar puzzles and ambiguities. Christianity, claimed Rousseau, caused conflict because it divided religion from the state. Since Jesus preached that a "spiritual kingdom" focuses on the world beyond, religion and state could not form a unit. This is also why a true Christian makes a bad citizen. Christians do not care about improving temporal society because they are interested only in a future one. Moreover, Christianity "preaches only servitude and submission,"[41] which would make Christians a good opportunity for tyrants, not to mention conquerors.

Rousseau, however, has trouble explaining the crusades. He tells us that the crusaders were not really Christians, but rather "soldiers of the priests" and "citizens of the Church."[42] The crusaders were fighting for a "spiritual homeland, which it [the church] had in some strange way made temporal."[43] Since the Gospel does not advocate a national religion, then "holy war is impossible among Christians."[44]

Rousseau's plan for a peaceful society is to realize that there are three types of religion. One is the "religion of man," which is a private religion. Another is a sort of civil religion centered on the state. A third type of religion, identified with monasticism, advocates complete withdrawal from society. All of these religions have their defects. In fact, Rousseau sees civil religion as potentially inciting a lot of violence when people do not accept the gods of the state.

Yet, civil religion, when rightly framed, provides the best choice for Rousseau. His recommendation is that such religion be simple, consisting of a few "negative" and "positive" dogmas. The positive dogmas may be summarized as follows:

1. The existence of an omnipotent, intelligent divinity that foresees and provides for the general welfare;
2. The life to come;
3. The happiness of the just; and
4. The sanctity of the social contract.[45]

The negative dogma consists of simply rejecting intolerance. Furthermore, Rousseau rejects the idea of an exclusivistic state religion. One should tolerate all religions as long as they do not conflict with the duties of the citizen.

Rousseau's thesis is plagued with many internal contradictions, not to mention with a misreading of history. Because he does not see that religion creates scarce resources, he is unperturbed by the fact that his own "civil religion" endorses the same mechanisms he criticizes in other religions. Even the few dogmas he calls "positive" will cause conflict if others do not believe in them. These dogmas, moreover, are no less verifiable than those of any other religion.

Part of Rousseau's theory is based on a misreading of biblical texts. Rousseau, for example, argues that pagan gods generally did not cause interterritorial wars because the gods were seen as masters only of their own spaces. He then claims that Israel sometimes followed this precept as well, and quotes Judges 11:24 as proof: "'Is it not the possession of that which belongs to Chamos your God lawfully your due?' says Jephthah to the Ammonites. 'By the same title we possess the lands which our conquering God has taken.'"[46]

However, the Latin Vulgate, on which his translation depends, poorly translates the Hebrew, which is better translated as "Is it not right that whatever your god Chemosh expropriates for you [*yorisheka*], you should possess; and that everything that Yahweh our God expropriates for us, we should possess?"[47] In other words, this biblical passage refers to the right of each god to give land taken by conquest to the respective worshipper, whereas Rousseau assumes that the biblical author is referring only to a right to maintain land boundaries of land already taken.

Of course, Rousseau had no access to Moabite religious thought. Our main piece of evidence for Moabite religion is called the Moabite Stele, (or Moabite Stone) discovered in the late nineteenth century. That monument alone would have dismantled Rousseau's interpretation. For in line 14 of the Moabite Stele, we find the god Chemosh ordering his king, "Go, take Nebo, from Israel."[48] In fact, almost every ancient Near Eastern religion, including that of ancient Israel, had the taking of land as a usual component of its theology. So even among the most critical Enlightenment figures, faulty translations sometimes became the basis for flawed arguments about the relationship between religion and violence.

It is toward the end of the Enlightenment period that we begin to see writers attributing violence to religion or specific forms of religion. A good example is found in reason number 7 of "The Memorial and Remonstrance" of James Madison, who states:

> Because experience witnesseth that ecclesiastical establishments, instead of maintaining the purity and efficacy of Religion, have had a contrary operation. During almost fifteen centuries has the legal establishment of Christianity been on trial. What have been its fruits? More or less in all places, pride, and indolence in the Clergy, ignorance and servility in the laity, in both, superstition, bigotry, and persecution.[49]

It should be added that by the late nineteenth century the field of peace studies was emerging. Such studies, exemplified by, among others, Louis Bara's *The Science of Peace* (*La science de la paix*, 1872), sought to place peace on a scientific footing.[50] The renowned anarchist philosopher Pierre-Joseph Proudhon (1809–1865), author of *War and Peace* (*La guerre et la paix*, 1861) promised that science would solve the problem of war.[51] Proudhon was among several philosophers who argued that reliance on religion was not the answer to conflict.

The science of peace wanted to establish objective goals for peace. For example, some wanted land to be apportioned according to fertility and population, with the idea that people would be content if their resources matched their needs. Such ideas, of course, rightly recognized that scarce resources cause conflict. However, they also were unrealistic in thinking about how quickly science could bring this utopia into existence. This utopian view of scarce resources, moreover, was dealt a massive blow by World War I.[52] In our concluding sections, we will wrestle with the question of whether science can ever establish a nonviolent world.

SUMMARY

It is not surprising to see that most ancient writers did not see religion itself as a cause of violence. The social effects of belief in the gods was not "problematized" in the manner that modern academics see problems. Marsilius does come close to seeing that religious beliefs can be manufactured to serve political purposes, but he mostly sees those purposes as benign. Machiavelli sees that religious figures act just as politically and ruthlessly as secular rulers. It is not until the Enlightenment that some begin to discuss how certain religious frameworks can cause violence (e.g., Rousseau and polytheism). No premodern author, however, sees that religion can create scarce resources, and thereby violence.

NOTES

1. Iliad 1.1.: Τίς τ' ἄρ σφωε θεῶν ἔριδι ξυνῆκε μάχεσθαὶ. Our text is from Homer, *The Iliad*, trans. A. T. Murray, 2 vols., LCL (Cambridge, MA: Harvard University Press, 1924).

2. See also Robert Vacca, "The Theology of Disorder in the Iliad," *Religion and Literature* 23, no. 2 (1991): 1–22.

3. Plato, *Phaedo*, trans. H. N. Fowler, LCL (1914; reprint, Cambridge, MA: Harvard University Press, 1982), p. 66c: καὶ γὰρ πολέμους καὶ στάσεις καὶ μάχας οὐδὲν ἄλλο παρέχει ἢ τὸ σῶμα καὶ αἱ τούτου ἐπιθυμίαι. διὰ γὰρ τὴν τῶν χρημάτων κτῆσιν πάντες οἱ πόλεμοι γίγνονται, τὰ δὲ χρήματα ἀναγκαζόμεθα κτᾶσθαι διὰ τὸ σῶμα.

4. Lucretius, *De Rerum Natura*, trans. and ed. W. H. D. Rouse and M. F. Smith, LCL (Cambridge, MA: Harvard University Press, 1982), 5.1430–35.

5. Philo, *The Decalogue*, trans. F. H. Colson, LCL (1937; reprint, Cambridge, MA: Harvard University Press, 1984), 28.153: πάντες μιᾶς πηγῆς ἐρρύησαν, ἐπιθυμίας ἢ χρημάτων ἢ δόξης, ἢ ἡδονῆς. My adapted translation.

6. See further Martin Dibelius, *James: A Commentary of the Epistle of James*, rev. Heinrich Greeven (Philadelphia: Fortress, 1981), pp. 215–17.

7. Origen, *Contra Celsum*, 8.73. For the English text, we depend on *The Ante-Nicene Fathers*, ed. Alexander Roberts and James Donaldson (1885–87; reprint, Grand Rapids, MI: Eerdmans, 1994), 4:395–669.

8. Augustine, *City of God* 5.22, trans. William M. Green et al., LCL (Cambridge, MA: Harvard University, 1963), 2:256–57. Latin text: "si ipsa non esset et vetere ritu numina colerentur . . . tanta celeriter bella confecit."

9. Examples of such revisionist histories include Susan Reynolds, *Fiefs and Vassals: The Medieval Evidence Reinterpreted* (Oxford: Clarendon, 1994); John Van Engen, "The Christian Middle Ages as an Historiographical Problem," *American Historical Review* 91, no. 3 (June 1986): 519–52.

10. Norman F. Cantor, *Inventing the Middle Ages* (New York: William Morrow, 1991).

11. Our citations of Aquinas's *Summa Theologica* are from the first complete American edition in three volumes, translated by Fathers of the English Dominican Province (New York: Benziger Brothers, 1947). We shall cite the divisions of the *Summa* itself, followed, after a slash, by the volume and pages from the Benziger Brothers edition.

12. Aquinas, *Summa*, part II–II, question 40/Benziger edition, 2:1359–63. For Augustine's general theory of war, see John Langan, "The Elements of St. Augustine's Just War Theory," *Journal of Religious Ethics* 12, no. 1 (1984): 19–38.

13. For an edition, see Alan Gewirth, ed. and trans., *Marsilius of Padua: The Defender of the Peace* (New York: Harper and Row, 1956). All of our citations are from this edition. See also Alan Gewirth, *Marsilius of Padua and Medieval Political Philosophy* (New York: Columbia University Press, 1951).

14. Gewirth, *Defender*, p. 3.

15. Ibid., p. 95.

16. Ibid., p. 19.

17. For an English edition, see Jacob Burckhardt, *The Civilization of the Renaissance in Italy*, trans. L. Goldscheider (London: Phaidon, 1955); for a German edition, see *Die Kultur der Renaissance in Italien* (1860; reprint, Stuttgart: Philipp Reclam, 1987). For a recent study of the Renaissance, see Lisa Jardine, *Worldly Goods: A New History of the Renaissance* (New York: Doubleday, 1996). For a useful anthology on contemporary issues in Renaissance studies, see Keith Whitlock, ed., *The Renaissance in Europe: A Reader* (New Haven, CT: Yale University Press, 2000).

18. Charles Homer Haskins, *The Renaissance of the 12th Century* (Cambridge, MA: Harvard University Press, 1927).

19. Elizabeth L Eisenstein, *The Printing Press as an Agent of Change: Communications and Cultural Transformations in Early-Modern Europe*, 2 vols. (New York: Cambridge University Press, 1979); *The Printing Revolution in Early Modern Europe* (Cambridge: Cambridge University Press, 1983), especially p. 145, where Eisenstein discusses most succinctly her definition of the Renaissance in the context of the printing revolution.

20. Niccolo Machiavelli, *The Prince*, ed. and trans. Lester G. Crocker (New York: Pocket Books, 1963); for the Italian text, we rely on Niccolo Machiavelli, *Il Principe*, ed. Giorgio Inglese (Turin: Einaudi Tascabili, 1995). For a wide-ranging study of the continuing influence of Machiavelli's theories, see E. A. Rees, *Political Thought from Machiavelli to Stalin: Revolutionary Machiavellism* (Aldershot, England: Ashgate, 2004).

21. For Rousseau's *The Social Contract*, we cite the English translation of Maurice Cranston (Harmondsworth, UK: Penguin, 1968). The French text is from the edition of Bruno Bernárdi, ed., *Rousseau: Du contrat social* (Paris: Flammarion, 2001). Rousseau says the following in *The Social Contract*, 3.6 (note): "Machiavelli was an honest man and a good citizen, but being attached to the house of Medici, he was forced, during the oppression of his fatherland, to disguise his love for liberty"/*Contrat*, p. iii (note): "Machiavel était un honnête homme et un bon citoyen; mais attaché à la maison de Médicis il était forcé dans l'oppression de sa patrie de déguiser son amour pour la liberté." My adapted translation is more literal, as Cranston translates "honnête homme" as "gentleman" and "patrie" as "country." For evidence that *The Prince* was not meant as satire, see Crocker's remarks, *The Prince*, pp. xx–xxi.

22. Machiavelli, *The Prince*, p. 72/*Il Principe*, p. 110: "è molto piú sicuro essere temuto che amato."

23. Machiavelli, *The Prince*, p. 77.

24. Ibid., p. 107.

25. Ibid., p. 113–14.

26. Machiavelli, *The Prince*, p. 77/*Il Principe*, p. 118: "parere piatoso, fedele, umano, religioso." Adapted from Crocker's translation.

27. Hugo Grotius, *The Law of War and Peace*, trans. Francis W. Kelsey (Indianapolis: Bobbs-Merrill, 1925). The numeration for our citations is as follows: Book.Chapter.Section.Paragraph (page number of Kelsey's edition). For the Latin text, we follow William Whewell, ed., *Hugonis Grotii De Jure Belli et Pacis Libri Tres*, 3 vols. (Cambridge: Cambridge University Press, 1853), which we cite by volume: page number.

28. Grotius, *Law of War*, 1.1.2.1 (p. 33)/*De Jure Belli*, 1:2: "status per vim certantium." My adapted translation, as Kelsey's translation renders "status" as "condition" rather than as "state."

29. Grotius, *Law of War*, 2.1.2.2 (p. 171)/*De Jure Belli*, 1:205: "defensionem, recuperationem rerum, et punitionem."

30. Grotius, *Law of War*, 1.2.1.4 (p. 52)/*De Jure Belli*, 1:32: "vitae membrorum conservatio, et rerum ad vitam utilium aut retentio aut acquisitio."

31. Grotius, *Law of War*, 3.4.9.1 (p. 648)/*De Jure Belli*, 3:80.

32. Ibid.

33. Grotius, *Law of War*, 3.1.6.1 (p. 605)/*De Jure Belli*, 3:13: "vis ac terror maxime propria bellorum."

34. Thomas Hobbes, *Leviathan*, ed. Richard E. Flathman and David Johnston, (New York: W. W. Norton, 1997), p. 62.

35. Ibid., p. 71.

36. Ibid., p. 69.

37. Rousseau, *Social Contract*, p. 46/*Contrat*, p. 52: "l'état de guerre ne pouvant naître des simples relations personelles, mais seulement des relations réelles."

38. Rousseau, *Social Contract*, p. 179.

39. Rousseau, *Social Contract*, p. 177/*Contrat*, pp. 169–70: "Chaque État ayant son culte propre aussi bien que son Gouvernement, ne distinguait point ses Dieux de ses lois. La guerre politique était aussi Théologique; les départements des Dieux étaient, pour ainsi dire, fixés par les bornes des Nations."

40. Rousseau, *Social Contract*, p. 178/*Contrat*, p. 170: "l'obligation de changer de culte étant la loi des vaincus."

41. Rousseau, *Social Conract*, p. 184/*Contrat*, p. 177: "Le Christianisme ne prêche que servitude et dépendance."

42. Rousseau, *Social Contract*, p. 185/*Contrat*, p. 177: "c'étaient des soldats du prêtre, c'etaient des Citoyens de l'Église."

43. Rousseau, *Social Contract*, p. 185/*Contrat*, p. 177: "ils se battaient pour son pays Spirituel, qu'elle avait rendu temporel."

44. Rousseau, *Social Contract*, p. 185/*Contrat*, p. 177: "comme l'Evangile n'établit point une Religion nationale, toute guerre sacrée est impossible parmi les Chrétiens."

45. Rousseau, *Social Contract*, p. 186.

46. Rousseau, *Social Contract*, p. 177/*Contrat*, p. 170: "La possession de ce qui appartient à Chamos, votre Dieu, disait Jephté aux Ammonites, ne vous est-elle pas légitiment due? Nous possédons au même titre les terres que notre Dieu vainqueur s'est acquises."

47. I accept here the translation of Robert G. Boling, *Judges*, Anchor Bible 6A (Garden City, NY: Doubleday, 1975), pp. 201 and 203–204.

48. For an edition, see Andrew Dearman, ed., *Studies in the Mesha Inscription and Moab* (Atlanta, GA: Scholars Press, 1989), with text, translation, and commentary supplied on pp. 93–130. The quoted portion of Moabite reads, in English transcription: *lk 'hz 't nbh 'l ysr'l.*

49. James Madison, "The Memorial and Remonstrance," reason number 7. We quote from the text in Robert S. Alley, ed., *James Madison on Religious Liberty* (Amherst, NY: Prometheus Books, 1985), p. 58.

50. For a review of the "science of peace," see Hans J. Morgenthau, *Politics among Nations: The Struggle for Power and Peace*, rev. Kenneth Thompson (Boston: McGraw-Hill, 1993), pp. 41–49.

51. For an edition, see Pierre-Joseph Proudhon, *La guerre et la paix; recherches sur le principe et la constitution du droit des gens* (1861; reprint, New York: Garland, 1972).

52. For a study of the effect of World War I on the philosophical optimism for peace, see Barbara Tuchman, *The Proud Tower: A Portrait of the World before the War, 1890–1914* (New York: Macmillan, 1966).

CHAPTER 2

MODERN THEORIES OF VIOLENCE

The most intensive and expansive wars in history were fought in the twentieth century. That century also saw the rise of more ambitious efforts to explain aggression. Part of the reason is that the rise of science and technology made research more feasible and war even more frightening. At the same time, new findings were expanding our knowledge of human biology and behavior. All these factors made for a slew of new theories about the causes of violence and war. Nonetheless, most of these theories still show a neglect or misunderstanding of the role of religion in violence.

SCIENTIFIC METHOD AND RELIGIOUS VIOLENCE

On a methodological level, a recurrent problem in the scientific study of violence is the paucity of interdisciplinary research on science and the role of religion in violence. In part, this is endemic in that few, if any, researchers can master all of the literature of other fields. But we see more specifically the following obstacles to good interdisciplinary work from scientists: (1) lack of common or adequate definitions of religion, a problem also in religious studies per se; and (2) lack of acquaintance with the field of religious and biblical studies.

To illustrate how even the most critical and skeptical scientists can fall into common traps because of their lack of acquaintance with religious studies, we feature here the work of Michael Shermer, author of *The Science of Good and Evil* (2004).[1] Shermer seems broadly acquainted with the scientific literature, but not with that of the anthropology of religion or biblical studies. For example, note how Shermer describes the evolution of human religions: "As bands and tribes coalesced into chiefdoms and states animistic spirits gave way to anthropomorphic and polytheistic gods, and in the eastern Mediterranean the anthropomorphic gods of the pastoral people there lost out to the monotheistic God of Abraham."[2]

Shermer's theory of the evolution of religion reflects that of Edward Burnett Tylor's (1832–1917) outdated unilineal model of religious evolution, which posited the following stages: animism > polytheism > monotheism.[3] This unilineal scheme was already beginning to be dismantled with fieldwork at the start of the twentieth century, because high gods could be found among some "tribal" people, and animism could be found in the most "civilized" states.

Likewise, Shermer is at least a half century out of date in biblical studies. Most critical biblical scholars no longer see Abraham as a historical figure, and we do not know if he was a monotheist.[4] Shermer cites not a single source for these claims. And the biblical records portray Abraham himself as believing in quite an anthropomorphic god who walks, converses, and eats with Abraham in the tents of Mamre (see Genesis 18). Nor did the anthropomorphic gods of pastoral people die out, if one regards Jesus as an embodied god.

Shermer's definition of "religion" suffers from apparently assimilating Christian views of religion uncritically. His definition is this: "a social institution that evolved as an integral mechanism of human culture to encourage altruism and reciprocal altruism, to discourage selfishness and greed, and to reveal the level of commitment to cooperate and reciprocate among members of the community."[5]

But where does Shermer derive the notion that religion is meant to encourage altruism? Does being an ascetic hermit who believes in God count as altruistic behavior? What is altruistic about killing others who do not believe the same set of precepts? In at least some circumstances, religion could be interpreted as maladaptive, not as altruistic.

That Shermer has assimilated Christian notions is more evident in his statement about the difference in morality between the Old and New Testaments: "This may represent the difference between Old Testament and New Testament morality: inflexible moral principles versus contextual moral guidelines—a stricter draconian God versus a kinder, gentler God."[6] As we shall show in chapter 9, some New Testament authors actually advocate the eternalization and intensification of violence. Christian authors, in fact, may advocate a much more violent approach to life and our future compared to what is found in the Old Testament.

Shermer's view of Christianity is related to his evolutionary scheme for the Golden Rule, which is also not conversant with the dating of biblical sources. Thus, Shermer's Table 1 (a chronology of "The Historical and Universal Expression of the Golden Rule") cites Leviticus 19:18, which he dates to 1000 BCE, as the first occurrence of the Golden Rule. However, the dating for this section of Leviticus, usually called the Holiness Code, is hotly contested, with most dates ranging from the eighth century BCE to the fourth century BCE.[7] Shermer apparently is not conversant with the literature that argues that the Golden Rule may represent a selfish political dictum.

In sum, a simple lack of acquaintance with the literature of religious and biblical studies seems to have led Shermer far afield in his attempt to explain the role of religion in violence. Our conclusion, of course, is completely the opposite of Shermer's in that we try to show that religion often creates new scarce resources rather than creating some sort of altruistic ethos. But Shermer must be given credit for at least reaching out across fields, even if not successfully. We, of course, will be vulnerable to similar objections. But dialogue among vastly different fields and disciplines may be how progress is made in understanding religious violence.

Nonetheless, scientific explanations still can be useful, and we now turn our attention to how our thesis relates to them. In general, we can identify the following categories of scientific explanation, which may be visualized as progressing from the most basic aspects of individual organisms to their broader life as groups: (1)biological/evolutionary, (2) psychological, (3) sociological, and (4) anthropological. We also treat violence from the perspectives of political and military sciences.

BIOLOGICAL/EVOLUTIONARY THEORIES

With the advent of the theories of Charles Darwin (1809–1882), there was a renewed attention to the view of life as a competition for survival. It is in this context that many of the theories of violence began to be framed in modern times. Perhaps one of the best-known theorists of violence from a biological perspective is Konrad Lorenz (1903–1989), the father of ethology, author of *On Aggression* (1963), and winner of a Nobel Prize in 1973.[8] Lorenz believes that many nonhuman species are equipped ("imprinted") with instinctive aggressive impulses but also with inhibitory feedback mechanisms. Thus, lions playfully fight and wrestle, but seldom injure each other. Aggression has served an evolutionary purpose in helping animals survive. Human beings have inherited the aggressive impulses, but lack control of the inhibitory mechanisms.

Overall, Lorenz seems to be an updated version of Hobbes and Freud. More important, for purposes of our thesis, Lorenz comments very little on religion. Lorenz's theories have come under severe scientific scrutiny in recent years. Some critics noted his factual errors regarding animal behavior.[9] Some social theorists objected to his social policies, which blame permissiveness by society for outbreaks of criminal violence. Moreover, some doubted that what might explain aggression in animals also explains human aggressive behavior.[10]

An updated version of Lorenz's thesis is provided by Luigi Valzelli's *Psychobiology of Aggression and Violence* (1981). Following a thorough review of the literature, Valzelli concludes that aggression developed as a useful mechanism for the preservation of species. Most aggression, he argues, can be traced to the area of the brain that is identified with the reptilian phase of evolution.[11] He provides an overall definition as follows:

> Aggressiveness is: that component of normal behavior which, under different stimulus-bound and goal-directed forms, is released for satisfying vital needs and for removing or overcoming any threat to the physical and/or psychological integrity subserving the self- and species-preservation of a living organism, and never, except for predatory activity, initiating the destruction of the opponent.[12]

However, he says, human evolution has brought a paradoxical result in that aggressive behavior is leading "toward self- and species annihilation."[13] One can see Lorenz's influence here.

Yet Valzelli also simply repeats benign views of religion without much criticism. For example, he claims that "more than casual comment should be given to recall the importance of religion in counteracting violence."[14] He documents this sweeping assertion with reference to a single sociological study by Christopher Kirk Hadaway.[15] The article cited, however, does not discuss violence at all, but rather focuses on the relationship between religion and "life satisfaction" in a select group of Americans. Hadaway himself rightly cautions that such a relationship must be tested in "various ethnic groups, different religious traditions, and other collectivities where religion may have a different meaning."[16]

Unfortunately, Valzelli's lack of rigor and superficial documentation is sometimes repeated by better-known scientists.[17] Edward O. Wilson, the putative father of sociobiology, has brought about a renewed emphasis on the biological basis of behavior.[18] Although he does not develop a full-fledged theory for the biological origin of religion, he does indicate that hypertrophy, the exaggerated growth of preexisting structures (e.g., elephant tusks), may hold the key to the emergence of civilization.[19] Wilson's theory received much resistance from some anthropologists, notably from Marshall Sahlins, a heavyweight in anthropology.[20]

In general, Wilson sees religion as hypertrophic in that it represents the growth and transmutation of simpler hunter-gatherer practices. But whatever one thinks of Wilson's theory, at least one of his examples of human violence undermines confidence that hypertrophy is a key mechanism in religious violence.[21] At issue is Aztec human sacrifice and cannibalism, a type of religious violence that Wilson links to the scarcity of meat.[22] For Wilson, the simple carnivorous practices of our Stone Age ancestors grew to the elaborate forms of human sacrifice and cannibalism found among the Aztecs.

While not impossible, this claim is based on a single citation from Marvin Harris, who is famous for materialistic explanations of behavior.[23] Unfortunately, Wilson seems unaware of the mordant critiques against Harris, beginning with the lack of explanation of why such hungry people would carry bodies long distances to temples if they could have eaten them at the point the victims were killed.[24] Wilson does indicate explicitly that anthropology, rather than just biology, may hold the key to the origin of religion.[25]

Biologist Richard D. Alexander has tried to develop a more detailed case for the sociobiological origin of morals in human beings, much of it inspired by Wilson, at least in a general sense. Given upcoming examples where people will commit violence to maintain some perceived religious benefit for themselves, we concur with Alexander, who says "that people are in general following what they perceive to be their own interests is, I believe, the most general principle of human behavior."[26] Alexander sees the idea of God as invented "to extend the notion that some have greater rights than others."[27] Such beliefs, in turn, aid human beings in intergroup competition, which is another general trait Alexander sees in humans.

Although we do not make any claims here about how or why religion evolved, we should note that a few evolutionary theorists have seen religion as maladaptive or purely epiphenomenal. Stephen Jay Gould (1941–2002), among others, has argued that many features in our evolution did not evolve for a purpose but rather we found a purpose for a preevolved feature. He prefers the term "exaptation" to "preadaptation."[28]

A more developed view of religion as maladaptive is found in the work of biologist Richard Dawkins, who has increasingly turned his attention to explaining religion from an evolutionary perspective. In his well-known book *The Selfish Gene*, Dawkins argues that human behavior can be explained by how it benefits genes.[29] However, such a view poses obvious problems for explaining religion, as some of the effects of religion seem to be counterproductive to the survival of genes. For example, how does executing a suicide bombing for religious reasons help to further the transmission of the suicide bomber's genes?

Dawkins's latest comments on religion, found in a two-part series in the secular humanist publication *Free Inquiry*, seek to answer that question.[30]

Therein he observes that religion is a universal phenomenon. He specifically argues against the idea, represented by David Sloan Wilson among others, that religions such as Christianity can result in greater group survival, a phenomenon fully compatible with Darwinian selection.[31]

On the contrary, Dawkins argues that religion may be more akin to the phenomena one sees in moths who steer themselves into flames, even if that flame extinguishes their genes. Why would moths do that? Dawkins explains that moths long ago developed a mechanism to steer by the light of celestial objects, but now that same mechanism induces them to steer right into flames. Similarly, Dawkins theorizes that early human beings found certain behaviors useful (e.g., obeying orders from more experienced adults to ensure survival), but now that feature is being co-opted by religion. And who benefits? Dawkins concludes, "The benefit, if there is any, is to religion itself."[32]

Our review of biological/evolutionary theories shows two general themes. One is that violence is a beneficial adaptation for group survival; the other is that it is a sort of maladaptation. As it pertains to our thesis, we would argue that human behavior may indeed be more complex than can be explained on the basis of genetic fitness.[33] But given the destructiveness of religion, we tend to see it as more akin to an exaptation, an epiphenomenon, or an outright maladaptation. More important, we note that regardless of how religion originated in our evolutionary past, many of these biological theories acknowledge that competition for scarce resources can drive violence, whatever the reason people compete for a particular resource.

PSYCHOLOGICAL THEORIES

As with the biological theories, not all of the best known psychological theories of aggression have focused on religion.[34] In a recent survey, psychologist Robert Emmons found that in a cumulative total of more than three thousand pages in three comprehensive handbooks on social psychology, less than a single page is devoted to discussion of the influence of religion on behavior.[35] In part, the lack of focus on religion is a result of the search for more basic natural factors and impulses, especially within the burgeoning field of evolutionary psychology. Other times the omission of religion may be due to outright inability to study religion objectively. Here, we survey a small sample of psychological theories that focus on violence.

Despite Sigmund Freud's (1856–1939) seeming disrepute within the scientific community, it is important to understand some of his thoughts on violence. Freud's ideas underwent evolution, and so one must be careful to not portray his early ideas as his only or as his permanent ideas. In some of his early writings, Freud spoke of two opposing inborn instincts in human beings. One was a life instinct he called *eros*, and the other was a death instinct he called *thanatos*. According to Freud, the death instinct built up almost like a substance in the body, and then had to be released in a sort of hydraulic or cathartic process. Although the death instinct usually had the bearer as the target, catharsis sometimes was redirected at outsiders, manifesting itself as violence or aggression.[36]

Perhaps one of the most influential psychological theories of aggression is associated with John Dollard.[37] Dollard's study of human psychology led him to conclude that "aggression is always a consequence of frustration."[38] That is to say, when one's attempt to reach a goal is frustrated, aggression will likely result. A goal can be as simple as a child wanting ice cream or a country wanting land. Psychologist Leonard Berkowitz points out that perceived frustration can be just as important a factor in aggression as an actual obstacle to some goal.[39] Likewise, aggression can be displaced toward a scapegoat, which can then be used to satisfy an aggressive impulse. Dollard makes only one indexed reference to religion, which he defines as "the belief that overt gratification is not obtainable at the moment but is deferred ultimately for the future."[40]

Dollard's theory has a number of commonalities with ours. We hold that the desire for scarce resource X can be frustrated, thereby causing violence. However, Dollard's definition of religion is quite defective. Religion should not be defined solely by the belief in some future reward. In fact, we can find many cases in which religion causes violence precisely because it promotes the belief in an immediate reward. Likewise, Dollard's definition misses the point of how unverifiability, which is an essential feature of religious belief, can itself cause frustration because there are no means to adjudicate disputes.

Our theory of scarce resources shares some commonalities with Walter Garrison Runciman's (1934–) theory of the role of relative deprivation as a source of aggression. The term "relative deprivation" refers to the idea that deprivation is always comparative. Runciman expounds the idea as follows: "If A, who does not have something but wants it, compares himself to B, who does have it, then A is 'relatively deprived with reference to B.'"[41] A more extended version of this idea is outlined as follows: "A is relatively deprived of X when (i) he does not have X (ii) he sees some other persons . . . as having X . . . (iii) he wants X, and (iv) he sees it as feasible that he should have X."[42]

Runciman is actually more interested in perceptions of social justice than in the causes of aggression, although he feels that such perceptions of deprivation can lead to violence. In a similar manner, Crane Brinton notes that revolutions often begin not with people who are impoverished or poor, but rather with elite members of society who grow to expect more after a period of rising standards of living.[43] Such persons perceive deprivation when in fact they are doing quite well by other standards. Thus, the well-to-do elite of America and France in the late eighteenth century initiated the American and French revolutions, while the Irish potato famine of the 1840s produced no revolution on the part of starving farmers.

In our case, we hold that fear of loss of scarce resource X—not just merely the desire to acquire X—can be a motivator for violence. My postulate is meant to supplement Runciman's statement that the value of religion lies in that it can sometimes help "restrict aspirations." In other words, Runciman holds that religion can make a person not want something, and presumably this restriction of aspirations would suppress any aggression caused by the desire for X. In addition, Runciman sees that "knowledge" of an inequality can "create relative deprivations where they did not exist before."[44] At the same time, Runciman should be supplemented by Abraham Maslow's (1908–1970) idea of a hierarchy of needs and "metamotivations" that go beyond simple biological needs and can encompass, in our theory, needs created by religion.[45]

SOCIOLOGICAL THEORIES

While psychology often deals with the behavior of individuals, sociologists focus on the behavior of human groups, though we also see overlap in the field of "social psychology."[46] And, in contrast to the field of psychology, sociology has focused extensively and intensively on the role of religion in human institutions. "Conflict perspectives" have formed one of the persistent models for explaining the behavior of groups. Such conflict perspectives are often juxtaposed to "functionalist" perspectives that see society as striving for stability. We will discuss briefly some of these and other perspectives that impinge on the study of violence.

Of recent importance is the work of Richard B. Felson and James Tedeschi, advocates of the "social interactionist" approach to explaining violence.[47] This approach does not place much importance upon identifying inner forces or biological components (e.g., hormonal or neurobiological) as the main indicators of aggression. Instead, aggression is considered an instrument to achieve certain goals or values. This approach focuses on situations and the context in which actors engage in aggressive behavior. This theory also emphasizes the existence of norms and the sense of justice as being important in moving actors into aggression. Thus, perceived injustice can be the cause of much of the aggressive behavior we see.

Our theory is compatible with at least some of the concepts of the social interactionist perspective. We certainly see violence as an instrument to achieve certain goals, namely, the securing of scarce resources or defense against the loss of scarce resources. Most of these researchers have not paid much attention to how certain religious goals figure in violence. Felson and Tedeschi's *Agression and Violence* (1993), for example, does not have a single indexed reference to "religion."

Our thesis is more critical of those versions of social interactionist perspectives advocated by Michael R. Gottfredson and Travis Hirschi, who believe that "aggressive or violent acts are explicable as acts that produce immediate benefits and entail long-term social costs for the actor. Such acts are usually defined as criminal by the state and as deviant by society and are the very acts that social control theory is designed to explain."[48] Such a concept does not explain violence sanctioned by states, including genocide, well. Nor does it explain religious violence in which the perceived benefit and social cost are deemed equal. For example, many medieval Christians thought that anti-Jewish violence both conferred an immediate benefit and had no necessary long-term social costs for perpetrators, especially when their status increased because of such violence.

Albert Bandura represents the "social learning" approach to explaining aggression, which is virtually synonymous with violence.[49] Bandura believes that "a full explanation of aggression must consider both injurious behavior and social judgements."[50] Accordingly, "aggression is defined as injurious and destructive behavior that is socially defined as aggressive on the basis of a variety of factors, some of which reside in the evaluator rather than in the performer."[51] Bandura's definition encompasses both psychological and physical.

Our thesis agrees with Bandura insofar as we are the evaluators of what counts as violence. However, using his definition, one also would have to conclude that certain societies have not historically considered religious violence to be "aggression" because those societies sanctioned it themselves. That is to say, the performer and the evaluator were sometimes the same entity. As we shall note in our upcoming discussion of anthropology, David Riches provides a corrective on Bandura's approach.

ANTHROPOLOGICAL THEORIES

Anthropology (the study of human beings as a species) and sociology overlap to such an extent that there exists a separate field called social anthropology. We confine ourselves here to anthropology as the study of institutions of the human species, especially as seen from an evolutionary perspective. Historically, anthropology has concerned itself with the observation of non-Western societies.[52] Currently, there is a reassessment of anthropology as a field and its role in the social sciences, but such reassessments are as old as academia.[53]

Unlike biological explanations, which have often shunned discussion of religion in violence, anthropology has been concerned with religion from its earliest history, and the anthropology of religion is a distinct discipline within the field.[54] Much of early anthropology, for instance, was permeated by collection of religious myths and lore in the persons of Sir James Frazer (1854–1941), Franz Boas (1858–1942), Bronislaw Malinowski (1884–1942), and A. R. Radcliffe-Brown (1881–1955). We cannot do justice to all of anthropology here, so we will concentrate on recent work in sociology and anthropology that is relevant to our thesis.

Although some theories of religion and violence appear to be new, many have their beginnings in anthropological theory. One illustrative example is the theory of René Girard (1923–), whose work we will analyze in more detail. Girard's idea of the scapegoat as key to violence has precedence in, among other sources, the work of anthropologist Clyde Kluckhohn (1905–1960), who argues that war was a concomitant of intragroup aggression.[55] When there is a danger that internal fighting will destroy a group, that group displaces its aggression on some outside group (cf. Freud).

If one studies the statistical chart provided by R. Brian Ferguson and Leslie E. Farragher's review of the study of warfare in anthropology, one sees a veritable explosion of interest in the 1960s.[56] For example, in 1958 the number of studies published is listed as fewer than twenty. In 1968 the number of studies is listed as at least seventy-five. The Vietnam War, of course, may be part of the explanation. But we also see more than seventy studies in 1975, 1979, and 1986. This compares to fewer than five in 1900. Explaining this increase beginning in the 1960s is difficult, though some may speculate that such statistics illustrate how the interests of academics center on how the study of war may serve their own interests (e.g., increased government funding for research on war) rather than because war became more common in the 1960s or 1970s.[57]

Having been trained formally as an anthropologist, I may be a bit more cautious about the limitations of anthropology. This is particularly important as there has been an overenthusiastic application of "anthropological" approaches in biblical studies that are, in fact, sometimes forays not cognizant of the complexities of internal arguments in the field. In fact, such an enthusiasm for anthropological approaches is ironic insofar as Ferguson and Farragher note that provincialism has been a persistent problem within the anthropological study of violence. Thus, anthropologists who study war among Native Americans of the Southwest may not communicate even with those researching in the Northeast.

It is just as important to urge caution in the use of ethnographies to make conclusions about violence. Having done some elementary fieldwork, I am very skeptical of ethnographic reports I cannot verify, and few can be verified. Ethnographers may present distorted descriptions of any particular group because of a number of factors, including their own prejudices, the selection of informants, and the fact that informants may behave differently in the presence of an outsider. As Pierre Bourdieu notes, sometimes instead of recording actual "facts" about meaningful interaction within a group, the ethnographer is simply recording a group's interaction with the ethnographer.[58] We only have to think about past scandalous controversies about the true origins of the Chumash Indians of California, or about the alleged misdeeds of Margaret Mead or Napoleon Chagnon, to appreciate this lesson.[59]

Although anthropology is perhaps famous for championing the idea that culture influences behavior more than biology does, we find historically that anthropology has representatives on both sides of the issue, and everywhere in between. In part, this is related to the perennial issue of how "scientific" anthropology should be. One can see this shift in the nomenclature: The courses I used to take under the rubric of "physical anthropology" are now often labeled "biological anthropology" or "bioanthropology."[60]

On the biological side of anthropological explanations for violence, we find Marvin Harris, who proposes that Aztec warfare is related to protein and meat deficiencies. Similarly, we find another biological determinist view in Irenaus Eibl-Eibesfeldt, author of *The Biology of Peace and War* (1979).[61] A more subtle but still materialistic explanation is represented by Roy A. Rappaport, who has integrated religion into his studies of the function of war as a mechanism for population control, especially in New Guinea.[62]

Territoriality has been identified as a main cause of aggression by Robert Ardrey.[63] For Ardrey, most animals—including human beings—possess a biological need to maintain and defend bounded spaces. In the field of international politics, Ardrey's work should perhaps be juxtaposed with that of John H. Hertz, who argued for the waning importance of territoriality in the 1950s.[64] Our theory holds that sacred space is indeed one of the main factors in religious violence. It is not so much our objective to prove that there is some sort of instinct to territoriality as it is to show how religion can manufacture the value of a territory that would have no value by other standards (e.g., economics, food production, etc.).

Since anthropologists often see their domain as the entire biological order of "primates," many anthropologists have focused their work on observing nonhuman primates for lessons about human violence. Of particular interest has been the work of Jane Goodall, who discovered that under certain circumstances, chimpanzees would engage in "wars."[65] A strong variable seemed to be the fission of a group of chimpanzees into subgroups, who then may come into conflict at the boundaries of their territories.[66]

More recently, primatologists such as Ellen J. Ingmanson and Takayoshi Kano have argued that bonobos, known also as pygmy chimpanzees (*Pan paniscus*), are basically peaceful when compared to regular chimpanzees.[67] Ingmanson and Kano argue that species do not always have to compete for scarce resources, but can learn to cooperate to make the most of scarce resources. They conclude that "[t]oday, bonobos offer proof that a species can survive by cooperating rather than constantly struggling for dominance."[68]

However, other primatologists opine that we should be more cautious in making such generalizations about bonobos.[69] First, many of the observations about bonobos are from captive pools; the animals may behave quite differently in the wild. Second, it took years to discover the extent of chimpanzee "wars," and Igmanson and Kano's own reports show how difficult it is to observe bonobos in the wild. Different subpopulations of bonobos have also reportedly shown different patterns of behavior.[70]

Perhaps more relevant to our methodology is the work of David Riches, who has been influential in arguing that studies of violence must carefully distinguish three viewpoints: (1) victim, (2) perpetrator, and (3) observer (meaning here a scholar of violence).[71] Each of these viewpoints may have different explanations for the legitimacy of violence even if they agree on the definition of violence. In the study of religious violence, this seems to be a germane observation. As we shall see, sometimes the scholar will assume the presuppositions of the perpetrator without making such an acceptance explicit. Other times, we will see the perpetrator's accounts of violence taken at face value without the countervailing narrative of the victims.

For the time being, we will pass over other anthropological theories of violence, especially as we will integrate discussion of them as we reach relevant sections of our book. The important lesson of this survey of social science approaches is that many recognize that scarce resources and competition for scarcities may be a cause of violence. However, there is still no realization or contemplation of the possibility that religion can create new scarce resources that may become a main factor in many instances of violence.

MILITARY THEORIES OF VIOLENCE

It may be supposed that military scholars would have much to say about religion in violence, but it is surprising how little some of the most important studies of military violence and theory even consider religion. When they do consider religion, they often misunderstand it. In this regard, military and political science has followed most of the examples we have examined above.

We will examine only briefly some of the major theories we believe are relevant to our hypothesis about religious violence.

Perhaps the most famous theorist of war was Carl von Clausewitz (1780–1831), author of *On War* (*Vom Kriege*), which was published posthumously.[72] Clausewitz was a Prussian soldier who actually fought in the Rhine campaigns (1793–94) against France. From 1818 to 1830 he served as director of the military academy in Berlin. As Anatol Rapoport notes, Clausewitz was able to see the transition between the international system of 1648–1789, which was racked by religious wars, and the beginning of the international system of 1815–1914, which culminated in the First World War.[73]

For Clausewitz, religion bears no role in explaining the cause of war or in resolving wars. War is a legitimate and rational means to effect national policy. To reproduce his famous adage, "War is a mere continuation of politics by other means."[74] Clausewitz in fact adopted a most extreme version of Rousseau's "civil religion," wherein the state becomes the paramount decision maker in a person's life and death. Clausewitz defines war as "an act of violence intended to compel our opponent to fulfil our will,"[75] and posits two motives for war: "hostile instinct and hostile intention."[76] According to Clausewitz, "civilized" (*Gebildeten*) people sometimes do not differ much from "savages" (*rohende Völkern*) insofar as war may be seen as a reaction to feelings. He explains that "this reaction depends not on the degree of civilization, but upon the importance and duration of the interests involved."[77] The instinctive need to destroy what we hate drives war. Psychologist Erich Fromm (1900–1980) would later echo this idea.[78]

From our perspective, of course, Clausewitz fails to see (or is not interested in seeing) the role of religion in conflict. His use of instinctive hostility as an explanation falls short in explaining why people group themselves into hostile camps in the first place. He has defined *nation* as a territory whose only goal is power, but the kinds of power do matter. While we can agree that power is probably one of the most important scarce resources in existence, we would argue that Clausewitz fails to see how power differentials can be manufactured by religion.

The first significant study of war from a statistical and scientific perspective was probably that of biologist Frederick Adams Woods and political scientist Alexander Baltzly. After six years of collecting data, they published *Is War Diminishng?* in 1915.[79] Woods and Baltzly compiled a list of wars between 1450 and 1900 but ultimately, they could not provide any definitive "causes" for wars. Empirical study of the causes of war took a big step with Quincy Wright's two-volume *A Study of War* (1942). Wright compiled a list of 278 wars between 1480 and 1940 in an effort to find causes of such conflict.[80] He classified four different types of war as follows: (1) balance of power, (2) civil war, (3) defensive war, and (4) imperial war. In the final analysis, Wright did not see how religion could create the rationale for "defense" or "imperialism."

Perhaps the most ambitious project of all was initiated by J. David Singer, a professor at the University of Michigan, in 1963. The effort, known as the Correlates of War Project (COW Project),[81] was motivated by the fact that Wright and other researchers had not produced refined categories for study nor a solid basis for casualty figures.[82] Consequently, Singer decided to produce a detailed data set that includes variables such as the length of conflicts, number of casualties, etc. The project has issued a series of publications, including a *Statistical Handbook* (1972) with a list of ninety-three wars and attributes (intensity, severity, duration) between 1816 and 1965, though the data sets have been updated to the near present.[83]

A key feature of the data collected in the COW *Statistical Handbook* revolves around classifying units that fought in wars. Nations are classified by membership in three systems, as follows:

1. The international system, which requires that a state be legally recognized by the United Nations or have a population of at least half a million people.
2. The central system, which requires that a nation "be active and influential in European-centered diplomacy."[84]
3. The major power system, which refers to membership in the most exclusive club of nations (e.g., the United States after 1945).

For the COW Project, it is important, then, to seek correlations of war by whether a member fought other members within a system or fought with members from outside a particular system. It seeks to account for wars with colonial entities, and not just with major nations.

The COW Project has become a key source for much research on war in the decades following its initiation. As noted by R. L. Merritt and Dina A. Zinnes, "Research reported in fifteen key journals that focus on quantitative international politics found that from 1974 to 1986, COW was the most frequently cited data project."[85] The COW Project Web site reports that it has helped to generate more than 150 journal articles and book chapters, and more than a dozen books.[86]

However, for all of its effort, the COW Project has produced very meager "causal" findings (e.g., "power transitions between two leading powers lead to war.").[87] By 1990, supporters of the COW Project were commenting that "the Correlates of War findings to date have not produced the kind of clear and unambiguous signals that would tell foreign policy makers what to do with foreign policy."[88] Even later modification that sought to include more attention to decision-making behavior did not seem to help much.[89] As we shall see, however, some of the strongest correlations are linked with scarce resources.

And, judging by the COW Project's data, religion plays no role in war. Of the ninety-three wars listed in the *Statistical Handbook*, one will be hard-pressed to find one that is correlated with religion. A search of keywords in what is presumably the most complete bibliography available does not turn up a single study with the words "religion" or "religious" in the title.[90] Thus, if religion plays any role in war, we could not tell much from the data sets of the COW Project, which, for example, does not record the type of religious violence leveled against Jews in pre-Nazi Europe. And because the COW Project focuses on "nations," transnational entities, such as al Qaeda, which play a role in religious violence, would not be included in such data sets. It certainly would be shortsighted to assume that the COW Project's omission of religion proves that religion is not a factor in war and violence.

THE BBC WAR AUDIT

Much of what the average person thinks about religion and war comes not from scholarly studies but from the media. In this regard, we should mention at least one case in which scholars, using data akin to the COW Project, have sought to prove that most wars are not religious.[91] The most well-known case is a study commissioned by the British Broadcasting Company that was meant to supplement a documentary called *What the World Thinks about God*, which was broadcast in February 2004. The study, titled "God and War: An Audit and Exploration," was completed by Greg Austin of the Department of Peace Studies at Bradford University in West York, England, along with Todd Kranock and Thom Oommen.

The main database for the study is presented in tables that list major wars from the middle of the second millennium BCE through the twentieth century CE. It ranks the intensity of "religious factors" in each war on a scale from 0 (no religious factors/intensity) to 5 (most religious factors/intensity). Table 1 in the study, for example, lists forty-two wars from 1469 to the end of the eighteenth century. The first sixteen wars—including the First Battle of Megiddo in 1469 BCE, the Roman Conquests of 498–272 BCE, and the Greek Persian Wars of 499–488 BCE—are listed as having 0 religious factors/intensity.

The flaws of this war audit are easy to detect for any serious historian of the ancient Near East. For example, the table assigns the Battle of Megiddo a religious component of 0. However, the Battle of Megiddo is mainly attested in one Egyptian text (*The Annals of Tuthmosis III*), and that text is replete with religious motives. For example, the reason given for the conquest of Megiddo is that it was land that "his father Re [a god] had given him."[92] If so, how can this be listed as having *zero* religious factors?

Other wars listed on Table 1 are simply too poorly attested to make any judgment. For example, we do not really know all that much about Roman Conquests of 498–272 BCE, yet Table 1 claims 0 religious factors here. Indeed, most of the first sixteen wars listed are either poorly attested in terms of their motives, or religious reasons can be found in a thorough reading of the relevant texts.

Likewise, there are methodological problems in the BBC study's claim (p. 17) that "Atheistic totalitarian states (Stalin's Russia and Mao's China) have perpetrated more murder than any state dominated by religious faith." However, note that the BBC study unduly combines "atheistic" and "totalitarian," and so credits to atheism many deaths that are best attributed to totalitarian violence. This undue combination of "atheistic" and "totalitarian" is especially noteworthy because the BBC study's criterion for judging a war as "religious" is the degree to which "religious ideas or justification were central." The BBC study does not use an equivalent criterion for Stalinist Russia and Maoist China. A proper opposite category of "religious ideas or justification" would be "atheistic ideas or justification." Yet, the BBC study never documents where Stalin justified his killing by appealing to "atheistic ideas" (e.g., "There is no God, therefore act of violence Y"). As we shall show in chapter 13, Stalinist violence has less to do with atheism than it has to do with communism and totalitarianism, both of which can exist in religious form.

As we shall show more thoroughly in chapter 12, if we used the BBC war audit's criteria, we would have to include Hitler under "religious" on the following statement alone: "Hence today I believe that I am acting in accordance with the will of the Almighty Creator; by defending myself against the Jew, I am fighting for the work of the Lord."[93] Nor does the war audit note that Hitler's plan for the Jews was simply a modern version of the plan outlined by Martin Luther in 1543. In short, the BBC war audit minimizes the effects of religion on violence and is not very careful in its methodology.

SUMMARY

We have encountered the idea that scarce resources can generate violence in the research of different fields. Biological theories about genes, territoriality, and food have been mentioned. Some psychological theories speak of deprivation as a source of aggression. Sociological and anthropological theories often repeat some of these themes. Political and military theories focus on power as the valued resource that causes conflict. Most of these scientific theories still do not focus on religion, and many scientific researchers still uncritically assimilate religious doctrines of the value of religion and its role in violence. Our theory, therefore, aims to correct these deficiencies in previous scientific theories of the role of religion in violence.

NOTES

1. Michael Shermer, *The Science of Good and Evil: Why People Cheat, Gossip, Care, Share and Follow the Golden Rule* (New York: Times Books, 2004). See also his earlier book, *How to Believe: Science, Skepticism, and the Search for God*, 2nd ed. (New York: Owl Books, 2003). Shermer sees religion as a "universal" feature of humanity (*Science of Good and Evil*, pp. 60–64), and he has been influenced in this idea by Donald E. Brown, *Human Universals* (Boston: McGraw-Hill, 1991).

2. Shermer, *Science of Good and Evil*, p. 46. For Tylor's views, see Edward Burnett Tylor, *Religion in Primitive Culture* (1871; reprint, New York: Harper and Row, 1958). This is actually part 2 of his book *Primitive Culture* (London: Murray, 1871).

3. For a recent view of this unilineal scheme, see Fiona Bowie, *The Anthropology of Religion* (Oxford: Blackwell, 2000), pp. 14–16.

4. See, for example, John Van Seters, *Abraham in History and Tradition* (New Haven, CT: Yale University Press, 1975).

5. Shermer, *Science of Good and Evil*, p. 46.

6. Ibid., p. 84.

7. For some representative arguments that date the Holiness Code, see Jacob Milgrom, *Leviticus 17–22* (Garden City, NY: Doubleday, 2000); *Leviticus 1–16* (Garden City, NY: Doubleday, 1992), p. 27; Israel Knohl, *The Sanctuary of Silence: The Priestly Torah and the Holiness School* (Minneapolis: Fortress, 1995); Avi Hurvitz, *A Linguistic Study of the Relationship between the Priestly Source and the Book of Ezekiel* (Paris: Gabalda, 1982); "The Evidence of Language in Dating the Priestly Code," *Revue biblique* 81 (1974): 24–56.

8. Konrad Lorenz, *On Aggression*, trans. Marjorie Kerr Wilson (New York: Bantam Books, 1966).

9. For one critique, see R. B. Zanovic, "The Zoomorphism of Human Collective Violence," in *Understanding Genocide: The Social Pyschology of the Holocaust*, ed. Leonard S. Newman and Ralph Erber (New York: Oxford University Press, 2002), pp. 222–38.

10. See further Pierre Karli, *Animal and Human Aggression*, trans. S. M. Carmona and H. Whyte (New York: Oxford University Press, 1991).

11. On the reptilian phase as one of three evolutionary steps toward the human brain, see P. D. MacLean, "The Triune Brain, Emotion, and Scientific Bias," in *The Neurosciences, Second Study Program*, ed. Francis O. Schmitt et al. (New York: Rockefeller University Press, 1970), pp. 336–49.

12. Luigi Valzelli, *Psychobiology of Aggression and Violence* (New York: Raven, 1981), p. 64.

13. Ibid., p. 63.

14. Ibid., p. 165.

15. Christopher Kirk Hadaway, "Life Satisfaction and Religion," *Social Forces* 57 (1978): 636–43.

16. Ibid., p. 641.

17. For a general critique of scientific studies purporting to find positive relationships between religion and the quality of life, see Hector Avalos, "Is Faith Good for You?" *Free Inquiry* 17, no. 4 (1997): 44–46.

18. See Edward O. Wilson, *On Human Nature* (Cambridge, MA: Harvard University Press, 1978), especially pp. 93–95. For a more recent and popular treatment of his views on morality, including his plea that empiricism be an important part of ethics, see his "The Biological Basis of Morality," *Atlantic Monthly* 281, no. 4 (April 1998): 53–70.

19. Ibid., p. 95.

20. Marshall Sahlins, *The Use and Abuse of Biology: An Anthropological Critique of Sociobiology* (Ann Arbor: University of Michigan Press, 1976).

21. For another critique from an anthropologist, see Jerome Barkow, "Culture and Sociobiology," *American Anthropologist* 80, no. 1 (1978): 5–20.

22. Wilson, *On Human Nature*, pp. 93–94.

23. Marvin Harris, *Cannibals and Kings: The Origins of Culture* (New York: Random House, 1977), pp. 147–68.

24. See discussion by David Carrasco, *City of Sacrifice: The Aztec Empire and the Role of Violence in Civilization* (Boston: Beacon, 1999), pp. 167–69; Bernard R. Ortiz de Montellano, "Aztec Cannibalism: An Ecological Necessity?" *Science* 200, no. 4342 (1978): 611–17. Carrasco prefers the more contextual explanations associated with Stanely Tambiah, *Culture, Thought and Action* (Cambridge, MA: Harvard University Press, 1985).

25. Wilson, *On Human Nature*, p. 95.

26. Richard Alexander, *The Biology of Moral Systems* (New York: de Gruyter, 1987), p. 34.

27. Ibid., p. 207.

28. Stephen Jay Gould, *The Structure of Evolutionary Theory* (Cambridge, MA: Harvard University Press, 2002), especially pp. 1231–35.

29. His latest book is *A Devil's Chaplain: Reflections on Hope, Lies, Science and Love* (Boston: Houghton Mifflin, 2003). See also his earlier works, *The Blind Watchmaker: Why the Evidence of Evolution Reveals a Universe without Design* (New York: W. W. Norton, 1986); and *The Selfish Gene* (Oxford: Oxford University Press, 1976).

30. Richard Dawkins, "What Use Is Religion? Part 1," *Free Inquiry* 24, no. 4 (June/July 2004): 13–14, 56; "What Use Is Religion? Part 2," *Free Inquiry* 24, no. 5 (August/September 2004): 11–12.

31. David Sloan Wilson, *Darwin's Cathedral: Evolution, Religion, and the Nature of Society* (Chicago: University of Chicago Press, 2003).

32. Dawkins, "What Use Is Religion? Part 2," p. 12.

33. For critiques of Dawkins by evolutionary geneticists, see R. C. Lewontin, Steven Rose, and Leon J. Kamin, *Not in Our Genes: Biology, Ideology and Human Nature* (New York: Pantheon, 1984), especially pp. 8 and 76. For another view, see Bradley A. Thayer, *Darwin and International Relations: On the Evolutionary Origins of War and Ethnic Conflict* (Lexington: University Press of Kentucky, 2004).

34. For some older surveys of research on aggression, see V. J. Konečni, "Methodological Issues in Human Aggression Research," in *Aggression in Children and Youth*, ed. R. M. Kaplan, V. J. Konečni, and R. W. Novaco (The Hague: Nijhoff, 1984), pp. 1–43.

35. See Robert A. Emmons, "Religion in the Psychology of Personality: An Introduction," *Journal of Personality* 67, no. 6 (December 1999): 873–88. The works surveyed were R. Hogan, J. Johnson, and S. Briggs, eds., *Handbook of Personality Psychology* (San Diego: Academic, 1997); L. A. Pervin, *Handbook of Personality: Theory and Research* (New York: Guilford, 1990); and D. T. Gilbert, S. T. Fiske, and G. Lindzey, eds., *Handbook of Social Psychology*, 4th ed. (Boston: McGraw-Hill, 1997).

36. On the death and life instincts in Freudian theory, see Frank J. Sulloway, *Freud, Biologist of the Mind: Beyond the Psychoanalytic Legend* (Cambridge, MA: Harvard University Press, 1992). For a Freudian approach to violence in anthropology, see A. I. Hollowell, *Culture and Experience* (Philadelphia: University of Pennsylvania Press, 1955). See further Richard D. Sipes, "War, Sports, and Aggression: An Empirical Test of Two Rival Theories," *American Anthropologist* 75, no. 1 (1973): 64–86.

37. John Dollard et al., *Frustration and Aggression* (New Haven, CT: Yale University Press, 1939).

38. Ibid., p. 1.

39. Leonard Berkowitz, "Aversive Conditions as Stimuli to Aggression," *Advances in Experimental Social Psychology* 15 (1982): 249–88. For his more comprehensive views, see *Aggression: Its Causes, Consequences, and Control* (Philadelphia: Temple University Press, 1993).

40. Dollard et al., *Frustration*, p. 169.

41. W. G. Runciman, *Relative Deprivation and Social Justice: A Study of Attitudes to Social Inequality in Twentieth-Century England* (London: Routledge and Kegan Paul, 1966), p. 10.

42. Ibid.

43. Crane Brinton, *The Anatomy of Revolution* (New York: Vintage, 1965), especially pp. 32–66.

44. Runciman, *Relative Deprivation*, p. 25.

45. See Abraham H. Maslow, *The Farthest Reaches of Human Nature* (Harmondsworth, UK: Penguin, 1971), especially pp. 289–309. See also his *Religions, Values, and Peak-Experiences* (New York: Harper and Row, 1970).

46. Alex Thio, *Sociology: An Introduction*, 3rd ed. (New York: HarperCollins, 1992).

47. See Richard B. Felson and James T. Tedeschi, eds., *Aggression and Violence: Social Interactionist Perspectives* (Washington, DC: American Psychological Association, 1993).

48. Michael R. Gottfredson and Travis Hirschi, "A Control Theory Interpretation of Psychological Research on Aggression," in ibid., pp. 63–64.

49. See Bandura, *Aggression*.

50. Ibid., p. 5.

51. Ibid., p. 8. For a perspective from cognitive psychology that integrates Bandura's theories, see Aaron T. Beck, *Prisoners of Hate: The Cognitive Basis of Anger, Hostility and Violence* (New York: Perennial, 1999). The latter also emphasizes heavily the role of the ego and perception of status, which can also be interpreted as a scarce resource in our society.

52. See William Sax, "The Hall of Mirrors: Orientalism, Anthropology, and the Other," *American Anthropologist* 100, no. 2 (1998): 292–308. Sax argues specifically against the thesis of Edward Said (*Orientalism* [New York: Random House, 1978]), who argued that the "Orient" was actually a hegemonically motivated construct of Western scholars. Despite its biases and early date, a useful earlier history of anthropology may be found in Marvin Harris, *The Rise of Anthropological Theory: A History of Theories of Culture* (New York: Harper and Row, 1968).

53. For a critical view of anthropology's status, see Immanuel Wallerstein "Anthropology, Sociology, and Other Dubious Disciplines," *Current Anthropology* 44, no. 4 (2003): 453–65.

54. For some representative studies, see Bowie, *Anthropology of Religion*; Stephen D. Glazier, ed., *Anthropology of Religion: A Handbook* (Westport, CT: Praeger, 1999); and Brian Morris, *Anthropological Studies of Religion: An Introductory Text* (Cambridge: Cambridge University Press, 1988).

55. Clyde Kluckhohn, *Mirror for Man: A Survey of Human Behavior and Social Attitudes* (Greenwich, CT: Fawcett World Library, 1960), p. 177.

56. R. Brian Ferguson and Leslie E. Farragher, *The Anthropology of War: A Bibliography* (New York: Harry Frank Guggenheim Foundation, 1988), p. i.

57. Patrick Wilcken (*Anthropology and the Intellectual in the Gulf War* [Cambridge: Prickly Pear Press, 1994]) makes this point about the role of anthropologists in the Gulf War.

58. Pierre Bourdieu, *Outline of a Theory of Practice*, trans. Richard Nice (Cambridge: Cambridge University Press, 1977), especially pp. 37–38. For comments on ethnography as it pertains to work in the Middle East, see Lila Abu-Lughod, "Zones of Theory in the Anthropology of the Arab World," *Annual Review of Anthropology* 18 (1989): 267–306.

59. See Nicole J. Grant, "From Margaret Mead's Field Notes: What Counted as 'Sex' in Samoa?" *American Anthropologist* 97, no. 4 (1995): 678–82; Derek Freeman, *Margaret Mead and the Heretic* (New York: Penguin, 1996); Lowell Holmes, *Quest for the Real Samoa: The Mead/Freeman Controversy and Beyond* (South Hadley, MA: Bergin & Garvey, 1987); Patrick Tierney, *Darkness in El Dorado: How Scientists and Journalists Devastated the Amazon* (New York: Norton and Norton, 2000); C. S. Mann, "Misconduct Alleged in Yanomamo Studies," *Science* 289 (September 29, 2003): 2252–53; and Brian D. Haley and Larry R. Wilcoxon, "Anthropology and the Making of Chumash Tradition," *Current Anthropology* 38, no. 5 (1997): 761–94.

60. For comments on this nomenclature, see Michael Alan Park, *Biological Anthropology: A Reader* (Mountain View, CA: Mayfield, 1998), p. 1.

61. Irenaus Eibl-Eibesfeldt, *The Biology of Peace and War: Men, Animals, and Aggression* (New York: Viking, 1979).

62. Roy A. Rappaport, *Pigs for the Ancestors: Ritual and Ecology of a New Guinea People*, rev. ed. (New Haven, CT: Yale University Press, 1985).

63. Robert Ardrey, *The Territorial Imperative* (New York: Atheneum, 1966).

64. John H. Hertz, "The Rise and Demise of the Territorial State," *World Politics* 9, no. 4 (July 1957): 473–93.

65. For a comprehensive study, see Jane Goodall, *The Chimpanzees of Gombe: Patterns of Behavior* (Cambridge, MA: Harvard University Press, 1983).

66. See also, Richard Wrangham and Dale Peterson, *Demonic Males: Apes and the Origins of Human Violence* (Boston: Houghton Mifflin, 1996).

67. Ellen J. Ingmanson and Takayoshi Kano, "Waging Peace," in *Biological Anthropology: A Reader*, ed. Park, pp. 8–11.

68. Ibid., p. 11.

69. Craig B. Stanford, "The Social Behavior of Chimpanzees and Bonobos: Empirical Evidence and Shifting Assumptions," *Current Anthropology* 39, no. 4 (1998): 399–420.

70. Gottfried Hohmann and Barbara Fruth, "Culture in Bonobos? Between-Species and Within-Species Variation in Behavior," *Current Anthropology* 44, no. 4 (August–October 2003): 563–71.

71. See David Riches, ed., *The Anthropology of Violence* (Oxford: Blackwell, 1986). For an extension of Riches's model, see Pamela J. Stewart and Andrew Strathern, *Violence: Theory and Ethnography* (New York: Continuum, 2002).

72. Carl von Clausewitz, *On War*, trans. Arnolo Rapoport (London: Penguin, 1968). For the German text, we depend on *Vom Krieg*, ed. Ulrich Marwedel (Stuttgart: Universal-Bibliothek, 1994). For some representative studies of Clausewitz, see Gert de Nooy, *The Clausewitzian Dictum and the Future of Western Military Strategy* (Leiden: Brill, 1997); Peter Paret, *Clausewitz and the State* (New York: Oxford, 1976).

73. Clausewitz, *On War*, p. 17.

74. *On War*, p. 119/*Vom Kriege*, p. 39: "Der Krieg ist eine blosse Forsetzung, der Politik mit andern mitteln." This succinct adage actually occurs as a heading of a section of Clausewitz's book.

75. *On War*, p. 101/*Vom Kriege*, p. 17: "Der Kriege ist auch ein Akt der Gewalt, um der Gegner zur Erfüllung unseres Willens zu zwingen."

76. *On War*, p. 102: *Vom Kriege*, p. 19: "Der Kampf zwischen Menschen besteht eigentlich aus zwei verschiedenen Elementen, dem feindseligen Gefühl und der feindseligen Absicht." My adapted translation, as Rapoport's translation does not repeat properly Clausewitz's use of the adjective "feindseligen."

77. *On War*, p. 103/*Vom Kriege*, p. 19: Dieses [Gemüt] Mehr oder Weniger hängt nicht von dem Grade der Bildung, sondern von der Wichtigkeit und Dauer der feindseligen Interessen ab."

78. Erich Fromm, *The Anatomy of Human Destructiveness* (New York: Holt, 1973).

79. Frederick Adams Woods and Alexander Baltzly, *Is War Diminishing? A Study of the Prevalance of War in Europe from 1450 to the Present Day* (Boston: Houghton Mifflin, 1915).

80. Quincy Wright, *A Study of War*, 2 vols. (Chicago: University of Chicago Press, 1942).

81. For a summary and critique of the COW Project up to the 1980s, see John A. Vasquez, "The Steps to War: Toward a Scientific Explanation of Correlates of War Findings," *World Politics* 40 (October 1987): 108–45.

82. J. David Singer and Melvin Small, *The Wages of War 1816–1965: A Statistical Handbook* (New York: Wiley, 1972), p. 8.

83. For the now numerous examples of these studies, see the COW Web site bibliography, http://www.correlatesofwar.org (accessed February 22, 2005).

84. Singer and Small, *Handbook*, p. 22.

85. J. David Singer and Paul F. Diehl, *Measuring the Correlates of War* (Ann Arbor: University of Michigan Press, 1990), p. ix.

86. See http://www.umich.edu/~cowproj/history.html (accessed June 2, 2004).

87. See Wayman and Singer, "Evolution and Directions," p. 248.

88. Ibid., p. 253.

89. The Behavioral Correlates of War project (BCOW) began in 1970 with the intention of adding behavioral data. See further Russell J. Leng and J. David Singer, "Militarized Interstates Crises: The BCOW Typology and Its Applications," *International Studies Quarterly* 32 (1988): 115–74; reprinted in Singer and Diehl, *Measuring the Correlates of War*, pp. 223–44.

90. See http://www.correlatesofwar.org (accessed February 22, 2005).

91. The study, titled "God and War: An Audit and Exploration," was commissioned by the British Broadcasting Company and can be accessed on the BBC Web site: http://news.bbc.co.uk/2/hi/programmes/wtwtgod/3518375.stm (accessed June 4, 2004). The full article, in PDF format, is found at http://news.bbc.co.uk/1/shared/spl/hi/programmes/wtwtgod/pdf/god_and_war.pdf, and we quote its page numbers.

92. For the text of this inscription, see Miriam Lichtheim, *Ancient Egyptian Literature*, vol. 2, *The New Kingdom* (Berkeley and Los Angeles: University of California Press, 1974), pp. 29–35.

93. Adolf Hitler, *Mein Kampf*, trans. Ralph Manheim (Boston: Houghton Mifflin, 1971), p. 65/German: "So glaube ich heute im Sinne des allmächtigen Schöpfers zu handeln: Indem ich mich des Juden erwehre, kämpfe ich für das Werk des Herrn." Our German text is from *Mein Kampf* (München: Müller, 1936), p. 70. Henceforth, when we quote *Mein Kampf*, we cite this German edition as "German (page number)" after a slash following the citation of the English translation source.

CHAPTER 3

PREVIOUS THEORIES OF RELIGIOUS VIOLENCE

W hile most theories of violence have focused on political, economic, psychological, and other sorts of natural causes, there have been a few notable attempts to link religion and violence. Still fewer focus on explaining the precise mechanism by which religion can result in violence. In this chapter, we comment on some theories that represent important viewpoints, as well as on theorists who have not enjoyed the credit deserved.

RENÉ GIRARD

The work of René Girard on violence cannot be overestimated, at least in the amount of discussion it has aroused. Born in Avignon, France, in 1923, Girard has been most closely associated with Stanford University. His influence towers above that of most theologians and philosophers who have theorized about violence. The basis of Girard's influence in religious studies rests chiefly on his *Violence and the Sacred*, which was first published in 1972.[1] His theories have been widely discussed in biblical studies as well.[2]

Some biblical scholars and scholars of religion have accepted Girard's theories as an advance in our understanding of violence.[3] Others decry Girard's theories as nothing but thinly disguised Christian apologetics. Thus, Marilyn Katz opines, "Girard's theory . . . has not commanded wide acceptance by specialists in the fields of either anthropology or Classics."[4] The anthropologist, Luc de Heusch, for instance, concludes that Girard's theory shows little acquaintance with the practice of sacrifice in many cultures.[5]

Heusch adds that Girard's theory is "is based on a dogmatic bias" and is "a neo-Christian, somewhat heretical theology."[6]

Girard, in general, sees religion as an essential component of humanity. He claims that "of all social institutions, religion is the only one to which science has been unable to attribute a genuine objective, a real function."[7] Moreover, Girard claims that "there is no society without religion because without religion society cannot exist."[8] At the same time, he proclaims that "we are reluctant to admit that violence and the sacred are one and the same thing."[9]

As it pertains to conflict, Girard's initial premise is that "there is ... hardly any form of violence that cannot be described in terms of sacrifice."[10] A society inflicts on a sacrificial victim the violence that would otherwise be turned toward the members of that society. Sacrifice becomes a preventive instrument against violence. Girard believes that religion "invariably strives to subdue violence,"[11] even if it sometimes paradoxically uses violence to end violence.

Girard argues that all sacrificial rituals require two substitutions. A community identifies a victim upon whom it will exhaust its aggression. However, such a victim, being a member of the community, usually is not actually sacrificed. Instead, a ritual or surrogate victim from outside the community substitutes for the original victim, who then represents all the members of the community.[12] For example, in Genesis 22, Abraham is told to sacrifice Isaac. However, Isaac is not sacrificed, and an animal is substituted instead. Isaac is the "insider," and the animal is the "outsider" that substitutes for Isaac. The outsider can also be seen as a monstrous double of the insider victim.

But what causes conflict and the need for sacrifice in the first place? Girard tells us that "rivalry does not arise because of the fortuitous convergence of two desires on a single object; rather *the subject desires the object because the rival desires it.*"[13] This imitating of a desire Girard terms "mimesis." Conflicts arise because people want things *because others want them*. Desire is itself mimetic.

Although Girard's *Violence and the Sacred* does not make many explicit pronouncements about Christianity, his later works declare that Christianity is superior to other traditions in its ability to manage and expose violence. Girard claims that, in contrast to scapegoating in non-Christian "myths," in Christianity the victim is truly innocent, and the persecutors are guilty.[14] Girard adds:

> Our religious tradition [Judeo-Christianity] is more genuinely scientific than our science of mythology. The biblical revelation (exposure) of mythology is no "mystical" insight. It rests on commonsensical observa-

tions. It requires no religious commitment to be understood. This anthropological vindication of the Judeo-Christian tradition is the first and foremost consequence of the mimetic theory."[15]

He predicts that "[i]f and when the Judeo-Christian deconstruction of mythology becomes common knowledge, the whole post-enlightenment culture of naive contempt for our Judeo-Christian heritage will crash to the ground."[16] Girard proclaims the uniqueness of the Hebrew Bible in that there "God sides with the victims against their persecutors."[17] In short, we see Girard revealing himself as a frank apologist for Christianity and the Bible.

While Girard has identified one mechanism of violence and explained how it works, if it is meant to outline the most fundamental mechanisms for religious violence, Girard's theory has numerous flaws. Sacrifice, we hope to show, is a secondary mechanism, not a fundamental one. Religious sacrifice depends on certain prior religious beliefs that have created a need for sacrifice. Any sort of secular sacrifice, moreover, may not always be morally equivalent to religious sacrifice, as we will also show.

Girard's theory also fails in its application to the very biblical texts he seeks to explain on the basis of his theory. He offers a superficial and arbitrary reading of biblical texts. For example, noting that Amos, Isaiah, and Micah denounce the Hebrew sacrificial system, Girard adds that "the eroding of the sacrificial system seems to result in the emergence of reciprocal violence."[18] Such a conclusion is refuted by a mound of evidence. For example, reciprocal violence was enshrined in the Code of Hammurabi, at least a thousand years earlier than these Hebrew prophets.[19] Yet the Code of Hammurabi was thoroughly embedded in a culture that had an extensive sacrificial system.[20] Conversely, some of the most violent episodes described in the Hebrew Bible occur in books (e.g., Deuteronomy 7 and 18) that advocate sacrifice.

Job, as read by Girard, becomes a moral farce. He tells us that "God sides with the victims against their persecutors," and then uses Job as an example.[21] Girard forgets that the narrator says that God allows Satan to torture Job, who is held to be "blameless and upright" (Job 1:1). In Job 2:3, God himself comments to Satan about Job: "He still persists in his integrity, although you incited me against him, to destroy him for no reason." Thus, even God admits he is siding with the torturer against the victim; God admits that he is allowing Job to be tortured "for no reason."[22]

As it pertains to his work on the New Testament, Girard's work has also been criticized by those who otherwise accept the main thrust of his theories. John A. Darr, for example, outlines how, in analyzing the passion narratives, Girard "is clearly attempting to read these Gospels as a monolithic entity, or, in his words, as 'the total' gospel."[23] While Girard tells us that Christ's sacrifice had the effect of "raising humankind once and for all above the culture of scapegoating,"[24] we see Jesus himself vowing to come back to exact revenge upon those that do not follow him (Matt. 25:31–46). In Matthew 10:34–37, Jesus says he comes not to bring peace but a sword, which seems to contradict Girard's supposition about God's purposes. Thus, Girard picks and chooses proof-texts just as the so-called fundamentalists do.

In sum, Girard's theory is neither as novel nor as effective in explaining religious violence as some would think. There may indeed be some cases in which scapegoating provides a good explanation for violence. But we shall argue that Girard misses a more fundamental and persistent mechanism of religious violence. For the same reasons, we do not see the sacrifice of Christ as any sort of acme in dealing with religious violence. Empirically and historically, we will show that the idea of God's sacrifice contributes to more violence rather than the reverse.

In sum, Girard is working with an essentialist paradigm that sees Christianity as the acme of peace and love, concepts that are misunderstood by Girard and many Christian apologists. Girard's reading of the Hebrew and Christian scriptures is idiosyncratic and superficial, not to mention interlaced with unverifiable theological premises. Girard represents simply another Christian apologist seeking to minimize the violent premises on which Christianity is based and to tout Christianity as humankind's greatest achievement.[25]

CHARLES Y. GLOCK AND RODNEY STARK

Some may place the beginning of the modern study of religion and violence with Emile Durkheim's treatise on suicide in 1897.[26] In more recent times, Charles Y. Glock and Rodney Stark have been the pioneers in the study of violence from the perspective of the sociology of religion. In 1966 Glock and Stark published a study, using statistical surveys, on how Christian belief influenced anti-Semitism.[27] The pair saw a correlation between conflict and religious traditions that are "particularistic," meaning "the belief that only one's own religion is legitimate . . . to the particularistic mind there are not faiths, but one true faith."[28] Religious particularism is very likely to result in religious hostility, but it does not necessarily always do so.[29] If there is a causal chain, it is one in which religious dogmatism and religious particularism may result in anti-Semitic beliefs only when other beliefs (e.g., that Jews are responsible for the crucifixion of Jesus) are added to the causal chain.

The work of Glock and Stark brought a much-needed empirical methodology to the study of whether religious beliefs can cause conflict and violence. However, in the end, they substitute other theological terms and premises that underlie conflict because they are not cognizant of how scarce resources are being created by "particularism." By not being cognizant of the linkage between particularism and a scarcity of resources, they themselves fall prey to creating new scarce resources in the search for a solution.

Particularism and exclusivism are only partly causes of violence. All religions have beliefs that others do not, otherwise one would not be able to distinguish one religion from another. Thus, particularism is too ambiguous a term to explain violence. Rather, religion can produce violence when it creates a belief in a scarce resource, a resource that is deemed so valuable that violence is needed to prevent its loss or to acquire it. Such scarce resources may also lead to violence by other rationales, as we shall show more clearly with the belief in the death of Christ.

In addition, Glock and Stark believe that "Christian ethics" are part of the solution to anti-Semitic violence. They conclude that "if the faithful would heed the message 'Love thy neighbor as thyself,' an account such as ours could not have been written."[30] Ironically, Stark, in particular, later became a very vocal advocate for the overall benefits of religion, and of monotheism in particular.[31]

As with other cases, the selection of texts Glock and Stark count as being essential to "Christian ethics" is flawed. By selecting texts that support "Christian ethics" rather than other texts that may say the opposite, Glock and Stark are creating new scarce resources (e.g., a canon within a canon). As we shall show more thoroughly, Glock and Stark also overlook how meaningless and/or flexible the idea and theology of "love" can be in Christianity.

MARTIN MARTY: THE FUNDAMENTALISM PROJECT

Although not specifically attempting to formulate a single theory of religious violence, Martin Marty, as head of the Fundamentalism Project, has helped to frame much of the discussion about the religious violence associated with so-called fundamentalists. The Fundamentalism Project is notable for its attempt to involve an interdisciplinary team that includes sociologists, psychologists, political scientists, and scholars of religion.[32] On the positive side, the project has brought together a wealth of information and interesting case studies illustrating what the authors call "fundamentalism," which Marty defines, in part, as "a strategy or set of strategies, by which beleaguered believers attempt to preserve their distinctive identity as a people or group."[33]

On the other hand, the Fundamentalism Project is permeated by "religionism." Marty does not believe that the unverifiability of religious beliefs is the major problem in religious violence, but rather the violence, for Marty, is mostly due to "fundamentalist" versions of religion. Marty's project also continues the common theme that "fundamentalist violence" is a response to modernity, changing global economics, and shifting political relationships. From a more cynical perspective, this focus on "fundamentalist violence" allows religionists to attempt to retain the value of "religion," while deflecting the more fundamental mechanisms to which all religions are susceptible to some extent.

We do not deny that many Muslim militants are reacting against colonialism or secularization, but our theory argues that such militants do so because modernism and secularization threaten fundamental scarce resources (e.g., salvation, sacred space) that have been manufactured by their Islamic belief system. To see modernity as the main or only factor in Muslim violence, therefore, overlooks more basic mechanisms of religious violence that we see recurring from the beginning of recorded history.

PHIL ZUCKERMAN

An intense and detailed study of a single case of religious conflict can tell us much about the role of social and economic status, even as we must also acknowledge methodological limitations. As we have indicated, sometimes it is difficult to distinguish politics and economics from religious strife. Is economics masquerading as religious conflict, or is religious conflict masquerading as economic conflict? This, of course, was the classic confrontation between Karl Marx and Max Weber. However, there is no reason to deny that both causal chains can be at work in different cases or at different times in a single case, however that is defined.[34]

Phil Zuckerman studied a single, socially homogeneous group of Jews in Willamette, Oregon, noting that "while previous research shows that religious schism is often the result of preexisting nonreligious or nonideological factors, there can be exceptions; sometimes ideological differences are the determining factors in a religious schism."[35] Despite their similar economic and social status, the members of Temple Am Israel, a liberal congregation, became bitterly divided over Zionism and the extent to which the congregation would follow orthodoxy or more liberal forms of Judaism. At the center was Rabbi Moishe Kohner, who advocated Palestinian and gay rights. Although Zuckerman does not use "scarce resource" vocabulary, some of the issues he has identified involve what we call "inscripturation" and "group privileging," which are some of the main scarce resources we will investigate more thoroughly.

TIMOTHY GORRINGE/WALTER STEPHENS

Of particular importance, but still not widely recognized among biblical scholars, is research that shows how specific theological dogmas have generated violence on a smaller scale within societies (as opposed to generating large-scale violence against outsiders as in war). In a magisterial study, Timothy Gorringe has argued that Anselm's theory of the atonement, in particular, had wide influence on violent justice systems in Europe. He notes that the need to hang or torture criminals was never self-evident, and there were often debates about the necessity of such practices. However, when such punishments were upheld, it was often because of allusions to Anselm's theory or New Testament ideas of the atonement. As Gorringe phrases it, "The theology of satisfaction, I contend, provided one of the subtlest and most profound of such justifications, not only for hanging but for retributive justice in general."[36]

In a similar, and perhaps even more fascinating case, Walter Stephens argues that debates about the nature of the Eucharist eventually led to the form of religious violence known as witch-hunting.[37] The Eucharist, an important Catholic sacrament by which a believer partakes of the flesh and blood of Christ, is premised on the idea that the bread and wine transubstantiate, respectively, into the true body and blood of Christ. In the early Middle Ages, not all Catholic theologians believed that transubstantiation was an authentic phenomenon. But belief in transubstantiation eventually became a Catholic orthodox creed promulgated by the Fourth Lateran Council (1215) and reaffirmed at the Council of Trent (1551).

Nonetheless, there was growing skepticism about transubstantiation in the 1400s and 1500s. Orthodox theologians feared that if people could not be convinced that spiritual substances can transubstantiate into material substances, then the belief in the Eucharist itself could be jeopardized. Stephens says, "Witchcraft narratives became necessary because theories of sacramental efficacy were increasingly difficult to believe when stated in the scientific terms of Scholastic theology."[38] Therefore, proving that a spiritual substance could become corporeal became an obsession for orthodox theologians. Sex was regarded as the ultimate proof that spiritual beings such as demons could become corporeal. Religious violence resulted from the attempts to coerce, and even torture, witches into providing such proof of sex with demons. For orthodox witch-hunters, such confessions by witches meant that the Eucharist, and the benefit of Christian salvation, could be preserved. We also hope to link other finer points of Christian theological dogmas with violence.

REGINA M. SCHWARTZ

Regina M. Schwartz, a professor of English and religious studies at Northwestern University, comes closest to articulating our thesis that religion creates scarce resources. Her main book on the subject is the *Curse of Cain* (1997), in which she concentrates on monotheism. She begins by relating her experience teaching a course on the Bible. Schwartz was raised in a Jewish home, but became troubled by the violence in the Bible. She relates her principal discovery as follows: "But why the violence? Why is claiming a distinctive collective identity important enough to spawn violence? I found an answer to this question in a principle of scarcity that pervades most thinking about identity. When everything is in short supply, it must be all competed for—land, prosperity, power, favor, even identity itself."[39] She goes on to observe that: "Scarcity is encoded in the Bible as a principle of Oneness (one land, one people, one nation) and in monotheistic thinking (one Deity), it becomes a demand of exclusive allegiance that threatens with the violence of exclusion."[40]

About a century and half before Schwartz, Arthur Schopenhauer (1788–1860) suggested something similar: "Indeed, intolerance is essential only to monotheism; an only God is by nature a jealous god, who will not allow another to live."[41] Monotheism automatically creates a group of insiders and outsiders: Those who believe in Yahweh are accepted, and those who don't are heterogenized. For Schwartz, the creation of outsiders is itself a violent act.

Needless to say, our entire thesis is built on the conviction that Schwartz is on the right track, despite the pleas made by Diana V. Edelman, among others, for acknowledgment of the existence of "inclusive monotheism"[42]— the idea that sometimes Yahweh, along with other gods, can be seen as variant forms of one supreme deity. If so, it is unclear why we should label this as inclusive monotheism without clearer evidence that other gods were regarded as legitimate variants of one supreme deity.

In some ways, Schwartz continues the idea of Stark and Glock that particularism is responsible for conflict. As she notes, "This book is about violence. It locates the origins of violence in identity formation, arguing that imagining identity as an act of distinguishing and separating from others, of boundary making and line drawing, is the most frequent and fundamental act of violence we commit."[43] But neither Stark nor Glock connect scarcity and competition for resources as part of religion.

Where we differ with Schwartz is in the scope of the scarcity and in arguing that religion—not just monotheism—is fundamentally engaged in the creation of scarce resources. While Schwartz focuses on identity, we elaborate on how scriptures, salvation, and sacred space are scarce resources created by religion, not just by monotheism. More important, we provide an ethical framework to compare religious and nonreligious violence. But we owe a lot to the insights of Schwartz, and the rest of this book can be seen as natural expansion and adaptation of ideas that she has proposed.

POST-SEPTEMBER 11

Since September 11, 2001, there has been renewed attention to the link between religion and violence.[44] In part this reflects the ethnocentrism of Western scholarship. Violence, after all, occurred in monstrous proportions and forms throughout the 1990s, as the genocides of Rwanda and the Balkans readily attest. However, it was September 11 that apparently galvanized the Western academy in renewed attempt to explain the role of religion and violence. Much of this, however, simply reviews and rehearses old platitudes about violence. Here we can do no more than review a few examples that will illustrate the contrast with our secular humanist approach.

At the 2003 Annual Meeting of the American Academy of Religion, two books were singled out for study. One was Marc Gopin's *Holy War, Holy Peace* (2002) and the other was Charles Kimball's *When Religion Becomes Evil* (2002).[45] These books, while useful in many ways, overlook some basic mechanisms by which religion can generate violence. Kimball and Gopin, for all of their insights, continue to legitimize and/or overlook the scarce resources created by religion.

Gopin, for example, suggests that "[g]estures of regret, honor and rededication should be made in every religious space that has been violated in Israel and Palestine. This includes the Dome of the Rock."[46] While such a gesture may provide a short-term solution, it fails to address the more fundamental problem of the creation of the scarce resource called *sacred space*. Gestures of honor, in the long run, simply continue the legitimization of sacred space over which conflict arises in the first place.

Kimball's book draws on the experience of Muslim-Christian relations, in which he is an expert. However, his discussion of scriptures does not address the scarce resource that is created by the very act of inscripturation. His attention, instead, turns to what he deems the abuse of scripture.[47]

Moreover, his effort to bring rapprochement between Abrahamic traditions seems to minimize very real differences in the conception of God by each tradition. Thus, Kimball criticizes American Christian fundamentalists for insisting that "Allah is not the same God."[48] However, this judgment itself presumes that a particular definition of God, in this case a homogenizing one, is the "truest" definition, thus continuing the legitimization of yet another scarce resource ("the true understanding of God").

In both books there are major gaps in attention to theories of violence. Thus Kimball nowhere mentions Schwartz's *The Curse of Cain*, even though Kimball's work is particularly focused on monotheistic traditions. And while acknowledging the problems posed by scriptural warrants for genocide, Gopin cannot seem to admit that scriptures that endorse genocide should receive no more tolerance than what we would expect to grant Nazi textbooks.[49] Neither seems familiar with critiques of other well-known theories such as those of Girard, whose work on scapegoating also cannot explain all types of violence created by religion.

JESSICA STERN

Billed as "the foremost U.S. expert on terrorism," by her publisher, Jessica Stern is a lecturer at the Kennedy School of Government at Harvard University. Her *Terror in the Name of God: Why Religious Militants Kill* (2003) works mainly from the angle of psychology and international relations.[50] The value of her work lies in the detailed interviews she has conducted with terrorists, who tell her some of the reasons why they commit their actions. These interviewees range from former Christian Identity believers (Kerry Noble of the Covenant, Sword and Arm of the Lord) to Muslim militants. She does recognize the importance of territoriality and humiliation as important elements in the motivation of those who commit religious violence. Her portraits provide a vivid reminder of how social ills figure in religious violence.

However, Sterns's view of religion, despite her secularist stance, remains within an essentialist perspective. Thus, one of her final recommendations is that "[w]e should encourage the condemnation of extremist interpretations of religion by peace-loving practitioners."[51] As we shall argue, such a stance fails to see that neither the "peace-loving" nor the "extremist" interpretation is ultimately verifiable. It also overlooks the flexible and relativistic manner in which "peace" is conceived by religions. "Peace" and "love" have consciously entailed violence, from Jesus to bin Laden. Stern fails to see that peace can be simply a code word for hegemony, a description of the conditions in the best interest of the proponent of peace.

MARK JUERGENSMEYER

Mark Juergensmeyer has attempted a global survey of religious violence in his *Terror in the Mind of God: The Global Rise of Religious Violence*, which provides a post–September 11 update of the work first published in 2000.[52] His book is divided into two parts, the first of which catalogues dramatic instances of religious violence ranging from Catholic-Protestant strife in Belfast to the Aum Shinrikyo assault on the Tokyo subway system.

Juergensmeyer's work is notable because he is one of the few scholars who consciously attempt to outline differences between religious and secular violence. He observes, for example, that religious wars may have longer time lines than secular wars; religious violence can be carried indefinitely into the future.[53] He notes that religious violence may be fostered by the certainty that the believer knows the mind of God.[54] Another common trait among religious warriors is the belief that contemporary religions are corrupted and so one must fight for a restoration of the "true" religion. In this respect, Juergensmeyer is close to some of the opinions attributed to Dawkins about "certainty" as a cause for religious conflict (to be discussed below).

However, Juergensmeyer ultimately concludes that much of modern religious violence is a reaction against secularization. Thus, Osama bin Laden is conducting a jihad against the United States, which bin Laden sees as the core of a secularizing empire. Aum Shinrikyo was disillusioned with the better life promised by technology and other purely secular means. If the state is often seen as the enemy of religion, this is because in many ways it is. The post-Enlightenment state has historically tried to confine religion to the private sphere. Consequently, Juergensmeyer concludes that "the cure for religious violence may lie in a renewed appreciation for religion itself."[55]

I ultimately disagree with Juergensmeyer's assessment. While it is true that the feeling of certainty can lead to violence, that is not what is the crucial differentia about religious violence. While Juergensmeyer has rightly alerted us to the fact that much of religion is a reaction against secularism, the fact remains that religious violence occurred long before secularization became an issue in the world. Christians often thought they were replacing a corrupt Judaism, and Islam thought both Christianity and Judaism were corrupt forms of the "true religion." Yet these feelings have little to do with "secularism" or the reaction toward the privatization of religion. Thus, our theory aims to provide a more fundamental mechanism for religious violence that both transcends and can explain reactions to specific circumstances such as "secularism."

J. HAROLD ELLENS

To date, the most voluminous treatment of violence and religion in the post–September 11 period is *The Destructive Power of Religion* (2004), edited by J. Harold Ellens, who is trained primarily in biblical studies and in ancient Near Eastern languages.[56] Ellens is a retired Presbyterian theologian and US Army colonel, as well as a licensed psychotherapist. The book is a collection of articles, a few of which were previously published, authored by prominent biblical scholars and scholars from a variety of areas.

Despite the title, the four volumes of *The Destructive Power of Religion* are described by Desmond Tutu, who wrote the preface, as being "urgent in their emphasis upon the positive power-religions' power for healing and redemption of personal and worldwide suffering and perplexity—as they are boldly setting forth the destructive side."[57] Likewise, Ellens tells us that despite the violence found in sacred texts, "the real God is a God of unconditional grace—the only thing that works in life, for God or for humans."[58]

In actuality, the essays do not have a consistent theory of violence. Ellens himself seems to favor a sort of Jungian approach in which the main root of violence is a view of a cosmic struggle between good and evil. His answer is that this "root hypothesis is erroneous. There is no reason to claim that there is such a thing as ontological evil in the world, and there is no evidence for a transcendental cosmic conflict."[59]

As we shall show in more detail later, scholars such as Ellens represent the continuation of an apologetic approach to religious violence. Religious violence is acknowledged but seen as unrepresentative, while "the real God" is described as being distorted by the human portrayal of violence. As we shall show, all religious viewpoints about the role of religion in violence perpetuate or endorse the very fundamental elements that create the violence; otherwise they do not recognize the elements that are responsible for the violence. In this case, speaking of "the real God" is simply trading one hegemonic view of God for another, with neither being verifiable.

SUMMARY

Our broad survey, as incomplete as it is, should demonstrate that a variety of factors have prevented natural scientists, social scientists, and scholars of religion from appreciating how religion can create new scarce resources. Regina Schwartz, who is primarily a scholar of English, has perhaps been more insightful than a mass of scholars of religion who still view religion as "essentially" good, and violence as a deviation of it. Even skeptics such as Michael

Shermer seem to have uncritically assimilated the benign views of religion advocated by religionists. If a new theory of religious violence is to be successful, it will have to directly address the deeply entrenched view that "true" religion is primarily designed for peaceful and altruistic purposes.

NOTES

1. René Girard, *Violence and the Sacred*, trans. Patrick Gregory (Baltimore: Johns Hopkins University Press, 1977); the original French text is from *La violence et le sacré* (Paris: Bernard Grasset, 1972).

2. For Girard's impact on biblical studies, see Andrew J. McKenna, ed., "René Girard and Biblical Studies," *Semeia* 33 (1985); Robert North, "Violence and the Bible: The Girard Connection," *CBQ* 47 (1985): 1–27; and Hans J. L. Jensen, "Desire, Rivalry and Collective Violence in the 'Succession Narrative'" *Journal for the Study of the Old Testament* 55 (1992): 39–59.

3. For an example of acceptance, see Ted Grimsrud, "Scapegoating No More: Christian Pacifism and New Testament Views of Jesus' Death," in *Violence Renounced: René Girard, Biblical Studies and Peacemaking*, ed. Willard M. Swartley (Telford, PA: Pandora Press; Scottdale, PA: Herald Press, 2000), pp. 49–69. A feminist perspective that integrates Girardian theory may be found in Tina Pippin, *Death and Desire: The Rhetoric of Gender in the Apocalypse* (Louisville, KY: Westminster/John Knox, 1992). See also P. J. Watson, "Girard and Integration: Desire, Violence, and the Mimesis of Christ as Foundation for Postmodernity," *Journal of Psychology and Religion* 26, no. 4 (1998): 311–21.

4. Marilyn A. Katz, "Problems of Sacrifice in Ancient Cultures," in *The Bible in Light of Cuneiform Literature*, ed. William W. Hallo, Bruce Williams Jones, and Gerald L. Mattingly, Scriptures in Context III (Lewiston, NY: Edwin Mellen Press, 1990), p. 97. See also Luc de Heusch, *Sacrifice in Africa: A Structuralist Approach*, trans. Linda O'Brien and Alice Morton (Bloomington: Indiana University Press, 1985), pp. 15, 17.

5. Heusch, *Sacrifice in Africa*, pp. 16–17.

6. Ibid.

7. Girard, *Violence and the Sacred*, p. 92/*La violence*, p. 135: "De toutes les intitutions sociales, la religieux est la seule à laquelle la science n'a jamais réussi à attribuer un objet réel, une fonction veritable."

8. Girard, *Violence and the Sacred*, p. 221; *La violence*, p. 303: "Il n'y a pas de société sans religion parce que sans religion aucune société ne serait possible."

9. Girard, *Violence and the Sacred*, p. 262/ *La violence*, p. 363: "Nous répugnons à admettre l'identité de la violence et du sacré."

10. Girard, *Violence and the Sacred*, p. 1; *La violence*, p. 1: "N'y a guère de violence . . . qui ne puisse se décrire en termes de sacrifice."

11. Girard, *Violence and the Sacred*, p. 20/*La violence*, p. 38: "Le religieux vise toujours à apaiser la violence."

12. Girard, *Violence and the Sacred*, p. 102.

13. Ibid., p. 145, Girard's emphasis; *La violence*, p. 204: "La rivalité n'est pas le fruit d'une convergence accidentelle des deux désirs sur le même objet. *Le sujet désire l'objet parce que le rival lui-même le désire.*"

14. René Girard, "Violence Renounced: Response by René Girard" in *Violence Renounced*, ed. Willard M. Swartley (Telford, PA: Pandora Press; Scottdale, PA: Herald Press, 2000), pp. 312–13.

15. Ibid., p. 313.

16. Ibid., p. 314.

17. Ibid., p. 319.

18. Girard, *Violence and the Sacred*, p. 43; *La violence*, p. 68: "L'usure du système sacrificiel apparaît toujours comme une chute dans la violence réciproque."

19. For comments on the Code of Hammurabi, see Jean Bottéro, *Mesopotamia: Writing, Reasoning, and the Gods*, trans. Zainab Bahrani and Marc van de Mieroop (Chicago: University of Chicago Press, 1992), pp. 156–84. The Code of Hammurabi has laws that endorse reciprocal injury (Laws 196–205) together with a preamble that touts the value of pure sacrifices (*zibi ellutim*). For an edition and translation of the Code of Hammurabi, see G. R. Driver and John C. Miles, eds., *The Babylonian Laws* (Oxford: Clarendon, 1955).

20. For a critique of Girard that integrates data from Mesopotamia, see Katz, "Problems of Sacrifice in Ancient Cultures," pp. 89–201.

21. Girard, "Violence Renounced," p. 319. See also René Girard, *Job: The Victim of His People*, trans. Yvonne Freccero (Stanford, CA: Stanford University Press, 1987).

22. For a sympathetic treatment of Girard's view of Job, see Baruch Levine, "René Girard and Job: The Question of the Scapegoat," *Semeia* 33 (1985): 125–33.

23. John A. Darr, "Mimetic Desire, The Gospels, and Early Christianity," *Biblical Interpretation* 1, no. 3 (1993): 362.

24. Girard, "Violence Renounced," p. 319.

25. Other assessments of Girard include Hent de Vries, *Religion and Violence: Philosophical Perspectives from Kant to Derrida* (Baltimore: Johns Hopkins University Press, 2002), which some may find to be more permeated by philosophical rhetoric than by historical applications.

26. See William Sims Bainbridge and Rodney Stark, "Suicide, Homicide, and Religion: Durkheim Reassessed," *Annual Review of the Social Sciences of Religion* 5 (1981): 33–56.

27. Charles Y. Glock and Rodney Stark, *Christian Belief and Anti-Semitism* (New York: Harper and Row, 1966).

28. Ibid., p. 20.

29. Ibid., p. 21.

30. Ibid., p. 212.

31. Rodney Stark, *One True God: Historical Consequences of Monotheism* (Princeton, NJ: Princeton University Press, 2001).

32. For a recent entry, see, Gabriel A. Almond, R. Scott Appleby, and Emmanuel Sivan, *Strong Religion: The Rise of Fundamentalisms around the World* (Chicago: University of Chicago Press, 2002). For the complete set, see Martin E. Marty and R. Scott Appleby, *The Fundamentalism Project*, 5 vols. (Chicago: University of Chicago Press, 1991–95).

33. Marty and Appleby, "Introduction," in *The Fundamentalism Project*, vol. 3, *Fundamentalisms and the State: Remaking Polities, Economies, and Militance*, p. 3.

34. See further M. Chaves and F. Kniss, "Analyzing Interdenominational Conflict: New Directions," *Journal for the Scientific Study of Religion* 34 (1995): 172–85.

35. Phil Zuckerman, *Strife in the Sanctuary: Religious Schism in a Jewish Community* (Walnut Creek, CA: Alta Mira Press, 1999), p. 230.

36. Timothy Gorringe, *God's Just Vengeance: Crime, Violence, and the Rhetoric of Salvation* (Cambridge: Cambridge University Press, 1996), p. 12.

37. Walter Stephens, *Demon Lovers: Witchcraft, Sex, and the Crisis of Belief* (Chicago: University of Chicago Press, 2002).

38. Ibid., p. 237.

39. Schwartz, *The Curse of Cain*, p. xi.

40. Ibid.

41. Arthur Schopenhauer, *Parerga and Paralipomena*, 2:15. For an English edition, see Arthur Schopenhauer, *Parerga and Paralipomena: Short Philosophical Essays*, trans. E. F. J. Payne, 2 vols. (Oxford: Clarendon, 1974), 2:358. For a German edition, see Arthur Hübscher, ed., *Arthur Schopenhauer: Sämtliche Werke*, 2 vols. (Wiesbaden: Brockhaus, 1966), 2:380: "In der Tat ist Intoleranz nur dem Monotheismus wesentlich; ein alleiniger Gott ist, seiner Natur noch ein eifersüchtiger Gott, der keinem andern das Leben gönnt."

42. See Diana V. Edelman, *The Triumph of Elohim: From Yahwisms to Judaisms* (Grand Rapids, MI: Eerdmans, 1996), pp. 24–25. For a more modern, though still mystical, and benign conception of monotheism, see Ellis Rivkin, *The Unity Principle: The Shaping of Jewish History* (Springfield, NJ: Behrman House, 2003).

43. Schwartz, *Curse of Cain*, p. 5.

44. See, for example, Bruce Lincoln, *Holy Terrors: Thinking about Religion after September 11* (Chicago: University of Chicago Press, 2003).

45. Marc Gopin, *Holy War, Holy Peace: How Religion Can Bring Peace to the Middle East* (New York: Oxford University Press, 2002); and Charles Kimball, *When Religion Becomes Evil* (San Francisco: HarperSanFrancisco, 2002).

46. Gopin, *Holy War, Holy Peace*, p. 191.

47. Kimball, *When Religion Becomes Evil*, pp. 52–53.

48. Ibid., p. 58.

49. For Gopin's discussion of scriptural problems, see *Holy War, Holy Peace*, pp. 70–71.

50. Jessica Stern, *Terror in the Name of God: Why Religious Militants Kill* (New York: HarperCollins, 2003).

51. Ibid., p. 296.

52. Mark Juergensmeyer, *Terror in the Mind of God: The Global Rise of Religious Violence* (Berkeley and Los Angeles: University of California Press, 2001). Juergensmeyer provides a pedagogical angle to his theory of religious violence in "Teaching about Religious Violence without Trivializing It," *Religious Studies News: Spotlight on Teaching* 18, no. 4 (October 2003): ii.

53. Ibid., p. 217.

54. Ibid., p. 219.

55. Ibid., p. 243.

56. J. Harold Ellens, ed., *The Destructive Power of Religion: Violence in Judaism, Christianity and Islam*, 4 vols. (Westport, CT: Praeger, 2004).

57. Ibid., 1:xvi.

58. Ibid., 1:xix.

59. Ibid., 1:8.

PART 2

A NEW THEORY OF RELIGIOUS VIOLENCE EXEMPLIFIED IN THE ABRAHAMIC RELIGIONS

The best general theories should be confirmed by broad and consistent results. Part 2 shows how our theory of scarce resources can be applied systematically to the so-called Abrahamic religions (Judaism, Christianity, and Islam), one of the largest complexes of religions that has ever existed. In particular, we illustrate how four main scarce resources (inscripturation, sacred space, group privileging, and salvation) have repeatedly generated violence from the earliest records of these religions to the present. We show that seemingly benign terms such as "peace" and "love" can have violent, hegemonic, and imperialistic features in all of the Abrahamic religions. Overall, Part 2 is a broad indictment of academic scholars who minimize or strive to maintain, through questionable hermeneutic strategies, the value of the Abrahamic religions despite the endorsement of violence in the foundational texts of these religions.

CHAPTER 4

SCARCE RESOURCE THEORY AND VIOLENCE

GENERAL OBSERVATIONS

Most of the explanations for violence that we have considered contain elements of scarce resource theory, which is defined here simply as the theory that scarce resources, real or perceived, are a major factor in violence. Religious theories of violence are still permeated by the idea that religion is essentially good, and that violence is a deviation. Regina Schwartz is among the few who recognize that scarcity is a key, but she restricts its influence to monotheism. Accordingly, here we establish the theoretical grounds for expanding the idea of scarcity to major components of religion. However, we provide first a more coherent history of the idea that scarce resources cause violence.

The idea that scarce resources are involved in violence is actually not so much new as it is simply undeveloped and implicit. In fact, scarcity is quite a common biblical theme, though one not often appreciated by biblical scholars. In Genesis 2–3, which relates the story of the first couple in the Garden of Eden, the god Yahweh Elohim purposely makes knowledge and eternal life scarce resources. Yahweh Elohim allows Adam and Eve to eat of any tree in the garden, except of the tree of knowledge of good and evil. In fact, Yahweh Elohim tells Adam and Eve that they will die "on the day" that they eat of the fruit from that tree (Gen. 2:17).

In chapter 3 a talking serpent tells Eve that Yahweh Elohim is lying. Indeed, Adam and Eve do not die "on the day" they eat of the tree. But, more important, Yahweh fears that the human couple will also now eat of the tree that provides an even scarcer resource, eternal life. The biblical author then explains why Yahweh Elohim must eject humans from the Garden of Eden:

Then the LORD God said, "See, the man has become like one of us, knowing good and evil; and now, he might reach out his hand and take also from the tree of life, and eat, and live forever"—

therefore the LORD God sent him forth from the garden of Eden, to till the ground from which he was taken. (Gen. 3:22–23)

The import of the story, often missed even by savvy readers, is difficult to understand without some knowledge of Near Eastern religions. In Near Eastern religions, immortality was one main feature that distinguished gods and human beings. Yahweh Elohim does not want human beings to have eternal life. It is a scarce resource, and seeking it caused of the Fall of humankind. Violence, in fact, is said to be one of the consequences, as the deity predicts enmity between the serpent and womankind, and prescribes pain for the woman on childbearing (Gen. 3:16). In this case, it is the deity, Yahweh Elohim, who is portrayed as defending and laboring to maintain the scarce resources of knowledge and eternal life for himself and his divine retinue.

Genesis also has a more transparent example in the story of Abraham and his nephew Lot. Abraham is an immigrant to the land of Canaan, which would later be given to his descendants. Abraham goes to Egypt, and returns with an increased amount of animals. However, the narrator says:

Now Lot, who went with Abram, also had flocks and herds and tents,

so that the land could not support both of them living together; for their possessions were so great that they could not live together,

and there was strife between the herders of Abram's livestock and the herders of Lot's livestock. At that time the Canaanites and the Perizzites lived in the land. (Gen. 13:5–7)

Thus, the biblical author makes a direct correlation between the scarcity of resources and the consequent strife between Abraham and Lot. We need not multiply many other examples to show that scarce resources were seen as a cause of conflict at least as far back as biblical times.

Likewise, in Islamic sources, we find hints that violence was caused by competition for valuable resources. On one occasion, it is reported that a tax collector brought a gift to Muhammad's community. Muhammad replied, "I am not afraid of your poverty but I am afraid that you will lead a life of luxury as past nations did, whereupon you will fight with each other for it [*fa-tanāfasū-hā*], as they fought for it, and it will destroy you as it destroyed them."[1] Thus, there seemed to be the recognition that desire for something will cause conflict.

MALTHUS AND SCARCE RESOURCES

The modern father of scarce resource theory is probably Thomas Malthus (1766–1834), author of *An Essay on the Principle of Population*, the first version of which appeared anonymously in 1798.[2] Malthus's essay is a protestation against the idea that human beings could live in a perfected state. He notes that from the earliest times, there has been a "prodigious waste of human life occasioned by this perpetual struggle for room and food."[3] Indeed, for Malthus, the world simply does not have enough resources to supply a growing population. This scarcity results in conflict.

Karl Marx criticized Malthus for offering "nothing more than a school-boyish, superficial plagiary of DeFoe" and other predecessors.[4] Later, Esther Boserup mounted a more formidable challenge to Malthus by claiming that scarcity sometimes drives increased production and cooperation to meet the challenge of scarce resources.[5] But Malthus, even if not completely original, exerted a great influence on modern thought.[6] In spite of Boserup and many other attempts to defeat Malthus's views, the ideas he represents have not disappeared.[7]

In fact, scarce resource theory has recrystallized beginning in the 1960s and 1970s. During the 1960s environmental studies pioneers Harold and Margaret Sprout contended that "most, if not all, human activity is affected by the uneven distribution of resources."[8] These sorts of studies continued into the 1990s. For example, in a brief survey of conflicts around the world, David Bishop and colleagues concluded that "there are significant causal links between scarcities of renewable resources and violence."[9]

Our discussion of the COW Project has shown that it is very difficult to identify general causes for war. Perhaps the strongest correlation, however, centers on scarce resources. A crosscultural survey completed by Melvin and Carol R. Ember concludes: "Bivariate test-results suggest an ecological explanation of war: Resource problems, particularly nonchronic resource problems created by aperiodic natural disasters, predict more war."[10] The Embers add that "fear of unpredictable scarcity may be more of a motive to go to war than known or expected scarcity."[11] So while the Embers still see fear as the common thread, there is no doubt that fear about scarce resources forms a strong motivator for violence.

As in the case of biological explanations of violence, territoriality has been of great importance in anthropological explanations. Rada Dyson-Hudson and Eric Alden Smith have attempted to develop a nuanced model of territoriality that takes into account resource density and resource predictability.[12] "Resource density" refers to the amount of a resource available per unit area, while "resource predictability" refers to the expectation that a resource will be available at particular times and places. Dyson-Hudson and

Smith believe that there is a correlation in the extent to which at least small groups of hunter-gatherers will be mobile or more territorial. In particular, they see a high degree of territoriality when both resource density and resource predictability are high; in that situation, territory becomes worth defending.

What this also means is that humans make choices about the value of space. As it relates to our theory, we also concur that people make choices about what spaces to defend. However, in the case of spaces whose value is purely religious, there are no verifiable reasons why the space should be valuable. That is to say, sometimes spaces devoid of any resources or possessing few resources become valuable. Territoriality here is difficult to explain on the basis of density of natural resources or predictability. We suggest that religion can create value that is just as powerful as any natural resource.

While many researchers blame the rise of the nationalistic state for war, there is much evidence that scarce resources are a more constant predictor of war, and that prestate wars may have been worse by different measures. Ember and Ember conclude that "where we have detailed information on the number of people killed over time, it appears that 'primitive' warfare might have been even more lethal *proportionately* than modern warfare."[13] Similarly, Steven LeBlanc provides a survey of conflicts among prehistoric and non-industrialized peoples ranging from the Mimbres culture of New Mexico to the people of New Guinea. LeBlanc concludes that all the conflicts he detected could be reduced to a single factor: "[P]eople seemed to be fighting over scarce resources."[14]

Scarce resources, whether expressed in Malthusian terms or in terms of other factors, is a powerful explanation for conflict. Today a Malthusian perspective is probably best represented in the work of Amartya Sen, the 1998 recipient of the Nobel Prize in Economics, which shows in great detail how food scarcities, in particular, result in conflict.[15] What is missing from the work of Malthus and Sen, not surprisingly, is that they do not see religion as a factor in creating new scarce resources.

SCARCITY IN THE FAMILY UNIT

Scarcity can be found at all levels of human organization. For example, consider the family, the smallest unit of human organization. Conflicts in the family can be varied in quality and quantity, and studies of families have recognized at least since the 1960s and 1970s that almost any aspect of family life can become a scarce resource. Many researchers of the family have explicitly used "resources" terminology in the study of conflict within the family.[16]

Power and status are two resources that are usually unevenly distributed in a family, thus causing conflict.[17] Birth order itself is a unique commodity that can create conflict.[18] The firstborn is often either privileged or burdened with responsibilities that subsequent siblings may not have. Conflict may ensue because younger siblings may resent the privileged status of the first-born. On the other hand, the firstborn may resent the responsibilities that go along with that birth position.

Divorce, of course, is a more final result of conflict between married couples. Competition between spouses may be the result of a scarce resource we call "status" or "privilege." Equality itself may be a scarce resource because it is not available in sufficient amounts, whether as a perception or as a reality. Where child custody is involved, time with the affected children may become a scarce resource, especially for the noncustodial parent.[19]

SCARCITY AT THE GROUP/NATIONAL SCALE

On a suprafamilial scale, scarce resources can result in conflict within and between groups. Criminologists have noted the importance of scarce resources in violent behavior in larger social units. Jack Levin and Gordana Rabrenovic are two researchers who have indeed turned their attention to religion.[20] One of their more relevant observations relates to an experiment performed in 1961 by Muzafer and Carolyn Sherif. These researchers separated boys of eleven and twelve years of age into two different groups in a summer camp after a period of undivided interaction. The researchers noted that aggression increased when the two groups participated in competitive games, including football and a treasure hunt. Levin and Rabrenovic conclude that "[w]hen the advantages of one group depend on the subordination of another group, then we might expect that intergroup competition will turn ugly. Thus, discrimination may have an economic basis, occurring when the members of one group seek to secure a larger share of the scarce resources of their society."[21]

We agree with this assessment if "economic" can also include rewards and losses that are believed to exist even if they do not. We contend that it is this sort of competition for scarce resources created by religion that is the key to understanding religious violence.

Ethnic conflicts have also been understood in terms of scarce resource theory. In a wide-ranging study of ethnic conflicts in Africa, Eastern Europe, and other parts of the globe, David Lake and Donald Rothchild conclude that "competition for scarce resources lies at the heart of ethnic conflict."[22] However, they also caution that competition for scarce resources is not always a sufficient cause for violence. Violence itself is costly, after all. What Lake and Rothchild miss, however, is the extent to which religion can "pay off." Indeed, they are thinking only of material and social benefits and costs, but religion offers transcendent benefits that can make violence appear profitable for ethnic groups.

Likewise, Lauren McLaren's study of immigration in Europe finds a strong link between anti-immigrant feelings and fear of losing valued resources.[23] As she notes, "the feeling of threat may relate to the resources of a group as a whole."[24] But McLaren's research also shows that researchers do not recognize other entities as constituting scarce resources. Thus, she classifies two types of threats found among those with anti-immigrant sentiments: (1) economic/status-based threats, and (2) cultural/symbolic threats. She labels the first "resource-based group level threats," and the second as "more symbolic or cultural threats," which can include religion and "way of life."[25] Both groups consist of resources in the sense of an entity that is considered useful for life; religion can be a resource that immigrants may be perceived to threaten.

We need little demonstration to see that national resources such as water, cultivable land, and energy supplies can cause conflict. Land disputes have been at the heart of many wars between nations in almost every part of the world. Within nations, water and cultivable land can create regional disputes, as in the western United States, where water from the Colorado River has figured in conflicts, even if not all outwardly violent.[26]

SCARCITY AT A GLOBAL SCALE

No one who has studied the field of international relations can escape the observation that scarcity drives much conflict on a global scale.[27] Studies that are adopting the "resource" nomenclature are beginning to appear with more frequency. Witness Michael Klare's *Resource Wars: The New Landscape of Global Conflict* (2002).[28] Not all nations have the same resources: Some do not have much cultivable land, while others lack significant oil reserves to meet their needs or wants.

It is important to note that almost any resource can be interpreted as scarce in almost any conflict. Stephen Van Evera, for instance, argues that "international politics is more competitive, hence more violent, when resources are more cumulative."[29] At first this would seem to refute our thesis about scarcity as a cause for conflict. However, one can see that "security of accumulated resources" itself is seen as a scarce resource over which conflict can ensue. Thus, even when one has accumulated a lot of resource

X, people can perceive that there is not enough security about resource X, and so security itself becomes the scarce resource.

Historically, fighting over resources on a global scale may be said to have begun with the arrival of the Europeans in the Americas, after which there was truly global interaction for the first time in human history.[30] The whole of these global power relations can be subsumed under the name "geopolitics," popularized by the Swedish geographer Rudolf Kjellen (1864–1922). During the late nineteenth century, territorial acquisition came to be seen frankly as a main obligation of states that were constantly searching for Lebensraum. Led by Friedrich Ratzel (1844–1904), many political theorists agreed that the unending search for living space was the constant factor in human conflict.[31] Nicholas Spykman (1893–1943), the famed professor of international relations at Yale University, viewed boundaries as temporary markers of expansion.[32]

Halford J. Mackinder (1861–1947) sought to interpret history as a struggle between sea power and land power. He was responding, in part, to Alfred Mahan (1840–1914), who claimed that the control of the sea was key to power. Mackinder rejoined with a dictum that was short-lived and refutable, but yet memorable:

- He who rules East Europe commands the Heartland,
- Who rules the Heartland commands the World Island (Eurasia),
- Who rules the World Island commands the World.[33]

This sort of rationale was an important factor in driving Nazi Germany's quest for domination of Russia. Eventually, nuclear weapons rendered the value of large territory for purely defensive purpose a moot commodity.

Accordingly, some recent theorists have moved from speaking of terracentric strategies to astrocentric strategies, in which space is the resource whose control determines control of the planet. The militarization of space has been a consequence of seeing space—or at least the ability to work in space—as a precious and scarce resource. Some, of course, credit Ronald Reagan's Strategic Defense Initiative (Star Wars) proposal as contributing to the fall of the Soviet Union. The expense required for acquisition of the scarce resource that may be considered the "ultimate defense" may have proven too costly for the Soviets.

Yet for all the talk about space, much of the current global conflict is not centered on terracentric or astrocentric resources. Rather, they are subterranean resources, most notably fossil fuels such as coal and oil. The latter, of course, has been the prime factor in many explanations for the 1991 conflict in the Middle East. Some researchers make the connection explicitly, for example, Stephen C. Pelletière's *Iraq and the International Oil System: Why*

America Went to War in the Gulf.[34] As we shall show, religion has created other scarcities in the Middle East that are every bit as powerful as oil.

SUMMARY

The idea that insufficiency is a major, if not the main, cause of conflict is not new. Whenever there is not enough of something that is valued, conflict is the likely result. We have demonstrated how such scarcities are related to conflict from the smallest social units to the largest sociopolitical entities. And while a broad spectrum of researchers see the importance of scarcities, none of them seems to appreciate fully how religion can create scarce resources over which conflict can occur.

What unites all of these scarcities, even those that are human-made, is that they exist or can exist. That is to say, available quantities of oil can really be insufficient to meet the needs or wants of people. Love and justice can really be insufficient in a family. But these scarcities differ in important ways from scarcities that are precipitated by religion. Those differences, we shall argue, render religion a more tragic source of violence. We shall now turn to explain the nature of these scarcities created by religion in more detail.

NOTES

1. Al-Bukhari, 3158/Book of Al-Jizya, 1/Darussalem Edition, 4.242. My translation of *tanāfasū-hā*. Dr. Khan's translation is "compete with each other for it." The sixth form of the verb *nafusa* can have either meaning, and others beside.

2. Thomas Malthus, *An Essay on the Principle of Population*, ed. Antony Flew (London: Penguin, 1970).

3. Ibid., p. 84.

4. Karl Marx, *Capital*, bk. 1, as extracted in *Karl Marx and Friedrich Engels on Religion* (New York: Schocken Books, 1964), p. 137.

5. Esther Boserup, *The Conditions of Agricultural Growth* (Chicago: Aldine, 1965).

6. A scathing critique of Malthus's originality may be found in Karl Marx's *Das Kapital*, bk. 1, as extracted in *Karl Marx and Friedrich Engels on Religion*, pp. 137–41.

7. For example, Lester R. Brown, Gary Gardner, and Brian Halweil, *Beyond Malthus: Nineteen Dimensions of the Population Challenge* (New York: W. W. Norton, 1999).

8. Harold Sprout and Margaret Sprout, *An Ecological Paradigm for the Study of International Politics* (Princeton, NJ: Center for International Studies, 1968). See also David Novick, *A World of Scarcities: Critical Issues in Public Policy* (London: Associate Business Programs, 1976), written in the aftermath of the Arab oil embargo.

9. David J. Bishop, F. Homer-Dixon, Jeffrey H. Boutwell, and George Rathjens, "Environmental Change and Violent Conflict," *Scientific American* 268, no. 2 (February 1993): 38–45.

10. Melvin Ember and Carol R. Ember, "Cross-Cultural Studies of War and Peace: Recent Achievements and Future Possibilities," in *Studying War: Anthropological Perspectives*, ed. S. P. Reyna and R. E. Downs (Amsterdam: Gordon and Breach, 1996), p. 190.

11. Ibid.

12. Rada Dyson-Hudson and Eric Alden Smith, "Human Territoriality: An Ecological Reassessment," *American Anthropologist* 80, no. 1 (1978): 21–41.

13. Ember and Ember, "Cross-Cultural Studies of War and Peace," p. 190.

14. Steven A. LeBlanc with Katherine E. Register, *Constant Battles: The Myth of the Peaceful, Noble Savage* (New York: St. Martin's, 2003), p. 9. For the use of mathematical models to explore the relationship between scarce resources and conflict, see John W. Maxwell and Rafael Reuveny,"Resource Scarcity and Conflict in Developing Countries," *Journal of Peace Research* 37, no. 3 (2000): 301–22.

15. See Amartya Sen, *Poverty and Famines: An Essay on Entitlement and Deprivation* (Oxford: Clarendon, 1981); and *The Political Economy of Hunger* (Oxford: Clarendon, 1995).

16. For one example, see H. Rodman, "Marital Power and the Theory of Resources in Cultural Context," *Journal of Comparative Family Studies* 3 (1972): 59–69.

17. Liat Kulik, "Equality in Marriage, Marital Satisfaction, and Life Satisfaction: A Comparative Analysis of Preretired and Retired Men and Women in Israel," *Families in Society: The Journal of Contemporary Human Services* 83, no. 2 (2002): 197–207; S. Beckman-Brindley and J. B. Tavormina, "Power Relationships in Families: A Social-Exchange Perspective," *Family Process* 17 (1978): 423–36.

18. Frank J. Sulloway, *Born to Rebel: Birth Order, Family Dynamics, and Creative Lives* (New York: Pantheon, 1997).

19. Ron Lehr and Peter MacMillan, "The Psychological and Emotional Impact of Divorce: The Noncustodial Fathers' Perspective," *Families in Society: The Journal of Contemporary Human Services* 82, no. 4 (2001): 373–82.

20. Jack Levin and Gordana Rabrenovic, *Why We Hate* (Amherst, NY: Prometheus Books, 2004).

21. Ibid., pp. 127–28.

22. David A. Lake and Donald Rothchild, "Containing Fear: The Origins and Management of Ethnic Conflict," *International Security* 21, no. 2 (Fall 1996): 41–75.

23. Lauren M. McLaren, "Anti-immigrant Prejudice in Europe," *Social Forces* 81, no. 3 (March 2003): 909–36.

24. Ibid., p. 918.

25. Ibid., p. 919.

26. For specific examples involving water, see Oregon State University's Transboundary Freshwater Dispute Database at http://www.transboundarywaters.orst.edu.

27. My discussion in this section is dependent on James E. Doughtery and Robert L. Pfaltzgraff Jr., *Contending Theories of International Relations: A Comprehensive Survey* (New York: Longman, 2001), especially pp. 188–230.

28. Michael Klare, *Resource Wars: The New Landscape of Global Conflict* (New York: Owl Books, 2002).

29. Stephen Van Evera, *Causes of War: Power and the Roots of Conflict* (Ithaca, NY: Cornell University Press, 1999), p. 108.

30. See Paul Kennedy, *The Rise and Fall of the Great Powers: Economic Change and Military Conflict from 1500 to 2000* (New York: Random House, 1987); and Immanuel Wallerstein, *The Modern World System*, 3 vols. (New York and San Diego: Academic, 1974–1989).

31. Friedrich Ratzel, *Anthropogeographie*, 2nd ed. (Stuttgart: J. Engelhorn, 1899), especially part 1, p. 2.

32. Nicholas J. Spykman, *The Geography of Peace* (New York: Harcourt, Brace, 1944).

33. See Halford Mackinder, *Democratic Ideals and Reality* (New York: Norton, [1962]), p. 150.

34. Stephen C. Pelletière, *Iraq and the International Oil System: Why America Went to War in the Gulf* (Washington, DC: Maisonneuve, 2004).

CHAPTER 5

HOW RELIGION CREATES SCARCE RESOURCES

*R*eligion is defined here as a mode of life and thought that presupposes the existence of, and a relationship with, supernatural forces and/or beings. Thus, our definition encompasses both those traditions that believe in a personal deity or those that do not or claim not to have such a belief (e.g., some varieties of Buddhism). As we have argued previously, we espouse a frank empirico-rationalist and naturalistic approach to religion. Religion can be explained on the basis of natural phenomena.

Believers often use the term "supernatural" to signify something that is beyond nature. In actuality, the term is meaningless, as we cannot know what something beyond nature would be. If we define "natural" as that which is detectable by one or more of the five senses and/or logic, then the supernatural must be unknown or unknowable. If we could detect it, it would be natural, not supernatural. If it is not natural, then it is nothing more than a concept whose reality cannot be verified. It is as meaningless as speaking of X without further specification of how we could identify X.

Since religion is based on belief in the existence of supernatural beings, it follows that religion is working from unverifiable premises or conclusions when it speaks of the supernatural. That is to say, we cannot verify the existence of anything supernatural. Thus, religious beliefs cannot be subject to public scrutiny, even if they often claim to be based on empirical evidence.

However, as with scarcities that are real, the scarcities generated by religion require only belief in them in order to "exist." And as with real scarcities, the competition for the scarce resource can cause conflict when the competitors feel that loss of control of the scarce resource will somehow threaten their well-being. For example, if in a particular circumscribed locale there is enough water only for one person, then conflict will probably arise whenever two or more persons inhabit that space. The fight for water is directly linked to well-being.

However, unlike water—which may actually be scarce—most scarcity generated or supported primarily by religious belief cannot be verified to be scarce at all. Thus, religious believers may die over a perceived scarcity that is not scarce in actuality. Conflicts that ensue over such scarcities are truly needless and not based on reality. This, we argue, is the tragedy of religious violence. Accordingly, in this section we will discuss four of the major scarce resources that are generated or supported primarily by religion. These are (1) access to divine communications, particularly through inscripturation; (2) sacred space; (3) group privileging; and (4) salvation.

INSCRIPTURATION

Inscripturation refers to the creation of a written account of what is believed to be authoritative information about or from supernatural forces and/or beings. William Schniedewind has recently written on the process of textualization, which generally refers to the process of transitioning from oral to written media.[1] However, our thesis holds that it is important to distinguish textualization from inscripturation, as the latter has more specific features beyond those borne by simply putting something into writing. A sacred scripture is created when someone puts into writing what readers believe to be the thoughts and actions of a deity or supernatural force. Inscripturation can occur long after some oral communication is textualized. By our definition, a written text may become scripture hundreds of years after it was first created; or it may enter and exit out of an inscripturated state.

All the major religions we discuss purport to have a record of supernatural revelations in some written form. For Jews it is the Tanakh. Muslims have the Qur'an as a basic document of revelation. Christians use both the Jewish Tanakh, reconceptualized as the "Old Testament," as well as what they call the New Testament. And as we shall see, some scholars claim that orality, not textuality, is predominant as authority in Islam.

As Schniedewind notes, words were believed to have magical powers in the ancient Near East.[2] God created the entire universe by speaking in Genesis 1. Blessings and curses were thought to have effects on the real world. Speech mystified many in the ancient world, as is also apparent in the whole doctrine of the *om* in Hinduism. The immateriality of echoes and memory was also a subject of discussion.

Writing was also believed to have magical power or to originate through supernatural processes. In the Enuma elish, the Mesopotamian creation story, Marduk possessed the heavenly tablets of destiny, which functioned as a sort of overall governance document for the universe. Changing a word or a number on a divine tablet could actually effect change in the real world. For example, Marduk changed the prophesied punishment of a city from seventy years to eleven years by simply changing the numbers on a tablet.[3]

In Exodus 34:1, God himself is said to have written at least part of the Bible: "The LORD said to Moses, 'Cut two tablets of stone like the former ones, and I will write on the tablets the words that were on the former tablets, which you broke.'" Many healing practices involved writing a document, which was itself thought to repel demons.[4] Simply writing down names could be a magical event.

Many of the consequences of inscripturation resemble those of the reported consequences of writing in general. Such consequences have been studied by, among others, Jack Goody and Walter Ong.[5] Some of their observations about orality have now been tested, and some have been found to be false, while others have been confirmed. For example, we know that accuracy in the memorization of long texts is much lower than early studies expected.

Some observations are almost certainly wrong, such as Ong's idea that dead people can convey messages through texts, but "spoken utterance comes only from the living."[6] Ong apparently fails to realize that audio recording makes this claim null and void. Other observations about the differences between orality and literacy are more difficult to test, and still rely on outdated ideas of "primitive" mind. As it applies to biblical studies, much of the research about orality and literacy has been superbly and acutely reviewed and critiqued by Patricia Kirkpatrick.[7]

We do not here consider the separate claimed effects of printing, which have been ably studied by Elizabeth Eisenstein.[8] However, it should be noted that Jean-Jacques Rousseau believed that one of the effects of printing was the permanence of bad writing. Whereas bad ideas expressed orally and in manuscripts could vanish, now they could remain forever in printed matter. Still to be explored, on a broader basis, is the extent to which we can apply the concept of "alternative literacies," as understood by Mesoamerican and Andean scholars, to the Near East.[9]

In terms of scarce resource theory, writing becomes a scarce resource when not everyone has access to the writings or to the ability to read. In the ancient Near East, most people never mastered the more complicated writing systems of Mesopotamia.[10] Most people would not be able to read anything regarded as sacred scripture. If these books are the basis of authority, then they are a scarce resource to those who cannot read them.

Before we outline in greater depth the effect of inscripturation on violence, we should note that many scholars have overplayed the differences between orality and textuality. More recent studies emphasize the dynamic interplay between orality and textuality. Martin Jaffee, for example, argues that the performative aspect of oral transmission, as well as the supposed importance of orality, can be modified and fictionalized after the creation of written texts.[11]

Yet what we continue to observe, as it pertains to violence, is how often scholars devalue those traditions that insist on textual fixity. While one can observe that empirically both emphases, textual and oral, exist, it is another thing for scholars to make the theological judgment that textual fixity is an illegitimate position, often labeled as "fundamentalist." The fact is that orality and textuality are often privileged whenever groups see some advantage in either modality. Thus, those who want to change a text may privilege the oral mode. Those who want to retain a cultural norm may insist on fixity. Hermeneutics can make pliable the most fixed of texts.

Of course, much of the dynamic between orality and textuality is paralleled in the purely secular realm as simply an aspect of any canon. In the United States Supreme Court, for example, there is a prestigious tradition of offering oral arguments before the bench. Yet, eventually, decisions are grounded in a text, whether it is a text of a preceding Supreme Court decision or as a portion of the Constitution itself.[12] So, in a manner of speaking, states and other sorts of organizations have privileged texts, even in secular societies.

But there are differences between secular privileged texts and sacred scriptures. Whereas we can verify that we decided to make the Constitution a privileged document, we cannot verify that a god decided to make any book his or her privileged mode of revelation. When divine communication is believed to reside in one book or set of books, and not in all books, then a sacred canon can be considered a form of sacred space, wherein the word of deities is embodied in those texts. Those who do not recognize that corpus as authoritative may become the object of aggression, especially when several books claim the same distinction. Nothing much would change if the exclusive authority were placed in an oral source. Verifiability, therefore, is the key difference in differentiating scarce resources generated by secular means versus religious textualization.

SACRED SPACE

All of the major world religions we study share the idea of sacred space. We may define "sacred space" as a bounded space whose value is placed above that of surrounding spaces for purely religious reasons. Since not everyone has access to, or can live in, a sacred space, it becomes a scarce resource. And because sacred space is a scarce resource, it is a potential center of conflict.

Mircea Eliade, one of the foremost theorists of comparative religion, relates sacred space to the notion of repeating a primeval hierophany (a manifestation of sacredness) or a kratophany (a manifestation of power).[13] That is to say, a space is believed to be a place where certain powers manifest themselves, so they become the place where human beings can share in that power. Eliade believes that the "the continuity of hierophanies is what explains the permanence of those sacred spots."[14] These manifestations can be as simple as the appearance of a plant repeatedly in a certain area in recurring seasons, or the identification of a place as the spot where some mythical event is thought to have occurred. In the case of Jerusalem, Eliade connects its sanctity with the notion of a center of the cosmos, where earth and sky communicate.

Eliade has an essentialist notion of religion and sacred space. For him, sacred space is not just found in every religion, but it is essential to it. So essential, in fact, that it seems human beings don't even have much choice in creating sacred space. As Eliade remarks, "the place is never 'chosen' by man; it is merely discovered by him."[15] Eliade's essentialist notion of sacred space has been contested by other scholars. In particular, Jonathan Z. Smith has faulted Eliade for misreading his sources or for not documenting his claims very well.[16] For example, Smith notes that *Dur-an-ki*, a Sumerian word rendered by Eliade as "the bond between heaven and earth," is actually a place of disjunction rather than conjunction between heaven and earth.[17]

Smith represents a social functionalist view that can be traced back at least to the social anthropologist Emile Durkheim (1858–1917), who sees religion as a mechanism that legitimizes social organizations and hierarchies.[18] Similarly, Smith sees sacred space in terms of a social cartography, wherein social power is expressed by means of physical boundaries. Thus, he points out how the temple of Jerusalem, as depicted in Ezekiel 44, has different levels of access for different layers of Israelite society.[19]

The holiest portion of the temple area—the Holy of Holies—was the inside of the temple itself, and this was only accessible to priests of the family called the Zadokites, who also had the widest range of access (Ezek. 44:15–16). The Levites, a group of temple assistants, had access to the courtyard of the temple (Ezek. 44:10–14). The Israelite people had the next level of access in the outer courtyard. Foreigners were not allowed to come into the temple at all (Ezek. 44:9). The royal prince seems to have had a level of access that is subordinate, and even ambiguous, relative to the Zadokite priest.

Neither Eliade nor Smith explain completely the origin of sacred space,[20] which may have more than a single cause. In some cases a space is deemed sacred because some miraculous occurrence is thought to have happened there. Other times, a space may be held sacred because actual historical events of religious significance are believed to have occurred there (e.g., the death/burial of a martyr). In many ancient Near Eastern religions, the idea of sacred space was related to the presence of the deity. A temple, for example, was believed to be literally the house of a god. As such, it was to be valued above the surrounding space.

However, Smith does provide an insight that we will discuss further: namely, that notions of sacred space can be flexible and evolving. That insight will prove useful when we seek solutions to the violence that can be linked to sacred space. And, indeed, some spaces may be sacralized primarily because they possess economic and political value. For the purposes of our thesis, we concentrate on cases where the value of the space is based on purely religious reasons—belief in unverifiable forces and/or beings—but we will discuss cases where space accrues economic and political significance because it has prior religious value.

GROUP PRIVILEGING

Closely linked to inscripturation and sacred space is the idea of group privileging, which refers to the fact that certain groups have privileges and rights not granted to those outside of the group. As such, those privileges become a scarce resource to outsiders.[21] In some cases, the privileges need not cause conflict if they are not valued at all by the outsider. For example, it is not necessary that all outsiders care that only priests can enter the Holy of Holies. To outsiders who live far away, it may not matter.

However, if belonging to a particular religious group means that one receives certain economic benefits that others in proximity don't, conflict may ensue. Economic benefits are now unequally distributed, constituting scarce resources. Thus, violence may follow attempts to acquire those benefits or attempts to prevent the loss of those benefits. Of course, group privileging can occur naturally, without any help from religion. This is demonstrated easily in animal behavior, as has been discussed in some of the studies we reviewed in chapter 2. But our thesis addresses examples where religion creates group privilege on unverifiable grounds.

A number of mechanisms for group privileging are readily apparent. One mechanism is through inscripturation itself. In ancient societies, not everyone was able to read and write, so elite groups had control over written information. In effect, the illiterate were denied access to writings believed to be divine revelation. Jeremy Bentham (1748–1832) is well aware of this mechanism when he remarks that the power of religious wonder-workers sometimes lies in some claimed special ability in "interpreting the divine decrees, to which no competitor has any access."[22]

Of course, illiterate people can come to believe that they have access to the divine without the need for written communication. But when the elite control society through what is believed to be divine communication in written form, illiterates do not have equal access to the divine. Bentham further observes that the power of an interpreter equals that of a legislator if the former retains "exclusive custody" of a text.[23] Virtually all the books in the Bible were probably written or compiled by elites, rather than by some marginalized peasants. But even if nonelites have their own religion, we can show that written communications are still contested or sought out by nonelites to enhance their authority.

In modern times, even with the spread of literacy, one still finds elites who control the interpretation of books. Thus, the Supreme Court is entrusted with providing the definitive interpretation of our Constitution. The hierarchy of the Catholic Church is still the authoritative interpreter of scripture for millions of people. Even among Protestants, famous for espousing the conscience of the individual in interpretation, there quickly develop elites who then are seen as the standard interpreters. In many parts of the Muslim world, women are still not able to read the Qur'an or become Imams. These privileges are primarily grounded in religious reasons.

SALVATION

The ultimate supernatural prize in many of these world religions is "salvation," a term that is highly complex and often ambiguous. Salvation, for our purposes, refers to the idea that one receives certain more permanent supernatural status or benefit by joining a particular religion. It is closely allied with group privileging, except that the reward called salvation is ultimately not tangible or verifiable. Salvation exists only insofar as people believe in it.

Salvation in Judaism is more physical, at least in the Hebrew Bible. Salvation means that God will defend one against a real enemy. Or it may mean that one is spared the wrath of Yahweh, that one attains immortality at the end of time. Christianity also speaks of salvation, but it has transformed earlier Jewish concepts. Salvation in Christianity could be a future state for those that believe that Jesus is the Messiah. Many Christians may speak of "salvation from sin," meaning that the Christian is saved from the ultimate destruction caused by sin. Salvation may also mean ultimately salvation from an eternal suffering in hell.

In any event, salvation is a scarce resource insofar as it is not available to everyone. It may be available only to those who join a particular group and pay a particular price, whether in terms of real finances or with other means. For example, we shall show that during the Crusades, martyrdom was believed to confer a virtual ticket to heaven. But not everyone was able to go on a Crusade, so this form of salvation constituted a scarce resource not equally available to all.

For purpose of our thesis, we focus on examples where belief in salvation results in violence. The mechanism can be quite diverse, but the commonality is that the path from the belief in salvation to a belief in violence is mainly the consequence of belief in unverifiable forces and/or beings. This may mean belief that certain modes of salvation require violence in order to be achieved or effected. As we shall show, orthodox Christianity is characterized by the belief that at least a priming act of violence, the torture and death of Christ, is essential and necessary to achieve salvation.

SUMMARY

Scarce resources are the main factors in most conflicts. A resource is anything that is believed to be necessary or advantageous to a certain mode of living. Religion can create conflict and violence when it creates scarce resources of such perceived value that people are willing to fight and die for them. The scarce resources are a necessary factor in violence when the loss of those valued scarce resources is thought to be imminent or when someone else attempts to acquire those scarce resources.

Four of the scarce resources created by religion can be identified as consistent factors in violence. The first of these is access to the divine will, manifested concretely in inscripturation. Sacred space relates to the scarce resource created when a bounded space is declared more valuable than surrounding space or when access to that space is not granted equally to all. Group privileging is a scarce resource because the privileges are not available to all. Salvation, as a set of valued benefits, may be a scarce resource when it is not available to everyone or when its cost is too high for some to accept. Our task now is to show concrete examples in which Judaism, Christianity, and Islam have precipitated violence by creating belief in these scarce resources.

NOTES

1. William Schniedewind, *How the Bible Became a Book* (Cambridge: Cambridge University Press, 2004).

2. See also Gerald L. Bruns, "Canon and Power in the Hebrew Scriptures," *Critical Inquiry* 10, no. 3 (March 1984): 462–80; and Frederick Moriarty, "Word as Power in the Ancient Near East," in *A Light Unto My Path; Old Testament Studies in Honor of Jacob M. Myers*, ed. Howard N. Bream, Ralph D. Heim, and Carey A. Moore (Philadelphia: Temple University Press, 1974), pp. 345–62.

3. On Marduk changing a prophecy, see Hector Avalos, "Daniel 9:24–25 and Mesopotamian Temple Rededications," *JBL* 117, no. 3 (1998): 507–11.

4. See also Michael D. Swartz, "Scribal Magic and Its Rhetoric: Formal Patterns in Medieval Hebrew and Aramaic Incantation Texts from the Cairo Genizah," *Harvard Theological Review* 83, no. 2 (1999): 163–80.

5. Jack Goody, *The Domestication of the Savage Mind* (Cambridge: Cambridge University Press, 1977); *Literacy in Traditional Societies* (Cambridge: Cambridge University Press, 1968); and Walter Ong, *Orality and Literacy: The Technologizing of the Word* (London: Routledge, 1982). See also Eric A. Havelock, *The Literate Revolution in Greece and Its Cultural Consequences* (Princeton, NJ: Princeton University Press, 1982).

6. Ong, *Orality and Literacy*, p. 102.

7. Patricia G. Kirkpatrick, *The Old Testament and Folklore Study* (Sheffield, UK: Sheffield Academic Press, 1988). See also Deborah Tannen, ed., *Spoken and Written Language: Exploring Orality and Literacy* (Norwood, NJ: Ablex, 1982).

8. Eisenstein, *The Printing Press as an Agent of Change*.

9. See Elizabeth Hill Boone and Walter Mignolo, eds., *Writing without Words: Alternative Literacies in Mesoamerica and the Andes* (Durham, NC: Duke University Press, 1994).

10. See further Giuseppe Visicato, *The Power and the Writing: The Early Scribes of Mesopotamia* (Bethesda, MD: CDL Press, 2000).

11. See Martin S. Jaffee, *Torah in the Mouth: Writing and Oral Tradition in Palestinian Judaism 200–400 CE* (New York: Oxford University Press, 2001). Other works on Hebrew scriptures include Moshe Halbertal, *People of the Book: Canon, Meaning, and Authority* (Cambridge, MA: Harvard University Press, 1997); and Barbara A. Holdredge, *Veda and Torah: Transcending the Textuality of Scripture* (Albany: State University of New York Press, 1996).

12. For discussions of American secular "sacred" texts, see Jaroslav Pelikan, *Interpreting the Bible and the Constitution* (New Haven, CT: Yale University Press, 2004); Pauline Maier, *American Scripture: Making the Declaration of Independence* (New York: Vintage, 1997); and Sanford Levinson, *Constitutional Faith* (Princeton, NJ: Princeton University Press, 1988).

13. Mircea Eliade, *Patterns in Comparative Religion* (New York: Meridian, 1958), pp. 367–87.

14. Ibid., p. 368.

15. Ibid., p. 369.

16. Jonathan Z. Smith, *To Take Place: Toward Theory in Ritual* (Chicago: University of Chicago Press, 1987), especially pp. 1–23.

17. Actually, Smith (ibid., p. 16) is a bit imprecise himself here, as he calls this word "Babylonian," which is a different language from Sumerian.

18. For a discussion of Smith's view of religion, see Sam Gill, "No Place to Stand: Jonathan Z. Smith as *Homo Ludens*, The Academic Study of Religion *Sub Specie Ludi*," *JAAR* 66, no. 2 (Summer 1998): 283–312.

19. Smith, *To Take Place*, pp. 47–65.

20. For a critique of Smith, see Ronald L. Grimes, "Jonathan Z. Smith's Theory of Ritual Space," *Religion* 29 (1999): 261–73.

21. For a classic treatment of group privilege, see Gerhard E. Lenski, *Power and Privilege: A Theory of Social Stratification* (Chapel Hill: University of North Carolina Press, 1984). Lenski, however, still sees Judaism and Christianity as providing a "basis for an ethical criticism of the existing order" (p. 39). He therefore still has assimilated uncritically benign views of how Judaism and Christianity create and maintain privilege.

22. Jeremy Bentham, *The Influence of Natural Religion on the Temporal Happiness of Mankind* (1822; reprint, Amherst, NY: Prometheus Books, 2003), p. 147. See also Delos B. McKown, *Behold the Antichrist: Bentham on Religion* (Amherst, NY: Prometheus Books, 2004).

23. Bentham, *The Influence of Natural Religion*, p. 150.

CHAPTER 6

JUDAISM AND THE HEBREW BIBLE

BASIC OVERVIEW

The Hebrew Bible, as represented in the modern Protestant canon, consists of thirty-nine books written probably no earlier than the first millennium BCE and no later than about 160 BCE, if the book of Daniel is considered to be the latest book of the Hebrew Bible.[1] Traditional Jews and Christians believe that Moses wrote the Pentateuch (also called the Torah), the first five books of the Bible, somewhere around 1400 BCE. However, most modern biblical scholars consider the Pentateuch and most of the Bible to have been composed by anonymous authors, with the Pentateuch itself being a composite from different time periods. The latest books, by traditional dating, would be those written after the return of the Jews from the Babylonian exile, beginning around 538 BCE.[2]

Modern critical scholars have established that even the oldest portions of the Bible (e.g., the Song of the Sea in Exodus 15) may not date much earlier than 1000 BCE. More radical "minimalists" would argue that the Hebrew Bible was almost wholly written in the postexilic era (after 586 BCE) as a nationalistic series of manifestos and collection of ethnic stories. Thus, for minimalists, most of the Bible is fiction that grew in much the same way as the corpus of stories relating to King Arthur.[3]

It would be simplistic to homogenize all the different authors and subcultures represented in the Hebrew Bible into one coherent theology. Most efforts to formulate a consistent picture of biblical theology largely have been failures.[4] These unsuccessful efforts include the famous ones associated with Gerhard von Rad, Walter Eichrodt, and Brevard Childs.[5] However, those failures can also be traced, in part, to the fact that theologies have been constructed mostly by Christians and Jews, whose links to the Bible result in inevitable selection bias based on unverifiable theological grounds.

For the purposes of our study of violence, we concentrate on that part of the Hebrew Bible known as the Deuteronomistic History (DtrH), an influential concept popularized by Martin Noth.[6] Briefly, Noth believed that all the books in the Hebrew Bible from Deuteronomy through 2 Kings were the product of a single author or editor.[7]

Noth believed that DtrH was written to explain the catastrophic fall of Jerusalem, the capital of Judah, in 586 or 587 BCE.[8] After the reign of Solomon, the kingdom had been divided into a northern half, comprising ten tribes, and a southern half, consisting of Judah and Benjamin, though it was just sometimes called Judah. The Northern Kingdom had fallen prey to the Assyrian Empire around 721 BCE, but Judah had survived and grown confident that Yahweh would protect it. That is why 586 BCE was even more shattering for Judah than September 11 was for the United States: Not only was the Judean capital destroyed, but many Jews were exiled to Babylonia. We acknowledge that DtrH is itself largely a modern construct, but there are sufficient commonalities among the books to detect some themes about violence.

PRELIMINARY COMMENTS ON SCHOLARSHIP

Scholarship on violence in the Hebrew Bible has been marked by at least two positions. The first position views the violence as historically accurate and morally defensible. The second position denies that the violence actually occurred or minimizes its importance. For example, the violence could have a purely literary or rhetorical function. The violence could be meant purely as a warning to insiders rather than an actual agenda meant for outsiders. For the moment, we will not consider those Christian scholars who reject the violence by devaluing the place of the Hebrew Bible in the Christian canon.[9]

If we first consider more carefully the outright defense of Hebrew violence, we also see that it can be subdivided into at least two categories. One type of defense relies on frankly theological explanations, as does Gleason Archer, who once served as professor of Old Testament at Trinity Evangelical Divinity School: "Just as the wise surgeon removes dangerous cancer from his patient's body by use of the scalpel, so God employed the Israelites to remove such dangerous malignancies from human society."[10]

Another frank defense relies on cultural relativism and political motives. In such a case, the violence is seen in the context of war practices in the ancient Near East. Such writers may assert that Israel was no worse than others, while paradoxically maintaining that the Hebrew religion represents the pinnacle of religious and ethical achievements for humankind. Here we often find works that specialize in biblical "ethics."[11] Those who deny that any actual violence occurred rely on modern critical approaches, which undermine the historicity of biblical narratives. Main representatives of these positions include Joel Kaminsky and Lori Rowlett, whose work we will study more carefully below.

Among the foremost of those who minimize or overlook the violence altogether stands Steven T. Katz, whose massive survey of genocide relegates the Hebrew genocide against the Amalekites to a footnote.[12] Katz, whose main thesis is that the Nazi genocide was unique in history, justifies this omission of an "extended analysis" of the Amalekite genocide by casting doubt on the idea that the Amalekites were all actually exterminated. Katz apparently fails to note that not all Jews were exterminated by the Nazis, but that does not count as a reason for omitting discussion of the Holocaust. In any case, we shall critique more carefully some of Katz's discussion of genocide later.

At the same time, there are also notable dissenters who see that the Bible has functioned as an instrument to legitimize violence. Foremost among some of the more recent entries into the discussion is John J. Collins, who was president of the Society of Biblical Literature in 2002. In that year in Toronto, he delivered his presidential address to the society, the largest organization of academic biblical scholars in the world. His address was published in the first issue of the *Journal of Biblical Literature* in 2003, and has now been published as a short book.[13] Therein, Collins notes that the story of the liberation of the Israelites became the story of the oppression of the Canaanites by the Israelites. He also describes how "biblical narratives have been a factor in the Zionist movement in Israel . . . providing powerful precedents for right-wing militants. Biblical analogies also provide the underpinning for support of Israel among conservative scholars."[14]

Nonetheless, Collins does not go as far as we will propose. He concludes that "perhaps the most constructive thing a biblical critic can do toward lessening the contribution of the Bible to violence in the world, is to show that certitude is an illusion."[15] As we shall argue, there is actually no necessary reason to maintain the authority or value of the biblical text at all in the modern world. We must acknowledge how inscripturation itself is a generator of violence. Moreover, Collins's claim that the Bible does not demand paradigms for all times and places seems to be itself an arbitrary judgment.

C. S. Cowles, a self-described evangelical Christian, has proposed to devalue the Hebrew Bible in the Christian canon.[16] Such a proposal is a slightly milder version of one that can be traced back to a man named Marcion (d. ca. 160), whose anti-Judaism led him to reject the entire Hebrew Bible and retain only a part of what we know as the New Testament. But no less than Marcion's proposal, Cowles's proposal is premised on the idea that Christianity is somehow less violent than Judaism. As we shall demonstrate, the New Testament at times actually endorses a more violent form of religion.

Another development, still in its infancy, is a plea for a shift away from the Zionist underpinnings of biblical scholarship itself. The most notable spokesperson is perhaps Keith Whitelam, author of *The Invention of Ancient Israel: The Silencing of Palestinian History*. Despite some of the problems that have been noted in his work, Whitelam has issued an important call to go beyond using archaeology as means to authenticate the presence of Israel on the land it now claims.[17]

In any case, the bulk of the academic profession is still engaged in the enterprise of maintaining the value of the biblical text despite the endorsement of violence, whether actual or not. Even among those who recognize the violent nature of the Hebrew Bible, there is usually no recognition that religion itself creates scarce resources over which people fight. We therefore now turn our attention to how the Hebrew Bible and the religions it represents has created the four scarcities we are studying: inscripturation, sacred space, group privileging, and salvation.

INSCRIPTURATION AS A SCARCE RESOURCE

Saint Thomas Aquinas, the influential medieval Catholic theologian, states that prior to Christianity, God revealed himself only to the Jews.[18] In fact, access to the divine will is characterized as a scarce resource through much of the Hebrew Bible, as Yahweh reveals himself to only a few people. Thus, Noah is saved from the Flood because God speaks to him (Gen. 6:8, 13). All communications to others are through Noah. Likewise, Yahweh speaks to Abraham, but to no one else, about the fate of Sodom.

The point at which the Hebrew Bible became an authoritative text is difficult to determine. Recently, William Schniedewind has proposed that "[t]he Bible as we know it began to take shape in Jerusalem in the late eighth century B.C.E., in the days of Isaiah, the prophet, and Hezekiah, the king of Judah."[19] He suggests that urbanization and centralization of the government and religion in Jerusalem were main factors.

In contrast to the writing systems of Mesopotamia, which were cumbersome and required specialists to manage them, writing in ancient Israel was already alphabetic. This meant that relatively more people could read and write. One example is found in the so-called Letter of a Literate Soldier at Lachish, a town near Jerusalem that was destroyed around 586 BCE. The soldier complains about a reprimand that questioned his ability to read. He protests that "never has any man had to read a letter to me." In other words, he asserts that he is fully literate.[20]

By the time of Josiah (642–609 BCE), there was an effort to install a mono-Yahwistic religion, at least according to the biblical accounts. A book is said to be discovered that the king should follow (2 Kings 22). Most scholars believe this book is some version of what we now know as Deuteronomy. According to Schniedewind, "Writing is central to the revelation in Deuteronomy."[21] Thus, Deuteronomy 27:2–3:

> On the day that you cross over the Jordan into the land that the LORD your God is giving you, you shall set up large stones and cover them with plaster.
>
> You shall write on them all the words of this law when you have crossed over, to enter the land that the LORD your God is giving you, a land flowing with milk and honey, as the LORD, the God of your ancestors, promised you.

What is envisioned is some sort of public monument that everyone can read. Moreover, the author expects that all Israelites will have at least some of Yahweh's words written on the doorposts of their homes (Deut. 6:9).

Deuteronomy also is quite insistent on the fixity of the text. For example, in Deuteronomy 4:2: "You must neither add anything to what I command you nor take away anything from it, but keep the commandments of the LORD your God with which I am charging you." Taken most literally, of course, if one does not add or subtract from a text, then the text will remain immutable. The eternity of this law is also at issue when Yahweh is quoted as saying: " If only they had such a mind as this, to fear me and to keep all my commandments always, so that it might go well with them and with their children forever!" (Deut. 5:29) Once God's word is reduced to a written text, we are told that Israel is to concentrate on that text. One must meditate on the law, day and night (Ps. 1).

VIOLENCE RESULTING FROM INSCRIPTURATION

The idea that a god reveals himself only within a select corpus of texts and to a select group of people already was causing problems within the Hebrew Bible. Not everyone agreed that certain entities were the only conduits to God. Others disagreed on the interpretation of texts, even if they agreed that those texts were the only conduits of divine communication.[22]

One example of a conflict about the proper conduit of divine communication is found in Numbers 12:2. The story begins when Aaron and Miriam, siblings of Moses, contemptuously ask: "'Has the LORD spoken only through Moses? Has he not spoken through us also?' And the LORD heard it." This story is premised on the idea that God does not reveal himself equally to all, and it definitely shows the conflict that ensues directly from this inequality.[23] The narrator explains that Yahweh struck Miriam for her insolence, and then proceeded to reiterate that he indeed does not reveal himself equally to all:

> And he said, "Hear my words: When there are prophets among you, I the LORD make myself known to them in visions; I speak to them in dreams.
>
> Not so with my servant Moses; he is entrusted with all my house.
>
> With him I speak face to face — clearly, not in riddles; and he beholds the form of the LORD. Why then were you not afraid to speak against my servant Moses?" (Num. 12:6–8)

The solution here is not to make revelation more abundant to all. The story endorses the idea that violence is a legitimate means to solve disputes resulting from the scarcity of revelation.

The problem of recognizing a divine communication was treated at some length in Deuteronomy 18, which provides criteria for recognizing a communication from Yahweh. The fact that violence and disagreements about who has the correct divine communication is most clear in Deuteronomy 18:20: "But any prophet who speaks in the name of other gods, or who presumes to speak in my name a word that I have not commanded the prophet to speak—that prophet shall die." Divine communication is a scarce resource, and violence must be used to maintain access to what is perceived to be the right conduit.

The main criteria for knowing if a word came from Yahweh is whether it is fulfilled (Deut. 18:22). Of course, this criterion was of only limited value, and could result in contradictory conclusions. For example, let us suppose that a prophet of Baal predicted that it would rain in the next few days, and that a prophet of Yahweh also predicted the same thing. If rain comes, then the criterion of fulfillment would not be sufficient to distinguish a false prophecy from a true prophecy.

At this point in Deuteronomy, we may pause to consider the astounding claims by Charles Mabee, who argues that "the ascendance of textual Yahwism" resulted in a detoxification of violence.[24] Along with other pacifists, whom we shall critique later, Mabee argues that "Yahweh removes the entire activity from the hands of the human despot and places it into the hands of Yahweh, subject to his initiation."[25] Mabee cites Deuteronomy 20 as a sign of just such an advance in thinking about violence.

To understand how superficial Mabee's claim is, let us consider Deuteronomy 20, which outlines the treatment of those towns that are "near" versus towns that are "far" from the Israelite living space. The Israelites are allowed to kill all males in the "far" towns, and keep women and children as booty (20:13–14). The towns that are "near," however, get the following treatment:

> But as for the towns of these peoples that the LORD your God is giving you as an inheritance, you must not let anything that breathes remain alive.
>
> You shall annihilate them—the Hittites and the Amorites, the Canaanites and the Perizzites, the Hivites and the Jebusites—just as the LORD your God has commanded,
>
> so that they may not teach you to do all the abhorrent things that they do for their gods, and you thus sin against the LORD your God. (Deut. 20:16–18)

How "textualization" means less violence for Mabee here is unclear. Certainly, Mabee's claim that at this point decisions about violence have been transferred from king to prophet is not supported by the text. Verses 5 and 9 still speak of "officials," not prophets, making important decisions. In fact, here textualization results in the genocidal rationales found in Deuteronomy 20 gaining permanence and currency for the next twenty-five hundred years. Deuteronomy 7 and 20, in particular, have been among the most often used to promote violence in both Christianity and Islam.

Moreover, Mabee's idea assumes that prophets bear God's true commandments about violence. But even if we grant Mabee's claim that prophets now decide, as conduits of Yahweh, on genocidal policies, it means that divine revelation remains a scarce resource, as only a few "prophets" become the conduit for Yahweh's revelation. Knowing when God has spoken, or to which prophet he has spoken becomes an issue that results in more violence. In any case, the average Israelite still ends up trusting a human being, a prophet who *claims* to speak for Yahweh, to decide when to slaughter whole towns.

In fact, some biblical authors seem to subsequently acknowledge that other criteria needed to be developed. In Jeremiah, the criterion of simple fulfillment was refined by restricting it to only the more improbable fulfillment.

> The prophets who preceded you and me from ancient times prophesied war, famine, and pestilence against many countries and great kingdoms.

> As for the prophet who prophesies peace, when the word of that prophet comes true, then it will be known that the LORD has truly sent the prophet." (Jer. 28:8–9)

Of course, once divine communications were set into writing, further conflicts followed. This is perhaps most clear in Jeremiah 8:8–10:

> How can you say, "We are wise, and the law of the LORD is with us," when, in fact, the false pen of the scribes has made it into a lie?

> The wise shall be put to shame, they shall be dismayed and taken; since they have rejected the word of the LORD, what wisdom is in them?

> Therefore I will give their wives to others and their fields to conquerors, because from the least to the greatest everyone is greedy for unjust gain; from prophet to priest everyone deals falsely. (Jer. 8:8–10).

First, note that the author concedes that not all scripture contains Yahweh's word. Schniedewind plausibly argues that the conflict here is between orality and textuality. That is to say, Jeremiah argues that any written Torah is false, while the oral law is genuine. If so, then the author is saying that no written text contains God's authoritative word. In either case, the author premises the whole diatribe on the idea that violence is a proper recourse when different ideas about divine communication disagree.

The book of Jeremiah is indeed replete with violence that centers on disagreements about who has access to divine communications. In a famous story in Jeremiah 28, a prophet named Hananiah disputes whether Jeremiah has access to genuine communications from Yahweh. Hananiah's punishment is death. Jeremiah (31:33) sees the problem of scarcity and proposes a solution: God will write his revelation in every Israelite's heart, but that will be in a utopian future. Overall, these examples foreshadow what will continue to be main themes in religious conflict: orality versus inscripturation; fixity versus flexibility.

But if violence involving inscripturation can be found within a religious tradition, it can also be found between religious traditions, or at least between traditions that claim to serve different deities. An example of such violence can be found during the reign of Antiochus IV Epiphanes (175–164 BCE), a member of the Seleucid Dynasty, which appropriated the area roughly corresponding to modern Syria in the aftermath of the death of Alexander the Great.

The main source for Antiochus's actions is found in the first book of Maccabees. The author tells us that Antiochus used force in order to prompt Jews to abandon their dietary laws, among other customs. Antiochus wanted forced assimilation to create a homogeneous identity that would serve his purposes. Eventually, he even desecrated the Jewish temple by setting up an "abominating sacrilege" thought to be a statue of a Greek god. But the catalogue of misdeed also includes the following:

> The books of the law that they found they tore to pieces and burned with fire.
>
> Anyone found possessing the book of the covenant, or anyone who adhered to the law, was condemned to death by decree of the king. (1 Macc. 1:56–57)

Of course, it is difficult to know Antiochus's reasoning. Here is a case in which Antiochus could have destroyed scripture because it was part of his goal to achieve cultural uniformity. However, the fact that he perceived scriptures to be a threat is most likely due to the denial of the idea that divine communication was not to be found uniquely or in any measure in the Jewish scriptures. Judaism claimed that Jewish scriptures contained the only revelation of God, and perhaps this threatened Antiochus's power to dictate his brand of religion.

Interestingly, the destruction of Hebrew sacred scriptures was carried out by Antiochus. As 1 Maccabees 1:44 states: "And the king sent letters by messengers to Jerusalem and the towns of Judah; he directed them to follow customs strange to the land." The reference to his evil writings continues in 1 Maccabees 1:51: "In such words he wrote to his whole kingdom. He appointed inspectors over all the people and commanded the towns of Judah to offer sacrifice, town by town." Antiochus, in other words, has substituted his writings as the prime authority in his domain.

That Antiochus was portrayed as attempting to replace God is found in the thinly veiled criticisms of Antiochus found in Daniel 7:25: "He shall speak words against the Most High, shall wear out the holy ones of the Most High, and shall attempt to change the sacred seasons and the law; and they shall be given into his power for a time, two times, and half a time." This description also shows that the author took textual fixity seriously. As in Deuteronomy, Yahweh's written words are not to be changed.

If the "true" conduit of divine revelation is regarded as a scarce resource, then we have here a fight for that scarce resource. Antiochus wished to be seen as the proper conduit for divine revelation, while the Maccabees fought equally hard to preserve the status of their divine scriptures, among other things. Antiochus, therefore, was trying to make the true source of divine revelation scarce by destroying rival scriptures. Conversely, the Maccabees were attempting to preserve the scarce resource that they believed held God's revelation.

Inscripturation has also figured in violence between Christianity and Judaism. In general, the conflict between Christianity and Judaism has much to do with the status of the corpus that Christians call the Old Testament, and which Jews call the Tanakh. For orthodox Judaism, the Tanakh is eternal and not to be superseded. For Christianity, the Tanakh is the "Old Testament," which was superseded by the new covenant (New Testament) upon the death of Jesus.

An example of violence between Christianity and Judaism on the issue of holy scripture can be found in the Hebrew chronicles of anti-Jewish violence in 1096, during the movements associated with the Crusades.[26] Emicho of Leinigen was the leader of the anti-Jewish mobs, which rampaged through a number of Jewish communities, including those in Cologne, Mainz, and Worms. The Chronicle of Solomon bar Simson tells what happens when a Christian ("an errant one") destroys the Torah of a Jewish household:

> There was also a Torah Scroll in the room; the errant ones [Christians] came into the room, found it, and tore it to shreds. When the holy and pure women, daughters of kings, saw that the Torah had been torn they called in a loud voice to their husbands: "Look, see, the Holy Torah is being torn by the enemy!" . . . "Alas, the Holy Torah, the perfection of beauty, the delight of our eyes, to which we used to bow in the synagogue, honoring it; our little children would kiss it. How has it now fallen into the hands of these impure uncircumcised ones?"
>
> When the men heard the words of the these pious women, they were moved with zeal for the Lord, our God, and for his holy and precious Torah . . . They found one of the errant ones in the room, and all of them, men and women, threw stones at him till he fell dead.[27]

It is very seldom that we have such a detailed rationale for violence perpetrated because of the perceived holiness of a text. The example certainly can be reduced to the form: "Belief X, therefore Act of Violence Y." In this case, the belief that the Torah is holy and cannot be desecrated is explicitly stated as the reason for the killing of the Christian who desecrated that text. At the same time, the Christian desecrated the Torah because he did not regard it as holy.

The attacks upon Jewish scriptures continues today. According to a report posted on the CNN Web site on April 1, 2002, a synagogue in Marseilles, France, was attacked: "'All the religious objects, books, the Torah, all of it burned,' Sydney Maimoun, the synagogue's president, told The Associated Press, adding there's 'really nothing left.'"[28] Most of the perpetrators were thought to be Muslims, and we shall examine the conflict over scriptures between Muslims and Jews more carefully in the chapter on Islam.

SACRED SPACE

Sacred space in Israel, as depicted in the Hebrew Bible, normally relates to at least three areas that can be visualized as concentric rings. The innermost ring is the holiest portion of the Temple of Yahweh. This ring is surrounded by the city of Jerusalem, which is to be seen as the "navel of the earth."[29] Jerusalem, in turn, is surrounded by the land of Israel, often called "the Holy Land" by Jews and Christians alike. In truth, different parts of the ring have alternated in their degree of sacredness throughout history. For example, for many years there was no temple in Israel, so its sacredness lived more in the imagination than in reality.

From a geophysical perspective, the land of Israel has very few natural resources that would render it valuable. Even Alan Dershowitz, author of a recent defense of Zionism, comments: "Nor was the land they [Jewish settlers] sought to cultivate rich in natural resources such as oil or gold, or strategically positioned as a trade route. It was a materially worthless piece of real estate in a backwater of the world whose significance to Jews was religious, historical and familial."[30]

Israel's location has somewhat more value to its neighbors. Israel constitutes a sort of land bridge between Africa and southwest Asia. But even here, the value of this passageway does not explain its holiness. The more valuable part of the land bridge is the coastal area, not the hill country in which Jerusalem is situated. Many areas of the world are passageways; few become holy. Thus, the nearby Suez Canal, one of the most important passages on the planet, is not regarded as sacred space. Its economic value is real, and it forms an actual scarce resource for those who wish to go around Africa in an efficient manner.

Accordingly, one can argue that the value of the Holy Land is almost entirely the creation of religion. That is to say, the belief that God has rendered this space more holy or valuable than other spaces best explains how it acquired those traits that render it "holy" in the eyes of many. The entire value of the so-called Holy Land was created by religion and is sustained by religion.[31] The material and political value it has acquired derives from its religious value, rather than the reverse.

The earliest occurrence of the actual term "holy land" or "holy ground" may be in Zechariah 2:12 (Hebrew Bible, 2:16): "The LORD will inherit Judah as his portion in the holy land ['*adamat haqqodesh*], and will again choose Jerusalem." According to the traditions codified in the Hebrew Bible, the land that came to be known as the Holy Land is part of an allotment given by God to Abram, whose name was later changed to Abraham. In Genesis 12:1, God appears to Abram, then residing in Mesopotamia, and tells him to go to Canaan. When Abram arrives in Canaan, Yahweh says: "To your offspring I will give this land" (Gen. 12:7). Abram then builds an altar there.

In some cases, the idea of sacred space is hardly distinguishable from a nationalistic ideology. For example, when Naaman, the Syrian general, looks for a cure for his leprosy, he is told to go to Israel and dip himself seven times in the Jordan river. He finds the earth of Israel so valuable that he takes some of Israel's dirt back to Syria (2 Kings 5:17). Earlier Elijah had admonished Ahaziah, king of Judah, for going outside Israel to receive health care:

> "Is it because there is no God in Israel that you are sending to inquire of Baal-zebub, the god of Ekron? Therefore you shall not leave the bed to which you have gone, but shall surely die." (2 Kings 1:6)

But while the land of Israel was seen as more valuable than surrounding areas by biblical authors, Jerusalem was seen as even holier. The origins of the place that became known as Jerusalem are unclear, but Jane M. Cahill advocates a date in the Chalcolithic period in the fourth millennium for the earliest occupation.[32] In contrast to many of the prominent archaeologists of the twentieth century (e.g., W. F. Albright and Yigael Yadin), many of today's prominent archaeologists (e.g., David Ussishkin and Israel Finkelstein) hold that Jerusalem was a rather small town at the time of David in the tenth century. Few, if any modern archaeologists uphold the idea that Jerusalem under Solomon (David's son) was the majestic center of the Near East that the accounts in 1 Kings 10 seem to envision.

The idea that Jerusalem, and, more specifically, Zion, was holy because of its association with Yahweh is often called the "Zion theology." As Jon Levenson notes, "Zion" may have referred originally to "the ridge on the [southeast] section of Jerusalem which lies between the Wadi Kidron and Tyropoeon Valley."[33] The meaning was later expanded to include all of Jerusalem. J. J. M. Roberts, who has written extensively on the Zion theology, includes a number of specific elements in this belief system, which we have simplified as follows: (1) Yahweh is the great king; (2) He chose Jerusalem as his dwelling place; (3) He protects Jerusalem from its enemies; (4) The nations acknowledge Yahweh's suzerainty; and (5) Inhabitants share the blessings of Yahweh's presence and must be fit to live in his presence.[34] Roberts traces this theology to the Davidic period, a time frame that is debatable, at best.

While elements of the Zion theology certainly evince continuities with pre-Israelite literature, documents that speak about Jerusalem in the fourteenth century BCE, when it was not yet in Israelite hands, show no awareness that this city was valued for religious reasons. Whenever any Zion theology began, it is clear that it was in place by the time certain Psalms and parts of Isaiah were written. The favoritism toward Israel and Zion is evident in a number of passages. For example, in Psalm 76:1–2: "In Judah God is known, his name is great in Israel. His abode has been established in Salem, his dwelling place in Zion." The connection between an imperialistic vision and the value of Jerusalem is clear in Psalm 46:5–10:

> God is in the midst of the city; it shall not be moved; God will help it when the morning dawns.

> The nations are in an uproar, the kingdoms totter; he utters his voice, the earth melts.

> The LORD of hosts is with us; the God of Jacob is our refuge.

> Come, behold the works of the LORD; see what desolations he has brought on the earth.

> He makes wars cease to the end of the earth; he breaks the bow, and shatters the spear; he burns the shields with fire.

> "Be still, and know that I am God! I am exalted among the nations, I am exalted in the earth." (Ps. 46:5–10)

The psalm makes clear that "peace" includes domination by Yahweh, a point to which we will return when we examine more critically the concept of "peace" (*shalom*) in the Hebrew Bible.

Others date the full flowering of the Zion theology at the time of the Deuteronomistic History (between the eighth and sixth centuries, depending on the scholar or portion).[35] The DtrH promoted Jerusalem as the only place of worship for all of Israel. Whereas other traditions could allow sacrifices at almost any place, the authors of DtrH sought to centralize worship for reasons that have been debated. Some scholars theorize that the Assyrian invasions made it important to protect the capital, so all resources were directed toward Jerusalem.[36]

Nonetheless, by the time the Hebrew scriptures became codified as the primary religious authority in the Second Temple period (with the second temple being rebuilt during the Persian Empire by the mid-fifth century), the value of Jerusalem still rested almost entirely on religious grounds, with political and economic value being derivative.[37] Chronicles echoes these religious sentiments:

> "Since the day that I brought my people out of the land of Egypt, I have not chosen a city from any of the tribes of Israel in which to build a house, so that my name might be there, and I chose no one as ruler over my people Israel;

> but I have chosen Jerusalem in order that my name may be there, and I have chosen David to be over my people Israel." (2 Chron. 6:5–6)

The main reason for its sacredness is still that the Temple of Jerusalem is to be located there. The Temple of Jerusalem, then, becomes the primary and innermost concentric ring of sacred space. The fact is that one can even subdivide the temple itself into a gradient of sacrality. The innermost room (*debîr*) is the most sacred, and only the High Priest can enter it. Outside the temple, laypersons can approach for sacrifice. Those with certain diseases (e.g., so-called leprosy) cannot enter the temple. In short, gradations in "holiness" function as an expression of social ranking.

Other extracanonical Jewish works placed Jerusalem at the center of the earth, as does Jubilees 8:19. In the Dead Sea Scrolls we find writings that are even more extreme in the degree of exclusion of the sick from Jerusalem. For example, the famous Temple Scroll says that the blind and the lame may not enter Jerusalem.[38] This is not a case where there was not enough physical space for the blind and lame; rather, we see space being created as a scarce resource on the basis of religious belief.

Many earlier Hebrew authors believed that the holiness of Israel and Jerusalem would be something finally guaranteed in the future. Isaiah 52:1 expresses the following sentiment: "Awake, awake, put on your strength, O Zion! Put on your beautiful garments, O Jerusalem, the holy city; for the uncircumcised and the unclean shall enter you no more." A more bureaucratic and hierocratic vision of the future is found in Ezekiel, wherein degrees of holiness map out a social hierarchy.

> In the holy district you shall measure off a section twenty-five thousand cubits long and ten thousand wide, in which shall be the sanctuary, the most holy place.
>
> It shall be a holy portion of the land; it shall be for the priests, who minister in the sanctuary and approach the LORD to minister to him; and it shall be both a place for their houses and a holy place for the sanctuary.
>
> Another section, twenty-five thousand cubits long and ten thousand cubits wide, shall be for the Levites who minister at the temple, as their holding for cities to live in.
>
> Alongside the portion set apart as the holy district you shall assign as a holding for the city an area five thousand cubits wide, and twenty-five thousand cubits long; it shall belong to the whole house of Israel.
>
> And to the prince shall belong the land on both sides of the holy district and the holding of the city, alongside the holy district and the holding of the city,

on the west and on the east, corresponding in length to one of the tribal portions, and extending from the western to the eastern boundary. (Ezek. 45:3–7)

The view of Israel and Jerusalem as sacred space continued into post-biblical Judaism. Thus, in the Talmudic tractate Kelim (5b), we have the following frank assertion: "The Land of Israel is holier than all other lands."[39] The tractate explains that there are actually ten grades of holy space, with the temple mount having an even higher degree of holiness than the land of Israel as a whole. As in Leviticus, the holiness is related to access for different groups of people. Thus, the tractate says that the temple mount is holier because men with discharges and menstruating women cannot enter it.

In short, there is a persistent tradition in the Hebrew Bible that declares that Israel is the type of privileged space we call "sacred." It receives the special favor of the god, Yahweh. Even more sacred are the city of Jerusalem and its temple. There is a close relationship between ethnic privileging and sacred space. Whatever the direction of any causal arrow, both ethnic privileging and sacred space are ultimately based on unverifiable premises ("Yahweh's favor," "holiness") that produced the scarce resource many call "the Holy Land."

VIOLENCE RESULTING FROM SACRED SPACE

Sacred space is inherently a scarce resource. It does not exist everywhere, and it is not accessible to all. There usually are more people than could live or participate in a sacred space. At its largest extent, "the nucleus of Israel's inheritance actually encompasses no more than 10,330 square miles."[40] As we have seen, Israel has been considered sacred space by varying groups for about twenty-five hundred to three thousand years, depending on whether one is a historical minimalist or a maximalist. However, the most sacred space within Israel is Jerusalem, and its temple. And, as expected under our theory, these entities have been the focus of violence in Israel.

Letters written by Jerusalem's ruler, Abdi-Heba, provide a glimpse of life at Jerusalem in the fourteenth century BCE. These letters were written to Akhenaten, the Egyptian pharaoh famous for introducing a sort of monotheism. The correspondence shows that Jerusalem was indeed involved in conflict then, but there is no mention of its holiness. We receive just a sliver of evidence in the following statement: "And now as for Jerusalem, if this land belongs to the king, why is it [not] of concern to the king like Hazzatu [land]?"[41] Note here that defense is solicited on political grounds (the land belongs to the king), and Abdi-Heba wants to incite the king to defend it as well as he appears to defend Hazzatu, another of the king's lands.

Although it is precarious to judge by absence, we should note that nowhere in any of this correspondence is there mention that Jerusalem is holy or sacred. The letters are all as practical and political as the one quoted above. The king should defend Jerusalem because it is his land, not because it is holy to some god whose existence cannot be verified. The putative owner, Akhenaten, actually exists. Abdi-Heba plays to the overlord's pride and fears of losing territory. Nowhere does Abdi-Heba say one must commit violence because a god said so. For this type of religious rationale pertaining to Jerusalem, we need to wait for the Hebrew Bible, and later Christianity and Islam.

If we return to the Hebrew Bible, we see that "sacred space" begins to be invoked as a rationale for exclusion and violence. The link between sacrality and violence is clear already in a story set in the time of Rehoboam, son of Solomon. According to 1 Kings 14:25–26, the Egyptian king, Shishak, went up to Jerusalem and "took away the treasures of the house of the LORD and the treasures of the king's house; he took everything. He also took away all the shields of gold that Solomon had made." Even if one argues that Shishak was mainly motivated by the monetary value of the treasure, it is clear that the material value was occasioned by the religious value of the place. That is to say, because it had religious value, material goods accrued to that sacred space, which resulted in it becoming a target for violent action by opponents.

Sacred spaces also figure in the violence that ensued in the rupture of the monarchy, as depicted in 1 Kings 12. Again, one must keep in mind that the episode is written from the viewpoint of the DtrH, which favored a single temple at Jerusalem. When the kingdom split, the northern ten tribes became a separate kingdom ruled first under Jeroboam. Judah and Benjamin, often referred to as Judah or the Southern Kingdom, were ruled by Rehoboam.

However, 1 Kings 12:26–33 says that Jeroboam feared the fact that the one temple was in Jerusalem. This meant that most of the tribute and offerings would be channeled to Judah's temple. So, as a countermeasure, Jeroboam established two shrines in the northern kingdom, at Bethel and Dan. In truth, the shrines at Bethel and Dan probably had a longer history, but we are looking at these shrines through the eyes of DtrH.

Amos, the prophet from Judah, is said to have spoken against the northern shrines:

> "the high places of Isaac shall be made desolate, and the sanctuaries of Israel shall be laid waste, and I will rise against the house of Jeroboam with the sword."

> Then Amaziah, the priest of Bethel, sent to King Jeroboam of Israel, saying, "Amos has conspired against you in the very center of the house of Israel; the land is not able to bear all his words." (Amos 7:9–10)

Although Amos is speaking of the actions of the Assyrians against these shrines, it is clear that the Hebrew author believes that violence is deserved. The Assyrians are simply instruments of God. The violence is deserved because the sacred spaces are not being used as the author would wish.

A more systematic kind of violence against rival sacred spaces is attributed to Hezekiah, king of Judah. During the reign of Hezekiah, the holiness of Jerusalem is said to have prompted another form of violence, but this time it was from within Israel rather than from an outsider. Hezekiah was faced with a threat from the rapacious Assyrian empire centered in Mesopotamia. The Assyrians had come all the way to Jerusalem in an attempt to take the city by force. This attempt is documented by Assyrian sources.[42]

What is interesting, for our purposes, is that 2 Kings 18 contains a speech attributed to an Assyrian official. The speech is meant to excite the citizens of Jerusalem against Hezekiah. One curious taunt addressed to Hezekiah and the inhabitants of Jerusalem was as follows: "But if you say to me, 'We rely on the LORD our God,' is it not he whose high places and altars Hezekiah has removed, saying to Judah and to Jerusalem, 'You shall worship before this altar in Jerusalem'?"

Indeed, Hezekiah appears to have destroyed other shrines dedicated to his own deity, Yahweh, in order to elevate the temple of Jerusalem to supremacy. Of course, this story seems to support the DtrH's emphasis that there should be only one legitimate temple for the entire nation of Israel, and that is the temple at Jerusalem. Hezekiah is portrayed as faithfully achieving this program of centralization by destroying temples of Yahweh located anywhere else. Violence, again, seems motivated, at least in part, by the idea that the temple of Jerusalem is more sacred and valuable than those at other places.

Later, Josiah, king of Judah, undertakes a systematic cleansing of the Temple of Jerusalem because it was not "holy" enough. That is to say, the temple was being used to worship other gods. Josiah's response, in part, is as follows:

> The king commanded the high priest Hilkiah, the priests of the second order, and the guardians of the threshold, to bring out of the temple of the LORD all the vessels made for Baal, for Asherah, and for all the host of heaven; he burned them outside Jerusalem in the fields of the Kidron, and carried their ashes to Bethel. (2 Kings 23:4)

As we have mentioned above, Josiah's actions were prompted by the belief that a sacred book had been discovered. That book directed Josiah to commit violence to maintain mono-Yahwism and to maintain or restore the privilege of the sacred space of Yahweh, the Temple at Jerusalem. Thus we see the violent link between inscripturation, sacred space, and group privileging.

By the postexilic period (after 538 BCE) Jerusalem was deemed by many to be uninhabitable, and special policies were enacted to repopulate it (see Neh. 7:4–5). As Nehemiah notes:

> Now the leaders of the people lived in Jerusalem; and the rest of the people cast lots to bring one out of ten to live in the holy city Jerusalem, while nine-tenths remained in the other towns.

> And the people blessed all those who willingly offered to live in Jerusalem. (Neh. 11:1–2)

In summary, the idea that Israel (and more specifically Jerusalem and its temple) is sacred space is primarily a religious idea. Jerusalem and Israel generally have not been endowed with rich natural resources. We see biblical authors endorse violence to defend Jerusalem's sanctity and we see enemies of Israel assailing it because it is regarded as sacred. We do not see such rationales for violence pertaining to Jerusalem before the Hebrew Bible (e.g., in the Amarna letters). Even if such prebiblical rationales for violence existed for Jerusalem or other cities, it is clear that Western ideas about the holiness of Jerusalem derive most directly from the biblical text and not from any other prebiblical source.

JERUSALEM AND MODERN ZIONISM

The modern conflict in Israel is complex. As with many of the conflicts we have studied, there are at least two viewpoints regarding the role of religion in the conflict. One side sees the conflict as primarily political, with religion forming a sort of sideshow.[43] In this scenario, the conflict began when Zionist Jews began to displace Palestinians in order to create a Jewish homeland. The conflict intensified in 1948, when perhaps between 472,000 and 900,000 Palestinians were made refugees in almost one fell swoop.[44]

Proponents of this side of the argument point to the fact that most Jews in Israel are secular, not religious. From one Palestinian perspective, the conflict in Israel may be seen as a symptom of colonial-imperialistic politics. For example, the conflict may be rooted in, among other political factors, the efforts of France and Britain to retain control of the Suez Canal. By controlling Palestine as a base, the British could monitor the canal.[45] From this perspective, religious rhetoric may simply be a symptom of politics.

The second perspective, and one we defend here, is that the type of Zionism that centers on Israel as the essential homeland for Jews ultimately rests on a religious belief in scriptural claims. In the absence of scripture or belief that God had given the land to the Hebrew people, this conflict may never have continued into the present. Thus, far from being mainly a political problem, modern Zionism represents the recrudescence of religious claims first enunciated in the Hebrew Bible.

To understand our argument, one need only look briefly at the life and correspondence of Theodor Herzl (1860–1904), the father of modern Zionism. Herzl's life has been the subject of recent revision, particularly the result of Jacques Kornberg's *Thedor Herzl: From Assimilation to Zionism*.[46] Kornberg argues against an older thesis, represented most thoroughly by the biography of Alex Bein, who believed that Herzl developed his Zionist idea after the infamous trial of Alfred Dreyfus in France in 1894.[47] Dreyfus was a French army officer who was accused of spying for Germany. Many saw the trial of Dreyfus, whom many consider to have been unjustly convicted and executed, as proof that anti-Semitism would never disappear despite the seeming assimilation of Jews into European society.

Kornberg shows that Herzl's idea of Zionism had crystallized before the Dreyfus affair. The legend that the Dreyfus affair was the catalyst for Herzl's Zionism can be traced to Herzl himself. Kornberg sees Herzl as engaging in a sort of revisionist autobiography, which can be refuted by studying Herzl's private correspondence predating the Dreyfus affair.

Moreover, Kornberg shows that Herzl was quite a secularized Jew. Born on May 2, 1860, in Budapest, Hungary, Herzl actually came to identify himself as an Austrian German. His yearning for assimilation while at the University of Vienna led him to join Albia, a German nationalist organization with an anti-Jewish animus. In a letter discussing his religious activities during a congress on Zionism in Basel, Herzl described his own diluted Judaism as follows: "I am no Rabbinic, and I attended temple in Basel only on the sabbath of the Congressweek. There I saluted the God of my fathers more than my own. I can worship my own God without Rabbis or prescribed prayers."[48]

However, Herzl eventually learned that his efforts at assimilation were all for naught. He would never be accepted as a real German, no matter how much he might mimic German customs. The idea that Germanism was in "the blood" was firmly rooted at the time of Herzl, and when expressed later by Hitler and other Nazi ideologues, the notion proved to be disastrous for Jews. Language and custom had little to do with being German; Jews would always be seen as a foreign element.

Seeing that assimilation would never be a permanent solution, Herzl proposed his modern version of Zionism in the First Zionist Congress, held in Basel, Switzerland, in 1897. While Herzl was already thinking of Palestine as a homeland for Jews, his secularism led him not to propose Israel as the *only* or *necessary* homeland of the Jews. In his famous 1895 Zionist manifesto,

Der Judenstaat (The Jewish State), Herzl in fact proposed Argentina as one of two options for a Jewish homeland.[49]

In a letter written in English and dated 1906, Herzl goes even further in considering options for a Jewish homeland:

> Jews will therefore be satisfied with any country be it ever so disadvanta-geous to ordinary immigrants, provided there can be fulfilled for them two conditions: firstly that white men be able to subsist there at all—and it is well known that Jews adapt themselves quickly to almost every climate—secondly that the administration of the proposed settlement, while even completely subject in every way to existing rule, shall be of such a Jewish "atmosphere" as to secure for them as Jews, liberty, safety, and justice.[50]

He held this view despite the fact that the idea for Jewish colonization of Palestine had been proposed by, among others, Moses Hess (1812–1875) and Zebi Hirsch Kalischer (1795–1874).[51]

However, sentiments similar to those of Herzl can be found among other more secularized Jews. Thus, Abraham Geiger (1810–1874), a Jewish theologian who advocated the abandonment of strict adherence to biblical and Talmudic laws, remarked that "[t]he present heap of ruins, Jerusalem, is, for us, at best, a poetic and melancholy memory. . . . Jerusalem is a thought for us, not a spatially limited place."[52]

So what happened? We suggest that Herzl's initial flexible position was eventually defeated by those Zionists, both Jewish and Gentile, who were inspired by the Bible. The insistence that Palestine be the *only, preferred,* or *essential* Jewish homeland, therefore, reflects a case where a modern ongoing conflict has been generated not because Zionists became more secular about a Jewish homeland, but rather because they came to accept certain biblical and fundamentally religious interpretations about the role of Palestine in Jewish life *despite* any secularism.[53]

In order to illustrate how the Bible permeated the renewed emphasis on Palestine as the Jewish homeland, let us look at two different types of professions represented in the Zionist movement: politicians and scientists. We begin with the politician Lord Arthur James Balfour (1848–1930), associated with now-famed author of the Balfour Declaration issued on November 2, 1917. The declaration, addressed to Lord Lionel Walter Rothschild, bears repetition:

> I have much pleasure in conveying to you, on behalf of His Majesty's Gov-ernment, the following declaration of sympathy with Jewish Zionist aspira-tions which has been submitted to, and approved by, the Cabinet:
>
> "His Majesty's Government view with favour the establishment in Palestine

of a national home for the Jewish people, and will use their best endeavours to facilitate the achievement of this object, it being clearly understood that nothing shall be done which may prejudice the civil and religious rights of existing non-Jewish communities in Palestine, or the rights and political status enjoyed by Jews in any other country." I should be grateful if you would bring this declaration to the knowledge of the Zionist Federation.[54]

Lord Balfour was born of Scottish ancestry in 1848.[55] Because of his brilliance and family connections, he rose quickly through the ranks of Parliament. At the time of the Balfour Declaration, he was foreign secretary. Balfour's motivations can be gauged from numerous writings he left, not to mention a biography by his niece, Blanche Dugdale, herself an ardent Zionist. In a speech delivered to a Bible society, Balfour made it clear that he regarded the Bible, even in the light of newer critical theories of its origin, as even a more "valuable source of spiritual life now than it could ever have been in the precritical days."[56]

Although he claimed to advocate democracy and self-determination, he made an exception in the case of Palestinians. He was frank in stating that if the Palestinians were to vote or even be consulted "they would unquestionably give an anti-Jewish verdict."[57] Overall, our assessment certainly agrees with that of Barbara Tuchman when she writes that "in Balfour the motive was biblical rather than imperial."[58]

But the British politicians were not alone in appealing to the Bible to support Zionism. During February 1944, the Seventy-eighth Congress of the United States held hearings on resolutions "relative to the Jewish National Home in Palestine," which were then published by Ktav, a well-known press for Jewish studies.[59] Although most of the senators and congressmen noted the Nazi atrocities as a cause for establishing a Jewish homeland, one can also see the role of the Bible in providing a justification. For example, Congressman John D. Dingell of Michigan, in an address to a synagogue in Detroit, argued as follows:

> From my earliest childhood I have always been taught to believe that Palestine was the ancestral, the historic, and the God-given land to the Jews; and I was taught moreover, that it was ordained by God that some day the Jews of the world would return to their homeland. . . . The Balfour Declaration clarified and gave additional substance to a practical, though not a new idea.[60]

Perhaps even more imperialistic and racist was the opinion voiced by Henry Cabot Lodge, a senator from Massachusetts. He explains his support for the Balfour Declaration as follows:

> You may smile when I tell you that, although, as I child I read my Bible, both the Old and New Testaments, I got my first idea of the present condition of Palestine and of the Mohammedan possession from two of Scott's novels. . . . I had of course intense sympathy with the Crusaders, and it seemed to me a great wrong that Jerusalem should be beneath the Muslim rule. . . . That Jerusalem and Palestine, sacred to the Jews, who had fought through the centuries to hold their city and their temple, a land profoundly holy to all the great Christian nations of the West should remain permanently in the hands of the Turks has seemed to me for many years one of the great blots on the face of civilization that ought to be erased [*sic*].[61]

Lodge made these statements after noting that "[t]he Turks were of a race generally regarded as related to the Mongols, who had come down from Asia and invaded the Empire of Byzantium. If they ever did anything of value to mankind history does not disclose it."[62] Needless to say, both Dingell and Lodge are recorded as voting for the resolutions supporting a Jewish homeland in Palestine.[63] As Yehuda Bauer notes, "[I]t would be unwise to ignore the tremendous influence of Christian religious attitudes that accepted the Jews as the rightful owners of the Holy Land."[64]

If politicians may have religious motives, certainly we would expect scientists to be free of religious motives. But science is sometimes contaminated with biblical agendas. One such example is the work of Walter Clay Lowdermilk (1888–1974), whose scientific findings were used to promote the Zionist argument for a Jewish homeland.[65] In 1939 Lowdermilk visited Palestine in his capacity as assistant chief of the United States Soil Conservation Service in the Department of Agriculture. Part of his mission was to survey the Near East "in the interests of land conservation in the United States."[66] However, Lowdermilk soon found himself entangled in a mission to develop the Jordan Valley Authority (JVA), an irrigation project modeled after the Tennessee Valley Authority.

The JVA had been prompted by efforts, reaching as far back as 1918, to irrigate a large area of Palestine using water from the Litani River. Such an irrigation project was necessary if Zionists were to make a case that Palestine was able to support large influxes of immigrants. However, most plans had failed until Lowdermilk made his proposal. He made a detailed report, and published his findings in semipopular form in his book *Palestine: Land of Promise*, published in 1944. He concluded that "full utilization of the Jordan Valley depression for reclamation and power will in time make possible the absorption of at least four million Jewish refugees from Europe, in addition to the 1,800,000 Arabs and Jews already in Palestine and Transjordan."[67]

Many anti-Zionists questioned not only Lowdermilk's motives, but also his scientific findings.[68] His main hypothesis, that the land could sustain more agriculture than it did currently, was based on the tenuous claim attributed to Moses in Deuteronomy 8:7–8, which speaks about God giving Israel: "A land of water brooks and fountains that spring out of valleys and depths, a land of wheat and barley of vines, figs and pomegranates, of olive oil and honey, a land in which thou shalt eat bread without scarceness, thou shalt not lack anything in it."[69]

Based, in part, on this description, Lowdermilk reasoned that "the Land of Israel was capable of supporting and actually did support at least twice as many inhabitants as at present."[70] It did not occur to Lowdermilk that biblical references to the abundance of Palestine may have been literary hyperbole or empty propaganda meant to incite Babylonian exiles to return to Israel. Nor did Lowdermilk select biblical texts that complain about miserable agricultural productivity in ancient Israel (e.g., Hag. 1:6).

Regardless of the validity of Lowdermilk's scientific findings, it is clear that his choice of study was motivated by the Bible. He did not give equal attention to all the lands he was sent to survey (e.g., North Africa and Europe). We can gauge further the extent of the Bible's influence on Lowdermilk by the biblical quotations at the heads of some of his book's chapters, as in the following examples:

> Chapter IV, Palestine in Ancient Times
> "A land wherein thou shalt eat bread without scarceness, thou shalt not lack anything in it" (Deut. 8:7–9).

> Chapter V, New Farmers in a Neglected Land
> "The Wilderness and the solitary place shall be glad for them" (Isa. 35:1).

Lowdermilk himself spoke of the influence that the Bible exerted on his selection of Palestine as an area worthy of scientific study, writing:

> Palestine was of special interest to me because the Bible presents the most authentic and longest written record of any nation except China. Indeed, the peoples of these sacred lands of the Near East are responsible for much that makes the religious, political, and educational institutions of the Western Hemisphere full of meaning for us.[71]

Lowdermilk, in fact, saw himself as reenacting the biblical Exodus as he traveled from Egypt to Israel: "In February, 1939, we, like the Children of Israel, left the land of Egypt before daylight . . ."[72] Lowdermilk, for all of his scientific expertise, still relies on uncritical acceptance of biblical history, as in his statements that

[t]he movement for establishing a Jewish homeland in Palestine is one of the most remarkable records of a people's struggle for national survival and self expression. It began about four thousand years ago in Ur of the Chaldees, when Abraham, prompted by divine inspiration left the plains of Mesopotamia to establish a new people on the Land of Canaan.[73]

Lowdermilk assumed not only the historicity of the biblical claim about Abraham's migration to be true, but further stated that Abraham was divinely inspired.

The historicity of Abraham, not to mention the historicity of the entire patriarchal period, has suffered devastating critiques in the last half century. Even some of the more conservative academic scholars can only content themselves with trying to establish the general historical context of patriarchal history. But even this seems to be a tenuous claim. In any case, Lowdermilk repeated his biblical claims as he testified before Congress in the resolutions of 1944 discussed above.[74]

And if we believe secular Jews do not use the Bible to support their case, we only need to see the example of Alan Dershowitz, a professor at Harvard Law School. In his recent book *The Case for Israel*, Dershowitz makes the shocking statement that "[h]istorians believe that the Hebrews arrived in present-day Israel sometime in the second millennium B.C.E. Under Joshua, and later King David and his successors, independent Hebrew kingdoms existed."[75]

In fact, there is no prominent Christian, Jewish, or secular historian who argues that an independent Hebrew kingdom ever existed under Joshua. Never does the Bible claim that Joshua was a king or had a kingdom. The Bible assigns the honor of being the first king to Saul (1 Sam. 10:17–26). We have no record of any non-Israelite kingdom that recognized Joshua as having an independent kingdom. We have no demographic data to support the claim that Jews formed the main part of the population for most of the sixteen hundred years between 1000 BCE and 636 CE. Dershowitz cites an atlas by Martin Gilbert, who is not a biblical historian, for this claim.[76] (Dershowitz's citation actually refers to a small information box in Gilbert's book, which provides no documentation for the claim.)

By most counts, tens of thousands of people have died violently since Israel became a nation. Figures published by Israel's Ministry of Foreign Affairs indicate that some 1,895 Israelis have died as a result of hostile action between 1948 and 1999.[77] Numbers for Palestinian deaths are more difficult to gauge, but most place them in the tens of thousands since 1948. Whatever one thinks of who owns what specific piece of land in Israel, it is fair to say that this conflict would not exist if it were not for the belief that God had given the land to Israel. The conflict would not exist if Jews did not see themselves as different from Muslims, and vice versa.

In sum, it is untenable to see the conflict between Palestinians and Jews as simply a secular or political fight for land. The main argument for Palestine as a Jewish homeland is inspired by religious claims from the Bible. Muslims counter with their own scriptural and religious arguments. Theodor Herzl, a secular Jew, did not propose in his Zionist manifesto of 1895 that Palestine was the only acceptable homeland for Jews. As late as 1906, Herzl still did not seem to believe that Palestine was the only acceptable homeland for the Jews.

It is true, as Pappe notes, that some of the more traditional rabbis ironically also resisted Israelite Zionism because of the biblical belief that Jews would remain in exile until the advent of the Messiah. It is also true that some liberal Jewish groups (e.g., the American Council for Judaism) rejected an essential link between Judaism and a given territory.[78] However, Pappe and other historians still downplay the biblical basis for most Zionists' eventually settling on the idea that Israel was the proper Jewish homeland.[79] And unlike the case of some of the orthodox Jews who used the Bible to reject political Zionism, there was no secular reason that made it *necessary* to have a Jewish homeland in Palestine.[80] The idea of Palestine as an "essentially" Jewish homeland cannot be understood except as a rebiblicalization of Zionist politics.[81]

GROUP PRIVILEGING

The ancient Israelites probably lived amidst a variety of ethnic groups. This is indicated by the Hebrew Bible itself. Thus, we are told that there are Hivites, Perizzites, Moabites, and Ammonites living in and around the land of Israel. External historical records also testify to the variety of groups that lived in and around Israel. New studies of ethnicity in ancient Israel and the ancient world are also stressing the ways in which people construct their identities and the way in which ethnic constructions related to imperialism, colonialism, and/or broader core-periphery relationships.[82]

The construction of identity in ancient Israel revolved around genealogical relationships, fictional or not. Identity was almost always transferred through the male line. Women sometimes were not identified even by name. The idea that the Hebrews were to maintain genealogical purity is evident throughout the Hebrew Bible. For example, in Genesis 24, when Abraham seeks to find a wife for Isaac, he instructs his servant as follows:

> "and I will make you swear by the LORD, the God of heaven and earth, that you will not get a wife for my son from the daughters of the Canaanites, among whom I live,

but will go to my country and to my kindred and get a wife for my son Isaac." (Gen. 24:3-4)

Likewise, there were specific injunctions against allowing certain ethnic groups to join the Israelite community for a variety of reasons. Thus, Deuteronomy 23:3–6 says:

No Ammonite or Moabite shall be admitted to the assembly of the LORD. Even to the tenth generation, none of their descendants shall be admitted to the assembly of the LORD,

because they did not meet you with food and water on your journey out of Egypt, and because they hired against you Balaam son of Beor, from Pethor of Mesopotamia, to curse you.

(Yet the LORD your God refused to heed Balaam; the LORD your God turned the curse into a blessing for you, because the LORD your God loved you.)

You shall never promote their welfare or their prosperity as long as you live.

Belonging to the genealogical collective called Israel conferred certain privileges related to space. In the case of the land of Israel, it is clear that biblical authors believed that Yahweh had given them a special privilege to live there:

For you are a people holy to the LORD your God; the LORD your God has chosen you out of all the peoples on earth to be his people, his treasured possession. (Deut. 7:6)

The mythology of Israel's chosen status is also reflected in a passage now somewhat obscured by English translations of:

When the Most High apportioned the nations, when he divided humankind, he fixed the boundaries of the peoples according to the number of the gods;

the LORD's own portion was his people, Jacob his allotted share. (Deut. 32:8–9)

The mythological context of this passage has become better understood in light of the monumental discoveries of texts at Ugarit in 1929. Ugarit was a city that flourished in the fourteenth century BCE. In 1929 archaeologists discovered the remains of this ancient city at Ras Shamra, in modern Syria.

The city also yielded a mountain of texts in Ugaritic, a language heretofore unknown to modern scholars.[83]

Ugaritic texts revealed that some of the names for Israel's deities probably derived from Canaanite precursors. Israel's god, Yahweh, could now be understood as a development of the mythology reflected, at least in part, at Ugarit. In Ugaritic mythology, the high god was named El or Elyon, and he had children. Thus, Deuteronomy 32:8–9 seems to reflect a polytheistic pantheon. Translations obscure the fact that "the Most High" is actually Elyon, a god superior to—and separate from—Yahweh. In fact, Yahweh appears to be Elyon's son. Elyon divides up the earth, and Yahweh is simply one of the sons of Elyon—who receives the portion of the earth that came to be known as Israel.[84]

But whereas in Deuteronomy 32 we find Yahweh to be simply one of many gods sharing the earth, the situation changes in Psalm 82.[85]

> God has taken his place in the divine council; in the midst of the gods he holds judgment:
>
> "How long will you judge unjustly and show partiality to the wicked?
>
> Give justice to the weak and the orphan; maintain the right of the lowly and the destitute.
>
> Rescue the weak and the needy; deliver them from the hand of the wicked."
>
> They have neither knowledge nor understanding, they walk around in darkness; all the foundations of the earth are shaken.
>
> I say, "You are gods, children of the Most High, all of you;
>
> nevertheless, you shall die like mortals, and fall like any prince."
>
> Rise up, O God, judge the earth; for all the nations belong to you! (Ps. 82:1–8)

In short, Yahweh has moved from being a national god to having a worldwide empire, or at least an empire that covered the world that was then known to the Hebrews. As we shall see, the imperial nature of Israelite religion is sometimes sanitized in scholarship and theology as a benign universalism, but it entailed ideas about violence and genocide that were paralleled repeatedly throughout history.

In fact, sometimes texts that endorse group privileging have been misunderstood to mean something more inclusive and "universal." Sometimes these texts even are used to support pacificism. As we pointed out, the sociologists Glock and Stark concluded their study of anti-Semitism with the recommendation "if the faithful would heed the message 'Love thy neighbor as thyself,' an account such as ours could not have been written."[86] This oft-cited proverb is first found in Leviticus 19:18, which reads in whole: "You shall not take vengeance or bear a grudge against any of your people, but you shall love your neighbor as yourself: I am the LORD."

However, as Harry M. Orlinsky, the prominent scholar of Hebrew, has deftly noted, the Hebrew term *re 'eka*, which translates as "your neighbor," is actually best understood as "your fellow Israelite."[87] The verse's final instruction to love your fellow Israelite as yourself, therefore, follows logically on the instruction not to hate anyone of your kin (*benê 'ammeka*) in the first half of the verse. Thus, the verse does not obligate universal love, but, in fact, is premised on privileging love for fellow Israelites over love for non-Israelites.

Similarly misunderstood is Malachi 2:10, which says: "Have we not all one father? Has not one God created us? Why then are we faithless to one another, profaning the covenant of our ancestors?" However, the terms "we" and "us" refer to Hebrews, not to everyone else. The prophet is specifically addressing the priest at the beginning of the chapter: "And now, O priests, this command is for you." These priests have been mistreating nonpriestly Hebrews. The prophet, therefore, urges these priests to see all Hebrews as members of the same covenant community. Again, this verse is premised on the idea of group privileging (Hebrews), and not a universalist text.

In a series of works Peter Machinist has attempted to emphasize the flexible nature of ethnic relations in the ancient Near East.[88] While we recognize that there were complex relationships between cultures that sometimes allowed for more interaction than what texts showed, it is also true that these texts served to reinforce differences. In any case, it was genealogy that was of utmost importance in reinforcing identity for Hebrew authors. This importance is still extant, as evident from some precarious recent attempts to establish genetic linkages with ancient Hebrew priestly families.[89]

VIOLENCE RESULTING FROM GROUP PRIVILEGING

The idea that Israel was a chosen group created conflicts that are evident already within the Hebrew Bible. The "chosenness" of Israel is most clear in Deuteronomy:

> It was not because you were more numerous than any other people that the LORD set his heart on you and chose you—for you were the fewest of all peoples.

It was because the LORD loved you and kept the oath that he swore to your ancestors, that the LORD has brought you out with a mighty hand, and redeemed you from the house of slavery, from the hand of Pharaoh king of Egypt.

Know therefore that the LORD your God is God, the faithful God who maintains covenant loyalty with those who love him and keep his command-ments, to a thousand generations, . . . (Deut. 7:7–9)

One obvious concomitant of seeing oneself as chosen is that it instantly creates insiders and outsiders. Outsiders do not have equal access to the empowered group's privileges, so potential conflict is inherent in the very fact of group privileging. Conflicts related to group privileging can be divided into two broad categories:

1. Those in which the privileged group commits violence to maintain its position.
2. Those in which a nonprivileged group fights to improve its position.

These two situations fulfill the conditions we described in the introduction. Briefly, we hold that scarce resource X created by religion may cause violence when at least one of two or more groups (1) desire X and/or believe that they are uniquely entitled to X; and/or (2) violence is used as a method to acquire and/or defend against the loss of X.

Of course, these categories can be found even when group privileging is not religious in nature. But, as our argument holds, group privileging resulting from religious motives is more wasteful in the violence it produces because the premise on which the privilege is granted is ultimately unverifi-able.

At the smallest level of social organization and at the lowest level of vio-lence, group privileging results in the fragmentation of families. For example, Ezra 10:3–44 details a major dissolution of families based on group privileging. After the Babylonian exile, the Jews return to Israel. However, the priestly author of Ezra favors a policy that Jews must not marry non-Jews. The author insists that those who had married foreign wives send them away together with their children (Ezra 10:44). The same passage details opposition to this family-fissioning policy. As we have mentioned, this idea can already be found in the case of Abraham's search for a spouse for his son Isaac. In anthropological terms, Ezra favored endogamy over exogamy.

When this privilege is attributed to supernatural forces and/or beings, then we may say that religious belief has generated a scarce resource called group privilege. And when a privileged group feels threatened, then it may take violent measures to preserve that privilege or extend that privilege. Thus, religious belief can be said to be a main factor in generating this violence.

At the most extreme level of violence, group privileging results in the extermination of at least some groups of people that are seen to threaten the privileged group in power. This is most clear in a number of passages, such as the following:

> When the LORD your God brings you into the land that you are about to enter and occupy, and he clears away many nations before you—the Hittites, the Girgashites, the Amorites, the Canaanites, the Perizzites, the Hivites, and the Jebusites, seven nations mightier and more numerous than you and when the LORD your God gives them over to you and you defeat them, then you must utterly destroy them. Make no covenant with them and show them no mercy.
>
> Do not intermarry with them, giving your daughters to their sons or taking their daughters for your sons,
>
> for that would turn away your children from following me, to serve other gods. Then the anger of the LORD would be kindled against you, and he would destroy you quickly.
>
> But this is how you must deal with them: break down their altars, smash their pillars, hew down their sacred poles, and burn their idols with fire.
>
> For you are a people holy to the LORD your God; the LORD your God has chosen you out of all the peoples on earth to be his people, his treasured possession. (Deut. 7:1–6).

Note that this passage links the "chosenness" of Israel with the destruction of the particular outsiders. Note that destruction of others is attributed to Israel's "holiness."

According to subsequent narratives, this policy was put into effect in the conquest of Canaan by Joshua and his successors. Thus, at the beginning of Joshua, we are told:

> After the death of Moses the servant of the LORD, the LORD spoke to Joshua son of Nun, Moses' assistant, saying,
>
> "My servant Moses is dead. Now proceed to cross the Jordan, you and all this people, into the land that I am giving to them, to the Israelites.
>
> Every place that the sole of your foot will tread upon I have given to you, as I promised to Moses.

> From the wilderness and the Lebanon as far as the great river, the river Euphrates, all the land of the Hittites, to the Great Sea in the west shall be your territory.

> No one shall be able to stand against you all the days of your life. As I was with Moses, so I will be with you; I will not fail you or forsake you.

> Be strong and courageous; for you shall put this people in possession of the land that I swore to their ancestors to give them. (Josh. 1:1–6)

Then, beginning with Jericho, we see Joshua and his troops doing what Deuteronomy said. Note, for example, the summary of actions against Jericho: " Then they devoted to destruction by the edge of the sword all in the city, both men and women, young and old, oxen, sheep, and donkeys" (Josh. 6:21).

When they reach the northern city of Hazor, Joshua is said to put his policy of genocide into effect again:

> And they put to the sword all who were in it, utterly destroying them; there was no one left who breathed, and he burned Hazor with fire.

> And all the towns of those kings, and all their kings, Joshua took, and struck them with the edge of the sword, utterly destroying them, as Moses the servant of the LORD had commanded. (Josh. 11:11–12)

Most of these violent episodes occur in the DtrH, and have been linked with what has been called "Holy War" or "Yahweh War." The term "Holy War," first popularized by Gerhard von Rad, actually goes at least as far back as Friedrich Schwally's work on Semitic warfare.[90] The Hebrew institution that corresponds to these terms is usually called *herem*.

The term "divine war" has also been advocated by Sa-Moon Kang, but for reasons based, in part, on an unclear contrast with Islamic jihad.[91] Kang argues that, in contrast to jihad, which he views as a Muslim effort "to spread their faith," Yahweh war is "a war for Israelites' existence as a people."[92] Kang cites not a single Islamic source for this statement. As we shall show more clearly in our upcoming discussion of jihad, the latter can also be seen as defensive war undertaken for the sake of the existence of Muslims as a people. Jihad can be interpreted as an imperialist effort to bring the whole world under Allah's dominion. In this sense, the repeated notions that Yahweh will conquer the entire world do not differ much from some conceptions of jihad.

Most scholars today acknowledge that many of the specific practices mentioned in the biblical materials are paralleled by war practices in other

Near Eastern cultures.[93] These features include encouragement to the warriors not to fear. The annihilation of people as a gift or sacrifice to a god is also part of many of these traditions. The idea that a god is giving land or victory permeates these traditions as well.

But not all of the violence can be reduced to a military *herem*. Clearly, also endorsed is mass killing by individuals who are not portrayed as being connected with the military. One particular example is found in 1 Kings 18, where Elijah, the Yahwistic prophet, engages in a contest with the priests of Baal. The contest consists of seeing which god will answer by fire when called upon. A sacrificial bull is prepared, and the priests call upon Baal. Their god does not answer. Elijah calls upon Yahweh, who answers with fire. As a result, Elijah butchers 450 prophets of Baal (1 Kings 18:40). Again, the author sees violence as the proper response to competition for group privileging based on religious beliefs.

The notion of group privileging is often closely bound up with the idea of holiness. As we have already observed, the concept of "holiness," which has acquired a rather benign metaphysical connotation in Western culture, is actually quite an exclusivistic and violent concept, which is often diluted in academic treatments of "holiness."[94] Usually, something "holy" has a special value, as we saw with land. In terms of people, "holy" simply privileges a group in relation to others. Since it has no verifiable origin in any divine process, it is simply a way to privilege a favored group. So holiness is simply another idiom in the discourse of power.

Of course, the group in an inferior position will often commit violence in order to improve its position or defend itself. This type of violence is also justified on religious grounds in the Hebrew Bible. Thus, in Exodus 1 it is the Egyptians who seek to maintain their privilege in the face of a growing population of Hebrew slaves. The Exodus ensues, and, of course, Yahweh is said to drown a whole Egyptian army.

SALVATION

As we have mentioned, "salvation" is the name we give to a set of benefits and status achieved through supernatural means. In ancient Israel salvation could mean that one was protected from real physical harm. But to "save" could sometimes be seen in purely human terms, as people could also be said to "save" others, as is the case with Saul in 1 Samuel 10:27: "But some worthless fellows said, 'How can this man save us?'"

However, for the purpose of explaining violence, the main form of salvation that concerns us is that attributed to supernatural causes, and principally to the work of Yahweh. The Israelite god was the master of his people, who are viewed as his slaves. As the slavemaster of his people, Yahweh bears the role of protector as well. Thus, he says:

> Because the LORD your God travels along with your camp, to save you and to hand over your enemies to you, therefore your camp must be holy, so that he may not see anything indecent among you and turn away from you. (Deut. 23:14)

It is also clear throughout the Hebrew Bible that salvation is not a resource that is equally distributed. The author of John perceives this uneven distribution of salvation when he quotes Jesus saying to the Jews: "You worship what you do not know; we worship what we know, for salvation is from the Jews" (John 4:22). Indeed, the Hebrew Bible indicates that Yahweh has a special relationship with his people, and so mainly restricts salvation to Israel:

> Now then bring it about; for the LORD has promised David: Through my servant David I will save *my people* Israel from the hand of the Philistines, and from all their enemies. (2 Sam. 3:18)

In some cases, Yahweh is portrayed as providing salvation only because of a special relationship with individuals, as in 2 Kings 19:34: "For I will defend this city to save it, for my own sake and for the sake of my servant David."

Of course, salvation can be scarce for the Israelites if they fail to do as their divine master says:

> They looked, but there was no one to save them; they cried to the LORD, but he did not answer them. (2 Sam. 22:42)

Salvation can also be purely for the purpose of showing the glory of Yahweh to non–Yahweh worshippers:

> So now, O LORD our God, save us, I pray you, from his hand, so that all the kingdoms of the earth may know that you, O LORD, are God alone. (2 Kings 19:19)

Salvation is available if one prays to the temple of Yahweh:

> "If disaster comes upon us, the sword, judgment, or pestilence, or famine, we will stand before this house, and before you, for your name is in this house, and cry to you in our distress, and you will hear and save." (2 Chron. 20:9)

Salvation is particularly reserved for Yahweh's territorial possessions, as indicated in Psalm 69:35: "For God will save Zion and rebuild the cities of Judah; and his servants shall live there and possess it." Similarly, Isaiah 45:20 indicates that salvation is to be found only in Yahweh, and other gods cannot save anyone: "Assemble yourselves and come together, draw near, you survivors of the nations! They have no knowledge—those who carry about their wooden idols, and keep on praying to a god that cannot save."

If people believe in a supernatural salvation—in this case, a protection wrought by supernatural entities or processes—then there naturally arises the question of which supernatural process or entity actually provides protection. If salvation is thought to reside in only one particular supernatural being and/or process, then it becomes a scarce resource because it is not available to those who do not engage in such a process or worship such a god. When a group lives in isolation, such notions of protection are probably of no great consequence for intergroup conflict. But when groups feel that scarce resource threatened by outsiders, then violence will likely ensue.

VIOLENCE RESULTING FROM SALVATION

When groups with radically different notions of salvation interact, then conflict can ensue if the means of salvation used by one group somehow infringes on the salvation process of another group. For example, if worship of Yahweh is the only way to bring salvation, this protection becomes a scarce resource if some group becomes an obstacle to obtaining the favor of Yahweh.

Indeed, suppose a group believes that salvation resides in Baal, not Yahweh. By itself this fact may not produce conflict. However, when the worship of Baal is feared to produce wrath from Yahweh, then the worship of Baal will be seen as interfering with the salvation process of the Yahweh worshipper. Salvation is a scarce resource, and attempting to secure that scarce resource becomes conflictive.

We indeed see this very process in the case of the Hebrew Bible, where worship of Baal and other gods was thought to degrade the opportunity to gain the scarce commodity called "salvation" by the Israelites. For example, in Numbers we are told that some Israelites feared that the worship of the Baal of Peor will incite Yahweh against all of Israel.

> Thus Israel yoked itself to the Baal of Peor, and the LORD's anger was kindled against Israel.
>
> The LORD said to Moses, "Take all the chiefs of the people, and impale

them in the sun before the LORD, in order that the fierce anger of the LORD may turn away from Israel." (Num. 25:3–4)

Likewise, in Judges 2:13–15, we are told that Yahweh became angry when the Israelites abandoned him to worship Baal. The result was predictable; "Whenever they marched out, the hand of the LORD was against them to bring misfortune, as the LORD had warned them and sworn to them; and they were in great distress."

Averting loss of Yahweh's favor and salvation from Yahweh's wrath could lead to the rationale that the cause of the problem had to be eliminated. This is what we see in the narratives concerning King Jehu.

Then Jehu entered the temple of Baal with Jehonadab son of Rechab; he said to the worshipers of Baal, "Search and see that there is no worshiper of the LORD here among you, but only worshipers of Baal. . . ."

As soon as he had finished presenting the burnt offering, Jehu said to the guards and to the officers, "Come in and kill them; let no one escape." So they put them to the sword. The guards and the officers threw them out, and then went into the citadel of the temple of Baal.

They brought out the pillar that was in the temple of Baal, and burned it.

Then they demolished the pillar of Baal, and destroyed the temple of Baal, and made it a latrine to this day. Thus Jehu wiped out Baal from Israel. (2 Kings 10:23, 10:25–28)

One could argue that the conflict between Baal and Yahweh was not about scarce resources at all. Political factors were at work, couched in religious terms. But this does not explain why Baal worship is seen as evil. In order for Baal worship to be seen as evil, a religious belief must be at work. Accordingly, we can say that these are all authentic instances of religious violence, in theory or in practice.

"BENIGN" VIOLENCE AND SALVATION

While we have already discussed cases in which a belief can cause the believer to perpetrate violence on members of other religions, we can also find examples of how religious belief X can lead one to submit to an act of violence against oneself or to commit an act of "benign" violence upon members of one's own religion. By "benign" violence, I mean an act of violence thought to be for the good of the victim rather than because he is regarded as an enemy. Such benign violence can still be subsumed under the rationale Religious Belief X, therefore Act of Violence Y.

Benign violence can be illustrated with the events of 1096, when groups of Christians unleashed some of the most significant anti-Jewish violence of the Middle Ages. The main historical sources for these attacks on Jews consist of three Hebrew narratives, one of which is anonymous. The other two are attributed to Solomon bar Simson, whom we have already met, and Rabbi Eliezer bar Nathan. According to these sources, a group of lay crusaders, led by a German man named Emicho, were mainly responsible.[95]

One case pertains to Master Isaac, who was about to set his own house on fire in order not to be taken alive by the rampaging Christians. He asked his family if they wished to become a sacrifice with him, and exclaimed, "My children, my children, Our God is the true God— there is none other!"[96] He then proceeded to take his children to the synagogue at midnight.

The narrator tells us that while in front of the Holy Ark, "he slaughtered them, in sanctification of the Great Name. Who has commanded us not to forsake pure fear of Him for any other belief, and to adhere to his Holy Torah with all our heart and soul."[97] Master Isaac added, "May this blood expiate all my transgressions!"[98] In the final scene of the story, as the Christians offer to rescue him, we receive indication for his refusal: "'Wicked Man, escape the flame; you can still save yourself.' They extended a pole toward him in order to draw him from the flames, but the saintly man did not want to grasp it, and died in the flame, an innocent, just, and God-fearing man. And his soul has found shelter in the precincts of righteousness in the Garden of Eden."[99]

Salvation is a scarce resource in Judaism because it can only be acquired through very specific means that are not available to outsiders. Worshipping the Christian god, for example, is not a way to achieve salvation in Judaism. Only by retaining one's Judaism can one be saved. Master Isaac's greater reward is to enter paradise.

Other very specific rationales for violence can also be found in these Chronicles. The Chronicle of Solomon bar Simson, for instance, says that some of the Jews gave the following reason for their submission to martyrdom:

> The Holy One . . . has commanded us to allow ourselves to be killed and slain in witness to the Oneness of his Holy Name. Happy are we if we fulfill his will, and happy is he who is slain or slaughtered and who dies attesting the Oneness of His Name. Such a one is destined for the World-to-Come, where he will sit in the realm of the saints—Rabbi Akiba and his companions, pillars of the universe, who were killed in witness to his name.[100]

In short, martyrdom is believed (1) to be commanded by God, and (2) to confer supernatural rewards, which we call salvation. One ought only to be too happy to be killed by this logic. This is indeed a case that can be summarized as Religioius Belief X, therefore Act of Violence Y. In these cases the acts of violence are being performed by believers upon themselves or by proxy, or by default.

CIRCUMCISION AS INTERNAL VIOLENCE

Part of our argument has involved the observation that treatises on violence focus on military activities. By doing so, many religions can be evaluated as being mostly peaceful. However, our definition of violence as any act that modifies the body in order to express power differentials, encompasses circumcision, the removal of the foreskin of the penis. Circumcision may be seen as part of a larger class of genital modification that can also include female genitalia. For the moment, however, we concentrate on the most commonly known practice in Judaism.

It should be noted first that circumcision was probably not originally a Hebrew custom, because there is an apparent depiction of circumcision from as early as 2400 BCE (Fifth Dynasty) in a bas relief from Saqqara, Egypt.[101] But within Jewish tradition, circumcision is traced to the "mark" of the covenant outlined in Genesis 17:[102]

> God said to Abraham, "As for you, you shall keep my covenant, you and your offspring after you throughout their generations.
>
> This is my covenant, which you shall keep, between me and you and your offspring after you: Every male among you shall be circumcised.
>
> You shall circumcise the flesh of your foreskins, and it shall be a sign of the covenant between me and you.
>
> Throughout your generations every male among you shall be circumcised when he is eight days old, including the slave born in your house and the one bought with your money from any foreigner who is not of your offspring.
>
> Both the slave born in your house and the one bought with your money must be circumcised. So shall my covenant be in your flesh an everlasting covenant.
>
> Any uncircumcised male who is not circumcised in the flesh of his foreskin shall be cut off from his people; he has broken my covenant." (Gen. 17:9–14)

At least two features emerge from this institution. First, it is a practice commanded by Israel's lord, Yahweh (see also Exod. 4:24–25). It is not voluntary insofar as it is imposed on children and on slaves.

The "original" motive for circumcision is poorly understood, but one plausible scenario is that it originated as a slave mark. Briefly, the argument for such an origin is that: (1) persons do not normally submit to such a procedure without some coercion; (2) modification of the anatomy is a known method of slave marking, as indicated in Exodus 21:6: "his master shall pierce his ear with an awl; and he shall serve him for life"; and (3) a test of loyalty by a slave for a master would most naturally require an action that would be otherwise undesirable for a slave. That is to say, if a master wanted to test whether a new slave would be obedient and loyal, then the master could require the slave to mutilate himself as a test (see also Gen. 34:21–25).

While Jon Levenson, among other modern Jewish scholars, still defends the practice as "essential" to Jewish life, there is a growing number of other Jewish authors who see circumcision as an unnecessary and even barbaric practice that should end.[103] Among the most vocal opponents is Ronald Goldman.[104] In brief, Goldman notes that there are no significant health benefits from the practice, which is affirmed by an important statement of the American Academy of Pediatrics published in 1999.[105]

The belief that God commanded circumcision certainly qualifies as a religious belief, and the mutilation of the penis in this manner certainly qualifies as violence. Accordingly, circumcision as justified in the Hebrew Bible, and in almost every Abrahamic tradition, would qualify, from our perspective, as violence of the type Religious Belief X, therefore Act of Violence Y. The practice can be related to the scarcities we associate with group privilege and salvation, especially as the Talmud (Aboth 3:11) suggests the belief that one may not enjoy paradise without circumcision. Therefore, circumcision also qualifies as another type of "benign" internal violence that is often overlooked or sanitized in the Abrahamic religions.

SUMMARY

As in the other so-called Abrahamic religions we will study, ancient Israelite religion does indeed record conflicts resulting from the four scarce resources on which we focus. Which authorities and texts contained God's word was a subject of conflict repeatedly (e.g., Numbers 12, Deuteronomy 18, Jeremiah 8:8). The creation of the sacred space called Jerusalem and the Temple of Yahweh resulted not only in strife within Israel, but also made that space a resource targeted by external enemies. Group privileging, based on genealogy, can be seen as related to the genocidal policies in Deuteronomy 7 and 20, among other places. Salvation could mean that one had to mutilate penises or kill one's own family to maintain, or defend against the loss of, Yahweh's favor. As we shall see, these same scarce resources will continue to foment violence of varying intensity in Christianity and Islam.

NOTES

1. The academic study of the Hebrew Bible is being reconfigured and consensus is difficult to achieve on any single theme. We can recommend only cautiously the following representative surveys of the Hebrew Bible. Norman Gottwald, *The Hebrew Bible: A Socio-Literary Introduction* (Philadelphia: Fortress, 1985) has a Marxist liberation theology angle. Brevard Childs, *Introduction to the Old Testament as Scripture* (Philadelphia: Fortress, 1979) has a more conservative critical bent. A more elementary survey is provided by Barry L. Bandstra, *Reading the Old Testament: An Introduction to the Hebrew Bible*, 3rd ed. (Belmont, CA: Wadsworth, 2004).

2. Biblical "history" is also undergoing a drastic revision. A standard brief history is provided by J. Maxwell Miller and John H. Hayes, *A History of Ancient Israel and Judah* (Philadelphia: Westminster, 1986). A more exhaustive history, with a heavy emphasis on archaeology, is that of Gösta W. Ahlström, *The History of Ancient Palestine* (Minneapolis: Fortress, 1993). Revisionist histories may be found in Keith Whitelam, *The Invention of Ancient Israel: The Silencing of Palestinian History* (London: Routledge, 1996); and Niels Peter Lemche, *Ancient Israel: A New History of Israelite Society* (Sheffield, UK: JSOT, 1990). For a review of the historiographical problems, with various viewpoints, see the collection of essays in V. Philips Long, ed., *Israel's Past in Present Research: Essays on Ancient Israelite Historiography* (Winona Lake, IN: Eisenbrauns, 1999).

3. "Minimalist" works include Philip Davies, *In Search of "Ancient Israel"* (Sheffield, UK: JSOT Press, 1992); *Whose Bible Is It Anyway?* (Sheffield, UK: Sheffield Academic Press, 1995); and Thomas L. Thompson, *The Mythic Past: Biblical Archaeology and the Myth of Israel* (London: Basic Books, 1999). For a response to the "minimalists" from an archaeologist, see William G. Dever, *What Did the Biblical Writers Know and When Did They Know It? What Archaeology Can Tell Us about the Reality of Ancient Israel* (Grand Rapids, MI: Eerdmans, 2001).

4. See James Barr, *The Concept of Biblical Theology* (Minneapolis: Fortress, 1999).

5. Gerhard von Rad, *Old Testament Theology*, trans. D. M. G. Stalker, 2 vols. (London: SCM Press, 1975); Walter Eichrodt, *Theology of the Old Testament*, trans. J. A. Baker, 2 vols. (Philadelphia: Westminster, 1961); Brevard Childs, *Biblical Theology of the Old and New Testaments* (London: SCM Press, 1992); Bernhard W. Anderson, *Contours of Old Testament Theology* (Minneapolis: Fortress, 1999).

6. Martin Noth, *Überlieferungsgeschichtliche Studien* (Halle: Max Niedermeyer Verlag, 1943); for an English edition, see *The Deuteronomistic History*, trans. Jane Doull and John Barton (Sheffield, UK: Sheffield Academic Press, 1981). For an

assessment of Noth's theory, see Mark O' Brien, *The Deuteronomistic History Hypothesis: A Reassessment* (Göttingen: Vandenhoeck & Ruprecht, 1989).

7. We specify "Hebrew Bible" because the order of books is different in the Protestant canon, which includes Ruth between Judges and 1 Samuel. Using the Hebrew Bible, the books that are part of DtrH are Deuteronomy, Joshua, Judges, 1 Samuel, 2 Samuel, 1 Kings, and 2 Kings.

8. There is a debate about whether the correct date for the destruction of Jerusalem by the Babylonians is 586 or 587. For the latter date, see Henri Cazelles, "587 ou 586?" in *The Word of the Lord Shall Go Forth: Essays in Honor of David Noel Freedman in Celebration of His Sixtieth Birthday*, ed. Carol L. Meyers and M. O'Connor (Winona Lake, IN: Eisenbrauns, 1983), pp. 417–35.

9. One example would be C. S. Cowles, "The Case for Radical Discontinuity," in *Show Them No Mercy: 4 Views on God and Canaanite Genocide*, ed. Stanley N. Gundry (Grand Rapids, MI: Eerdmans, 2003), pp. 13–44.

10. Gleason Archer, *Encyclopedia of Bible Difficulties* (Grand Rapids, MI: Zondervan, 1982), p. 121.

11. Some examples include Daniel Friedmann, *To Kill and Take Possession: Law, Morality, and Society in Biblical Stories* (Peabody, MA: Hendrickson, 2002); Gordon J. Wenham, *Story as Torah: Reading the Old Testament Ethically* (Edinburgh: T & T Clark, 2000); Douglas A. Knight, ed., "Ethics and Politics in the Hebrew Bible," *Semeia* 66 (1995); Eckert Otto, *Theologische Ethik des Alten Testaments* (Stuttgart: Kohlhammer, 1994).

12. Steven T. Katz, *The Holocaust in Historical Context*, vol. 1, *The Holocaust and Mass Death before the Modern Age* (New York: Oxford University Press, 1994), p. 147n75.

13. John J. Collins, "The Zeal of Phinehas"; Collins, *Does the Bible Justify Violence?* (Minneapolis: Fortress, 2004). See also Carol Delaney, *Abraham on Trial: The Social Legacy of Biblical Myth* (Princeton, NJ: Princeton University Press, 1998).

14. Collins, "The Zeal of Phinehas," p. 14. See also Delaney, *Abraham on Trial*; and Cheryl Kirk-Duggan, ed., *Pregnant Passion: Gender, Sex, & Violence in the Bible*, Semeia Studies 44 (Atlanta, GA: Society of Biblical Literature, 2003).

15. Ibid., p. 21.

16. Cowles, "The Case for Radical Discontinuity."

17. For an earlier important treatment of the relationship between Zionism and archaeology, see Neil Asher Silberman, *Digging for God and Country: Exploration, Archaeology, and the Secret Struggle for the Holy Land, 1799–1917* (New York: Knopf, 1982).

18. *Super Evangelium Johannis*, 4.2: Ideo vera notitia de Deo habebatur solum a Iudaeis." Latin text in John Y. B. Hood, *Aquinas and the Jews* (Philadelphia: University of Pennsylvania Press, 1995), p. 127n6.

19. Schniedewind, *How the Bible Became a Book*, p. 64.

20. Ibid., pp. 101–102.

21. Ibid., p. 109.

22. See also Tikva Frymer-Kensky, "Revelation Revealed: The Doubt of Torah," in *Textual Reasonings: Jewish Philosophy and Text Study at the End of the Twentieth Century*, ed. Peter Ochs and Nancy Levene (Grand Rapids, MI: Eerdmans, 2002), pp. 68–75.

23. For other comments on Miriam as an authority figure, see Susan Ackerman, "Why Is Miriam Also among the Prophets? (And Is Zipporah among the Priests?)," *JBL* 121, no. 1 (2002): 47–80; Rita J. Burns, *Has the Lord Indeed Spoken Only through Moses? A Study of the Biblical Portrait of Miriam*, SBL Dissertation Series 84 (Atlanta, GA: Scholars Press, 1987).

24. Charles Mabee, "Text as Peacemaker: Deuteronomic Innovation in Violence Detoxification," in *Violence Renounced: René Girard, Biblical Studies, and Peacemaking*, ed. Willard M. Swartley (Telford, PA: Pandora, 2000), pp. 70–84.

25. Ibid., p. 77.

26. For an edition of these chronicles, we depend on Shlomo Eidelberg, *The Jews and the Crusaders: The Hebrew Chronicles of the First and Second Crusades* (Madison: University of Wisconsin Press, 1977).

27. Ibid., p. 37.

28. "French, Belgian Synagogues Burned," CNN.com, April 1, 2002, http://edition.cnn.com/2002/WORLD/europe/04/01/synagogue.attacks/?related (accessed July 14, 2004).

29. For the "navel of the earth" concept and its application to Jerusalem (beginning with the Second Temple period), see Michael Tilly, *Jerusalem—Nabel der Welt: Überlieferung und Funktionen von Heiligtumstraditionen im antiken Judentum* (Stuttgart: W. Kohlhammer, 2002).

30. Alan Dershowitz, *The Case for Israel* (Hoboken, NJ: Wiley, 2003), p. 15.

31. For some critical comments on the supposed biological need for territory, see W. D. Davies, "Reflections on Territory in Judaism," in *Sha'arei Talmon: Studies in the Bible, Qumran, and the Ancient Near East Presented to Shemaryahu Talmon*, ed. Michael Fishbane and Emanuel Tov (Winona Lake, IN: Eisenbrauns, 1992), pp. 339–43.

32. Jane M. Cahill, "Jerusalem at the Time of the United Monarchy: The Archaeological Evidence," in *Jerusalem in Bible and Archaeology: The First Temple Period*, ed. Andrew G. Vaughn and Anne E. Killebrew (Atlanta, GA: Scholars Press, 2003), p. 19.

33. Jon Levenson, "Zion Traditions," in *The Anchor Bible Dictionary*, ed. D. N. Freedman (New York: Doubleday, 1992), 6:1098.

34. J. J. M. Roberts, "Zion in the Theology of the Davidic-Solomonic Empire," in *Studies in the Period of David and Solomon and Other Essays*, ed. Tomoo Ishida (Winona Lake, IN: Eisenbrauns, 1982), p. 94. Most recently, "Solomon's Jerusalem and the Zion Tradition," in *Jerusalem in Bible and Archaeology*, ed. Vaughn and Killebrew, pp. 163–70.

35. Some scholars subsequent to Noth have argued for a preexilic and exlic or postexilic editions. See further, Richard D. Nelson, *The Double Redaction of the Deuteronomistic History* (Sheffield, UK: JSOT Press, 1981).

36. Oded Borowski, "Hezekiah's Reforms and the Revolt against Assyria," *Biblical Archaeologist* 58, no. 3 (September 1995): 148–55. For a contrasting view, which argues that centralization was independent of any Assyrian threat, see Lynn Tatum, "Jerusalem in Conflict: The Evidence for the Seventh-Century B.C.E. Religious Struggle over Jerusalem," in *Jerusalem in Bible and Archaeology*, ed. Vaughn and Killebrew, pp. 291–306.

37. See also Carol L. Meyers and Eric M. Meyers, "Jerusalem and Zion after the Exile: The Evidence from First Zechariah," in *Sha'arei Talmon*, ed. Fishbane and Tov, pp. 121–35.

38. For a study of the exclusions in the Temple Scroll and further bibliography, see Hector Avalos, *Illness and Health Care in the Ancient Near East: The Role of the Temple in Greece, Mesopotamia, and Israel*, Harvard Semitic Monographs 54 (Atlanta, GA: Scholars Press, 1995), pp. 323–24.

39. All of our citations of the Babylonian Talmud are from Isidore Epstein, ed., *Hebrew-English Edition of the Babylonian Talmud* (London: Soncino Press, 1988–1994).

40. Barry Beitzel, *Moody Atlas of Bible Lands* (Chicago: Moody, 1985), p. 25.

41. El Amarna letter 286:32–43. We follow the edition and translation of William L. Moran, *The Amarna Letters* (Baltimore: Johns Hopkins University Press, 1992), p. 326.

42. Miller and Hayes, *A History of Ancient Israel and Judah*, pp. 346–65. See also Mordechai Cogan, *Imperialism and Religion: Assyria, Judah, and Israel in the Eighth and Seventh Centuries, B.C.E* (Missoula, MT: Scholars Press/Society of Biblical Literature, 1974).

43. For representatives of the conflict as primarily political, see Baylis Thomas, *How Israel Was Won: A Concise History of the Arab-Israeli Conflict* (Lanham, MD: Lexington Books, 1999).

44. These numbers have ranged from 472,000 to 900,000, as noted by Dershowitz, *The Case for Israel*, p. 85.

45. On these sentiments about the Suez Canal, see comments in Thomas, *How Israel Was Won*, p. 6.

46. Jacques Kornberg, *Theodor Herzl: From Assimilation to Zionism* (Bloomington: Indiana University Press, 1993).

47. Alex Bein, *Theodore Herzl: A Biography*, trans. Maurice Samuel (New York: Atheneum, 1970); *Theodor Herzl: Biographie* (Vienna: Fiba Verlag, 1934).

48. Thedor Herzl, *Briefe und Tagebucher, Briefe 1903–1904* (Frankfurt: Propyläen, 1995), 7:76: "Ein Rabbiner bin ich auch jetzt nicht, u[nd] in den Tempel gehe ich nur in Basel am Samstag der Congresswoche. Dort grüsse ich auch mehr den Gott meiner Väter als meinen eigenen. Denn mit meinem Gott kann ich auch ohne Rabbiner u[nd] vorgeschriebene Gebete verkehren." For a more recent view from an assimilated Jew, see Richard Rubenstein, "The Temple Mount and My Grandmother's Paper Bag: An Essay on Inter-religious Relations," *Dialogue and Alliance* 41, no. 1 (Spring/Summer 2000): 76–99.

49. For an English edition, see Theodor Herzl, *The Jewish State: An Attempt at a Modern Solution of the Jewish Question*, trans. Sylvie D'Avigdor (London: Pordes, 1967), p. 29.

50. Herzl, *Briefe und Tagebucher*, 7:29.

51. See H. I. Bach, *The German Jew: A Synthesis of Judaism in Western Civilization, 1730–1930* (London: Oxford University Press, 1985), pp. 153–54.

52. Abraham Geiger, *Unser Gottesdienst: Eine Frage, die dringend Lösung verlangt* (Breslau: Schletter'sche Buchhandlung, 1868), p. 18: "Der gegenwärtige Trümmerhaufe Jerusalem ist für uns höchtens eine poetische wehmüthige Erinnerung … Jerusalem ist für uns ein Gedanke, keine räumlich begränzte Stätte." See further,

Jacob Petuchowski, *New Perspectives on Abraham Geiger: An HUC-JIR Symposium* (Cincinnati, OH: Hebrew Union College Press, 1975), p. 45. For a more recent study of Geiger, see Susannah Heschel, *Abraham Geiger and the Jewish Jesus* (Chicago: University of Chicago Press, 1998).

53. For similar observations about the reappropriation of the Bible by secular Jews, see Michael Karpin and Ina Friedman, *Murder in the Name of God: The Plot to Kill Yitzhak Rabin* (New York: Metropolitan Books, 1998), p. 35.

54. My text is from Ronald Sanders, *The High Walls of Jerusalem: A History of the Balfour Declaration and the Birth of the British Mandate of Palestine* (New York: Holt, Rinehart and Winston, 1983), pp. 612–13.

55. James Tomes, *Balfour and Foreign Policy: The International Thought of a Conservative Statesman* (Cambridge: Cambridge University Press, 1997).

56. Wilfrid M. Short, ed. *Arthur James Balfour as Philosopher and Thinker: A Collection of the More Important and Interesting Passages in His Non-Political Writings, Speeches and Addresses 1879–1912* (London: Longmans, Green, 1912), p. 60.

57. Quoted in Tomes, *Balfour and Foreign Policy*, p. 212.

58. Barbara W. Tuchman, *Bible and Sword: England and Palestine from the Bronze Age to Balfour* (1956; reprint, New York: Ballantine Books, 1984), p. 311.

59. The record of the hearings were published, with additional materials, under the opaque title *The Jewish National Home in Palestine* (New York: Ktav Publishing House, 1970). The House resolutions at issue were numbered 418 and 419.

60. US Congress, *The Jewish National Home in Palestine*, p. 304.

61. Ibid., pp. 375–76.

62. Ibid., p. 376.

63. For the full roster, see ibid., pp. 370–72.

64. Yehuda Bauer, *Rethinking the Holocaust* (New Haven, CT: Yale University Press, 2001), p. 254.

65. See Rory Miller, "Bible and Soil: Walter Clay Lowdermilk, the Jordan Valley Project and the Palestine Debate," *Middle Eastern Studies* 39, no. 2 (April 2003): 55–81.

66. Walter Clay Lowdermilk, *Palestine: Land of Promise* (New York: Harper and Brothers, 1944), p. 2.

67. Ibid., p. 227.

68. See Miller, "Bible and Soil," pp. 67–70.

69. For the revisionist argument that the phrase "land of milk and honey" actually refers to the less fertile and uncultivated grazing areas of land, see Etan Levine, "The Promised Land of Milk and Honey," *Estudios Bíblicos* 58 (2000): 145–66.

70. Lowdermilk, *Land of Promise*, p. 21. Lowdermilk also claims in this section to be basing himself on his own study of soils, archaeological findings, and present-day climate.

71. Ibid., p. 2.

72. Ibid., p. 3.

73. Ibid., p. 6.

74. US Congress, *The Jewish National Home in Palestine*, pp. 175–92.

75. Dershowitz, *The Case for Israel*, p. 15.

76. Martin Gilbert, *The Routledge Atlas of the Arab-Israeli Conflict*, 7th ed. (London: Routledge Taylor & Francis, 2002), p. 1.

77. See article on "Terrorism Deaths in Israel 1920–1999" on the Web site for the Israel Ministry of Foreign Affairs: http://www.mfa.gov.il/MFA/MFAArchive/2000 _2009/2000/1/Terrorism%20deaths%20 in%20Israel%20-%201920-1999.

78. US Congress, *The Jewish National Home in Palestine*, pp. 124–26.

79. Pappe (*History of Modern Palestine*, p. 37), for example, simply alludes to the fact that "the visionaries carried the day" as opposed to Jews who did not see Palestine as the only homeland. But Pappe does not explain where that vision derives.

80. For a study of anti-Zionism and Zionism among orthodox Jews, see Eliezer Don-Yehiya, "Nationalism and Religion in Jewish and Moslem Fundamentalism," *Dialogue and Alliance* 14, no. 2 (Spring/Summer 2000): 41–75. For a study of how modern apocalyptic views influence Zionism and control of Jerusalem's sacred spaces, see Gershom Gorenberg, *The End of Days: Fundamentalism and the Struggle for the Temple Mount* (New York: Free Press, 2000).

81. For insightful comments on Zionism and biblical narratives, see Collins, "The Zeal of Phinehas," p. 14; Whitelam, *The Invention of Ancient Israel*.

82. Examples of recent studies include, Kenton Sparks, *Ethnicity and Identity in Ancient Israel: Prolegomenon to the Study of Ethnic Sentiments and Their Expression in the Hebrew Bible* (Winona Lake, IN: Eisenbrauns, 1998); and R. Christopher Heard, *Dynamics of Deselection: Ambiguity in Genesis 12–36 and Ethnic Boundaries in Post-Exilic Judah* (Atlanta, GA: Society of Biblical Literature, 2001). For the idea that the DtrH was composed in order to solidify an ethnic identity, see E. Theodore Mullen Jr., *Narrative History and Ethnic Boundaries: The Deuteronomistic Historian and the Creation of Israelite National Identity* (Atlanta, GA: Scholars Press, 1993).

83. For a general introduction to Ugaritic studies, see Dennis Pardee, "Ugaritic Studies at the End of the 20th Century," *BASOR* 320 (November 2000): 49–86; and Gordon D. Young, ed., *Ugarit in Retrospect: Fifty Years of Ugarit and Ugaritic* (Winona Lake, IN: Eisenbrauns, 1981). For a more thorough technical survey, see W. G. E. Watson and N. Wyatt, eds., *Handbook of Ugaritic Studies* (Leiden: Brill, 1999).

84. E. Theodore Mullen Jr., *The Assembly of the Gods*, Harvard Semitic Monographs 24 (Atlanta, GA: Scholars Press, 1980), pp. 202–205. Attempts to invalidate the polytheism in this passage are based on speculative solutions from evangelical scholars, including David Stevens, "Does Deuteronomy 32:8 Refer to 'Sons of God' or 'Sons of Israel'?" *Bibliotheca Sacra* 154 (1997): 131–41; and Michael S. Heiser, "Deuteronomy 32:8 and the Sons of God," *Bibliotheca Sacra* 158 (2001): 52–74. For a brief exposition of the propolytheistic reading, see Emanuel Tov, *Textual Criticism of the Hebrew Bible* (Minneapolis: Fortress, 1992), pp. 269–70.

85. See Mullen, *The Assembly of the Gods*, pp. 228–31.

86. Glock and Stark, *Christian Belief*, p. 212.

87. Harry M. Orlinsky, "Nationalism-Universalism and Internationalism in Ancient Israel," in *Translating and Understanding the Old Testament: Essays in Honor of Herbert Gordon May*, ed. Harry Thomas Frank and Willliam L. Reed (Nashville, TN: Abingdon, 1970), pp. 206–36, especially 210–11.

88. See Peter Machinist, "On Self-Consciousness in Mesopotamia," in *The Origins and Diversity of Axial Age Civilizations*, ed. S. N. Eisenstadt (Albany: State University of New York Press, 1986), pp. 183–202, 511–18; "The Question of Distinc-

tiveness in Ancient Israel: An Essay," in *Ah, Assyria . . . Studies in Assyrian History and Ancient Near Eastern Historiography Presented to Hayim Tadmor*, ed. Mordechai Cogan and Israel Eph'al (Jerusalem: Magnes Press, 1991), pp. 196–212. See also Robert D. Miller, "Popular, Ideological, and Textual Dimensions of Postexilic Judean Culture,"*Estudios Biblicos* 60 (2002): 337–50.

89. Karl Skorecki et al., "Y Chromosomes of Jewish Priests," *Nature* 385 (January 2, 1997): 32; and Mark Thomas et al., "Origins of Old Testament Priests," *Nature* 394 (July 9, 1998): 138–39. While genetics is beyond our expertise, we should note that some of Skorecki's presuppositions seem unduly confident about the nature of historical data. In "Y Chromosomes" (p. 32), for example, Skorecki says that his team "determined the designation of each subject as a member of the priesthood by direct questioning. Subjects who were not sure of their designation or who identified themselves as 'Levite' (a separate junior priesthood, based on less-well-defined patrilineal lineage) were not included in the current analysis." Their samples, therefore, do not seem to acknowledge the complex histories of Hebrew priesthoods that are admitted even in the Hebrew Bible. Skorecki also seems to ignore how flexible genealogies were, as anyone comparing the genealogies Matthew 1 and Luke 3 can attest. For a recent study of the male-specific region of the Y chromosome, see Helen Skaletsky, "The Male-Specific Region of the Human Y Chromosome of Discrete Sequence Classes," *Nature* 423 (June 2003): 825–37.

90. Gerhard von Rad, *Der heilige Krieg im alten Israel* (1926; reprint, Göttingen: Vandenhoeck & Ruprech, 1969); and Friedrich Schwally, *Semitische Kriegsaltertumer I: Der heilige Krieg im alten Israel* (Leipzig: Dietrich, 1901).

91. Sa-Moon Kang, *Divine War in the Old Testament and in the Ancient Near East* (Berlin: de Gruyter, 1989). See also Gwilym H. Jones, "'Holy War' or 'Yahweh War'?" *Vetus Testamentum* 25, no. 3 (1975): 642–58.

92. Kang, *Divine War*, p. 2.

93. Some representative studies of "Holy War" or "Yahweh War" are as follows: Lori Rowlett, *Joshua and the Rhetoric of Violence: A New Historicist Analysis* (Sheffield, UK: Sheffield Academic Press, 1996); Susan Niditch, *War in the Hebrew Bible: A Study in the Ethics of Violence* (New York: Oxford University Press, 1993); K. Lawson Younger, *Ancient Conquest Accounts: A Study in Ancient Near Eastern and Biblical History Writing* (Sheffield, UK: JSOT Press, 1990); Gwilym H. Jones, "The Concept of Holy War," in *The World of Ancient Israel*, ed. R. E. Clements (Cambridge: Cambridge University Press, 1989), pp. 299–321; and Peter C. Craigie, *The Problem of War in the Old Testament* (Grand Rapids, MI: Eerdmans, 1978). For a view that is more critical of biblical ethics, see Gerd Lüdemann, *The Unholy in Holy Scripture: The Dark Side of the Bible*, trans. John Bowden (Louisville, KY: Westminster/John Knox, 1997), pp. 33–54.

94. Representatives include Jo Bailey Wells, *God's Holy People: A Theme in Biblical Theology* (Sheffield, UK: Sheffield Academic Press, 2000); and John G. Gammie, *Holiness in Israel* (Minneapolis: AusburgFortress, 1989).

95. See further Robert Chazan, *In the Year 1096: The First Crusade and the Jews* (Philadelphia: Jewish Publication Society, 1996). The narratives, in English translation, may be found in Eidelberg, *The Jews and the Crusaders.*

96. Eidelberg, *The Jews and the Crusaders*, p. 40.

97. Ibid.

98. Ibid.

99. Ibid., p. 41.

100. Ibid., p. 31.

101. David L Gollaher, *Circumcision: A History of the World's Most Controversial Surgery* (New York: Basic Books, 2002), pp. 1–2. See also Jack M. Sasson, "Circumcision in the Ancient Near East," *JBL* 85 (1966): 473–76.

102. For source criticism of texts dealing with circumcision, see William H. Propp, "The Origins of Infant Circumcision in Israel," *Hebrew Annual Review* 11 (1987): 355–70.

103. See Jon Levenson, "The New Enemies of Circumcision," *Commentary* 109, no. 3 (March 2000): 29–36.

104. Ronald Goldman, *Questioning Circumcision: A Jewish Perspective* (Boston: Vanguard, 1998). See also essays in Elizabeth Wyner Mark, ed., *The Covenant of Circumcision: New Perspectives on an Ancient Jewish Rite* (Hanover, NH: University Press of New England/Brandeis Univesity Press, 2003).

105. American Academy of Pediatrics, "Circumcision Policy Statement," *Pediatrics* 103, no. 3 (March 1999): 686–93.

CHAPTER 7

ACADEMIC DEFENSES OF VIOLENCE IN THE HEBREW BIBLE

Throughout the history of biblical interpretation, there have been various attempts to mitigate the violence found in the Hebrew Bible, and in the Deuteronomistic History, in particular. Of course, most interpreters prior to the mid-twentieth century had no concept of the DtrH, as it is now called, and so defenses usually were more often generalized to "God's people" or to specific books of the Bible in which the violence is found. However, as Louis H. Feldman shows, by at least the first century, Jewish interpreters were trying to explain and/or defend biblical violence to Jews and non-Jews.[1]

The privileging of Israel's violence can be seen in works by many Christian writers, even if they no longer held all of the Old Testament laws and practices as being in force. Thus, Aquinas says, "The Jewish people were chosen by God so that Christ might be born of them . . . even their wars and deeds are to be expounded mystically; not so the wars and deeds of the Assyrians or Romans."[2]

In book 3 of his *Law of War and Peace*, Hugo Grotius attempts to wrestle with the implications of biblical genocide for international laws of war in his time. He sets up his defense by urging readers to consider that certain actions (e.g., deceit) must be performed to bring about a greater good. Such actions, he says, "though evil in themselves, may be so modified by particular occasions, as to lose their criminality in consideration of the good, to which they lead."[3]

On a more subtle line of argumentation, Grotius urges readers not to use biblical genocide to infer that it is the custom of nations to kill women and children. Grotius, as Jean-Jacques Rousseau observed, often submits what nations practice in fact as "proof of right."[4] Grotius's aversion to using the

Bible as a warrant has less to do with the actual permissibility of killing women and children than it does with finding better examples for that warrant. For Grotius, the trouble with many biblical examples is that they are commanded by God, and so Grotius seeks to prove that killing women and children has been held permissible on the basis of other texts, biblical and classical, in which human beings act without a divine command.

Grotius then finds his warrant in, among other examples, Psalm 137: "The Psalmist's expression of the Babylonian children being dashed against the stones is a much stronger proof of the custom commonly prevailing among nations, in the use of victory, to which the language of Homer bears a close resemblance, where the poet says, that 'bodies of infant-children dashed upon the ground, while ruthless war all things affrights.'"[5]

Some things have changed since Grotius, and some have not. The historicity of the narratives in the Deuteronomistic History, not to mention the rest of the Bible, is increasingly under criticism. The rise of the so-called minimalists has meant that even the most seemingly established "facts" are no longer such.[6] We see, for example, the increasing skepticism about the existence of a Solomonic kingdom of any substance; or even of David himself.[7] However, this skepticism has also allowed some apologists to say that biblical genocide probably did not occur either.

In light of this increased critical and skeptical approach, scholarly defenses of violence in the Hebrew Bible take the following approaches, some of which show no less ingenuity than shown by Grotius: (1) the "greater good" theory; (2) the allusions to war are primarily rhetorical, and so there was no actual violence; (3) belief that Yahweh was Israel's warrior can result in nonviolence; (4) countertraditions and subversive readings are possible for violent texts; and (5) *Shalom*, often translated as "peace," is the true ideal. We will examine an illustrative case of each of these defenses.

THE "GREATER GOOD" THEORY

One recent example of the "greater good" theory of Israel's violence is Joel Kaminsky's 2003 article, "Did Election Imply Mistreatment of Non-Israelites," in the prestigious *Harvard Theological Review*.[8] In reality, Kaminsky uses another version of theodicies that posit a "greater good" explanation for evil.[9] Thus, when defending Israel's exclusivism, Kaminsky tells us that "[o]ne must measure the loss that would be sustained by discarding such a central idea—central to both Judaism and Christianity—against the gain to be had by deposing of it."[10] Indeed, Kaminsky seemingly encourages humanity to be grateful for Israel's election because, as he argues,

"While this theological idea may seem arbitrary and unfair, it may be taken as a sign of God's close and merciful relationship towards humanity as a whole, and of his profoundly personal character."[11]

Interestingly, Kaminsky explicitly tries to disassociate the policies advocated by some biblical authors with those of Nazi Germany. His main argument is:

> While some have compared the anti-Canaanite polemic to certain Nazi policies, no biblical text ever advocated the pursuit and slaughter of Canaanites who lived outside of Canaan or fled its bounds. The condemnation of the Amalekites, however, is phrased in terms of a cosmic battle between Israel's God, YHWH, and Amalek that will last throughout time (Exod. 17:14–15).[12]

This argument is somewhat puzzling because it presumes that slaughter within the borders of Canaan somehow is a mitigating factor. Would Kaminsky argue that the slaughter that took place within German borders is somehow more justified? Secondly, the first sentence in the quote above seems to contradict the second since seeing something as a "cosmic" battle would, by definition, transcend national borders.

The fact is that not only are such attitudes of biblical authors quite parallel to Nazi policy, but Nazi policy can be seen as simply one of the most tragic applications of policies enunciated in the Bible. Indeed, Hitler saw the struggle between German and Jew as a cosmic struggle: "Hence today I believe that I am acting in accordance with the will of the Almighty Creator; by defending myself against the Jew, I am fighting for the work of the Lord."[13] Moreover, Hitler explicitly saw Judaism not as a religion, but as a worldwide (i.e., cosmic) phenomenon: "The Jewish state was never spatially limited in itself, but universally unlimited as to space, though restricted in the sense of embracing but one race."[14]

Hitler saw Marxism as a Jewish instrument, and certainly cosmic in its scope. Indeed, he spoke of a "Marxism whose goal is and remains the destruction of all non-Jewish national states."[15] He saw German ethnicity as part of a cosmic struggle when he said, "Blood sin and desecration of the race are the original sin in this world and the end of a humanity which surrenders to it."[16] Hitler also declared, "To bring about such a development is, then, nothing else but to sin against the will of the eternal creator."[17] In sum, Nazi policy was no less "cosmic" than what may be reflected concerning Amalek, and we would not hold Nazism in less moral contempt because its violence was part of some "cosmic" vision.

Kaminsky also argues that the election of Israel was not absolute because an insider such as Achan was executed, and an outsider such as Rahab the prostitute was made part of the community.[18] Thus, obedience to Yahweh, more than ethnicity, is the mark of community membership. However, Rahab becomes an insider only by helping perpetuate the genocidal policies of Joshua. Thus, she says to Joshua, "I know that the LORD has given you the land, and that dread of you has fallen on us, and that all the inhabitants of the land melt in fear before you" (Josh. 2:9). If anything, Rahab is a victim of effective terrorism, and now plans to help Joshua enact the slaughter that is about to befall Jericho. If this is a sign of Hebrew benevolence toward an outsider, it is parallel to allowing Jewish collaborators to live because they may have helped to destroy their fellow Jews in Nazi Germany.

Achan's case does indeed prove that being an Israelite does not mean that one is allowed to live outside the code in force. Achan is punished because he steals items that were dedicated to Yahweh—items that should be in the custody of priests. The fact that the biblical author regards his execution as legitimate proves to be no more inclusive than Nazis executing their own for disobeying orders.

In sum, Joel Kaminsky's case that group privileging has more benefits than drawbacks is certainly not proven by his appeal to the Joshua narratives. The benefits are for members of Joshua's community, while extermination is the general policy toward many "outsiders" in Joshua. Kaminsky exacerbates the weakness of his own case by appealing to some mystical relationship between Israel and her god, Yahweh, that is somehow supposed to benefit others. Certainly, the biblical record indicates that such benefits would accrue only by submission to the religious and political goals of Israel. As such, Joshua is an excellent example of how group privilege, as a scarce resource in itself, can be the cause of violence.

THE PRIMARILY RHETORIC ARGUMENT

As have many scholars before him, Kaminsky attempts to argue that the genocide in Joshua was more rhetorical than real.[19] In particular, Kaminsky appeals to the study of Lori L. Rowlett, who believes Joshua is nothing more than a thinly disguised version of Josiah, the king of Israel who sought to centralize and homogenize Israelite identity through the worship of Yahweh. Rowlett argued that the rhetoric of violence in Joshua is not meant "to incite literal violence against a particular group. The text of Joshua is concerned with voluntary submission to a set of rules and norms; it is primarily directed at Josiah's own subjects; not at real (ethnic) outsiders, but at insiders who pose a threat to the hierarchy being asserted."[20]

As insightful as Rowlett's study is otherwise, I disagree with her main conclusion. First, she treats as mutually exclusive what need not be such. The rhetoric of violence can terrorize outsiders as much as it seeks to consolidate power within a group of insiders. Rowlett does not explain why Joshua cannot be primarily directed at "real (ethnic) outsiders." Saying that outsiders should be killed can indeed result in outsiders being killed. Nor does it eliminate the possibility that *herem* was practiced on insiders, as argued by Yoshihide Suzuki.[21]

Rowlett holds, as do most scholars today, that Joshua is part of the Deuteronomistic History, which, according to Martin Noth, stretches from Deuteronomy through 2 Kings (with the exception of Ruth in the canonical order of Christian Bibles). We have seen that this corpus also outlines very specific rules for dealing with outsiders such as the Moabites and Ammonites, who were real historical entities.

Rowlett's comparisons of biblical war rhetoric with the war rhetoric of neighboring cultures also would be evidence that this war rhetoric could be meant to be implemented against "outsiders." The Assyrian, Egyptian, and Hittite examples of war rhetoric that she adduces were often actually applied to outsiders, and so why should Israel be different? Many of the Assyrian war inscriptions are also written within the home country, and so why can it not be the case that they were also meant for in-house consumption?

The Moabites provide an instructive case of how violent rhetoric can be meant for in-house consumption while not excluding actual violence toward outsiders. Moabites were identified as an ethnic group and constituted a kingdom east of Israel. The Moabite king, Mesha, left behind a very famous stele in the ninth century.[22] The Moabite Stele mentions how Chemosh, Mesha's main god, ordered the latter to fight Israel and take part of Israel's land. This, of course, is directly parallel to what Joshua is commanded to do. The Moabite Stele mentions how the captives were slaughtered as part of a "consecration" or "ban," and the Moabite uses a word root (*hrm*) that is identical to the Hebrew root used for this practice of slaughtering the enemy as a sort of sacrifice for the national deity.[23]

The enmity between Israel and Moab is confirmed by each other's narratives, and so we can be confident that there was an actual historical enmity even as we concede that posthumous inscriptions can be written that may not be factual in every detail.[24] Since the Moabite Stele possesses many of the rhetorical features of violence we find in biblical records, one could just as well argue that the Moabite Stele was being used to consolidate a national identity. One could also argue that Mesha was also communicating with his own people in a way that Josiah was communicating with his own people. The Moabite Stele, after all, was written in Moabite, not in Hebrew. Thus, even if the Joshua narratives are meant for in-house consumption, the rhetoric is still premised on principles and policies that were were probably carried out against actual people.

YAHWEH AS A WARRIOR

Millard Lind believes that Israel's concept of Yahweh as a warrior could minimize violence.[25] The reason is that if Yahweh is regarded as the only warrior, as stated in Exodus 15:3 and other passages, then logically this means that Israelites need not fight; Yahweh will fight for them. Lind says regarding his thesis, "Basic to all that follows is the first point, that is, the testimony that Yahweh the warrior fought by means of miracle, not through the armies of his people."[26] He then quotes Joshua 24:12: "I sent the hornet ahead of you, which drove out before you the two kings of the Amorites; it was not by your sword or by your bow." Lind argues further that this tradition was early, not late, in Israel's history.

Similarly, Paul Keim argues that "[i]t is because Yahweh is a warrior that we can be peacemakers."[27] In fact, argues Keim, "[T]o say Yahweh is a warrior is to say, in the parlance of biblical theology, that Yahweh is a deliverer. Yahweh's desire is for the dignity and sacredness of human life."[28] As part of the argument, Keim selects the concept of God that favors peace as follows: "I believe in a God who, because of love and a healing strategy for creation, is constrained in the way God acts in the world. Any depictions of God's acts in conflict with these constraints must be understood as false."[29] In addition, Keim objects to those that use "selective proof-texting of almost comical proportions" to promote a violent image of God, especially in the aftermath of September 11.[30]

But the arguments of both Lind and Keim are quite problematic. First, the reasons for choosing a peaceful conception of God are no more verifiable than the reasons for choosing a violent conception. Thus, for example, Keim's idea that any vision of God contrary to the one he has constructed is "false" rests on no better ground than if someone constructed a violent conception of God and then declared that peaceful visions of God "must be understood as false." This arbitrariness again underscores the selective use of empirico-rationalism to establish a favored theological concept.[31]

On a moral level, Lind and Keim must explain why violence by proxy (since Yahweh hurts and kills our enemies, we don't have to) should be less morally reprehensible than if individuals avoided violence because they knew some gunman would surely do the work for them. And if one is to argue that God, but not a human being, has a right to take human life or commit violence, then this is itself a human conception of God that is no less arbitrary than the conception that God allows human beings to commit violence.

It is also arbitrary to say that Yahweh as a warrior actually refers to Yahweh's desire for "the dignity and sacredness of human life." First it rests on a homogenizing view of what counts as "the parlance of biblical theology." One could just as well argue that Yahweh as warrior reflects his character as a ruthless killer "in the parlance of biblical theology." For example, Exodus 15:3–4 reads: "The LORD is a warrior; the LORD is his name. Pharaoh's chariots and his army he cast into the sea; his picked officers were sunk in the Red Sea." How does killing a whole army, whether by "natural means" or not, reinforce the concept that Yahweh has respect for the dignity of human life? Is this the same Yahweh who, earlier in Exodus (11:4–5), said he would kill all firstborn Egyptian infants, who were otherwise innocent? In fact, Yahweh is not portrayed so much as favoring "human life" as much as he is portrayed favoring Hebrew lives.

Selective proof-texting is still part of the techniques of both Lind and Keim. For in deciding what counts as a "true" representation of God, they must base their selections on the premise that certain texts are authoritative (e.g., passages with Jesus as peacemaker). But this selection is no more verifiable than the choice of any so-called fundamentalist who chooses a violent Jesus as authoritative. In sum, both Lind and Keim overlook the fact that the very unverifiability of any claim about God is the problem. At the very least, Keim must explain why we could not make the following conclusion just as well: "It is because God commands violence from human beings in 1 Samuel 15:3 that we can reject peacemaking."

On a more practical level, while it is true that believing that a god is the only combatant can lead logically to human nonviolence, the fact is that this is not usually the case with Israel. The idea of a god who fights for his people is known from neighboring cultures that were quite warlike. Lind himself cites one example from Assyrian materials: "Not by my own power, not by the strength of my bow—by the power of my gods, by the strength of my goddesses, I subjected the lands . . . to the yoke of Assur."[32] This rhetoric did not prevent Assyrians from effecting horrible carnage on their enemies.

Robert the Monk, a chronicler of the First Crusade, provides us with a case in Christianity in which the belief that God is the one fighting is fully compatible with the fact that human beings are doing actual combat. Robert the Monk cites David's attribution of his victory to God in order to argue that Christians should not glory in armies, but in the power of God.[33] Yet this did not prevent real fighting by real people. Similarly, the Qur'an (Sura 8:17) says, "It was not you who slew them; it was Allah who slew them" (*falam taqtulūhum wa-lākinna allaha qatalahum*).[34] Believing that war is won through the action of a god is simply part of magical thinking, much like the belief that medicines are actually given their affectivity by a god.

Even if it were the case that such a belief in God as warrior renders the believer nonviolent, this does not mean that no violence will occur because of this belief. On the contrary, attackers who know of this belief in an opponent may be more willing to commit violence against such believers because they know that retaliation will not follow. Furthermore, the motives of such rhetoric need not be as benign as Lind makes them appear. Believers in Yahweh's warrior status can credit him with the most violent acts, simply substituting their powerlessness for what they would love to do to their enemies if they could.

Lind's assertion that the pre-Mosaic materials and depictions of the patriarchal traditions are "pacifistic" is not quite accurate.[35] Violence is fully sanctioned in the narratives about Sodom and Gomorrah (Genesis 19), where Yahweh kills women and children for reasons that are not explained clearly by the biblical author. Even if these narratives are meant to explain the infertility of the areas southeast of the Dead Sea, the author has no qualms in seeing violence as appropriate and even divine.

Intertribal warfare was said to begin even before birth in the case of Jacob and Esau, who represented Israel and Edom, respectively:

> The children struggled together within her; and she said, "If it is to be this way, why do I live?" So she went to inquire of the LORD.

> And the LORD said to her, "Two nations are in your womb, and two peoples born of you shall be divided; the one shall be stronger than the other, the elder shall serve the younger." (Gen. 25:22–23)

Note again how group privileging (Yahweh favors Jacob, not Esau) is largely responsible for the struggle. As Genesis 27:41 describes it: "Now Esau hated Jacob because of the blessing with which his father had blessed him, and Esau said to himself, 'The days of mourning for my father are approaching; then I will kill my brother Jacob.'"

But this also parallels Yahweh's own group privileging, as indicated by Malachi 1:2–3:

> I have loved you, says the LORD. But you say, "How have you loved us?" Is not Esau Jacob's brother? says the LORD. Yet I have loved Jacob but I have hated Esau; I have made his hill country a desolation and his heritage a desert for jackals.

The conflict between Israel and Edom is not simply the result of group privileging: Group privileging is seen as appropriate despite the conflict that inevitably results. On a historical level, Edom and Israel probably did fight over territory. In sum, the biblical authors knew that group privileging brought conflict, but they were still willing to see it as appropriate and even of divine origin.

COUNTERTRADITIONS AND SUBVERSIVE READINGS

Another strategy to defend biblical violence has its origins in literary studies, although one could argue that such readings have always existed within the biblical text.[36] In brief, the claim that countertraditions exist revolves around the idea that biblical authors did not agree on many issues. For every author advocating genocide, there was one advocating peace with the neighbors. For every author advocating exclusion, there was one who advocated inclusion.

Much of the interest in this type of reading was initiated by feminist scholars who set out not just to critique patriarchal structures in the Bible but to demonstrate that masculine readings of those texts has obscured positive images of women. Regarding the New Testament, the most prominent of such scholars is Elizabeth Schüssler-Fiorenza, who has spent much of her career at Harvard Divinity School.[37] For the Hebrew Bible, Phyllis Trible and Mieke Bal would be some main representatives.[38] At least one other scholar, Ilana Pardes, has surveyed the movement as well as participated in it.[39]

The recognition of countertraditions and subversive readings is indeed a positive development when countering those who believe in a unitary interpretation of the Bible. However, sometimes the claim of countertraditions rests on methods and premises that are no better epistemologically than those of the so-called fundamentalists. Likewise, sometimes the countertraditions can themselves be subject to a subversive reading that can undermine them. Thus, Pardes claims that Bal, who is otherwise a keen interpreter, uses sexist models when dealing with Ruth.[40]

Laura Donaldson, in particular, has brilliantly critiqued studies that purport to show that the book of Ruth provides a countertradition to the relatively more exclusivistic positions concerning Moabites found in the DtrH.[41] Ruth, after all, is portrayed as a Moabite who is allowed to join the Hebrew community, and eventually figures in the genealogy of David. Donaldson, however, notes that Ruth's incorporation comes at the price of losing her culture. The book of Ruth, thus, turns into a story of deculturation rather than integration.

As it pertains to violence, Thomas Römer, a professor at the University of Lausanne, France, illustrates a recent attempt to re-read violent narratives in the context of imperialism. [42] Although Römer seems to accept some of the violence in the Bible as factual, more often he attempts to explain it as a response to empire or as a form of resistance. Thus, he acknowledges that Yahweh demands love, just as an Assyrian king might demand love from his vassals. However, within the context of Assyrian oppression, we can see that Deuteronomy is expressing its resistance to Assyrian hegemony by asserting that Yahweh, not the Assyrian oppressor, is the true object of love. Thus, Deuteronomy has "an anti-Assyrian subversive meaning."[43]

Slightly more subtle subversive readings have been attempted by Susan Niditch, author of *War in the Hebrew Bible*. She cites a case in which "relations between Israelites can provide a model of reconciliation for less closely related opponents in war as seen in the treatment of foreign prisoners in 2 Kgs 6:22-23."[44] This passage is part of a story in which Arameans, close linguistic cousins of the Hebrews, come to Israel to seize Elisha, the prophet of God they suspect is feeding intelligence to the Israelite king. God strikes the Aramean army with blindness, and Elisha tricks them into entering the town of Samaria, where the Arameans find themselves surrounded once their eyes are reopened.

Thereupon, the Hebrew king asks Elisha if he should kill all of the Arameans.

> He answered, "No! Did you capture with your sword and your bow those whom you want to kill? Set food and water before them so that they may eat and drink; and let them go to their master."

> So he prepared for them a great feast; after they ate and drank, he sent them on their way, and they went to their master. And the Arameans no longer came raiding into the land of Israel. (2 Kings 6:22–23)

At first, this seems benign, even if self-interest rather than just selfless hospitality is clearly expressed. The food and drink are meant to pacify the enemy, much like the conciliatory tactics advocated by some of the Greek thinkers we will discuss in chapter 9. In any case, read in a broader context, and specifically in light of the events narrated immediately afterward, this whole episode seems to set up an excuse to slaughter the Arameans.

In fact, in the very next verse, and in seeming contradiction to verse 23, it is said: "Some time later King Ben-hadad of Aram mustered his entire army; he marched against Samaria and laid siege to it" (2 Kings 6:24). And are the Arameans grateful for the food that they had received? Absolutely, not. In fact, the Arameans make food so scarce in Israel that we have the following miserable scene:

> As the siege continued, famine in Samaria became so great that a donkey's head was sold for eighty shekels of silver, and one-fourth of a kab of dove's dung for five shekels of silver.

> Now as the king of Israel was walking on the city wall, a woman cried out to him, "Help, my lord king!"

> He said, "No! Let the LORD help you. How can I help you? From the threshing floor or from the wine press?"

> But then the king asked her, "What is your complaint?" She answered, "This woman said to me, 'Give up your son; we will eat him today, and we will eat my son tomorrow.'
>
> So we cooked my son and ate him. The next day I said to her, 'Give up your son and we will eat him.' But she has hidden her son." (2 Kings 6:25–29)

What follows is the defeat of the Arameans by Yahweh, and the capture of the Aramean food supply, which is then used to feed the previously starving Israelites. Far from being a model for how to treat Aramean prisoners, the larger story is that it may not pay to be nice to Arameans.

SHALOM AS HEGEMONY

Self-serving translations are mostly responsible for representing the Hebrew *shalom* as "peace" in many instances in the Hebrew Bible. The idea that *shalom* means little more than "domination" is already found in Johannes Pedersen, who is criticized by Niditch for this idea.[45] Pedersen, however, seems to restrict his remarks to ancient periods when he writes, "In the olden time peace is not in itself the opposite of war."[46] Pedersen could be echoing Clausewitz's putative view that "peace is continuation of struggle only by other means."[47] In fact, it can be shown that both the etymology and the use of *shalom* in the Hebrew Bible is often consistent with an imperialistic approach to the world rather than with the benign and self-serving portrayals we find in Walter Brueggemann's *Peace* and in the works of other religionist scholars.[48]

The root *shalom* has been studied quite thoroughly by Gillis Gerleman, who actually criticizes Pedersen for having too soft a view of *shalom*.[49] Gerleman notes that the piel intensive, with some 90 occurrences in the Hebrew Bible, is the most frequent of all the verb forms of the root. The normal Qal (ground) form occurs 8 times, and the Hiphil (causative) form about 13 times. The noun form occurs some 240 times. The overwhelming meaning, whether as a verb or as a noun, is usually "repayment," "reward," or "retaliation."[50]

Many translations, such as "healing" or "peace," can be understood in the sense of reward or payment. Thus, Job 22:21, which is translated as "Agree with God, and be at peace," is better understood as something akin to "settle accounts with Him and be satisfied." A more retributive meaning may be found in Deuteronomy 32:35: "Vengeance is mine, and recompense [*shillēm*], for the time when their foot shall slip; because the day of their calamity is at hand, their doom comes swiftly."[51] The hegemonic aspect of *shalom* can be seen more clearly here:

When you draw near to a town to fight against it, offer it terms of peace.

If it accepts your terms of peace and surrenders to you, then all the people in it shall serve you at forced labor. (Deut. 20:10–11)

The terms of "peace" are clearly Israel's terms for peace, and the narrative makes clear that peace involves the enslavement of the people with whom Israel is at peace.[52]

Solomon's empire, even if is more fictional than not, is portrayed as living in peace in 1 Kings 4:24: "For he had dominion over all the region west of the Euphrates from Tiphsah to Gaza, over all the kings west of the Euphrates; and he had peace on all sides." Here, peace is linked with imperialistic power. Peace is linked with Yahweh's empire in Job 25:2: "Dominion and fear are with God; he makes peace [*shalom*] in his high heaven."

Even the supposedly more peaceful utopia envisioned in some portions of Isaiah, one finds hegemony and peace linked: "His authority shall grow continually, and there shall be endless peace for the throne of David and his kingdom. He will establish and uphold it with justice and with righteousness from this time onward and forevermore. The zeal of the LORD of hosts will do this" (Isa. 9:7). But what is envisioned is a kingdom ruled by Yahweh on his terms and with everyone in slavery to him and his kingdom or paying tribute to him.

SUMMARY

Despite the seemingly critical stance of the authors we have discussed, they all seem to share the idea that the scriptures should be maintained in our culture and tradition. Some scholars expunge or reinterpret the objectionable portions. Some scholars find countertraditions that express the parts they favor. We concede that many of these efforts can make positive contributions to showing that a violent view is not the only view found in the Bible. However, ultimately, all of these defenses are premised on selectivity that is no more arbitrary than that of so-called fundamentalists. The fact is that we can no more verify that God meant to be violent than we can that he did not. We cannot verify that the seemingly peaceful sayings represent God's thoughts anymore than the warlike ones. It is this unverifiablity that becomes the most scarce resource of all, and a prime generator of violence.

NOTES

1. Louis H. Feldman, *"Remember Amalek!" Vengeance, Zealotry, and Group Destruction in the Bible according to Philo, Pseudo-Philo, and Josephus* (Cincinnati, OH: Hebrew Union College Press, 2004).

2. Aquinas, *Summa,* I–II 104.2 ad 2: "Populus Iudaeorum ad hoc electus erat a Deo, quod ex eo Christo nasceretur . . . etiam bella et gesta illius populi exponuntur mystice; non autem bella vel gesta Assyriorum vel Romanorum."

3. Grotius, *The Law of War and Peace,* 3.4.9.1 (p. 648)/*De Jure Belli,* 3.80. For a detailed survey of the legal materials pertaining to biblical homicide in light of neighboring cultures, see Pamela Barmash, *Homicide in the Biblical World* (Cambridge: Cambridge University Press, 2005).

4. Rousseau, *The Social Contract,* p. 51/*Du Contrat,* p. 46: "Sa plus constante manière de raisonner est d'etablir toujours le droit par le fait."

5. Grotius, *The Law of War and Peace,* 3.4.9.1 (p. 648). Citing Homer's *Iliad* 22.63.

6. For some recent discussions, see John Van Seters, "Is There Any Historiography in the Hebrew Bible? A Hebrew-Greek Comparison," *Journal of Northwest Semitic Languages* 28, no. 2 (2002): 1–25.

7. See Gary N. Knoppers, "The Vanishing Solomon: The Disappearance of the United Monarchy from Recent Histories of Ancient Israel," *JBL* 116, no. 1 (Spring 1997): 19–44.

8. Joel S. Kaminsky, "Did Election Imply Mistreatment of Non-Israelites?" *Harvard Theological Review* 96, no. 4 (2003): 397–425.

9. For a recent discussion of theodicy, including "greater good" arguments, see the essays in Daniel Howard-Snyder, ed., *The Evidential Argument from Evil* (Bloomington: Indiana University Press, 1996).

10. Kaminsky, "Did Election Imply Mistreatment of Non-Israelites?" p. 425. For a similar version of of the "greater good" theory, see also R. D. Nelson, "Herem and the Deuteronomic Social Conscience," in *Deuteronomy and Deuteronomic Literature: Festschrift C. H. W. Brekelmans,* ed. M. Vervenne and J. Lust (Leuven: Peeters/Leuven University Press, 1997), pp. 39–54.

11. Kaminsky, "Did Election Imply Mistreatment of Non-Israelites?" p. 425.

12. Ibid., p. 404.

13. Adolf Hitler, *Mein Kampf,* trans. Ralph Manheim (Boston: Houghton Mifflin, 1971), p. 65; German edition (Munich: Müller, 1936), p. 70: "So glaube ich heute im Sinne des allmächtigen Schöpfers zu handeln: Indem ich mich des Judenerwehre, kämpfe ich für das Werk des Herrn."

14. *Mein Kampf,* p. 150/German p. 165: "Der jüdische Staat war nie in sich räumlich begrenzt, sondern universell unbegrenzt auf den Raum, aber beschränkt auf die Zusammenfassung einer Rasse."

15. *Mein Kampf,* p. 168/German, p. 185: "Der Marxismus, dessen letztes Ziel die Vernichtung aller nichtjüdischen Nationalstaaten ist und bleibt."

16. *Mein Kampf,* p. 249/German, p. 272: "Die Sünde wider Blut und Rasse ist die Erbfünde dieser Welt und das Ende einer sich ihr ergebende Menschheit."

17. *Mein Kampf,* p. 286/German, p. 314: "als sunde treiben wider den Willen des ewigen Schöpfers."

18. See further, Joel S. Kaminsky, "Joshua 7: Reassessment of Israelite Conceptions of Corporate Punishment," in *The Pitcher Is Broken: Memorial Essays for Gösta Ahlström*, ed. Steven W. Holloway and Lowell K. Handy (Sheffield, UK: Sheffield Academic Press, 1995), pp. 315–46.

19. We do not treat here the more sweeping claim that nothing in the Torah is historical, but rather allegorical, as argued by David Sperling, *The Original Torah: The Political Intent of the Bible's Writers* (New York: New York University Press, 1998).

20. Rowlett, *Joshua and the Rhetoric of Violence*, p. 183.

21. Yoshihide Suzuki, "A New Aspect of [ḥrm] in Deuteronomy in View of an Assimilation Policy of King Josiah," *Annual of the Japanese Bible Institute* 21 (1995): 3–27.

22. See Dearman, *Studies in the Mesha Inscription and Moab*.

23. See Philip Stern, *The Biblical [Ḥerem]: A Window on Israel's Religious Experience* (Atlanta, GA: Scholars Press, 1991).

24. For a recent discussion of the historicity of the Moabite Stone, see J. A. Emerton, "The Value of the Moabite Stone as an Historical Source," *Vetus Testamentum* 52, no. 4 (2002): 483–92. Although Emerton makes a good effort, we cannot quickly dismiss the construction of "autobiographies" after the death of a king. See further, Thomas L. Thompson, *The Bible in History: How Writers Create a Past* (London: Jonathan Cape, 1999), pp. 8–15; and Simon B. Parker, "Appeals for Military Intervention: Stories from Zinjirli and the Bible," *Biblical Archaeologist* 59, no. 4 (1996): 213–24.

25. Millard Lind, *Yahweh Is a Warrior: The Theology of Warfare in Ancient Israel* (Scottsdale, PA: Herald, 1980). For another study that is cognizant of the prebiblical roots of the Divine Warrior imagery, see Patrick D. Miller Jr., *The Divine Warrior in Early Israel*, Harvard Semitic Monographs 5 (Cambridge, MA: Harvard University Press, 1973).

26. Lind, *Yahweh Is a Warrior*, p. 23.

27. Paul Keim, "Is God Non-Violent?" *Conrad Grebel Review* 21, no. 1 (Winter 2003): 27. This is a quote from a header in Keim's article.

28. Ibid., pp. 26–27.

29. Ibid., p. 27.

30. Ibid., p. 29.

31. The same objection can be leveled at Harry Huebner, whom Keim cites as an influence. Huebner ("Christian Pacifism and the Character of God," in *The Church as Theological Community: Essays in Honor of David Schroeder*, ed. Harry Huebner [Winnipeg, MB: CMBC Publications, 1990], p. 270), for example, claims that "the defenceless, suffering, Christ of the gospels is the embodiment of the character of God." However, Huebner's version of God is no more verifiable than a "fundamentalist" or nonpacifistic version of God. Since all claims about God are equally unverifiable, then the difference between so-called pacificists and so-called fundamentalists mainly lies in *which* texts they choose to take literally.

32. Lind, *Yahweh Is a Warrior*, p. 30.

33. RHC, 3.748: "non gloriemur in armis sive in viribus nostris, sed in Deo potentiore omnium, quoniam ipsius est bellum nostrum, et ipse dominabitur gentium." Apparently, the sermon is alluding to variant quotations of 1 Samuel 17:47 and Psalms 22:29 (21:29).

34. Unless noted otherwise, all of our translations of the Qur'an are from the edition of A. Yusuf Ali. Here I use my adapted translation, as Ali omits a repetition of the root *q-t-l* (the second "slew").

35. Lind, *Yahweh Is a Warrior*, p. 45.

36. Some bibical examples can be seen in Jesus' use of scriptures to counter Satan's use of scripture (see Matt. 4:1–11).

37. Elizabeth Schüssler-Fiorenza, *In Memory of Her: A Feminist Theological Reconstruction of Christian Origins* (New York: Crossroad, 1983).

38. Phyllis Trible, *God and the Rhetoric of Sexuality* (Philadelphia: Fortress, 1978); *Texts of Terror: Literary and Feminist Readings of Biblical Narratives* (Philadelphia: Fortress, 1984); Mieke Bal, *Lethal Love: Feminist Literary Interpretations of Biblical Love Stories* (Bloomington: Indiana University Press, 1987); *Murder and Difference: Gender, Genre, and Scholarship on Sisera's Death* (Bloomington: Indiana University Press, 1988); and *Death and Dissymetry: The Politics of Coherence in the Book of Judges* (Chicago: University of Chicago Press, 1988).

39. Ilana Pardes, *Countertraditions in the Bible: A Feminist Approach* (Cambridge, MA: Harvard University Press, 1992).

40. Ibid., p. 6.

41. Laura Donaldson, "The Sign of Orpah: Reading Ruth through Native Eyes," in *Ruth and Esther: A Feminist Companion to the Bible*, 2nd series, ed. Athalya Brenner (Sheffield, UK: Sheffield Academic Press, 1999), pp. 130–44.

42. Thomas Römer, *Dieu Obscur: Le sexe, la cruauté, et la violence dans l'Ancien Testament* (Geneva: Labor et Fides, 1998). This work has not yet been translated into English, but is discussed in Lüdemann, *The Unholy in Holy Scripture*, pp. 49–51. All quotations are from the French original.

43. Römer, *Dieu Obscur*, p. 82: "une signification subversive, antiassyriene" (my translation). For similar explanations of war ideologies in the Hebrew Bible, see Paul D. Hanson, "War and Peace in the Hebrew Bible," *Interpretation* 38 (1984): 341–62; "War, Peace, and Justice in Early Israel," *Bible Review* 3 (1987): 32–45; and Norbert Lohfink, "'Holy War' and the 'Ban' in the Bible," *Theology Digest* 38, no. 2 (Summer 1991): 109–14.

44. Niditch, *War in the Hebrew Bible*, p. 136.

45. Ibid., p. 135.

46. Johannes Pedersen, *Israel: Its Life and Culture* (London: Oxford University Press, 1973), 2:311.

47. See Rapoport in Clausewitz, *On War*, p. 14.

48. Walter Brueggemann, *Peace* (St. Louis, MO: Chalice, 2001).

49. Gillis Gerleman, "Die Wurzel [*šlm*]," *Zeitschrift für die Altestamentliche Wissenschaft* 85 (1973): 1–14. For a more pacifistic view, Shemaryahu Talmon, "The Signification of [Shalom] and Its Semantic Field in the Hebrew Bible," in *The Quest for Meaning: Studies in Biblical Intertextuality in Honor of James A. Sanders*, ed. Craig A. Evans and Shemaryahu Talmon (Leiden: Brill, 1997), pp. 75–115; Howard Jacobson, "LXX Genesis 42:23: ἵλεως ὑμῖν," *Textus* 20 (2000): 39–41; and Irene Nowell, "Jerusalem: City of Peace," *TBT* 40 (2002): 12–18.

50. Gerleman, "Die Wurzel," p. 4: "Alle Erscheinungen der Wurzel, nominale wie verbale, liegen . . . innerhalb des Sinnbereiches des Bezahlens und Vergeltens."

51. The pair, "*naqam we-shillēm*" ("vengeance and recompense"), may be understood as a hendiadys (one meaning through two words), and so are to be seen as synonymous.

52. For another study of "shalom" that acknowledges the possibility of domination, see John Keber, "Shalom in the Hebrew Bible," *Listening: Journal of Religion and Culture* 29 (1996): 7–23.

CHAPTER 8

CHRISTIANITY AND THE NEW TESTAMENT

BASIC OVERVIEW

By Christianity, we refer to the array of groups that claim to base their religion on the teachings of Christ as portrayed in the New Testament.[1] According to some counts, in the year 2000 there were some 33,820 Christian denominations and paradenominations.[2] Before elaborating on the definition of "Christian," we should certainly recognize the existence of groups who also claim to be following "Christ" but do not base their beliefs on what is now generally called the New Testament. In fact, scholars are increasingly recognizing the existence of alternative Christianities whose writings are not in the canon. This idea has recently been popularized by Dan Brown's *The Da Vinci Code* (2003), which otherwise simply constructs its own version of early alternative Christianities.[3]

Perhaps the most well-known of groups that did not acknowledge what most Christians today call the New Testament are subsumed under the name "Gnostics."[4] Some of these groups opposed the embodied conceptions of Christ found in the New Testament and/or saw the god of the Hebrew Bible as evil. Nonetheless, it remains accurate to say that what has come to be known as Christianity acknowledges the authority of the teachings of Jesus, as portrayed in the New Testament, in some form or another.

In reality, we cannot identify anyone as a Christian if that word is taken to mean a follower of the actual teachings of Jesus. The reason is that we do not really know what Jesus taught. He left nothing written in his own hand, as far as we can determine. Nothing that we know about Jesus can be shown to be anything more than the account of other authors. This much was acknowledged by Rudolf Bultmann, the great New Testament scholar, when he stated, "Thus, theological thinking—the theology of the New Testament—begins with the kerygma of the earliest Church, and not before."[5]

The problem is compounded by the nature of our source materials. Despite some recent claims that a manuscript containing 1 Corinthians, a letter attributed to Paul, can be dated to the first century, the oldest manuscript of the New Testament is still acknowledged to be P52, which dates from the second century.[6] It contains only a few verses from John 18. Most complete manuscripts of the New Testament are dated no earlier than the third and fourth centuries. Thus, we cannot verify that any or all of the words found in those third- and fourth-century manuscripts actually represent what Jesus said. In fact, passages such as Mark 16:9–20 and 1 John 5:7, which were regarded as original portions of the New Testament just a century ago, are no longer held to be such.

Since we cannot say that someone is a Christian on the basis of agreement with the actual words and thoughts of Jesus, this chapter will show that ultimately the supposed differences between fundamentalists and more liberal segments of Christianity are based on equally subjective and "essentialist" selections of what constitutes the true thoughts of Jesus. Second, we sometimes do not understand what a portrayed teaching of Jesus was on the basis of the language and context of certain New Testament passages. As we shall see, these issues are particularly refractive when dealing with the teachings about "love" and violence in the New Testament.

PRELIMINARY COMMENTS ON SCHOLARSHIP

Very few scholars argue that Christianity is a violent religion. Those works that do argue systematically for the violent history of Christianity are usually relegated to the margins of academia. One case in point is Karlheinz Deschner's *Kriminalgeschichte des Christentums* (The criminal history of Christianity; 1986), a massive multivolume narrative about the history of Christianity written as a "criminal history."[7] While Deschner provides a catalogue of Christian violence, he does not seek to explain how or why Christianity generates violence in any novel manner. A more balanced assessment, which shows that the New Testament espoused both peace and violence, is represented by Michael Desjardins.[8]

Usually, it is the opposite. Christianity is portrayed as a religion of love and peace. Often this emphasis on love and peace is juxtaposed with the vengeful god of the Old Testament. In his book *Does Christianity Cause War?* (1997), David Martin provides us with one study that concludes that Christianity need not be seen as violent.[9] In particular, Martin argues against

Richard Dawkins's assertion that "religion causes wars by generating certainty."[10] Martin argues that conflicts usually pegged as "religious" are in fact the result of a variety of factors, one of them being nationalism. Once one separates the political from the religious, according to Martin, one sees that religion cannot be called an important factor at all.

Martin provides very few close readings of any Christian text, least of all the New Testament. Instead, he offers this more generalized counterargument:

> In giving an account of the Christian code I tried to lay out the theo-logic and the socio-logic behind the text "The Kingdom comes not by violence." The Lord tells his servant Peter to "put up" his sword and explains that his servants do not fight. At the very least, this suggests that Dawkins's theory of the inherent bellicosity of religion is the reverse of what the Gospels actually teach, and Dawkins would need to explain why this is so.[11]

As we shall show below, Martin not only misinterprets the texts he uses (and for which he gives no precise biblical citation) to support a pacifistic view of Christianity, but he also ignores many other Christian texts that are unequivocal in their endorsement of violence. Accordingly, Martin is selective in the passages he believes are representative of "what the Gospels actually teach."

Similarly, we have *Revelation, The Religions, and Violence* (2000), a recent treatise by Leo D. Lefebure.[12] Lefebure does engage in a comparative discussion of religions and their scriptures, apparently acknowledging that "[t]he biblical heritage not only supports contemporary notions of liberation; it also justifies slavery and calls for the extermination of entire populations."[13] He seems to confront the frank violence of many biblical passages. Lefebure does not analyze the precise mechanisms for violence, although he does include a critique of René Girard.

In the end, however, Lefebure chooses to ignore the violence and proclaims: "For Christians, the heart of revelation is that God is infinite, overflowing love, love without measure, love beyond reason, love like a fountain that flows and flows and flows until the water floods everything all around."[14] Forgotten are passages where Jesus tells us to hate parents (Luke 14:26), and where he promises a vengeful judgment on those who do not cater to his needs (Matt. 25:40–46). Thus, we are offered a neomystical interpretation to erase all the violence.

This chapter will show how Christianity, beginning with the New Testament authors, has an ambivalent stance toward violence. Some passages indeed enjoin peaceful responses, but we shall show that even these responses can be interpreted as tactical, meaning that they are intended for utilitarian purposes. Other times authors said to espouse nonviolence actually believe in a type of "deferred violence" that they would like to see heaped upon their current enemies. We shall argue that the foundational event of Christianity, the sacrifice of the son of God, is a violent act that has led to violence on a wider scale. Only a selective reading of the New Testament can yield a vision of Christianity as a religion of nonviolence. As in all the religions we are studying, the main mechanisms of violence involves the creation of scarce resources.

SACRED SPACE

Most of the New Testament was written at a time when Rome had power over the Jewish Holy Land and after it had destroyed the temple. The destruction of the temple was a traumatic event for Judaism, but it did not destroy this religion. Rather, Judaism found new ways to survive this temple destruction, much as it survived the first destruction of the temple by the Babylonians around 586 BCE.[15]

While one can argue that the destruction of the Jewish temple was primarily a political act by the Romans, we also have evidence that the very notion that a temple was sacred made it a target of the Romans. In fact, Josephus tells of a debate among the officials of Titus, who is credited with destroying the temple, as to how to calculate the religious role and value of the temple in the conquest of Palestine.[16] One official opined that if the Jews used it as a fortress, then it was no longer a temple, and it was permissible to burn it. The Christian apologist Tertullian had a more generalized notion of how the Romans treated temples, and observes that, for the Romans, "the plunder of wealth is the same whether it is sacred property or that of laymen."[17]

The destruction of the Jewish temple meant that Jews and early Christians had to rethink the role of the temple in their religious life. As P. W. L. Walker notes, for the most part, early New Testament Christianity devalued Jerusalem and the temple as sacred spaces.[18] In Mark, for instance, the witness to the resurrection is in Galilee, not in Jerusalem. Matthew describes Jesus teaching on different mountains, not just on Mount Zion. Luke and Acts relate the story Christianity's migration from its old center to Rome, its new center. Paul has reconceived the temple entirely as being embodied in a believer. Thus, 1 Corinthians 3:17 says, "If anyone destroys God's temple, God will destroy that person. For God's temple is holy, and you are that temple." Revelation 21:22 speaks of how the future temple will be God himself.

But early Christians did not give up the idea of sacred space altogether.

Matthew (4:5; 27:53) still calls Jerusalem "the Holy City." Likewise, the author of 2 Peter 1:18 still refers to the divine commissioning of Jesus on "the holy mountain." The author of Revelation has not given up on the special role of Jerusalem when he says: "And I saw the holy city, the new Jerusalem, coming down out of heaven from God, prepared as a bride adorned for her husband" (Rev. 21:2).

And sometimes, a supposed lack of territoriality is attributed to Jesus on the basis of texts that could be read otherwise. For example, in the famous Sermon on the Mount, in which Jesus doles out blessings (beatitudes) for various good virtues, one finds the following statement: "Blessed are the meek, for they shall inherit the earth" (Matt. 5:5).[19] At first glance, it appears that Jesus is enlarging the space allotted to his favored group, as the whole "earth" should be sufficient for all. However, "the earth," in the sense of our whole planet or even all the land known at the time of Jesus, is probably not what was meant.

The Greek term, *gē* ("earth") is most likely a translation of the regular Hebrew term *'aretz*, which is often used to designate the land of Israel. Supplementary evidence comes from Psalm 37:11, which has a parallel blessing: "But the meek shall inherit the land" (the Greek translation has *gē*). Earlier in that same Psalm, the promise is made, "Trust in the LORD, and do good; so you will live in the land" (Ps. 37:3). Since everyone is already assumed to live on the earth in the most general sense, then the clause, "so you will live in the land," can only refer to a more restricted space, namely, Israel. The New American Bible, therefore, comes closest to the original sense with its translation of "the land" in Matthew 5:5.

In other ways, Christianity multiplied sacred spaces. Perhaps the most influential sacred space, now occupied by the Vatican, came to be in Rome, whose rise as a center of Christianity can already be seen in Acts. Eventually, of course, the Lateran Palace and Saint Peter's Basilica would become the center of Christianity and be seen as sacred space. Christianity did not share sacred space easily with other religions; Christians often built their temples on top of previous non-Christian temples. In this manner, Christianity diminished other religions' sacred spaces, rendering the ones left even a scarcer resource.

Despite the relative devaluation of Jerusalem in the early Christian centuries, the idea of Israel and Jerusalem being a holy space has resurfaced repeatedly in Christian history.[20] At the Council of Nicea, which enshrined the doctrine of the trinity as part of orthodoxy, one finds a reference to the privilege that should be accorded to the Bishop of Aelia, which probably refers to Jerusalem. In his *Institutes of the Christian Religion* (first published in 1536), John Calvin (1509–1564) expresses this sentiment succinctly: "Israel was made holy; the others profane."[21] This privileging of Jerusalem and

Israel made the space they occupied a scarce resource over which various groups competed for its acquisition through violence.

VIOLENCE DUE TO SACRED SPACE IN THE NEW TESTAMENT

Conflicts over sacred space can be seen already in the New Testament. Perhaps the most famous case involves Jesus himself. As related in John, Jesus' violence is described as follows:

> In the temple he found people selling cattle, sheep, and doves, and the money changers seated at their tables.
>
> Making a whip of cords, he drove all of them out of the temple, both the sheep and the cattle. He also poured out the coins of the money changers and overturned their tables.
>
> He told those who were selling the doves, "Take these things out of here! Stop making my Father's house a marketplace!"
>
> His disciples remembered that it was written, "Zeal for your house will consume me." (John 2:14–17)

Relative to the other Gospel accounts of this episode, John adds the use of a whip, an instrument that would certainly inflict bodily injury, even if mild.[22] The account in Luke 19:46 gives one motivation as follows, "It is written, 'My house shall be a house of prayer'; but you have made it a den of robbers." John portrays the disciples as connecting Jesus' use of violence to a biblical text (Ps. 69:9).

Ronald Sider, a self-described pacifist, attempts to devalue this text by claiming that "Jesus certainly did not kill the moneychangers. Indeed I doubt he even used the whip on them."[23] He provides no documentation for the claim that Jesus did not use a whip, and yet he does not hesitate to declare historical the pacifistic statements of Jesus. And Sider here seems to indicate that violence short of killing is acceptable. This indicates that many self-described pacifists are no less arbitrary than fundamentalists in choosing what counts as a true representation of Jesus.

The episode also shows that Jesus thinks the temple was a scarce resource, not available to all or for every type of activity. Jesus uses violence to acquire control of the space or to redefine what he views to be the proper use of the space. Since Jesus is a paradigm of Christian conduct, his actions came to influence some of the violence linked to sacred spaces that we see in later Christian history.

At the same time, we see non-Christians using violence to counter assaults by Christians on sacred space. One example is the story of the arrest of Stephen, who was later stoned to death. Note the role of sacred space and scripture in outlining the reason's for Stephen's execution: "They set up false witnesses who said, 'This man never stops saying things against this holy place and the law'" (Acts 6:13).

In sum, already in the New Testament we have instances of violence related to the acquisition or maintenance of sacred spaces known as the temple and Jerusalem. The New Testament already shows us a basic paradigm for the violence that is to beset the acquisition of, or the maintenance of control over, the sacred spaces called the temple, Jerusalem, and the Holy Land.

THE FIRST CRUSADE AND SACRED SPACE

In Christian history, the Crusades constitute perhaps the most significant conflicts related to the idea that the Holy Land was sacred space. Although some scholars dwell primarily on the political side of the Crusades, we will argue that the idea of sacred space was a primary factor in at least the First Crusade, and that political and economic forces were derivative.

The most commonly accepted narrative of the First Crusade can be summarized as follows.[24] On November 27, 1095, Pope Urban II (1035–1099), speaking at Clermont (France), called for a Crusade in response to a request by the Byzantine emperor Alexius (1081–1118). Alexius was alarmed by the increasing territory being won by Islamic Turkish armies, which by that time had also captured Jerusalem. The first expeditions left in the spring of 1096, and were largely composed of laypersons who wreaked havoc on many European towns on their eastward route. Most of these early groups of crusaders met defeat by the Turks, disease, or groups of European Christians who resisted their depredations.

The more successful groups of the First Crusade left later in 1096, led by French princes, including Raymond of Toulouse, Godfrey of Bouillon and his brother Baldwin of Boulogne, Stephen of Blois, Bohemond of Taranto, and his nephew, Tancred. Despite many factional conflicts and logistical setbacks, they eventually conquered Jerusalem on July 15, 1099. Godfrey of Bouillon became the first king of Jerusalem, though he preferred the title "advocate of the Holy Sepulchre."

But this basic narrative belies the fact that the study of the Crusades is extremely complex. Within Crusade scholarship, two broad schools have been identified. One school, called traditionalist and represented by Hans Eberhard Mayer, sees the Crusades quite narrowly as those expeditions authorized by the pope to recapture the Holy Sepulchre.[25] Since at least the time of Georg Christoph Müller's 1709 dissertation on the Crusades, these expeditions have been numbered, and Müller himself numbered five (1096, 1147, 1190, 1217–29, and 1248).[26] Mayer ends his history of the Crusades in 1291, with the fall of Acre to the Mamluk Muslims. The word *crusade* was not used to describe any of these expeditions until the thirteenth century.

The other school, sometimes called the pluralist school, is represented by N. J. Housley, K. M. Setton, and Jonathan Riley-Smith.[27] This school views the Crusades as part of a long history of Western aggression against "the other" that has lasted into modern times. By this definition, the persecution of the Albingensians would be a Crusade (1209–29), as would perhaps President George W. Bush's self-described war on terrorism.[28]

Whichever school one deems to be more accurate in its assessment of the Crusades, there is no doubt that at least some part of the Crusades was directly attributed by its promoters to the idea of sacred space. Indeed, both schools can be seen as centering on holy space of different levels. The traditional school sees the holy space as quite small, comprising the Holy Sepulchre or Jerusalem. The pluralist school is actually working with a Christian holy space that is larger. As such, it is actually a larger version of the concentric structure of sacred space that we encountered in parts of the Hebrew Bible.

In any case, some of the clearest examples of the relationship between violence and sacred space may be found in the First Crusade and the propaganda meant to incite Christians to join it. The speech delivered by Urban II at Clermont has not been directly preserved, but we do have various accounts of it from supposed witnesses or recorders. These include the versions of Fulcher of Chartres (1101), Robert the Monk (1107), the anonymously written *Gesta Francorum* (deeds of the Franks), Balderic of Dol (1108–10), and Guibert of Nogent (ca. 1109). These testimonies are all gathered in the monumental *Recueil des Historiens des Croisades* (RHC), which still forms a basic source for all studies of the early Crusades.[29]

We must be cautious in representing these testimonies as a stenographic record of the speech and thought of Urban II. Rather they are to be seen, in part, as retrospective narratives colored by regionalism and the success of the First Crusade.[30] Fortunately, we have supplementary evidence that can help us establish the likelihood of certain aspects of Urban's thought. Otherwise, these testimonies constitute evidence of what the authors understood to be the motives for the First Crusade.

According to Mayer's chronology, Fulcher of Chartres is closer to the actual event of the speech.[31] Urban's motivation for this Crusade is clear in the following: "Therefore, on this matter deserving prayer, not I, but the Lord, beseech you as Christ's heralds to publish this edict everywhere and to persuade people of whatever rank, knights and foot-soldiers, rich and poor, to aid promptly to those Christians and to destroy this vile race from our lands."[32]

Israel is to be seen as holy space that has been invaded and rendered impure by Muslims. The motivation of sacred space is even clearer in the version of Robert the Monk: "Let the holy sepulchre of the Lord our Saviour, which is possessed by unclean nations, especially incite you, and the holy places which are now treated shamefully and irreverently soiled with their filthiness."[33]

But the most systematic case for the First Crusade on the basis of sacred space is the version of Guibert of Nogent. This version begins by arguing that not all space is of equal value:

> If among the churches spread over the whole world some, because of persons or location, deserve reverence above others (for persons, I say, since greater privileges are accorded to apostolic sees; for places, indeed, since the same dignity which is accorded to persons is also shown to regal cities, such as Constantinople), we owe most to that church from which we accepted the grace of redemption and the source of all Christianity.[34]

The speech subsequently outlines the various reasons why Jerusalem is holy. Not one of the reasons is economic or outwardly political. Instead, the speech harkens to scriptural warrants for declaring Jerusalem holy. Note the following argument:

> If this land is spoken of in the sacred pages of the prophets as the inheritance and the holy temple of God before ever the Lord walked about in it, or was revealed, what sanctity, what reverence has it not acquired since God in His majesty was there clothed in the flesh, nourished, grew up, and in bodily form there walked about, or was carried about; and, to compress in fitting brevity all that might be told in a long series of words, since there the blood of the Son of God, more holy than heaven and earth, was poured forth, and His body, its quivering members dead, rested in the tomb. What veneration do we suppose it deserves?[35]

In short, if the city was holy before Jesus walked its streets, it should even be holier after that. Yet Jesus need not have even lived or died in Jerusalem to render it holy. As the speech argues: "Let us suppose, for the moment, that Christ was neither dead nor buried, and had never lived even for a moment in Jerusalem. Surely, if all this were lacking, this fact alone ought still to incite you to go to the aid of the land and city—the fact that 'Out of Zion shall go forth the law and the word of the Lord from Jerusalem![36]

After showing the sacred status of Jerusalem, the speech goes on to use that sanctity as a reason to fight and die:

> If in ancient times the Maccabees attained to the highest praise of piety because they fought for the ceremonies and the Temple, it is also justly granted you, Christian soldiers, to defend their liberty of your country by armed endeavor. If you also consider that the abode of the holy apostles and any other [saints] should be striven for with such effort, why do you refuse to rescue the Cross, the Blood, the Tomb? . . . We now hold out to you wars which contain the glorious reward of martyrdom, which will hold that title of praise now and forever.[37]

Despite these testimonies, Carl Erdmann, a prominent historian of the Crusades, propounded in 1935 an influential thesis that Urban II did not have Jerusalem as a principal objective. However, Erdmann's thesis been effectively refuted by H. E. J. Cowdrey, who draws on five further types of sources to supplement the extant versions of Urban's speech.[38] These supplementary sources leave little doubt that Urban had Jerusalem as his main goal all along.

All versions contain explicit religious directives. Thus, in Fulcher's version, Urban II proclaims: "Moreover, Christ commands it."[39] A more popular general cry became "God wills it" (*Deus vult*).[40] Any misgivings related to leaving the family behind are countered by scriptural quotations, such as in the following argument portrayed by Robert the Monk: "But if you are detained by love of children, parents and wives, recall what the Lord says in the Gospel, 'He that loves father or mother above me, is not worthy of me.'"[41]

The compensation for going on the First Crusade was likewise mostly religious rather than material.[42] Some people actually gave up material goods to take part in these Crusades. Godfrey of Bouillon is said to have sold all of his possessions and surrendered his territories in order to facilitate his expedition.[43] Payment was in the form of indulgences, or promised forgiveness of sins. A previous pope, Gregory VII (ca. 1020–1085), had tried to mount an expedition to Palestine in 1074, but with little success, probably because the concept of indulgences for crusading was not yet widely accepted.

The development of indulgences for participation in the Crusades developed with great alacrity around the eleventh century. As James Brundage, a specialist in medieval canon law, observes, "[A]n indulgence is satisfaction for the temporal punishment required by God in satisfaction for sin."[44] Hostiensis (d. 1271), the celebrated Italian medieval canon lawyer, seems to have been even more extensive in his view of an indulgence, apparently equating it with an unqualified remission of all sins.[45] Hostiensis links the papal power to grant an indulgence directly with the pope's right over the Holy Land, which is sacred because it is the place of the birth, preaching, and death of Christ: "Thus, the Pope renders legitimate and has just cause to grant of an indulgence to those who go to recover the Holy Land, and to declare war on the infidels who posses it; and wherein Mohammed, and not Christ is worshipped, even though that [land] is consecrated because of the birth, preaching, and death of Jesus Christ."[46]

Whatever the exact nature of these indulgences were, they were thought to be an effective motivator. Urban's innovation seems to have been the combining of armed pilgrimage with spiritual remuneration. These religious motivators had dire consequences for the inhabitants of Jerusalem.

Most of the chroniclers relay with little remorse the news that the crusaders slaughtered the inhabitants of Jerusalem. The account of Raymund of Agiles notes that the blood reached up to the bridles of the horses (*et usque ad frenos equorum*).[47] Neither women nor children were spared. The justification for such violence was biblical; the *Gesta Francorum*, for instance, invoked I Samuel 15:8 in order to justify this wholesale massacre.[48] Recall that in this biblical passage, Saul was instructed by God to kill all the men, women, and children of the Amalekites. Saul failed to keep his promise and incurred the wrath of God. Raymund of Agiles calls the massacres a just punishment because the inhabitants blasphemed God.[49]

The idea of sacred space can also be found in some of the later Crusades. In particular, the Third Crusade was initiated by Pope Gregory VIII (d. 1187). Though, he reigned for only a couple of months, Gregory VIII outlined the motives for the Crusade in his *Audita tremendi* (Awesome news). To be sure, many of the Crusades also involved political and economic motives, especially among the elite leaders. However, heavenly remuneration was the only economic benefit most of the common Crusaders would ever hope to receive. Sylvia Schein has argued effectively against the view that the propaganda for regaining the Holy Land was mainly disseminated among the upper classes after the First Crusade.[50]

In short, we have shown here that sacred space has been singled out as a prime motivator for violence in Christianity. The bounded space called Jerusalem receives its sanctity from belief in biblical tradition, especially that concerning Jesus Christ. All the propaganda meant to motivate people to fight was permeated by the idea that holy space existed and that it could not be inhabited by everyone. The belief that Jerusalem was special, a sacred space, was based on belief in unverifiable forces and/or beings (holiness, God's commands). Thus, fighting for this sacred space during the Crusades constitutes a prime example of religious violence. If we were to schematize this more crudely, it would be as follows:

Belief that Jerusalem is sacred space
+ Belief that this sacred space belongs to Christians, not non-Christians
+ Promise of transcendent rewards

= Violence in order to regain Jerusalem

In chapter 10, we will show how the idea of Jerusalem as sacred space still fuels religious violence in the modern world.

INSCRIPTURATION

The New Testament of the Protestant and Catholic canons consists of twenty-seven books. Four Gospels tell the story of Jesus. The book of Acts centers on the nascent church as it spread from the margins of the Roman Empire to its very center in Rome. The Pauline corpus purports to collect the letters of Paul, perhaps the most influential Christian in orthodox traditions. Other epistles (e.g., Peter; Philemon; 1, 2, and 3 John) address various problems besetting various groups of Christians at the end of the first century and the beginning of the second. Finally, the book of Revelation presents us with a sort of revenge novel, and becomes one of the most violent visions in history.[51]

The belief that the New Testament is inspired by God has been supported by a number of arguments. One comes from some New Testament authors themselves, for example, 2 Timothy 3:16: "All scripture is inspired by God and is useful for teaching, for reproof, for correction, and for training in righteousness." A variety of interpretations are possible of the word "inspiration."[52] The Greek word for "inspired" (*theopneustos*) may be translated even more literally as "god-breathed." And the most inclusivistic reading could mean that "all writings" *pasa graphē*, whether Christian or not, are inspired and useful in some way. But most Christian groups have understood "all scripture" to mean all the writings they regard as inspired, which, of course, is a self-serving and circular criterion.

The fact is that we do not know how or why the books in the New Testament canon were selected. As we have noted already, many other self-described Christian writings not found in the current canon could just as well be considered as God's word. In any case, the importance of scripture in Christianity is not to be doubted. Much of what is known as Christianity claims that the word of God is not equally distributed in every book or set of books. Accordingly, the New Testament constitutes or contains a scarce resource, the word of God.

VIOLENCE RESULTING FROM INSCRIPTURATION

Clues to conflict resulting from inscripturation can be found within the New Testament itself. Note, for example, Acts 19:19: "A number of those who practiced magic collected their books and burned them publicly; when the value of these books was calculated, it was found to come to fifty thousand silver coins." The premise of such burning is that the so-called magic books did not contain God's word, and joining Christianity meant destroying rival scriptures.

Some four hundred years later, Pope Leo I (440–461) is said to be doing the same thing with rival scriptures: "And the apocryphal scriptures, which under the names of the Apostles, form a nursery-ground for many false-hoods, are not only to be proscribed, but also taken away altogether and burnt to ashes in the fire."[53] We have other tantalizing clues about inter-Christian conflict that may have involved rival scriptures. In Galatians, Paul makes the following remarks:

> I am astonished that you are so quickly deserting the one who called you in the grace of Christ and are turning to a different gospel—
>
> not that there is another gospel, but there are some who are confusing you and want to pervert the gospel of Christ.
>
> But even if we or an angel from heaven should proclaim to you a gospel contrary to what we proclaimed to you, let that one be accursed! (Gal. 1:6–8)

A "gospel" here may simply mean an oral proclamation of beliefs. But we can reasonably infer that those following a given proclamation would have written it down, creating rival written gospels. This seems to be what is at issue in 1 Peter 1:21–2:1:

> First of all you must understand this, that no prophecy of scripture is a matter of one's own interpretation,
>
> because no prophecy ever came by human will, but men and women moved by the Holy Spirit spoke from God.
>
> But false prophets also arose among the people, just as there will be false teachers among you, who will secretly bring in destructive opinions. They will even deny the Master who bought them—bringing swift destruction on themselves.

Here we see that the author is concerned about false teachings that are juxtaposed with "true" scripture. The author argues that true scripture can be identified because it is generated by the Holy Spirit. The author suggests that the movement from orality to inscripturation seems immediate for utterances regarded as being divine. However, the problem is that the so-called false prophets likely claimed the same divine origin for their scriptures or teachings.

And one did not need to disagree about which texts contained the word of God in order to create a conflict. Interpretation of texts created its own conflict, which has proven to be a far more prevalent source of conflict. In terms of scarce resource theory, an interpretation of a text constitutes a scarce resource when it is held to be the only representation of the mind of God.

THE TALMUD AND ANTI-JEWISH VIOLENCE

The Talmud, the main repository of oral law in traditional Judaism, was a violent issue in the early Christian world. Traditional Judaism holds that the oral tradition is just as authoritative as the Hebrew Bible in outlining the right way to live (*halakah*). The most authoritative edition of the Talmud, called the Babylonian Talmud, is thought to have been edited around 500 CE.[54] One of its main portions, called the Mishna, may have already been edited by 200 CE. The Mishna actually consists of some sixty-three tractates that treat special themes in Jewish life, ranging from rules about how to observe the Sabbath to a treatise about idolatry (*Aboda zara*).

During the Middle Ages, many Christians believed it was proper to force Jews to convert on the basis of the Hebrew Bible and the Talmud. Such use of the Talmud was facilitated by a compilation called the *Pugio Fidei* (Dagger of Faith) credited to Raymond Marti, a thirteenth-century Dominican monk. Earlier, Pablo Christiani, a converted Jew, joined the Dominican order and preached in Provence and Aragon during the 1250s and 1260s. Being quite familiar with the Hebrew scriptures and the Talmud, Christiani compiled a list of biblical passages that he believed pointed to Jesus being the Messiah. If Jews did not accept this interpretation of the Hebrew Bible and Talmud, they were actually rejecting their own sacred texts, and so became candidates for forced conversion.[55]

More specifically, Jews were often seen as engaging in bad business practices. In part, this was the result of Christian codes that forbade Christians from engaging in money lending. Thus, it was left to Jews to provide these services, which then engendered complaints from those who thought the charging of interest was either extortionate or morally wrong. However, other sources of these stereotypes can be traced to the rules of conduct described in the Talmud itself. Stereotypes about bad Jewish business practices came not so much from actual experience but from Christians reading Talmudic passages that seemed to allow less scrupulous behavior when dealing with Gentiles.[56]

Ironically, attention to the Talmud's anti-Gentile statements often was brought by Jewish converts. Thus, in 1236 Nicholas Donin, who had converted from Judaism, presented Pope Gregory IX (ca. 1170–1271) with a list of anti-Christian statements found in the Talmud.[57] For example, in Baba Kama 113b, one encounters a discussion about whether robbery of non-Jews is permitted. Rabbi Simeon the pious opines that while robbery is prohibited, it is permissible to retain lost articles. (Actually, Simeon qualifies this opinion by saying that robbery is permitted in the time of war, but not during peacetime.) However, retaining lost articles is justified even in the following situation:

> It is permissible, however, to benefit by his [a non-Jew's] mistake as in the case when Samuel once bought of a heathen a golden bowl under the assumption of it being made of copper for four *zuz*, and also left him minus one *zuz*. R[abbi] Kahana once bought of a heathen a hundred and twenty barrels which were supposed to be a hundred while he similarly left him minus one *zuz* and said to him: "See that I am relying upon you."

In part, Rabbi Kahana's practice can be justified by an appeal to Deuteronomy 22:3: "and with all lost things of thy brother's." However, "thy brother" here means a fellow Hebrew, not a Gentile. Thus, the privilege of having lost items returned applies to Hebrews, not to non-Hebrews. This is also a case in which a practice X is justified by appeal to divine communication Y. This, therefore, qualifies as a rule of conduct "caused" by religion.

So, in practice, if a Gentile sold an object for less than it was worth by mistake, a Jew was under no obligation to tell the seller. Of course, not all Jews followed such injunctions.[58] The point, however, is that anti-Jewish persecution on charges of fraudulent dealings originated in the very scriptures used by many Jews as a code of conduct. This code of conduct, whether meant to be defensive or not, was perceived by many Christians as conferring group privileges of the most unscrupulous sort, which tended to work toward the disadvantage of Jews when Christians learned of it. Sometimes the alleged Jewish lack of business scruples was linked to the story of the despoiling of the Egyptians as the Hebrews left Egypt.[59]

An actual case of anti-Jewish violence involving destruction of sacred scriptures is found in 1096, as part of one group of Crusaders:

> When they heard that the [Jewish] communities had been killed, they all fled to gentile acquaintances. They remained there for the two days of Shavuot.

> On the third day, as morning dawned, there were rumblings, and the enemy
> rose up against them. They broke into houses, taking spoil and seizing booty.
> They destroyed the synagogue and took out the Torah scrolls and desecrated
> them. They gave them over to trampling them on the streets.[60]

Physical violence related to inscripturation is not difficult to find in the history of Christianity. Perhaps one of the most famous instances is found in Martin Luther's (1483–1546) tract "On the Jews and Their Lies."[61] Luther envisions a seven-part program against Jews that includes the following: "Third, I advise that all their prayer books and Talmudic writings, in which such idolatry, lies, cursing, and blasphemy are taught, be taken from them."[62]

Other directives enjoin Christian leaders to burn synagogues and even kill rabbis who persist in teaching their religion. Luther prefaces his remarks with the following motivation: "This is to be done *in honor of our Lord* and Christendom, so that God might see that we are Christians, and do not condone or knowingly tolerate such public lying, cursing, blaspheming of his son and of his Christians."[63]

Clearly, to Luther, the only authoritative scripture is the canon known as the Old and New Testaments; the Jewish Talmud does not contain God's authoritative truth. The Protestant Luther believes he must destroy competing claims of God's scripture much as the Catholic pope Leo I did before him. The motives are expressly religious and so constitute examples of religious violence when put into practice.

GROUP PRIVILEGING

In Galatians 3:28 the author writes, "For there is neither male nor female, neither Jew nor Greek." This usually is the text often cited to show that Christianity has dissolved the ethnocentricity of Judaism. In fact, it has been claimed that this text eventually resulted in the abolition of slavery and the rise of women's rights.[64] However, such readings of Galatians 3:28 are no less selective and biased than those that use the New Testament to maintain rigid group privileging.[65]

Indeed, the dissolution of ethnocentricity in New Testament Christianity is quite superficial; Christianity has actually substituted a different type of group privilege. Whereas ethnocentricity in the Hebrew Bible is founded on genealogy, Christianity has created a new ethnos based on devotion to Christ. But this can be read as an imperialistic practice, wherein allegiance to family is transferred to allegiance to Christ, who often functions as simply the Christian version of the Roman emperor. In short, Christianity simply uses a new set of features to define the in-group and out-group.

The clearest cases for the new grouping are found in the Gospels, as in the following passage:

> "Do not think that I have come to bring peace to the earth; I have not come to bring peace, but a sword.
>
> For I have come to set a man against his father, and a daughter against her mother, and a daughter-in-law against her mother-in-law;
>
> and one's foes will be members of one's own household.
>
> Whoever loves father or mother more than me is not worthy of me; and whoever loves son or daughter more than me is not worthy of me;
>
> and whoever does not take up the cross and follow me is not worthy of me." (Matt. 10:34–38)

This passage is often misinterpreted to mean that the result of following Jesus is conflict within the family. However, the original Greek, especially in verse 35 (*ēlthon gar dichasai*),[66] is best understood to mean that *the purpose* of Jesus is to bring conflict. *Purpose*, rather than *result*, is the most accurate grammatical meaning of the clause. Nonetheless, a stronger statement of hate is found in Luke 14:26-27:

> "Whoever comes to me and does not hate father and mother, wife and children, brothers and sisters, yes, and even life itself, cannot be my disciple.
>
> Whoever does not carry the cross and follow me cannot be my disciple."

The stridency of these statements is often softened by Christian apologists.[67] However, it is clear that all of these efforts ignore the plain meaning of the text and/or create new problems in semantic logic that would render "love passages" vulnerable.

These sentiments, moreover, are parallel to what is expected of slaves and imperial subjects. In Exodus 21:4, for example, we find the following law concerning a slave who wishes to leave a slave master's household: " If his master gives him a wife and she bears him sons or daughters, the wife and her children shall be her master's and he shall go out alone." Again, loyalty to the master is placed above loyalty to the biological family of the slave; the slave master is either punishing the slave for leaving or coercing him into staying by holding his family hostage.

The bulk of the New Testament is sufficient to refute a common Christian apologetic argument that the "imperial" church began with Constantine.[68] By making Christianity the state religion, so this argument goes, Constantine created a set of privileges that were more oppressive than Jesus would have wished. The reality is that the New Testament already bears the roots of the imperial aspirations Constantine made into a reality. New Testament Christianity already patterns itself on the imperialism and hierarchy of the Roman Empire, even as Christians are trying to counter Roman oppression.[69] In chapter 16, we examine more thoroughly the idea that Christianity was modeled on imperialistic and slave societies.

GROUP PRIVILEGE AND ANTI-JEWISH VIOLENCE

Anti-Judaism has precipitated the most persistent violence involving group privileging in Christianity. I use the term "anti-Judaism" specifically because I see "anti-Semitism" as a misnomer that should be avoided despite its historical use as synonymous with hostility toward Jews. The term "anti-Semitism" should be reserved for hatred of all Semitic people, of which Jews form only a small group. The literature on anti-Judaism is now quite extensive and complex.[70] Our mission here is to show that one can argue plausibly that anti-Judaism in Western civilization has been primarily religious in origin, with political and economic motives being ancillary.

In general, at least two types of explanations for anti-Judaism can be identified in scholarship.[71] One type of explanation, which can be labeled "essentialist," sees anti-Judaism as a permanent part of Jewish relations with others. According to this view, Judaism, as a monotheistic faith with peculiar traditions, will always be seen as different. The main evidence comes from pre-Christian history, which shows that anti-Jewish sentiment existed apart from Christianity. Since pre-Christian and non-Christian anti-Judaism is well documented, it also serves to shift responsibility away from Christianity.

Another view can be described as "functionalist," arguing that various religious and social contexts are quite accepting of Judaism. Thus, anti-Judaism depends on context rather than on some inevitable hatred. The scholar of anti-Judaism, Peter Schäfer, numbers Elias Bickerman and Martin Hengel among the representatives of functionalism, though he admits that these scholars also espouse elements of the essentialist model.[72] In any case, one can see that both categories also parallel, even if in a dilute form, the tensions between biological/natural and cultural explanations for violence. Schäfer himself prefers a combination of the two approaches, especially in light of the fact that neither model is ever found in pure form.

With regard to Christian anti-Judaism, some hold Christianity to be essentially and uniquely anti-Jewish, and some do not. An example of the former position is Rosemary Ruether, who argues that "the special virulence of Christian anti-Semitism can be understood only from its source in a religious fraternity in exclusive faith turned rivalrous."[73] According to Reuther, pagan anti-Judaism had little, if any, effect on Christian anti-Judaism; the central event in the break between Judaism and Christianity was the "raising up of faith in Messiah Jesus as a supersessionary covenantal principle."[74] That is to say, one was not part of God's people unless one adopted the idea that Jesus was the Messiah in conjunction with the principle that this superseded the policies in what Christians call the Old Testament.

John G. Gager is among those who do not consider Christianity to be essentially negative toward Judaism.[75] His survey of both non-Christian and Christian sources leads him to conclude "that neither in paganism nor in Christianity is there evidence for a consistently negative understanding of Judaism."[76] Instead, Gager sees anti-Judaism as arising out of conflicts about Judaism within early Christianity. He adds that "eventually the anti-Jewish side won. Its ideology became normative, not just for subsequent Christianity but, through the formation of the New Testament, for our perception of earlier Christianity as well."[77]

The roots of this violence between Christians and Jews reach back to the New Testament. While Christianity ostensibly began as a sect of Judaism, by the end of the first century it is clear that the distance between traditional Judaism and Christianity has grown to violent proportions. The Gospels, which are some of the latest books produced in the New Testament, already provide a conflict between Jesus and traditional Jewish authorities represented by the Pharisees and Scribes. In John 8:44 Jesus tells the Jews, "You are from your father the devil, and you choose to do your father's desires. He was a murderer from the beginning and does not stand in the truth, because there is no truth in him. When he lies, he speaks according to his own nature, for he is a liar and the father of lies."

Likewise, some New Testament authors see "the Jews" as responsible for the violence against Jesus.

> For this reason *the Jews were seeking all the more to kill him*, because he was not only breaking the Sabbath, but was also calling God his own Father, thereby making himself equal to God. (John 5:18)

> After this Jesus went about in Galilee. He did not wish to go about in Judea because *the Jews were looking for an opportunity to kill him*. (John 7:1)

> "*You that are Israelites*, listen to what I have to say: Jesus of Nazareth, a man attested to you by God with deeds of power, wonders, and signs that God did through him among you, as you yourselves know—

this man, handed over to you according to the definite plan and foreknowl-
edge of God, *you crucified and killed* by the hands of those outside the law.
(Acts 2:22–23)

The fact that traditional Judaism rejects the major aspect of Christianity, the
Messiahship of Jesus, led dominant Christian groups to deny Jews any rights
and privileges otherwise granted to Christians.

By late antiquity there developed systematic laws that affirmed status differences between Jews and Christians. Canon Sixteen of the Council of
Elvira (ca. 306), for instance, prohibits marriage between Christians and
Jews. Canon Forty prohibits secular and clergy from eating with Jews.[78] Yet
this can be seen as simply an extension of the directive found in 2 John
10–11: "Do not receive into the house or welcome anyone who comes to you
and does not bring this teaching; for to welcome is to participate in the evil
deeds of such a person." Followers of Christ were already discriminating
against those who did not follow the teachings as outlined by New Testament
authors.

Augustine, the foremost theologian of late antiquity, actually thought
the Jews should be tolerated, although this belief was based on premises that
were quite negative toward Judaism. Augustine argued that the dispersal of
the Jews among the nations was a just recompense, at least in part, for their
killing of Christ. However, their dispersal actually served Christianity insofar
as the Jews could at least attest to the existence of the Old Testament, which
Christians were using to support Christianity. As Augustine commented, at
least now, nonbelievers could not argue that the Old Testament was a Christian invention (*a nobis putaretur esse confictum*).[79]

At the same time, Augustine could not envision equal rights for Jews
because of their religious views. Augustine, in fact, proposed that slavery was
the just station of Jews in return for crucifying Christ and refusing to accept
the Gospel. Overall, Augustine argued that slavery was the result of the Fall,
and this was an institution that accorded with nature. Laws that maintained
slavery, therefore, were in full accordance with "natural law" (*naturalem
ordinem*).[80]

Jerome, who often disagreed with Augustine about the role of the
Hebrew scriptures, had quite paradoxical attitudes toward Judaism. On the
one hand, he studied with learned Jews, and absorbed many of their exegetical traditions. On the other hand, he saw the continued existence of the Jews
as an affront to Christ. John Chrysostom (344–407), author of *Discourses
against the Jews*, was a most virulent anti-Jewish writer. His writings broach
the idea of killing Jews for their unbelief, among other perceived moral
depravities.[81]

While group privileging generally resulted in anti-Jewish violence throughout Christian history, it is in the Middle Ages that one sees some of the most brutal and systematic attacks on Jews.[82] In part, the codification of Canon Law was responsible for more uniform policy toward the Jews.[83] Despite signs of tolerance shown in Canon Law at times, the reality is that Jews were expelled from England in 1290 under Edward I (1272–1307). In 1306 France expelled the Jews, and, of course, by 1492, Spain also expelled the Jews.

In any event, the First Crusade led the way in a new wave of systematic anti-Jewish violence. As noted, the First Crusade was proclaimed in 1095, and the first contingents began to make their way eastward in 1096. These first contingents, composed mostly of laypersons and peasants, were held responsible for most anti-Jewish violence, which is reported by both Christian and Jewish sources. Those sources indicate that the hordes of crusaders moved into towns such as Cologne, Mainz, and Worms, some of the main centers of Jewish population. Many of the Jews caught in those pogroms refused to convert to Christianity. According to one Jewish chronicle, the following was considered a rationale for suicide:

> After all things, there is no questioning the ways of the Holy One, blessed be He . . . Who has given us His Torah and has commanded us to allow ourselves to be killed and slain in witness to the Oneness of His Holy Name. Happy are we if we fulfill His will and happy is he who is slain or slaughtered and who dies attesting to the Oneness of His Name. Such a one is destined for the World-to-Come, where he will sit in the realm of the saints, the pillars of the universe. . . . Moreover, for such a one a world of darkness is exchanged for a world of light, a world of sorrow for one of joy, a transitory world for an eternal world.[84]

One explanation for the rise of violence against the Jews at this time is that Christian policies toward Jews had become much more systematic. One example was the *Sicut Iudaeis* (Constitutions for the Jews) attributed to Pope Calixtus II (1119–1124). Although these directives counsel against forcing Jews to convert, they are still premised on the idea that their main moral deficiency is being obstinate in not believing that Jesus is the Messiah. Again, the division between Christians and Jews consists in religious differences.

Martin Luther, the father of Protestantism, at first seemed to be tolerant of Jews. But eventually he spouted forth a plan of action for the Jews that became the blueprint of the Nazi holocaust. For this reason, it bears repeating at length:

> First, to set fire to their synagogues or schools and to bury and cover with dirt whatever will not burn, so that no man will ever again see a stone or cinder of them.

This is to be done *in honor of our Lord and Christendom*, so that God might see that we are Christians, and do not condone or knowingly tolerate such public lying, cursing, blaspheming of his son and of his Christians . . . .

Second, I advise that their houses also be razed and destroyed . . .

Third, I advise that all their prayer books and Talmudic writings, in which such idolatry, lies, cursing, and blasphemy are taught, be taken from them.

Fourth, I advise that their rabbis be forbidden to teach henceforth *on pain of loss of life* and limb . . .

Fifth, I advise that safe-conduct on the highways be abolished completely for the Jews.

Sixth, I advise that usury be prohibited to them, and that all cash and treasures of silver and gold be taken from them for safekeeping . . .

Seventh, I recommend putting a flail, an ax, a hoe, a distaff, or a spindle into the hands of young strong Jews and Jewesses and letting them earn their bread in the sweat of their brow, as was imposed on the children of Adam (Gen. 3 [:19])[85]

Note that Luther's murderous plan has mainly religious motives as justification. The plan, he says, is to be enacted in honor of Christ and Christendom. He targets the religious literature of Jews, and the Talmud in particular.

In sum, as best we can ascertain, the original meaning of Christian brotherhood applied best to other Christians in the New Testament. Outsiders were admitted only if they gave up their own religion. Those that did not accept Jesus, the Christian version of the emperor, would be tortured or killed upon his return. This has not changed much through most of Christian history, and the Jews have been the most prominent victims of Christian group privileging that goes all the way back to the earliest portrayals of Jesus that we can date.

SALVATION

As in the Hebrew Bible, salvation has a wide range of meanings in the New Testament. The primary Greek verb *sōzō*, translated as "save," can indeed apply to being rescued from physical danger, as in the case of Paul's shipwreck in Acts 27:20: "When neither sun nor stars appeared for many days, and no small tempest raged, all hope of our being saved was at last abandoned." In this case, "being saved" is clearly related to surviving or evading drowning. One can be "saved" from illnesses and other oppressive situations (e.g., Mark 1:34 and Luke 8:48). The latter concept is not unusual, as Asclepius, a main Greek healing god, is also called "savior" (*sōtēr*).[86]

Beyond the more mundane level of poverty and illness, many New Testament authors also speak of more transcendental forms of salvation. Here we can differentiate at least two concepts of transcendental salvation that have an important impact on violence: salvation that is achievable in the present, and salvation that will be granted in the future.

Salvation that is achievable in the present can include salvation from sin, a concept that is particularly developed in letters attributed to Paul. In Romans 6:6–7 he says: "We know that our old self was crucified with him so that the body of sin might be destroyed, and we might no longer be enslaved to sin. For whoever has died is freed from sin." It is here that we also encounter many of the pneumocentric approaches to salvation that result in the devaluation of the body. Thus, one must die, even if symbolically, to be saved from sin. Such a death results in a new creation (2 Cor. 5:17).

A more future-oriented approach to salvation means that we must work in this lifetime to collect the reward, which often is the privilege of living in a utopia. Jesus is quoted as espousing this more eschatological approach to salvation in Matthew 24:13: "But the one who endures to the end will be saved." Likewise, works attributed to Paul also speak of salvation being in the future. Other scholars point to the existence of a "realized eschatology," meaning that some New Testament authors believed that the end of time had come. In this manner the Kingdom of Heaven had arrived, or was "within" believers (Luke 17:21).

In any case, salvation is portrayed as a scarce resource, a valuable commodity that may be attained or maintained through violence. Thus, Jesus is quoted as saying: "For many are called, but few are chosen" (Matt. 22:14). Matthew 24:13, quoted above, follows an extensive discourse on the suffering that Jesus' followers must endure before they can achieve salvation. Moreover, salvation is often pneumocentric, meaning that what is important is to save the soul, not the body. As Jesus is quoted as saying, "Do not fear those who kill the body but cannot kill the soul; rather fear him who can destroy both soul and body in hell" (Matt. 10:28).

Within the Catholic tradition there developed the concept of *Extra Ecclesiam nulla salus* (Outside of the church there is no salvation). As Hans Küng notes, the Council of Florence (1442) was unequivocal: "The Holy Roman Church . . . firmly believes, confesses and proclaims that outside the Catholic Church no one, neither heathen nor Jew nor unbeliever nor schismatic will have a share in eternal life, but will, rather, be the subject to everlasting fire."[87]

Since Vatican II, the Catholic Church has seemingly softened its exclusive stance on salvation. But as soon as seemingly more inclusive theologies are adopted, we meet with new ones to exclude. Thus, William E. Phipps, who welcomes a more ecumenical attitude among Catholics toward Muslims and Jews, goes on to devalue New Age movements as follows: "Much of what is called New Age spirituality, with its attention to self-deification, horoscopes, crystal gazing, seances and other irrational magic, is just a current phase of Old Age superstition that is global in scope."[88]

This assumes, of course, that the Eucharist, salvation, and prayer to the Christian god do not constitute equally unverifiable "superstitions." In short, even this more "inclusive" theology simply results in the maintenance of the scarce resource called "salvation" as presumably New Age techniques would not be considered salvific.[89]

VIOLENCE AND THE ATONEMENT

The idea that salvation and violence are linked historically in Christian theology received graphic testimony in Mel Gibson's 2004 feature film *The Passion of the Christ*. According to an interview with Bill O'Reilly, Gibson wanted shocked viewers to "find the beauty" in the bloodbath of Jesus' torture.[90] Gibson hopes that his film will raise our appreciation for the suffering of Christ, and perhaps convert a few hard-hearted nobelievers to his version of Christianity. It would be a mistake simply to dismiss Gibson as a fanatic who has distorted Christianity.

It is true that some theologians (e.g., Duns Scotus, ca. 1266–1308) believe that God, being omnipotent and sovereign, could have chosen any means, even blasphemous ones, to achieve salvation. It is also true that there have been a variety of other theories of the atonement (the process of salvation through Christ's death) in Christian history. However, it remains accurate to say that the dominant Christian soteriological theory is premised on the idea that Jesus had to die and/or endure bodily torture in order for Christians to achieve salvation. We find some of these ideas in the New Testament book of Hebrews (9:22), which provides one of the earliest systematic theories regarding the necessity of Christ's death: "Indeed, under the law almost everything is purified with blood, and without the shedding of blood there is no forgiveness of sins." The author adds in 9:26: "But as it is, he has appeared once for all at the end of the age to remove sin by the sacrifice of himself."

The author argues that blood must be shed in order for sins to be forgiven. Being that animal sacrifice can purify only a finite number of sins, a higher being must be sacrificed to effect to overturn an infinite number of sins or to purify entities of a higher order. Thus, the sacrifice cannot simply be animal; it now must be one who is higher than human beings on the onto-logical plane. The author of Hebrews does not believe that Jesus is God, but rather that he is a divine just below God in stature.

In any case, the idea that Christ had to die for our sins became linked with the idea that he had to be tortured before he died. This idea derives from a Christian interpretation of Isaiah 53, which becomes the epigraph seen at the beginning of Mel Gibson's *The Passion*:

> Surely he has borne our infirmities and carried our diseases; yet we accounted him stricken, struck down by God, and afflicted.
>
> But he was wounded for our transgressions, crushed for our iniquities; upon him was the punishment that made us whole, and by his bruises we are healed . . .
>
> He was oppressed, and he was afflicted, yet he did not open his mouth; like a lamb that is led to the slaughter, and like a sheep that before its shearers is silent, so he did not open his mouth . . .
>
> Yet it was the will of the LORD to crush him with pain. When you make his life an offering for sin, he shall see his offspring, and shall prolong his days; through him the will of the LORD shall prosper.
>
> Out of his anguish he shall see light; he shall find satisfaction through his knowledge. The righteous one, my servant, shall make many righteous, and he shall bear their iniquities. (Isa. 53:4–5, 7, 10–11)

Since medieval times, the more dominant theories of soteriology were ones associated with Anselm and Thomas Aquinas. Anselm (1033–1109), in his famous *Cur Deus Homo* (Why God became man), held that sin violates the infinite honor and majesty of God. The most proportionate punishment would be infinite, something man could not satisfy. The only way to satisfy this violation would be for God himself to become man. By sharing our nature, he becomes the worthy substitute for human beings. By being infi-nite, he provides the infinite satisfaction for sin.[91]

Likewise, Aquinas believed that it was necessary for God to become flesh.[92] More importantly, Aquinas addressed quite directly whether Christ had to endure violence in order for salvation. One issue, in particular, is whether a natural death would have been more suitable than a violent death. Aquinas claimed that Christ had to suffer and die for at least five reasons, the first being that man "knows thereby how much God loves him."[93] This was rooted in passages such as John 3:16: "For God so loved the world that he gave his only Son, so that everyone who believes in him may not perish but may have eternal life." This link between love and violence would come to have strong repercussions in the history of Christian violence.

The thought of Anselm and Aquinas has been dominant even among Protestant theologians. Thus, the Westminster Confession of Faith (1648), which was followed by the Puritan fathers who settled America, stated that Christ willingly suffered, as our mediator, the "most painful sufferings in His body."[94] Likewise, if one examines the writings of Reformed American theologian Charles Hodge (1797–1878), one finds that he also wrote that Christ had to suffer so that God could show his love for humankind.[95]

Nor have pacifistic groups necessarily abandoned the idea that violence was part of God's salvation plan. Thus, the Quaker catechism authored by Robert Barclay (1648–1690) grants that "Christ also suffered for us, leaving us an Example, that we should follow his Steps [1 Pet. 2:21] *For we are to* bear about in the Body the dying of the Lord Jesus, that the Life also of Jesus might be made manifest in our body."[96] The Confession of Faith in a Mennonite Perspective, adopted in 1995, proclaims in Article 8: "We believe that, through the life, death, and resurrection of Jesus Christ, God offers salvation from sin and a new way of life to all people."[97]

Newer theories of the atonement have criticized the sacrificial models as rooted in patriarchal and masculine cultures. One of the most discussed is that proposed by Gustaf Aulén, the Swedish theologian and author of *Christus Victor*.[98] Aulén believes that Anselmian theories are late accretions on Christianity, while the most authentic traditions see the atonement as an example of God's love, not a punishment for sin. Jesus' resurrection showed Satan that he was indeed the master of the universe, and so his is the "Christus Victor" in this sense.

In the end, Aulén does not completely evade the violence of the atonement, only the seeming "necessity" of it. Likewise, J. Denny Weaver, who uses Aulén as a model in *The Nonviolent Atonement* (2001), affirms that Jesus' death is not "needed," as in the Anselmian version. Yet Weaver accepts that Jesus did die. His theory thus turns Jesus' death into a case of even more needless violence.[99] Far from rejecting any violence, Aulén and Weaver turn violence yet again into part of the act of "love."[100]

In sum, despite many alternative theories of the atonement that have been proposed throughout history and in modern times, the idea that Christ suffered and died in order to express God's love, needlessly or not, has reinforced the idea that violence was necessary to gain this greater benefit called "salvation." Most of what is known as Christianity in the modern world is premised on the idea that violence was experienced, necessarily or not, in order to solve a perceived human problem (e.g., sinfulness, the wrath of God, etc.).

VIOLENCE FOR THE SAKE OF SALVATION

In contrast to the idea of René Girard, who argues that the sacrifice of God effected the overthrow of scapegoating violence, the notion that salvation of humankind had been achieved through such a trauma to the deity has spawned a number of rationales for violence, whose consequences echo in many forms. In a magisterial study, Timothy Gorringe has argued that Anselm's theory of the atonement, in particular, had wide influence on violent justice systems in Europe. He notes that the need to hang or torture criminals was never self-evident. The necessity of such practices was often debated. However, when they were upheld it was generally because of allusions to Anselm's theory or New Testament ideas of the atonement. As Gorringe phrases it, "[T]he theology of satisfaction, I contend, provided one of the subtlest and most profound of such justifications, not only for hanging but for retributive justice in general.[101]

As it pertains to our thesis, a most persistent rationale for violence used the violent death of Christ to justify forcing the conversion of others. Since God made such a great sacrifice, it behooves human beings to be grateful. Refusal to convert after learning of the suffering of the Christ means that one is ungrateful. This lack of gratefulness must be punished, as indicated in Hebrews 10:29: "How much worse punishment do you think will be deserved by those who have spurned the Son of God, profaned the blood of the covenant by which they were sanctified, and outraged the Spirit of grace?"

Paradoxically, another rationale for violence used the death of Christ as an occasion to blame his killers. This rationale was often used against Jews, as is evident in the Chronicle of Solomon bar Simson's description of Godfrey of Bouillon's actions against Jews during the First Crusade. According to the Chronicle, Godfrey was bent on "avenging the blood of the crucified one by shedding Jewish blood."[102] Likewise, the same Chronicle portrays crusading Christians as using the following rationale for killing Jews on their way to Jerusalem: "Look now, we are going a long way to seek out the profane shrine and to avenge ourselves on the Ishmaelites [= Muslims], when here, in our very midst, are the Jews—they whose forefathers murdered and crucified him for no reason."[103]

Ironically, Solomon bar Simson indicates that Christians cited an apparent death sentence passed upon the Jews by Jesus, who is quoted as saying "there will yet come a day when my children will come and avenge my blood." Schlomo Eidelberg, an expert on violence against Jews during the Crusades, believes that this is an allusion to Matthew 27:25, in which Jews seemingly pass a death sentence upon themselves: "Then the people as a whole answered, 'His blood be on us and on our children!'"[104]

Christian anger also was driven, in part, by some of the Jewish descriptions of Christ as a man "despised, abominated, and held in contempt in his own generation, a bastard son conceived by a menstruating and wanton mother."[105] Such an opinion of Christ directly threatened notions of Christian salvation. For if Christ was not God, but a mere man, then Christian salvation would be nullified.

If the idea of salvation refers to being rescued from the wrath of God, then it is clear that Christians often feel free to inflict violence on those that were not willing to be saved or who were seen as unsavable. This rationale is attributed to the Knights Templar, the famous order of fighting monks established in the twelfth century. Stephen Howarth, a historian of the Knights Templar, comments: "One of the main objectives of the Crusades was unification of eastern and western Christendom, and one of the basic principles of the time was that religious belief . . . could be effectively established by force."[106]

The use of coercion to effect conversions was discussed quite intensely during the Middle Ages, especially in the case of Jews. There were strong arguments voiced on both sides. Gratian, perhaps the most important canonical lawyer in Catholicism, compiled a vast compendium of church law. One of his decretals prohibited the forced conversion of Jews.[107] The premise for such a prohibition was that faith is supposed to be voluntary in order to be efficacious. On the other side was Duns Scotus, who advocated the forced baptism of all Jewish children. The main argument was that the salvation of souls takes precedence over the rights of parents.

Thomas Aquinas, the most influential theologian of the Middle Ages, used rationales for violence that were linked to the maintenance and expansion of the scarce resource we call salvation. He also seems to have been ambivalent on the use of force. On the one hand, Aquinas argued that one should not force Jews to convert if they had not received the faith. However, once Jews had received the faith then "they ought to be compelled to keep it."[108]

One way Aquinas justified the use of force to retain Jewish converts appealed to the concept of contractual law. He reasons that "[j]ust as taking a vow is a matter of will . . . keeping the faith once one has received it, is a matter of obligation."[109] Two biblical examples also serve to justify force and killing those that retracted their conversion. Following Augustine, Aquinas uses Paul's conversion as an example. Augustine observed that Paul was compelled before he was taught to follow Christ. A second example is that of Absalom, whose killing was necessary for the sake of David's kingdom (1 Sam. 18:9–14). Accordingly, Aquinas, again following Augustine, reasons that the church "heals the sorrow of her maternal heart by the delivery of so many nations."[110] In short, the church can liberate the nations from hell by means of violence.

But the main reason Aquinas gives for waging war and imprisoning unbelievers is not so that those unbelievers will convert, but rather so that those unbelievers do not hinder the salvation of others.[111] Here we can clearly see how salvation is a scarce resource, unavailable except through sanctioned means. Violence may be used in order to allow or maintain access to this scarce resource.

Aquinas likewise favored bodily compulsion for heretics who strayed from Christianity. One of the main biblical texts used by Aquinas, among others, to sanction such compulsion is Luke 14:23: "Then the master said to the slave, 'Go out into the roads and lanes, and compel people to come in, so that my house may be filled.'" This instruction is part of a parable given by Jesus, who is speaking of a rich man who gave a feast, but the invitees did not come. The master of the house told his servants to force people off the street into the banquet. By analogy, if Christians are the servants, and Jesus is the master of the house, then Christians must compel nonbelievers to enter the kingdom of God.

But it is here that Aquinas becomes inconsistent because he seems to be disregarding the use of force for the salvation of souls in the case of some groups, and yet advocating it in the case of others. Heretics and converted Jews can be compelled, but not necessarily everyone else. Yet, throughout Aquinas's discussion of force in conversions, it seems that the lack of acceptance of the Christian notion of salvation threatens the entire notion of salvation itself. That is to say, lack of acceptance may lead others to believe that salvation is false, so this scarce resource must be protected from the skeptics.

Another policy based on the suffering of Christ dealt with how to suffer violence as a Christian. This idea can be found already in 1 Peter:

Slaves, accept the authority of your masters with all deference, not only those who are kind and gentle but also those who are harsh.

For it is a credit to you if, being aware of God, you endure pain while suffering unjustly.

If you endure when you are beaten for doing wrong, what credit is that? But if you endure when you do right and suffer for it, you have God's approval.

For to this you have been called, because Christ also suffered for you, leaving you an example, so that you should follow in his steps.

"He committed no sin, and no deceit was found in his mouth."

When he was abused, he did not return abuse; when he suffered, he did not threaten; but he entrusted himself to the one who judges justly.

> He himself bore our sins in his body on the cross, so that, free from sins, we might live for righteousness; by his wounds you have been healed. (1 Pet. 2:18–24)

Here, the Passion of Christ serves as part of a rationale to maintain violence. Slaves are to suffer and not revolt against even harsh slave masters. Suffering gains the approval of God, while rejection of suffering earns no credit.

Of course, many will argue that this policy originally served to protect Christians in an environment of persecution. Christians would survive if they did not revolt and if they were not seen as troublemakers. But the results would remain the same: Suffering was to be seen as good, and therefore violent oppression would not be defeated. Slavery, for example, which was a violent institution itself, would be maintained if slaves were told to obey slave masters.

The types of rationales seen in these medieval examples have not disappeared. In part, these rationales now fuel violence between Protestants and Catholics in many parts of the world. One such example is in Mexico. According to a report from the US Department of State: "On August 27, 1998, indigenous Catholics in Mitziton, Chiapas, took 23 evangelicals hostage and threatened to eject them from the community if they did not convert to Catholicism. Catholic and state authorities intervened to obtain their release. In addition, a number of Catholic churches were burned in Chiapas, but the authorities made no arrests."[112]

In sum, the theory of salvation in orthodox Christianity could lead logically to violence against others and to the maintenance of violence against Christians. The common theme is that salvation is a scarce resource, not easily achievable, and not available through every means. Thus, it sometimes has behooved Christians to force conversions on others in order to save them. Other times, violence was necessary in order to remove obstructions that would allow nonbelievers access to this resource. Finally, salvation is a resource scarce enough that one might have to suffer and not overthrow violent regimes in order to attain more intangible supernatural rewards.

SUMMARY

Christianity adapted some of the scarce resources found first in the Hebrew Bible and in Judaism, but it also created additional scarce resources. The New Testament supersedes or devalues the Hebrew Bible as the eternal locus of divine authority. Sacred spaces multiply, though Jerusalem resurfaces as a primary sacred space throughout Christian history, sometimes with violent consequences, as in the Crusades. Group privileging continues, though now it is defined by allegiance to Jesus, the new emperor, rather than on the basis of biological genealogy.

But perhaps the most persistent violence generated by Christianity relates to the scarce resource called "salvation" through the violent death of the son of God. Anthropologists are not certain why people came to believe that sacrifice or the shedding of blood was necessary for absolution from sin. One theory, espoused notably by Walter Burkert, traces sacrifice to Paleolithic hunting practices.[113] Such hunting practices taught human beings that killing sustains life, as the dead animal becomes the means by which human beings live. These ideas have yet to be firmly established in the paleoanthropological record.[114] Likewise, there was a tradition that gods ate, and perhaps also were kept alive by, animals killed by human beings. We have just such an indication in Genesis 8:21, where Yahweh is said to smell the pleasing sacrifice offered by Noah after the Flood. The Near Eastern scholar William Hallo has proposed that sacrifice originated in the attempt to sanctify the very act of consumption.[115]

The idea that one must shed blood to neutralize sins is rooted in a long prebiblical tradition of the ancient Near East. Already in the Enuma elish, the creation story from Mesopotamia (ancient Iraq), we have a god named Kingu who is sacrificed so that human beings can be made from his blood. In effect, this is a god sacrificed to give life to humans.[116]

Ultimately, however, any notion that sacrifice is necessary for our collective health is neither empirically proven nor helpful for overcoming violence. Burkert, in fact, comes close to indicating that notions of collective sacrifice and guilt are good. Those Christians who favor nonviolent theories of the atonement must do so by either disregarding the New Testament or by reinterpreting it in a manner no less arbitrary or unverifiable than the techniques used by fundamentalists to maintain interpretations that maintain a violent atonement.

And it is in studying the effects of the belief in the sacrifice of God that Girard's theory is exposed for all its impotence. Contrary to Girard's theory, the belief in sacrifice can create new rationales for violence rather than result in the final overthrow of mimetic or scapegoating violence. The supposed uniqueness of the sacrifice of Christ has been associated with a complex of soteriological ideas that generated a new scarce resource over which to fight. If the only way to salvation is through Christ, anything that threatens a person's salvation now becomes the object of violence. It is Girard's theory that should be at least partially sacrificed in academia.

NOTES

1. For histories of the rise of Christianity, see W. H. C. Frend, *The Rise of Christianity* (Philadelphia: Fortress, 1984). A more unconventional view may be found in John Dominic Crossan, *The Birth of Christianity: Discovering What Happened in the Years Immediately after the Execution of Jesus* (San Francisco: HarperSanFrancisco, 1998). For a sociological perspective, see Rodney Stark, *The Rise of Christianity: A Sociologist Reconsiders History* (Princeton, NJ: Princeton University Press, 1996). For the idea that Christianity began, in part, as a health care reform movement, see Hector Avalos, *Health Care and the Rise of Christianity* (Peabody, MA: Hendrickson, 1999).

2. David B. Barrett, George T. Kurian, and Todd M. Johnson, *World Christian Encyclopedia: A Comparative Survey of Churches and Religions in the Modern World*, 2nd ed. (New York: Oxford University Press, 2001), 1.10. For criticisms of the counts and methodology of this authoritative encyclopedia, see Michael McClymond, "Making Sense of the Census, or, What 1,999,563,838 Christians Might Mean for the Study of Religion," *JAAR* 70, no. 4 (2002): 875–90.

3. Dan Brown, *The Da Vinci Code* (New York: Doubleday, 2003).

4. See Bart D. Ehrman, *Lost Christianities: The Battle for Scripture and the Faiths We Never Knew* (New York: Oxford University Press, 2003). For a recent treatment of Gnosticism, see Karen King, *What Is Gnosticism?* (Cambridge, MA: Harvard UniversityPress/Belknap Press, 2003). King argues that "Gnosticism," as such, did not exist, but is more of a modern construct. See also the older treatment of Elaine Pagels, *The Gnostic Gospels* (New York: Random House, 1979).

5. Rudolf Bultmann, *Theology of the New Testament*, trans. Kendrick Grobel (New York: Charles Scribner's Sons, 1951), 1:3.

6. Y. K. Kim, "Paleographical Dating of p46 to the Later First Century," *Biblica* 69 (1988): 248–57. My own forthcoming study of Kim's data shows that many of the letter forms that he has identified as first century also occur in later centuries. See further, David Alan Black, ed., *Rethinking New Testament Textual Criticism* (Grand Rapids, MI: Baker Academic, 2000).

7. Karlheinz Deschner, *Kriminalgeschichte des Christentums* (Hamburg: Rowohlt, 1986).

8. Michael Desjardins, *Peace, Violence and the New Testament* (Sheffield, UK: Sheffield Academic Press, 1997).

9. David Martin, *Does Christianity Cause War?* (Oxford: Clarendon, 1997).

10. Ibid., p. 22.

11. Ibid., p. 163.

12. Leo D. Lefebure, *Revelation, The Religions, and Violence* (Maryknoll, NY: Orbis, 2000).

13. Ibid., p. 58.

14. Ibid., p. 201.

15. For a recent history of the Second Temple, see Lee I. Levine, *Jerusalem: Portrait of the City in the Second Temple Period (538 B.C.E.–70 C.E.)* (Philadelphia: Jewish Publication Society, 2002).

16. Josephus, *The Jewish War*, trans. H. St. J. Thackeray, LCL (Cambridge,

MA: Harvard University Press, 1928), 6.237–242. For variant versions that place the blame squarely on Titus, see Levine, *Jerusalem*, p. 409.

17. Tertullian, *Apologeticus*, trans. T. R. Glover and G. H. Randall, LCL (Cambridge, MA: Harvard University Press, 1977), 25.14–15: "Nec dissimilis rapinae sacrarum divitiarum et profanarum."

18. P. W. L. Walker, *Jesus and the Holy City: New Testament Perspectives on Jerusalem* (Grand Rapids, MI: Eerdmans, 1996).

19. For a general treatment of the Beatitudes, see Hans D. Betz, *Essays on the Sermon on the Mount*, trans. L. L. Welborn (Philadelphia: Fortress, 1985), especially pp. 17–36; Neil J. McElaney, "The Beatitudes of the Sermon on the Mount/Plain," *CBQ* 43, no. 1 (1981): 1–13; and Roland H. Worth, *The Sermon on the Mount: Its Old Testament Roots* (Mahwah, NJ: Paulist Press, 1997). For the possibility that Jesus' beatitudes have precursors in the Dead Sea Scrolls, see Emile Puech, "4Q525 et les pericopes des béatitudes en Ben Sira et Matthieu," *Revue Biblique* 98 (1991): 80–106; and Benedict T. Viviano, "Beatitudes Found among the Dead Sea Scrolls," *Biblical Archaeology Review* 18 (1992): 53–55, 66. For a detailed survey of connections with the Hebrew Bible and rabbinical sources, see W. D. Davies, *The Setting of the Sermon on the Mount* (Cambridge: Cambridge University Press, 1966).

20. Edward Y. Yarnold, "Who Planned the Churches at the Christian Holy Places in the Holy Land?" *Studia Patristica* 18, no. 1 (1986): 105–109.

21. John Calvin, *Institutes of the Christian Religion* (first published in 1536; reprint, Grand Rapids, MI: Eerdmans, 1972), 1:396. It is also true that many biblical and postbiblical traditions also thought of areas (e.g., Sinai) outside of Israel proper as special places for God, on which see Jon Levenson, *Sinai and Zion: An Entry into the Jewish Bible* (San Francisco: Harper and Row, 1985).

22. For a more extensive study of this passage and comparison to parallel accounts in other Gospels, see Raymond E. Brown, *The Gospel According to John 1-XII* (Garden City, NY: Doubleday, 1983), pp. 114–25.

23. Ronald Sider, *Christ and Violence* (1979; reprint, Eugene, OR: Wipf and Stock, 2001), p. 47.

24. The standard narrative of the First Crusade is represented by, among others, Jonathan Riley-Smith, ed. *The Illustrated History of the Crusades* (New York: Oxford University Press, 1995), pp. 1–2, 34–36; and Hans Eberhard Mayer, *The Crusades*, trans. John Gillingham (New York: Oxford University Press, 1972), pp. 41–62. More comprehensive histories of the Crusades include Steven Runciman, *A History of the Crusades*, 3 vols. (Cambridge: Cambridge University Press, 1951–54).

25. Mayer, *The Crusades*, p. 11.

26. Georg Christoph Müller, *Dissertatio Inauguralis De expeditione Cruciatis Vulgo von Kreutz Fahrten* (Nuremburg: Literis Jodici Wilhelmi Kohlesii, 1709), pp. 3–6, 11, 20, 25–27, 33. For a discussion of Müller's contribution, see Christopher Tyerman, *The Invention of the Crusades* (Toronto: University of Toronto Press, 1998), pp. 111, 155n40. We restore the first two words of the title of Müller's work that were omitted by Tyerman's otherwise insightful treatment.

27. Representative works include Riley-Smith, *The Illustrated History of the Crusades*, especially pp. 8–12; N. J. Housely, *The Italian Crusades: The Papal-Angevin Alliance and the Crusades against Christian Lay Powers, 1254–1343* (New York: Oxford

University Press, 1986); *The Later Crusades, 1274–1580* (New York: Oxford University Press, 1986); and Kenneth M. Setton, *The Papacy and the Levant (1204–1571)*, 4 vols. (Philadelphia: American Philosophical Society, 1976–84). For the idea that the Crusades are more of a modern scholarly construct, see Tyerman, *The Invention of the Crusades*. For the so-called Peace of God movements just prior to the First Crusade, see Tomaz Mastnak, *Crusading Peace: Christendom, the Muslim World, and Western Political Order* (Berkeley and Los Angeles: University of California Press, 2002). However, even Mastnak (*Crusading Peace*, p. 11) acknowledges that "[t]he peace movement did not ban war altogether." Indeed, the main issue was how to limit the use of arms.

28. President George W. Bush used the word "crusade" in a statement released on September 16, 2001. He said, "This crusade, this war on terrorism is going to take a while." The statement remains on the White House Web site, and may be found at http://www.whitehouse.gov/news/releases/2001/09/20010916-2.html (accessed July 12, 2004). Although Bush was widely criticized for using that word, it is still part of the vocabulary of some of the president's supporters. Thus, the *Boston Globe* reported in 2004 on a "March 3 letter, which Bush-Cheney Campaign Chairman Marc Racicot sent to new campaign charter members in Florida, lauded the Republican president for 'leading a global crusade against terrorism.'" "Bush letter Cites 'Crusade' against Terrorism," *Boston Globe*, April 18, 2004, http://www.boston.com/news/politics/ president/bush/articles/2004/04/18/bush_letter_cites_crusade_against_terrorism/ (accessed July 12, 2004).

29. *Recueil des Historiens des Croisades*, 16 vols. (Paris: L'Académie impériale des inscriptions et Belles-Lettres, 1841–1906; hereafter RHC), from which all our Latin citations are drawn. The report of Fulcher of Chartres is available in English as *A History of the Expeditions to Jerusalem, 1095–1127*, trans. Frances Rita Ryan and ed. Harold S. Fink (New York: W. W. Norton, 1969).

30. See further, Mayer, *The Crusades*, pp. 10–11; Tyerman, *Invention of the Crusades*, pp. 8–29.

31. Mayer, *The Crusades*, p. 11.

32. RHC, 3.324: "Qua de re supplici prece hortor, non ego, sed Dominus, ut cunctis cujuslibet ordinis tam equitibus quam peditibus, tam divitibus quam pauperibus, edicto frequenti vos, Christi praecones, suadeatis, ut ad id genus nequam de regionibus nostrorum exterminandum tempestive Christocolis opitulari satagant." (My adapted translation of Ryan's translation.)

33. Ibid., 3:728: "Praesertim moveat vos sanctum Domini Salvatoris nostri Sepulcrum, quod ab immundis gentibus possidetur, et loca sancta, quae nunc inhoneste tractantur et irreverenter eorum immundiciis sordidantur."

34. Ibid., 4.137: "Si inter ecclesias toto orbe diffusas alieae prae aliis reverentiam pro personis locisque merentur; pro personis, inquam, dum apostolicis sedibus privilegia majora traduntur, pro locis vero, dum regiis urbibus eadem quam personis dignitas, uti est civitas Constantinopolitana, praebetur: illi potissimum ecclessiae deberemus ex qua gratiam redemptionis et totius originem Christianitatis accepimus."

35. Ibid., 4.137–138: "Si enim haec terra Dei haereditas et templum sanctum, antequam ibi obambularet ac pateretur Dominus, in sacris et propheticis paginis

legitur, quid sanctitatis, quid reverentiae obtinuisse tunc creditur, quum Deus majestatis ibidem incorporatur, nutritur, adolescit, corporali, vegetatione hac illacque perambulat aut gestatur; et, ut cuncta quae longo verborum gyro narrari possunt, digna brevitate constringam, ubi Filii Dei sanguis, coelo terraque sanctior, effusus est, ubi corpus, paventibus elementis mortuum, in sepulchro quievit? quid putamus venerationis emeruit?"

36. Ibid., 4.138: "Ponamus modo in Iherusalem Christum neque mortuum, nec sepultum, nec ibidem aliquando vixisse. Certe, si haec deessent omnia, solum illud ad subveniendum terrae et civitati vos excitare debuerat, quia de Syon exierit lex et verbum Domini de Iherusalem."

37. Ibid., 4.138: "Si Machabaeis olim ad maximam profuit pietatis laudem quia pro cerimoniis et Templo pugnarunt et vobis, o milites Christiani, legitime conceditur, ut armorum studio libertatem patriae defendatis. Si limina etiam sanctorum apostolorum vel quorumlibet aliorum tanto sudore petenda putatis, quid crucem, quid sanguinem, quid monumentum eruere, quid visitare, quid pro his eruendis animarum pretia impendere detrectatis? . . . Nunc vobis bella proponimus quae in se habent gloriosum martyrii munus, quibus restat praesentis et aeternae laudis titulus."

38. Carl Erdmann, *Die Enstehung des Kreuzzungsgedankens* (Stuttgart, W. Kohlhammer, 1935); and H. E. J. Cowdrey, "Pope Urban's Preaching of the First Crusade," *History* 55 (1970): 177–88, republished in Thomas F. Madden, ed., *The Crusades: The Essential Readings* (Oxford: Blackwell, 2002), pp. 16–29. Cowdrey's supplementary evidence consists of "(i) chronicles providing contemporary evidence for 1096; (ii) charters of 1096; (iii) contemporary letters; (iv) the *excitatoria* by which men were urged to rally to the Crusade; and (v) letters and other rulings of Urban himself" (*The Essential Readings*, p. 20).

39. RHC 3.324: "Christus autem imperat."

40. As recorded in the *Gesta Francorum* (ibid., 3.515), the war cry *Deus adjuva, Deus vult* ("God help us, God wills it") was uttered, at among other occasions, as Christians rampaged through Jerusalem. This also shows that, contrary to some of the arguments about the suppression of human agression by the appeal to God's help, it is fully concomitant with human aggression.

41. Ibid., 3.728: "Quod si vos carus liberorum and parentum et conjugum detinet affectus, recolite quid in Evangelio dicat Dominus: Qui amat patrem aut matrem super me, non est me dignus." The scripture cited here is Matthew 10:37.

42. For some notable exceptions, especially in later crusades, see the chronicle of Alberic of Trois Fontaines in Alfred J. Andrea, *Contemporary Sources for the Fourth Crusade* (Leiden: Brill, 2000), p. 293.

43. Mayer, *The Crusades*, p. 45.

44. James A. Brundage, *The Crusades, Holy War, and Canon Law* (Hampshire, UK: Variorum, 1991), p. 119.

45. Hostiensis, *Lectura* to X 5.7.13, no. 17 (Venice 1581, vol. 5, fol 34[rb]) as cited in Brundage, *The Crusades, Holy War, and Canon Law*, p. 137 n 146: "[Indulgentia] quae est remissio omnium peccatorum. . . . "

46. Hostiensis, *Lectura* to X.3.34.8, no. 17–18 (Venice, 1581, vol. 3, fol 128[va]) as cited in Brundage (*The Crusades, Holy War, and Canon Law*, p. 137 n 144): "Quod autem papa illis qui vadunt ad defendendum et recuperandam Terram Sanctam dat

indulgentias et infidelibus Terram possidentibus bellum indicit, licite facit papa en iustam causam habet, cum illa consecrata sit natiuitate, conuersatione, et morte Iesu Christi, en in qua non colitur Christus, sed Machometus" (my translation).

47. RHC, 3.300.

48. Ibid., 3.515: "neque feminis, neque parvulis pepercerunt."

49. Ibid., 3.300: "Justo nimirum judicio, ut locus idem eorum sanguinem exciperet, quorum blasphemias in Deum tam longo pertulerat."

50. Sylvia Schein, *Fideles Crucis: The Papacy, the West, and the Recovery of the Holy Land, 1274–1314* (New York: Oxford University Press, 1991). On the effects of propaganda among the masses, see also Antony Leopold, *How to Recover the Holy Land: The Crusade Proposals of the Late Thirteenth and Early Fourteenth Centuries* (Aldershot, UK: Ashgate, 2000).

51. General treatments of the New Testament writings include Bart D. Ehrman, *The New Testament: A Historical Introduction to the Early Christian Writers*, 3rd ed. (New York: Oxford University Press, 2000); *The Orthodox Corruption of Scripture: The Effect of Early Christological Controversies on the Text of the New Testament* (New York: Oxford University Press, 1993). See also Harry Y. Gamble, "The Canon of the New Testament," in *The New Testament and Its Modern Intepreters*, ed. Eldon J. Epp and Geroge W. MacRae (Philadelphia: Fortress, 1989), pp. 201–43.

52. For a useful summary of various views of "inspiration," see Norman L. Geisler and William G. Nix, *A General Introduction to the Bible* (Chicago: Moody, 1986), pp. 113–90. Geisler, of course, is an advocate of inerrancy. For the perspective of a critical scholar, see Paul J. Achtemeier, *Inspiration and Authority : Nature and Function of Christian Scripture* (Peabody, MA: Hendrickson, 1999). Also useful, but dated, is Bruce Vawter, *Biblical Inspiration* (Philadelphia: Westminster, 1972).

53. Philip Schaff and Henry Wace, eds., *The Nicene and Post-Nicene Fathers* (1886–89; reprint, Grand Rapids, MI: Eerdmans, 1997), 12:25.

54. For a general introduction, see Jacob Neusner, *The Formation of the Babylonian Talmud* (Leiden: Brill, 1970); *The Talmud of the Land of Israel: A Preliminary Translation and Explanation* (Chicago: University of Chicago Press, 1982–89); and Adin Steinsaltz, *The Essential Talmud*, trans. Chaya Galai (New York: Basic Books, 1976). For an older and still useful technical introduction, see Mielziner, *Introduction to the Talmud*.

55. See further, Robert Chazan, *Daggers of Faith: Thirteenth-Century Christian Missionizing and Jewish Response* (Berkeley and Los Angeles: University of California Press, 1989); David Berger, "Mission to the Jews and Jewish Christian Contacts in the Polemical Literature of the High Middle Ages," *American Historical Review* 91 (1986): 576–91; and Hood, *Aquinas and the Jews*, pp. 36–37.

56. On the Talmud and the church, see Solomon Grayzel, "The Talmud and the Medieval Papacy," in *Essays in Honor of Solomon B. Freehof*, ed. Walter Jacob, Frederick C. Schwartz, and Vigdor W. Kavaler (Pittsburgh, PA: Rodef Shalom Congregation, 1964), pp. 220–45.

57. Hood, *Aquinas and the Jews*, p. 35.

58. See further Jacob Katz, *Exclusiveness and Tolerance: Studies in Jewish-Gentile Relations in Medieval and Modern Times* (West Orange, NJ: Behrman House, 1961), pp. 57–63.

59. For an older, but still insightful study of this episode, see Julian Morgenstern, "The Despoiling of the Egyptians," *JBL* 68 (1949): 1–28.

60. Chazan, *In the Year 1096*, p. 41.

61. Martin Luther, *On the Jews and Their Lies*, trans. Martin H. Berman, in *Luther's Works: The Christian in Society IV*, ed. Franklin Sherman (Philadelphia: Fortress, 1971), pp. 123–306.

62. Ibid., p. 269.

63. Ibid., p. 268 (italics mine).

64. For egalitarian readings, see Rebecca Merrill Groothius, *Good News for Women: A Biblical Picture of Gender Equality* (Grand Rapids, MI: Baker, 1997); Eung Chun Park, *Either Jew or Gentile: Paul's Unfolding Theology of Inclusivity* (Louisville, KY: Westminster/John Knox, 2003). For antiegalitarian readings from a self-described evangelical Christian perspective, see Richard Hove, *Equality in Christ: Galatians 3:28 and the Gender Dispute* (Wheaton, IL: Crossway Books, 1999).

65. For a detailed scholarly commentary, see Hans Dieter Betz, *Galatians* (Philadelphia: Fortress, 1979), pp. 189–201.

66. The Greek word *dichasai* is a first aorist active infinitive of *dichazō* that is best associated with "purpose" or "final" clauses. For the grammar, see Blass and A. Debrunner, *A Greek Grammar of the New Testament and Other Early Christian Literature*, trans. Lawrence Johnson (New York: Paulist, 1999), p. 390.

67. For the argument that these family dissensions are envisaged as happening near the end of the world, see Rudolf Schnackenburg, *The Moral Teaching of the New Testament* (London: Burns and Oates, 1975), p. 143. This interepretation again fails to address the Greek grammar, not to mention the fact the Jesus presents himself as the instigator of this dissension regardless of when it is supposed to take place.

68. Representatives of the view that "imperial Christianity" began with Constantine are too numerous to mention, but they are found in many introductory textbooks, such as that of Willard Oxtoby, *World Religions: Western Traditions*, 2nd ed. (New York: Oxford University Press, 2002), p. 223. See also Desmond O'Grady, *Beyond the Empire: Rome and the Church from Constantine to Charlemagne* (New York: Crossroad, 2001).

69. For a revisionist history of the relationship between Christianity and the Roman Empire, see Marta Sordi, *The Christians and the Roman Empire*, trans. Annabel Bedini (Norman: University of Oklahoma Press, 1994). Sordi argues that the notion of Christianity as opposing the Roman Empire on political grounds is weak. Likewise, a relentless persecution of Christians by the Roman Empire is partly a later construct. Sordi argues that the main conflicts between Christianity and the Roman Empire were religious.

70. See Charlotte Klein, *Anti-Judaism in Christian Theology*, trans. Edward Quinn (Philadelphia: Fortress, 1978); John G. Gager, *The Origins of Anti-Semitism: Attitudes toward Judaism in Paganism and Christian Antiquity* (New York: Oxford University Press, 1983); and Rosemary Ruether, *Faith and Fratricide: The Theological Roots of Anti-Semitism* (New York: Seabury, 1979).

71. For more details on these types of approaches, see Peter Schäfer, *Judeophobia: Attitudes toward the Jews in the Ancient World* (Cambridge, MA: Harvard University Press, 1997), especially pp. 2–8; and Robert S. Wistrich, *Antisemitism: The Longest Hatred* (New York: Schocken Books, 1991).

72. Schäfer, *Judeophobia*, p. 5.

73. Ruether, *Faith and Fratricide*, p. 30.

74. Ibid., p. 56.

75. Gager, *The Origins of Anti-Semitism*.

76. Ibid., p. 268.

77. Ibid., p. 269.

78. On the Council of Elvira, see Louis H. Feldman, *Jew and Gentile in the Ancient World: Attitudes and Interactions from Alexander to Justinian* (Princeton, NJ: Princeton University Press, 1993), pp. 373, 380, 398.

79. Augustine, *City of God*, trans. William M. Green et al., LCL (Cambridge, MA: Harvard University Press, 1963), 4.34. For the Latin text, we depend on the edition of T. E. Page et al., 6 vols., LCL (Cambridge, MA: Harvard University Press, 1957–72).

80. Ibid., 19.15.

81. See further, Robert L. Wilken, *John Chrysostom and the Jews: Rhetoric and Reality in the Late Fourth Century* (Berkeley and Los Angeles: University of California Press, 1983). For the views of earlier church fathers, see Judith Lieu, *Image and Reality: The Jews in the World of the Christians in the Second Century* (Edinburgh: T&T Clark, 1996).

82. For a Catholic scholar's view of this period, especially in light of Vatican II, see Edward A. Synan, *The Pope and the Jews in the Middle Ages* (New York: Macmillan, 1965).

83. Hood, *Aquinas and the Jews*, p. 25.

84. Eidelberg, *The Jews and the Crusaders*, p. 31.

85. Luther, *On the Jews and Their Lies*, pp. 268–72. Sherman himself observes, "It is impossible to publish Luther's treatise today, however, without noting how similar his proposals were to the actions of the Nationalist Socialist regime in Germany in the 1930's and 1940's" (p. 268 n 193). See further, Peter F. Wiener, *Martin Luther: Hitler's Spiritual Ancestor* (Cranford, NJ: American Atheist Press, 1999).

86. For a study of Asclepius, see Avalos, *Illness and Health Care in the Ancient Near East*, pp. 37–98.

87. Hans Küng, *Christianity and the World Religions: Paths to Dialogue with Islam, Hinduism, and Buddhism* (New York: Doubleday, 1986), p. 23.

88. William E. Phipps, *Muhammad and Jesus: A Comparison of the Prophet and Their Teachings* (New York: Continuum, 1996), p. 214.

89. Küng, *Christianity and the World Religions*, p. 23.

90. *The O'Reilly Factor*, Fox News, February 27, 2004.

91. For some representative studies of Anselm's theory of atonement, see Brian Leftow, "Anselm on the Necessity of the Incarnation," *Religious Studies* 31, no. 2 (June 1995): 167–85; and Joan M. Nuth, "Two Medieval Soteriologies: Anselm of Canterbury and Julian of Norwich," *Theological Studies* 53, no. 4 (1992): 611–45.

92. Aquinas, *Summa*, part 3, question 1, article 2/Benziger 2:2026–27.

93. Ibid., question 46, article 3, objection 3/Benziger 3:2267.

94. Westminster Confession of Faith, 8.3 (Philadelphia: Great Commission Publications, n.d.), p. 7.

95. Charles Hodge, *Systematic Theology* (Grand Rapids, MI: Eerdmans, 1973), 3.540.

96. Robert Barclay, A Catechism and Confession of Faith, 3rd ed., chap. 16, article 6, available online at http://www.qhpress.org/texts/barclay/catechism (accessed July 10, 2004).

97. *Confession of Faith in a Mennonite Perspective* (Scottdale, PA: Herald, 1995), also available online at http://www.mennolink.org/doc/cof/art.8.html (accessed July 10, 2004).

98. Rodger's treatment juxtaposes Anselm with the soteriology proposed by Gustaf Aulén, for which see the latter's *Christus Victor: An Historical Study of the Three Main Types of the Idea of Atonement*, trans. A. G. Hebert (New York: Macmillan, 1969). For a critique from a self-described orthodox perspective, see Symeon Rodger, "The Soteriology of Anselm: An Orthodox Perspective," *Greek Orthodox Review* 34, no. 1 (1989): 19–43.

99. J. Denny Weaver, *The Nonviolent Atonement* (Grand Rapids, MI: Eerdmans, 2001), p. 72.

100. For a Jewish perspective on the atonement, see Jon Levenson, *The Death and Resurrection of the Beloved Son: The Transformation of Child Sacrifice in Judaism and Christianity* (New Haven, CT: Yale University Press, 1993).

101. Gorringe, *God's Just Vengeance*, p. 12.

102. Eidelberg, *The Jews and the Crusaders*, p. 25.

103. Ibid., p. 22.

104. Ibid., pp. 25, 147 n 42.

105. Ibid., p. 32.

106. Stephen Howarth, *The Knights Templar* (New York: Dorset Press, 1982), p. 179.

107. See Hood, *Aquinas and the Jews*, pp. 86, 132 n 27.

108. Aquinas, *Summa*, part II–II, question 10, article 8, reply objection 2/Benziger, 2:1219.

109. Ibid., reply objections 3/Benziger, 2:1219.

110. Ibid., reply objections 3 and 4 /Benziger 2:1219.

111. Ibid., objection 4/Benziger 2.1219: "They should be compelled by the faithful, if it be possible to do so, so that they do not hinder the faith by their blasphemies, or by their evil persuasions, of even by their open persecutions."

112. US Department of State Report on International Religious Freedom for 1999 (Washington, DC: Bureau for Democracy, Human Rights, and Labor, 1999), also available online at http://www.state.gov/www/global/human_rights/irf/irf_rpt/1999/irf_mexico 99.html (accessed May 25, 2004).

113. Walter Burkert, *Homo Necans: The Anthropology of Ancient Greek and Sacrificial Ritual and Myth*, trans. Peter Bing (Berkeley and Los Angeles: University of California Press, 1983). Burkert himself acknowledges his debt to Konrad Lorenz, and seems to mourn the destruction of collective rituals by the emergence of modern individualism. See also Margo Kitts, "Sacrificial Violence in the *Iliad*," *Journal of Ritual Studies* 16, no. 1 (2002): 19–39.

114. Although he uses outdated anthropological reports, Jonathan Z. Smith makes similar observations about Burkert in "The Domestication of Sacrifice," in *Violent Origins: Walter Burkert, René Girard, and Jonathan Z. Smith on Ritual Killing and Cultural Formation*, ed. Robert G. Hamerton-Kelly (Stanford, CA: Stanford University Press, 1987).

115. William W. Hallo, "The Origins of the Sacrificial Cult," in *Ancient Israelite Religion: Essays in Honor of Frank Moore Cross*, ed. Patrck D. Miller Jr., Paul D. Hanson, and S. Dean McBride (Philadelphia: Fortress, 1987), pp. 3–13.

116. Despite the need for an update, a good edition of the Enuma elish may be found in Alexander Heidel, *The Babylonian Genesis* (Chicago: University of Chicago Press, 1951). For the Kingu episode, see especially tablet 6, and pp. 36–47.

CHAPTER 9

ACADEMIC DEFENSES OF CHRISTIAN VIOLENCE

Our thesis stresses that many modern academic scholars defend violence or attempt to maintain the value of the biblical corpus despite its violence. In relation to the New Testament, such defenses have been particularly prominent among self-described pacifists such as Walter Wink, John Howard Yoder and Ronald Sider, but they actually encompass to some degree the works of most Christian scholars.[1] Thus, here we examine the basis for the claim that Christianity is essentially a religion of peace and love.

Historically, Christian theologians and scholars have often contrasted Christianity with the Old Testament, which presumably has more hate and wrath in it. Rudolf Schnackenburg presents the standard view:

> The Early Church, and with it, Christianity, was profoundly convinced that the greatest of Jesus' achievements in the moral sphere was the promulgation of the chief commandment of love of God and one's neighbour. The message of Christian *agape*, the model and highest expression of which is the mission of the Son of God to redeem the sinful human race, brought something new into the world, an idea and reality so vast and incomprehensible as to be the highest revelation of God, and quite inconceivable apart from revelation.[2]

The idea that Christianity brought a whole new concept of love to the world is so powerful that even some of the most skeptical thinkers have accepted it without much scrutiny. Thus, Michael Shermer, one of the leading popular skeptics today, repeats this commonplace Christian view when he says, "This may represent the difference between Old Testament and New Testament morality: inflexible moral principles versus contextual moral guidelines—a stricter draconian God versus a kinder, gentler God."[3] Accordingly, our response will center on showing that, in regard to the New Testament and Christianity: (1) hate is also enjoined by Jesus; (2) love can entail violence in the New Testament and in Christian exegesis; (3) love can be tactical rather than substantive; (4) forgiveness is an ambiguous concept; and (5) peace can be interpreted as a form of Christian hegemony.

In brief, our discussion will center on the fact that any interpretation that sees the New Testament or Jesus as essentially advocates of love, peace, and forgiveness must rely on an ultimately unverifiable rationale for the selection of what counts as representative texts. Such a selection is no more verifiable than the selection of violent views, and the ultimate theological grounds for pacifist actions by Christians are no more verifiable than the grounds for violent ones.

JESUS COMMANDS HATE

Arbitrary selectivity and interpretation is the main reason that the New Testament is so often viewed as preaching only or essentially love. However, the existence of violence in Christianity cannot be explained unless it is also recognized that Jesus also preached "hate." One of the prime examples of hate speech attributed to Jesus is found in Luke:

> Now large crowds were traveling with him; and he turned and said to them,
>
> "Whoever comes to me and does not hate father and mother, wife and children, brothers and sisters, yes, and even life itself, cannot be my disciple.
>
> Whoever does not carry the cross and follow me cannot be my disciple. (Luke 14:25–27)

Although the text seems as clear an expression of hate as any text found anywhere, Christian apologists have attempted to erase or lessen its negative connotations. Thus, John Vernon McGee, a fundamentalist Christian broadcaster and commentator, says: "The verses are simply saying that we should put God first. A believer's devotedness to Jesus Christ should be such that, by comparison, everything else is hated."[4] *The Good News Bible* completely omits the word "hate," and translates the verse as follows: "Whoever comes to me cannot be my disciple unless he loves me more than he loves his father and his mother, his wife and his children, his brothers, and his sisters and himself as well." Likewise, Wayne Meeks, author of a study on early Christian ethics, omits Luke 14:26 from his index.[5]

This interpretation of Luke 14:26 is achieved by assuming that a parallel saying in Matthew 10:37 constitutes the proper meaning of Luke 14:26. Briefly, Matthew 10:37 says: "Whoever loves father or mother more than me is not worthy of me; and whoever loves son or daughter more than me is not worthy of me." We may label this "the comparative interpretation," which can be summarized more schematically as follows: "Hate X = Love Y more than X."

The first problem with this comparative interpretation is that the Greek word for "hate," *miseo*, never means "to love Y more than X" in any biblical text. In fact, *miseo* is interpreted as the opposite of love everywhere it occurs in Greek biblical texts. To understand our argument, it is necessary that we begin with an examination of the basic relevant grammatical structure of a crucial portion of Luke 14:26:

Verb	+	**object(s) of verb**	+	**reflexive pronoun**
Hate		the father . . .		("his own")
μισεῖ		τὸν πατέρα		ἑαυτοῦ . . .

The first obvious issue is that we need to establish the most accurate meaning of the Greek word (μισέω; pronounced *miseo*) translated as "hate." There are at least two basic procedures for establishing the meaning of words in any ancient language: (1) seek contrastive expressions involving the word in question, and (2) compare translations into other languages.[6]

If we use the first procedure, then we note that in every instance where we find "*miseo* + object of hate," there is every reason to take it as the opposite of love. For example:

So Samson's wife wept before him, saying, "You *hate me*; you do not really love me. (Judg. 14:16)

Hate evil and love good, and establish justice in the gate; it may be that the LORD, the God of hosts, will be gracious to the remnant of Joseph. (Amos 5:15)

No slave can serve two masters; for a slave will either *hate the one* and love the other, or be devoted to the one and despise the other. You cannot serve God and wealth." (Luke 16:13)[7]

In every case, "hate X" means the absence of any love for X, the opposite of love, and/or even hostility toward X.[8]

Luke 16:13 is particularly important as it shows the usage of the word by presumably the same author of Luke 14:26. Luke 16:13: says: "No slave can serve two masters; for a slave will either hate the one and love the other, or be devoted to the one and despise the other. You cannot serve God and wealth." The author clearly indicates here that "hate" = "absence of love." One *cannot* have both love and hate for the same person. You either love one or the other. Thus, we can develop a linguistic and semantic rationale for our interpretation of *miseo* in Luke 14:26:

1. Since *miseo* is interpreted literally as the opposite of love (= "hate") *everywhere* in the Bible,
2. and since there is no other indication that *miseo* is not literal in Luke 14:26,
3. then *miseo* probably means the opposite of love in Luke 14:26.

In fact, the main problem with interpreting the grammatical structure "*miseo* + object of hate" as a comparative expression is that it is no such thing grammatically. Greek has very specific modes of constructing comparative expressions, and no indicators of comparison are present here.[9]

The comparative interpretation of Luke 14:26 actually creates a number of logical and semantic problems. For example, if we accept the proposition that "hate X" actually means "to love Y more than X," then we should note the odd reading generated by such an equation in Amos 5:15 : "Hate evil" = "Love good more than evil." However, it is clear that the author of Amos 5:15 is exhorting listeners to not love evil at all. In sum, there are no linguistic grounds to interpret Luke 14:26 as meaning anything other than to have no love or to have the opposite of love for parents in order to be a disciple of Jesus.

The arbitrary nature of Christian apologetics in Luke 14:26 can also be gauged by an unwillingness to treat occurrences of "love" in the same manner. That is to say, few, if any, of the same interpreters who want to treat "hate" comparatively in Luke 14:26 will do so for "love." But we could just as well posit that "love X = Hate Y more than X." Indeed, there is a great circularity at work in saying that Jesus cannot mean hate in Luke 14:26 because he preaches "love" elsewhere. But we can reverse this rationale and argue that Jesus probably did not mean "love" literally elsewhere because he clearly meant "hate" in Luke 14:26.

Any grounds for a comparative interpretation probably would have to be moral—for example, Jesus could not possibly have meant "hate your father," as that would seem immoral. However, this imposes our morality upon the author, when most Christian interpreters would insist that we derive our morality from the author's words. Moreover, using this procedure we could change the meaning of all texts we find immoral for us. Linguistic meanings must be established on linguistic grounds, not moral grounds.

There are also cogent reasons for not using Matthew 10:37 to establish the meaning of Luke 14:26. One reason is quite simple. *One cannot assume that Luke's readers had read Matthew at the time Luke was written.* At the time Luke was being written, the New Testament, as we know it, did not exist. It was not complete, and this quite likely applies to all four Gospels. Therefore, it is unlikely that the author of Luke would use the word "hate" and hope that someone would have read Matthew in order to explain what Luke meant. That is not a reasonable expectation.[10] Rather, one would expect that Luke would use words the audience would understand *from the way that those words are used in the language of the reader.* The Greek word *miseo* has as consistent and as strong a meaning as any word in the entire Greek lexicon. It does not vary and is not subject to as much flexibility as other words may be.

Matthew's reading can also be explained without having to change the meaning of the word *miseo* in Luke. Matthew may not have liked the strong and harsh tone of Luke 14:26, so he changed it. Indeed, the Catholic biblical scholar Joseph Fitzmyer explicitly suggests this when he says, "Matthew has softened the demand of Jesus by his redactional wording 'loves . . . more than me.'"[11] We know that Matthew changed, added, or used other sources relative to Luke (compare the genealogies in Matthew 1 and Luke 3).

Similarly, the fact that *The Good News Bible* (GNB) substitutes "love" for "hate" in Luke 14:26 does not mean that the definition of the word "hate" has changed; it just means that the GNB has changed the meaning of the passage altogether. Similarly, Matthew's action does not redefine the word *miseo* in Greek; Matthew may be changing the meaning of Luke altogether by providing different words.

Since the passage seems to be clear, sometimes Christian apologists will resort to "recontextualization" or "modernization" to maintain the value of this text. John Howard Yoder, a leading pacifist author, says:

> Modern psychologizing interpretation of Jesus has been bothered largely with whether the word *hate* here should be taken seriously or not. This is certainly to miss the point of the passage. The point is rather that in a society characterized by very stable, religiously undergirded family ties, Jesus is here calling into being a community of voluntary commitment, willing for the sake of its calling to take upon itself the hostility of a given society.[12]

Yoder's violence to the plain meaning of the text is as arbitrary as any encountered from fundamentalists. Indeed, how does one come to understand "the point" of a passage except by understanding the meaning of the words in a passage? If "hate" is the opposite of "love," as we have amply demonstrated, then why can't the point of the passage be that you must hate your family to follow Jesus? Instead, Yoder invents his own point, which has nothing to do with anything mentioned in the text or context. This also leads to another question: If Jesus wanted to make the point that you should actually *hate* your family, what other, stronger word would he have used?

And why does Yoder invert the object of hate so that the passage becomes centered on a "community" taking upon itself "the hostility of a given society"? The grammatical objects of "hate" are "parents" and "family," and so why does Yoder not see parents and family as the community which becomes the object of Jesus' hostility? This indeed, is to deny the victimhood of the family, and to condone the clearly hateful words of Jesus.

Likewise, why does Yoder suppose that Jesus cannot be doing both, creating a so-called voluntary organization *and* asking joiners to hate their families? As in the case of other pacifistic readings, Yoder's claim ends up as nothing less than an effort to maintain the value of violent texts and hate speech by pretending or claiming that Jesus did not mean what he said. Such arguments are no less arbitrary than those used by fundamentalists, and they expose the fact that Yoder's pacifism is based on privileging violent texts by pretending they are not.

But a hopeful sign is that recent critical scholarship has focused on the antifamilial nature of some of Jesus' injunctions.[13] Often these are assigned to the early strata of Gospel materials. However, the problem remains that any interpretation that sees Jesus as essentially loving and peaceful will center on choosing one text, whether early or late, as representative of the preaching of Jesus. But if one assumes that the antifamilial passages are indeed closer to the historical Jesus, then it is the advocates of a more violent portrayal of Jesus who may have a greater claim to approximating any "essential" message of Jesus.

LOVE CAN ENTAIL VIOLENCE

As most students of New Testament Greek realize, there are three main Greek words that are translated as "love" in English.[14] Love centered on sexual passion is *eros*, which is usually identified with erotic love. However, this word does not occur in the New Testament. A common word that is found in the New Testament is *phileo*, which is often identified with the love of friendship or between family members (e.g., Matt. 6:5, 10:37).

The highest form of love mentioned in the New Testament is often said to reflect the Greek word *agape*. A main exponent of this idea was Anders Nygren (1890–1978) in his *Agape and Eros*.[15] For Nygren, *agape* was selfless love, and it typified Christianity, in opposition to the Old Testament. Even in the face of new research showing some of the Greek and Near Eastern roots of *agape*,[16] most Christian theologians and scholars of the New Testament continue to affirm that Christian love is one of the most essential and valuable gifts bestowed upon the world by Christianity.[17] So momentous is this supposedly new concept that some scholars have even tried to explain its development sociologically.[18]

Agape is the word used in one of the most famous love passages, John 3:16: "For God so loved the world that he gave his only begotten son so that you may not perish but have eternal life." And, of course, *agape* is the Greek word used in what are portrayed as Jesus' new commandments:

> I give you a new commandment, that you love one another. Just as I have loved you, you also should love one another.
>
> By this everyone will know that you are my disciples, if you have love for one another." (John 13:34–35)

First Corinthians, a letter usually attributed to the apostle Paul, likewise extols the value of *agape* in its famous passage about the virtues of love:

> Love is patient; love is kind; love is not envious or boastful or arrogant
>
> or rude. It does not insist on its own way; it is not irritable or resentful;
>
> it does not rejoice in wrongdoing, but rejoices in the truth.
>
> It bears all things, believes all things, hopes all things, endures all things.
>
> Love never ends. But as for prophecies, they will come to an end; as for tongues, they will cease; as for knowledge, it will come to an end. (1 Cor. 13:4–8)

Yet the suspicion that the rhetoric of "love" might be self-serving was already being questioned in the New Testament itself, as in 1 John:

> We know love by this, that he laid down his life for us—and we ought to lay down our lives for one another.
>
> How does God's love abide in anyone who has the world's goods and sees a brother or sister in need and yet refuses help?
>
> Little children, let us love, not in word or speech, but in truth and action. (1 John 3:16–18)

The author of this letter undertakes elaborate discussions on what love really means, which presumes that he did not deem it clear to his addressees. The author's concept of *agape* did not agree with those he was trying to persuade. Those criticized by the author were apparently using the rhetoric of love, but not performing actions that suited the author's definition of it. In more recent times Friedrich Nietzsche remarked: "Not their love of humanity, but the impotence of their love, prevents the Christians of to-day—burning us."[19]

Indeed, emerging particularly in the last half century is the realization that "love" can sometimes be part of the discourse of master-slave or lord-vassal relationships. Far from being mutual or selfless, *agape* may describe behavior that entails violence and other hierarchical phenomena. Part of the reason for this change is that previous scholars were too eager to divorce the New Testament use of *agape* from corresponding words and concepts found in the Hebrew Bible. After all, Christianity was thought to be bringing something radically new.

The word "love" often designates the attitude and set of behaviors that a lord expects from his vassal in the ancient Near East. Especially instructive in this regard are the Assyrian lord-vassal "treaties" of Esarhaddon (ca. 681–669 BCE), king of Assyria.[20] One commandment to a vassal, for example, reads: "(You swear) that you will love Ashurbanipal, the crown prince, son of Essarhaddon, king of Assyria, your lord as (you do) your-selves."[21] Likewise, a vassal is commanded to "fight and (even) die for him [the lord]."[22] This, of course is not that different from what Jesus commands his own disciples to do in Luke 14:26: "Whoever comes to me and does not hate father and mother . . . even life [Greek: *psyche*] itself, cannot be my disciple." Curses were applied to those who did not obey the Assyrian king's commandments.

The hint that lord-vassal language is important in understanding the New Testament concept of love was already noted more than forty years ago by the brilliant Harvard Near Eastern scholar William L. Moran, who said, "[I]f the old sovereign-vassal terminology of love is as relevant as we think it is, then what a history lies behind the Christian test of true *agape*—'If you love me, you will keep my commandments!'"[23] Moran's insight, while bringing a new understanding, has remained confined largely to the Hebrew Bible. The similarity of New Testament language to lord-vassal treaties, when commented upon, is often expressed only obliquely.[24]

More recently, Susan Ackerman has made a case that the Hebrew words *'aheb*, a verb, and *'ahabah*, the related noun, which are usually translated with the relevant forms of *agape*, almost always reflect an inequality in power in the Hebrew Bible.[25] She argues that while there may be overlap between inter-personal "love" and political "love," the former still indicates a one-sided use in the Hebrew word. Thus, Jacob is described as loving Rachel (Gen. 39:18, 20, 30), but it is never said that Rachel loved Jacob. The same is true in the description of numerous other relationships between men and women.

Ackerman believes that *'ahēb/'ahâbâh* is an action performed by the superior party relative to an inferior party (male > female, parent > child, Yahweh > human being, etc.). Only once is it said that a man (Solomon) loves Yahweh (1 Kings 3:13), whereas the reverse is the norm (Yahweh loves X). In cases where gods seem to be the object of human love in Jeremiah (2:25 and 8:2), Ackerman interprets this as a satirical reversal that reflects Jeremiah's view of those gods as inferior to human beings.

While we are convinced that Ackerman seems to have found a pattern, it does leave another question: Why is it only the superior party that is described as performing this act? This is especially puzzling because, as Moran had noted, it is usually the inferior party who owes "love" to the master in the relationship. I believe this puzzle can be solved if we add one more element to this hierarchical and political view of love: individual privileging. Love functions as a means of expressing status differences in which a superior party selects an object of love, who can only give gratitude, affection, and service in return. Inferior parties cannot or do not select their superiors, masters, or parents.

The idea that the superior party selects the inferior one is repeatedly found in the Hebrew Bible, as in Deuteronomy 7:6: "For you are a people holy to the LORD your God; the LORD your God has chosen you out of all the peoples on earth to be his people, his treasured possession." And this selection can be acknowledged as simply arbitrary, as in Romans 9:13, "As it is written, I have loved Jacob, but I have hated Esau."

If one compares the Hebrew Bible to the New Testament, one will see that a reversal has actually taken place in the latter. Far from indicating mutuality or even lack of self-interest, *agape* has often become even more hierarchical, demanding, and servile in the New Testament relative to that in the Hebrew Bible. Although Nygren does not locate *agape* in the context of Near Eastern imperial rhetoric, his translator, Philip Watson, actually seems to acknowledge the slavish nature of *agape* when he says: "But the love of man for God of which the New Testament speaks is of quite a different stamp. It means whole-hearted surrender to God, whereby man becomes God's willing slave, content to be at His disposal, having entire trust and confidence in Him, and desiring only that His will be done."[26]

More importantly, New Testament notions of *agape* also obligate and even enjoin violence. One example is put on the lips of Jesus:

> I will no longer talk much with you, for the ruler of this world is coming. He has no power over me;

but I do as the Father has commanded me, so that the world may know that I love the Father. Rise, let us be on our way. (John 14:30–31)

As becomes apparent at the crucifixion, Jesus' demonstration of his love for the father means the willingness to be tortured and be killed.

In fact, love means that a friend should be willing to die for his comrade (John 15:13). Jesus says that "[t]hose who love their life lose it, and those who hate their life in this world will keep it for eternal life" (John 12:25). Paul Ramsey, one of the foremost Christian ethicists of the twentieth century, also observes that love for one's neighbor has been used to argue for the necessity of war.[27] We have already seen how Luke sees love for Jesus as entailing hatred for one's parents, and parallels the idea that the servant's love for the master is paramount. Matthew 10:34–37 says that love for Jesus entails violence among family members.

Nor is the notion of *agape* very inclusive. While Jesus commands disciples to "love one another," the benefits of salvation are available only to those who obey Jesus' view of God. Thus, John 14:6: "Jesus said to him, 'I am the way, and the truth, and the life. No one comes to the Father except through me.'" As portrayed here, Jesus is generating a scarce resource by promulgating this belief, which itself will generate violence in later history.

While Paul expounds on the virtues of love in 1 Corinthians 13, he elsewhere recommends violence upon the body for the sake of salvation.[28] Thus, in 1 Corinthians 5:5, Paul is reported to give the following instruction to correct the case of a man who has committed a sexual sin: "You are to hand this man over to Satan for the destruction of the flesh, so that his spirit may be saved in the day of the Lord." Most readers fail to appreciate that Paul is likely speaking of the killing of the person.[29] The author reflects again the idea that the spirit is much more important than the body, so any violence that results in bettering the spirit is a form of love. "Love" means love toward someone's soul, not toward his body.[30]

And the view of *agape* in 1 Peter shows how easily violence and "love" can be combined:

Honor everyone. Love the family of believers. Fear God. Honor the emperor.

Slaves, accept the authority of your masters with all deference, not only those who are kind and gentle but also those who are harsh.

For it is a credit to you if, being aware of God, you endure pain while suffering unjustly. (1 Pet. 2:17–19)

The history of postbiblical interpretation shows that "love" could also be interpreted in such a way as to allow almost any act of violence. We can see how this works in the writings of Augustine, the preeminent theologian of Western Christendom. In his "Reply to Faustus," Augustine attempts to answer non-Christian objections to the violence in the Bible.[31] Faustus, an unbeliever, cites cases in which violent acts do not seem compatible with love, as when Moses commanded the killing of some three thousand Israelites because they had committed idolatry with the Golden Calf (Exodus 32).

Augustine, however, sees this as a case of love because idolatry hurts the soul, whereas Moses only hurt the bodies of the idolaters. Indeed, the idea that the soul could benefit from bodily punishment has biblical roots in Matthew 10:28: "Do not fear those who kill the body but cannot kill the soul; rather fear him who can destroy both soul and body in hell." Again, a pneumocentric view of humanity is at the root of corporeal violence.

Augustine makes a similar argument in his commentary on the Sermon on the Mount.[32] Therein he explains that physical punishment (*vindicta*) is not incompatible with love. Beating a child, for example, is an act of love. The proper attitude of the recipient of punishment, therefore, should be happiness. He then cites as an example Elijah, who punished with death the worshippers of Baal, the rival of Yahweh, so that the living might "be struck with salutary fear."[33] In other words, the creation of fear, otherwise called "terrorism," is a just and legitimate instrument for God and his prophet.

Likewise, for Augustine, turning the other cheek still allows for retaliative violence. The idea that "love" of God should entail the willingness to endure physical violence without retaliation can be traced back to Jesus' injunction to turn the other cheek. However, Augustine says that it is intentionality and inward disposition that makes the difference. Thus, if we intend to turn the other cheek, our external bodily response need not match that inward disposition.[34]

In order to illustrate the difference between inward dispositions and outward actions, Augustine specifically cites an apocryphal story in which the apostle Thomas is struck by a servant. Thomas curses the man, who is then mauled by a lion. However, since Thomas secured a pardon for the servant in the next world, this violent retaliation in this world should not be seen as evil. Augustine concludes concerning Thomas, "Inwardly he preserved a kindly feeling, while outwardly he wished the man to be punished as an example."[35]

Grotius has an even more ingenious explanation for Jesus' injunction of turning the other cheek. In fact, he resorts to an argument that is found among Islamic hermeneuticians when discussing jihad. Grotius explains that a specific statement restricts a more general statement. In the case of turning the other cheek, we ought to interpret this as literally as possible, meaning that Christ is encouraging nonretaliation only when one is struck on those specific body parts, namely, the cheeks.[36]

Retaliation, therefore, is not prohibited by Christ against any other body parts. In fact, the selection of "cheeks" for this injunction shows that Jesus intended nonretaliation for only the lightest sorts of injury rather than for more severe injuries. Grotius appeals to supposed Hebrew customs to opine that "turning the cheek" could be entirely figurative. In addition, Grotius argues that Christ is not addressing magistrates, who may have a duty to retaliate when the larger national body is attacked.

Grotius's legalistic mind was able to counter at least two other arguments used by pacifists. Jesus' injunction to walk an extra mile, Grotius argues, simply shows that Jesus chose actions that would least inconvenience a Christian. It would be different if Jesus had obliged us to walk a thousand miles. Jesus' injunction (Matt. 5:40/Luke 6:29) to turn over a cloak when someone demands only a coat comes under Grotius's scalpel as well. Grotius notes that a coat or a cloak should not be held equivalent to means of subsistence. War, therefore, is permissible for defense of one's food supply or country under Jesus' injunctions. Grotius also believes that the injunction about the cloak refers only to not pursuing some sort of lawsuit in court.[37]

Among modern authors, we also find that "love" can explain acts of the most brutal violence. One example comes from R. A. Torrey, one of the contributors to *The Fundamentals*, a series of tracts that helped popularize the name "fundamentalist." Torrey argues that "[t]he extermination of the Canaanite children was not only an act of mercy and love to the world at large; it was an act of love and mercy to the children themselves."[38] The reason is that if these children grew up, they probably would end up suffering an eternity in hell. Slaughtering them in infancy ensured that their souls would go to heaven. Clearly, the slaughter, under this logic, is a loving act.

LOVE AS TACTICAL

Of particular importance in discussions about the teachings of Jesus is the so-called Golden Rule, which has been seen as the acme of pacifist injunctions. As it is stated in Matthew 7:12, the rule reads as follows: "In everything do to others as you would have them do to you; for this is the law and the prophets." As is the case with many other key passages, what seems obvious at first sight in this passage becomes complicated once examined in light of ancient cultures.

First, it should be noted that the Golden Rule is neither unique nor original to Christianity. We can trace its various versions to Greek authors hundreds of years before Jesus. Marcus Borg, a well-known member of the Jesus Seminar, claims that he has found it in Buddhist scriptures.[39] As we have noted, Michael Shermer lists the Golden Rule as occurring in a number of cultures, though his dating of the first biblical injunction in Leviticus 19:18 is baseless. If one follows a more standard view based on literary-historical criteria, then a date no earlier than the late eighth century BCE is plausible. If we restrict ourselves to the actual extant hard copies of any portion of Leviticus 19, these are no earlier than the second/first centuries BCE.[40]

And, as the biblical scholar Alan Kirk notes, there are at least three ways to read this rule.[41] The first interpretation is that it represents a completely disinterested action, and so is the true paradigm of love. This interpretation is the one favored by many modern Christian interpreters, especially those with pacifist leanings. A second interpretation emphasizes a reciprocal or neutral stance, in which equality is more of an economic transaction. A third interpretation is that the Golden Rule is based on self-interest.[42] This interpretation has antecedents in Greek authors who see a more Machiavellian strategy to vanquish the enemy. Thus, Thucydides (IV.19.1–4) speaks of the wisdom of one who "vanquishes his foe by generosity."[43] Being good to an enemy may oblige the enemy to return the favor.

So which interpretation is the one favored by the Gospel writer? At first glance, it may seem as though the disinterested interpretation is indicated. However, this does not seem compatible with the violence Jesus plans for the enemies of Christians at the last judgment:

> Then he will say to those at his left hand, "You that are accursed, depart from me into the eternal fire prepared for the devil and his angels; for I was hungry and you gave me no food, I was thirsty and you gave me nothing to drink, I was a stranger and you did not welcome me, naked and you did not give me clothing, sick and in prison and you did not visit me."

> Then they also will answer, "Lord, when was it that we saw you hungry or thirsty or a stranger or naked or sick or in prison, and did not take care of you?"

> Then he will answer them, "Truly I tell you, just as you did not do it to one of the least of these, you did not do it to me."

> And these will go away into eternal punishment, but the righteous into eternal life. (Matt. 25:41–46)

It is here that we see, then, another view of the nature of Christian love. However, there is also good reason to suppose that the idea can be traced back to the earliest sources. Gordon Zerbe, author of an extensive treatise on nonretaliation in the New Testament, notes, "As in many early Jewish texts non-retaliation and good deeds in response to persecutors in Q is grounded in the hope of eschatological vindication and judgment."[44]

The idea that love has a utilitarian value reappears in the work of modern pacifists. Thus, William Klassen urges that Christians use love to convert enemies into friends.[45] In any case, Matthew indicates that Christians can afford to love their enemies now because Jesus will torture the enemies of Christians at the end of time. The judgment described in Matthew 25, after all, does not differ much from an act of revenge. At the very least, the author or editor of Matthew did not seem to see any incompatibility between the Golden Rule included in chapter 7 and the revenge that Jesus was to mete out in chapter 25.

CHRISTIANITY AND FORGIVENESS

The New Testament concepts of forgiveness can be deconstructed in a similar manner. As used in the New Testament, "forgiveness" represents a translation of a number of words. One word, *aphiēmi*, describes a literal releasing from a debt. This is the verb used, for example, in Matthew 6:12: "And forgive us our debts, as we also have forgiven our debtors." It is also the verb used in relation to sins in Matthew 9:6: "But so that you may know that the Son of Man has authority on earth to forgive sins."

In the Hebrew Bible, forgiveness relates to abstaining from retaliation for some perceived or actual wrong done to the forgiving party. For example, we find the concept in Genesis 50:17: "Say to Joseph: 'I beg you, forgive the crime of your brothers and the wrong they did in harming you.' Now therefore please forgive the crime of the servants of the God of your father." Joseph's brothers had attempted to kill Joseph and fool his father into thinking an animal had killed him. As practiced here, forgiveness indeed prevents any violence on the part of Joseph.

However, others would say that the Bible has a very inconsistent attitude toward forgiveness. In actuality, forgiveness is related to group privileging insofar as only certain people are forgiven, and others are not. For example, in Exodus 23:17, Yahweh himself says: "Keep far from a false charge, and do not kill the innocent and those in the right, for I will not acquit the guilty." Likewise, Yahweh is said to give the following instruction in Deuteronomy 24:16: "Parents shall not be put to death for their children, nor shall children be put to death for their parents; only for their own crimes may persons be put to death."

However, both of these instructions seem contradicted by the story of

David's adultery with Bathsheba as told in 2 Samuel 11–12. Briefly, in that story Bathsheba is married to Uriah, a non-Hebrew. One day, David sees Bathsheba bathing, and orders her brought to him. He impregnates her, and soon must try to hide his deed. He places Uriah at the battlefront, where the likelihood of death is highest. His plan succeeds, and Uriah dies.

Nathan, a prophet, comes to David and brings word that Yahweh is displeased with David's actions. In fact, in 2 Samuel 12:9, the author clearly indicates that Yahweh regards David as having committed murder: "Why have you despised the word of the LORD, to do what is evil in his sight? You have struck down Uriah the Hittite with the sword, and have taken his wife to be your wife, and have killed him with the sword of the Ammonites."

The penalty for adultery is execution, and intentional murder is definitely deserving of execution under Hebrew law. David seems ready to accept his death sentence, when Nathan exclaims, "Now the LORD has put away your sin; you shall not die" (2 Sam. 12:13). Instead, Yahweh decrees that David's child is to die (2 Sam. 12:14). Of course, God directly contradicts his own word that he would not acquit the guilty. Likewise, his actions violate his instruction in Deuteronomy 24:16. In short, authors of the Hebrew Bible pick and choose who deserves forgiveness based on the perceived value of the person.

The inconsistent policy of forgiveness in the Hebrew Bible does not change in the New Testament. The instruction to forgive others is given in a number of places by Jesus. For example:

And forgive us our debts, as we also have forgiven our debtors.

And do not bring us to the time of trial, but rescue us from the evil one.

For if you forgive others their trespasses, your heavenly Father will also forgive you;

but if you do not forgive others, neither will your Father forgive your trespasses. (Matt. 6:12–15)

When Peter asks Jesus how many times he should forgive an offender, Jesus responds, "seventy-seven times" (Matt. 18:22).

But exactly when to forgive is open to interpretations that have generated violence in Christian history. For example, consider the following injunction in Luke 17:4: "And if the same person sins against you seven times a day, and turns back to you seven times and says, 'I repent,' you must forgive." However, this could mean that if a person does not repent, then forgiveness is not obligatory. This became the basis for killing non-Christians who would not convert, because "repent" was interpreted to mean "convert."

Indeed, one finds Jesus presenting forgiveness as optional in John 20:23: "If you forgive the sins of any, they are forgiven them; if you retain the sins of any, they are retained." Other times, injunctions seem to be contingent on whether the person confessed to having sinned, as in 1 John 1:9: "If we confess our sins, he who is faithful and just will forgive us our sins and cleanse us from all unrighteousness." By implication, therefore, if one does not confess sins in this manner, then forgiveness may not be granted.

Romans 12:14 often is invoked as an example of Christian love toward enemies: "Bless those who persecute you; bless and do not curse them." However, the tactical and utilitarian aspect of this advice becomes clearer in verse 20: "[I]f your enemies are hungry, feed them; if they are thirsty, give them something to drink; for by doing this you will heap burning coals on their heads." The latter clause about "heaping burning coals on their heads," is an allusion to Proverbs 25:21–22. Read as a whole, the commandment to be nice becomes simply a way to build up the potential for violence against the opponent. The nicer one is to one's opponent, the more violence will be deserved by the opponent in the end.[46]

As is the case with Hebrew law, certain injunctions can be interpreted to apply only to fellow Christians, as in Colossians 3:13: "Bear with one another and, if anyone has a complaint against another, forgive each other; just as the Lord has forgiven you, so you also must forgive." As in the case of *agape*, the same texts that promote *agape* also premise nonretaliation on deferred violence. In other words, violence is not necessary now because it will surely come later.

In sum, Christianity, if it is meant to be a religion based on the New Testament, does not endorse a love open to all. Love was still primarily meant for other Christians. Christianity simply substituted creedal adherence for genealogical identity as basis for receiving love. Those who believe in Christ will receive eternal love. Those who do not believe will receive an eternal torture in a fiery lake. When authors portray Jesus as instructing his followers to love their enemies on earth, this instruction was premised on the idea that violence would be applied by Jesus at a later time on behalf of wronged followers. No New Testament or early Christian writer can be found who believes in complete nonviolence, and all can be seen to believe in a sort of deferred violence.

PEACE AS CHRISTIAN HEGEMONY

As in the Hebrew Bible, peace in the New Testament can often be interpreted to mean a set of conditions that are optimal for the proponent of peace. This, of course, includes all concomitants of peace, including justice.[47] Within the study of the New Testament and early Christianity, the division in scholarship has usually been between the pacifists and the antipacifists or nonpacifists. Debate sometimes centers around selecting a text or group of texts that represent the "true" or "essential" teachings of Christ and the New Testament. Others acknowledge a pluralistic approach, wherein both pacifistic and nonpacifistic views are recognized.[48] Equally important has been whether objections to military service have been based on ethical or religious grounds (e.g., fear of contamination with the idolatry customary in the Roman army).[49]

Those who advocate a purely pacifistic view of the New Testament usually cite the "love" verses discussed above. Those who advocate the view that military service was permissible in the New Testament may argue that the New Testament everywhere assumes that military service is permissible, and nowhere prohibits it explicitly.[50] Thus, in John 8:11, Jesus is portrayed as instructing the adulterous woman as desisting from sinning anymore. No such injunction is ever delivered to a soldier. In Acts 10:1–2, Cornelius, a centurion of the Italian cohort, is described as God-fearing and devout. In Luke 22:36, Jesus is quoted as saying: "But now, the one who has a purse must take it, and likewise a bag. And the one who has no sword must sell his cloak and buy one." This implies that an instrument of war could be part of a Christian's normal equipment.

Still others would say that ultimately, it does not matter what early Christians thought about the military, as social and historical contexts have changed throughout Christian history. Thus, Jesuit scholar Robert J. Daly, after a survey of early Christian views, concludes:

> The argument, for example, that the early church was pacifist, and thus we too should be pacifist, is indefensible. First . . . the evidence simply cannot support an unqualified statement that the early church was pacifist. But even if it were the case, it would in itself prove nothing for contemporary life. The early church accepted the institution of slavery. No theologian would argue that we should do the same today.[51]

A recurrent methodological flaw in studies on violence in early Christianity centers on the use of two overlapping assumptions: (1) military violence is the only type of violence that matters, and (2) being against military service or against military resistance is coterminous with being nonviolent. Among those categorized as pacifists in the early Christian period, we find Athenagoras, Origen, and Tertullian. Of these, Athenagoras has left too few writings to fully assess the extent to which he advocated nonviolence.

However, Origen's position on violence, as indicated by his famous treatise against the anti-Christian philosopher Celsus, is quoted as follows by David G. Hunter: "Moreover, we who by our prayers destroy all daemons which stir up wars, violate oaths, and disturb the peace, are of more help to the emperors than those who seem to be doing the fighting. We who offer prayers with righteousness . . . are cooperating in the tasks of the community."[52] This and other texts, then, are interpreted by Hunter to mean that Origen "reaffirms the Christians' loyalty to the Roman state while at the same time reasserting the traditional Christian commitment to nonviolence."[53]

However, Origen's "commitment to nonviolence" can be asserted only if we ignore other types of violence. For example, Eusebius reports that Origen castrated himself because he took very literally Jesus' comments in Matthew 19:12 ("there are eunuchs who have made themselves eunuchs for the sake of the kingdom of heaven").[54] Although Eusebius claims that this act was due to Origen's immaturity and youthfulness, Origen clearly thinks otherwise.[55] In *Contra Celsum*, Origen tries to clarify Celsus's observation that "men will contend unto death rather than abjure Christianity."[56] Origen responds, "But surely it is not without honor for the body to suffer for the sake of godliness, and to choose affliction on account of virtue."[57] So it is inaccurate to label Origen "nonviolent." Origen repudiates violence on behalf of the Roman Empire, but he believes in being obligated to endure or commit violence for the religious reasons he favors.

Tertullian's pacifism is repeatedly cited by pacifistic scholars as well as those who acknowledge a plurality of views on military service.[58] Tertullian, in general, was against Christians serving in the Roman military, but he was also intent on showing that Christians were not harmful to Roman society. A classic locus cited in Tertullian occurs in his *Apologeticus*: "If, as we said above, we are bidden to love our enemies, whom have we to hate? Again, if, when a man injures us, we are forbidden to retaliate, that the action may not make us alike, whom then can we injure?"[59] Tertullian, of course, omits the passage in which Jesus ordains followers to hate their parents. Nevertheless, even this passage does not mean that Tertullian is against violence.

In fact, Tertullian is best described as an advocate of "deferred violence," as is clear from his yearning for revenge at the end of his treatise against the participation of Christians in public amusements such as gladiator contests. Note his statements about his preferred entertainment:

> Yes, and there are still to come other spectacles—that last, that eternal Day of Judgement, that Day which the Gentiles never believed would come, that Day they laughed at, when this old world and all its generations shall be consumed in one fire. How vast the spectacle that day, and how wide! What sight shall wake my wonder, what my laughter, my joy and exultation? as I see all those kings, those great kings welcomed (we were told) in heaven,

along with Jove, along with those who told of their ascent, groaning in the depths of darkness! And the magistrates who persecuted the name of Jesus, liquefying in fiercer flames that they kindled against the Christians.[60]

Clearly, Tertullian did not think violence was wrong, even against enemies. His glee at the violence he believed to be coming against the enemies of the Christians certainly shows that he was not so much against violence as he was against perpetrating it himself under his current circumstances.

Tertullian's violent rhetoric shows again what many of these supposedly pacifistic writers have in mind: a temporary and tactical cessation of hostilities, much like Clausewitz envisions in his dictum that politics is war by other means. We can make similar arguments for most New Testament and early Christian authors who are often described as pacifists. These authors or characters usually advocate deferred violence, not nonviolence. Their vision of peace is always envisioned as being finalized under the absolute rulership of the Christian god. It is as hegemonic as anything envisioned by Clausewitz.[61]

SUMMARY

"Love," as a set of concepts described in the New Testament, is not really a good response to violence in our world. First, Christian *agape* can entail unrelenting violence, from the punishment of individuals to the Crusades.[62] Second, the definition of love is itself dependent on a scarce resource, namely access to God's mind and divine communication. Thus, the true definition of *agape* becomes a scarce resource in itself, which then provides the seeds of violence. Finally, the history of interpretation of *agape* provides empirical confirmation that the most violent ideologies could still be justified by an appeal to "love." This renders "love" in the New Testament a meaningless concept, or at least one no less relativistic than secular humanist approaches to love.

NOTES

1. John Howard Yoder, *The Politics of Jesus* (Grand Rapids, MI: Eerdmans, 1972); Sider, *Christ and Violence* (1979; reprint, Eugene, OR: Wipf and Stock, 2001) Walter Wink, *Jesus and Nonviolence: A Third Way* (Minneapolis: Fortress, 2003). The latter is a distillation of a larger series of books by Walter Wink (see our bibliography).

2. Rudolf Schnackenburg, *The Moral Teaching of the New Testament*, trans. J. Holland-Smith and W. J. O'Hara (London: Burns and Oates, 1975), pp. 90–91.

3. Shermer, *The Science of Good and Evil*, p. 84.

4. J. Vernon McGee, *Thru the Bible with J. Vernon McGee* (Pasadena, CA: Thru the Bible Radio, 1988), 4:311.

5. Wayne A. Meeks, *The Origins of Christian Morality: The First Two Centuries* (New Haven, CT: Yale University Press, 1993).

6. For a general treatment on the issues of establishing the meaning of words, see R. R. K. Hartmann, ed., *Lexicography: Principles and Practice* (New York: Academic, 1983); and Arthur Mettinger, *Aspects of Semantic Opposition in English* (New York: Oxford University Press, 1994).

7. Judges 14:16 and Amos 5:15 as cited in the Septuagint, the Greek translation of the Hebrew Bible. For an edition, see Alfred Rahlfs, *Septuaginta . . . Editio minor* (Stuttgart: Deutsche Bibelgesellschaft, 1979).

8. See also Joseph Fitzmyer, *The Gospel According to Luke X–XXIV* (Garden City, NY: Doubleday, 1985), p. 1063.

9. On comparative expressions, see Blass and Debrunner, *Greek Grammar*, pars. 60–62.

10. Note that just such flawed logic is used by Roland H. Bainton (*Christian Attitudes toward War and Peace: A Historiacal Survey and Critical Re-evaluation* [New York: Abingdon, 1960], p. 56) when he explains the use of the word "sword" in Matthew 10:34. Bainton argues that it must be "metaphorical" because Luke used a different word.

11. Fitzmyer, *The Gospel According to Luke X–XXIV*, p. 1063.

12. Yoder, *The Politics of Jesus*, p. 45.

13. See Elizabeth Clark, "Antifamilial Tendencies in Ancient Christianity," *Journal of the History of Sexuality* 5, no. 3 (1995): 356–80.

14. Fundamental studies of "love" in the New Testament include Ceslaus Spicq, *Agape in the New Testament*, trans. Sister Marie Aquinas McNamara and Sister Mary Honoria Richter, 3 vols. (St. Louis, MO: B. Herder, 1963–66); Spicq actually includes more detailed philological study in his earlier work, *Agapè: Prolégomènes a une étude de théologie néo-testamentaire* (Leiden: Brill, 1955); Anders Nygren, *Agape and Eros*, trans. Philip S. Watson (Philadelphia: Westminster, 1953). For a more recent brief survey, see William Klassen, "Love (NT and Early Jewish)," in *The Anchor Bible Dictionary*, ed. Freedman, 4:381–96.

15. Nygren, *Agape and Eros*. For a similar benign view, applied to modern ethical problems, see Gene Outka, *Agape: An Ethical Analysis* (New Haven, CT: Yale University Press, 1972).

16. Of special importance are the articles by Oda Wischmeyer, "Vorkommen und Bedeutung von *Agape* in der Ausserliche Antike," *Zeitschrift fur die Neutestamentliche Wissenschaft* 69, no. 3–4 (1978): 212–38; "Traditiongeschichtliche Untersuchung der Paulinischen Aussagen über die Liebe (*Agape*)," *Zeitschfirt für die Neutestamentliche Wissenschaft* 74, no. 3–4 (1983): 222–36. Wischmeyer shows that, contrary to some previous conclusions, *agape* was used in ancient Greek, but she argues that it received a whole new semantic development in Christianity, particularly with Paul.

17. For examples of scholars still influenced, implicitly or explicitly, by an idealized view of *agape*, see Glenn H. Stassen, "The Fourteen Triads of the Sermon on the Mount (Matt. 5:21–7:12)," *JBL* 122, no. 2 (Summer 2003): 267–308. For one critique

of Nygren, see Lowell D. Streiker, "The Christian Understanding of Platonic Love: A Critique of Anders Nygren's *Agape and Eros,*" *Chicago Studies* 47 (1964): 331–40.

18. Eugen Schoenfeld, "An Illusive Concept in Christianity," *Review of Religious Research* 30, no. 3 (1989): 236–45; and Paul Rigby and Paul O'Grady, "*Agape* and Altruism: Debates in Theology and Social Psychology," *JAAR* 57, no. 4 (1989): 719–37. For the argument that the concept of loving one's enemies constituted the principal part of Jesus' social revolution, see Richard Horsley, *Jesus and the Spiral of Violence: Popular Jewish Resistance in Roman Palestine* (Minneapolis: Fortress, 1993).

19. Friedrich Nietzsche, *Beyond Good and Evil*, trans. Helen Zimmern (1884; reprint, Amherst, NY: Prometheus Books, 1989), p. 91.

20. The common designation for these is "treaties," though this is most misleading if meant to convey some sort of mutuality. These documents were more like acknowledgements of surrender and capitulation. There was not much choice for the vassal whether to accept many stipulations. Again, the slave-master mentality is what is fundamental, and the kinship rhetoric is what is fictionalized.

21. Donald J. Wiseman, *The Vassal Treaties of Essarhaddon* (London: British School of Archaeology in Iraq, 1958), pp. 49–50: lines 266–68: The Assyrian crucial clause is *ki-i nap-šat-ku-nu la tar-'a-ma-ni* (= "you will love [Ashurbanipal] . . . as you do your own lives."). Note that the Assyrian word word for "life" here is *napshu*, which is cognate with Hebrew *nephesh*, the word usually translated with the Greek *psyche*, which is used in Luke 14:26 to translate "life."

22. Ibid., pp. 33–34: lines 50–51.

23. William L. Moran, "The Ancient Near Eastern Background of the Love of God in Deuteronomy," *CBQ* 25 (1963): 87. For a more expanded study of lord-vassal language, see Klaus Baltzer, *The Covenant Formulary in Old Testament, Jewish, and Early Christian Writings*, trans. David E. Green (Philadelphia: Fortress, 1971).

24. Thus, Luke T. Johnson (*The Writings of the New Testament: An Introduction* [Philadelphia: Fortress, 1986], p. 186) notes that the Beatitudes bear some similarities to the blessings and curses of Deuteronomy 27–28, but he does not elaborate on how this structure was part of lord-vassal terminology. Spicq (*Agapè: Prolégomènes*, pp. 122–24) mentions some of the hierarchical nature of related words, but never develops the connection with lord-vassal treaties.

25. Susan Ackerman, "The Personal is Political: Covenental and Affectionate Love' ['*Ahēb, 'Ahâbâh*] in the Hebrew Bible," *Vetus Testamentum* 52, no. 4 (2002): 437–58. For an earlier treatment of love as political in the Hebrew Bible, see J. A. Thompson, "The Significance of the Verb *Love* in the David-Jonathan Narratives in 1 Samuel," *Vetus Testamentum* 24 (1974): 334–38.

26. Nygren, *Eros and Agape*, p. viii. See also Bultmann's comments on the servile nature of *agape* in *Theology of the New Testament*, pp. 262–63, 343–45.

27. Paul Ramsey, "Justice in War," in *The Essential Paul Ramsey: A Collection*, ed. William Werpehowski and Stephen D. Crocco (New Haven, CT: Yale University Press, 1994), p. 64: "Love for neighbors threatened by violence, by aggression, by tyranny, provided the grounds for admiting the legitimacy of the use of military force."

28. On 1 Corinthians 13, see Emanuel Miguens, "1 Corinthians 13:8 Reconsidered," *CBQ* 37, no. 2 (1975): 76–97.

29. See Hans Conzelmann, *I Corinthians*, trans. James Leitch (Philadelphia: Fortress, 1975), p. 97 and nn. 35–36.

30. See also, Jennifer Glancy, "Boastings of Beatings (2 Corinthians 11:23–25)," *JBL* 123, no. 1 (Spring 2004): 99–135; N. Clayton Croy, "'To Die Is Gain' (Philippians 1:19–26): Does Paul Contemplate Suicide?" *JBL* 122, no. 3 (2003): 517–31. For a critical look at Paul's notions of inclusion, see Denise Kimber Buell and Caroline Johnson Hodge, "The Politics of Interpretation: The Rhetoric of Race and Ethnicity in Paul," *JBL* 123, no. 2 (Summer 2004): 235–51.

31. Augustine, "Reply to Faustus," 22.79 in *The Nicene and Post-Nicene Fathers*, ed. Philip Schaff and Henry Wace (1886–89; reprint, Grand Rapids, MI: Eerdmans, 1996), 4:303–304.

32. Augustine, "Our Lord's Sermon on the Mount," 1.20.63, in *The Nicene and Post-Nicene Fathers*, 6:27.

33. Ibid., 1.20.64.

34. Augustine, "Reply to Faustus," 22.76–79.

35. Ibid. This episode about Thomas is also mentioned in Augustine's "Sermon on the Mount"; in both, Augustine alludes to the noncanonical status of the story.

36. Grotius, *The Law of War and Peace*, 1.2.8.3 and 7 (pp. 71–74)/*De Jure Belli*, 1:63 and 1:66.

37. Grotius, *The Law of War and Peace*, 1.2.8.3 and 4 (pp. 71–72)/*De Jure Belli*, 1:63–65. Grotius anticipates a current argument that Matthew 5:40, whose context seems to be a Jewish court of law, is later than the context of the parallel saying in Luke 6:29. See Michael G. Steinhauser, "The Violence of Occupation: Matthew 5:40–41 and Q," *Toronto Journal of Theology* 8, no. 1 (1992): 28–37.

38. R. A. Torrey, *Difficulties in the Bible: Alleged Errors and Contradictions* (Chicago: Moody, n.d.), p. 60.

39. Marcus Borg, *Jesus and Buddha: The Parallel Sayings* (Berkeley, CA: Seastone, 1999), pp. 14–15. Borg quotes Dhammapada 10.1 for his Buddhist source.

40. Milgrom, *Leviticus 1–16*, p. 27; and Esther Eshel, "Leviticus, Book of," in *Encyclopedia of the Dead Sea Scrolls*, ed. Lawrence Schiffman and James VanderKam (New York: Oxford University Press, 2000), pp. 490–91. A more technical report may be found in Emanuel Tov, "4QLev^c,e,g (4Q25, 26a, 26b)," in *Pomengranates and Golden Bells: Studies in Biblical, Jewish, and Near Eastern Ritual, Law, and Literature in Honor of Jacob Milgrom*, ed. D. P. Wright, D. N. Freedman, and A. Hurvitz (Winona Lake, IN: Eisenbrauns, 1995).

41. Alan Kirk, "'Love Your Enemies,' The Golden Rule and Ancient Reciprocity (Luke 6:27–35)," *JBL* 122, no. 4 (2003) 667–86.

42. See Jeffrey Wattles, *The Golden Rule* (New York: Oxford University Press, 1996), especially pp. 64–66.

43. Thucydides, *History of the Peloponnesian War*, trans. C. F. Smith, LCL (1919–23; reprint, Cambridge, MA: Harvard University Press, 1975): καὶ ἀρετῇ αὐτὸν νικήσας.

44. Gordon M. Zerbe, *Non-Retaliation in Early Jewish and New Testament Texts: Ethical Themes and Social Contexts* (Sheffield, UK: JSOT Press, 1993), p. 210.

45. William Klassen, "Love Your Enemy: A Study of NT Teaching on Coping with an Enemy," *Mennonite Quarterly Review* 37 (1963): 147–71.

46. See further, Zerbe, *Non-Retaliation*, pp. 251–54.

47. For a recent more philosophical attempt to use the New Testament to establish some guidelines for justice, see Leroy H. Pelton, "Biblical Justice," *JAAR* 71, no. 4 (December 2003): 737–65.

48. For a concise review of scholarship, see David G. Hunter, "A Decade of Research on Early Christians and Military Service," *Religious Studies Review* 18, no. 2 (April 1992): 87–94; "The Christian Church and the Roman Army in the First Three Centuries," in *The Church's Peace Witness*, ed. Marlin E. Miller and Barbara Nelson Gingerich (Grand Rapids, MI: Eerdmans, 1994), pp. 161–81. See also Lisa Sowle Cahill, *Love Your Enemies: Discipleship, Pacifism, and Just War Theory* (Minneapolis: Fortress, 1994).

49. For the view that any rejection of military service had more to do with fear of idolatry than with obejctions to violence per se, see John Helgeland, "Christians and the Roman Army: AD 173–337," *Church History* 43 (1974): 149–63. A ritual fear of bloodshed among Christians is credited with pacificism by Michel Spanneut, "Horreur du sang et non-violence dans l'Église des premiers siècles," *Studia Patristica* 18, no. 1 (1985): 71–76.

50. See John J. O'Rourke, "The Military in the NT," *CBQ* 32 (1970): 227–36. See also John Helgeland, Robert J. Daly, and J. Patout Burns, *Christians and the Military: The Early Experience* (Philadelphia: Fortress, 1985). For an older and classic treatment, see Adolf Harnack, *Militia Christi: The Christian Religion and the Military in the First Three Centuries*, trans. David McInnes Grace (Philadelphia: Fortress, 1981).

51. Robert J. Daly, "Military Service and Early Christianity: A Methodological Approach,"*Studia Patristica* 18, no. 1 (1985): 1–8.

52. Origen, *Contra Celsum*, 8.73, as cited in Hunter, "The Christian Church and the Roman Army," p. 175. For Origen's *Contra Celsum*, we depend on *The Ante-Nicene Fathers*, trans. Roberts and Donaldson, 4:395–669.

53. Hunter, "The Christian Church and the Roman Army," p. 175.

54. Eusebius, *Ecclesiastical History*, trans. J. E. L. Oulton, LCL (Cambridge, MA: Harvard University Press, 1980), 6.8.1–3.

55. Eusebius attributes Origen's actions to an immature and youthful mind (φρενὸς μὲν ἀτελοῦς καὶ νεανικῆς), but he also says another Christian named Demetrius approved of Origen's sincere act. On castration in early Christianity, see Mathew Kuefler, *The Manly Eunuch: Masculinity, Gender Ambiguity, and Christian Ideology in Late Antiquity* (Chicago: University of Chicago Press, 2001).

56. Origen, *Contra Celsum*, 8.48.

57. Ibid., 8.50.

58. See, for example, Stephen Gero, "*Miles Gloriosus*: The Christian and Military Service According to Tertullian," *Church History* 39 (1970): 285–98.

59. Tertullian, *Apologeticus*, pp. 166–67 (Latin): "Si inimicos, ut supra diximus, iubemur diligere, quem habemus odisse? Item si laesi vicem referre prohibemur, ne de facto pares simus, quem possumus laedere?"

60. Tertullian, *De Spectaculis*, trans. T. R. Glover and G. H. Rendall, LCL (Cambridge, MA: Harvard University Press, 1977), pp. 296–299 (Latin): "At enim supersunt alia spectacula, ille ultimus et perpetuus iudicii dies, ille nationibus insperatus,

ille derisus, cum tanta saeculi vetustas et tot eius nativitates uno igni haurientur. Quae tunc spectaculi latitudo! Quid admirer? Quid rideam? Ubi gaudeam, ubi exultem, tot spectans reges, qui in caelum recepti nuntiabantur, cum Iove ipso et ipsis suis testibus in imis tenebris congemescentes? Item praesides persecutores dominici nominis saevioribus quam ipsi flammis saevierunt insultantes contra Christianos liquescentes?"

61. For a sanitized and benign view of Christian imperialism, see Richard Horsley, *Jesus and Empire: The Kingdom of God and the New World Disorder* (Minneapolis: Fortress, 2003).

62. For the Crusades as an act of love, see Jonathan Riley-Smith, "Crusading as an Act of Love," in *The Crusades: The Essential Readings*, ed. Thomas F. Madden, pp. 32–50.

CHAPTER 10

ISLAM AND THE QUR'AN

BASIC OVERVIEW

Despite the claim of many Muslim historians that Islam is a religion born in the full light of history, the origins of Islam are shrouded in mystery. Much of what we see in textbooks simply repeats information from sources whose origin and reliability is increasingly questioned by modern scholars.[1] Everything from the historicity of the life of Muhammad to the reliability of the Qur'an and the traditions concerning the prophet known as the Hadith has come under renewed scrutiny.[2]

The diverse nature of what is called "Islam" is beyond the scope of our treatment. However, we may begin with one attested brief description of Islam found in Al-Bukhari's authoritative collection of Islamic traditions (Hadith), which we adapt and summarize as follows: Islam is based on five principles: (1) to testify that "there is no God but Allah and Muhammad is his messenger"; (2) congregational prayers (*Salat*); 3) the payment of a sacred tithe or tax (*Zakat*); (4) the pilgrimage to Mecca (the *Hajj*); and (5) fasting during the month of Ramadan (*Sawm*).[3] There are, of course, varying interpretations regarding the way each of these elements is to be carried out more specifically.

For the purpose of our study of violence in Islam, we will treat other major features of Islam as we assess how inscripturation, sacred space, group privileging, and salvation have figured in the violence found in Islamic cultures. After outlining some preliminary views of violence in Islam, we offer a brief biography of Muhammad, because much of the violence that is found in Islam can be traced to the use of Muhammad as a paradigm of behavior.

PRELIMINARY COMMENTS ON SCHOLARSHIP

It is not surprising to find Muslim writers who proclaim that Islam is a peaceful religion. Maulana Muhammad Ali, an Ahmadiyya Muslim, says "Islam is thus, in its very inception, the religion of peace."[4] Ali in particular cites belief in the unity of God and the unity of humankind as the essential feature of this peaceful impulse. Among the Qur'anic passages cited to support the peaceful agenda of Islam is Sura 2:256:

> Let there be no compulsion in religion; Truth stands out clear from error; whoever rejects Evil and believes in God hath grasped the most trustworthy Hand-hold, that never breaks. And God heareth and knoweth all things.[5]

Many Western non-Muslim scholars also have advocated a peaceful view of Islam in recent years. David Martin, who claims that religion is seldom the cause of war, argues as follows for Islam:

> However, this type of conflict has little to do with religion as such, since, as argued earlier, it occurs just as easily when the religious factor is absent. Turks, Iraqis, and Iranians can slaughter Kurds, and vice versa, with an enthusiasm entirely unaltered by the presence or absence of religious difference. In Turkey, Turks are largely Sunni, Kurds often Alawite. In Iraq Kurds are Sunni, like most Iraqis, and in Iran they are Sunni and the Iranians mostly Shia. But the degree of conflict remains fairly constant.[6]

Another formidable academic entry into the debate on Islamic violence is made by Carl Ernst, a professor at the University of North Carolina at Chapel Hill. Ernst's *Following Muhammad* (2003) begins by noting the problem of seeing Islam as non-Western.[7] Islam, in fact, derives from the Hebrew Bible, the New Testament, and the works of Greek philosophers that had become lost to medieval Christianity. He offers the familiar claim that Islamic fundamentalism is a response to European colonialism. He concludes that "[f]ollowing Muhammad . . . is the responsibility of those who consider themselves Muslim. It is the responsibility of non-Muslims to acknowledge the legitimacy of this enterprise."[8]

Bruce Lawrence is perhaps the most vocal recent academician to express the idea that Islam is not a violent religion. In his *Shattering the Myth: Islam Beyond Violence* (1998), Lawrence sets out to demonstrate "(a) that Islam is not inherently violent and (b) that the longer view of Muslim societies offers hope, rather that despair, about the role of Islam in the next century."[9] For Lawrence, "violence remains an aberration rather than the norm."[10]

While never providing an explicit definition of religion, Lawrence comes close when he tells us that "in the deepest sense, Islam remains a religion, since those who profess a belief in Allah and in Muhammad as His final prophet are marked with a distinctive set of rituals and laws."[11] Apparently, it is "rituals and laws" that constitute a religion for Lawrence. But Lawrence tells us also that Islam is an ideology that is subordinated to nationalism, the principal ideology of our time.[12]

Lawrence accepts the idea that Westerners have three views of Islam. The first is the popular Islam that has become the subject matter of anthropologists. The second is the public Islam, which is the domain of political scientists, journalists, and policy makers. Finally, there is the academic Islam, a favorite of historians, linguists, and scholars of religion. He concludes that "the principal reason for the negative view of Islam is the predominance of the second view: public Islam."[13] Lawrence then proceeds to repeat the well-known thesis that the type of violence we see in Islam represents a reaction against colonialism.

He identifies three broad-scale Islamic movements; revivalism, reform, and fundamentalism.[14] His definition of "fundamentalism" is peculiar insofar as he sees it as a third stage in Islamic relations with the West rather than as a constant feature found in any period of Islamic history. For Lawrence, the first type of Islamic reaction against colonial expansion in the eighteenth and nineteenth centuries was revivalism, which he never defines clearly. He does tell us that revivalist movements were all preindustrial. Revivalist movements attempted to contest control, in the name of Islam, of vital commodities being lost to Western expansionism. For example, the so-called Padris resisted the shifts in the Sumatran coffee trade that were taking place under Dutch control.

When revivalism failed, many Muslims tried reform, which was allied with nationalistic movements. During this phase, nationalistic governments with dictatorial models were a key feature. Islam was used to provide legitimation, but the state really dictated what constituted genuine Islam.[15] Fundamentalism emerged only after the failure of reform. Fundamentalists react against a nationalism that is seen as too Western and too secular. Islamic unity and militancy is seen as a necessary element of survival in a world still controlled by the West. As evidence, Lawrence quotes Mohamed Sakr, a Harvard PhD who believes that "the West is against us."[16]

In any event, Lawrence claims that these Islamic fundamentalist movements are all the result of interaction with European cultures. In fact, Lawrence argues that "there is no spontaneous Islamic movement after the colonial period; all are reacting to some forces, or series of forces, that emanates from the Western world, which is to say, first from Northern Europe and then from the United States."[17]

Lawrence underscores this by arguing that "[w]hat matters most for Muslims lies beyond Palestine. It is an economic rather than a territorial nightmare. It relates to the present uneven distribution of global resources."[18] We should see any Muslim violence as the result of many Muslims reacting against an apparent loss of socioeconomic status in the face of other global competitors who seemingly are advancing economically much faster. "All Muslim societies," he argues, were members of a sort of proto–Third World by the time this term was coined in the 1950s.[19] Lawrence's thesis is undergirded by an analysis of fundamentalism in Pakistan, Syria, Tunisia, Iran, and Saudi Arabia.

Both Ernst and Lawrence, of course, are also writing partly as a response to Samuel P. Huntington's notorious thesis that Islam has become the primary enemy of the West in the aftermath of the demise of the bipolar world.[20] We will return to Lawrence's arguments, in particular, after we survey the scarce resources created in Islam by inscripturation, sacred space, group privileging, and salvation. We will show that the notion of some phase of modern Islam called "fundamentalism," which supposedly emerged only after Western colonialism, not only is definitionally muddled, but also ignores the fact that Islam is premised, from the start, on the use of violence to achieve its ends.

BIOGRAPHY OF MUHAMMAD

That the life of Muhammad furnishes a paradigm for Islamic behavior is acknowledged by Muslim and non-Muslim scholars. Thus, Carl Ernst, who otherwise campaigns against the violent view of Islam, suggests that despite the difficulty in defining Islam, one must understand the "role of Muhammad as the central figure defining Islamic religiosity."[21] If Muhammad is the key to understanding Islam, then certainly it is fair to also examine the violent episodes attributed to Muhammad, something Ernst and other writers on Islamic violence often do not do.

As Ibn Warraq notes, the traditional biographies of Muhammad are called *Sira* or *al-Maghazi*.[22] The former term usually refers to the biography proper, while the latter originally referred to stories of the battles of Muhammad. Both are used somewhat synonymously. There is a growing amount of modern critical scholarship that has questioned the accuracy of these biographies, which contain many contradictions and historical anachronisms, not to mention a persistent problem of being unable to verify most of the reports on which these biographies are based.

But although many modern critical scholars no longer believe that these sources are very reliable, it is important to understand how these biographies function with regard to violence. Any violence based on the example of

Muhammad is based on the belief of Muslims that these biographies are accurate. As long as Muslims believe the biographies to be authoritative, they will function to influence violent behavior. These sources, therefore, also constitute another element of inscripturation.

Among the most authoritative traditional biographies of Muhammad is the one attributed to Ibn Ishaq (ca. 85/704–150/767). As Ibn Warraq notes, the original version of Ibn Ishaq's Sira is not extant, but we have two recensions and at least fifteen versions.[23] The recension of Ibn Hisham (d. 218/833) is perhaps the most authoritative, and it has been translated into English by Alfred Guillaume.[24]

M. A. Draz, a professor at Egypt's prestigious Al-Azhar University, presents a good example of a scholar who follows the traditional narrative that assumes that these biographies are accurate.[25] By this account, Muhammad was born on a Monday in the second week of the lunar month Rabi' Al-Awwal, during the Year of the Elephant, which corresponds to 571 in the Gregorian calendar. Muhammad's father, 'Abd Allah, died some seven months before Muhammad's birth. Amina, his mother, helped to educate him after he left the care of a wet nurse. An Abyssinian housekeeper named Umm Ayman is also said to have assisted Amina. Around the age of eight or nine, Muhammad was under the protection of his uncle, 'Abd Manaf, with the surname of Abu Talib.

At age twenty-five, Muhammad married a wealthy woman named Khadija, a middle-aged widow some fifteen years his senior. Muhammad remained married only to Khadija for twenty-five years. Muhammad fathered two boys, both of whom died, with Khadija. His four daughters (Zaynab, Ruqayya, Umm Kulthum, and Fatima) by Khadija had more significant roles in Islamic history. Fatima married Ali, who became the fourth caliph. Umm Kulthum and Ruqayya married Uthman, the third caliph, who is credited with sponsoring the authoritative edition of the Qur'an. Zaynab died two years before Muhammad, but left him a granddaughter, Umama, who became Ali's wife after the death of Fatima.

The beginning of the most important phase of Muhammad's life began on night of the seventeenth of Ramadan (February 610). On that night a strange figure, later to be recognized as the angel Gabriel, appeared to him in a cave. He claimed to have harbored doubts about his experience, the nature of the doubts becoming a source of contention later. Muhammad related his experience to Khadija, who reassured him that he was receiving a divine revelation. Khadija sent Muhammad to her cousin, a Christian convert named Waraqa bin Nawfal, who confirmed that Muhammad was receiving a revelation consistent with biblical revelatory traditions. A Hadith recorded by Al-Bukhari says that Aisha, Muhammad's favorite wife after the death of Khadija, described the first revelations as follows:

> The commencement of the (Divine) revelation to Allah's messenger was in the form of good righteous (true) dreams which came true like bright daylight, and then the love of seclusion was bestowed upon him. He used to go in seclusion in the cave of Hira' where he used to worship (Allah alone) continuously for many nights before returning to (or his desire to see) his family. He used to take with him the journey food for the stay and then come back to (his wife) Khadija to take his food likewise again till suddenly the Truth descended upon him while he was in the cave of Hira'.[26]

Muhammad returned to receive subsequent revelations and reassurances from Gabriel that he was not crazy.

By his forty-third lunar year, Muhammad had received a definitive commission to "arise and deliver thy warning" (Sura 74:2). Muhammad soon began to make converts—as well as enemies. Persecution became so fierce that he decided to move to Yathrib, now more commonly known as Medina. In the year 612, at which the Islamic calendar begins its count, Muhammad fled to Medina in an event called the Hijra. At Medina, Muhammad created the first effective Muslim community (*ummah*), and he died in that town in 632, aged exactly sixty-three lunar years. We shall treat other aspects of Muhammad's biography as we discuss how the four main scarce resources (inscripturation, sacred space, group privileging, and salvation) have precipitated violence in Islam.

INSCRIPTURATION

The most privileged deposit of God's revelation in Islam is called the Qur'an. As William Graham has noted, the primary meaning of the word is "recitation."[27] As a book, the Qur'an is divided into 114 Suras, which are subdivided into verses. The Qur'an is associated with the term *kitāb*, which is often translated as "book." Revelation is viewed as being sent down or as "coming down" (*nazala*) from heaven. The revelations of the Prophet were collected on various types of materials or in individual human memories, but no single written Qur'an was extant during the lifetime of the Prophet. According to one authoritative tradition, Uthman, Muhammad's son-in-law and the third caliph, is said to have provided the definitive edition of the Qur'an.[28]

In addition, Islam often appeals for authority to large collections of traditions not found in the Qur'an. Some of these collections, the Hadith, bear as much or more authority than the Qur'an. The most authoritative collection of Hadith, and the one we cite most often, is that of Al-Bukhari. These traditions are supposedly authenticated by a chain (*isnad*) of named transmitters who can be traced back to Muhammad. Critics who have questioned the reliability of the Hadith include Ignaz Goldziher, Joseph Schacht, Patricia Crone, and Michael Cook.[29]

The history of the exegesis of the Qur'an is quite complex, and here we follow a standard historiography of Qur'anic exegesis. *Ijtihad*, or private interpretation, seems to have been allowed in the earliest phases of Islam. The door of *ijtihad* was then closed, though how closed it is in actuality depends on the interests of interpreters. The idea of "consensus" (*ijma*) and "analogy" (*qiyas*) form other hermeneutic tools, not unlike those we find in Jewish and Christian exegesis. *Sharī'a* refers to the body of legal traditions that govern Muslims. Different schools disagree on specific interpretations of texts and on methodology.

If, as our thesis holds, inscripturation creates a scarce resource, then we must address at least some of the issues posed by Daniel Madigan, author of *The Qur'an's Self-Image* (2001).[30] Madigan minimizes the role of the Qur'an, as a bounded written entity, in Muslim life. He, in fact, says that "Islam is . . . characterized by an almost entirely oral approach to its scripture. . . . one finds no physical book at the center of Muslim worship."[31] A more radical version of this position was already voiced by Hugo Grotius and Blaise Pascal (1623–1662), who claimed that Islam and Christianity differed in that "Muhammad prohibited reading, while the Apostles commanded it."[32]

Although Madigan seems to resist John Burton's contention that the Qur'an was not considered a source of law until around 800 CE, he also contends that the earliest Muslim communities did not see codification as essential to the Qur'an.[33] Overall, Madigan elaborates and updates the work of Graham in emphasizing orality over textuality as the center of authority and practice in Islam.[34]

One crucial passage Madigan enlists to support his thesis is Sura 17:93, in which the following demand is made of Muhammad: "[S]end down to us a [*kitāb*] that we can read." This presupposes, argues Madigan, that Muhammad did not see a book as the primary locus for his authority.[35] Thus, for Madigan, the frequently used word *kitāb* does not always indicate a book in the Western sense of a bounded text. It is better translated as "writing," as a process, and as "book" only by extension.[36] Indeed, Madigan argues that other passages (e.g., Sura 6:7) seem to indicate that there is a distinction between "authority and physical writtenness."[37]

Madigan seems motivated by his own aversion to seeing the Qur'an as a closed corpus. It is one thing to say that the Qur'an holds itself to be "above canons and limits."[38] But it seems more subjective to argue that "[t]he too-easy adoption of the understanding of *kitāb* as 'book' is precisely what opens the way to fundamentalism, which identifies the limits of God's *kitāb* with the boundaries of the received text."[39] Here, Madigan has gone beyond describing the use of the word *kitāb* empirically and moved into adopting a particular definition in order to avoid fundamentalism. Madigan, therefore, must presume "fundamentalism" to be theologically or philosophically unacceptable. If so, then he is again working with an essentialist conception of Islam that would regard fundamentalism as illegitimate on other than empirical grounds.

While it is probably true that "Qur'an" originally referred to a varied oral and written phenomenon in the earliest phases of Islam, it is also true that the Qur'an came to be regarded as much a book as the Torah or the New Testament. Ibn Hisham's biography, in fact, indicates that oral recitation was sometimes not as authoritative as Madigan would lead us to believe. In one case, God is portrayed as reviling "gentiles, who do not know the book but merely recite passages."[40] Here, it does not seem that reciting is held to be as good an index of "knowledge" as reading the book.

Indeed, Madigan makes too much of the difference between the Qur'an's orality and that of other sacred books. Thus, Deuteronomy appears to emphasize the oral nature of God's word by its constant reference to hearing God's word. A primary credo of Deuteronomy is "Hear, O Israel, our Lord, is One." Yet Deuteronomy 4:2 also can declare the written form of what was heard to be fixed and inviolable. Then again, Deuteronomy 5 probably changed some of the text of the Ten Commandments found in Exodus 20.

Likewise, Jesus left nothing in writing, and all of his teaching was probably oral. Yet this does not mean that the texts that contain his presumed teachings are not also regarded as fixed at later points. Letters attributed to Paul are also ascribed to a revelation from Jesus rather than to some earthly transmission process. Despite the great textual divergences that probably existed in the first centuries following Christianity, the idea of fixity is no more verifiable than the importance of orality because the main sources for the importance of orality are texts that are later than the period about which they speak.

Madigan, in fact, ignores that the importance of orality can also be retrojected by a later written culture.[41] People can invent the supposed importance of orality just as they can invent the supposed importance of texts in the past. This is an issue Graham also does not address clearly, and some of his claims about orality in Hinduism are heavily dependent on precarious relative dating of Hindu texts.[42] In any event, flexible orality mixes and alternates with textual fixity in almost every major scriptural tradition.

A more realistic view of the relation between scripture and oral authority, including the Qur'an, can best address Madigan's seeming puzzlement over some notions of fixity in the Qur'an. One can see that both flexibility and fixity sometimes function within any religious community as instruments of legitimation for the maintenance or change of particular viewpoints. Textuality and orality can be seen as rhetorical and hermeneutic strategies for maintaining or changing power relations. Those who wish to maintain power based on a specific textual form or interpretation will usually insist on fixity. Those not satisfied with current allocations of power may insist on flexibility and oral sources of authority that are beyond the text. Yet both strategies are premised on the power of a text to enforce fixity, for one does not argue against fixity unless it is believed to have force.

Madigan's thesis also is weak on empirical grounds, insofar as we can easily find Muslims who do seem to believe that the Qur'an is a bounded object at the center of their worship. For example, in the narrative about Saladin's conquest of Jerusalem, the Muslim historian Imad Ad-Din tells how the sacred spaces were rededicated: "The pulpit was erected . . . readings of the revealed text given, and thus truth triumphed and error was cancelled out. The Qur'an was raised to the throne and the Testaments cast down."[43] If, as Madigan argues, Muslims do not see the Qur'an as being the center of their worship, then how should we regard this episode?

Indeed, Madigan seems to overlook how even more confining and bounded Qur'anic revelation can be at times. For example, the Hebrew Bible is acknowledged to contain the revelation of God to many authors. Certainly, Moses is quite privileged within the Hebrew Bible, but other authors, such as Isaiah, Jeremiah, and Daniel, have also received genuine revelation according to Judaism. No single human author or authority was behind the Hebrew Bible or the later repository of Jewish oral tradition known as the Talmud. Christianity is more dependent on the word of God being invested in one individual, Jesus, but other authors are also acknowledged to receive a revelation from God or from Jesus.[44]

In contrast, the Qur'an is now believed to be the word of God to Muhammad, not to anyone else. M. A. Draz, a professor of Islamic studies and himself a Muslim, says that "historically speaking the Qur'an is a Muhammadan phenomenon."[45] The Qur'an itself indicates that revelation is not equally distributed in Sura 42:51: "It is not fitting for a man that God should speak to him except by inspiration or from behind a veil, or by sending of a Messenger to reveal, with God's permission, what God wills; for He is Most High, Most Wise."[46] Earlier in the same Sura (42:7), it is clear that Muhammad is the fortunate recipient of one of these revelations:

> Thus have We sent by inspiration to thee an Arabic Qur'an that you may warn the Mother of Cities and all around her and warn (them) of the Day of Assembly of which there is no doubt; (When) some will be in the Garden, and some in the blazing fire. (My adapted translation.)

The very passage (Sura 17:93) that Madigan cites for his view of the flexibility of the Qur'an also seems to legitimize Muhammad on nothing more than his own word. Muhammad refuses to provide any sort of evidence, and responds in Sura 17:96 that God is "sufficient" (*kafā*) as Muhammad's witness between him and his detractors. Of course, Muhammad's listeners were simply left with no verifiable evidence that God was indeed Muhammad's witness. Muhammad's authority may have been based just as much on violence as on charisma.[47]

Another main component of Islamic scriptural authority, the Hadith, is also dependent on being traced to Muhammad. Muhammad is himself privileged, and, by extension, so is the record of his claimed revelations.[48] Thus, revelation is a scarce resource insofar as it is invested in a single person who then authorizes a single set of writings as the record of God's will. Even the doctrine of abrogation, which Madigan seems to use to support flexibility, is premised on the authority of a fixed text.

So rather than frame our entire debate with Madigan in terms of the oral versus the fixed nature of the Islamic view of the Qur'an, I wish to argue that the Qur'an is seen by many Muslims to be sufficiently inscripturated to create a scarce resource. The Qur'an can be seen as a discrete entity that contains God's revelations, even if all of God's revelations are not contained in the Qur'an (e.g., but also in the Hadith). Despite Madigan's protestations, we can still indeed demonstrate that the Qur'an, at least in the so-called Uthmanic version, is a privileged discrete entity compared to non-Muslim scriptures. Significant episodes of violence have resulted from maintaining the value of Muslim scriptures.

Among some of the earliest traditions about the nature of the Qur'an is the one about the authoritative version published by Uthman, the third caliph. From Al-Bukhari's version of this tradition, it becomes clear that at least some early Muslims thought of the Qur'an as inhabiting a discrete physical entity. Things were written on various media. But more important, Uthman felt the need to burn "all other Quranic materials."[49] If, as Madigan argues, the concept and the content of the Qur'an was so flexible, then why burn all but one version?

The fact that some early Muslims did think of a closed canon or tightly bounded set of scriptures can be seen in the following Hadith found in Al-Bukhari: "By Allah, we have no book to read except Allah's book (the Qur'an) and whatever is (written) on this scroll."[50] Another Hadith says:

> After the prophet, the Muslims used to consult the honest religious learned men in matters of law so that they might adopt the easiest of them, but if the Book (the Qur'an) or the Sunna (fa-'iḍa waḍaḥa al-kitāb 'awi as-sunna) gave a clear, definite statement about a certain matter, they would not seek any other verdict.[51]

What book or scriptures were these jurists consulting? They must have formed a discrete and identifiable entity: a bounded entity. This Hadith tells us that the text did provide the boundaries for what was allowable and what was not.

Indeed, one need not read much farther in M. Muhammad Ali's discussions of the Qur'an to see that he privileges the Qur'an. In another work, *Introduction to the Study of the Holy Qur'an*, M. Muhammad Ali says that "the transformation wrought by the Holy Qur'an is unparalleled in the history of the world, and thus its claim to being unique stands as unchallenged today as it did thirteen centuries ago."[52] For M. Muhammad Ali, the uniqueness of the Qur'an resides, in part, on its transformative power.

The Qur'an is also believed to be unique because of its textual purity, and M. Muhammad Ali says that "no copy differing in even one diacritical point is met with in the possession of one among four hundred million Muslims."[53] This supposed textual purity is compared with the Bible, which does indeed suffer from much textual variation. Textual purity constitutes, therefore, a sort of guarantee that Muslims have God's word exactly as revealed to Muhammad. Accordingly, M. Muhammad Ali can conclude that Islam is "the last" religion.[54] It also shows that the Qur'an is thought of as a fixed entity, at least textually.

The idea of *taḥrīf*, the "corruption" or "distortion" of previous scriptures, also has a role in establishing the superiority of the Qur'an. Thus Muslims may admit that previous biblical figures received a genuine revelation, but the scriptures produced eventually were corrupted and distorted. Those scriptures, therefore, are not to be held as authoritative when they disagree with the Qur'an.[55] The divine will is most perfectly embodied and contained in the Qur'an, as was argued by many Islamic apologists long before modern colonialism.[56]

Abu Ya 'ala (ca. 1066 CE) and other Muslim writers speak of a hierarchy of non-Muslim peoples that placed religions that had scriptures above those that did not (*lā kitāba lahum*).[57] This also caused some inequalities that determined the amount of violence to be used on "scriptural" versus "nonscriptural" religions. Moreover, the Qur'an would be in the Arabic language (*Qur'an 'arabi*). The Arabic language, as the privileged language of revelation, is also mentioned in Sura 26:192–195.

Thus, it is better to describe the Qur'an as a document that was originally meant to be heard, simply because most people could not read. Alternatively, we could argue that it is not mutually exclusive to regard a written document as bounded and fixed, and yet oral insofar as its transmission to the masses. Again, both Judaism and Christianity have a large corpus of nonbiblical interpretations (e.g., the Talmud in Judaism) that no more show the lack of fixity of the biblical text than any non-Qur'anic traditions necessarily negate the belief, as logically inconsistent as it may be, in the fixity and boundedness of the Qur'an.

In summary, the most privileged communications in Islam are located within the personhood of one man, Muhammad. No other scripture is as privileged as one thought to derive from Muhammad. In this regard, the Qur'an and its associated scriptural traditions form a scarce resource relative to the claims of divine communication among non-Muslims. As is the case with many resources regarded as scarce, violence is often believed to be necessary to defend against any perceived attack on the value of Muslim scriptures.

THE QURAYẒA MASSACRE AND INSCRIPTURATION

If we follow our general hypothesis that violence tends to result from competition for scarce resources, then the existence of two or more scriptures that claim to be sole depositories of God's revelation may lead to conflict. Some of the earliest traditions about the formation of the Qur'an indicate to us how intensive that competition was believed to be. As mentioned, some traditions hold that by the time of Uthman, there seemed to be the need to burn "all other Quranic materials."[58] This led to the so-called Uthmanic recension as the one deemed authoritative by most Muslims today.

In any event, the fact that inscripturation is involved in violence is illustrated by the frequent conflicts between Muslims and the "People of the Book" mentioned in the Qur'an, Ibn Hisham's biography of Muhammad, and the Hadith. The People of the Book usually refers to Jews and Christians, who had well-known sets of scriptures. In particular, inscripturation figures in the massacre of the Jewish tribe of Qurayẓa, one of the most disturbing episodes related in Ibn Hisham's biography of Muhammad. The massacre of Qurayẓa still figures in many scholarly discussions, ranging from attempts to defend it as a justifiable act against treason to outright denial of its historicity.[59] What is often missed, even in some of the most perceptive treatments, is the role of debates about scripture in the massacre.

In order to understand the massacre and its background in scriptural debates between Jews and Muslims, it is useful to summarize the basic relationships that Muslim traditions say existed in Medina during the time of Muhammad's arrival in 622. At this time, Medina harbored both Jewish and Arab tribes, according to Muslim writers. The Jews of Medina were divided into three main tribes that had formed alliances with two principal Arab tribes, the Khazraj and Aws tribes. We may summarize these relationships as follows at the time that Muhammad arrives in Medina.

Jewish Tribe	Allied Arab Tribe
Qaynuqa'	Khazraj
Naḍīr	Aws
Qurayẓa	Aws

Upon his arrival in Medina, Muhammad established an agreement known as the Covenant of Medina. This covenant seemingly provided the Jewish tribes with certain rights, including the right to practice their religion. In actuality, one can also read it as an instrument whereby Muhammad transfers allegiances from tribal family structures to himself, and so it is an instrument of incipient imperialism.

Soon, however, it becomes apparent that Muhammad's revelations are in conflict with the Jewish scriptures. Sometimes Muhammad is portrayed as very cognizant of how disputes about the proper conduit for a revelation from God can arise. For example, in Ibn Hisham's biography of Muhammad is a scene in which Muhammad is discussing the difficulty of having people believe that one has received God's revelation.[60] An inquirer asks Muhammad how he expects people to believe him when during the time of Moses people listened directly to the word of God, then changed it. The inquirer presumably assumed that all the Hebrews had listened to God's instructions about idolatry, but yet still constructed a Golden Calf (Exodus 32), completely disregarding what they had heard.

Muhammad quotes a scholar, who has explained that not all of the Hebrews actually listened to the word of God. Only a group (*parīq min-hum*) that accompanied Moses heard God speak.[61] The group could not accompany Moses the whole way up the mountain, so they stayed back a bit while a cloud enveloped Moses. That group, therefore, could only hear what God said. When Moses returned to the larger group, who had not heard God speak directly, Moses told them what God said. But this larger group "contradicted him and said that God had ordered something else."[62]

In another instance Muhammad reports that God is angry with the three main Jewish tribes of Medina: the Qaynuqa', Naḍīr, and Qurayẓa. Muhammad ridicules the Jewish tribes because they fought each other as allies of pagans. When the fighting was over, the Jews ransomed prisoners instead of killing them. Muhammad seems to think that this was contrary to the biblical injunctions to kill prisoners, especially in the story of the Amalekites related in 1 Samuel 15. Since the Jews do not seem to follow these injunctions, God then asks the Medinese Jews: "Will you believe in part of the scripture and disbelieve in another part?"[63]

In 627 Muhammad became displeased with the Qurayẓa tribe because they seemed to have assisted too little when the Muslims of Medina were being besieged by the Meccans. The Qurayẓa tribe is accused of breaking an earlier alliance agreement. After successfully surviving the onslaught from the Meccans, Muhammad moved against the Qurayẓa tribe. The movement was commanded by the angel Gabriel, who said: "God commands you, Muhammad, to go to Banu Qurayẓa. I am about to shake their stronghold."[64] Muhammad sent his trusty aide, Ali, to form an advance party.

Upon the approach to the strongholds of the Qurayẓa, Ali overheard the Qurayẓa insulting the Prophet. Ali returned to meet Muhammad and reported the insults. Thereupon, Muhammad exclaimed: "You brothers of monkeys, has God disgraced you and brought His vengeance upon you?"[65] Muhammad's remarks allude to a written tradition regarding Exodus 32, in which the Israelites build a Golden Calf. According to this extrabiblical tradition, God punishes the Israelites by turning them into apes. Muhammad, moreover, seems to have used that scripture as part of his rationale to attack the Qurayẓa, and he saw himself as an instrument of God's continuing vengeance on idolatrous Jews.[66]

Terrorism forms another explicitly stated instrument, as when Ibn Hisham relates that Muhammad besieged the Qurayẓa for twenty-five nights and that "God cast terror [ru'b] into their hearts" (*wa-qadafa 'allahu fi kulubihum al-ra'b*).[67] The concept of God as terrorist is fully accepted and endorsed here, and harks back to biblical traditions found in, among other places, Genesis 35:5, where God's aid of the Hebrews is described as follows: "As they journeyed, a terror from God fell upon the cities all around them, so that no one pursued them."[68] Similarly, in Exodus 23:27 God says: "I will send my terror in front of you, and will throw into confusion all the people against whom you shall come, and I will make all your enemies turn their backs to you."

A negotiation follows with Ka'ab b. Asad, leader of the Qurayẓa who reviews three options available to his tribe. The first option is as follows: "Follow this man [Muhammad] and accept him as true, for by God it has become plain to you that he is a prophet who has been sent and that it is he that you find mentioned in your scripture; and then your lives, your property, your women and children will be saved."[69] This should mean that Muhammad did not see whatever disloyalty or treachery done to him as necessarily meriting death or a lesser punishment. The main criterion for Muhammad's decision to punish them at this point was whether they accepted that Muhammad is the Prophet mentioned in the Hebrew Scriptures.

The Qurayẓa responded, "[W]e will never abandon the laws of the Torah" (*lā nafaraq ḥukma al-tāwrat 'abadan*).[70] They added that they would not change their laws. A second suggestion was to have the Qurayẓa kill their own women and children, and then come out to take whatever fate

Muhammad decided upon. The Jews rejected this as well, as they saw no point in living without their families.

The final option centers on the Sabbath. The Jews were said to be aware that the Muslims knew that the Sabbath law would prohibit Jews from fighting. However, the Muslims argued that as far as the Jews were concerned, "not a single man among you from the day of your birth has ever passed a night resolved to do what he knows ought to be done."[71] Thus, Muslims were presumably right to suspect that the Sabbath would be used as a ruse to surprise and kill Muslims.

After more tense negotiations, Muhammad agreed to let the fate of the Qurayẓa be decided by Saʿd b. Muʿadh of the Aws tribe, which had been friendly with the Qurayẓa tribe. It is evident, however, that Saʿd was bent on pronouncing a death sentence on the Qurayẓa. He thought he would die soon from a wound, and said that he now cared little for any man's censure concerning his decision. Upon hearing this, one of the Jews went back and announced the punishment that now seemed certain.

Saʿd's decision came soon enough: "I give judgment that men should be killed, the property divided, and the women and children taken as captives."[72] This seems to follow a practice found in the Hebrew Bible; in Deuteronomy 20, we find laws of war that make a distinction between treatment of towns that are near (within territory allotted to Israel) and those towns that are far. The towns that are "near" are to be annihilated completely. However, for a town that is "far," Deuteronomy 20 prescribes the following:

> When you draw near to a town to fight against it, offer it terms of peace.
>
> If it accepts your terms of peace and surrenders to you, then all the people in it shall serve you at forced labor.
>
> If it does not submit to you peacefully, but makes war against you, then you shall besiege it;
>
> and when the LORD your God gives it into your hand, you shall put all its males to the sword.
>
> You may, however, take as your booty the women, the children, livestock, and everything else in the town, all its spoil. You may enjoy the spoil of your enemies, which the LORD your God has given you.
>
> Thus you shall treat all the towns that are very far from you, which are not towns of the nations here. (Deut. 20:10–15)

The Qurayẓa Jews surrendered, and the biography of Muhammad tells us what happened next:

> Then he [Muhammad] sent for them and struck off their heads in those trenches as they were brought out to him in batches.[73] Among them was the enemy of Allah Huyayy b. Akhtab and Ka'b b. Asad their chief. There were 600 or 700 in all, though some put the figure as high as 800 or 900. As they were being taken out in batches to the apostle they asked Ka'b what he thought would be done with them. He replied: "Will you never understand? Don't you see that the summoner never stops and those who are taken away do not return? By Allah it is death!" This went on until the apostle [Muhammad] made an end of them.[74]

Huyayy accepted his fate by admitting that a person who forsakes God, as he has, will be forsaken. A final appeal to scripture is found in Huyayy's final exclamation: "A book and a decree and massacre have been written against the Sons of Israel."[75]

There are many aspects of this story that impinge on violent conflicts over scripture. The entire story can be seen, in large part, as an argument for Islamic supersessionism and legitimization as the true interpreters of the Jewish Torah. First, the violence inflicted on the Jews follows the assertion that the Jews no longer have the sole interpretational control over their own scriptures. The Jews do not recognize that Muhammad is mentioned in those scriptures, and this has delegitimized them as interpreters.

Equally important, the story makes clear that the Jews are accused of not following their own scriptures even when they do understand them. This has at least two consequences, the first being that Muslims are free to presume that Jews will not deal fairly with Muslims. After all, if Jews do not follow God's covenant, what should make Muslims believe that Jews will follow any covenant with human beings? This presumed faithlessness to God then allows Muhammad to punish the Jews preemptively for a treachery they will certainly commit, if they have not already.

Muhammad also executes a pious reversal on the Jews by showing that he aims to follow scripture better than Jews do. Note that Muhammad first offered terms of peace, an option stated in Deuteronomy 20:10–15 for "far cities," when he could have called for their total annihilation without first offering such terms. On the other hand, here may be a case in which Muhammad is himself guilty of believing parts of scripture and not others. Muhammad also follows the pattern of Elijah, the Hebrew prophet who himself killed 450 prophets of Baal (1 Kings 18:40).

As we have argued at the outset, a scarce resource X created by religion may cause violence when at least one of two or more groups desire X and/or believe that they are uniquely entitled to X. Under such circumstances, violence may be used to acquire X and/or defend against loss of X. In this case, the scarce resource is the Hebrew Bible. Both Muslims and Jews were vying for control of this scriptural entity. Jews insisted that they would "never abandon the laws of the Torah," and were willing to commit violence or suffer violence to retain this resource. Muhammad, on the other hand, aspired for control over this resource insofar as he claimed to have the correct interpretation and saw himself as being inscribed in the Torah. This is indeed a case in which conflicts over scripture played a major role in violence.

ACADEMICS AND THE QURAYẒA MASSACRE

It should be noted that the massacre at Qurayẓa is often sanitized by both Muslim writers and non-Muslim academics. In so doing, these scholars become complicit in endorsing religious violence or in not understanding the implications of their defense of Muhammad. For example, M. J. Kister, who does not seem to mention the tradition that Muhammad himself carried out the executions, emphasizes presumed treachery as the main motive. A sketch of the life of the prophet by Marmaduke Muhammed Pickthal omits any indication that Muhammad himself killed the men of Qurayẓa.[76] As we shall argue, omitting or minimizing Muhammad's role becomes part of an apologetics for violence.

In the popular media, one particularly egregious example of academics minimizing the moral horror of Muhammad's actions at Qurayẓa is found in *Muhammad: Legacy of a Prophet* (2002), a documentary that aired on PBS.[77] Celebrated writer and academic Karen Armstrong, for example, says in this documentary that:

> Muhammad had nothing against the Jewish people per se, or the Jewish religion. The Quran continues to tell Muslims to honor the People of the Book. And to honor their religion as authentic. And the Jewish tribes who had not rebelled, who had not given help to the Meccans, continued to live in Medina completely unmolested. Muhammad was not trying to exterminate Jews. He was just trying to get rid of very dangerous internal enemies.[78]

A close reading of the episode in the Arabic sources does not bear out her assessment. Muhammad insisted that the Jews convert to his religion. The story indicates that Muhammad would have let these Jews live if they had accepted his religion. The fact that Muhammad was willing to overlook the treachery in return for converting to Islam means that religion was a main variable in his decision to kill these Jews.

Moreover, Armstrong does not explain why exiling these Jews would not have been better than killing them. The idea that violating an agreement should be valued above human life is itself a principle that should be questioned. Finally, Armstrong presumes that the Qurayẓa have done and are everything that the Muslim sources characterize them to be. But we have no accounts from the Qurayẓa themselves, and this seems to violate basic standards of fairness.

But more startling in this PBS documentary is the reaction of M. Cherif Bassiouni, president of the International Human Rights Institute at DePaul University and a 1999 nominee for the Nobel Peace Prize. A prolific author and renowned expert on human rights law, Bassiouni says, concerning Muhammad's rules of war: "He makes it very clear to his soldiers that if they have the right to use force against the Qureīsh, that does not mean that they will do the same thing that has been done in pre-Islamic wars, in which women and children could be killed, in which no prisoners could be taken, no quarter given. No, No. He said Islam is a religion of law and spirituality."[79] Yet what law allows people to be beheaded for violating an agreement? What law allows women to be widowed and children to be made fatherless because they would not convert to another religion? Cherif Bassiouni, of course, is simply repeating a common apologetic that most empires employ. That is to say, most empires see themselves as helping put an end to disorder or to improve some lesser civilization.

And, of course, we have even starker reports about Muhammad's treatment of the enemy. In one episode found in the Hadith, Muhammad captures some former Muslims who killed a camel driver. The report says that "[t]he Prophet ordered that their hands and legs should be cut off and their eyes should be branded with heated pieces of iron, and that their cut hands and legs should not be cauterized, till they died."[80] Executing a murderer is one thing in our society, but torturing him until he dies is held to be a crime.

So if, as Carl Ernst and others claim, Muhammad is the essential paradigm for Islamic behavior, then why don't Muhammad's actions qualify as "essential" parts of Islam? More important, it is clear that Muslim theologians cannot have it both ways. They cannot say that Muhammad forms a paradigm of behavior for modern times, and yet overlook the fact that in modern times he would qualify as a war criminal and terrorist. Under the Geneva conventions, for example, one cannot torture prisoners.[81] The idea that one had to accept Muhammad's religion or be killed, a choice he apparently was willing to accept from the Qurayẓa tribe, only shows how intolerant and criminal his behavior could be regarded today.[82]

SCRIPTURE AND INTRA-MUSLIM VIOLENCE

While many scholars focus on Muslim violence against non-Muslims, one must also observe the violence that is advocated scripturally against fellow Muslims. One illustrative example comes from discussions of the use of violence against what are regarded as criminal offenses in some Muslim societies. In October 1976 a symposium was held in Riyadh, Saudi Arabia, and proceedings were published under the title of *The Effects of Islamic Legislation on Crime Prevention in Saudi Arabia*.[83] According to the organizers themselves, the symposium was meant to, among other things, "illustrate how the Islamic Sharī'a can overcome the crime problems in the modern world."[84] The Sharī'a, the collective name for Muslim law, of course, consists primarily of the Qur'an and other scriptural authorities.

Among the papers read was "Effect of Religion against Crime" by Sheikh Manna Khalil Al-Kattan. The author appeals to the Qur'an and the Hadith to provide the justification for specific punishments. For example, he quotes the Hadith in order to show that "[a]n unmarried adulteress shall be flogged with one hundred stripes and banished for one year and a married adulteress shall be flogged with one hundred stripes and stoned to death."[85] The author tells us that "it is incumbent upon Muslims to abide by the teachings and commandments prescribed in the Qur'an, the Sunnah, and the Sharia in order to eradicate the roots of crime."[86] This certainly meets our basic criterion for attributing a religious cause to an act of violence: Religious Belief X, therefore Act of Violence Y. The belief that the Hadith represents the divine guidance of Muhammad would result, for example, in the act of violence of stoning a woman to death.

In the same symposium, Mohammad Salam Madkour read a paper titled "Defining Crime Responsibility According to Islamic Legislation."[87] He tells us that Islamic legislation was "revealed in the interest of humanity. He adds that Islamic legislation is "broad and flexible . . . worldly and unworldly, individual and collective," especially because Islam encompasses both the religious and secular in life.[88] But "flexible" is a term that is relative, as demonstrated when Madkour says:

> As regards highway robbery and mischief on earth the Qur'an says: "The punishment of those who wage war against God and His Apostle and strive with might and main for mischief through the land is: Execution, or crucifixion; Or the cutting off of hands and feet from opposite sides, Or exile from the land: That is their disgrace in this world, and a heavy punishment is theirs in the hereafter; Except for those who repent before they fall into your power.[89]

The citation is from the Sura 5:36–37, which shows again that the belief in this scripture is used to support violence. As in Christianity, the violence can be eternalized into the hereafter rather than just restricted to this lifetime.

More interestingly, Madkour adds that "if these crimes are proven and legally substantiated by evidence the punishments are fixed and cannot be changed or modified."[90] Here Madkour speaks of the class of crimes known as Hudud, whose punishments are fixed as specified in the Qur'an. But if "flexible" is the opposite of "fixed," either we have a logical contradiction or there is much relativity about what will be treated flexibly and what will be treated as immutable. The decision is made on religious grounds, ultimately unverifiable.

This type of violence cannot be blamed simply on Saudi responses to modern secularism or colonialism because the appeal is to texts that predate modern secularism and colonialism. Early traditions and discussions exist that advocate this sort of violence, so those texts are not simply a modern retrojection by these Saudi officials and scholars. Accordingly, these modern Saudis can be seen as continuing a type of violence endorsed from what are believed to be the earliest scriptural traditions of Islam. They see colonialism, if anything, as posing a possible obstacle to that continuity. The symposium was organized as a sort of demonstration, to secularizing societies, of the superiority of continuing these early Muslim practices. They fear the world will coerce them into discontinuing these practices rather than installing such practices because of some reaction against modern secularism.

Likewise, it is difficult to argue that such violence simply denotes some arbitrary textual selectivity on the part of an Al-Khattan. All textual selections of the Qur'an or Hadith are based on religious grounds. Thus, a more peaceful Hadith is no more verifiable than a violent one. This, of course, raises the issue of how the term "crime" is in itself a value judgment caused by religion. Stoning to death an adulteress is not a "crime," but having sex outside of marriage is.

In many other ways, violence against human beings is premised on religious value judgments. A body is allowed to sustain injury if it will prevent injury to the larger collective body in some way. Such a view of Islamic law sees it as "good" to injure a person's body in order to save the person's soul. A body must sustain injury in order to deter the person from injuring other bodies. But unlike secular forms of punishment, the reasons are ultimately unverifiable.

Yet it is this type of "internal" religious violence—violence committed against members of one's own religion—that underscores the weakness of simply focusing on war or interstate disputes (e.g., the COW Project) in order to measure religious violence. Given the number of people who have been executed under these interpretations of Sharī'a in the last millennium, for example, one might indeed reach a number that approximates those killed in a smaller-scale war listed in the COW Project.

SACRED SPACE

Sacred space is a basic theme of Islam. *Ḥarām*, a primary lexeme translated as "holy" and "sacred," is found some twenty-six times in the Qur'an.[91] The related noun, *ḥaram*, is usually translated as "holy place," "sanctuary," or "asylum." Sacred spaces can come in various forms, and also differ by sect. For example, the towns of Karbela or Najaf are regarded as sacred spaces particularly by Shiites. Among some Sufi traditions, grave sites of Sufi masters may become sacred space. A holy space may be assigned or created by God, as indicated in Sura 5:100: "God made Ka'ba, the Sacred House, an asylum of security for men." Note the idea that the sacred space is or should be a place of protection.

As in the other Abrahamic religions, the idea of special value to the space is reflected in the amount and quality of access allowed to that space. Although one should not deny entrance to those eligible for admission (Sura 22:25), those deemed "unclean" (*najīs/'anjās*), such as polytheists (*mushrikūn*), should not be allowed entrance into the Sacred Mosque (Sura 9:28). Sura 9:18 states that, as a more general rule, "the mosques of God shall be visited and maintained by such that believe in God and the Last day, establish regular prayers, and practice regular charity, and fear none (at all) except God."

There are other rules found in the Hadith that pertain to behavior in a mosque or sacred spaces. For example, M. Muhammad Ali notes that "carrying on any kind of trade in the mosque is strictly prohibited, as is also the reciting of poems, and even sitting in circles and indulging in talk at the time of prayer."[92] As in the case of the Jewish temple, a Muslim sacred space could also be a place for sanctioned violence in the form of animal sacrifice.

Within Islam, the most sacred of spaces is Mecca. The sacredness of Mecca is proclaimed by Muhammad, when he is quoted as saying, "I have been commanded only to serve the Lord of this City, Him who has sanctified it (*ḥarrama-ha*)" (Sura 27:91). Indeed, one of the five pillars of Islam is a pilgrimage (*Hajj*) to Mecca. The proper direction (*qiblah*) a Muslim faces when praying is toward Mecca.

According to Muslim tradition, Mecca was sacred and a site for pilgrimage long before the time of Muhammad. Much of Muslim tradition would probably agree with M. Muhammad Ali's assessment that the sacredness of Mecca rests on the supposed connection to events in the lives of Abraham and Ishmael.[93]

Within Mecca, the most sacred value is bestowed upon the Ka'aba, called also the *al-bayti al-ma'muri* (House that is visited) in Sura 52:4. It is associated with the main mosque, called the *Masjid al-Ḥarām* (Sura 17:1). The term *Ka'aba* derives from a root meaning "swelled" or "exalted." According to Muslim traditions, it is the oldest place where Allah was worshipped. Other traditions says that this is the place where Ishmael was abandoned to die, following a tradition that can be traced back to Genesis 16. The place fell into disrepair and idolatry, but it was rebuilt and cleansed by Abraham and Ishmael (Sura 2:127).

Inside the Ka'aba rests a black stone (*Hajar al-Aswad*) whose significance is unclear. Many critical scholars see it as a remnant of pagan worship, while Muslims believe it to be of mysterious origin. M. Muhammad Ali, for example, says, "There is not the least indication to show where the stone came from and when it was placed there."[94]

Medina, the first town to come under Muslim rule, is also an important sacred space. Al-Bukhari reports that "Al-Madina is a sanctuary (*ḥaramun*). . . . Its trees should not be cut and no heresy should be innovated nor any sin should be committed in it."[95] Again, sacrality correlates with behaviors deemed correct by the Muslim masters of the sacred space. Freedom of religion does not seem to be allowed in Muslim sacred spaces.

Jerusalem is also sacred space for Muslims. In fact, Patricia Crone and Michael Cook have concluded that the Hijazi origins of Islam are a later invention meant to displace the preeminence of Jerusalem in the initial phases of Islam.[96] Many early Muslim sources acknowledge that earliest direction for proper prayer was Jerusalem or somewhere other than Mecca.[97] In any case, evidence for the value of Jerusalem for Muslims can be found from at least the time of the Crusades. For example, Ibn-Al Athir, a reputed witness of the Third Crusade, noted that after Saladin's conquest, "The Sultan ordered that the Dome of the Rock should be cleansed of all pollution, and this was done."[98]

The most sacred portion of Jerusalem for Muslims is enclosed within a compound called the Al-Haram Al-Sharif, which encompasses some thirty-five acres. Within this compound is the Dome of the Rock, which may be the earliest preserved example of Islamic architecture.[99] The building is attributed to Abd Al-Malik (685–705), and bears inscriptions that may reflect a variant text of the Qur'an. The Miraj, Muhammad's mystical ascent into heaven, is said to have occurred here. Also in this compound is "the farthest mosque" (*al-masjidi al-Aqsa* in Sura 17:1), which is dated to around 711–713.

We can also demonstrate empirically that the importance of Jerusalem is related to one's religiosity even today. A survey of Palestinians conducted by Naḍīr Izzat Sa'id finds that among those described as "very religious" the importance of Jerusalem from an Islamic religious perspective is 98 percent, but that drops to 58 percent among those described as "not religious."[100] The

Haram al-Sharif was "very important" to 99 percent of those Palestinians described as "very religious," but only to 78 percent of those described as "not religious." Likewise, the Al-aqsa mosque and Dome of the Rock were described as "very important" to 98 percent of the "very religious," but only to 79 percent of those who were "not religious."[101]

VIOLENCE DUE TO SACRED SPACE

Sacred space is inherently a scarce resource when more than one group desires it or when an underprivileged group does not have the same privileges and access to that space. The value of Jerusalem is almost entirely the creation of religion, and we have seen a repeated recorded conflict over that space since at least the Assyrian siege in the eighth century BCE. Like Christians, Muslims have engaged in violence in order to maintain or regain space considered sacred.

This violence is quite evident in the Crusades, of course. We have a Muslim perspective in the work of 'Imad ad-Din, who says:

> Islam wooed Jerusalem, ready to lay down lives for her as a bride-price, bringing her a blessing that would remove the tragedy of her state, giving her a joyful face to replace an expression of torment, making heard, above the cry of grief from the Rock, calling for help against its enemies, the reply to this appeal, the prompt echo of the summons, an echo that would make the gleaming lamps rise in her sky, bring the exiled Faith back to her own country and dwelling-place and drive away from al-Aqsa those whom God drove away with his curse. . . . Saladin marched forth . . . to remove the heavy hand of unbelief with the right hands of Faith, to purify Jerusalem of the pollution of those races, of the filth of the dregs of humanity.[102]

This passage shows that Muslims were simply using the mirror image of arguments we know well from the preserved Christian sources. Jerusalem was sacred space not because of its riches or economic resources, but because Muslim scriptural traditions associate crucial supernatural activities of Muhammad with that site. All such events associated with Muhammad at Jerusalem, however, are not verifiable.

In more recent times, sacred spaces in Iraq have been attacked in intra-Muslim wars between Wahhabis and Shiites. The Wahhabis, now represented by the ruling family of Saudi Arabia, believe that the veneration of Shiite martyrs and saints is nothing more than a form of idolatry.[103] The Wahhabis regard themselves as Muslims, and Shiites as non-Muslim or as practicing a perverted form of Islam.

In 1801 the Wahhabis laid siege to Najaf, a Shiite holy city in Iraq. In that same year, the Wahhabis sacked Karbala, where the Shiite martyr Al-Husayn lost his life in the aftermath of a war for the succession to Muhammad's leadership. Part of a report from the Wahhabi perspective on this violence in Karbala is as follows:

> Sa'ud set out with his divinely supported army and cavalry. . . . He made for Karbala and began hostilities against the people of the city of Al-Husayn. . . . The Muslims [= Wahhabis] scaled the walls, entered the city by force, and killed the majority of its people in the markets and in their homes. Then they destroyed the dome placed over the grave of Al-Husayn by those who believe in such things.[104]

By 1803 the Wahhabis began to conquer the Hijaz region of Saudi Arabia, and the burning of Shiite scriptures was among their activities. In 1925 the Wahhabis took Mecca and Medina and destroyed Shiite tombs.

In these cases, the Wahhabis were motivated by an attempt to clean out what they considered to be Shiite desecration of sacred space, or to expand the sacred space of Islam. On the other side, Shiites were willing to commit violence to defend their sacred spaces.[105] These examples also show that sacred space can be destroyed not so much because one group desires it, but because a group knows the space is valuable to its enemy. Nonetheless, it is the value of the space, a value created by religion, that renders it a target.

OSAMA BIN LADEN AND SACRED SPACE

The fight over sacred space is part of the stated grievance voiced by Osama bin Laden, regarded as the foremost enemy of the United States today.[106] In a declaration dated February 23, 1998, bin Laden and four of his cohorts issued a fatwa, an edict obligatory to all Muslims. The fatwa bears the title "Jihad against Jews and Crusaders," terms to which we will return below.[107]

The fatwa begins with a standard praise to Allah and a reference to the Qur'an. Specifically, it quotes Sura 9:5: "But when the forbidden months are past, then fight and slay the pagans wherever ye find them, seize them, beleaguer them, and lie in wait for them in every stratagem (of war)." This verse is one of the most prominent of the jihad verses, as we will see in our detailed discussion of jihad below.

Bin Laden's fatwa then goes on to list three facts that are used as the cause for war against the United States. The first fact is given as follows:

First, for over seven years the United States has been occupying the lands of Islam in the holiest of places, the Arabian Peninsula, plundering its riches, dictating to its rulers, humiliating its people, terrorizing its neighbors, and turning its bases in the Peninsula into a spearhead through which to fight the neighboring Muslim peoples.[108]

The fatwa complains about the humiliation being inflicted by the United States on Muslim countries, and then provides the third fact as follows:

Third, if the Americans' aims behind these wars are religious and economic, the aim is also to serve the Jews' petty state and divert attention from its occupation of Jerusalem and murder of Muslims there. The best proof of this is their eagerness to destroy Iraq, the strongest neighboring Arab state, and their endeavor to fragment all the states of the region such as Iraq, Saudi Arabia, Egypt, and Sudan into paper statelets and through their disunion and weakness to guarantee Israel's survival and the continuation of the brutal crusade occupation of the Peninsula.[109]

Of course, there are political reasons given for opposing the United States. However, bin Laden perceives the political to be an instrument of the religious. The United States is using political and military power in order to carry out what is essentially a religious or anti-Islamic agenda that is aligned with Zionism, which is all about sacred space for bin Laden.[110]

The fatwa goes on to state that the proper response to these actions by the United States is a jihad. In addition to the Sura cited at the opening of his fatwa, bin Laden's authority for declaring a jihad is that "the ulema through Islamic history have agreed that *jihad* is an individual duty if an enemy destroys the Muslim countries."[111] He cites Imam Bin-Qadamah and Imam al-Kisai, among others. Bin Laden goes on to describe more specifically that the fatwa includes Americans and their allies.

To our knowledge no commentator has noted that bin Laden's fatwa is very similar to the sermon attributed to Urban II at the start of the First Crusade. This may be significant, as bin Laden has specifically called the United States "crusaders" (*al-salibiyyun*). As in the case of Urban II's speech, bin Laden begins by noting that enemy forces are occupying the holy sites. Like Urban II, he cites holy texts. And both Urban II and bin Laden quote scripture to support the contention that dying for the recovery of holy space will be rewarded in heaven. Of course, it is difficult to prove that bin Laden patterned his speech specifically in light of knowledge of Urban II's speech. Perhaps more likely is that both followed a similar logic of violence.

GROUP PRIVILEGING

At the broadest level, most Muslims feel that they are privileged relative to non-Muslims. Such privileging is the result of a number of factors, but it involves the belief that one is in the possession of God's most perfect revelation and way to salvation. We can find examples easily in the Qur'an, as in Sura 3:85–87: "If anyone desires a religion other than Islam (submission to god), never will it be accepted of him; and in the Hereafter he will be in the ranks of those that have lost (all spiritual good)."

In Ibn Hisham's biography of Muhammad, we also find numerous indications of the types of privileging favored by the prophet. In contrast to the notion of some brotherhood of all human beings, Muhammad is sometimes portrayed as making agreements that are explicitly meant to create kinship bonds that center on insiders and outsiders. Thus, in the famous Covenant of Medina, between Muslims and Medinans made upon his arrival at Medina, Muhammad extols the idea that "believers are friends one to another to the exclusion of outsiders."[112]

Likewise, the Hadith are permeated by the feeling of superiority among Muslims. Thus, Al-Bukhari records one tradition in which the religious status of a boy is at issue. The boy has a non-Muslim mother and a Muslim father. A group of Muslims state that custody must be given to the Muslim parent. The episode concludes with the statement that "Islam is always superior and never inferior" (*al-Islām ya'lū wa lā yu'lā*).[113]

But although the claim that Muslims see themselves as bearing a superior religion seems beyond debate, recent works have focused on the extent to which Muslims actually are intolerant of, and violent toward, non-Muslim people who live within Muslim domains. One of the most wide-ranging recent studies of Muslim privileging was conducted by Yohanan Friedmann in his *Tolerance and Coercion in Islam*.[114] Friedmann focuses on the legal traditions of Islam that have a strong interest in delineating the rights and responsibilities toward people who live in areas controlled by Muslim rulers. In general, those non-Muslim inhabitants are called *dhimmis*.

Perhaps the most detailed treatise of Muslim policy toward *dhimmis* is found in *Aḥkām ahl-al dhimma* by Ibn Qayyim al-Jawziyya (1292–1350). As Friedmann notes, Ibn Qayyim's hierarchy has Islam at the top, followed by Christianity, Judaism, Zoroastrianism, and "polytheists."[115] The latter is usually designated by the term *mushrikūn*. The Hanafi legal tradition dictates that Muslims should be punished equally as *dhimmis* in cases of murder. In part, this is based on Sura 5:45 ("judge in equity between them"), which refers to a case where Jewish litigants come to a Muslim court for justice.

However, the Al-Shafi school could argue the opposite point by appealing to the same texts or to alternative traditions. Indeed, Al-Shafi could argue that one should never kill a Muslim for killing a non-Muslim regardless of the motive (e.g., robbery). The injunction, "judge in equity between them" in Sura 5:45, for example, could be interpreted to apply only to judgments between Jewish litigants and not between Muslims and non-Muslims. The law of "equality," then, really means the application of retaliation, as required by Jewish law, as indicated by Sura 5:48 ("We ordained therein for them [Jews]: 'Life for life . . . '").

The payment of *jizya*, which has been variously interpreted as a tribute or tax, also underscores differences between Muslims and non-Muslims. Payment of *jizya* is mentoned only once in the Qur'an, in Sura 9:29: "Fight those who believe not . . . until they pay the *Jizya* with willing submission and feel themselves subdued." However, much scholarly discussion has resulted on the meaning of the Arabic expression (*hatta yu'tū l-jizyata 'an yadin wa-hum ṣāgirūn*) translated in A. Yusuf Ali's version as "Until they pay the *jizya* with willing submission, while feeling themselves subdued." In addition, the term *jizya*, usually derived from the verb *jazā* ("to give satisfaction"), itself has been the subject of voluminous study.[116]

The benign explanation is usually that *jizya* is a contribution that helps provide for the common defense or some other benefit. Thus, M. Muhammad Ali chastises Western scholars who describe the *jizya* as some sort of "religious tax whose payment entitled certain non-Muslims to security of life under Muslim rule."[117] M. Muhammad Ali notes that such taxes were levied before Islam and are a normal part of all states. In fact, M. Muhammad Ali adds, "[I]t was an act of great magnanimity on the part of the Prophet to confer complete autonomy on a people after conquering them and a paltry sum of tribute (*jizyah*) in such conditions was not a hardship but a boon."[118]

Friedmann shows, however, that *jizya* could be viewed as a sign of humiliation and dominance, as was apparently the case with the tribe called the Taghlib.[119] This was a Christian Arab tribe, and discussions ensued over whether their status was to be centered on their ethnicity more than on their religion. In any event, the Taghlib argued that they should not be required to pay *jizya* because they were fellow Arabs, and so not subject to such mistreatment. At the extreme end of the spectrum was Umar b. al-Khattab, who argued that the Taghlib were not to be considered People of the Book, so killing them was permissible in case they did not convert to Islam.[120]

Similar issues of group privileging are raised by the phenomenon of slavery in Muslim cultures. Aside from the inherent nature of slavery as one that privileges masters over slaves, there is also the issue of whether slaves could be converted by force. The reason some interpreters (e.g., Tabari) thought slaves could be converted by force is because slaves and black people in particular, were not thought to have a religion (*lā dīna lahum, lā yu'lamu mā dīnuhum*).[121] Thus, some of the coercive practices that may have been prohibited against People of the Book were not prohibited against people that did not possessed sacred texts.

Within the legal traditions, one manifestation of the relationship between group privileging and violence was the nature of punishment for physical injuries inflicted on Muslims by non-Muslims, and vice versa. One tradition certainly held that the killing of a non-Muslim by a Muslim should not be punished in the same way as the killing of a Muslim by another Muslim. This tradition is found in Ibn Hisham's biography of Muhammad in the section on the Covenant of Medina. Briefly, Muhammad's agreement reads as follows: "A believer shall not kill a believer because of [his killing] an unbeliever."[122]

Some Islamic traditions allowed blood money to be paid on behalf of the killer, by which the killer could avoid being killed himself. Here, too, there was discussion about equality. Some traditions held that a *dhimmi* paid the same amount in blood money as a Muslim until the days of 'Umar b. 'Abd al-Aziz, who valued at half the blood money of a *dhimmi*.[123]

There are many other categories of group privileges that one could discuss as well. For example, apostates formed another group against whom violence could be perpetrated. Abu Hanifa, in particular, thought that apostates should be killed, and considered even asking them to repent prior to execution to be discretionary.[124] Overall, therefore, the fundamental texts of Islam support a variety of group privileges. Now that we have established that group privileging does exist in Muslims cultures, we can show how group privileging has resulted and continues to result in violence.

SAUDI ANTI-JUDAISM AND VIOLENCE

Group privileging, following our theory, leads to violence when those who possess the privilege attempt to guard against loss, and/or when those who do not have the privilege attempt to acquire it. Violence may also be a response to any perceived or real scarcities of justice caused by group privileging. As we have seen above, a privileged religious group may believe that God has sanctioned or even obligated it to commit violence on a nonprivileged group. The nonprivileged group may be seen as threatening the power of the privileged group in some manner.

In the case of Muslims, one of the nonprivileged groups on which violence is permitted is the Jews. These cases of anti-Judaism also help us to understand why, in particular, Lawrence's view of an essentially peaceful Islam is defective. In order to understand why Lawrence's thesis is defective, we will summarize one of his examples, that of Saudi Arabia, a bit more carefully. He begins his analysis of Saudi Arabian fundamentalism with a summary of the key historical events, which we adapt here as well from Lawrence:

1902–32	'Abd al-'Aziz ibn Sa'ud contests other Arab chiefs for control of the Arabian penninsula.
1927	Treaty of Jidda, by which the British recognize Abd al-'Aziz as King of Hijaz, and Najd
1932	Kingdom of Saudi Arabia consolidated
1933	First oil concession to Aramco
1953	Death of King 'Abd al-'Aziz
1953–64	King Sa'ud deposed, goes into exile, replaced by King Faisal
1975	King Faisal Assassinated
1975–82	King Khalid
1979	Mecca Mosque rebellion
1982–	King Fahd[125]

Lawrence then argues specifically that Saudi Arabia's espousal of fundamentalism does not go as far back as the country's birth in 1932. He says that an opposite conclusion is at least equally valid, namely, that "Saudi Arabia has become a viable nation-state not by implementing Muslim norms but by using religion as a mask. In the name of Islam, the state introduced changes that would otherwise be unacceptable to a population little prepared and even less inclined to engage the modern world."[126]

The Saudi government was perceived as so un-Islamic, argues Lawrence, that a little-known upstart named Juhayman ibn Sayf al-'Utayba, almost succeeded in overthrowing the regime in the 1970s. Juhayman promoted his brother-in-law as a the *mahdi*, a sort of Messiah figure. Juhayman managed to capture the grand mosque of Mecca in 1979, and held it for two weeks before the government captured and executed him. For Lawrence, the Saudi royal family simply "played the fundamentalist game without being fundamentalists."[127]

Lawrence's thesis has many defects that need more scrutiny. His view of fundamentalism obscures how often the Saudi royal family appealed to religious arguments and Muslim scripture to further policies that certainly meet the rationale Religious Belief X, therefore Act of Violence Y. And one of the best types of sources for discovering true religious motives are communications not meant to be widely disseminated. Such communications disclose religious rationales that would be dangerous or even embarrassing if widely known. On the other hand, historians also need to be cautious in authenticating materials said to come from private communications.

One particularly excellent case of a private communication that seems authentic comes from 'Abd al-'Aziz ibn Sa'ud, king of Saudi Arabia. It is important to understand the background of these statements in order to appreciate confidence in their authenticity. According to Elie Kedouri, the respected historian of the Middle East, the statements were made in 1937 to Col. H. R. P. Dickson, who had retired from his post as British political agent in Kuwait the previous year.[128] Dickson paid a visit to the king in Riyadh and made a report of three private conversations. The report of these conversations was sent to the government of India and is now catalogued as part of the Foreign Office File.[129]

In one of these conversations, Sa'ud expresses his dismay that the British would think of supporting the Zionist cause in Palestine. Saud's statements bear repeating in some length:

> Today we and our subjects are deeply troubled over this Palestine question. . . . God's Holy Book (the Qur'an) contains God's own word and divine ordinance, and we commend to His Majesty's Government to read and carefully peruse that portion which deals with the Jews and especially what is to be their fate in the end. For God's words are unalterable and must be. . . . Our hatred for the Jews dates from God's condemnation of them for their persecution and rejection of Isa (Jesus Christ), and their subsequent rejection later of his chosen Prophet. . . . Verily the word of God teaches us, and we implicitly believe this O Dickson, that for a Muslim to kill a Jew, or for him to be killed by a Jew ensures him immediate entry into Heaven and into the august presence of God almighty.[130]

Sa'ud goes on to say that he is an "Imam" and "Spiritual Leader" of Arabia, and so his interpretation of the Qur'an is authoritative for his subjects.

So what is the fate of the Jews in the Qur'an to which the Saudi official alludes? The Qur'an specifies a violent end for Jews, and there are at least two references to this. The Qur'an (Sura 2:80) taunts unfaithful Jews who say, "The fire shall not touch us." This statement is echoed in Ibn Hisham's biography of the Prophet, in an episode in which the Jews believe that they will not be in hell more than a week.[131] However, Muhammad assures them that this is not the case. Jews will burn in hell forever. How does this create violence? As the Saudi official indicates, violence against Jews in this life will have no effect on their afterlife. They are all doomed to hell anyway.

Sa'ud engages in political reasoning during this conversation. He denies that he has any designs on ruling Palestine. He adds that this would "be a solution, but God forbid that this should happen, for I have enough to spare as it is." He sees Italy, Germany, and Turkey as "ravening wolves today seeking whom they may devour" and adds that "political interest demands that I keep with the best of them, that is England."[132]

Recall that Lawrence has argued that Saudi Arabia's rulers were not fundamentalist as far back as the inception of the country. Rather, Saudi rulers are supposed to be using Islam as a mask. The private conversations recorded here indicate that at least by 1939 Saudi rulers were using rhetoric that harks back to the Qur'an. Seeing fundamentalism as a recent reaction against colonialism does not explain why Sa'ud repeats a charge against Jews that is found in the Qur'an. In other words, the same violent rhetoric and mentality against Jews existed in the earliest available Islamic records and so cannot be attributed solely to modern reactions to colonialism.

In sum, politics does not explain Sa'ud's hatred of the Jews. Religion does. Of course, one can argue that Sa'ud was simply using anti-Jewish rhetoric that he knew would be effective with a Christian. For example, Sa'ud may have known that Christians have historically retaliated against Jews for the killing of Christ. However, Sa'ud's rhetoric has been echoed in many early Islamic sources as well. There is no reason to believe that Sa'ud did not believe what he said. In any case, his arguments for hatred against Jews are all religious. He cites the Qur'an as his main authority, and his specific reasons are the Jews' rejection of Muhammad, not to mention Jesus. These are Muhammad's reasons as well.

SALVATION

We have emphasized that a resource may be judged to be scarce when it meets one or more of the following requirements: (1) it is not immediately available; and (2) accessing it, maintaining it, or acquiring it requires the expense of a significant amount of social or physical capital and labor. Indeed, this is the case with the Islamic view of salvation. Unlike Christianity, salvation in Islam does not necessarily involve being "saved" from sin in the sense of removing some metaphysical substance by accepting Jesus.

However, as in Judaism and Christianity, salvation in Islam does involve the element of protection from God's wrath and punishment. In this regard, Islamic salvation has an eschatological element in the sense that the punishment will take place in the afterlife. This aspect of salvation becomes a scarce resource insofar as it is not available through all means, and it is of sufficient value that any obstacles toward salvation may become cause for violence.

In fact, the whole of the Qur'an is premised on the idea that unbelief should be and will be punished violently. On a more transcendent level, this idea is embodied in the concept of hell. The main word translated "hell" in the Qur'an is *jahannam*, which is clearly derived from the New Testament "Gehenna" (e.g., Matt. 5:22), which in turn refers to the Valley of Hinnom at Jerusalem. That valley was a place where refuse was constantly burning.[133]

The description of hell is that of fiery abode in which sinners suffer violence, as is explicit in Sura 3:55–56:

> Behold! God said: "O Jesus! I will take thee and raise thee to myself and clear thee (of the falsehoods) of those who blaspheme; I will make those who follow thee superior to those who reject faith, to the Day of Resurrection: Then shall ye all return to me, and I will judge between you of the matters wherein ye dispute. As to those who reject faith, I will punish them with terrible agony ['*addibuhum* '*adāban*] in this world and in the hereafter. Nor will they have anyone to help.

The cognate repetition of the Arabic lexeme '*aduba* (Form 2: to afflict, to torture, to pain), "I will tortorously torture them," shows the intensity of this violence.

Equally important, it should be noted that this violence cannot be strictly for defensive purposes, as may be argued in some interpretations of jihad. The verse clearly says that the reason for the torture is that the ones to be tortured have rejected faith. A similar concept of punishment for unbelief is found in Sura 7:94, and even M. Muhammad Ali, who otherwise advocates a peaceful view of Islam, has to admit that "[i]t is clear from this that God brings down his punishment upon a sinning people in order that they might turn to Him, in other words, that they may be awakened to a higher life."[134]

A standard explanation for such torture is that it is remedial and meant to bring about a greater good. Yet this explanation means that the devotees of Islam who believe this also accept the premise that violence is essential or necessary for unbelievers to achieve a higher life. Violence, therefore, appears to be not only an instrument of good; it is also portrayed as an essential part of Islam here.

Just as Islam endorses the idea that divine violence is a legitimate instrument against unbelievers because of their unbelief, the Qur'an can be read as endorsing the idea that unbelief is in itself an offense against which violence is a permissible defensive action. One clear case is found in Sura 3:149–52:

> O ye who believe. If ye obey the Unbelievers they will drive you back on your heels, and ye will turn back (from faith) to your own loss. Nay, God is your protector, and He is the best of helpers. Soon shall We cast terror into the hearts of the Unbelievers, for that they joined companions with God,

for which He had sent no authority; their abode will be the Fire and evil is the home of wrong-doers!

Again, the passage shows that the basis of violence against these unbelievers rests on religious reasons rather than on fear of physical harm from the unbelievers. The reason given for casting "terror" (ru'b) is that the offenders joined companions with God, a reference to polytheism. It is not stated that the reason for casting terror upon unbelievers is because Muslims fear being killed by unbelievers.

Yet Sura 3:149–52 also indicates the flaw of overlooking how salvation here constitutes a scarce resource that Muslims fear losing. Muslims might lose their salvation or enjoyment of paradise if they obey or fall prey to unbelievers. By becoming an unbeliever, one risks hellfire. Therefore, in the face of such potential loss of salvation, violence is deemed a proper defensive means against unbelievers.

It is in this context that the work of Ayatollah Morteza Motahari, one of the most prominent modern theoreticians of jihad, becomes relevant.[135] According to one biography, Motahari was born in 1920 in the Khorasan province of Iran.[136] He undertook theological studies in Qom under, among other luminaries, Ayatollah Khomeini. A fierce anticommunist who feared that atheism would destroy Islam, Motahari served as the head of the Department of Theology at the University of Tehran. On May 1, 1979, he was assassinated, reportedly at the instigation of Forqan, a rival Muslim faction. Motahari actually became known in the West because many of his works were translated into English.

One of those works is *Jihad: The Holy War of Islam and Its Legitimacy in the Qur'an*.[137] Motahari begins his treatise on jihad by citing Sura 9:29:

> And Fight those who have not faith in God, nor in the Hereafter, and (who) forbid not what God and his prophet have forbidden and (who) are not committed to the religion of truth, of those who have been brought [sic] the book, until they pay tribute, and they are the low.[138]

Motahari uses this passage to illustrate the principle that whenever one finds two passages in which one seems conditional and the other unconditional the conditional interpretation ought to be applied to both passages. This leads to the conclusion that jihad is not to be applied unconditionally to any non-Muslim at any time.

Among the conditions under which fighting is permitted is included fighting Christians and Jews who do not believe in God, which means belief in the *tawhid*, the unity of God as defined by Motahari's view of Islam. Christianity, says Motahari, has "no Christian structure of society, no Christian legal system, and no Christian rules as to how society is to be formed."[139] This is why Christianity does not have laws equivalent to jihad. Motahari also rejects what he interprets as Christian pacifism on the charge that it is "weak and limpid, with no ground to stand on."[140] His objection is that such pacificism seems to invite oppression and surrender. Any society in which Muslims perceive themselves to be humiliated is not a society in a state of peace. Islam is different in that its "mandate is to reform the whole world."[141]

The theory of jihad advocated by Motahari holds that "defense" is not to be interpreted merely as a response to an attack on the borders of a Muslim country. Rather, it is the obligation of Muslims to liberate Muslims who find themselves in a state of subjugation and humiliation outside of the borders of one's country. He provides the following example from the Palestinians:

> If we do not save them, what we are doing in effect is helping that oppressor's oppression against the oppressed.
>
> We may be in a situation whereby a party has not transgressed against us but has committed some type of injustice against a group from another people, who may be Muslims, or who may be non-Muslims. If they are Muslims—like today's plight of the Palestinians who have been exiled from their homes . . . is it permissible for us in such circumstances to hurry to the help of those oppressed Muslims and deliver them, or is this not permissible? Certainly this too is permissible. In fact it is obligatory. It would not be a case of commencing hostilities, it would be rushing to the defense of the oppressed especially if they are Muslims.[142]

Motahari's notion of jihad shows at once the aspect of group privileging, wherein oppressed Muslims receive special cosideration over non-Muslims. But moreover, salvation is intepreted in real-world terms as deliverance from oppression. Violence can be used in the defense of Muslims anywhere in the world who may be oppressed. Under this theory, any attacks against Israel or those who help Israel oppress the Palestinians are not seen as aggressive attacks, but rather as defensive actions.

Another category of aggression that would legitimize an Islamic jihad concerns cases in which governments pose some obstacle to Islamic notions of salvation. Motahari undergirds this argument by citing the case of Rustam, a pre-Islamic tyrant of ancient Iran who asked Muslims what their goal was. Muslims replied that their goal was "to change the worship of worshippers from the worship of those who worship to the worship of God . . . Our aim is to free these creatures of God."[143]

In fact, Motahari has a hierarchy of holiness when classifying jihads. Defense of one's person is holy, but defense of a nation is "more holy." The holiest grade is given to a supranational "humanitarian cause." This can mean that if a nation adopts an officially polytheistic stance that poses a threat to the practice of Islam, then "if a people fight for tawhid to combat shirk (polytheism), their fight is motivated by defense."[144] Similarly, Motahari argues that jihad in "defense of chastity" is permissible because losing one's chastity could mean losing the opportunity to enjoy paradise.[145]

According to Motahari, one must not use jihad to force polytheists to convert. However, it is legitimate to "fight polytheists in order to uproot evil from that society. Ridding society of evil polytheistic beliefs is one thing, while imposing the belief in *tawhid* is another."[146] It is, of course, unclear how ridding a society of polytheistic beliefs is not equivalent to imposing monotheism.

Preemptive jihad is also allowable. Motahari deduces this from the Sura al-Tawba (Sura 9), which speaks of fighting polytheists who do not keep promises. Motahari reasons that a predictable characteristic of polytheists is that "they do not observe one of the essential principles of humanity— keeping one's promises."[147] Given such a characteristic, it is only reasonable to be vigilant for the violation of agreements with polytheistic nations. And if a Muslim senses that a nation intends to destroy Muslims, then a defensive war is necessary because "if we wait, they will destroy us."[148]

It is interesting that Motahari sees jihad as a form of therapy, and uses medical rhetoric not unlike what we have seen in the Hebrew Bible and in Christianity when characterizing what are classified as defensive violent responses. Motahari outlines a hypothetical case in which a medical institution may destroy a new medicine that would cure a disease simply because the existence of that cure would cause the medical institution to go out of business. In such a case, it would be right to defend against the loss of that new medicine. Likewise, a fight against those who aggress against spiritual values "is necessary for mankind's prosperity and happiness."[149]

THE SEPTEMBER 11 HIJACKERS

Motahari's theory of salvation and jihad and that of Osama bin Laden are not simply musings voiced in Islamic ivory towers. They are put into practice, as in the attacks of September 11, 2001. In order to understand how the 9/11 attacks relate to ideas of Islamic salvation and jihad, we only need to review briefly some of the statements and actions of the hijackers themselves.

Perhaps the best known of the 9/11 hijackers is Mohamed Atta. A graduate of the Technical University in Hamburg, Atta spent considerable time traveling around the United States. Official reports hold that he was on board American Airlines Flight 11, which roared into the north tower of the World Trade Center.[150] Dated 1996, the Last Will and Testament of Mohamed Atta gives a glimpse into his mindset.

In the name of God all mighty

Death Certificate

This is what I want to happen after my death, I am Mohamed the son of Mohamed Elamir awad Elsayed: I believe that prophet Mohamed is God's messenger and time will come no doubt about that and God will resurrect people who are in their graves. I wanted my family and everyone who reads this will to fear the Almighty God and don't get deceived by what is in life and to fear God and to follow God and his prophets if they are real believers. In my memory, I want them to do what Ibrahim (a prophet) told his son to do, to die as a good Muslim.[151]

As near as we can tell from such statements, Atta crashed into the World Trade Center because he believed in Islam. He adds toward the end of his testament:

I wanted the people who look at my will to be one of the heads of the Sunna religion. Whoever it is, I want that person to be from where I grew up or any person I used to follow in prayer. People will be held responsible for not following the Muslim religion. I wanted the people who I left behind to hear God and not to be deceived by what life has to offer and to pray more to God and to be good believers. Whoever neglects this will or does not follow the religion, that person will be held responsible in the end.[152]

There can be few statements as conclusive as this when determining whether Islamic beliefs can cause violence. Atta simply recorded reasons for violence that have been voiced from the earliest recorded history of Islam.

SUMMARY

Islam is many things, and violence has been part of its theology from the beginning. As is the case with Christianity and Judaism, Islam has created scarce resources that always have the potential for violence. Muslim scriptural traditions have been held to be sufficiently valuable to kill others who may challenge their authority as indicated by the Qurayza massacre. Sacred spaces have been created, and many Muslims feel that death is part of the price of defending them. Group privilege has resulted in oppression and violence toward non-Muslims. Salvation is premised on the existence of a tortorous and eternalized violence called hellfire. Above all, Muhammad, who is held to be the paradigm of Muslim behavior, committed acts of unspeakable violence that are still imitated today.

NOTES

1. For a standard history of Islam, see Marshall G. S. Hodgson, *The Ventures of Islam: Conscience and History in a World Civilization*, 2 vols. (Chicago: University of Chicago Press, 1974).

2. Excellent anthologies of modern criticism have been edited by Ibn Warraq in the following works: *The Quest for the Historical Muhammad* (Amherst, NY: Prometheus Books, 2000); *The Origins of the Koran: Classic Essays in Islam's Holy Books* (Amherst, NY: Prometheus Books, 1998); and *What the Koran Really Says: Language, Text, and Commentary* (Amherst, NY: Prometheus Books, 2002). Of particular note are the works of John Wansbrough (see our bibliography). For more recent periods, see Reinhard Schulze, *A Modern History of the Islamic World*, trans. Azizeh Adodi (New York: New York University Press, 2002).

3. Al-Bukhari, 8/Book of Belief, 2/Darussalam Edition, 1:58.

4. M. Muhammad Ali, *The Religion of Islam*, 6th rev. ed. (Columbus, OH: Ahmadiyya Anjuman Isha'at Islam, 1990), p. 4. Ahmadiyya Muslims have often been branded unorthodox by other Muslims. See further, Antonio R. Gualtieri, *Conscience and Coercion: Ahmadi Muslims and Orthodoxy in Pakistan* (Montreal: Guernica, 1989). M. Muhammad Ali, however, is seen as an authority by M. A. Draz (*Introduction to the Quran* [London: I. B. Tauris, 2000], p. 143 n 1), who utilizes the former's translation of the Qur'an.

5. This verse is cited by, among others, Carl Ernst, *Following Muhammad: Rethinking Islam in the Contemporary World* (Chapel Hill: University of North Carolina Press, 2003), p. 45.

6. Martin, *Does Christianity Cause War?* p. 204.

7. Ernst, *Following Muhammad*, especially pp. 5–10.

8. Ibid., p. 213.

9. Bruce Lawrence, *Shattering the Myth: Islam beyond Violence* (Princeton, NJ: Princeton University Press, 1998), p. 3. See also his *New Faiths, Old Fears: Muslims and Other Asian Immigrants in American Religious Life* (New York: Columbia University Press, 2002).

10. Lawrence, *Shattering the Myth*, p. 6.

11. Ibid., p. 9.

12. Ibid.

13. Ibid., p. 4.

14. Ibid., p. 33.

15. Ibid., p. 49.

16. Ibid., p. 55. For other representatives of the view that global economic forces are at the root of the problems between Islam and the West, see also Benjamin R. Barber, *Jihad vs. McWorld: Terrorism's Challenge to Democracy* (New York: Ballantine Books, 1995).

17. Lawrence, *Shattering the Myth*, p. 45.

18. Ibid., p. 35.

19. Ibid., p. 50.

20. Samuel P. Huntington, *The Clash of Civilizations and the Remaking of World Order* (New York: Simon & Schuster, 1996). For a recent response to Huntington, see

also Richard W. Bulliet, *The Case for Islamo-Christian Civilization* (New York: Columbia University Press, 2004).

21. Ernst, *Following Muhammad*, p. xviii.

22. Ibn Warraq, "Studies on Muhammad and the Rise of Islam," in *The Quest for the Historical Muhammad*, p. 24.

23. Ibid., p. 27. For a more general history of the Arab peoples, see Albert Hourani, *A History of the Arab Peoples* (Cambridge, MA: Harvard University Press, 1991). Hourani still repeats uncritically many of the stories about Muhammad found in Muslim sources.

24. Unless noted otherwise, all of our references to the biography of Muhammad will be to Ibn Hisham's version of Ibn Ishaq. For the Arabic text, we depend on 'Abd al-Malik Ibn Hishâm, *al-Sîrat al-Nabawîyah li-Ibn Hishâm*, 4 vols. (Beirut, Lebanon: Dar al-Kotob al-Ilmiyah, 2000). For a translation, see A. Guillaume, *The Life of Muhammad: A Translation of Ibn Ishaq's Sirat Rasul Allah* (London/Karachi: Oxford University Press, 1955). I follow Guillaume's translation except when noted otherwise.

25. Draz, *Introduction to the Qur'an*, pp. 3–11.

26. Al-Bukhari, 3/The Book of Revelation 1.3/Darussalam edition 1:46–47. See also M. Muhammad Ali, *A Manual of Hadith* (1941; reprint, Columbus, OH: Ahmadiyya Anjuman Isha'at Islam, 2001), pp. 3–4.

27. William A. Graham, *Beyond the Written Word: Oral Aspects of Scripture in the History of Religion* (Cambridge: Cambridge University Press, 1987), pp. 88–89. For a comparative study of scriptures in Islam, Christianity, and Hinduism, see the earlier and more ostensibly theological treatment of Ary A. Roest Crollius, *Thus They Were Hearing: The Word in the Experience of Revelation in the Qur'an and Hindu Scriptures* (Rome: Gregorian University, 1974). For a brief critical introduction to the Qur'an, see Michael Cook, *The Koran: A Very Short Introduction* (London: Oxford University Press, 2000).

28. Al-Bukhari, 4986–4987/Book of Virtues of the Qur'an, 3/Darussalam Edition 6.424–426. For the variety and contradictory traditions that existed among Sunni and Shiite traditions, see Hassein Modarressi, "Early Debates on the Integrity of the Qur'an: A Brief Survey," *Studia Islamica* 77 (1993): 5–39. See also Estelle Whelan, "Forgotten Witness: Evidence for the Early Codification of the Qur'an," *JAOS* 118, no. 1 (1998): 1–14.

29. Ignaz Goldziher, *Muslim Studies*, trans. S. M. Stern and C. R. Barber, 2 vols. (London: Allen and Unwin, 1967–71); Michael Cook, *Muslim Dogma: A Source Critical Study* (Cambridge: Cambridge University Press, 1981); Patricia Crone and Michael Cook, *Hagarism: The Making of the Islamic World* (Cambridge: Cambridge University Press, 1977); Joseph Schacht, *The Origins of Muhammadan Jurisprudence* (Oxford: Clarendon, 1950); and *An Introduction to Islamic Law* (Oxford: Clarendon, 1964).

30. Daniel A. Madigan, *The Qur'an's Self-Image: Writing and Authority in Islam's Scripture* (Princeton, NJ: Princeton University Press, 2001).

31. Ibid., p. 3.

32. Blaise Pascal, *Pensées*, ed. Gérard Ferreyrolles (Paris: Le livre de poche, 2000), p. 241: "Mahomet en défendant de lire, les apôtres en ordonnant de lire."

Pascal, in turn, was dependent on Hugo Grotius, *The Truth of Christianity* (*De la vérité de la Religion chrétienne*, 1627), 6.2.

33. See John Burton, *The Collection of the Qur'an* (Cambridge: Cambridge University Press, 1977); and Madigan, *The Qur'an's Self-Image*, pp. 32, 35.

34. Graham, *Beyond the Written Word*.

35. Madigan, *Qur'an's Self-Image*, pp. 54–55.

36. Ibid., pp. 82, 178.

37. Ibid., p. 56.

38. Ibid., p. 178.

39. Ibid.

40. Guillaume, *Life of Muhammad*, p. 252.

41. See Jaffee, *Torah in the Mouth*.

42. See Graham, *Beyond the Written Word*, p. 199 n 3.

43. Francesco Gabrieli, *Arab Historians of the Crusades*, trans. E. J. Costello (New York: Barnes & Noble, 1969), p. 164.

44. For a comparison of Muhammad and Jesus, see Phipps, *Muhammad and Jesus*.

45. Draz, *Introduction to the Qur'an*, p. 1.

46. On the question of whether Islamic theology had notions of inspiration akin to those in Christianity, see Josef van Ess, "Verbal Inspiration? Language and Revelation in Classical Islamic Theology," in *The Qur'an as Text*, ed. Stefan Wild (Leiden: Brill, 1996), pp. 177–94.

47. For a Weberian ("charisma" as a feature of leadership) treatment of Muhammad's authority, see Hamid Dabashi, *Authority in Islam: From the Rise of Muhammad to the Establishment of the Umayyads* (New Brunswick, NJ: Transaction, 2002), especially pp. 33–70.

48. For the view that the importance of extra-Qur'anic traditions are being diminished and Qur'anic hermeneutics increasing, see Reinhard Schulze, *A Modern History of the Islamic World*, trans. Azizeh Adodi (New York: New York University Press, 2002), p. 292.

49. Al-Bukhari, 4987/ The Book of Virtues of the Qur'an, 3/Darussalam edition 6:426.

50. Al-Bukhari, 7300/ Holding Fast to the Qur'an and the Sunna, 5/Darussalam edition, 9:245.

51. Al-Bukhari, 7368/Holding Fast to the Qur'an and the Sunna, 28/Darussalam edition, 9:282.

52. M. Muhammad Ali, *Introduction to the Holy Qur'an* (1936; reprint, Lahore, Pakistan: Ahmadiyya, 1992), p. 33.

53. M. Muhammad Ali, *Muhammad and Christ* (1921; reprint, Lahore, Pakistan: Ahmadiayya, 1993), p. 4.

54. Ali, *The Religion of Islam*, p. 5.

55. See further H. Lazarus-Yafeh, *Intertwined Worlds* (Princeton, NJ: Princeton University Press, 1992), pp. 19–35; Uri Rubin, *Between Bible and Qur'an: The Children of Israel and the Islamic Self Image* (Princeton, NJ: Darwin Press, 1999), especially pp. 205–206.

56. For example, see the extended comparison between the Christian/Jewish

scriptures and the Qur'an made by the Hanbali scholar Ibn Taymiyya (1263–1328). For the text, see Thomas F. Michel, ed., *A Muslim Theologian's Reponse to Christianity: Ibn Taymiyya's Al-Jawab Al-Sahih* (Delmar, NY: Caravan Books, 1984), especially pp. 350–69.

57. Ibn Qudama, *Al-Mughni*, vol. 6:296–298, cited in Yohann Friedmann, *Tolerance and Coercion in Islam: Interfaith Revelations in the Muslim Tradition* (Cambridge: Cambridge University Press, 2003), pp. 57–58 and n16.

58. Al-Bukhari, 4987/Book of the Virtues of the Qur'an, 3/Darussalam edition 6:426.

59. For a denial of the historicity of this episode, see W. N. Arafat, "New Light on the Story of the Banû Qurayza and the Jews of Medina," *JRAS* (1976): 100–107. Arafat's arguments have been ably refuted by M. J. Kister, "The Massacre of the Banû Qurayza: A Re-Examination of a Tradition," *Jerusalem Studies in Arabic and Islam* 8 (1986): 61–96.

60. Guillaume, *Life of Muhammad*, p. 251.

61. Ibn Hisham, *al-Sîrat*, 2:158.

62. Guillaume, *Life of Muhammad*, p. 251.

63. Ibid., p. 253. For views of Jews in Muslim traditions, see Rubin, *Between Bible and Qur'an*.

64. Guillaume, *Life of Muhammad*, p. 461.

65. Ibid.

66. See further, Kister, "The Massacre of the Banû Qurayza.

67. Ibn Hisham, *al-Sîrat*, 3:213.

68. וַיְ סָעוּ וַיְהִי ־חִתַּת אֱלֹהִים עַל־הֶעָרִים אֲשֶׁר סְבִיבֹתֵיהֶם

69. Guillaume, *Life of Muhammad*, p. 462.

70. Ibid., p. 462/Ibn Hisham, *al-Sîrat*, 3:214.

71. Guillaume, *Life of Muhammad*, p. 462.

72. Ibid., p. 464.

73. Even some scholars (e.g, Kister, "The Massacre of the Banū Qurayza") who otherwise present a frank discussion of this episode seem to omit or downplay the tradition that Muhammad himself did the beheading. However, Ibn Hisham (*al-Sîrat*, 3:218) leaves little doubt that Muhammad is meant because the verb (daraba="strike off [heads]") is singular, and no other grammatical subject is seen as an antecedent but Muhammad.

74. Guillaume, *Life of Muhammad*, p. 464.

75. Ibid.

76. Marmaduke Muhammed Pickthal, *Al-amin: Life Sketch of the Life of Muhammed* (New Dehli: Kitab Bhavan, 2003), p. 60. Similarly sanitized is the version offered by Tahia al-Ismail, *The Life of Muhammad: His Life Based on the Earliest Sources* (London: Ta Ha Publishers, 1988), pp. 169–70. A brief, but more speculative, apologetic is provided in W. Montgomery Watt, *Muhammad: Prophet and Statesman* (New York: Oxford University Press, 1961), pp. 173–74.

77. Alexander Kronemer and Michael Wolfe, *Muhammad: Legacy of a Prophet* (Kikim Media and Unity Production Foundation, 2002). Funding was credited to, among other sources, the Corporation for Public Broadcasting, Arabian Bulk Trade, El-Hibri Foundation, and the Qureishi Family Trust.

78. The quotation of Karen Armstrong is on page 44 of the PBS transcript, in

PDF format, at http://www.pbs.org/muhammad/transcripts/muhammad_script.pdf), which can be accessed through the PBS Web site: http://www.pbs.org/muhammad /film_transcripts.shtml (accessed on March 7, 2005). We have not used all capitals for some of the proper names in the transcript. See also her comments on the Qurayẓa massacre in Karen Armstrong, *Muhammad: A Biography of the Prophet* (New York: HarperCollins, 1992), pp. 206–10. Armstrong shows no acquaintance with the primary Arabic sources of the biography of Muhammad, as evidenced by her frequent citation of Arabic sources only through English translations.

79. The quotation from Bassiouni is from the PBS transcript at: http://www.pbs.org/muhammad/transcripts/bassiouni.html (last accessed on March 7, 2005). Another example of the idea that Islam came to "civilize" is found in John L. Esposito, *Unholy War: Terror in the Name of Islam* (New York: Oxford University Press, 2002), pp. 29–30.

80. Al-Bukhari, 6802/Book of Al-Hudud, 15/Darussalam edition, 8.415.

81. See especially articles 2 and 3 of the Geneva Convention Relative to the Treatment of Prisoners, adopted formally on August 12, 1949 by the Diplomatic Conference for the Establishment of International Conventions for the Protection of Victims of War. Available online at http://www.unhchr.ch/html/menu3/b/91.htm (accessed July 19, 2004).

82. See also article 2, which speaks of the right not be discriminated against because of religion, and article 18, which speaks of the right to change religion, in the Universal Declaration of Human Rights proclaimed by the United Nations in 1948. For the text, see Ian Brownlie, ed., *Basic Documents on Human Rights*, 3rd ed. (Oxford: Clarendon, 1992), pp. 22, 25.

83. *The Effect of Islamic Legislation on Crime Prevention in Saudi Arabia: Proceedings of the Symposium Held in Riyadh, 16–21 Shawal 1936 A. H. [9–13 October, 1976]* (Riyadh: Ministry of the Interior, Kingdom of Saudi Arabia, 1980).

84. Ibid., p. 369.

85. Al-Khattan, "Effect of Religion against Crime," in ibid., p. 212.

86. Ibid., pp. 212–13.

87. Ibid., pp. 89–145.

88. Ibid., p. 95.

89. Ibid., pp. 100–101.

90. Ibid., p. 101.

91. My count based on Hanna E. Kassis, *A Concordance of the Qur'an* (Berkeley and Los Angeles: University of California Press, 1983), p. 545.

92. Ali, *Manual of Hadith*, p. 58.

93. Ali, *The Religion of Islam*, p. 378. For a critical study of the role of the Abraham traditions in Islam, see Reuven Firestone, *Journeys in Holy Lands: The Evolution of the Abraham-Ishmael Legends in Islamic Exegesis* (Albany: State University of New York, 1990).

94. Ali, *The Religion of Islam*, p. 395.

95. Al-Bukhari, 1867/Virtues of Al-Madina, 1/Darussalam Edition, 3:68.

96. Crone and Cook, *Hagarism*.

97. For example, Guillaume, *The Life of Muhammad*, p. 258: "And when the *qibla* was changed from Syria to the Ka'ba. . . . "

98. Gabrieli, *Arab Historians of the Crusades*, p. 144. See also Carole Hillebrand, *The Crusades: Islamic Perspectives* (New York: Routledge, 2000).

99. See Oleg Grabar, *The Shape of the Holy: Early Islamic Jerusalem* (Princeton, NJ: Princeton University Press, 1996), pp. 52–116. For an earlier treatment, with observations about the state of this area in the early twentieth century, see Martin S. Briggs, *Muhammadan Architecture in Egypt and Palestine* (1924; reprint, New York: Da Capo, 1974), pp. 31–37.

100. Jerome M. Segal et al., *Negotiating Jerusalem* (Albany: State University of New York Press, 2000), p. 144, table 3.3.

101. Ibid., p. 146, table 3.4.

102. Gabrieli, *Arab Historians of the Crusades*, p. 147.

103. Hamid Algar, *Wahhabism: A Critical Essay* (Oneonta, NY: Islamic Publications International, 2002), p. 24. Algar cautions against seeing the Wahhabis as a group within Sunni Islam. Instead, Algar, believes that the Wahhabis should be seen as a separate sect. For the view that Wahhab, the founder, was more tolerant than what is now called Wahhabism, see Natana J. Delong-Bas, *Wahhabi Islam: From Revival and Reform to Global Jihad* (New York: Oxford University Press, 2004).

104. Adapted from Algar, *Wahhabism*, p. 24.

105. For accounts of Wahhabi attacks on Shiite holy sites, see Yitzhak Nakhash, *The Shi'is of Iraq* (Princeton, NJ: Princeton University Press, 1994), pp. 27–29, 155.

106. For a biography, see Yossef Bodansky, *Bin Laden: The Man Who Declared War on America* (Roseville, CA: Prima, 2001). For an official US view of bin Laden and his worldview, see *The 9/11 Commission Report: Final Report of the National Commission on Terrorist Attacks upon the United States* (New York: W. W. Norton, 2004), especially pp. 47–52.

107. English text of the fatwa is from the following Cornell University Web site: http://www.library.cornell.edu/colldev/mideast/wif.htm. For the Arabic text, we consulted that published in the periodical *Al-Quds al-Arabi*, a copy of which may also be found on the Cornell University Web site: http://www.library.cornell.edu/colldev/mideast/fatw2.htm (accessed August 8, 2004).

108. Ibid.

109. Ibid.

110. Ibid.

111. Ibid. See also Ahmed S. Hashim, "The World according to Usama Bin Laden," *Naval War College Review* 54, no. 4 (Autumn 2001): 11–36.

112. Guillaume, *The Life of Muhammad*, p. 232.

113. Al-Bukhari, 1353/Book of Funerals 79/Darussalam edition 2.250. Friedmann (*Tolerance and Coercion*, p. 35) translates this as "Islam is exalted and nothing is exalted above it."

114. Friedmann, *Tolerance and Coercion*.

115. Ibid., p. 38.

116. See, for example, Franz Rosenthal, "Some Minor Problems in the Qur'an," in *What the Quran Really Says: Language, Text and Commentary*, ed. Ibn Warraq (Amherst, NY: Prometheus Books, 2002), pp. 324–27; Meïr M. Bravmann, "The Ancient Background of the Qur'anic Concept of Al-Gizyatu 'Am Yadin," *Arabica* 13 (1960): 307–14 and *Arabica* 14 (1967): 90–91, as reprinted in *What the Koran Really*

Says, 350–63; and "A Propos de Qur'an IX.29: Ḥattā Yu'Ṭū L-Gizyata Wa-Hum Ṣagirūna," *Arabica* 10 (1963): 94–95, as reprinted *What the Koran Really Says*, pp. 348–49.

117. Ali, *The Religion of Islam*, p. 428.

118. Ibid.

119. Friedmann, *Tolerance and Coercion*, pp. 62–64.

120. Ibid., p. 63.

121. Ibid., p. 118.

122. Ibid., p. 40n146.

123. Ibid., p. 41.

124. Ibid., p. 127.

125. Lawrence, *Shattering the Myth*, p. 85.

126. Ibid., p. 85.

127. Ibid., p. 88.

128. Eli Kedourie, *Islam in the Modern World and Other Studies* (New York: Holt, Rinehart and Winston, 1980).

129. Text of Foreign Office File 3701/20822 E7201/22/31, as printed in ibid., pp. 70–74.

130. Ibid., pp. 71–72.

131. Guillaume, *The Life of Muhammad*, p. 252.

132. Kedourie, *Islam in the Modern World*, p. 72.

133. L. Bailey, "Gehenna: The Topography of Hell," *Biblical Archaeologist* 49 (1986): 187–91.

134. Ali, *The Religion of Islam*, pp. 229–30.

135. See Lawrence, *Shattering the Myth*, pp. 115–17, 175–78.

136. See the Iran Chamber Society Web site at http://www.iranchamber.com/personalities/mmotahari/morteza_motahari.php (accessed August 7, 2004).

137. Morteza Motahari, *The Holy War of Islam*, trans. Mohammad Salman Tawhidi; available at ibid. This was also the source of our brief biography.

138. Ibid.

139. Ibid., p. 4.

140. Ibid., p. 10.

141. Ibid.

142. Ibid., pp. 16–17, adapted.

143. Ibid., p. 17.

144. Ibid., p. 26.

145. Ibid., p. 23.

146. Ibid.

147. Ibid., p. 31.

148. Ibid., p. 32.

149. Ibid., p. 34.

150. For his brief biography, see *The 9/11 Commission Report*, pp. 160-61.

151. The will and testament is found on the PBS Web site: http://www.pbs.org/wgbh/pages/frontline/shows/network/personal/attawill.html (accessed on March 7, 2005).

152. Ibid.

CHAPTER 11

ACADEMIC DEFENSES
OF ISLAMIC VIOLENCE

As we have noted, there is no shortage of scholars—Muslim and non-Muslim—who promote the idea that Islam is essentially peaceful. The peaceful interpretation is represented by, among others, Mahmud Shaltut, author of *The Muhammedan Duty and Fighting in Islam (al-da'wah al-muḥammadiyah wa-al-qitāl fi al-Islām)*, which was published in 1948.[1] Likewise, M. Muhammad Ali also devotes a large section of his *The Religion of Islam* to promoting a defensive interpretation of jihad. Among Western academics, Bruce Lawrence and Carl Ernst have been recent vocal representatives of an "essentially" peaceful Islam.[2]

As we shall argue, many of the "peaceful" advocacy arguments are constructed in the same manner they would say Muslim fundamentalists construct their arguments. What remains at issue is that unverifiability rules both sides. In this chapter, we will argue that (1) speaking of an "essentially" peaceful Islam is philosophically unwarranted; (2) a purely defensive view of jihad is unwarranted; (3) "peace" can be deconstructed to mean a set of conditions that are favorable to Islam; and (4) colonialist explanations for Islamic violence are overly simplistic.

ESSENTIALISM AND THE "PEACEFUL" ISLAM

Many modern philosophers have rightly cautioned against committing acts of "essentialism."[3] The essentialist fallacy, usually traced at least as far back as Plato, claims that entities have unchanging characteristics that identify them as what they are. This has been at the root of racism, Orientalism, and myriad other "sins" in academia, not to mention in almost every other sector of society. However, it is precisely essentialism that is at the root of characterizations of Osama bin Laden as "hijacking" or "perverting" Islam. Such notions of "perversion," of course, are meaningless unless one has already decided what constitutes the "true" or "essential" Islam.[4]

As mentioned previously, Charles Kimball reflects this essentialism in his *When Religion Becomes Evil*.[5] Recall that Kimball criticizes American Christian fundamentalists for insisting that "Allah is not the same God."[6] Of course, Kimball presumes that a particular definition of God, in this case his homogenizing one, is the "truest" definition, thus continuing the legitimization of the same scarce resource ("the true understanding of God") that leads people to commit violence in the first place.

The contradiction of essentialism can be seen quite blatantly in Ernst's book *Following Muhammad*, which is premised on the idea that non-Muslims have imposed violent intepretations on Islam. At the conclusion of his book, Ernst says that "[f]ollowing Muhammad . . . is the responsibility of those who consider themselves Muslims. It is the responsibility of non-Muslims to acknowledge the legitimacy of that enterprise."[7]

Ernst would seem to invalidate the cries of oppression from former Muslims or Muslims who say that Islam is oppressing them. For example, many Muslim and former Muslim women argue that Islam has oppresssed them and they can provide an "insider's" perspective. Many critics of Islam also recognize the arbitrary nature of "peace" and "rights" in Islam. As Eleanor Abdella Doumato observes, "Islamic rhetoric can be manipulated to obfuscate what people actually mean when they talk about 'rights.'"[8] So how does letting Muslims speak for themselves about Islam validate these viewpoints?

More important, according to Ernst, the self-described Muslim known as Osama bin Laden is not following a legimate brand of Islam. Commenting on bin Laden, Ernst tells us that "[t]hose of us who have studied the text of the Qur'an, the writings of the great poets, and the history of Islamic civilizations, feel very keenly the distortion and perversion of Islamic symbols and authority perpetrated by these modern extremists."[9] But how is Ernst, himself a non-Muslim, acknowledging the legitimacy of bin Laden, a self-described Muslim, to define what following Muhammad means for him? Clearly, Ernst himself is working from an essentialist vision of what the true and unperverted Islam is.

It is likewise fatuous to argue that "consensus" determines what is essential in a religion. By this standard, a bin Laden may indeed not represent the true Islam. However, were we to apply this standard consistently, then anyone could be classified as "deviant" at the inception of any new religion. This would mean, for example, that Jesus' teachings would be deemed illegitimate since at the time these were introduced, they did not represent the consensus of Judaism. Likewise, Muhammad would have to be deemed illegitimate if we measured consensus by the number of adherents to the poly-theism portrayed as existing at the time of Muhammad's arrival. By the same token, bin Laden could argue that his deviation is no less legitimate, and he would be on no less verifiable grounds than any other understanding of Islam.

Indeed, we acknowledge that peaceful interpretations are possible in many Muslim texts. However, until non-Muslim and Muslim scholars allow that violent and offensive interpretations of Islamic texts are no less theological and verifiable than peaceful ones, the whole subject of violence in Islam still centers on essentialism. Scholars must either agree that they will apply empirico-rationalist criteria consistently or admit that they are as arbitrary and as theological as anyone deemed "deviant."

THE MYTH OF THE "DEFENSIVE" JIHAD

Much of the controversy about Islamic violence centers on the meaning of a single word, "jihad." It is important, therefore, to know some of the most basic linguistic issues in interpreting and translating this word. The root is *j-h-d*, which in the Arabic first form, *jahada*, means, according to Lane's standard lexicon, "He strove, laboured, or toiled."[10] Thus, Muslim writers say that it could just as well be used to describe a Muslim's struggle to live a righteous life. It is the third grammatical form of the Arabic verb that is used for a more violent physical fighting, but that in itself does not mean fighting is unjustified or not defensive.

Some Muslim thinkers urge a distinction between a "lesser jihad (*al-jihād al-āṣghar*), which refers to spiritual self-discpline, and the "greater jihad" (*al-jihād al-akbar*), which, depending on the intepreter, refers to war on behalf of Islam fought under strict regulations. In the case of the war on behalf of Islam, one sees the expressions "Jihad of the Sword" (*jihād al-sayf*) and "Jihad in the Path of God" (*Jihād fī sabīl Allah*). In any case, most traditionalist Muslim interpreters admit that jihad can be violent, even if justified.

Both Muslim and non-Muslim scholars who support a pacificistic or defensive notion of jihad focus on one or more of the following issues: (1) misunderstanding the meaning of the root *j-h-d*; (2) inattention to the chronology and abrogation of Qur'anic passages; (3) not understanding that when jihad does refer to fighting, it is defensive fighting; (4) generalizing what the Qur'an restricts; and (5) the forbidding in the Qur'an of coercion in religion.

In regard to the word "jihad," these authors would rightly note that the root *j-h-d* does not necessarily involve the infliction of physical injury to another person. The root meaning is "struggle," and this need not involve violence.

However, the fact that jihad does not always involve violence does not mean that jihad never involves violence. Indeed, even some of the defensive interpretations of jihad concede that violence is at least sometimes what jihad means.

Debatable readings of texts are sometimes elicited in support of the peaceful jihad. For example, M. Muhammad Ali quotes a Hadith in which Muhammad states that "the hajj [pilgrimage] is the most excellent of all *jihad*s."[11] However, it is not clear that as found in Al-Bukhari, this is a general statement that applies to both men and women.[12] The context is a question asked by Muhammad's wife Aisha. Prior to her question Al-Bukhari relates that the Prophet was asked which Muslim deed was the most important, and he answered that it was the *shahadah* (believing in Allah and his messenger).

When asked what deed was next in importance, Muhammad answered that it was "Jihad in Allah's cause" (*jihād fī sabīl 'Allahi*), which is certainly believed to be violent by most interpreters. However, Aisha remarked that "[w]e consider *Jihad* as the best deed. Should we not participate in *Jihad?*" It is only then that the Prophet said that the best jihad was the "Hajj-Mabrur" (*la-kunna 'afdalu al-jihādi hajj mabrur*). Thus, Muhammad's answer could be understood as saying that the best jihad *for women* is the Hajj-Mabrur. Otherwise, one must accept that Muhammad was wrong when he said that the second best deed was fighting for Allah.

A second argument for a defensive jihad is premised on the notion that the Qur'an was not written in strict chronological order, something critical scholars of the Qur'an would also admit. Thus, one must take into account the circumstances and relative dates when a particular Qur'anic passage was revealed. One also must make a distinction between the portions of the Qur'an written at Mecca, when the Prophet urged caution, and those portions written at Medina, where fighting became a defensive necessity. A whole corpus of literature called *asbab al-nuzul* was devoted to determining the relative chronology and circumstances that would aid in providing the proper interpretation to a passage.[13]

In his detailed linguistic study of jihad, Reuven Firestone opines that "the classic evolutionary theory" of war can be summarized as follows:[14]

Stage	Description	Representative passages
1	Nonconfrontation	15:94–95
2	Defensive fighting	2:190, 22:39–40
3	Intitated attack allowed with restrictions	2:217, 2:191
4	Unconditional command to fight all unbelievers	2:216, 9:5, 9:29

The chronological argument is usually coupled with the hermeneutical procedure called *naskh*, or abrogation. The idea is that one passage, usually a later one, cancels a contradictory instruction or revelation given in an earlier passage. The justification for this procedure is often based on a passage such as Sura 2:106: "Whatever message we abrogate or cause to be forgotten, we bring one better than it or one like it."[15]

However, some Muslim commentators deny that *naskh* means contradicting a previous revelation or instruction. For example, M. Muhammad Ali says that in Sura 2:106, "cause to be forgotten" means that "the world was made to forget."[16] But such a translation is ad hoc and grammatically unwarranted because the Arabic pronominal suffix-*hā* ("it"), attached to the verb "abrogate," refers back to "one of the messages [*ayat*]." Therefore "the world," a word nowhere mentioned in the text, cannot be the grammatical referent at all.[17]

Likewise, Sura 16:101 says, "When we substitute one revelation for another—and Allah knows best what He reveals (in stages)—they say: 'Thou art but only a forger.'" Since this Sura, argues M. Muhammad Ali, was revealed at Mecca, it cannot refer to previous Qur'anic revelations, as the Mecca revelations were the first. Thus, the abrogation most likely refers to the fact that the Qur'an "had taken the place of previous revelations," such as those found in the Bible.[18] But this abrogation also involves circular reasoning, as the only criterion for locating the Sura at Mecca is premised on the idea that abrogation cannot occur.

Sometimes M. Muhammad Ali admits that "it is an abrogation, but not an abrogation of words of the Qur'an; rather an abrogation of a misconception of their meaning."[19] A further argument against abrogation is that the Qur'an cannot contradict itself, and therefore there can be no such thing as a true abrogation. Again, both of these claims are based on circular reasoning or on dubious evidence.

The third argument for a defensive jihad does not deny that sometimes jihad refers to fighting non-Muslims. Rather, the argument is that jihad is permitted only for defense. Never is a jihad to be used to convert people to Islam. Such a notion is supported with texts such as Sura 10:99: "If it had been thy Lord's Will, They all would have believed,—All who are on earth! Wilt thou then compel mankind, against their will to believe?"

An offensive interpretation of jihad, on the other hand, can be readily sustained on the basis of very clear passages in the Hadith literature. One case in point is recorded in Al-Bukhari's *Book of Al-Jizya*. The report speaks of a convert named Al-Hurmuzan who is approached by Umar, the caliph. Umar says to Al-Humurzan, "I would like to consult you regarding these countries which I intend to invade."[20] One of these lands is Khosrau, and soon an expedition, led by An-Nu'man bin Murraqin, is on its way. However, upon arrival it becomes clear that the representatives of Khosrau do not know who these Muslims are; one of those unfortunate foreigners asks, "Who are you?" (*ma antum*). The Muslim answer is, "Our Prophet . . . has ordered us to fight you till you worship Allah alone or give *jizya*," a sure reference to Sura 9:29.[21] The Muslim envoy adds that any Muslim killed will enter paradise.

This story illustrates a number of points that refute any essentially peaceful view of Islam. First, the report itself makes clear that the expedition was not mounted because of any attack from the people of Khosrau. Indeed, the people of Khosrau are depicted as not even knowing who the invading Muslims are. Second, the story illustrates that the sole purpose expressed for this conquest is obedience to the command found in Sura 9:29. Third, this means that explanations such as that of M. Muhammad Ali, which restrict the command only to the time and place specifically mentioned in Sura 9:29, were not understood the same way by many early Muslims. Fourth, the idea that such expeditions are reactions to colonialism is not to be found here, as colonialism is portrayed here as a Muslim religious obligation.

A fourth argument for a defensive view of jihad is that the Qur'an explicitly forbids Muslims to convert non-Muslims by force. Ernst, M. Muhammad Ali, and others, usually cite as proof Sura 2:256:[22]

> Let there be no compulsion in religion; Truth stands out clear from error; whoever rejects Evil and believes in God hath grasped the most trustworthy Hand-hold, that never breaks. And God heareth and knoweth all things.

Surprisingly, Ernst and other defenders of the peaceful interpretation simply quote this text without much comment, as though it were self-explanatory or not open to any other interpretation.[23]

However, the expression "let there be no compulsion in religion (*lā ikrāha fī al-dīn*) is open to interpretations that are no less verifiable than the ones for an offensive jihad. Linguistically, the verse can also be understood as a simple description of a current state of affairs (e.g., "it is not feasible to enforce conversion at the moment") rather than as a command that prohibits coercion at any time (see also Sura 10:99). Rudi Paret, though acknowledging that it is possible to translate it as an expression of tolerance, regards as more likely the understanding that the Qur'an is not proclaiming tolerance, but rather expressing resignation.[24]

As Friedmann notes, the *asbāb al-nuzūl* literature, which attempts to provide the events corresponding to this passage, associates it with the expulsion of the Jewish tribe Banu Naḍīr, from Medina around 625 CE.[25] This expulsion hardly constitutes an example of tolerance. Moreover, the passage itself could be interpreted to be addressing only other Muslims. In fact, many early

Muslim interpreters argued that this verse has been abrograted by the more violent Sura 9:29, among others.[26]

A fifth argument for a defensive jihad centers on exegesis of the actual jihad passages themselves. M. Muhammad Ali, in particular, focuses on Sura 9:5, which was quoted by bin Laden for his fatwa against the United States. Thus, M. Muhammad Ali would disagree with bin Laden's interpretation of Sura 9:5 because bin Laden is applying to the United States what only applies to the specific historical actors mentioned in the text. M. Muhammad Ali explicitly states that it would be "a mistake to regard the order as including all idolatrous people living anywhere in the world or even in Arabia."[27]

For M. Muhammad Ali, any fighting mentioned in 9:5 is to be directed at the specific tribes that had violated an agreement with Muhammad. M. Muhammad Ali urges us to read 9:5 in light of the preceding verse, and so we present Sura 9:4–6 for the sake of providing context for the reader:

> (But the treaties are) not dissolved with those Pagans with whom ye have entered into alliance and who have not subsequently failed you in aught, nor aided any one against you. So fulfill your engagments with them to the end of their term. For God loves the righteous.

> But when the forbidden months are past, then fight and slay the pagans wherever you find them, and seize them, beleaguer them, and lie in wait for them, In every strategem (of war); But if they repent and establish regular prayers and practice regular charity, then open the way for them; For God is Oft-forgiving, Most Merciful.

> If one amongst the Pagans ask thee for asylum Grant it to him, so that he may hear the Word of God; and then escort him to where he can be secure. That is because they are Men without Knowledge.

The pagans being discussed here, M. Muhammad Ali contends, are the ones mentioned in 8:55–56: "For the worst of beasts in the sight of God are those who reject Him; They will not believe. They are those with whom you made a covenant. But they break the covenant every time, and they have not the fear (of God)." In sum, for M. Muhammad Ali, this Qur'anic passage cannot be used to justify any sort of violent treatment of unbelievers in modern times.

But one can see the inconsistency of arguing, as M. Muhammad Ali does, that because Sura 9:5 was supposedly speaking only about specific enemies on a particular historical occasion, it cannot be used to authorize violence today. Apparently, the premise is that one is not authorized to follow examples that took place in historical time. We can schematize this apparent rationale is as follows: *Any command to or about historical person X applies only to historical person X.*

However, M. Muhammad Ali and all other Qur'anic interpretation is premised, at one time or another, on the opposite hermeneutics. That is to say, all modern Muslim rules drawn from the Qur'an took place in a discrete or presumed historically bounded space and time in Muslim scriptural traditions. This does not prevent modern Muslims from taking those actions to serve as models for behavior today.

M. Muhammad Ali, for example, does not argue that because Muhammad was speaking to actual historical people when he recommended that they not practice polytheism, the prohibiton of polytheism only applies to those particular people. M. Muhammad Ali does not argue that because God was threatening specific unbelievers with hellfire in the seventh century, unbelievers should not feel similarly at peril today. M. Muhammad Ali's argument also contradicts the principle that the Qur'an teaches timeless moral truths. But if killing unbelievers in the seventh century was deemed just and good, then why is it not considered the same today? For example, unbelief alone was cited as the reason for punishment in authoritative texts we have cited (e.g., Sura 3:56–57, 149–52), not unbelief under conditions X, Y, or Z.

In sum, any view that jihad is essentially peaceful is based on premises and exegetical maneuvers that are no more consistent or verifiable than those that use the Qur'an to justify practices we would deem to be aggressive. If a violent jihad cannot be described as essentially part of Islam, a "peaceful" jihad cannot be described as essentially part of Islam either. The type of jihad selected is ultimately a theological and a value judgement that is not verifiable on empirico-rationalist grounds.

DECONSTRUCTING PEACE IN ISLAM

Our treatment of "love" in Christianity emphasized the flexibility of the concept, not to mention the fact that many Christian theologians conceive of violence as an expression of love. Likewise, some Islamic thinkers can conceive of "mercy" and "peace" as endorsing violence. Thus, just as the Christian R. A. Torrey could say that infanticide could be an act of love, Sayyid Qutb, sometimes called as the modern father of fundamantalist Islam, can say that "even the torment endured by the transgressors originates from Allah's mercy."[28]

Given our survey of Islamic exegesis, it also becomes clear that "peace" is a value-laden word. "Peace" means the state of affairs that best serves the interests of Islam. Thus, when the Qurayza tribe did not wish to surrender, Muhammad had no problem slaughtering them in batches. This could not have been a peaceful action from the viewpoint of the Qurayẓa. In fact, few actions reported in the Qur'an and Ibn Hisham's biography cannot be explained as instances of Islamic aggression and imperialism rather than self-less quests for peace.

In fact, from the viewpoint of many Christians of the early centuries of Islam, the latter was a fundamentally violent religion. For example, Hnan-isho', the East Syrian exegete (ca. 700), is quoted in the thirteenth century as saying that Islam "is a religion established by the sword and not a faith confirmed by miracles."[29] Even if this is not a historically accurate report of what Hnanisho' said, the perception of Islam as violent was sufficiently strong to use it as an argument by the thirteenth century, long before modern Western colonialism could be blamed.

When dicussing the meaning of the root *s-l-m*, which generates many of the words rendered as "peace" and its variants, Fazlur Rahman seems to gloss over the hegemonic and hierarchical nature of derivative forms. He tells us that the root *s-l-m* means "'to be safe,' 'whole' and 'integral,'" but he notes that the first form of the verb of that root is not found in the Qur'an.[30] Far more frequent is the fourth form of the verb, *aslam*, which means "he surrendered himself" or "gave himself up." Of course, the basic concept of the term "Islam" is submission, and "surrender to God's law" in particular, according to Rahman.[31] As we shall show later, all the Abrahamic religions originated as part of slave societies, which see "God" as a slavemaster who demands total obedience and submission.

It is in the context of this fundamental unverifiability of the entire system of Muslim hermeneutics that violence becomes not only possible but likely under certain definitions of "defense." If unbelievers are thought to pose a threat to the eternal well-being of a person, then it may be defensive to kill the threat. If unbelievers do not wish to pay the poll tax, that may threaten the security of an entire community, and so violence becomes defensive. If Islam cannot be described as essentially violent, it certainly cannot be described as essentially peaceful, either.

DISMANTLING COLONIAL EXPLANATIONS

The notion that modern colonialism is the key to Muslim violence is premised on the false notion that colonialism is a modern phenomenon. At the very least, this depends on how one defines "colonialism." In another study, we have defined colonialism as any form of social, political, or economic subjugation undertaken by a state and its allied institutions.[32] Colonialism is as old as recorded history if it is taken to mean the exploitation and subjugation of outsiders by organized states. The recognition that imperialism and colonialism extends long before the pre-Christian era is reflected in the work of Jon Berquist, among other biblical scholars, anthropologists, and historians.[33]

The Assyrian and Persian empires, for example, were not doing much that is different from the British or Americans, with the exception of improved technology and larger territories for the modern versions of empire. Nonetheless, the idea of exploiting the resources of conquered people, using them for cheap labor; the existence of a periphery and a core; and the imposition of cultural norms were all present then. Likewise, subjugated people reacted in ways that were similar to many modern peoples. They asserted their identities.[34] They fought back. They used subversive literature. They called on their gods to save them from the imperialist enemy.

Bruce Lawrence, whose views we introduced in chapter 10, misses the fundamentally imperialistic nature of Islam as depicted in the Qur'an, the Sira (Islamic biographies of Muhammad), and the Hadith. Lawrence quotes 'Abd al-'Aziz Khayyat to show that at least some Muslims think Sharī'a, prohibits "the elevation of country above God (nationalism)."[35] Of course, the other side is that many textual traditions can also be interpreted to assume that the goal of Islam is to bring the entire earth under Muslim rule. Thus, Muhammad is once reported to have preached to the Jews that "the earth belongs to Allah and His messenger" (*al-'arḍa llāhi wa-rasūlihi*).[36] This belief was then used to authorize the expulsions and dispossession the Jews of Beit-ul-Midras.

In fact, all three major Abrahamic religions have imperialism, control of the entire earth, as a fundamental goal if one judges by their basic sacred scriptures. The Hebrew Bible speaks of God's (Elohim) possession of all the earth (Psalm 82).[37] Jesus commands the spreading of Christianity over the entire world (Matt. 28:18–19), thus following the model of the Roman Empire long before the rise of Constantine. Islam, likewise, envisions the whole world under the command of Allah. If there is anything "essential" or "fundamental" in all of the Abrahamic religions it is the idea that the particular god each worships has or should have universal dominion.

It is difficult to maintain the argument that a bin Laden is simply part of a modern reaction against an imperialistic America when one considers a previous war between the United States and Muslim powers. Few Americans know that America fought against Islamic nations from 1801 to 1805 under Thomas Jefferson.[38] At that time, Tripoli, Algiers, Tunisia, and Morocco formed the so-called Barbary States, which had been harrassing American and European ships for years. Prisoners and ships were often taken, and ransom was routinely paid. In 1797 President John Adams ratified the Treaty of Tripoli, famous for having a clause explicitly stating that the government of the United States "is not in any sense founded on the Christian Religion." The treaty was supposed to bring hostilities to an end, but treaties soon were forgotten when Barbary leaders wanted more money.

Before becoming president, Jefferson had met with Abdrahman, the ambassador from Tripoli. Jefferson wanted to know why the ambassador regarded the United States as being at war with Tripoli, especially since the United States had neither declared nor threatened war. Jefferson, writing to John Jay, reports what Abdrahman responded, as follows:

> The Ambassador answered us that it was founded on the Laws of their prophet, that it was written in their Koran, that all nations who should not acknowledge their authority were sinners, that it was their right and duty to make war upon them wherever they could be found, and to make slaves of all they could take as Prisoner, and that every Musselman who should be slain in battle was sure to go to Paradise.[39]

In short, Abdrahman did not say anything we cannot find in the Qur'an, Muhammad's biography, or the Hadith. The United States was hardly a colonial power at this point, and it barely had anything that could be called a navy.[40] So, again, Lawrence seems selective in how he views colonialism and imperialism.

On another front, it is naive to think that imperialists do not see themselves as acting in self-defense. Most empires—whether the Assyrians, medieval Muslims, or Nazi Germany—see themselves as struggling to survive in the face of hostile neighbors. This is one reason that Hans Morgenthau, the famed advocate of political realism, postulated that any nation that seeks a favorable change in power status is, in fact, pursuing an imperialist policy, defensive or not.[41]

If one reads *Mein Kampf,* one will see that Adolf Hitler thought he was acting against colonialism of two types. One was a sort of internal colonialism that he attributed to Jews living in Germany who were working for the financial destruction of the nation. A second type, closer to classic colonialism, was also attributed to a global Jewish conspiracy, but involved an alliance of nations bent on destroying Germany. Thus, Hitler writes that "[t]oday we are not fighting for a position as a world power; today we must struggle for the existence of our fatherland,"[42] adding "[t]he Jew today is the great agitator for the complete destruction of Germany."[43]

Hitler thought only the possession of large tracts of territory could ensure a sufficient buffer to protect Germany. Like some Muslims who believe that they are a privileged people, Hitler thought Germans were a privileged people who were destined to subjugate non-Germans. Hitler characterized Jews and other non-Germans as "apes" (*Affe*),[44] and many traditions about Muhammad show that he, too, portrayed Jews as apes (*qirada*).[45] Such dehumanization was part of the reason that violence was permissible against Jews in both Nazi Germany and in some Islamic scriptural traditions.

It does not help the pacifist Islamic argument to say that Nazi Germany acted on false information about Jews. The sense of self-defense borne by Hitler's *Mein Kampf* is no less verifiable than the sort of reasons for defense given by a bin Laden or by Muhammad in Ibn Hisham's biography. Ultimately, therefore, the colonialist explanation for Muslim violence neither provides an excuse nor sheds much light on why Muslims can believe that almost anything that aims to stop the spread of Islam is cause for violent jihad.

Historically, Lawrence's thesis downplays the fact that Muslim imperialism and colonialism was well under way long before Europe invaded the Middle East.[46] By 732/3, Charles Martel was beating back Muslim encroachments into France. Muslims ruled much of Spain until their expulsion in 1492.[47] Islamic armies were fighting in the fields of Germany in the tenth century. So we could easily reverse the argument and say that Western colonialism was nothing more than a reaction against Islamic imperialism. In any case, modern European colonialism helps very little in explaining violent beliefs that go back to the birth of Islam.

Certainly, one reason Lawrence's theory is not viable is that he defines "fundamentalism" in an unclear manner that obscures much of the violence in Islam. It is as if the violence that matters is connected with fundamentalism. Once we see that any violence based on a religious belief should count as "religious violence," then fundamentalism, as defined by Lawrence, is of little help in explaining that violence.[48] For example, how does the idea that one should stone an adulterous woman change because "fundamentalism" is defined by Lawrence as a stage after revivalism or reform? Did this idea of stoning a woman to death not exist before colonialism or before revivalism? Of course it did. The important variable is the existence of a text or a divine revelation that has authorized this, regardless of one's colonial condition.

The Saudi scholars and government ministers of the 1976 Riyadh symposium (discussed in chapter 10) were not advocating the amputation of a hand on the basis of imitating a secular Western government. The Saudi scholars and officials were not advocating the killing of women on the basis that revivalism and reform had not worked. The Saudi officials and scholars in our example were quoting scriptures and religious beliefs in order to justify these violent actions. Those beliefs existed long before colonialism, they existed during colonialism, and they continue to exist after colonialism—simply because those principles are embedded in at least part of Islam itself.

The case of Osama bin Laden also refutes much of Lawrence's thesis.

Bin Laden, after all, tells us that he is fighting the United States because Americans have encroached on space that the Qur'an deems sacred. This space was deemed sacred before the United States existed. It was sacred during colonialism. And it is still sacred. We could surmise that bin Laden is lying or does not mean what he says. But we cannot deny that he is appealing to a tradition that exists in the most essential documents of Islam. In any case, bin Laden is using the same theological arguments used by Muslims from the beginning of their recorded traditions.

Empirically, Lawrence's thesis that bin Laden represents some deviant form of Islam also does not seem statistically warranted. For example, a recent poll published by CNN reports that "[a]lmost half of all Saudis said in a poll conducted last year that they have a favorable view of Osama bin Laden's sermons and rhetoric."[49] If a near majority of Saudis have a favorable view of bin Laden's violent rhetoric, then why can we not claim that a near majority of Saudis support a violent form of Islam, or at least a violent rhetoric? If what the majority of Muslims believe or practice is what counts as "essential" or "predominant," then certainly such empirical findings contradict an "essentially" peaceful Islam in Saudi Arabia.

SUMMARY

Islamic violence is neither solely a modern reaction against colonialism nor some aberrant feature of the religion. Rather, violence forms the initial premises of Islam, be it in the Qur'an or in the life of Muhammad, who continues to be a model for Muslim behavior. At the very least, violence was permitted to carry out the agenda of Muhammad, it is an allowable interpretation of certain passages in the Qur'an and the Hadith, and it is believed to be so by those who carry out violent acts today.

We have focussed on the views of Carl Ernst and Bruce Lawrence because they represent much of the way academics who defend a peaceful Islam do so on the basis of faulty historical premises, unclear definitions, and a lack of detailed attention to the perpetrators of violence. More importantly, they themselves promote "essentialist" versions of Islam while aiming to combat essentialism.

Ultimately, the fallacy of the peaceful essentialists is the result of a crisis of epistemology in the study of religion. On the one hand, it has become unfashionable to acknowledge that one is using empirico-rationalism to evaluate Islam, and so comes the idea that we should let Muslims speak for themselves. On the other hand, some of these same scholars do not hesitate to use empirico-rationalist approaches to declare that bin Laden is "deviating" from the true Islam. Ultimately, what is really happening is that these scholars are using empirico-rationalist epistemology to dismiss the portion of Islam that they do not favor.

Were these scholars epistemologically consistent, then they would need to conclude that no Islamic religious claim, peaceful or violent, is justified when evaluated on empirico-rationalist grounds. Only actions and conduct based on verifiable entities and phenomena are justified, and anything else is an appeal to vacuity. Alternatively phrased, no Islamic religious claim, peaceful or violent, can be deemed justified *unless* evaluated on empirico-rationalist grounds. And it is that lack of verifiability for any Islamic religious claim that ultimately allows the violent side to exert itself repeatedly and gain legitimacy within Muslim communities.

NOTES

1. We follow the English edition published by Rudolph Peters, *Jihad in Mediaeval and Modern Islam: The Chapter on Jihad from Averroes' Legal Handbook 'Bidayat al-Mudjtahid' and the Treatise 'Koran and Fighting' by the Late Shaykh Al-Azhar, Mahmud Shaltut* (Leiden: Brill, 1977).

2. Among more popular writers, we can also mention Karen Armstrong, *Holy War: The Crusades and Their Impact on the Modern World* (New York: Anchor Books, 2001), especially pp. 33–34, 46–47.

3. See Stephan Fuchs, *Against Essentialism: A Theory of Culture and Society* (Cambridge, MA: Harvard University Press, 2001).

4. For similar observations, see Wellman and Tokuno, "Is Religious Violence Inevitable?" p. 293.

5. Kimball, *When Religion Becomes Evil*.

6. Ibid., p. 58.

7. Ernst, *Following Muhammad*, p. 213.

8. Eleanor Abdella Doumato, "The Ambiguity of Shari'a and the Politics of 'Rights' in Saudi Arabia," in *Faith and Freedom: Women's Human Rights in the Muslim World*, ed. Mahnaz Afkhami (Syracuse, NY: Syracuse University Press, 1995), p. 137.

9. Ernst, *Following Muhammad*, pp. xvi–xvii.

10. Edward William Lane, *An Arabic-English Lexicon* (1863–1893; reprint, Beirut: Libraire du Liban, 1968), 2:473. Arabic has "forms" of verbs, which refers to a conjugational pattern. An Arabic verb may have different meanings depending on which "form" one uses.

11. Ali, *The Religion of Islam*, p. 408.

12. Al-Bukhari, 1519 and 1520/Book of Hajj, 4/Darussalam edition, 2:345–346.

13. For a critical look at this genre, see Andrew Rippin, "The Function of *Asbab al-Nuzul* in Koranic Exegesis," *The Quest for the Historical Muhammad*, ed. Warraq, pp. 392–419; originally published in *Bulletin of the School for Oriental and African Studies* 51 (1988): 1–20.

14. Reuven Firestone, *Jihad: The Origin of Holy War in Islam* (New York: Oxford University Press, 1999), pp. 51–65.

15. Translation in Ali, *The Religion of Islam*, p. 28.

16. Ibid., p. 29n25.

17. The pronominal suffix *-hā* grammatically agrees with "one of the *ayat* [revelation]." Thus, the translation "cause it to be forgotten" refers to the "revelation," not the world, a word nowhere mentioned in text.

18. Ali, *The Religion of Islam*, p. 28.

19. Ibid., p. 31.

20. Al-Bukhari, 3159/Book of Al-Jizya, 1/Darussalam 4:243.

21. Al-Bukhari, 3159/Book of Al-Jizya, 1/Darussalam 4:244.

22. Ernst, *Following Muhammad*, p. 45; Ali, *The Religion of Islam*, p. 410.

23. For example, there is no hint of even an alternate understanding in the citation given by Ernst, *Following Muhammad*, p. 45.

24. Rudi Paret, "Sure 2, 256: lā ikrāha fī d-dīni," *Der Islam: Zeitschrift für Geschichte und Kultur des islamische Orients* 45 (1969): 300: "Das Koranwort würde dann nicht Toleranz predigen, wäre vielmehr Ausdruck der Resignation." Otherwise, Paret indicates that an expression of tolerance could not have been formulated more simply than this in Arabic ("Und wie könnte mann es knapper formulieren . . . ?").

25. For a detailed discussion of various exegetical traditions pertaining to Sura 2:256, see Friedmann, *Tolerance and Coercion*, pp. 94, 100–107.

26. Ibid., p. 102.

27. Ali, *The Religion of Islam*, p. 414.

28. Sayyid Qutb, *In the Shade of the Qur'an* (New Delhi: Naida Printing Press, 2001), pp. 16–17. For a recent study of Qutb, see Sayed Khatab, "Hakimiyyah and Jahiliyyah in the Thought of Sayyid Qutb," *Middle Eastern Studies* 38, no. 3 (July 2002): 145–70. For a recent discussion about the supposed deviancy of "holy war" in Islam, see Khaled Abou El Fadl, *The Place of Tolerance in Islam*, ed. Joshua Cohen and Ian Lague (Boston: Beacon Press, 2002). Abou El Fadl notes (p. 23) that "it would be disingenuous to deny that the Qur'an and other Islamic sources offer possibilities of intolerant interpretation." Nonetheless, he believes that "the text does not command such intolerant readings."

29. For an English translation of the text, see Robert Hoyland, *Seeing Islam as Others Saw It: A Survey and Evaluation of Christian, Jewish, and Zoroastrian Writings on Early Islam* (Princeton, NJ: Darwin Press, 1997), p. 203.

30. Fazlur Rahman, "Some Key Ethical Concepts in the Qur'an," *Journal of Religious Ethics* 11, no. 2 (1983): 172.

31. See further, Jane Smith, *An Historical and Semantic Study of the Term Islam as Seen in Sequences of Qur'an Commentaries* (Missoula, MT: Scholars Press, 1975).

32. Hector Avalos, "The Gospel of Lucas Gavilan as Postcolonial Biblical Exegesis," *Semeia* 75 (1996): 88.

33. See Jon L. Berquist, *Judaism in Persia's Shadow: A Social and Historical Approach* (Minneapolis: Fortress, 1995). For the implications of imperialism on scripture-formation in ancient Israel, see Jon L. Berquist, "Postcolonialism and Imperial Motives for Canonization," *Semeia* 75 (1996): 15–35. For an earlier treatment of imperialism in the ancient Near East, see J. Nicholas Postgate, *The First Empires*

(London: Elsevier-Phaidon, 1977); "In Search of the First Empires," *BASOR* 293 (1994): 1–13; and Robert J. Wenke, "Elymeans, Parthians, and the Evolution of Empires in Southwestern Iran," *JAOS* 101, no. 3 (1981): 303–15. On colonization in the ancient Near East, see John Boardman, "Aspects of Colonization," *BASOR* 322 (2001): 33–42.

34. On asserting identity as a response to marginalization by an empire, see Peter Machinist, "The Question of Distinctiveness in Ancient Israel: An Essay." For a broader theoretical perspective see Richard H. Thompson, *Theories of Ethnicity: A Critical Appraisal* (New York: Greenwood Press, 1989); Wallerstein, *The Modern World System*, vol. 1, *Capitalist Agriculture and the Origins of the European World-Economy in the Sixteenth Century*, and *The Capitalist World Economy* (Cambridge: Cambridge University Press, 1979).

35. Lawrence, *Shattering the Myth*, p. 54.

36. Al-Bukhari, 3167/Book of Al Jizya, 6/Darussalam edition, 4:248. See also Sura 7:158.

37. For a recent discussion of the development of the cosmic view of the Israelite pantheon, see Lowell K. Handy, "The Appearance of the Pantheon in Judah," in *The Triumph of Elohim: From Yahwisms to Judaisms*, ed. Diana Vikander Edelman (Grand Rapids, MI: Eerdmans, 1996), pp. 27–43.

38. We are distilling the account found in Joseph Wheelan, *Jefferson's War: America's First War on Terror 1801–1805* (New York: Carroll and Graf, 2003).

39. Ibid., pp. 40–41.

40. Unfortunately, Wheelan cites no more than an encyclopedia article for his view of jihad, and so repeats the common apologetic view that the most authentic jihad is defensive and peaceful (ibid., p. 8).

41. See Morgenthau, *Politics among Nations*, pp. 50–51.

42. Hitler, *Mein Kampf*, p. 620/German, p. 699: "Heute aber kämpfen wir nicht für eine Weltmachtstellung, sondern haben zu ringen um den Bestand unseres Vaterlandes."

43. Hitler, *Mein Kampf*, p. 623/German, p. 702: "So ist der Jude heute der grosse Hetzer zur restlosen Zerstörung Deutschlands."

44. Hitler, *Mein Kampf*, p. 402/German, p. 445.

45. On the "ape" tradition in Islam, see Suras 2:265 and 7:166; Michael Cook, "Ibn Qutayba and the Monkeys," *Studia Islamica* 89 (1999): 43–74; Ilse Lichtenstadter, "'And become ye accursed apes,'" *Jerusalem Studies in Arabic and Islam* 14 (1991): 162–75. Licthenstadter traces this tradition to the Jewish Talmud (e.g., Sanhedrin 109a).

46. For some standard histories of Muslim colonialism and imperialism in Europe, see Bernard Lewis, *Islam and the West* (New York: Oxford University Press, 1993); *The Muslim Discovery of the West* (New York: Oxford University Press, 1993); Paul Coles, *The Ottoman Impact on Europe* (London: Thames and Hudson, 1968); Halil Inalcik, *The Ottoman Empire: The Classical Age 1300–1600*, trans. Norman Itzkowitz and Colin Imber (New York: Praeger, 1973). For a more popular survey, see also Paul Fregosi, *Jihad in the West: Muslim Conquests from the 7th to the 21st Centuries* (Amherst, NY: Prometheus Books, 1998).

47. See further Roger Collins, *The Arab Conquest of Spain, 710–797* (Oxford:

Blackwell, 1989); Joseph O'Callaghan, *Reconquest and Crusade in Medieval Spain* (Philadelphia: University of Pennsylvania Press, 2003).

48. For other examples of violence and oppression that occurs among Muslims, see Ibn Warraq, *Why I Am Not a Muslim* (Amherst, NY: Prometheus Books, 1995), especially pp. 172–350.

49. "Poll of Saudis Shows Wide Support for bin Laden's Views" (June 9, 2004) at http://www.cnn.com/2004/WORLD/meast/06/08/poll.binladen.

PART 3

SECULARISM AND VIOLENCE

Our thesis does not argue that secularism is completely peaceful or that only religion is violent. Since the root of violence is scarcity, violence will never disappear as long as something is perceived to be—or actually is—scarce. Our argument has been that scarcities caused by unverifiable propositions form a more tragic and preventable violence. One may not be able to do much about the scarcity of land, but one need not create a new scarcity of land by calling it "holy" on the basis of unverifiable claims.

Nonetheless, it behooves secular humanists to explain some of the main instances of violence that have been attributed to atheism or secularism. Our aim is not so much to deny that the violence is performed by secular institutions and individuals, but rather to show that secular philosophies are not as clear a motive for violence as is often supposed. Our discussion considers Nazism and Stalinism, two of the main supposed culprits of atheistic violence.[1] In addition, we address the issue of statism or nationalism, as that has been credited as one of the most violent phenomena attributed to secularization in recent history.

NOTE

1. For a treatment of Stalin and Hitler as a pair, see Alan Bullock, *Hitler and Stalin: Parallel Lives* (New York: HarperCollins, 1991).

CHAPTER 12

THE NAZI HOLOCAUST

The Nazi Holocaust is often paraded as an example of atheistic human values and/or the consequences of evolutionary theory. This charge is particularly prevalent among Christian apologists, as exemplified by John P. Koster's comment in a chapter titled "Adolf Hitler: Neo-Darwinism and Genocide," from his jeremiad against atheism:

> Two aspects of Hitler's life really have to be considered at this point. The first aspect is the way in which something resembling the atheist syndrome shaped Hitler's own savagely distorted personality. The second is the way in which Darwin and Huxley's picture of man's place in the universe prepared the way for the Holocaust.[1]

Koster portrays Hitler as anti-Christian, adding, "Having rejected Christianity for themselves, Hitler and the Nazis began efforts to undermine whatever elements of Christian culture were left in Germany."[2]

Two practical consequences of Nazi ideology are noted by Koster. One is the passage of the Nuremberg Laws, which prohibited marriage between Jews and Aryan Germans. Another, outlined in the famous Wannsee Conference of 1942, began the large-scale movement of Jews to labor camps, where only the hardiest were to survive. The labor camps were seen as living laboratories for Charles Darwin's concept of the survival of the fittest.

Koster's views are, of course, not unique. Views like his are disseminated repeatedly in the popular media. Thus, Rush Limbaugh tells us that if we destroy faith in God, something nefarious will take its place. He proclaims that "throughout history that substitute for faith has been a belief in a man-made god called the state. Untold crimes have been committed in its name, Hitler and Stalin being the most bloody recent examples."[3] Commenting on the seeming attack on moral absolutes in the movie *Saved* (2004), William Donohue, president of the Catholic League, commented on the *Today Show* that "if there are no moral absolutes, then we're back to different strokes for different folks. We put pizza in the oven in this country. They put Jews into ovens in Nazi Germany."[4]

In short, Koster, Limbaugh, and Donohue represent on a popular level the view of many Christian apologists that Christianity was not involved in Nazism, and that Nazism was an atheistic or non-Christian phenomenon. It would be easy to dismiss these remarks as the work of amateurish Christian apologists, except that they do reflect some or all of the work of some respected academic historians, John Conway being one example.[5]

Contrary to these views, we will argue that the Holocaust neither was primarily grounded in atheism nor used atheism for its justification. In fact, we shall argue that the Holocaust has its roots in biblical traditions that advocate genocide. Those roots continue in Christian and Muslim traditions. The main factor contributed by modern science was the technology to implement efficiently what some biblical authors had in mind for groups of people deemed inferior.

In order to construct our argument, we have to understand some basic issues in Holocaust studies. As is the case with most significant world events, the study of the Holocaust is immensely complex. We certainly cannot do justice to it here. But there are some basic positions about its causes and roots that can be identified in the scholarly literature.[6] For our purposes, we can divide Holocaust studies into those that see (1) primary responsibility in religious factors, and particularly in Christianity; and (2) religion as a peripheral or negligible factor.

RELIGIOUS OR SOCIAL CAUSES?

Among scholars who do not see religion as a primary factor is Ernst Nolte, who represents the view that Nazism was mainly an anti-Bolshevik reaction.[7] Another position, represented by François Furet, sees both Communism and Nazism as a rejection of liberalism, meaning primarily capitalistic individualism.[8] Within this tradition, there are studies that focus on whether the Holocaust is rooted in factors that are distinctly German or fall within a wider scope we call "Western civilization." In particular, Daniel J. Goldhagen recently argued that the German people were willing participants in Hitler's genocidal program.[9] For Goldhagen, the fault lies mainly within Germany.

Enzo Traverso, on the contrary, argues that the Nazi Holocaust cannot be seen as particularly Germanic, but rather represents a complex synthesis drawn from elements of Western civilization on a broader scale. These elements include colonialism, the industrialization of death, social Darwinism, and the anxieties and displacements produced by the dissolution of the Hapsburg Empire. He places little, if any, responsibility on religious factors. In fact, Traverso is emphatic in claiming that "the 'regenerative' anti-Semitism of Nazism cannot be reduced to fulfillment of Christian Judeophobia, in a predetermined drama in which Nazism undertakes the final assault against the Antichrist."[10] For Traverso, "[a] historically unique aspect of the Jewish genocide is that it was perpetrated for the specific purpose of a biological remodeling of the human race."[11]

A slightly different angle revolves around the uniqueness of the Holocaust. Its main representative is Stephen T. Katz, author of the massive *The Holocaust in Historical Context*, a projected trilogy, the first volume of which was published in 1994.[12] Katz has a very singleminded thesis: "The Holocaust is phenomenologically unique by virtue of the fact that never before has a state set out, as a matter of intentional principle and actualized policy, to annihilate physically every man, woman, and child belonging to a specific people.[13] Katz criticizes Hyam Maccoby and other scholars who see a continuity between Christian anti-Semitism and Nazi ideology.[14]

And, indeed, there are those who see Nazi ideology as a sort of natural consequence of Darwinism. One example is an anthology edited by Götz Aly, Peter Chroust, and Christian Pross, titled *Cleansing the Fatherland: Nazi Medicine and Racial Hygiene* (1994).[15] Such scholars emphasize the ways in which racist biological theories were often expressed as medical problems. Thus, the Aryan body was being sickened by a sort of Jewish cancer that had to be expunged.

Another group of researchers sees religion as a major factor in Nazi policies. Here we can identify at least two positions. One position sees Nazi religion as pagan rather than as a form of Christianity. As such, this link to paganism has served to shift responsibility away from Christianity and toward non-Christian origins. In this regard, the work of Nicholas Goodrick-Clarke has been seminal. In at least two tomes, he has tried to uncover the pagan roots of Nazi ideology in the works of Guido von List and Jörg Lanz von Liebenfels, and in organizations such as the Order of the New Templars and the Thule Society.[16] Yet even he concedes, "The Nazi crusade was indeed essentially religious in its adoption of apocalyptic beliefs and fantasies including a New Jerusalem."[17]

A second position lays responsibility much more squarely in the lap of Christianity. This position can be traced as far back as the works of Guenter Lewy and Gordon Zahn.[18] A principal current representative of this position is Richard Steigmann-Gall.[19] Steigmann-Gall notes that many of Hitler's anti-Christian sentiments were based on supposed private conversations recorded in, among other sources, Herman Rausching's *Hitler Speaks*, a book that has been widely discredited as fraudulent.[20] After surveying a mass of documents, Steigmann-Gall concludes, "Christianity, in the final analysis, did not constitute a barrier to Nazism. Quite the opposite: For many of the subjects of this study, the battles waged against Germany's enemies constituted a war in the name of Christianity. . . . They were convinced that their movement did not mean the death of God, but the preservation of God.[21]

Within this set of writers who see Christianity as bearing major responsibility for the Holocaust are those who have laid responsibility on the Catholic Church in particular. John Cornwell began a new, furious round of debate in this regard with the publication of *Hitler's Pope: The Secret History of Pius XII* (1999).[22] Since then, a flurry of arguments in support and refutation have been offered by both Jewish and Catholic scholars.[23]

DEFINING RACISM

A second manner in which atheism has been blamed for the Nazi Holocaust rests on the assumption that atheistic scientists initiated or promoted evolutionary and biological concepts of race. Indeed, there is a predominant idea that "race" is a modern invention. The anthropologist Audrey Smedley tells us confidently that "[r]ace as a mechanism of social stratification and as a form of human identity is a recent concept in human history. Historical records show that neither the idea of or ideologies associated with race existed before the seventeenth century."[24] Part of the historical record Smedley explicitly deems free of racism are the Old and New Testaments. Such a notion has allowed many to miss the similarities in racial attitudes found in Nazi Germany and in the Hebrew Bible.

Part of the problem in comparing biblical racism and racism in modern times is the very unstable definition of "race" in academic circles. Commenting on a textbook on cultural anthropology, Eugenia Shanklin rightly complains that "the word *race* is used in several contexts with different meanings and without bothering to define it in the text."[25]

If one surveys a recent issue devoted to race in *American Anthropologist*, the premier journal of anthropology, one finds a similar variety of definitions. Kamala Visweswaran states that "race is a concept which signifies and symbolizes social conflicts and interests by referring to different types of human bodies."[26] Another definition analyzed by Matt Cartmill is as follows: "geographically delimited conspecific populations characterized by regional phenotypes."[27]

Milford Wolpoff, one of the most prominent theorists of race in modern anthropology, defines race as "a group of individuals geographically (and for humans, also culturally) determined who share a common gene pool and varying combinations of distinguishing characteristics."[28] Wolpoff traces modern racism back to Platonic ideas of "essentialism," wherein ideal and immutable types form a standard by which existing models are measured. Wolpoff concludes that "Nazi Germany was the first political organization based on an explicit biopolicy." Specifically, he identifies three main features of Nazi racial ideology: (1) the human races are different species; (2) some are more advanced than others; (3) competition among them is the main mechanism of their evolution.[29]

We do not deny that Nazism had "scientific" forefathers. Shanklin credits the famous theorist of race Arthur Compte de Gobineau (1816–1882) with adding "a hierarchical dimension to the study of racial differences, proclaiming that there were 'superior and inferior' races and that the majority of races were incapable of civilization."[30] Houston Stewart Chamberlain (1855–1927), an Englishman by birth, is also considered one of the notorious forefathers, though more from the philosophical and historical side.

The main villain is often said to be Ernst Haeckel (1834–1913), one of the most popular evolutionary theorists and writers at the turn of the twentieth century. Wolpoff asserts, "There was virtually nothing in the Nazi doctrines that was not put forth by Haeckel and well known and accepted by educated Germans when Hitler was still a housepainter."[31] Haeckel's *The Riddle of the World* (*Die Welträtsel*) sold some one hundred thousand copies in 1899. Haeckel favored an extreme version of polygenism, which asserted that the human "races" each evolved from a different species of ape-man. In addition, Haeckel saw the extermination and exploitation of superior and inferior racial groups as a positive and natural consequence of Darwinism. Haeckel was extolled in official publications of the Nazi Party.[32]

Christian apologists have not been idle in popularizing these claims. Sometimes such writers distort even the most basic facts to push Hitler even more strongly into an evolutionary stance. For example, Vance Ferrell, author of the notoriously inaccurate antievolution handbook *The Evolution Cruncher* (2001), says, "Adolf Hitler's *Mein Kampf* was based on evolutionary theory. . . . The very title of the book was copied from a Darwinian expression; it means "My Struggle" [to survive and overcome]"[33] Of course, anyone who has seen the earliest editions of *Mein Kampf* knows that the struggle to which the title refers had nothing to do with evolutionary theory. The earliest version of Hitler's book was titled *Four and a Half Years of Struggle against Lies, Stupidity, and Cowardice* (*4 1/2 Jahre Kampf gegen Lüge, Dummheit, and Feigheit*). It was only later that this politically permeated title was shortened, perhaps at the behest of publisher Max Amman.[34]

As we shall see, the definition of racism espoused by Wolpoff and many other modern anthropologists is deeply flawed because it does not address ancient sources very directly. The idea that race was tied to geographical location does not work well in the case of Nazi Germany. *Mein Kampf*, in fact, shows that one of the main features that bothered Hitler about the Jews was their lack of geographical rootedness. For Hitler, it was precisely *because* Jews were not tied to a country that they were dangerous. In his own words, Hitler explains: "Since the Jew never possessed a state with definite territorial limits and therefore never called a culture his own, the conception arose that this was a people which should be reckoned among the ranks of the nomads. This is a fallacy as great as it is dangerous."[35] Hitler continues to explain that Jews go from country to country as parasites seeking a new host. Hitler does not believe Jews behave the way they do because of some specific geographic origin.

Clearly, then, the notion of race has a more basic feature that may include, but is not restricted to, geography. Accordingly, we agree more closely with Benjamin Isaac, who has made a powerful case that racism existed in classical antiquity. He says that the "essence of racism is that it regards individuals as superior or inferior because they are believed to share imagined physical, mental, and moral attributes with the group to which they are deemed to belong, and it is assumed that they cannot change these traits individually."[36] Geographical racism is one of many types of group privileging that may exist. In sum, most modern definitions of race do not fully address the sources of the ancient world, and so are not working with a complete data set. For instance, Smedley, who sees the Old and New Testaments as devoid of racialist thinking, cites no primary source in the original language before making her pronouncements. Once we understand that racism is one type of a more fundamental phenomenon of group privileging, comparisons between ancient and modern racism become more useful and clear. Accordingly, we must now turn our attention to the ideas of race among the Nazis and compare them to what we find in the ancient world, and particularly to those in the Bible.

THE BIBLICAL ROOTS OF NAZI RACISM

The fact that Nazi ideologues saw themselves as religious refutes the idea that Nazism was necessarily, or actually, based on atheism. While we certainly can find seemingly anti-Christian or even agnostic statements among Nazi ideologues, the main theoreticians saw themselves as religious. To illustrate this religious context, we shall examine the work of one proto-Nazi and one Nazi ideologue. We shall treat Hitler's own religious racism more thoroughly in a following section.

The work of Jörg Lanz von Liebenfels illustrates the extent to which the Bible was used to support the notion of race and Aryan supremacy.[37] Lanz was born on July 19, 1874, in Vienna-Penzig to what appears to be a middle-class family. He seems to have harbored dreams of aristocracy and a knightly ancestry in his youth. By 1893 he had joined the Cistercian Order, and was interned at the Heiligenkreuz Abbey near Vienna.

Lanz eventually left (or was dismissed from) the Cistercian Order for reasons that are unclear. In any case, Lanz had extensive knowledge of Hebrew and Near Eastern languages. He began to be captivated by some of the discoveries originating in the ancient Near East. Among these discoveries were the monuments of the Assyrian Empire, which ruled much of the Near East in the first half of the first millennium BCE. He was also fascinated by new discoveries of primate and dinosaur fossils.

He combined these interests with his religious ones in a book called *Theozoology (Theozoologie)*, published in 1905. *Theozoology* argued that intercourse between the first humans and animals was responsible for the racial deteriorations he associated with the Fall. This seemingly odd ideology can be traced to his exegesis of Genesis 3, in which the serpent seems to be overly friendly with Eve.

Lanz also noted that people who were hated by the Hebrews were described in animalistic terms in the Bible. For example, Esau is described as being hairy in Genesis 27:11,[38] and God himself says that he hates Esau. Psalm 137:9 says the following about the Edomites: "Happy shall they be who take your little ones and dash them against the rock!" Lanz argues that this hate seems arbitrary unless one assumes that Esau is the product of these bestial miscegenations. These beast-men are also notorious for their perverted sexual practices, and Lanz believes that they constituted the inhabitants of Sodom. These ape-men (*Affenmensch*), argues Lanz, are what we encounter in the fossil record as Neandertals.

Lanz's characterization of Jews and non-Germans was not that different from characterizations of Jews in many Islamic traditions. Well-known in Islam is the tradition that God turned the Jews into apes because of idolatry. This idea can be found in Sura 2:65: "Those amongst you who transgressed in the matter of the Sabbath; We said to them 'Be ye apes'" (*qirada*). Likewise, Ibn Hisham's biography of Muhammad, relates an episode in which Muhammad speaks of how God made (*ja 'ala-hum*) some of the Hebrews into "apes" (*qirada*) for their sins.[39] As Michael Cook demonstrates, the fact that this tradition was taken seriously is illustrated by efforts among Islamic scholars to determine whether these apes had borne progeny that exist into the present day.[40]

Ilse Lichtenstadter has traced this idea of devolving into apes to the Jewish Talmud. In Sanhedrin 109b, we find the curious story of what happened to the folks God dispersed after the attempt to build the Tower of Babel (Genesis 11). The groups building the tower were classified into three groups: (1) those who wanted to live in heaven, (2) those who wanted to worship stars (*kokabim*),[41] and (3) those who wanted to wage war, presumably against God. The last group was turned into apes (*kophim*). In short, Jewish exegetical traditions acknowledged the existence of inferior and bestial races.[42]

In actuality, we can trace the idea of likening people deemed inferior or "outsiders" to apes all the way back to the end of the third millennium BCE. A Sumerian text called the Curse of Agade, contains the story of a king named Naram Sin who angered certain gods, apparently because he did not observe religious traditions properly. As revenge, these gods brought down a people called the Gutians upon Naram Sin's capital city, Agade. The description of the Gutians is as follows: "Gutium, a people who do not recognize limits, with human instincts, but canine intelligence and apes' features."[43]

In any case, for Lanz, the war between these bestial beings and the pure stock (the blond Germanic race) is a cosmic struggle. Jews are identified as being of these inferior races. Lanz accordingly suggests young good-for-nothings (*jugendliche Taugenichtse*) be castrated and sterilized (using the newly discovered radiation) in order to avoid a racial catastrophe for the blond race.[44]

We have counted at least one hundred biblical references in *Theozoologie* cited to support Lanz's racist ideology. By contrast, there are only a handful of references to scientific works on anthropology and paleontology. From a modern critical viewpoint, Lanz's reading of the Bible is certainly tendentious and his philology is flawed. However, he is no more mistaken in his reading of Hebrew than Glock and Stark were mistaken in their interpretation of "love your neighbor." And Lanz is correct about the depiction of disfavored people in bestial terms in the Bible. This dehumanization and bestialization of Jews, after all, was a large factor in the depiction of other races under Nazi Germany.

In fact, the Bible was certainly the first great popularizer of racist descriptions of the other in the ancient Near East. Despite the fact that we find depictions of enemies in bestial terms, Jerrold S. Cooper observes that "Mesopotamian sources of all periods are surprisingly free of racist ideology."[45] Peter Machinist also notes that "nowhere in Mesopotamian literature is there anything like a systematic ethnography of a foreign group or a treatise on Mesopotamian national character."[46] Machinist does, however, find regional assertions of cultural identity. It is not until the Bible comes on the scene, therefore, that we truly have a consistent and persistent authority for racism in Western civilization.

Alfred Rosenberg, regarded as a premier theorist of race in Nazi Germany, also used parts of the Bible as support in *The Myth of the Twentieth Century: An Assessment of the Psychical-Spiritual Struggle of our Time*, first published in 1930.[47] The subtitle alone shows that Rosenberg was no atheist, but rather followed a religious outlook on life. Rosenberg's book, which was his main opus, sold an estimated half million copies by the end of 1936, and about 1 million copies were in print in 1944. It was second only to Hitler's *Mein Kampf* in sales and reputation.[48]

Rosenberg was born in Reval (Tallin), Estonia, on January 12, 1893, of Estonian and Lithuanian heritage.[49] Rosenberg's main duty during the Nazi period was to serve as Reich Minister for the Eastern Occupied Territories, a job in which he supervised the labor and extermination camps. Rosenberg was tried at Nuremberg and was executed by hanging on October 16, 1946.

Some biographies of Rosenberg speak of his denouncement of Christianity for maintaining a Semitic religious heritage. However, Rosenberg is best described as being against Christendom, the organized religions such as Catholicism that had departed from what he believed to be the true teachings of Jesus. Rosenberg sought to purify Christianity by going back to its Nordic roots. In this he was supported by the well-known biblical scholar Ernest Renan (1823–1892).[50] Thus, Rosenberg did not repudiate Christianity insomuch as he thought he was following the true and original teachings of Christ.[51]

For example, Rosenberg believed that Christ's life is what should be meaningful for Germans.[52] Rosenberg repudiated the idea of Christ's sacrifice as a Jewish corruption, and saw Jesus as a great figure, whose true work, the love of one's race, was distorted by Christendom into some universal love. Rosenberg thought that the Gospel of John best preserved some of the teachings of Jesus: "The Gospel of John, which still bears an aristocratic spirit throughout, strove against the collective bastardization, orientalization and Judaization of Christianity."[53] Rosenberg then praises Marcion (second century), the Gnostic Christian who repudiated the Old Testament entirely and promoted a canon consisting only of an expurgated Gospel of Luke and some of Paul's epistles.

Indeed, Rosenberg syncretized Christian concepts found in the New Testament with Germanic myths, as well as myths of his own creation or adaptation. But how does Rosenberg's biblical exegesis and syncretism differ from what other self-described Christians have done throughout history? Many scholars argue precisely that the New Testament authors combined Hellenistic with Jewish ideas. In short, if we use the same logic used by Christian recontextualists, we could also argue that Rosenberg does not represent so much an anti-Christian movement as a recontextualization of Christianity. In fact, he called it "positive Christianity" (*positive Christentum*), as opposed to the one represented by the Asiatic clergy.[54]

The Myth of the Twentieth Century is replete with biblical quotations. Rosenberg also had a familiarity, though superficial and flawed, with the Talmud. Some of his interpretations of the Bible were ones with which even Jewish scholars could agree. He notes that Leviticus 25:17, which states "thou shalt not take advantage of thine neighbor," refers to fellow Hebrews, and not to everyone else.[55] As we have noted, this is also precisely the interpretation of Harry M. Orlinsky, the great Jewish biblical scholar. In fact, Rosenberg and other Nazi theoreticians utilized and understood well the work of many authoritative biblical scholars, including Ernest Renan, Paul Anton De Lagarde, and Gerhard Kittel.[56]

The idea that the Hebrews were to maintain genealogical purity is evident throughout the Hebrew Bible. For example, in Genesis 24, when Abraham seeks to find a wife for Isaac, he instructs his servant as follows:

> and I will make you swear by the LORD, the God of heaven and earth, that you will not get a wife for my son from the daughters of the Canaanites, among whom I live,
>
> but will go to my country and to my kindred and get a wife for my son Isaac. (Gen. 24:3–4)

Long before the Nuremberg Laws or the marriage laws of the Council of Elvira, Deuteronomy was promulgating laws against intermarriage with other ethnic groups:

> No Ammonite or Moabite shall be admitted to the assembly of the LORD. Even to the tenth generation, none of their descendants shall be admitted to the assembly of the LORD,
>
> because they did not meet you with food and water on your journey out of Egypt, and because they hired against you Balaam son of Beor, from Pethor of Mesopotamia, to curse you.
>
> (Yet the LORD your God refused to heed Balaam; the LORD your God turned the curse into a blessing for you, because the LORD your God loved you.)
>
> You shall never promote their welfare or their prosperity as long as you live. (Deut. 23:3–6)

Yet such a notion of race can also fit that which we find among some early Muslim writers. For example, Abu al-Fida comments that "[t]he community of Yahud is more inclusive than that of the Banu Isra'il because many

Arabs, Byzantines, Persians and others become Jews without being of the Banu Isra'il."[57] Thus it is clear that for al-Fida, Banū Israel corresponds to an ethnic designation conferred by genealogy.

And just as some can find social Darwinism in Nazi Germany, we can also find the notion that people could be killed for their physical attributes in ancient Israel. In one episode, David is said to put the following policy into effect: "He also defeated the Moabites and, making them lie down on the ground, measured them off with a cord; he measured two lengths of cord for those who were to be put to death, and one length for those who were to be spared. And the Moabites became servants to David and brought tribute" (2 Sam. 8:2). In other words, David kills the strongest, and spares those who would pose the least threat. Those saved, however, are kept as slaves. Susan Niditch comments that it seems "as if David were employing genetic selection to weaken Moabite stock."[58] Would Wolpoff say that this is a sort of biopolicy?

In sum, Lanz and Rosenberg illustrate that there was a long tradition, traceable to Muslim, Hebrew, and Near Eastern sources, that saw groups of people as being inferior or meriting violence on the basis of genealogical identity.[59] All of these sources posited the existence of bestial races who posed a danger to the privilcgcd group. In Hebrew traditions the privileged group was the Israelites; in Nazi traditions the privileged group was the blond Germans. Different groups may have played the superior or inferior partner in this hierarchy, but the idea of a hierarchy based on genealogy and physical constitution is parallel.

MEIN KAMPF AND RACE

But even if Lanz and Rosenberg may be dismissed as eccentrics who had little influence on Hitler, we can still make the case that Hitler's own version of racism has as much or more in common with biblical racism than with some version of atheistic evolutionary theory. Our main source here is Hitler's *Mein Kampf*, which outlined much of his racial ideology. We need to undertake our own independent study of this work in order to test various readings of it by anthropologists and Christian apologists.

First, *Mein Kampf* provides clear evidence that Hitler was not an atheist. For example, Hitler says: "Hence today I believe that I am acting in accordance with the will of the Almighty Creator; by defending myself against the Jew, I am fighting for the work of the Lord."[60] Hitler also states that he sees Protestantism as a great ally of German nationalism: "Protestantism as such is a better defender of the interests of Germanism, insofar as this is grounded in its genesis and later tradition."[61] Hitler claims Martin Luther as one of his heroes.[62]

So what is race for Hitler? One of the clearest definitions may be the following: "Race, however, does not lie in the language but exclusively in the blood, which no one knows better than the Jew, who attaches very little importance to the preservation of his language, but all importance to keeping his blood pure."[63] As we have noted, for Hitler, "[b]lood sin and desecration of the race are the original sin in this world and the end of a humanity which surrenders to it."[64] Expressing a belief reminiscent of one found in Leviticus 17:11–14, Hitler exclaims that "in the blood alone resides the strength as well as the weakness of man."[65]

Hitler sees Judaism not as a religion, but as a race that uses religion as an instrument to preserve itself.[66] Accordingly, Hitler's version of the state is a defensive one, and the state is an instrument to promote the welfare of a race, not an end in itself.[67] Hitler certainly sees races as being involved in a struggle guided by natural law. And one of the greatest weapons for the destruction of Germany is the contamination of blood, which comes through exogamy, marriage outside of the German kin group, which is seen as a "foreign virus."[68] It is not the case that Hitler thought that race was immutable. On the contrary, he thought that one had to guard the race because it might mutate into something undesirable.

Thus, to the extent that it remained consistent, race, for Hitler, meant a biological relationship, a genealogical relationship. Race was in the blood, in genealogy, not necessarily in geographical location. This was combined with the ranking of races from superior to inferior. In sum, Hitler's concept of racism meant the belief that genealogical groups were not all equal. Hitler does refer to "superior, but less ruthless races," and "culturally inferior but more active men."[69] The blond race was the highest genealogical group. If we understand racism, then, as the idea that genealogical groupings determine rankings of rights and privileges, then biblical racism and Nazi racism are indeed parallel.

GENEALOGICAL/BLOOD PURITY

Nazi Germany was not the first to use medical rhetoric to discriminate against Jews. Long before any Darwinian theories may have been applied in Nazi Germany, ancient pre-Christian authors used health scares in order to pursue anti-Jewish policies or to portray Jews negatively. Thus, Lysimachus (second or first century BCE), one of the most anti-Jewish authors of the pre-Christian world, alleged that the Jews had been kicked out of Egypt because they had leprosy.[70] Even if the charge of leprosy is unhistorical, it shows that the author thought that perceived medical conditions could justify the expulsion of a whole group of people.

The specific idea of blood purity did not begin with Darwin or evolutionary theory. Such a notion was already present in Christian ideas about Jews. For example, Juan Martinez Siliceo, the archbishop of Toledo, proposed legislation in 1547 based very specifically on what is called *limpieza de sangre* ("cleanliness of blood," "purity of blood").[71] Statutes enacted in Toledo in 1449 also focused on blood purity as a means to discriminate against Jews who had converted but were not Spaniards by "blood."

Some of Hitler's specific terminology for "purity of the blood" (e.g., "Reinhaltung des Blutes") corresponds quite closely to the terminology applied against Jews in sixteenth-century Spain. Likewise, in Islam we find that blood is also believed to be the locus of genealogical relationships. Thus, one Hadith speaks of Allah making blood sacred (*harrama . . . dimā'a*).[72] Hitler, therefore, probably mirrors Christian or Islamic ideas more than Darwinian ones here.

The idea of blood purity was, in turn, dependent on even older notions that one's genealogy was located in the blood. This idea may be found in Judaism, as is evident in comments found in Jewish literature concerning the story of the murder of Abel by his brother Cain. According to Genesis 4:10, Yahweh tells Cain that he knows of Abel's murder because the "bloods of your brother [Abel]" are crying from the ground. The Hebrew text literally has the plural, "bloods of your brother" (*demey 'āhīkā*), an odd fact commented upon in the Talmud (Sanhedrin 37b) as well as in the commentary of the great medieval Jewish scholar, Rashi, on Genesis 4:10.[73] One of the explanations recorded in those sources is that "bloods" refers to the "descendants" of Abel.[74]

In fact, we can argue that at least parts of the Hebrew Bible constitute the principal exponents of the most systematic ideology of genealogical purity inherited by Western civilization. One example is found in the story of Ezra's shock at the Jews having mixed with foreigners while in Babylon:

> After these things had been done, the officials approached me and said, "The people of Israel, the priests, and the Levites have not separated themselves from the peoples of the lands with their abominations, from the Canaanites, the Hittites, the Perizzites, the Jebusites, the Ammonites, the Moabites, the Egyptians, and the Amorites.

> For they have taken some of their daughters as wives for themselves and for their sons. Thus the holy seed has mixed itself with the peoples of the lands, and in this faithlessness the officials and leaders have led the way." (Ezra 9:1–2)

Even if the Hebrew author did not understand modern genetics, it is clear that the author understands that the mixing of "seed" is a physical process. Likewise, the author seems to think of "pollution" in material terms in prohibiting miscegenation:

> which you commanded by your servants the prophets, saying, "The land that you are entering to possess is a land unclean with the pollutions of the peoples of the lands, with their abominations. They have filled it from end to end with their uncleanness.
>
> Therefore do not give your daughters to their sons, neither take their daughters for your sons, and never seek their peace or prosperity, so that you may be strong and eat the good of the land and leave it for an inheritance to your children forever." (Ezra 9:11–12)

Ezra believed that this miscegenation would bring the wrath of God (10:14). The solution was to send away the wives, even with children (Ezra 10:3). Thus, family values here are subordinate to ethnic values. This is racism if "race" is defined as the idea that one genealogically related group is superior to others.[75] It is no surprise, therefore, that Samuel Goitein, author of a massive study of Jews in Mediterranean society, finds that in the medieval Jewish group he studied, "the bonds of blood were stronger than the ties of marriage."[76]

Seen in this light, we can return to Koster's claim that the Nuremberg Laws are a consequence of the acceptance of Darwinian race theory. On the contrary, the Nuremberg Laws are simply a continuance of Christian and biblical concepts. The marriage of Christians and Jews was already forbidden by the Council of Elvira in the fourth century, as we have mentioned previously. Koster cites the Wannsee Conference's plan to place Jews in labor camps, then ignores that this labor idea is the last point of Martin Luther's seven-point plan for the Jews. Koster and his like-minded cohorts ignore the ancient and predominant tradition against Jews in Christian history.

GENOCIDE MEDICALIZED

We have already discussed how group privileging is related to the genocide of the Canaanites and Amalekites. The purpose here is to show that the Nazi policy of genocide was based on premises quite similar to those in the Hebrew Bible. In Nazi Germany, Jews were seen as contaminants that had sickened the German collective body. Hitler expressed his fear that Jews would seduce and contaminate Aryan women; genocide was seen as the "cure."

"Medicalized" rationales for cleansing the Fatherland can be found in the Hebrew Bible itself.

> Praise, O heavens, his people, worship him, all you gods! For he will avenge the blood of his children, and take vengeance on his adversaries; he will repay those who hate him, and cleanse the land for his people. (Deut. 32:43)

> You shall not defile the land in which you live, in which I also dwell; for I the LORD dwell among the Israelites. (Num. 35:34)

As mentioned above, the Hebrew Bible frequently spoke of foreign nations in terms of "contamination." Likewise, the disease was supposed to be cut off. The fact that this sort of biblical mentality has force in modern rationales is clear in the justification provided by Gleason Archer, a fundamentalist apologist, for biblical genocide: "Just as a wise surgeon removes dangerous cancer from the patient's body by use of the scalpel so God employed the Israelites to remove such dangerous malignancies from human society."[77]

Seen in this light, we may argue that Hitler hated Judaism not so much because he perceived Judaism to have a racist ideology, but because he saw it as a racist ideology that was successful. This is most clear in the following passage, in which Hitler comments on the amorphous idea of a Jewish "state": "It is one of the most ingenious tricks that was ever devised, to make this state sail under the flag of 'religion,' thus assuring it of the tolerance which the Aryan is always ready to accord a religious creed. For actually, the Mosaic religion is nothing other than a doctrine for the preservation of the Jewish race."[78] For Hitler, therefore, the solution was to assert a racist ideology that would match and overcome the Jewish one. Rivalry, after all, implies equality at some level.

At the same time, Hitler saw racism as compatible with religion, as do many biblical authors. Even Haeckel, who is often maligned for supposedly introducing scientific grounds for genocide, saw himself as simply reexpressing biblical concepts in scientific language. Note, for example, Haeckel's comments on his vision of Utopia: "The future morality, free from all religious dogma, and grounded in a clear knowledge of nature's law, teaches us the ancient wisdom of the Golden Rule . . . through the words of the Gospel: 'Love your neighbor as yourself.'"[79] As in Christian and Jewish texts, "your neighbor" originally meant a fellow member of your in-group. Thus, Haeckel's interpretation of "neighbor," even if exegetically flawed, was based on the same concept of insider and outsider that is present in the earlier religions.

So from Haeckel to Hitler, Nazis did not see themselves as opposing biblical principles so much as they thought that modern science could be used to support, purify, and update those biblical principles. Nazis were often more like the scientific creationists of today who believe their pseudoscience supports the Bible. Of course, one can argue that Hitler was not so sophisticated a biblical exegete as to detect that there were also biblical traditions that spoke against any sort of strict ethnocentrism. But ultimately, what he did was not more theologically selective in biblical exegesis than many Jews and Christians who are held as paradigms (e.g., Luther).

SUMMARY

Nazi racism is a synthesis of modern pseudoscience and biblical concepts of ethnocentrism and genealogical purity. In many cases, biblical claims were misunderstood, and in other cases biblical claims in fact had a racist basis. In this regard, Nazi ideology is similar to creationist ideology, which believes that scientific findings support the biblical stories of Creation and the Flood.

We may summarize these parallels between Nazi racial policy and the genealogical policies of some authors in the Hebrew Bible:

	Nazism	Hebrew Bible
Ethnic purity commanded	Yes	Yes
Endogamy encouraged	Yes	Yes
Foreigners as contaminants	Yes	Yes
Genocide as a solution	Yes	Yes

Determining the causes of the Holocaust usually involves the examination of the main factors for anti-Judaism in Western culture. As we have already observed, some scholars view the conflict between Judaism and Christianity as inevitable or in essentialist terms. Others do not see anything inherent in Christianity that precipitates anti-Jewish violence, the Holocaust being the most extreme instance. We believe that both sides have some truth, and yet both miss the fact that the Nazi Holocaust represents the synthesis of attitudes found in both the New Testament and the Hebrew scriptures.

In a study of ethnocentrism in the Bible, the Jewish theologian Jon Levenson concluded, "Jews would do well to consider that the factors which impeded the banishment of Christian stereotypes are not quite without their counterparts in Judaism."[80] Stephen T. Katz, the scholar of religion, and Milford Wolpoff, the anthropologist, fail to see the parallels between certain practices that they have identified as unique or characteristic of the Nazis and certain practices promulgated in the Hebrew Bible itself. Indeed, the supreme tragic irony of the Holocaust is that the genocidal policies first systematically enunciated in the Hebrew scriptures were reversed by the Nazis. Nazi ideology simply had better technology to do what biblical authors had said they would do to their enemies.

Whatever mix of causal factors one manages to find in the primary sources, it is quite clear that atheism is the most difficult to find. Nowhere does Hitler say that he hates Jews because he is an atheist, nor does he ever claim to carry out some atheist agenda. Many of the anti-Christian statements that have been attributed to him have been disputed by respectable historians. If Hitler was guilty of anything, he was not scientific enough in his view of humanity.[81] Wherever we can trace his racist ideology, it goes back to the conflict between Christianity and Judaism.

The bulk of the evidence indicates that Nazism was indeed a synthesis of Christian anti-Judaism, Israelite ethnocentrism, anti-Christian paganism, and pseudoscientific thinking. Religion was a necessary precursor to this synthesis. The reason the Jews were identified as a distinct group had predominantly religious rationales in European history. Christianity, which began with a group of Jewish sectarians, eventually saw itself becoming different from traditional Judaism. Jews became the group that did not accept Jesus as the Messiah. This distinction probably took racial/ethnic overtones within generations. Hitler saw himself as trying to counteract Hebrew racism, which he saw as the main counterpart and enemy of the German race.

NOTES

1. John P. Koster, *The Atheist Syndrome* (Brentwood, TN: Wolgemuth and Hyatt, 1989), p. 142.

2. Ibid., p. 150.

3. Rush Limbaugh, *The Way Things Ought to Be* (New York: Pocket Books, 1992), p. 281.

4. Interview with Lester Holt, *Today Show Saturday*, NBC, June 12, 2004.

5. John Conway, *The Nazi Persecution of the Churches, 1933–1945* (London: Weidenfield and Nicolson, 1968).

6. For some of the seminal work, see Saul Friedländer, *Nazi Germany and the Jews*, vol. 1, *The Years of Persecution, 1933–1939* (New York: HarperCollins, 1997).

7. Ernst Nolte, *Der europäische Bürgerkrieg 1917–1945: Nationalsozialismus und Bolschewismus* (Berlin and Frankfurt: Propyläen/Ullstein, 1987).

8. François Furet and Ernst Nolte, *Fascism and Communism*, trans. Katherine Golsan (Lincoln: University of Nebraska Press, 2000), which contains correspondence outlining the differences between the two scholars.

9. Daniel J. Goldhagen, *Hitler's Willing Executioners: Ordinary Germans and the Holocaust* (New York: Little, Brown, 1996).

10. Enzo Traverso, *The Origins of Nazi Violence* (New York: New Press, 2003), p. 146.

11. Ibid., p. 3.

12. Katz, *The Holocaust in Historical Context*, vol. 1, *The Holocaust and Mass Death before the Modern Age*.

13. Ibid., p. 28.

14. Ibid., p. 17 n 38.

15. Götz Aly, Peter Chroust, and Christian Pross, *Cleansing the Fatherland: Nazi Medicine and Racial Hygiene*, trans. Belinda Cooper (Baltimore: Johns Hopkins University Press, 1994). See also Sheila Weiss, "The Race Hygiene Movement in Germany, 1904–1945," in *The Wellborn Science*, ed. Mark B. Adams (New York: Oxford University Press, 1990), pp. 8–68.

16. Nicholas Goodrick-Clarke, *The Occult Roots of Nazism: Secret Aryan Cults and Their Influence on Nazi Ideology* (New York: New York University Press, 1992).

17. Ibid., p. 203.

18. Guenter Lewy, *The Catholic Church and Nazi Germany* (New York: McGraw-Hill, 1964); and Gordon Zahn, *German Catholics and Hitler's Wars: A Study in Social Control* (New York: Sheed and Ward, 1962).

19. Richard Steigmann-Gall, *The Holy Reich: Nazi Conceptions of Christianity, 1919–1945* (Cambridge: Cambridge University Press, 2003).

20. Ibid., p. 28.

21. Ibid., p. 261.

22. John Cornwell, *Hitler's Pope: The Secret History of Pius XII* (New York: Viking, 1999).

23. Indeed, the literature on the role of Catholicism in Nazi Germany can now fill a library of its own. Examples that place responsibility on the Catholic Church include David Kertzer, *The Popes against the Jews: The Vatican's Role in the Rise of Modern Antisemitism* (New York: Knopf, 2001); Michael Phayer, *The Catholic Church and the Holocaust, 1930–1965* (Bloomington: University of Indiana Press, 2000); and Robert P. Erickson and Susannah Heschel, *Betrayal: German Churches and the Holocaust* (Minneapolis: Fortress, 1999). These studies have their counterparts in Pierre Blet, *Pope Pius XII and the Second World War: According to the Archives of the Vatican*, trans. Lawrence Johnson (New York: Paulist, 1999); and José M. Sánchez, *Pius XII and the Holocaust: Understanding the Controversy* (Washington, DC: Catholic University of America Press, 2002).

24. Audrey Smedley, "'Race' and the Construction of Human Identity," *American Anthropologist* 100, no. 3 (1999): 690. For a more thorough treatment of race as a modern phenomenon, see also Ivan Hannaford, *Race: The History of an Idea in the West* (Washington, DC: Woodrow Wilson Center Press, 1996).

25. Eugenia Shanklin, "The Profession of the Color Blind: Sociocultural Anthropology and Racism in the 21st Century," *American Anthropologist* 100, no. 3 (1999): 672. Shanklin is more specifically complaining about the textbook by Emily A. Schultz and Roberta Lavenda, *Cultural Anthropology: A Perspective on the Human Condition* (Mountain View, CA: Mayfield, 1995).

26. Kamala Visweswaran, "Race and the Culture of Anthropology," *American Anthropologist* 100, no. 1 (1998): 77.

27. Matt Cartmill, "The Status of the Race Concept in Physical Anthropology," *American Anthropologist* 100, no. 3 (1998): 651.

28. Milford Wolpoff and Rachel Caspari, *Race and Human Evolution: A Fatal Attraction* (New York: Simon & Schuster, 1997), p. 406.

29. Ibid., p. 136. My numeration of the three features has been added for convenience.

30. Shanklin, "The Profession of the Color Blind," p. 669.

31. Wolpoff and Caspari, *Race and Human Evolution*, p. 136.

32. For examples, see Ute Deichman, *Biologists under Hitler*, trans. Thomas Dunlap (Cambridge, MA: Harvard University Press, 1996), pp. 259–60.

33. Vance Ferrell, *The Evolution Cruncher* (Altamont, TN: Evolution Facts, 2001), p. 817.

34. See "Mein Kampf," in Louis L. Snyder, ed., *Encyclopedia of the Third Reich* (New York: Marlowe, 1976), p. 224.

35. Hitler, *Mein Kampf*, pp. 303–304/German pp. 332–33: "Da der Jude niemals einen Staat mit bestimmter territorialer Begrenzung besass und damit auch nie ein Kultur sein eigen nannte, enstand die Vorstellung, als handle es sich hier um ein Volk, das in die Reihe der Nomaden zu rechnen wäre. Dies ist ebenso grosser wie gefährlicher Irrtum."

36. Benjamin Isaac, *The Invention of Racism in Classical Antiquity* (Princeton, NJ: Princeton University Press, 2004), p. 23.

37. My biography of Lanz is indebted to Goodrick-Clarke, *The Occult Roots of Nazism*, pp. 90–122. The readings and translations of *Theozoologie* are my own, unless otherwise noted.

38. Jörg Lanz von Liebenfels, *Theozoologie* (1905; reprint, Deutschherrenverlag, 2001), p. 10: "Esau ist ein solcher haariger sá'ir mensch (Gen. xxvii, 11). Mit diesen affenmenschen trieben der Bewohner Palästinas Unzucht, und Gott muss Lev. xvii, 7 diese Buhlerei strenge verbieten."

39. Guillaume, *Life of Muhammad*, p. 251/Ibn Hisham, *Al-Sirah*, 2:158.

40. Cook, "Ibn Qutayba and the Monkeys"; Lichtenstadter, "'And Become Ye Accursed Apes.'" See also William H. C. Propp, "Acting Like Apes," *Bible Review* 20, no. 3 (June 2004): 34–40, 46.

41. The Soncino English edition translates the Hebrew term *kokabim* as "idols," but I prefer "stars," which is more literally accurate, for two other reasons: (1) Worshipping stars is most compatible with the idea of building a tower that reached heaven; and (2) building a tower was not otherwise necessary to worship idols.

42. For another study of the bestial depiction of "the other," including Jews and Muslims in medieval times, see John Block Friedman, *The Monstrous Races in Medieval Art and Thought* (Syracuse, NY: Syracuse University Press, 2000); and Sara Higg Strickland, *Saracens, Demons, and Jews: Making Monsters, in Medieval Art* (Princeton, NJ: Princeton University Press, 2003).

43. Jerrold S. Cooper, *The Curse of Agade* (Baltimore: Johns Hopkins University Press, 1983), pp. 56–57. My translation of the Sumerian is adapated from Cooper. "Apes" is here ^{ugu}ugu$_4$–bi. For depictions of apes in the ancient Near East, see the richly illustrated study of Azad Hamoto, *Der Affe in der altorientalischen Kunst* (Münster: Ugarit-Verlag, 1995).

44. Lanz, *Theozoologie*, p. 148: "Jugenliche Taugenichtse wären ohne Gnade zu kastrieren, oder sterilisieren (durch Strahlung)."

45. Cooper, *Curse of Agade*, p. 30.

46. Machinist, "On Self-Consciousness in Mesopotamia," p. 184.

47. Our citations are from the following edition: Alfred Rosenberg, *Der Mythus des 20. Jahrhunderts: Eine Wertung der seelische-geistigen Gestalentkämpfe unserer Zeit* (Munich: Hoheneichen Verlag, 1938).

48. For sales figures, see "Rosenberg, Alfred," in Snyder, *Encyclopedia of the Third Reich*, p. 300.

49. For Rosenberg's biography, see Snyder, *Encyclopedia of the Third Reich*, pp. 299–301. An older, and still useful, treatment is found in Albert Chandler, *Rosenberg's Nazi Myth* (Ithaca, NY: Cornell University Press, 1945). Chandler translates *seelige* as "mental," and we believe "psychical" better captures Rosenberg's idea of a "soulish" element in life. Extracts have been translated into English as Alfred Rosenberg, *Race and Race History and Other Essays*, ed. Robert Pois (New York: Harper and Row, 1970).

50. Levy Smolar, "Ernest Renan's Interpretation of Biblical History," in *Biblical and Related Studies Presented to Samuel Iwry*, ed. Ann Kort and Scott Morschauer (Winona Lake, IN: Eisenbrauns, 1985), pp. 237–57.

51. We also disagree partly with the following statement by David Redles ("Nazism and Holocaust," *Encyclopedia of Religion and War*, ed. Gabriel Palmer-Fernandez [New York: Routledge, 2004], p. 325) for similar reasons: "Many historians still today mistakenly equate Nazi anti-Christian views with an overall anti-spiritual perspective." But, just as in the case of Rosenberg, much of what is called "anti-Christian" in Nazi literature may best be classified as "anti-Christendom," or Christianity as reflected in dominant organized institutions such as Catholicism, which is seen by Rosenberg as a corrupt version of the "true" Christianity.

52. Rosenberg, *Der Mythus*, p. 74.

53. Ibid., p. 75. My translation of the German: "Gegen diese gesamte Verbastardierung, Verointalisierung und Verjudung des Christentums wehrte sich bereits das durchaus noch aristokartischen Geist atmende Johannesevangelium." Pois's edition (*Race and Race History*, p. 70) translates *Johannesevangelium* as "evangelical teachings of St. John," which obscures Rosenberg's more specific reference to the book we call the Gospel of John.

54. Rosenberg, *Der Mythus*, p. 78.

55. Rosenberg, *Race and Race History*, p. 180.

56. Rosenberg, in particular was a devoted reader of the renowned biblical scholars Ernest Renan and Paul Anton De Lagarde (1827–1897), whom he eulogizes in *Der Mythus*, p. 458. For the case of Gerhard Kittel, another famous biblical scholar associated with supporting the Nazi cause, see Robert P. Ericksen, *Theologians under Hitler: Gerhard Kittel, Paul Althaus, and Emanuel Hirsch* (New Haven, CT: Yale University Press, 1985), pp. 28–78; and Max Weinreich, *Hitler's Professors: The Part of Scholarship in Germany's Crimes against the Jewish People* (1946; reprint, New Haven, CT: Yale University Press, 1999), especially pp. 40–43, 215–16.

57. Abu al-Fida as cited in Friedmann, *Tolerance and Coercion*, pp. 68–69.

58. Niditch, *War in the Hebrew Bible*, p. 130.

59. We need not go as far back as the Neanderthals for the origin of racism, as

the speculative theory of Ferren MacIntyre ("Was Religion a Kinship Surrogate?" *JAAR* 72, no. 3 [2004]: 660) claims. We have no real data on how Neanderthals saw other groups of hominids.

60. Hitler, *Mein Kampf*, p. 65/German, p. 70: "So glaube ich heute im Sinne des allmächtigen Schöpfers zu handeln: Indem ich mich des Judenwehre, kämpfe ich für das Werk des Herrn."

61. Hitler, *Mein Kampf*, p. 112/German, p. 123: "Der Protestantismus vertritt von sich aus die Belange des Deutschtums besser, soweit dies in seiner Geburt und späteren Tradition überhaupt schon begründet liegt."

62. Hitler, *Mein Kampf*, p. 213: "Beside Frederick the Great stands Martin Luther as well as Richard Wagner"/German, p. 232: "Neben Friedrich der Grossen stehen hier Martin Luther sowohl als wie Richard Wagner."

63. Hitler, *Mein Kampf*, p. 312/German, p. 342: "Die Rasse aber liegt nicht in der Sprache, sondern ausschliesslich im Blute, etwas, das niemand besser weiss als der Jude, der gerade auf die Erhaltung seiner Sprache nur sehr wenig Wert legt, hingegen allen Wert auf die Reinhaltung seines Blutes."

64. Hitler, *Mein Kampf*, p. 249/German, p. 272.

65. Hitler, *Mein Kampf*, p. 338/German, p. 372: "Im Blute allein liegt sowohl die Kraft als auch die Schwäche des Menschen begründet."

66. Hitler, *Mein Kampf*, p. 151/German, p. 165.

67. Hitler, *Mein Kampf*, p. 151/German, p. 165.

68. Hitler, *Mein Kampf*, p. 339/German, p. 372: "fremden Erreger."

69. Hitler, *Mein Kampf*, p. 135/German, p. 148.

70. Menahem Stern, ed., *Greek and Latin Authors on Jews and Judaism* (Jerusalem: Israel Academy of Sciences and Humanities, 1974), 1:384.

71. See further, Linda Martz, "Pure Blood Statutes in Sixteenth-Century Toledo: Implementation as Opposed to Adoption," *Sefarad* 61, no. 1 (1994): 91–94; Albert Sicroff, *Los estatutos de limpieza de sangre: Controversias entre los siglos xv y xvii*, translated from French into Spanish by Mauro Armiño (Madrid: Taurus ediciones, 1985); Henry Kamen, *The Spanish Inquisition: A Historical Revision* (London: Weidenfeld and Nicolson, 1997), especially pp. 242–54; and *Philip of Spain* (New Haven, CT: Yale University Press, 1997), pp. 33–34.

72. Ali, *A Manual of Hadith*, p. 316.

73. Rashi, *Chumash: With Rashi's Commentary*, ed. A. M. Silberstein, 5 vols. (Jerusalem: Silberman Family, 1934).

74. Sanhedrin 37b has more literally "seeds" (*zr'wtyw*), which is translated "descendants." The German Jewish scholar, Abraham Geiger (*Was hat Mohammed aus dem Judenthume aufgenommen?* [Bonn: F. Baaden, 1833], pp. 104–105) also notes that this Jewish interpretation is probably to be found, in less obvious form, in the Qur'an. Geiger translates the relevant form of the Hebrew *zera'* as "nachkommen" ("descendants"), as well.

75. For another perspective, focusing on marriage of priests with Jewish women, see Martha Himmelfarb, "Levi, Phinehas, and the Problem of Intermarriage at the Time of the Maccabean Revolt," *Jewish Studies Quarterly* 6 (1999): 1–24.

76. Samuel D. Goitein, *A Mediterranean Society: The Jewish Communities of the World as Portrayed in the Documents of the Cairo Geniza* (Berkeley and Los Angeles:

University of California Press, 1999), 3:1. See also Tzvi Abusch, "Blood in Israel and Mesopotamia," in *Emanuel: Studies in the Hebrew Bible, Septuagint, and Dead Sea Scrolls in Honor of Emanuel Tov*, ed. Shalom M. Paul et al. (Leiden/Boston: Brill, 2003), pp. 675–84.

77. Archer, *Encyclopedia of Bible Difficulties*, p. 121.

78. Hitler, *Mein Kampf*, p. 150/German, p. 165: "Er gehört zu den genialsten Tricks, die jemals erfunden worden find, diesen Staat als "Religion" segeln zu lassen und ihn dadurch der Toleranz zu versichern, die der Arier dem religiösen Bekenntnis immer zuzubilligen bereit ist. Denn tatsächlich ist die mosaische Religion nichts anderes als eine Lehre der Erhaltung der judischen Rasse."

79. Ernst Haeckel, *Die Lebenswunder: Gemeinverständliche Studien über biologische Philosophie* (Leipzig: Alfred Kröner Verlag, 1925), p. 369: "Die vervollkommete Moral, frei von allen religiösen Dogma und auf die klare Erkenntnis der Naturgesetze gegründet, lehrt uns die alte Weisheit der goldenen Regel . . . mit den Worten des Evangeliums: 'Liebe deinen Nächsten als dich selbst.'"

80. Jon Levenson, "Is There a Counterpart in the Hebrew Bible to the New Testament Antisemitism?" *Journal of Ecumenical Studies* 22, no. 2 (1985): 260.

81. As Steven Pinker (*The Blank Slate: The Modern Denial of Human Nature* [New York: Viking, 2002], p. 155) astutely observes, Nazism and Stalinism had opposing views of psychology and biology.

CHAPTER 13

STALINISM

I f Hitler does not qualify as an atheist, Stalin certainly does in the eyes of many. Moreover, it has been claimed that Stalinist terror provides a primary example of how violence can be caused by atheism. Vance Ferrell, author of the antievolution compendium *The Evolution Cruncher*, tells us that "Lenin was an ardent evolutionist and so was Stalin. In fact, it was the message he read in Darwin's book that turned Stalin into the bestial creature he became."[1] In general, such statements are poorly documented or come from secondhand sources.

Our discussion will show that Stalin's reign of terror had as much to do with politics as it did with atheism. Stalin, in fact, had a complex relationship with religious institutions in the Soviet Union. Much of our discussion will be documented with archival materials that have been brought to light only since the arrival of glasnost and fall of Communism.

Josef Stalin (1879–1953) was the steely leader of the Soviet Union from 1924 to 1953. According to standard biographies, Stalin was born Josif Dzhugashvili to illiterate peasant parents in Gori, Georgia.[2] His mother envisioned him as a priest in the Russian Orthodox Church, and Stalin actually pursued religious studies until he was about twenty. He began his activities with socialists around 1899, and took part in the Bolshevik Revolution that toppled Czar Nicholas II (1868–1918) in 1917. He was named "Stalin" ("steel") after the revolution. After the death of Vladimir Lenin (1870–1924), the prime mover of the revolution, Stalin rose to power after a series of struggles with other Communist leaders. In the wake of the Great Purge of his rivals in 1936–38, Stalin ruled virtually as sole dictator of the Soviet Union until his death in 1953.

THE POLITICS OF THE GREAT TERROR

Until about a decade ago, most scholars actually knew very little about Josef Stalin's private thoughts on much of anything, as many of the principal documents remained unavailable. As late as 1990 Walter Laqueur, the prominent biographer of Stalin, lamented, "Stalin's private papers have not been discovered so far and no one can say for sure whether they still exist."[3]

This situation did not deter those who claimed that Stalin is a prime example of the evil atheism can cause. John Blanchard, author of a compendium against atheism, says of Stalin, "[H]is contempt for God was especially demonstrated in his vicious persecution of believers, many of whom died for their faith in the course of a vicious purge which, in one authority's estimate, led to the systematic slaughter of some ten million people."[4]

With the advent of the Gorbachev era, archives became more accessible to scholars. The late 1990s saw the publication of important collections of Stalin's personal correspondence and documents concerning the Great Terror, as the purges under Stalin came to be called. Of special importance is the correspondence preserved with Vyacheslav M. Molotov (1890–1986) and Lazar Kaganovich (1893–1957), two of Stalin's adjutants in the 1920s and 1930s.[5] Equally important was the documentation concerning the period between 1932 and 1939.[6]

Despite the new disclosures, Stalin's motives for the Great Terror are still very difficult to discern. As J. Arch Getty and Oleg V. Naumov comment concerning these newly revealed documents:

> They do not tell us exactly when Stalin became convinced that mass terror was necessary, nor do they fully illuminate his thoughts. They do not prove whether there was a plan to conduct terror or the extent to which conscious plans were made to facilitate it. Scholars and readers will still have to make their own judgements about such questions, but at least now they have more to go on.[7]

Indeed, we cannot find any direct evidence that Stalin's own personal agenda killed because of atheism. That is to say, Stalin never justified any actions with direct statements such as, "I do not believe in God, therefore I am committing violent act X." As we have shown previously, the same is not the case with many of the actions attributed to the religious actants in our examples. In many of those cases, we can indeed find direct statements of the form: "I believe God wants X, therefore I am committing violent act Y."

However, we also said that inference was also an allowable method to establish causation, and we can do the same with Stalin. Stalin did follow many antireligious policies that can reasonably be attributed to his atheism.

Much evidence for this has been collected in the works of Dimitry Pospielovsky.[8] Persecution of churches included their closures, destruction, imprisonment, and murder of clergy. Such actions can indeed be reduced to the form: "I do not believe in God, therefore I am committing violent act X."

Pospielovsky's work also supports the argument that not all of the anti-religious activity was violent. For example, some of the activity took the form of conferences and books, such as the one on the Dead Sea Scrolls. Some of the violence against churches needs to be qualified by the fact that sometimes the Soviets were favoring pro-Soviet churches or pro-Soviet believers. Churches that cooperated with the Communist agenda were sometimes allowed to operate, while churches that were not cooperative were usually repressed violently. In some ways, this is no different than church-state relations in the rest of Europe.[9]

Other violent aspects of what is denominated as the Great Terror under Stalin can be shown to be primarily political rather than atheistic. In order to understand this, we have to distinguish between two distinct, although related, types of violent agendas during the Stalin era. One was directed at the kulaks, the general name for wealthy farmers or for almost anyone that opposed his agricultural policies. The other violent campaign was internal, and directed at Communist bureaucrats who were deemed inimical to Stalin or to his agenda.[10]

The liquidation of the kulaks is quite well documented. Stalin himself spoke of the "liquidation of the Kulaks" as part of his agenda. However, this had little to do with atheism. The action against the kulaks can be traced to Stalin's first Five-Year Plan, announced in 1929. Stalin envisioned a rapid pace of industrialization and the collectivization of farms. The rapid modernization of agriculture was necessary because kulaks produced the food that would be consumed by the workers moving toward a full-blown collective economy.

The kulaks, naturally, were opposed to being dispossessed of their land. It was this resistance that led to the mass execution of many kulaks. A number of crucial documents allude to this process. One is a speech given by Nicolai Bukharin (1888–1938), a close associate of Stalin and, for a time, head of a section of the Supreme Council for the National Economy of the Soviet Union. Bukharin addressed a plenary session of the Soviet Central Committee on December 19, 1930, and remarked, "In my opinion, the destruction of the kulaks constitutes, in the first place, a decisive, and, if I may speak frankly, painful process entailing a direct break with the old structure, a process of refashioning [*peredelka*] the petty peasant economy on the basis of socialist collectivization."[11]

A memo from Kaganovich and M. F. Shkiriatov also indicates the nature of the resistance being suppressed by Stalin's officials. The memo speaks of a counterrevolutionary organization called "The People's Community Party." According to the memo, "The objective of this counterrevolutionary organization was the overthrow of Soviet power, the dissolution of the kolkhozy and the restoration of individual farming [*edinolichnoye khoziaistvo*] as the predominant form of agriculture."[12] The memo goes on to urge resistance to this organization because it favored using anti-Semitic propaganda and the organization of "Hitlerite pogroms."[13]

Even Stalin's most vocal critics did not attribute his violence to atheism, but rather to a misguided zeal for rapid industrialization and collectivization. Perhaps the most frank critic of Stalin during the Stalinist period was M. N. Riutin (1890–1937), who served as a member of the Presidium for the Supreme Council for the National Economy. In 1932 he published what has come to be known as the Riutin Platform, a document that was suppressed. The Riutin Platform is a scathing critique of Stalin, and it discussed the kulaks. Riutin notes that Stalin's plan had actually proven to be a disaster, commenting,

> Stalin's slogan, "the liquidation of the kulaks as a class" cannot possibly lead to any real definitive liquidation of the kulaks, since the basis for this slogan—"all-out collectivization"—is not founded on a genuine "turn among the broad masses of the countryside toward socialism." On the contrary, it is founded on the most direct and indirect form of the most severe coercion, designed to force the peasants to join the kolkhozy. It is founded not on an improvement in their condition but on their direct and indirect expropriation and massive impoverishment.[14]

Note that, as Riutin understood it, the "liquidation of the kulaks as a class" was to involve their transition from the kulak class to the class of the kolkhozy (collective farms). This was supposed to result in the betterment of the former kulaks. However, the unintended result of Stalin's plan was detrimental to the kulaks. Ironically, Riutin sees Stalin as helping incite a civil war that was contrary to the true essence of Communism. Riutin, in fact, refuses to group Stalin with great Communist leaders such as Marx and Lenin.

Although Riutin credits Stalin personally with destruction of the kulaks, one can also find evidence that Stalin could not control overzealous officials who were directly responsible for the violence against the kulaks. As Getty and Naumov note, Stalin even called for a "halt to forced collectivization and ordered a reduction in the use of violence against peasants" in a March 2, 1930, article in *Pravda*.[15]

A secret decree, now published, shows that the destruction of the kulaks can be seen, in part, as one in which lower echelons went farther than the upper echelons intended. This decree, issued by the Central Committee and dated May 8, 1933, instructs lower-level officers to cease arresting people "for no reason" and to stop the practice of "arrest first, ask questions later."[16] The decree goes on to state:

> These comrades do not understand that the method of mass, disorderly arrests, if this can be considered a method—represents, in light of the new situation, only liabilities, which diminish the authority of Soviet power. They do not understand that making arrests ought to be limited and carried out under strict control of the appropriate organs. They do not understand that the arrests must be directed solely against active enemies of Soviet power.[17]

Getty and Naumov note the hypocrisy of this decree in light of the fact that these officials were trying to reverse violence that they themselves had sanctioned. Nonetheless, the point remains that none of these directives against the kulaks can be linked solely to atheism. The actions can be seen as part of a misguided and brutal effort to force collectivization upon the masses.

STALIN AND THE CHURCH

Recent revelations also help to elucidate Stalin's complex relationship with the Russian Orthodox Church (ROC). Of particular importance has been the work of Tatiana A. Chumachenko, who teaches in the Department of Modern Russian History at Chelyabinsk State University. Her *Church and State in Soviet Russia: Russian Orthodoxy from World War II to the Khrushchev Years* appeared in English in 2000.[18] More recently, Steven Miner has provided a study of a crucial period between 1941 and 1945.[19]

Chumachenko's work was mostly archival, the main source being the collection of the Council for Russian Orthodox Church Affairs. The important feature of these archives is that they had never been removed or purged. Two groups of documents can be identified, according to Chumachenko. The first group consists of high-level documents from the council itself. Within this group, Chumachenko encountered formerly top-secret Memoranda of Instructions by Members of the Government Relating to the Activity of the Russian Orthodox Church, which have now proven invaluable.[20] A second group consists of documents that speak of the relationship between the council and regional commissaries.

The work of Mikhail I. Odintsov also bears mentioning, as he has helped to provide a periodization for church-state relations in the former Soviet Union.[21] For Odintsov, the period between 1943 and 1948–49 was crucial. On September 4, 1943, Stalin met with bishops of the ROC. Georgi Karpov, the chairman of the Council for Russian Orthodox Church Affairs, wrote a report on the meeting which became public only in 1989. The Russian text was published by Odintsov.[22]

The meeting resulted in a normalization of relations with the ROC. This normalization led to Decree 1095, issued on October 7, 1943.[23] The decree outlined the duties of the Council for Russian Orthodox Church Affairs, which functioned as the official liaison between the government and the Patriarch of Moscow. The council had, among other duties, the review of issues and requests raised by the Patriarch of Moscow, as well as overseeing regulation of laws pertaining to church issues. In short, the normalization under Stalin meant that the church became a government organ.

But for the average Russian it meant the sight of "overflowing churches on Orthodox holidays, the possibility of conducting religious rites in homes, ringing bells to call believers to services, and festive religious processions with large crowds of people."[24] The number of open churches more than doubled (from 207 to 509) between 1944 and 1945.[25] The number of churches and chapels reported open by the Council for Russian Orthodox Church Affairs went from 9,829 in October 1943, about the time Stalin normalized relations with the ROC, to 14,187 in January 1948.[26] In 1944 about 148,000 people went to Easter services in Moscow churches.[27] In a single church in the city of Kuibyshev, 22,045 baptisms were recorded in 1945, and 5,412 were recorded in the first three months of 1946 alone.[28]

Stalin promised financial assistance to the ROC in the meeting of 1943, and records show a resulting growth in income for the ROC. The income for all the Moscow churches was 550,000 rubles in 1946, and 3,150,000 rubles in 1947.[29]

What these documents also indicate is that provincial authorities sometimes disobeyed Stalin's orders for more tolerance toward the ROC. In 1947 the council received 2,033 complaints about opposition from authorities to the opening of churches.[30] Some officials refused to open theological institutions despite orders signed by Stalin himself.[31]

But churches were not completely powerless, even against some bureaucrats. In 1944 in the Riazan region, a regional executive committee tried to demolish a building that was to be used as a church. The official explanation was that it was unsafe. The bureaucrats met resistance from workers in the collective farms, and eventually the building was declared "in good condition."[32]

The ROC also cooperated with the government in suppressing rival denominations. One example is the renovation movement, known also as the Living Church, which attempted to combine Bolshevism with Orthodox Christianity. The Living Church, led by Metropolitan Alexander Vvedenskii, was considered schismatic, especially as it allowed married clergy. Correspondence, including some with Stalin's notations, show that there was an active campaign to bring about the demise of the renovationists. The movement lost much power after the death of Vvedenskii in 1946, though some churches continued to be active until at least 1948.[33]

In any case, the study of church-state relations under Stalin show both an atheistic reign of terror against religion and a more conciliatory stance when it served Stalin's political purposes. Rather than representing some radical atheistic innovation, Stalin's normalization was more akin to the church-state unions common in many Western Christian countries.[34] Rather than showing Stalin's reign of terror as simply an atheistic plot, the new documents show that the ROC continued its pre-Communist alliance, though tenuous and complex, with the elite powers. In fact, the new question should be the extent to which the ROC cooperated with the government to suppress rival denominations.

COMMUNISM IN THE BIBLE

The crediting of atheism for Stalin's crimes usually can be tied to a simplistic and false equation: "Communism = atheism and atheism = communism. In fact, communism, if defined as a form of social organization based on collective ownership of property, need not be atheistic at all. Significant movements (e.g., liberation theology) and noted groups (e.g., Hutterites) exist that identify as Christian but still espouse communism in some form. And the violence caused by Stalin's forced collectivization can be found on a smaller scale in the biblical case of forced collectivization discussed below.

Indeed, readers of the Bible seem to ignore that one of the first enunciations of communism is in the New Testament.[35] The book of Acts relates the story of one of the first forms of an ideal society formed by early Christians. Acts 4:32–35 tells us about the communistic nature of this society:

> Now the whole group of those who believed were of one heart and soul, and no one claimed private ownership of any possessions, but everything they owned was held in common.

> With great power the apostles gave their testimony to the resurrection of the Lord Jesus, and great grace was upon them all.

> There was not a needy person among them, for as many as owned lands or houses sold them and brought the proceeds of what was sold.

> They laid it at the apostles' feet, and it was distributed to each as any had need.

Moreover, this attempt at collective ownership was accompanied by violence and coercion in the story that immediately follows in Acts 5.

According to Acts 5:1–11, Ananias and Sapphira were a married couple who had sold their property as part of this collectivization process. However, unlike a man named Levi, who had given all of the proceeds of his sale to the apostles, Ananias held some of the profit from the apostles. The apostle Peter immediately confronted Ananias, and rendered the following indictment:

> "Ananias," Peter asked, "why has Satan filled your heart to lie to the Holy Spirit and to keep back part of the proceeds of the land?
>
> While it remained unsold, did it not remain your own? And after it was sold, were not the proceeds at your disposal? How is it that you have contrived this deed in your heart? You did not lie to us but to God!"
>
> Now when Ananias heard these words, he fell down died. And great fear seized all who heard of it. (Acts 5:3–5)

About three hours later, Sapphira, who knew of Ananias's retention of profits, encountered Peter. The latter pronounced God's death sentence on her, and she died. The story ends in Acts 5:11 with the following note: "And great fear seized the whole church and all who heard of these things."

The story in Acts has two elements paralleled in Stalinist policy, insofar as we understand it. First, there was a stated goal of collectivization. Second, those found not to be cooperating with collectivization were the objects of violence. The numbers of people killed may have been different, but the principle is similar: Violence is a proper method of dealing with those who do not cooperate with collectivization.

Arguing that Ananias's crime was lying or backing out on a promise to God does not mitigate the principle we have identified as parallel. The author still endorses the idea that a promise to enjoin collectivization can be enforced through violence. The one main difference, of course, is that God's orders and wishes are not verifiable, as the author of Acts claimed. Any people killed under these premises truly would have suffered for a violation of a promise to a nonexisting entity or at least an entity not known to exist, whereas the violence under Stalin violated the rules of a person who actually did exist, however unjustified those rules may have been.

SUMMARY

The idea that atheism was responsible for the mass terror under Stalin is partly true. Atheism was certainly a part of the reason for antireligious violence throughout the Soviet era. The larger factor, however, seems to be political. Stalin's actions against the kulaks represents an instance of a policy of forced collectivization rather than an atheistic policy. Other repressive actions could be tied to the creation of a Pan-Soviet identity.[36] To what extent the action against the kulaks was carried out by overzealous officials and to what extent any mass violence represents what Stalin initially and personally intended is disputable. Such forced collectivization would probably lead to violence whether one believes in God, as in the case of Ananias and Sapphira, or not, as in the case of Stalinism.

NOTES

1. Vance Ferrell, *The Evolution Cruncher* (Altamont, TN: Evolution Facts, 2001), pp. 820–21.

2. Our biography of Stalin is distilled from Walter Laqueur, *Stalin: The Glasnost Revelations* (New York: Scribner's, 1990).

3. Ibid., p. 337.

4. John Blanchard, *Does God Believe in Atheists?* (Auburn, MA: Evangelical Press, 2000), p. 68. For a review of Blanchard's book, see Hector Avalos, *Free Inquiry* (Fall 2002): 69–70.

5. Lars T. Lih, Oleg Naumov, and Oleg V. Khlevniuk, eds., *Stalin's Letters to Molotov* (New Haven, CT: Yale University Press, 1995); R. W. Davies, Oleg V. Khlevniuk, and E. A. Rees, *The Stalin-Kaganovich Correspondence 1931–36* (New Haven, CT: Yale University Press, 2003).

6. J. Arch Getty and Oleg V. Naumov, *The Road to Terror: Stalin and the Self-Destruction of the Bolsheviks, 1932–1939* (New Haven, CT: Yale University Press, 1999).

7. Ibid., p. 25.

8. Dimitry V. Pospielovsky, *A History of Soviet Atheism in Theory and Practice and the Believer*, 3 vols. (London: Macmillan, 1987–88). See also Stephen K. Batalden, ed., *Seeking God: The Recovery of Religious Identity in Orthodox Russia, Ukraine, and Georgia* (DeKalb: Northern Illinois University Press, 1993).

9. Examples are numerous, and include notably Henry VIII (1509–1547) and "Bloody" Mary I (1553–1558). See further, Peter A. Dykema and Heiko Oberman, eds., *Anticlericalism in Late Medieval and Early Modern Europe* (Leiden: Brill, 1993).

10. See further, Robert W. Thurston, *Life and Terror in Stalin's Russia 1934–1941* (New Haven, CT: Yale University Press, 1996).

11. Getty and Naumov, *The Road to Terror*, p. 47.

12. Ibid., p. 65.

13. Ibid.

14. Ibid., p. 57.

15. Ibid., p. 109.

16. Ibid., p. 115.

17. Ibid.

18. Tatiana A. Chumachenko, *Church and State in Soviet Russia: Russian Orthodoxy from World War II to the Krushchev Years*, trans. Edward E. Roslof (Armonk, NY: M. E. Sharpe, 2002), p. 11. The original title is *Gosudartsvo, pavoslavnaia tserkov, veruiushchie, 1941–1961* (Moscow: AIRO-XX, 1999).

19. Steven Merritt Miner, *Stalin's Holy War: Religion, Nationalism, and Alliance Politics 1941–1945* (Chapel Hill: University of North Carolina Press, 2003).

20. Chumachenko, *Church and State*, p. 11.

21. Mikhail I. Odintsov, *Russie patriarkhi XX veka: Sud'by Otechestva i Tserkvi na stranitsakh arkhivnykh dokumentov* (Moscow: RAGS, 1999).

22. Ibid., pp. 283–91. It appears as document number 34 in Odintsov's collection of documents.

23. For an English translation, see Chumachenko, *Church and State*, pp. 17–18.

24. Ibid., p. 190.

25. Ibid., p. 59, table 1.1.

26. Ibid., p. 67, table 1.3.

27. Ibid., p. 85.

28. Ibid.

29. Ibid.

30. Ibid., p. 61.

31. Ibid., pp. 71–72.

32. Ibid., p. 62.

33. Ibid., p. 39.

34. For Stalin's policy toward Jews, see Robert Weinberg, *Stalin's Forgotten Zion: Birobidzhan and the Making of a Soviet Jewish Homeland, An Illustrated History, 1928–1996* (Berkeley and Los Angeles: University of California Press, 1998); and Gennadi Kostyrchenko, *Out of the Red Shadows: Anti-Semitism in Stalin's Russia.* (Amherst, NY: Prometheus Books, 1995). For other treatments of Soviet Jewry, see Allan Laine Kagedan, *Soviet Zion: The Quest for a Russian Jewish Homeland* (New York: St. Martin's, 1994); and Nora Levin, *The Jews in the Soviet Union since 1917*, 2 vols. (London: I. B. Taturis, 1990).

35. For a classic application of Marxism to the Bible, see José P. Miranda, *Marx and the Bible: A Critique of the Philosophy of Oppression*, trans. John Eagleson (Maryknoll, NY: Orbis, 1974).

36. For one study of how indigenous Kazakh religious and healing practices were affected by the drive toward a Pan-Soviet identity, see Paula A. Michaels, *Curative Powers: Medicine and Empire in Stalin's Central Asia* (Pittsburgh: University of Pittsburgh Press, 2003). For policy toward Muslims, see Alexandre Bennigsen and S. Enders Wimbush, *Muslims of the Soviet Empire: A Guide* (Bloomington: Indiana University Press, 1986).

CHAPTER 14

THE NATION-STATE AND SECULAR HUMANIST VIOLENCE

If secularism is to be blamed for violence, then some scholars claim that such secularism comes in the form of statism or nationalism. On a popular level, we have already encountered it in Rush Limbaugh's bombastic proclamation that "throughout history that substitute for faith has been a belief in a man-made god called the state. Untold crimes have been committed in its name, Hitler and Stalin being the most bloody recent examples."[1] The same sentiment can be found in more scholarly assessments, as the following from Michael Freeman: "[N]ationalism is like religion in that it can be the ultimate source of value and consequently motivate extraordinary actions."[2] Likewise, Bruce Lawrence observes that nationalism can also be a form of "mimetic religion."[3]

But perhaps one of the most self-assured assaults on the state as a secular form of violence comes from William T. Cavanaugh, a professor of religious studies at the University of St. Thomas, who argues explicitly that much of what appears to be religious violence is in fact fueled by secularist statism that transfers religion to the private sphere.[4] More specifically, Cavanaugh argues against the thesis that the state was a response to the religious wars of the sixteenth and seventeenth centuries in Europe. On the contrary, he argues, the state was not thrust as peacemaker into religious wars, but rather religious wars were caused and encouraged by the rise of the state.

But the most radical part of Cavanaugh's thesis is that religion as a distinct category of consciousness actually did not exist prior to the rise of the state. Cavanaugh, in fact, proposes that "'Wars of Religion' is an anachronism, for what is at issue in these wars was the very creation of religion as a set of privately held beliefs without direct political relevance."[5] For Cavanaugh, what are called religious wars were actually precipitated by a state's efforts to create "a set of private beliefs which is defined as personal conviction and which can exist separately from one's public loyalty to the State." Sometimes he speaks of just "the creation of religion," as if religion did not exist before this time.[6] In so doing, of course, he can avoid crediting religion with any violence, as "religion" does not exist before the sixteenth and seventeenth centuries.[7] Cavanaugh seems unaware that, by his own logic, religion cannot be credited with any good if religion did not exist (at least prior to the sixteenth and seventeenth centuries).

By making religion a private issue, Cavanaugh contends, the state allowed itself a monopoly on the use of violence. Thomas Hobbes is seen as a main architect of the modern state, and the Saint Bartholomew's Day Massacre becomes a main example of state-instigated violence. Cavanaugh concludes that since "the separation of the Church from power did nothing to stench the flow of blood" the solution is to make religion more public again so that it can act as the antidote to statist violence.[8] In short, Cavanaugh provides another plea for more public use of religion to quell violence.

Our purpose here is to demonstrate that Cavanaugh's examples of political wars cannot be blamed only on the rise of the state. Cavanaugh, in fact, has an idiosyncratic definition of "religion," and seems unaware of more complex views of the role of religion and state in the sixteenth and seventeenth centuries. Indeed private religion can be found in ancient Mesopotamia, without any apparent conflict with the state.[9] Finally, we will concede that a secular state can mimic the violent effects of religion because it too can create scarce resources. However, we will argue that a secular approach can still solve the problem of nationalism and statism better than religion can.

THE ORIGINS OF THE MODERN STATE

Cavanaugh's assertions must be seen in light of larger debates on the origin of modern states. As noted by Philip Gorski, the standard view of the rise of the modern state locates the beginning in the seventeenth and eighteenth centuries.[10] The establishment of England's constitutional monarchy and the French Revolution are seen as two key events. The hallmark of the modern state included the secular monopoly of power. Personal identity was linked with the nation rather than with a religion, and each state was independent.

However, many scholars are challenging this historiography, finding the roots of nationalism much earlier. First, and as Anthony W. Marx has pointed out brilliantly in his revisionist history of the rise of nationalism, it is useful to distinguish nationalism from statism. Nationalism is "the political sentiment of popular solidarity intended to coincide with states."[11] One can have feelings of solidarity or nationalism without states, and one can have states without nationalism. States, Marx says, are "institutions claiming a legitimate monopoly of coercion and rule."[12] Once seen in this manner, it is possible to see that the church itself can constitute a "state" that can create large-scale violence.

But the definition of a "state" is itself problematic. The recent round of conflict over the definition can be traced at least as far back as the competing theories of anthropologists Morton Fried and Elman Service. Fried thought the rise of the state was usually violent and coercion was always involved.[13] Service, on the other hand, thought the state originated mainly in the attempt to manage the allocation of resources. In such a management system mutual benefit, rather than force, can be a motive for initiating suprakinship organizations known as "states."[14] Whichever view one chooses, it is clear that more scholars are realizing that entities similar to states and empires can be found all the way to the dawn of recorded history, as writing and the state seem to be linked.[15]

Moreover, it seems clear that there were a variety of pathways to the modern state that cannot be all lumped together.[16] Marx notes that the process can be bidirectional, with "religious identity secularized by states, and states shaped by religion."[17] For example, Marx argues that popular religious solidarity, not privatization of religion, resulted in a state such as that of the Restoration in England. There, Charles I (1625–1649) planned for Catholics to be very much a part of the public expression of religion, in opposition to popular anti-Catholic sentiment. Because of this, the anti-Catholic populace helped dethrone him.[18] In other cases, the imposition of a generalized and public religion was enforced by a state, as in the case of Spain, where the Inquisition sought to impose public religious uniformity.

THE SAINT BARTHOLOMEW'S DAY MASSACRE

But even if we were to disagree with Marx's analysis of the rise of the state, it is clear that there are serious flaws in Cavanaugh's analysis of particular historical examples. One case in point is the famous Saint Bartholomew's Day Massacre of 1572. The events surrounding this massacre are complex, but most historians agree that the massacre is related to an attempted assassination of Gaspard de Coligny, an admiral who was the main representative of the French Huguenots.[19] Coligny was shot on August 22, 1572, allegedly by a Catholic named Maurevert. Coligny was subsequently assassinated as he was recovering from his wounds. Claiming the fear of revenge by

Huguenots, Catholic leaders apparently launched a preemptive and generalized massacre of Huguenots in Paris on August 24 and in other towns in subsequent days. The death toll has been variously placed between two thousand and some seventy thousand.

Cavanaugh argues that this massacre was really part of a political plot by the Queen Mother, Catherine de Medici (1519–1589). She had a large influence on her son, Charles IX (1550–1574), who was only twenty-two when he took the throne. Specifically, Cavanaugh claims that "[t]he Queen Mother who unleashed the massacre . . . was not a religious zealot but a thoroughgoing *Politique* with a stake in stopping the nobility's challenge to royal pretensions toward absolute power."[20] The motive, argues Cavanaugh, was her frustration with the inability to create a state church that would unite both Protestant Huguenots and Catholics.

But Cavanaugh cites at most two sources for this indictment of Catherine de Medici, and both are secondary studies.[21] Cavanaugh otherwise shows no familiarity with primary source material surrounding the massacre,[22] though the source material available at the time that Cavanaugh wrote noted the difficulty in identifying the specific chain of responsibility. Some sources blame Catherine, while others blame Guise, a Catholic official.[23]

When one looks at the correspondance of King Charles IX himself, one finds that he is either in the dark or is feigning ignorance on the day of the massacre. In a letter dated August 24, Charles IX writes to the governor of Lyon, François de Mandelot, saying: "I will do everything possible to verify the facts and punish those culpable" for the assault on Admiral Coligny.[24] Other interpreters of the same correspondence see much more premeditation on the part of Charles and his mother.[25] The comments of James Smither best summarize our quandary: "The question of who was responsible for which aspects of the massacre is not entirely clear and perhaps never will be."[26]

POPE GREGORY XIII AND THE MASSACRE

A most telling piece of evidence for the religious nature of the massacre, and one passed over in silence by Cavanaugh, is the reaction of Pope Gregory XIII. Far from condemning the massacre as the work of political intrigue, he celebrated the massacre and commissioned the artist Giorgio Vasari (1511–1574), to create commemorative murals in the Sala Regia of the Apostolic Palace at the Vatican. As Robert Kingdon notes, "It has almost certainly become something of an embarrassment to the Vatican in this more ecumenical age; the Sala Regia is no longer regularly open to the general public as part of the Vatican Museum."[27]

Likewise, a commemorative medallion commissioned by the pope provides no hint that he thought that the massacre was a purely political mishap. The medallion, an exemplar of which is stored at the British Museum, bears the legend "Gregorius XIII" on one side, and "*Ugonottorum strages*" (Huguenot conspirators) on the other.[28] Depicted on the latter side is an avenging angel with a cross in one hand and a sword in the other. Interestingly, an illustration of the medallion was omitted from the English translation of Philippe Erlanger's well-known history of the massacre.[29]

Why Cavanaugh neglects to mention these facts is a mystery,[30] but it is clear that Cavanaugh is simply following a long apologetic tradition found in *The Catholic Encyclopedia* of 1912. In an article in that reference work, Georges Goyau provides an official view of the Catholic Church, noting that he sees the massacre as rooted in "the half-pagan doctrine of Machiavellism," which allowed political murder.[31] Cavanaugh, as we have seen, blames Thomas Hobbes's ideas. Both Cavanaugh and Goyau deny that Catholic beliefs are at all responsible for the massacre.

But both Machiavelli and Hobbes can be read in different ways. For example, Machiavelli himself did not think he was merely imitating paganism in his view of statescraft. On the contrary, two of his specific examples of effective governors were Popes Julius II and Alexander VI. In fact, Machiavelli said that he once discussed governance with the Archbishop of Rouen, who was questioning the ability of Italians to make war. Machiavelli indignantly replied "that the French did not understand statesmanship; for if they understood it they would never have allowed the Church to attain such greatness."[32] Machiavelli did not see a big difference between church and state.[33] Perhaps it was precisely *because* Machiavelli thought that those religious figures acted no better than secular ones that he became convinced that power is at the root of governing, regardless of whether or not one is religious.

The available sources also clearly refute another attempt to minimize the religious nature of the assaults on Protestants. While acknowledging the celebratory nature of Gregory XIII's reaction (as well as mentioning the medallion and Vasari's murals), *The Catholic Encyclopedia* also claims that such a celebratory mood ceased when details of the massacre as a heinous political act became clearer.[34] In particular, Goyau claims that Pope Gregory XII's refusal in October 1572 to receive Maurevert, who was accused of shooting Coligny on August 22, meant that the pope had come to see the massacre as a criminal act. Goyau concludes:

> As to the congratulations and the manifestations of joy which the news of the massacre elicited from Gregory XIII, they can only be fairly judged by

assuming that the Holy See, like all Europe and indeed many Frenchmen, believed in the existence of a Huguenot conspiracy of whose overthrow the Court boasted and whose punishment an obsequious parliament had completed.[35]

However, a thorough study of the source material pertaining to the massacre refutes all of these assertions, as well as some of the Cavanaugh's main arguments. One such study was undertaken by Robert Kingdon.[36] Four sources, in particular, are sufficient to show the religious nature of the events surrounding the massacre. We have undertaken our own independent study of each of these sources.

The first important source consists of the official instructions given in 1571 to Antonio Maria Salviati, the papal nuncio to France under both Pope Pius V and Gregory XIII. He served as nuncio at the time of the massacre.[37] Particularly instructive is the correspondence between Salviati and Tolomeo Cardinal Galli, secretary to Pope Gregory XIII. Much of this correspondence instructs Salviati to complain about the increased power given to Huguenots, and especially to Coligny. At the same time, many parish churches were being instructed to carry out anti-Protestant activities.[38]

The idea that the pope did not know of the savagery of the massacre is contradicted by Salviati's report, dated August 24 and 27, to Galli, which notes, "The entire city is up in arms, and the homes of Huguenots are besieged and attacked, many people assaulted, and the mob is sacking with incredible zeal."[39] He goes on to note that he does not think a single Catholic was killed or injured.[40] Galli indicates having received Salviati's report in a letter dated September 8, 1572, the same day the pope celebrated the massacre with an elaborate service in Rome. Galli added that the pope was overjoyed at the prospect of "purging the Kingdom of France of the Huguenot plague."[41]

Nor do we see any regret in the weeks following the massacre. In a letter dated September 10, 1572, Galli expresses his wish that the king of France use liberal authority against heretics in his diocese "in order to purge it from heresy and in order that we may enact the decrees of the Council of Trent."[42] In a letter dated October 6, 1572, Galli tells Salviati that the pope is quite pleased with the "joyous progress that with the Grace of God . . . his majesty has achieved in actions against the Huguenots."[43]

The murals of Vasari tell us that the pope was not regretful after Goyau tells us he was. We have Vasari's correspondence regarding the murals.[44] In a letter dated November 17, 1572, Vasari comments on the pope's request for a mural about the "Huguenot affair" (*la cosa degli Ugonotti*), and indicates that he had not yet begun the murals.[45] By December 12, he seems to have a plan for organizing the murals.[46] Vasari reports that by January 30, 1573, the pope had seen the outlines of the murals that were to be painted. These murals show that, except in one case, all the victims were unarmed. Women and children are depicted being literally butchered. There is no hint of regret, and much sense of satisfaction in Vasari's description of the pope's reactions.

A pair of instructions provided to later nuncios constitutes evidence for papal attitudes years after the massacre. A set of nearly identical instructions were given to Giovanni Battista Castelli in 1581 and Girolamo Ragazzoni in 1583. Far from indicating that Pope Gregory XIII had come to see the massacre as some sort of criminal act by October of 1572, these instructions urged the continuance of war against the Protestants. As Kingdon remarks, "Instructions to later nuncios to France make it clear that whenever the French crown was considering a choice between peace and internal religious war, the official representative of the papacy was to urge war."[47]

Our own study of this correspondence confirms Kingdon's assessment. Thus, instructions to Ragazzoni specifically say that when it comes to choosing between war and peace with the Huguenots, then the advice is "to prefer always war rather than peace because with the enemies of God one must never have peace."[48] Indeed, these sources also devastate Cavanaugh's claim that the state was responsible for this anti-Protestant war, while the church would have made a suitable peacemaker.

It is remarkable that Pierre Hurtubise, the Catholic scholar who edited Salviati's correspondence, concludes: "[W]hen we consider the attitude of Rome toward the Protestants in sixteenth-century France, we remember that the belief in 'violence pays,' had a very important counterpart: 'reform pays.'"[49] That reform, we submit, was the rise of the secular state, which, though not perfect, managed to minimize at least some of the religious conflict that had proven so devastating to Europe.

Contrary to the apologetic efforts of Cavanaugh and Goyau, the Saint Bartholomew's Day Massacre shows how deeply involved the church was in fomenting rhetoric and policies that made such a massacre probable. In fact, massacres against Protestants had already been accomplished at, among other places and dates, Pont Notre Dame in December of 1570 and in Orange in February of 1571. If Catherine de Medici, or any other politician, was able to unleash anything, it is because religious hatred was already there to begin with. Had there been no steady drumbeat of violent anti-Protestant rhetoric and instructions from the Vatican and its allied institutions, there would have been no reason for Catholic populations to behave the way they did against their neighbors.

A statement about the Saint Bartholomew's Day Massacre was finally issued by Pope John Paul II in 1997. It read, in part: "On the eve of 24 August we cannot forget the sad Massacre of Saint Bartholomew's Day, an event of very obscure causes in the political and religious history of France.

Christians did things which the Gospel condemns."[50] However, the causes are not all that obscure to anyone who reads correspondence between the Vatican and France. The causes are not obscure to those who see Vasari's murals. And, by saying "Christians" instead of "Catholics," the pope seems to neglect Salviati's observations that it was specifically Catholics, not all Christians, who were doing most of the attacking on that day.

In sum, Cavanaugh's theory that religious wars in the sixteenth and seventeenth centuries were mainly caused by the states's efforts to privatize religion are fatally flawed. Sometimes states attempted to privatize religion because of preexisting religious factionalism. Sometimes states used preexisting religious differences for their own purposes. Sometimes popular religiosity managed to mold the state for its purposes. Cavanaugh's idea that more public religious participation by citizens is the cure for statism is certainly not borne out by the example provided by the Saint Bartholomew's Day Massacre.

SUMMARY

This chapter has shown that some famous instances of violence attributed to the rise of secularized states are, in fact, the result of religious factors. For example, the massacre of the Huguenots was mostly the result of religious divisions and tensions, not the result of some increased secularization of France, as argued by Cavanaugh. The religious factors in what looks like purely statist violence are often missed because religionist apologists are not familiar with primary sources. This is not to deny that nationalism and statism cannot cause violence. However, religionist apologists often have too monolithic a view of a secular state.

Nationalism and statism can certainly cause violence on their own.[51] States may create scarce resources for which people will compete and die. For example, a state may control territory and not allow outsiders, much like religions create sacred space and do not allow outsiders inside. Similarly, nationalism may create group privileges that can then be used to oppress outsiders. States may claim a monopoly on violence in a manner that is not beneficial to outsiders or the world at large, as witnessed by the threat of nuclear armaments.

On the other hand, secular states also have been successful in deterring religious violence in pre- and postindustrial societies. E. E. Evans-Pritchard, in his study of tribal warfare among the Nuer of Africa, observed, "To-day such fights are less common because fear of Government intervention acts as a deterrent."[52] Likewise, the more secularized democracies such as the

United States, Iceland, Norway, and Sweden see much less religious violence than is found in the Middle East and other less secularized regions.

And it would be inaccurate to equate the state with the only form of organization envisioned by secular humanism. Alternative ideas to the nationalist state have been proposed since antiquity. Cynics in ancient Greece, for example, flouted the conventions of humanity, including the notion of states. Today, we see scholars taking an interdisciplinary approach to creating alternatives to the state. A group called the Subaltern Studies Group, composed of many Latin American scholars, states as a main part of its agenda: "De-nationalization is simultaneously a limit and a threshold of our project. The 'de-territorialization' of the nation-state under the new permeability of frontiers to capital-labor flows merely replicates, in effect, the genetic process of implantation of a colonial economy in Latin America in the sixteenth and seventeenth centuries."[53]

Similarly, Amitai Etzioni has argued that a global community may eventually be recognized as in the best interests of our planet's inhabitants.[54] Whatever form of social organization is chosen, however, we shall demonstrate in our next chapter that involving religion in decision making is never a good idea if the goal is to eliminate or at least minimize violence.

NOTES

1. Rush Limbaugh, *The Way Things Ought to Be* (New York: Pocket Books, 1992), p. 281.

2. Michael Freeman, "Religion, Nationalism, and Genocide: Ancient Judaism Revisited," *Archives européennes de sociologie* 35 (1994): 259–82.

3. Bruce Lawrence, *Shattering the Myth: Islam Beyond Violence* (Princeton, NJ: Princeton University Press, 1998), p. 13.

4. William T. Cavanaugh, "'A Fire Strong Enough to Consume the House': The Wars of Religion and the Rise of the State," *Modern Theology* 11, no. 4 (1995): 397–420.

5. Ibid., p. 398.

6. Ibid., p. 403.

7. Ibid.

8. Ibid., p. 414.

9. See Muhammad Dandamayev, "State Gods and Private Religion in the Near East in the First Millennium, B.C.E.," in *Religion and Politics in the Ancient Near East*, ed. Adele Berlin (Bethesda, MD: University of Maryland Press, 1996), pp. 35–45.

10. Philip S. Gorski, "The Mosaic Moment: An Early Modernist Critique of Modernist Theories of Nationalism," *American Journal of Sociology* 105, no. 5 (March 2000): 1428–68.

11. Anthony W. Marx, *Faith in Nation: Exclusionary Origins of Nationalism* (New York: Oxford University Press, 2003), p. 8.

12. Ibid., p. 22.

13. Morton Fried, *The Evolution of Political Society: An Essay in Political Anthropology* (New York: Random House, 1967).

14. Elman Service, *The Origins of the State and Civilization: The Process of Cultural Evolution* (New York: W. W. Norton, 1975). For review of state formation theories, including a critique of Algaze, see the anthology of Gary M. Feinman and Joyce Marcus, *Archaic States* (Santa Fe, NM: School of American Research Press, 1998).

15. One important representative of this view of early state formation is Guillermo Algaze, *The Uruk World System* (Chicago: University of Chicago Press, 1993). For an updated view, see his "The Prehistory of Imperialism: The Case of Uruk Period Mesopotamia," in *Uruk Mesopotamia and Its Neighbors: Cross-Cultural Interactions in the Era of State Formation*, ed. Mitchell Rothman (Santa Fe, NM: School of American Research, 2001), pp. 27–83.

16. See Liah Greenfield, *Nationalism: Five Roads to Modernity* (Cambridge, MA: Harvard University Press, 1992).

17. Marx, *Faith in Nation*, p. 37.

18. Ibid., pp. 94–112.

19. For some general accounts, see Robert M. Kingdon, *Myths about the St. Bartholomew's Day Massacres, 1572–1576* (Cambridge, MA: Harvard University Press, 1988); and Philippe Erlanger, *St. Bartholomew's Night: The Massacre of Saint Bartholomew*, trans. Patrick O'Brien (New York: Pantheon, 1962). As we shall show, this is a slightly sanitized version of the French original, *Le massacre de la Saint-Barthélemy* (Paris: Gallimard, 1960).

20. Cavanaugh, "Wars of Religion," p. 402.

21. Ibid., p. 401. His only source cited for the quoted passage on Catherine de Medici in his footnote 19 is pages 24–26 of Richard S. Dunn, *The Age of Religious Wars: 1559–1689* (New York: W. W. Norton, 1970). But pages 24–26 do not speak of the massacre, and Cavanaugh apparently is speaking of pages 34–36, which do speak of the massacre. Dunn, however, follows a standard history, and he does not seem to be engaged with the primary sources. In footnote 23, Cavanaugh also cites pages 189–90 of J. H. M. Salmon, *Society in Crisis: France in the Sixteenth Century* (New York: St. Martin's, 1975; Cavanaugh lists another place and publisher) for his statements about the Queen Mother. However, in regard to Catherine de Medici being a Machiavellian, Cavanaugh seems to accept as fact what Salmon attributes to Huguenot propaganda.

22. For some important sources, see Alfred Soman, ed., *The Massacre of St. Bartholomew: Reappraisals and Documents* (The Hague: Nijhof, 1974). See further, Babara Diefendorf, "Prologue to a Massacre: Popular Unrest in Paris, 1557–1572," *American Historical Review* 90, no. 5 (December 1985): 1067–91.

23. See further, James D. Tracy, *Europe's Reformations, 1450–1650* (Lanham, MD: Rowman and Littlefield, 1999), pp. 146–51.

24. *Correspondance du roi Charles IX et du sieur de Mandelot, gouverneur de Lyon, pendant l'anneé 1572, époque du massacre de Saint-Barthélemy, Monuments inédits de l'histoire de France 1* (Paris: Crapelet, 1830), p. 39: "j'estois aprés pour faire tout ce qui m'estoit possible pour la vériffication du faict et chastiment des coulpables."

25. James R. Smither, "The St. Bartholomew's Day Massacre and Images of Kingship in France: 1572–1574," *Sixteenth Century Journal* 22, no. 1 (1991): 31.

26. Ibid., p. 29.

27. Kingdon, *Myths*, p. 46.

28. For a study of the medallion, see Josephe Jacquot, "Medailles et jetons de la Saint-Barthélemy," *Revue d'Histoire litteraire de la France* 73, no. 5 (September–October 1973): 791–72. See further, Erlanger, *La massacre de la Saint-Barthélemy*, plate 30; and Kingdon, *Myths*, p. 46.

29. In the French version of Erlanger's book, an illustration of the Medallion appears as plate 30 right after p. 224. No explanation is given for its omission in the version of Erlanger's book translated by Patrick O'Brien. An actual medallion appears on the Web site of the Huguenot Society of South Africa: http://www.geocities.com/hugenoteblad/hist-hug.htm (accessed July 17, 2004). There are also variant readings of the word corresponding to "Huguenot" on the inscription on the Medallion. Fehl ("Vasari's 'Extirpation of the Huguenots,'" p. 264) reads "Ugunottorum" while the Web site transcribes it as "Hugonotorium." However, the "H" does not appear in the inscription of the Medallion shown on that Web site. Philipp P. Fehl, "Vasari's 'Extirpation of the Huguenots': The Challenge of Pity and Fear," *Gazette des beaux-arts* 84 (1974): 257–84.

30. Dunn (*Age of Religious Wars*, p. 35) gives one sentence to the pope's celebration, and so Cavanaugh should have been aware of at least this much.

31. Georges Goyau, "St. Batholomew's Day," in *The Catholic Encyclopedia* (1912), also available online at http://www.newadvent.org/cathen/13333b.htm (accessed July 17, 2004).

32. Machiavelli, *The Prince*, p. 13/*Il Principe*, p. 24: "che' franzesi non si intendevano dello stato; perché, s'e' ne'ntendessino, non lascerebbono venire in tanta grandezza la Chiesa." My adapted translation, as Crocker's translation adds "and power," which is not in the Italian text we cite.

33. Rousseau, in a note added to the edition of 1782, also had observed that "Rome's court strongly prohibited the book . . . since it is that Court he depicts most clearly."/*Du contrat*, p. 111: "La Cour de Rome a sévèrement défendu son livre . . . c'est elle qui'l dépeint le plus clairement." My translation. For another translation, see Cranston, ed., *Social Contract*, p. 118.

34. See Goyau "Saint Bartholomew's Day."

35. Ibid.

36. Robert M. Kingdon, "The Reaction in Geneva and Rome," in *The Massacre of St. Bartholomew*, ed. Soman, pp. 25–49, especially pp. 41–46.

37. Pierre Hurtubise, *Correspondance du Nonce en France: Antonio Maria Salviati (1572–1578)*, Acta Nuntiaturae Gallicae 12 (Rome: Université Pontificale Grégorienne/École Française de Rome, 1975). Hurtubise also commented on Kingdon's article on pages 50–51 of Soman, *The Massacre of St. Bartholomew*.

38. For a study of the propaganda surrounding the massacre, see Kingdon, *Myths*.

39. Pierre Hurtubise, *Correspondance du Nonce*, p. 204: "La città tutta se'è messa in arme, et le case degl'Ugonotti sono state assediate, et combattute, et ammazzati molti huomini, et dalla plebe saccheggiate con avidità incredible."

40. Ibid., p. 204: "Nessun Catolico s'intende esser né morto né ferito."

41. Ibid., p. 225: "purgare il regno di Francia de la pesta ugonottica."

42. Ibid., p. 230: "purgarlo da le heresie et mettano in opera li decreti del Consilio Tridentino." My translation.

43. Ibid., p. 259: "il felice progresso che con la gratia di Dio . . . fa l'esecutione contra ugonotti." My translation.

44. The relevant correspondence is provided by Fehl, "Vasari's 'Extirpation of the Huguenots,'" p. 278, app. I.

45. Ibid., "I intend to attend to pursuing this work." (*Io intendo a seguitare quest'-opera*). My translation.

46. Vasari's letter to Francesco de'Medici, as provided in ibid., A.4.

47. Kingdon, "Reactions in Geneva and Rome," p. 44.

48. Pierre Blet, ed., *Girolamo Ragazzoni, évêque de Bergame, nonce en France: correspondance de sa nonciature (1583–1586)*, Acta Nuntiaturae Gallicae 2 (Rome: Université Pontificale Grégorienne/École Française de Rome, 1962), p. 137: "avvertirà d'inclinar sempre più a la guerre che a la pace, perché con li nimici di Dio non si doverebbe mai tener pace." My translation.

49. Hurtubise, "Comments" on Kingdon's article, in Soman, *The Massacre of St. Bartholomew*, pp. 51–52.

50. Pope John Paul II's statement is found on the official Vatican Web site: http://www.vatican.va/holy_father/john_paul_ii/travels/documents/hf_jp-ii_spe_23081997_vigil_en.html (accessed July 17, 2004).

51. See further, Jonathan Friedman, *Globalization, the State and Violence* (Walnut Creek, CA: AltaMira Press, 2003).

52. E. E. Evans-Pritchard, *The Nuer: A Description of the Modes of Livelihood and Politcal Institutions of a Nilotic People* (New York: Oxford University Press, 1940), p. 152.

53. Latin American Subaltern Studies Group, "Founding Statement," *Dispositio/n* 19, no. 46 (1994 [published 1996]): 8.

54. Amitai Etzioni, *From Empire to Community: A New Approach to International Relations* (New York: Palgrave Macmillan, 2004).

PART 4

SYNTHESIS

Religion is inherently prone to violence. This does not mean, of course, that all religions result in violence or that religions cannot proclaim peace. Rather, what we mean is that the fundamental characteristic of religion as a mode of life and thought is predicated on the existence of unverifiable forces and/or beings. This means that disputes and claims are not easily settled by verifiable means, and violence is often the means to settle disputes and claims.

We have identified the main mechanism for religious violence in the creation of new scarce resources. However, unlike the secular scarce resources that result in violence, the scarce resources created by religion may not be—and often are not—scarce at all. Given these realities, this part of our book will explore the ethics of religious violence, as well as some possible solutions from both a religious and secular humanist perspective. We will also examine the implications of our thesis for American foreign policy in order to demonstrate its practical applications.

CHAPTER 15

A COMPARATIVE ETHICS OF VIOLENCE

Our treatment has not argued that *all* violence is caused by religion. Our thesis fully admits that purely secular pursuits can, and do, cause violence. If scarcity is the key to understanding violence, then violence itself will not totally disappear unless scarcities disappear. Given our finite amount of space and resources, this is probably unlikely. Even given these admissions, however, we will argue that religious violence is more immoral than secular violence.

As such, our discussion may be seen as part of the field of "comparative ethics," though, in the field of religious studies, scholars usually compare religions rather than religion and secularism.[1] As mentioned previously our argument may be framed in the form known as a fortiori argument, and *kol wahoma* in rabbinic argumentation:[2] Briefly, such an argument attempts to show that if the truth for one claim is judged to be evident, then another claim ought to be more evidently true. Before we provide the full form of this argument, it may be relevant to outline our basic position on ethics.

MORAL RELATIVISM

Moral relativism has a negative connotation in common discourse. It has, however, a long and distinguished career in philosophy. We can trace it as far back as Plato's *Protagoras*, who is famous for the dictum that man is the measure of all things.[3]

We certainly find it in Hobbes's *Leviathan*, where he succinctly says:

> But whatsoever is the object of any mans Appetite or Desire; that is it, which
> he for his part calleth Good; And the object of his Hate, and Aversion, Evill.
> ... For these words of Good, Evill, and Contemptible, are ever used with
> relation to the person that useth them. There being nothing simply and
> absolutely so; nor any common Rule of Good and Evill.[4]

Likewise, we can see it expressed today among major secular humanist philosophers such as Paul Kurtz and Kai Nielsen.[5] Gil Harman and David Wong may be the most prominent exponents in recent years.[6] From the religious perspective, Joseph Fletcher ignited a storm of controversy with his version.[7] In anthropology, Melville Herkovits has provided a systematic overview, which is important in showing the extent to which different cultures advocate different moralities.[8] Neil Levy, another philosophical exponent of relativism, is useful because some of his work on moral relativism was written in the aftermath of September 11.[9]

According to Levy, one can distinguish three types of moral relativism.[10] The first is denominated as "descriptive relativism," which simply means the acknowledgement that different fundamental moralities exist, regardless of their justification. This idea has been contested by, among others, those who argue that what seem to be different principles or morality are not actually so upon closer inspection.[11] Thus, one person may say that giving money to charity is bad, and another that giving money to charity is good. However, upon closer inspection, they both are ruled by the principle that helping the poor is good, and differ only on method.

A second type is "moral requirement relativism," which Levy defines as "the view that what is morally required of individuals varies from group to group, culture to culture, and so forth."[12] Finally, there is "meta-ethical relativism," which mainly focuses on analyzing the meaning of moral statements. For example, what does it mean to say "Murder is wrong"? Once analyzed, one may see that "murder" simply refers to a killing not authorized by a particular group. Thus, capital punishment may not be considered "murder" in some societies, but abortion may be.

Despite these different types of relativism identified by Levy, we claim that all theorists of ethics can still be categorized into two groups: (1) those who acknowledge they are moral relativists and (2) those who do not acknowledge that they are moral relativists. Indeed, we do see all ethics as relativistic, even the ones that claim absolutes. For example, let us consider a practitioner of a more "absolutist" neo-Kantian ethics, such as Alan Gewirth. As did Immanuel Kant, Gewirth wishes to formulate some rational means to establish rules of ethics that can be universal.

In an effort to establish a sort of categorical imperative to aid the needy, Gewirth begins by arguing that "every agent must hold that he has generic rights on the ground or for the sufficient reason that he is a prospective agent who has purposes he wants to fulfill."[13] The foremost of these rights are "freedom and well-being," because one cannot be a viable purposive agent without them. Therefore, it is necessary to recognize that we cannot interfere with someone's right to freedom and well-being. Eventually, this leads Gewirth to believe that a nation with a surplus of food has the duty to give any excess to a needier nation in order to help that nation's inhabitants exercise their freedom and possess well-being.

But, as in all versions of Kantian ethics, the initial premise is always relative. Thus, we can ask why we should think it an absolute moral right for purposive agents to have "freedom and well-being." All we are doing is stating again what we would like to have for ourselves, but that is itself a relativistic judgment. And it is just as relativistic to hold that "rational" principles should be the mark of any morality, even as we hold that empirico-rationalism does and should guide our moral judgments to one extent or another in order to best fulfill our interests.

We can further extend our argument for moral relativism with the observation, outlined most elegantly by Nielsen, that all ethical judgments are human judgments, even if one believes in God.[14] Basically, any statement of the type "X is good because God says so" is still a human judgment. At the outset this may seem simple, but in reality there are only two choices in a world in which ethics involve a deity. To understand this dilemma, we need to consider a variant of Euthyphro's Dilemma as found in Plato's *Euthyphro*.[15] We can briefly summarize the argument here:

Things are either good in themselves;
or
They are good because God says so.

If one says that something is good or evil in itself, then God becomes unnecessary for morality. That something is good would be as obvious as the fact that a triangle has three sides. One does not need a god to make a triangle have three sides, and so God would be unnecessary to establish such a moral principle.

If one says that something is moral because God says so, then this still renders us the judge of morality, for we are the ones making the judgment that "whatever God calls good is what shall be called good." Even if one says that God planted our sense of goodness in us, we must still judge that something God planted in us is good. There is no way to escape this circle. Consequently, every moral judgment is ultimately a human judgment, and so God remains irrelevant as an ultimate source of morality.

INTEREST AS THE ULTIMATE ARBITER

If God is no better a standard of morality than human judgment, then how do we judge what is moral? My answer is: The way we have always judged it—by interest. Thus, Hobbes is right in observing that "bad" or "evil" describes nothing more than what is against our individual and/or group interests, real or perceived. Such a fundamental feature of morality would not change whether we believed in God or not, and it applies to what would seem to be the most absolutely wrong things of which we can conceive, the killing of infants being one of them. As we have demonstrated, some biblical authors had no problem killing children because they were afraid those children would grow up to contaminate Israel. Thus, killing children was not considered wrong because their existence threatened Israel's perceived interests.

Likewise, consider the idea that inflicting unnecessary pain is wrong. Aside from the definitional problem that will render "unnecessary" just as relative a term as anything else, we also have another self-interested premise. This premise centers on the idea that the nerve activity we associate with "pain" is somehow valuable. But this is valuable only because pain is something we, as possessors of nervous systems that are electrochemically constituted to experience pain, do not like. Even then we value the electrochemical experience we call "pain" in human beings, but not necessarily in animals. Even if one believes in God, we can show that the noninfliction of pain is a relative value.

On the other hand, there also degrees of moral relativity. Moral rules based on verifiable premises are less relativistic and arbitrary than moral systems wherein verifiability comes into play to the extent that it can influence value judgments. For example, we can verify that we cannot verify that demons possess people we would otherwise consider mentally ill. Therefore, we do not consider demons when making any value judgments about mentally ill people. Having a god in a moral system does not inherently change it, except to add another scarce resource and bureaucratic layer to our moral decision making, rendering morality even more relativistic.

The foregoing should not be construed to mean that we do not believe in any system of moral rules. We simply affirm that all moralities must recognize the self-interest involved in their construction. We adhere to the moral system that best suits our interests, whether we acknowledge this or not. We also affirm that if one accepts empirico-rationalism as providing reliable data, then empiricism and logic should be components of any moral system that purports to make judgments that can be verified.

What makes moral systems relevant is the involvement of two or more persons who interact. A lone individual's morality is irrelevant. Morality comes into play only when someone else is affected. The interplay between the individual and the collective with whom an individual interacts is the basis of all moral systems. Moral systems identify common interests and try to impose them on individuals. Individuals accept these systems to the extent that the collective rules serve their self-interest.

Self-interest, however, need not mean that individuals cannot act for the benefit of others. For example, an individual's psycho-biological constitution is such that he cannot stand pain and suffering in others. This is also self-interest, as his mental well-being is linked to the welfare of others. In order to avoid the pain of seeing others in pain, he helps others diminish their suffering. To the extent that this aversion to pain in others is cultural and valued, it is a value that can be transmitted to others. To the extent that other people have the same sympathies, there will be agreement. To the extent that they do not, there will never be agreement. This is a reality that is not going to change in either theistic or atheistic systems of ethics.

RELIGIOUS VIOLENCE IS ALWAYS IMMORAL

Within a moral relativistic frame that accepts empirico-rationalism as providing reliable data, our argument that religious violence is always immoral begins by positing the seemingly obvious proposition that what exists has more value than what does not exist. Only what exists can be said to have any value. If that is the case, then life, as an existent phenomenon, must have more value than what does not exist. We can schematize our rationale as follows:

1. What exists is worth more than what does not exist.
2. Life exists.
3. Therefore, life is worth more than what does not exist.

Accordingly, we may deem immoral any action that places the value of life as equal to or below the value of nothing. Therefore, it is always immoral to kill for something that has no actual value.

We can also extend this argument to what cannot be proven, on empirico-rationalist grounds, to exist. For example, if one were to say that she was killing because undetectable Martians have declared it obligatory to kill, the argument would be regarded rightly as absurd. But the fact is that the possibility of undetectable Martians existing is not what would render such a statement absurd; it is perfectly possible that undetectable Martians exist and order people to kill other people. The main reason that we would not accept this rationale as moral is that we, as observers, cannot verify that undetectable Martians exist, and so we would regard the perpetrator's claims as absurd.

In fact, we can argue that killing because undetectable Martians said so is equivalent to killing for no reason or to killing for nothing, even if the person doing the killing believes herself to have a just reason. Here, as observers and members of the larger society, we are judging the perpetrator based on the empirico-rationalist verifiability of the claim. And here is where the utility of David Riches's triad of victim-perpetrator-observer in evaluating violence comes into play. Since we cannot verify that undetectable Martians exist, we judge the perpetrator's claim to be without merit, and the killing to be unjustified. Any act of killing not justified or authorized is called "murder" in our society.

Accordingly, we can propose that just as it is always immoral to kill for something that does not exist, killing for something that cannot be proven to exist is equally immoral. And since religion is, by our definition, a mode of life and thought premised on the existence of and/or relationship with unverifiable supernatural forces and/or beings, then it follows that killing for religious reasons is always immoral. We can make a similar argument for any act of violence. Therefore, we recapitulate our proposition as follows: *It is always immoral to commit any act of violence for religious reasons.*

We can also make our case against religious violence within the framework of scarce resource theory. When religious violence is compared to secular violence resulting from scarce resources, the a fortiori argument would be as follows: If acts of violence caused by actual scarcities are judged as immoral, then acts of violence caused by scarcities that do not actually exist are even more immoral. We may say that any act predicated on the acquisition or loss of a nonexistent resource is morally wrong because a life was traded for a nonexistent gain.

We may illustrate this with a more concrete, if fanciful, example. Suppose that male twins, who are otherwise equal, are the sole survivors of a boating accident. The twins are fortunate to encounter a helicopter with room for only one person to be rescued. The scarce resource is space on the helicopter. The choices that these twins encounter logically include: (1) One twin gives up his life for the other; or (2) one fights the other for the space in that helicopter. Fighting for one's life may be considered justifiable, if tragic.

However, let us say that it is not true that there is room for only one more person on that helicopter. In that case, such loss of life would be wasteful. That is to say, the loss of life is sustained on the false premise that only one could be saved. But while this violence may be wasteful, it still might be justified if the surviving twin did not know that there was, in fact, room for both twins.

The situation would be different if the surviving twin could have verified that there was room, but did not. In this case, we may hold his actions to be unjustified. The reason again is that a life would be traded for a nonexistent scarcity. And what exists is always more valuable than what does not exist.

But let us say now that the only reason that one twin killed the other is that the surviving twin believed that an invisible Martian had told him that only one seat was available, or that only one twin had the privilege to enter the helicopter even though two seats were actually available. In this case, we would hold the killer to be unjustified, if we did not hold him to be mentally ill. The reason is that we cannot verify that invisible Martians exist or communicate with any individual. Just as a jury in Texas convicted Andrea Yates in 2002 for killing her children, even as she claimed it was on God's orders, we would not allow the perpetrating twin to claim communication from an undetectable Martian as justification for his killing.[16]

We can extend this argument to religious beliefs. Let us say that population X has declared a certain bounded space was given to them by a god, who communicates only with members of population X. While there may be enough physical space for the community, the space has now been made scarce solely because of the belief that a god has declared it to be his property. Any loss of life resulting from that scarcity would be completely wasteful if that god did not in fact exist. Any violence resulting from this belief would be judged wasteful and/or immoral.

If the morality of any act of violence is measured in proportion to verifiability, then we can judge some specific acts of historical violence as more immoral than others. To begin with, an act of violence based on scarcities that do not actually exist would be more immoral than an act of violence based on scarcities that actually do exist. Thus, Muhammad's killings would be deemed more immoral than killings resulting from fighting over a piece of land that is actually too small for two warring populations to live upon. Likewise, any killing by Christians or Jews based on biblical commands would be more immoral than any killing done because of actually existing scarce resources.

SUMMARY

Secular violence certainly may be immoral sometimes; perhaps even most of the time. Killing for something that is not necessary to human existence, for example, may be deemed immoral. Killing to create an empire may be deemed immoral. But killing for nonreligious reasons is not always immoral. Killing in self-defense is usually not considered immoral. Killing when there is no other way to survive is not considered immoral. If a person needs a basic resource (e.g., food or water) to survive, then it may be morally permissible to fight and kill for it.

In contrast, violence for religious reasons is *always* immoral. Killing over scarcities that do not actually exist is certainly always immoral, because one is trading a life for a nonexistent gain. Committing an act of violence over scarcities that cannot be verified to be scarce is likewise always immoral because bodily well-being should never be traded for a gain that cannot be verified to exist. The fact that religious violence is *always* immoral, and that nonreligious violence is *not always* immoral, is the fundamental ethical distinction between religious and nonreligious violence.

NOTES

1. See, for example, David Little and Summer B. Twiss, *Comparative Religious Ethics* (New York: Harper and Row, 1978).

2. See Moses Mielziner, *Introduction to the Talmud*, 5th ed. (New York: Boch, 1968), p. 251.

3. See also, Lawrence C. Becker and Charlotte B. Becker, *A History of Western Ethics* (New York: Garland, 1992), pp. 13–14.

4. Thomas Hobbes, *Leviathan*, ed. Richard E. Flathman and David Johnston (New York: W. W. Norton, 1997), p. 32.

5. Paul Kurtz, *In Defense of Secular Humanism* (Amherst, NY: Prometheus Books, 1993), pp. 65–67; and Kai Nielsen, *Ethics without God*, rev. ed. (Amherst, NY: Prometheus Books, 1990).

6. David B. Wong, *Moral Relativity* (Berkeley and Los Angeles: University of California Press, 1984). Wong provides further clarifications of his work in "Pluralistic Relativism," *Midwest Studies in Philosophy* 20 (1996): 378–400.

7. Joseph F. Fletcher, *Situation Ethics: The New Morality* (Philadelphia: Westminster, 1966).

8. Melville J. Herskovits, *Cultural Relativism: Perspective in Cultural Pluralism* (New York: Random House, 1972).

9. Neil Levy, *Moral Relativism: A Short Introduction* (Oxford: Oneworld Publications, 2002).

10. Ibid., pp. 19–22. Levy is adapting categories found in Richard Brandt, "Ethical Relativism," in *Moral Relativism: A Reader*, ed. Paul K. Moser and Thomas L. Carson (New York: Oxford University Press, 2001), pp. 25–31.

11. One representative of such an antirelativist argument is Michele M. Moody-Adams, *Fieldwork in Familiar Places: Morality, Culture and Philosophy* (Cambridge, MA: Harvard University Press, 1997).

12. Levy, *Moral Relativism*, p. 20.

13. Alan Gewirth, "Aid for the Needy," in *Ethics: Theory and Practice*, ed. Manuel Velasquez and Cynthia Rostankowski (Englewood Cliffs, NJ: Prentice-Hall, 1985), pp. 353–74.

14. Nielsen, *Ethics without God.*

15. For other variants and a critique of the use of Euthyphro's Dilemma, see Richard Joyce, "Theistic Ethics and the Euthyphro Dilemma," *Journal of Religious Ethics* 30, no. 1 (2002): 149–75.

16. For an overview of the Andrea Yates case, see Suzanne O'Malley, *"Are You There Alone?" The Unspeakable Crime of Andrea Yates* (New York: Simon & Schuster, 2004).

CHAPTER 16

SOLUTIONS

If religious violence is always immoral, then how do we solve the problem of religious violence? Two obvious logical choices present themselves: (1) Retain religion, but modify it so that scarcities are not created; or (2) remove religion from human life. Each of these choices has advantages and disadvantages. We will discuss arguments for both choices as we discuss solutions related to the four scarcities that have been central to our thesis: inscripturation, sacred space, group privileging, and salvation.

First, note that we indicate "minimization" is the key, as violence cannot be eliminated for the simple reason that scarce resources will probably always exist. Competing interests will always exist. In some cases, violence should not be eliminated, as self-defense, for example, is a legitimate use of violence. Minimization means that we concentrate on ridding ourselves of unnecessary violence.

Since religious violence is caused mainly by competition for resources, then part of the solution must involve making religious believers aware of how they have created scarce resources. Nonbelievers must challenge believers to explain why they believe in such resources in the first place. We should challenge believers to explain why they believe certain spaces are sacred. Nonbelievers should challenge believers to explain how their notion of salvation is any more verifiable than the notions offered by other religions. Of course, it is naive to expect believers will automatically examine their beliefs and abandon them. However, making believers aware of how religion can create scarce resources must be a starting point if there is a solution at all.

One can object that eliminating the notions of salvation, sacred space, divine revelation, and group privileging would eliminate religion itself. This is only the case if one judges religion to essentially consist of these elements. Of all of these elements, however, we believe divine revelation is the only essential feature of all religions. That is to say, a person who believes that there is some sort of god or transcendent force must have some notion that he or she is able to perceive that entity. Sacred space, salvation, and group privileging are not so clearly essential, though they certainly may seem so.

At the same time, there are degrees of sacredness and other complexities that may render any notion of sacred space or salvation to be so diluted that it does not effectively create a scarce resource. And recent efforts to redefine many key Christian concepts at least theoretically render them less exclusivistic and less likely to generate violence. What we need to remember is that the notion of the Holy Land has been redefined or abandoned throughout history by many Jews and Christians who still called themselves "religious" at some level. Such redefinitions, in effect, sometimes made competition for a physical space irrelevant.

SCRIPTURE: A ZERO-TOLERANCE ARGUMENT

Even if we do not eliminate religion from human life, an argument can be made to eliminate any scripture that contains religious violence from religious life. A zero-tolerance argument means the rejection of any scripture that contains any religious violence in any portion. Thus, even if religion is retained, we can remove such scripture as a whole genre of religious experience.

We begin our zero-tolerance argument with *Mein Kampf*, a book that is held to be the paradigm of evil in modern society. Imagine that a new religious group were to call themselves the Hitlerian Church, and that the main text would be *Mein Kampf*. Certainly, the name "Hitlerian" by itself would arouse anger and suspicion. The reason, of course, is that Hitler is rightly held responsible for the murder of millions of people.

So the question can be posed: Would one act of genocide advocated in *Mein Kampf* be enough to repudiate the name "Hitlerian" from our church? What if the acts of genocide were on a smaller scale? Let us suppose Hitler had advocated killing only a few hundred people, just as Muhammad is said to have done at Qurayẓa. Would we still repudiate the label? I would guess that most people in our society would rightly repudiate the Hitlerian Church label even if we were to somehow prove that Hitler actually ordered a few killings, while the rest could be attributed to out-of-control operatives at the local and lower levels.

But suppose now that someone argued that there were *some* good things within *Mein Kampf.* Hitler, after all, said he stood for family values. He said he was following God's wishes. He said he loved his fellow community members. I would speculate that most people would still not be convinced that we should keep any part of *Mein Kampf,* even if there were "good" chapters. The genocide committed under Hitler is so heinous that it would outweigh any supposed good in *Mein Kampf.*

This is why an analogous proposal made by C. S. Cowles for the Bible fails. Cowles believes that the genocide in the Hebrew Bible is morally repugnant. His proposal, however, is unclear. He denies he wants to eject the Old Testament from the canon, as did Marcion, the second-century apologist. But when it comes to omitting genocidal texts from the canon, Cowles seems to endorse the idea that "in practice this is precisely what the church has done."[1] Cowles, however, never comes to terms with the even greater and more eternalized violence of the New Testament, nor does he give any verifiable reason why we must keep only the "good" parts of the Bible.

Similar approaches in Islam are insufficient. In a recent study of the New Islamists in Egypt, Raymond W. Baker shows that indeed there are many Muslim intellectuals who seek ways to eschew violence.[2] According to Baker, "[T]he energizing faith of the New Islamists is anchored in the foundational belief that the Qur'an and the Sunnah of the Prophet provide the spiritual inspiration for a distinctive Islamic vision of human community."[3] But the New Islamists still do not address the real problem, which is that their selection of particular parts of the Hadith or the Qur'an as authoritative representations of Islam are ultimately no more verifiable than those of the so-called fundamentalists. Thus, violence may become the way to adjudicate disputes, just as in Christianity.

In sum, just as we should reject all of *Mein Kampf* because of its racist and genocidal policies, we should reject the Bible for any genocidal policies it ever endorsed. We should reject other scriptures if they also ever advocate any sort of violence. In fact, *Mein Kampf* does not contain a *single* explicit command for genocide equivalent to those found in the Hebrew Bible. Yes, *Mein Kampf* describes the Jews as an evil to be expelled from Germany, but nowhere in *Mein Kampf* is there anything as explicit as the policy of killing Canaanites in Deuteronomy 7 and 20 or 1 Samuel 15. Thus, if all of *Mein Kampf* is to be rejected simply for its *implied* genocidal policies, we should certainly reject all of the Bible for some of its explicit and blatant genocidal policies.

THE FOLLY OF REAPPROPRIATION

One solution that may work in part, and for the wrong reasons, is reappropriation. The main goal or reappropriation is to retain the value of scripture. This is an idea that permeates the history of Jewish, Christian, and Muslim exegesis. Methodologically, reappropriation means that it is legitimate to deviate from the "original meaning" of a text in order to apply it to another cultural or temporal context. For example, such scholars may argue that we need not take literally the six-day creation of Genesis 1. We can render Genesis 1 meaningful today by regarding it as an expression of God's loving care for humanity.

The moral reprehensibility of this practice can be shown by the simple fact that any good textual exegete could reappropriate *Mein Kampf* and turn it into a text meaningful for today. All we have to do is divest it of the meaning it had in its original context, and—*poof*—the text becomes relevant for us. For example, we could pretend that "family" and "fellow community members" in *Mein Kampf* now mean "everybody." We can pretend that "Jews" are a symbol that should not be taken seriously. If two thousand years from now most historical proof of a Holocaust were lost, perhaps we could even argue that *Mein Kampf* was meant for in-house consumption, and none of its ugly thoughts were ever carried out in real life.

So why don't scholars do that? Because they apply empirico-rationalist hermeneutics selectively. For example, there are excellent linguistic and contextual markers to determine what the original meaning of "German" as a racist term meant for Hitler. It now would be ludicrous to reinterpret Hitler's "German" to mean "everybody." The "original meaning" of whatever Hitler said is sufficient to judge his book on moral grounds. The same should apply to the Bible. Once we think we have established an original meaning for a biblical passage, then reappropriation is a morally sordid game, just as reappropriation of *Mein Kampf* would be. Reappropriation, therefore, is a morally reprehensible charade that should end.

Indeed, any reappropriation of biblical texts is vacuous, for it does not explain why we are investing so much effort in maintaining a book that we can do without. Societies existed before the Bible, so there is no logical reason why they cannot exist without it. Maintaining the Bible is another form of "essentialist" thinking. My analogies with Hitler and *Mein Kampf* are deliberate here, for I see very little difference in the techniques used by biblical scholars and theologians to maintain the relevance of a text that we otherwise believe meant something completely different or violent in its original context.

THE FUTILITY OF COUNTERTRADITIONS HERMENEUTICS

The recent reemphasis of countertraditions to make the Bible relevant is simply a variant of the reappropriation technique. We certainly can show that perhaps some biblical authors did not advocate genocide or exclusion of the same kind or degree as what we have discussed. However, choosing one countertradition as the "essential" or "true" understanding of the Bible is inevitably no more justified than picking one portion of *Mein Kampf* that seems to contradict another, and calling that our authority for action. Countertraditions, therefore, are ultimately meaningless because they do not answer the question of why we should care that the Bible has countetraditions in the first place.

Even if we were not secular humanists, an argument could be made that scriptural religions are a cause of more violence than their sacrality is worth. All scriptures produce ambiguities that themselves generate new conflicts. The distance between their production and our reading of them is, of course, a major generator of ambiguity. Even within a single corpus or book we can find ambiguous statements that might lead one to act in one manner, and another to act the opposite. Given that we likely can never absolutely determine the meaning of most biblical texts, what a nonfundamentalist scholar is doing here differs very little from a so-called fundamentalist.

But can't we say the same about all texts? That is to say, are we not, as Hans-Georg Gadamer argued, recreating any text every time we read it?[4] Perhaps, but there are still important differences between sacred scripture and secular reappropriation. I do not advocate a secular countertradition because of an unverifiable belief in a god. I do not equate my reappropriation with that of a communication from a god; I recognize it for what it is. With texts such as the US Constitution, we can at least agree on verifiable procedures for reappropriation or for countertraditions. It is a more democratic process (relatively speaking) and of a different quality from the rationale "Countertradition X is best because it accords with the mind of unverifiable being Y."

But if that is the case, then how does retaining this illusion differ from simply ejecting these scriptures altogether? The answer, of course, is that it does not. The result would be the same insofar as we do not deem the original meaning of those scriptures as authoritative when we reappropriate them. But the result of abandoning the original meaning of a text is no different from disregarding the authority of the text altogether. For example, if an individual chose not to interpret Jesus' commandment to hate one's parents literally or as originally meant, then the result is no different than if he rejected the Bible as authoritative altogether: Either way, he would not hate his parents.

We have shown that some portions of the Bible advocate genocidal policies. Whether they were carried out historically or not is not as important as
the fact that they are endorsed as a good thing. We should judge them just
as harshly as we would if Hitler had never actually carried out what he said
he would do. We have shown that Jesus endorsed hate sometimes. For those
reasons alone, we should not hold the Bible as sacred. Just as Hitler's appeal
to God and a higher motive would not be cause to render *Mein Kampf* sacred,
the fact that the Bible also claims a higher authority should not be cause to
maintain its sacrality. The advocacy of a single episode of religious violence
should be sufficient to void all claims of divine origin for both the Qur'an
and the Bible.

AESTHETICS AS APOLOGETICS

The superiority of the Bible is being maintained through aesthetics. That is
to say, having given up on the idea that we can maintain the Bible as the word
of God or as a historical record, some scholars have increasingly encouraged
the appreciation of the Bible for its "literary" and "aesthetic" merits. This
shift can already be seen in the celebrated 1753 lectures of Bishop Robert
Lowth (1710–1787), who remarked that in regard to Hebrew poetry, "the
human mind can conceive of nothing more elevated, more beautiful, or more
elegant."[5]

Hermann Gunkel (1862–1932), the father of "form criticism," which
sought to identify the earliest and most basic literary units of biblical texts,
had a thinly veiled motivation for privileging the poetic side of the Bible, as
the following passage shows:

> But legends are not lies; on the contrary, they are a particular form of
> poetry. Why should not the lofty spirit of the Old Testament religion, which
> employed so many varieties of poetry, indulge in this form also? For religion
> everywhere, the Israelite religion included, has especially cherished poetry
> and poetic narrative, since poetic narrative is so much better qualified than
> prose to be the medium of religious thought. Genesis is a more intensely
> religious book than the Book of Kings.[6]

Gunkel's arguments are located squarely within his discussion of the historical factuality of biblical narratives. He is speaking in the aftermath of devastating attacks on the historicity of the Pentateuch. The idea that Genesis is
more religious than 1 Kings also shows that Gunkel is actually creating a
canon within a canon.

Now there is a cottage industry in the "literary" approach to the Bible, and its main representatives are Robert Alter, Meir Sternberg, and Frank Kermode.[7] The apologetic intent is sometimes quite frank, as in the case of Alter's comment on how ancient and modern readers have approached the Hebrew Bible:

> Subsequent religious tradition has by and large encouraged us to take the Bible seriously, rather than enjoy it, but the paradoxical truth of the matter may well be that by learning to enjoy the biblical stories more fully as stories, we shall also come to see more clearly what they mean to tell us about God, man and the perilously momentous realm of history.[8]

Even violence is sometimes regarded with aesthetic delight by scholars. For example, Susan Niditch speaks of a "bardic" tradition describing war as follows: "The bardic tradition, so called because of the beautiful traditional-style narration in which much of the material is preserved, presents a view of war that glorifies warriors, their courage, daring, leadership, in skill."[9] She includes as part of this "bardic" tradition the story of the beheading of a man (David and Goliath) and other acts of murder and mayhem.

In actuality, there is nothing that can be objectively defined as beautiful in scripture. Beauty is a value judgment. Such value judgments, however, should be exposed when they purport to be based on some sort of objective criteria. Usually beauty is located in episodes that cannot be called such when taking into account the violence and other forms of human devaluation that they entail.

That aesthetics functions as apologetics can be seen in the sheer fact that so much of the Bible consists of mangled, nearly incomprehensible text. David J. A. Clines, perhaps the foremost Hebrew lexicographer alive, has estimated that perhaps "one in every two words in the Hebrew Bible may be corrupt."[10] If this is correct, and we are not even evaluating an uncorrupted text, then how are we to judge beauty? How are episodes condoning violence, slavery, and misogyny beautiful? Are there nonbiblical texts that are more beautiful?

In order to solve the problem of religious violence, believers must become aware of how aesthetics functions to keep violent texts alive. Once we see that the biblical text is not necessarily any more beautiful then any other text, there is no longer any justification to privilege the Bible on aesthetic grounds. And since aesthetics are relative, our judgment that the Bible is also an ugly text, especially in its more violent episodes, paves the way toward morally obligating us to move beyond this text.

THE FATUITY OF ESSENTIALISM

Despite the fact that critical scholarship has exposed the lack of consensus about almost any issue in scriptural studies, there still persists the claim that the "essential" message of Christianity can be used for "peace building." Thus, a recent attempt by Andrea Bartoli to show the value of Christianity in peace building is premised on the myth that "many communities within Christianity continued seeking a closer relation with the original message of Jesus."[11] We have pointed to similar conceptions in Islam and Judaism.

Such an approach is doomed to failure. Not only can we never verify what "the original message of Jesus" was, but our collective culture has spent probably millions of person-hours trying to find "the original message of Jesus"—when that time could have been spent actually peace building. More tragically, the very idea that there is any such thing as "the original message of Jesus" creates a scarce resource over which conflicts have historically occurred and will continue to occur. Peace building cannot be based on mythology, but on real solutions to real problems. A better solution, there-fore, is to abandon all pretense to finding the "original message" of anybody in antiquity.

DESACRALIZING SPACE

Religions are capable of modifying views of sacred space. We have seen such modification in both Christianity and Judaism. Many Jews, such as Geiger and Herzl, did not believe that Judaism should be tied to a particular space. As Jonathan Z. Smith points out, the sacrality of Jerusalem was actually flex-ible and underwent an evolution. Philip Schaff, a superb historian and con-servative Christian by modern standards, observed: "The Crusades also fur-nish the perpetual reminder that not in localities is the Church to seek its holiest satisfaction." Christians, Jews, and Muslims can indeed redefine sacred space so that it is not as much of a scarce resource.[12]

However, note that this lesson has still not been learned, as evident from Marc Gopin's recommendations for deescalating the Palestinian-Israeli con-flict.

> Gestures of regret, honor and rededication should be made in every reli-gious space that has been violated in Israel and Palestine. This includes the Dome of the Rock, Joseph's tomb, Hebron, Jericho, in addition to various synagogues, mosques, and gravesites. Such gestures should be bilateral organized by a variety of interfaith organizations but endorsed publicly by leading political figures on both sides.[13]

While such a gesture may provide short-term alleviation, it fails to address the more fundamental problem of the creation of sacred space. Gestures of honor, in the long run, simply continue the legitimization of sacred space over which conflict has arisen. A longer-term solution would involve dialogue about how religion creates sacred space. Desacralizing space is ultimately the best solution, as it eliminates at least one scarce resource over which people fight.

DEPRIVILEGING GROUPS

If privileging groups creates scarce resources, then an obvious solution is to advocate the depriveging of those groups. Imagine, for example, no hierarchy of claims to have privileged access to God, whose existence cannot be verified and who may not exist at all. Of course, the major objection is that the result will be chaos, as we will lose the authorities that guide our morality.

Our response is that we already do have chaos. Christianity, for example, has been alive for two thousand years or so, and religious hierarchies and privileges have not brought us any closer to peace, which is usually defined as a set of conditions for the privileged group in the first place. If any hierarchy is undesirable, then hierarchies based on unverifiable premises have to be worse.

SALVATION AS A COMMON GOOD

The idea of a supernatural resource that results in security or some sort of permanent benefit has caused a great deal of violence throughout history. The obvious solution is to dismantle this idea. To some extent, some are trying with new models for the atonement. But these models do not go far enough. First, the idea that anyone needs supernatural salvation is unverifiable. Second, the concept that God or God's son or anyone else has to die to be saved is not only unverifiable but can be seen as a continuation of ancient violent ideas about blood magic and sacrifice that simply have no place in the modern world. The idea that God died not because it was necessary, but simply to show his love, is equally misguided. The idea that violence is an expression of love is the problem.

Walter Wink is only partly correct when he says that for Christians, "[t]he issue is not 'What must I do in order to secure my salvation?' but rather, 'What does God require of me in response to the needs of others?'"[14] By appealing to what "God requires," Wink propagates a fundamental engine of conflict: now time must be spent arguing about exactly what God requires. By allotting millions of person-hours to saving souls, we are neglecting real needs and real solutions for the living bodies that inhabit our planet.

Moreover, nonexistent beings cannot save anyone. If there are saviors, they are human beings. Accordingly, our solution is to make sufficiently abundant those resources that people are actually lacking. These include food, shelter, justice, and so on. We can see that people want education and opportunity. We can verify that people are dying of hunger and disease. Empirico-rationalist epistemology is the key to determining what people actually need to live.

A COST-BENEFIT ARGUMENT

At first sight, one of the most persuasive arguments for the value of religion in bringing peace to the world is a long list of conflicts whose resolution Wink attributes to nonviolent religious activity. Examples include the Solidarity movement in Poland, Martin Luther King's struggles for civil rights in America, and Ghandi's ouster of the British in India.[15] So let's grant for the moment that all of those conflicts were solved by religious beliefs such that we could schematize them as "Religious Belief X, therefore Peaceful Action Y." Indeed, we do not claim that religious beliefs cannot result in acts that benefit human beings.

Our argument is rather more subtle. First, we hold that it is not ethical or moral to bring good based on myth or premises that cannot be verified. The easiest illustration of this is a somewhat crude analogy. Let us pretend that a child behaved in a good way because of her belief in Santa Claus. She performed acts of kindness because of that belief. She cleaned her room because of that belief. Yet all the while we know that Santa Claus cannot be verified to exist.

Surely, we would not continue to espouse the Santa Claus myth for the sake of enhancing the child's behavior. It is unethical because we are asking the child to give us a tangible service in return for a nonexistent reward (Santa Claus's existence and his benefits). In other words, the child is working on the basis of false premises. Second, when the child learns that Santa Claus does not exist, it may have a deleterious effect on why she behaves well, which would not serve our self-interest. Compelling or encouraging good behavior should be based on appreciation of the value of verifiable causes and consequences to behavior.

We hold that any beneficial acts of religion are in the same category. Believers may behave because of rewards that do not exist or cannot be verified to exist. Such unverifiable rewards include heaven, salvation, and God's favors. Those supernatural rewards do not remove self-interest, they simply channel it in a different direction. It is immoral to encourage anyone to behave well if we realize that the supernatural rewards are no more verifiable than the belief in the existence of Santa Claus. Since no one acts against his perceived self-interest, only those actions that are based on verified or verifiable rewards and consequences are moral.

However, we hold that the potential acts of good caused by religion can never exceed those that cause violence. This is particularly the case if one assumes that religion encourages altruistic behavior (as Michael Shermer does, for example). In fact, there is no such thing as altruistic behavior in some absolute sense, because all actions are performed for some perceived benefit to the agent. This is the case even if the effect is, by our judgment, counterproductive to the agent. For example, those slamming into the World Trade Center lost the opportunity to further propagate their genes if they were childless. This might seem to be altruistic from the perspective of someone that shared their religious beliefs.

However, if Atta and his cohorts believed they were going to paradise, that is self-interest. If they thought they were helping to build a better Muslim world, it is self-interest insofar as they were building the vision of Islam that makes them happy. Indeed, if acts of altruism make us feel good, that is a perceived benefit to us, psychologically if not genetically or somatically. Interest is relative, but it is always self-interest.

Self-sacrifice is immoral if the benefit does not actually exist. One would be trading one's life for nothing. Likewise, any act of love based on religion is immoral. Given that the worth of all people is theoretically equal, any loss of life caused by an unverifiable belief would be immoral or unnecessary. For example, let's say that out of religious reasons someone actually lays down his life for his friends, as stated in John 15:13 (e.g., Jesus dying on a cross to bring a supernatural reward called "salvation"). But since his body is equal in value to that of his friend, there really has been no net gain in life. There has instead been a net loss of life. One person died who did not need to die. Such an act would be immoral because it caused the death of one person when none needed to die in the first place.

This argument can be extended to less drastic and more benign levels. If we say, for example, that the Christian notion of *agape* causes us to love others, then there is no reason why such a notion must be interpreted in religious terms. First, by interpreting "love" in religious terms, one is not acting with any less self-interest than for nonreligious reasons. Second, when one does it for religious self-interest, one is again trading nonexistent or nonverifiable benefits for existent ones. Third, the creation of any scarce resource by a religious version of *agape* or love could be an unnecessary side effect that would not occur if we encouraged secular versions of love.

HOW MUCH CREDIT IS DUE?

Less well appreciated is that many of the benefits attributed to religion are intended to reverse problems caused by religion itself. For example, the abolition movement can be seen as a departure from biblical view of slavery rather than obedience to some New Testament prohibition of slavery. That slavery was accepted and endorsed throughout the Bible needs little demonstration, as is widely acknowledged by Christian writers (see Eph. 6:5, 1 Pet. 2:18).[16]

Having generally endorsed slavery for some nineteen hundred of the last two thousand years, Christianity can claim little credit for abolishing something that it could have abolished almost two millennia years earlier. In fact, it is because the Bible was considered an authority that the abolition of slavery was retarded in the first place. The first Christians apparently had no trouble overturning many other age-old institutions, and so it also is not very cogent to argue that Christianity could not speak against slavery in the first century.

The same can be said of many icons of charity. Mother Teresa (1910–1997), for example, opposed contraception on religious grounds. Thus, on the one hand, she indeed helped many poor people, but on the other hand, she advocated policies that helped to generate the very pool of poor people she was attempting to help. Religious beliefs are largely responsible for arguments against contraception, which helps to perpetuate poverty and conflicts over scarce resources. So in the end, did Mother Teresa help more people than were harmed by her religious belief?[17]

THE SLAVERY MODEL AND ABRAHAMIC RELIGIONS

Samir Amin, a noted Marxist theoretician, observed that the Abrahamic religions, among others, originated during a period in which a tributary economic system was in place. These religions were meant to legitimize that tributary system.[18] A similar proposal was made by Karl Jaspers regarding the so-called Axial Age, when many of the most influential religions were born, presumably to help legitimize the state.[19] It is indeed intriguing that many of the world's major religions emerged between about 500 BCE and 600 BCE.

We can modify these ideas by observing that all the Abrahamic religions were born in slave model societies, wherein slavery was endorsed and/or seen as an important part of the economy. The Hebrew Bible, for example, sees the history of the Israelite people as a history of former slaves. Yet the Hebrew Bible also endorses slavery of people subjugated by the Israelites

(Lev. 25:44). Christianity was born in the Roman Empire, which was a slave society.[20] Islam developed amid a slave society and a vigorous slave trade.[21]

If there is anything "essential" about the Abrahamic religions, it is that they still are permeated by a slave mentality. All Abrahamic religions see God as the master of the universe. Israelite worshippers refer to themselves as "servants" of Yahweh, and circumcision was originally likely seen as a sort of slave mark demanded by God. Christ often appears to be nothing more than the Christian version of a Roman emperor. The meaning of the very term "Islam"—submission—describes nothing less than becoming a slave of Allah.

SUMMARY

We acknowledge that some Jewish, Christian, and Muslim theologians accept, especially in more recent times, that some of their theologies are violent. But they do not seem able to surrender general religious traditions that are no more well grounded than the religiously violent ones. In fact, until the Abrahamic religions overthrow the master-slave model in which they were born, we see little progress to be made. Since all religious beliefs are ultimately unverifiable, the greatest scarce resource of all is verifiability. And one way to remedy or minimize unverifiability in any decision-making process, especially that leading to violence, is to eliminate religion from human life altogether.

NOTES

1. C. S. Cowles, "The Case for Radical Discontinuity," in *Show Them No Mercy: Four Views on God and Canaanite Genocide*, ed. Stanley N. Gundry (Grand Rapids, MI: Eerdmans, 2003), p. 36.

2. Raymond W. Baker, *Islam without Fear: Egypt and the New Islamists* (Cambridge, MA: Harvard University Press, 2003). For examples of modern Islamic thinkers who question the applicability of some Islamic practices in the modern world, see Abdullah Saeed and Hassan Saeed, *Freedom of Religion: Apostasy and Islam* (Aldershot, England: Ashgate, 2004).

3. Ibid., p. 273.

4. Hans-Georg Gadamer, *Truth and Method*, trans. Joel Weinsheimer and Donald G. Marshall, 2nd rev. ed. (1753; reprint, New York: Crossroad, 1989).

5. Robert Lowth, *Lectures on the Sacred Poetry of the Hebrews* (1839; reprint, Whitefish, MT: Kessinger, 2004), p. 18.

6. Hermann Gunkel, *The Legends of Genesis: The Biblical Saga and History*, trans. W. H. Carruth (1901; reprint, New York: Schoken Books, 1974), p. 3.

7. Robert Alter and Frank Kermode, eds., *The Literary Guide to the Bible* (Cam-

bridge, MA: Harvard University Press, 1987); Robert Alter, *The Art of Biblical Narrative* (New York: Basic Books, 1981); and Meir Sternberg, *The Poetics of Biblical Narrative: Ideological Literature and the Drama of Reading* (Bloomington: Indiana University Press, 1987). See also, J. Cheryl Exum and David J. A. Clines, eds., *The New Literary Criticism and the Hebrew Bible* (Valley Forge, PA: Trinity Press International, 1993).

8. Alter, *The Art of Biblical Narrative*, p. 189.

9. Susan Niditch, *War in the Hebrew Bible: A Study in the Ethics of Violence* (New York: Oxford University Press, 1993), p. 153.

10. D. J. A. Clines, "One in Every Two Words in the Hebrew Bible May Be Corrupt" (paper presented at the Annual Meeting of the Society of Biblical Literature (Atlanta, GA: November 2003). I was present at this lecture, and I am quoting from *Abstracts 2003: Annual Meetings: American Academy or Religion/Society of Biblical Literature, Atlanta, Georgia, November 22–25* (Atlanta, GA: American Academy of Religion/Society of Biblical Literature, 2003). To be fair, Dr. Clines may moderate his assessment in the near future.

11. Andrea Bartoli, "Christianity and Peacebuilding," in *Religion and Peacebuilding*, ed. Harold Coward and Gordon S. Smith (Albany: State University of New York Press, 2004), p. 161.

12. Philip Schaff, *The History of the Christian Church* (AP&A, [1889]), 5:128.

13. Marc Gopin, *Holy War, Holy Peace: How Religion Can Bring Peace to the Middle East* (New York: Oxford University Press, 2000), p. 191.

14. Walter Wink, *Jesus and Nonviolence: A Third Way* (Minneapolis: Fortress, 1992), p. 6.

15. Ibid., pp. 1–3.

16. For a recent discussion see, Stephen Haynes, *Noah's Curse: The Biblical Justification of American Slavery* (New York: Oxford University Press, 2000).

17. For critiques of Mother Teresa's work, see Susan Shields, "Mother Teresa's House of Illusions: How She Harmed Her Helpers as Well as Those They 'Helped'" *Free Inquiry* 18, no. 1 (1998), also available online at http://www.secular humanism.org/ library/fi/shields_18_1.html; and Christopher Hitchens, *The Missionary Position: Mother Teresa in Theory and Practice* (London: Verso, 1995).

18. See Samir Amin, "The Ancient World-Systems versus the Modern Capitalist System." *Review* (Fernand Braudel Center) 14, no. 3 (1991): 349–85; and *Class and Nation: Historically and in the Current Crisis*, trans. Susan Kaplow (New York: Monthly Review Press, 1980).

19. See essays in S. N. Eisenstadt, ed., *The Origins and Diversity of the Axial Age Civilizations* (Albany: State University of New York Press, 1986).

20. Keith Bradley, *Slavery and Society at Rome* (Cambridge: Cambridge University Press, 1994).

21. Daniel Pipes, *Slave Soldiers and Islam: The Genesis of a Military System* (New Haven, CT: Yale University Press, 1981).

CHAPTER 17

FOREIGN POLICY IMPLICATIONS

Carl von Clausewitz may have cared little for the role of religion in war, but that outlook is certainly changing, especially following 9/11. Therefore, it behooves foreign policy makers to understand the implications of our thesis. First, our thesis should make clear that foreign policy must never be based on an appeal to unverifiable forces and/or beings. We have enough existing scarce resources over which to fight without creating unverifiable ones. On the other hand, understanding groups and states in which religion does play a role is an important tool in foreign policy. Here we survey some ideas and problems that are at issue in dealing with the explosive mixture of religion and foreign policy.

BUSH'S FOREIGN POLICY

As noted by Richard Clarke, "To the extent that religion was a political force during the Cold War, it was a weak one promoted by the United States as a counterpoint to the anti-religious ideology of the Soviet Union."[1] There is a resurgence of religious ideology in the foreign policy of George W. Bush.[2] Although the roles of oil and economics have been viewed by some as the primary factors in Bush's foreign policy on terrorism, it seems clear that religion also has an important role.[3] Bush, like many of the scholars we have discussed, is an essentialist when it comes to Islam. He believes that Islam is essentially good, and that Osama bin Laden is practicing a deviant form of Islam.

Bush's essentialism was most clear in his address on September 20, 2001, to a joint session of Congress in the aftermath of September 11. Concerning

Islam, he stated: "It's practiced freely by many millions of Americans, and by millions more in countries that America counts as friends. Its teachings are good and peaceful, and those who commit evil in the name of Allah blaspheme the name of Allah. The terrorists are traitors to their own faith, trying, in effect, to hijack Islam itself."[4]

Ironically, Bush's critics have also accepted essentialism when it comes to Islam. Thus, Clarke, in his *Against All Enemies*, severely criticizes Bush's obsession with Iraq. Clarke served as the nation's first National Coordinator for Security, Infrastructure Protection, and Counterterrorism under Bill Clinton. On September 11, 2001, he was serving as the manager of the Situation Room in the White House. Despite his long career studying al Qaeda, he provides the following description for that organization: "Al-Qaeda is a worldwide political conspiracy masquerading as a religious sect. It engages in murder of innocent people to grab attention. Its goal is a fourteenth-century-style theocracy in which women have no rights, everyone is forced to be a Muslim, and the Sharia legal system is used to cut off hands and stone people to death."[5]

So on the one hand, al Qaeda is not really a religious sect, and on the other hand, al Qaeda's main goal is forced theocracy. Clarke suggests that Bush "should have launched a concerted effort globally to counter the ideology of al-Qaeda and the larger radical Islamic terrorist movement with a partnership to promote *the real Islam*."[6] Likewise, *The 9/11 Commission Report* speaks of America opposing "a perversion of Islam."[7]

Given the unverifiability of the ultimate premises, promotion of the "real" version of any religion only regenerates conflict. Religious conflicts cannot be settled by any objective means, and this is where the danger of violence is ever present just underneath the surface of even the most pacifistic of religions. So in contrast to the essentialist solutions, which promote the "good Islam," foreign policy should center on exposing the fact that *all* versions of Islam—or any religion—are based on equally unverifiable premises. Foreign policy should seek to counteract, through aggressive and nonviolent educational programs, all modes of thought that are premised on the existence of supernatural beings and/or forces.

THE MECCA OPTION

The fact that our foreign policy makers do not see the potential use of belief in sacred space to quell violence is most obvious in the apparent impasse between the United States and al Qaeda. The rise of transnational militant groups such as al Qaeda has made deterrence even more problematic, as there is no national territory that may be targeted by the United States to counteract these groups. These difficulties have been outlined by, among other national security specialists, Paul K. Davis and Brian Michael Jenkins of the RAND Institute.[8] Davis and Jenkins are interested in the religious components of al Qaeda, and they cite John Esposito as one of their sources on Islamic religion.[9]

Briefly, Davis and Jenkins want to pursue a policy of influence combined with the threat of force as a main deterrent. Thus, they suggest:

> Draw a line and credibly announce that anyone crossing that line by possessing or supporting the acquisition of WMD for terrorist purposes will be pursued relentlessly—forever, if necessary—with all the means necessary and with the United States willing to lower its standards of evidence, presume guilt, violate sovereignty, attack preemptively, and so on.[10]

They add that a deterrent strategy should focus on what the enemy values:

> An important theme dating from the mid-1970s consisted of determining what the Soviet Union's leaders held dear and "holding it at risk," a euphemistic way of saying that in the event of an attack on the United States, whatever the Soviet leaders valued (rather than what U.S. system analysis might imagine they should value) would be destroyed. Nuclear targeting, then, might have the objective of destroying the communist party's control structure, not just destructive devices such as missiles. Targeting might include attacks on the leaders themselves, even if they were in deep underground shelters.[11]

Davis and Jenkins certainly recognize that one of the most crucial issues in foreign policy during the nuclear era was deterrence.[12] Nuclear weapons meant that the world could be destroyed. Consequently, a policy of deterrence evolved as different sides shifted in advantage. According to the Harvard Study Group, the United States was "substantially invulnerable to attack through the mid-1950s"[13] By the mid-1970s a rough parity existed that still favored the offensive side, even though neither side could eventually hope to win. We had arrived at the era of mutually assured destruction (MAD) as a state of affairs, even if not as a policy.[14]

The Soviet Union, the United States' main opponent during the nuclear era, was constantly reminded that any nuclear strike would be returned with one that would result in the obliteration of the Soviet Union, if not the planet. It was, therefore, not in the best interest of either side to use nuclear weapons. This stalemate became so costly to maintain that some believe it figured in the collapse of the Soviet Union. But the demise of the bipolar world meant that deterrence had to be reconfigured.[15]

However, Davis and Jenkins do not see the logical implications of their observations. Given the value of sacred space for Muslims, Davis and Jenkins fail to see that targeting what the opponent values could logically lead to a policy advocating the destruction of Mecca. Indeed, one of the things that all Muslims—including, presumably, the members of al Qaeda—value most is the sacred space called Mecca. The *Hajj* to Mecca is one of the five pillars of Islam. Osama bin Laden's proclamation of war speaks of the damage already being done to sacred space. Clearly bin Laden values sacred space.

Accordingly, the deterrent most analogous to that identified by Davis and Jenkins as effective against the Soviet Union is the potential destruction or occupation of Mecca. Announcing the possibility of the "Mecca Option" would be as good a deterrent as MAD. All Muslim militants would be put on notice that any attack on the United States would be met with the destruction or occupation of their most sacred site. If that did not deter them, few other things would work.

However, unlike MAD, the Mecca Option need not result in loss of life, because it is the space itself that is valued. Unlike the situation with the Soviet Union, a rapid response against Mecca would not be crucial, because attacks are unlikely to come directly from Mecca. Destroying Mecca immediately would have no tactical value, so occupants could be evacuated prior to attack. The Mecca Option would also be cost-effective, as it would require very little military force or loss of American lives to destroy the most sacred areas of Mecca.

But what would be the consequences of an extension to Mecca of the hypothetical proposals made by Davis and Jenkins for the Soviet situation? The cost, of course, is enmity of the Muslim world. To what extent military theorists will be willing to pursue such a new way of thinking about sacred space is the big question to be answered. Ultimately, such strategists will need to weigh the cost of Muslim enmity against the potential destruction of our society. If Machiavelli had any insight at all perhaps it is best paraphrased by this question: It is better to be feared than loved if it deters our destruction, or are sacred spaces more valuable than human lives? This is the type of new question that emerges from the rethinking of the value of sacred space in foreign policy.

JERUSALEM AND ISRAEL

Jerusalem's sacred value has been created by religion, and its political and economic value derives from its religious value. Given that situation, the United States must decide whether supporting the state of Israel is in our national best interest. Here one finds at least two camps. One camp says that our relationship with Israel is in our national interest, while the other camp would argue that it is not. We look briefly here at each side.

Among those who support the idea that Israel is in our national interest are those who see Israel as a stable democracy on which we can rely in the Middle East. Advocates of such a policy include Nadav Safran and, most recently, Alan Dershowitz.[16] To one degree or another, this has been the foreign policy of the United States since the birth of Israel in 1948.

Among those who say that Israel does not provide enough benefit to outweigh the hostility of the Muslim world are Jewish as well as non-Jewish theoreticians. Cheryl A. Rubenberg, who supports a two-state solution, nonetheless argues against the common assumptions that Israel is of strategic value to the United States and that Israel demonstrates enlightened democratic values that are consistent with those of the United States. Basing himself more on moral grounds, Marc Ellis, a Jewish theologian, has also questioned the support that the United States has given to Israel.[17]

Our survey of the relationship between religion and violence indicates that Islamic violence against the West will not be resolved unless the Israel situation is resolved. The idea that Jews are the enemy is very deeply ingrained in Muslim history and philosophy. It goes back to first biographies of the prophet Muhammad, who serves as a paradigm of Muslim behavior. This hatred has existed before colonialism, during colonialism, and in our supposedly postcolonial world.

As long as Jerusalem and Israel continue to be regarded as sacred space, it will continue to be a problem. A pessimist would predict that violence in Jerusalem will continue indefinitely. An optimist would point to the fact that many Jews in Europe have indeed come to see Jerusalem and Israel as something best left in the past or in poetry (e.g., Geiger).[18] If we can descripturalize the argument and desacralize the space, there may be a slight glimmer of hope for resolution.

SUMMARY

Gilles Kepel has argued vigorously that terrorist "Islamist" movements, as he calls them, are in decline.[19] The attacks of September 11, he observes, have failed to mobilize the Islamic world in the manner Osama bin Laden expected. Far from showing their vitality, the attacks show the desperation and frustration of Islamist movements to unite the Muslim world against the West. We hope that this is the case.

However, there are also grounds for pessimism. First, it does not take many Islamic terrorists to bring down a superpower. September 11 had an incredibly negative impact on the US economy. Second, it is unclear whether the current wars in Iraq and Afghanistan are helping to disband Muslim militants or creating more of them. The latter scenario has a precedent in the Soviet invasion of Afghanistan, which some scholars see as a turning point in the globalization of Islamic militancy.[20] Third, our government is still very misinformed about religion. By seeking to promote "good" religion, it overlooks the inherent danger in all religion—the use of unverifiable propositions to further an agenda.

Solving political and economic problems is a very important part of our foreign policy. In fact, we have not argued that religion is the only problem in the Middle East. Certainly we must address educational, economic, and political problems. However, a sound foreign policy must recognize that disputes about ultimately unverifiable beliefs are a prime factor in religious violence. An effective foreign policy, therefore, must include an educational program that convinces world citizens that violence about resources that do not exist, or that cannot be verified to exist, is against their own interest. Ultimately, such a strategy would be in everyone's best interest.

NOTES

1. Richard A. Clarke, *Against All Enemies: Inside America's War on Terror* (New York: Free Press, 2004), p. 71.

2. Joseph J. Martos, *May God Bless America: George W. Bush and Biblical Morality* (Tucson, AZ: Fenestra Books, 2004).

3. For the role of oil in American foreign policy in the first Gulf War, see Micah L. Sifry and Christopher Serf, *The Gulf War Reader: History, Documents, Opinions* (New York: Random House, 1991); and Daniel Yergin, *The Prize: The Epic Quest for Oil, Money, and Power* (New York: Simon & Schuster, 1992). For the view that Eisenhower marks the beginning of a systematic policy based on oil, see Nathan J. Citino, *From Arab Nationalism to OPEC: Eisenhower, King Sa'ud, and the Making of U.S.-Saudi Relations* (Bloomington: Indiana University Press, 2002). Citino (p. 95) sees Eisenhower as naive about Islam.

4. Our text is from http://www.americanrhetoric.com/speeches/gwbush911joint sessionspeech.htm (visited on June 23, 2004).

5. Clarke, *Against All Enemies*, p. 218.

6. Ibid., p. 247. For others who argue for the value of religion in settling disputes, see also Jonathan Fox and Shmuel Sandler, *Bringing Religion into International Relations* (New York: Palgrave Macmillan, 2004), and Beverly Milton-Edwards and Peter Hinchcliffe, *Conflicts in the Middle East since 1945*, 2nd ed. (London: Routledge, 2001), p. 116.

7. *The 9/11 Commission Report*, p. 363.

8. Paul K. Davis and Brian Michael Jenkins, *Deterrence & Influence in Counter-*

terrorism: A Component in the War on al Qaeda (Santa Monica, CA: Rand, 2002). See also Rafael Bonoan et al., *Deterring Terrorism: Exploring Theory and Methods*, Institute for Defense Analyses Paper P-3717 (Washington, DC: Institute for Defense Analyses, 2002).

9. John L. Esposito, *Unholy War: Terror in the Name of Islam* (New York: Oxford University Press, 2002).

10. Davis and Jenkins, *Deterrence & Influence*, p. 75.

11. Ibid., p. 79.

12. For some representative views of deterrence just before the fall of the bipolar configuration, see Albert Carnesale et al., *Living with Nuclear Weapons* (New York: Bantam, 1983), especially pp. 82–101; Graham T. Allison, Albert Carnesale, and Joseph S. Nye Jr., eds., *Hawks, Doves and Owls: An Agenda for Avoiding Nuclear War* (New York: W. W. Norton, 1985); and Richard K. Betts, "Conventional Deterrence: Predictive Uncertainty and Policy Confidence," *World Politics* 37, no. 2 (January 1985): 153–79.

13. Carnesale et al., *Living with Nuclear Weapons*, p. 100.

14. A plea for the distinction between MAD as policy and as a condition is found in Allison, Carnesale, and Nye, *Hawks, Doves and Owls*, p. 228.

15. For some current discussions of foreign policy in the post-Soviet world, see Zbigniew K. Brzezinski, *The Choice: Global Domination or Global Leadership?* (New York: Basic Books, 2004); John Lewis Gaddis, *Surprise, Security, and the American Experience* (Cambridge, MA: Harvard University Press, 2004); and Joseph S. Nye, *Soft Power: The Means to Succeed in World Politics* (New York: Public Affairs, 2004).

16. Nadav Safran, *Israel: The Embattled Ally* (Cambridge, MA: Harvard University Press, 1981); and Dershowitz, *The Case for Israel*.

17. Cheryl A. Rubenberg, *Israel and the American National Interest* (Urbana and Chicago: University of Illinois Press, 1986); Marc H. Ellis, *Beyond Innocence and Redemption: Confronting the Holocaust and Israeli Power* (San Francisco: Harper and Row, 1990); and *Unholy Alliance: Religion and Atrocity in Our Time* (Minneapolis: Fortress, 1997).

18. For a review of possible future scenarios, see A. Hareven, "Towards the Year 2030: Can a Civil Society Shared by Jews and Arabs Evolve in Israel?" *International Journal of Intercultural Relations* 26 (2002): 153–68.

19. Gilles Kepel, *Jihad: The Trail of Political Islam* (Cambridge, MA: Harvard University Press, 2002), especially pp. 375–76.

20. Esposito, *Unholy War*, p. 157.

CONCLUSION

Religion, as a mode of life and thought that is premised on relationships with supernatural forces and/or beings, is fundamentally prone to violence. Violence in religion may indeed be akin to a "recessive gene," as Kelton Cobb has described it.[1] The violence, first and foremost, resides in the unverifiability of a religion's basic premises and any consequences that follow. Since there are no objective means to adjudicate unverifiable claims, conflict and violence ensue when counterclaims are made. As such, the potential for violence is part of every religious tradition, though we have concentrated only on the Abrahamic traditions.[2]

We have embedded our critique of religious violence within the framework of scarce resource theory of violence. Within this framework, scarce resources, real or perceived, are a major mechanism for conflict. This is particularly the case because, by nature, religion creates scarcities. Any time someone says that he has received a revelation from God, a scarce resource has been created. Any time a group declares that it is the receptor, transmitter, and rightful custodian of written divine communication, scarce resources are created in the form of inscripturation and group privileging. Any time one physical space is declared to be more valuable than another, another scarce resource has been created—especially if others are competing for that same space.

Most scholars of religion and biblical scholars have been complicit in creating and propagating the value of violent texts at one time or another. Some may acknowledge that the mission of academics is to help faith communities in a benign and inclusivistic way, as does Charles Cosgrove, who thinks it is scholarship's mission to establish the "viability of other faith interpretations" (i.e., those outside of "Western theological academe").[3] Anne

Clark tells us that "the sympathetic treatment of Judaism or indeed any other non-Christian faiths, in schools, will benefit children from all faith communities."[4] Most academic scholars are not so frank in acknowledging that their scholarship is an apologetic enterprise.

Given the violence in the scriptures we have examined, I would suggest that the opposite should be our mission. Our job as biblical scholars is to undermine the value of any scripture that endorses violence. We become complicit in violence when we attempt to maintain the value of a book whose main truth claims can never be verified. We are complicit when we maintain the value of violent scriptures by focusing on "aesthetics" that exist no more than the "aesthetics" of *Mein Kampf*. We need to ask ourselves, as academics, why the Bible and the Qur'an, among other scriptures, are worth privileging at all. Our final mission, as scholars of these scriptures, must be to help humanity close the book on a long chapter of human misery.

NOTES

1. Kelton Cobb, "Violent Faith," in *September 11: Religious Perspectives on the Causes and Consequences*, ed. Ian Markham and Ibrahim M. Abu Rabi' (Oxford: Oneworld Publications, 2002), pp. 158–59. For a scientist's view of the persistently violent consequences of religious belief, see also Sam Harris, *The End of Faith: Religion, Terror, and the Future of Reason* (New York: W. W. Norton, 2004).

2. See, for example, the study of violence in Buddhism in John D'Arcy May, *Transcendence and Violence: The Encounter of Buddhist, Christian, and Primal Traditions* (New York: Continuum, 2003).

3. Charles H. Cosgrove, *Appealing to Scripture in Moral Debate: Five Hermeneutical Rules* (Grand Rapids, MI: Eerdmans, 2002), p. 169. See also Daniel Patte, *Ethics of Biblical Interpretation: A Reevaluation* (Louisville, KY: Westminster/John Knox, 1995).

4. Anne Clark, "Why Teach Judaism?" in *Christian-Jewish Relations through the Centuries*, ed. Stanley E. Porter and W. R. Pearson (Sheffield, UK: Sheffield Academic Press, 2000), p. 482.

BIBLIOGRAPHY

Abou El Fadl, Khaled. *The Place of Tolerance in Islam*. Edited by Joshua Cohen and Ian Lague. Boston: Beacon Press, 2004.

Abu-Lughod, Lila. "Zones of Theory in the Anthropology of the Arab World." *Annual Review of Anthropology* 18 (1989): 267–306.

Abusch, Tzvi. "Blood in Israel and Mesopotamia." In *Emanuel: Studies in the Hebrew Bible, Septuagint, and Dead Sea Scrolls in Honor of Emanuel Tov*, edited by Shalom M. Paul, Robert A. Kraft, Lawrence H. Schiffman, and Weston W. Fields, 675–84. Leiden/Boston: Brill, 2003.

Achtemeier, Paul J. *Inspiration and Authority: Nature and Function of Christian Scripture*. Peabody, MA: Hendrickson, 1999.

Ackerman, James S., with Jane Stouder Hawley. *On Teaching the Old Testament as Literature: A Guide to Selected Biblical Narratives for Secondary Schools*. Bloomington: Indiana University Press, 1967.

Ackerman, Susan. "The Personal Is Political: Covenental and Affectionate Love ['Aḥēb, 'Ahâbâh] in the Hebrew Bible." *Vetus Testamentum* 52, no. 4 (2002): 437–58.

———. "Why Is Miriam among the Prophets? (And Is Zipporah among the Priests?)." *JBL* 121, no. 1 (2002): 47–80.

Ahlström, Gösta W. *The History of Ancient Palestine*. Minneapolis: Fortress, 1993.

Alexander, Richard. *The Biology of Moral Systems*. New York: de Gruyter, 1987.

Algar, Hamid. *Wahhabism: A Critical Essay*. Oneonta, NY: Islamic Publications International, 2002.

Algaze, Guillermo. "The Prehistory of Imperialism: The Case of Uruk Period Mesopotamia." In *Uruk Mesopotamia and Its Neighbors: Cross-Cultural Interactions in the Era of State Formation*, edited by Mitchell Rothman, 27–83. Santa Fe, NM: School of Amrerican Research, 2001.

———. *The Uruk World System*. Chicago: University of Chicago Press, 1993.

Ali, A. Yusuf. *The Holy Qur'ān: Text, Translation, and Commentary*. Brentwood, MD: Amana, 1983.

Ali, M. Muhammad. *Introduction to the Holy Qur'an*. 1936. Reprint, Lahore, Pakistan: Ahmadiyya, 1992.

————. *A Manual of Hadith*. 1941. Reprint, Columbus, OH: Ahmadiyya Anjuman Isha'at Islam, 2001.

————. *Muhammad and Christ*. 1921. Reprint, Lahore, Pakistan: Ahmadiyya, 1993.

————. *The Religion of Islam*. 6th rev. ed. Columbus, OH: Ahmadiyya Anjuman Isha'at Islam, 1990.

Alles, Gregory. "Toward a Genealogy of the Holy: Rudolf Otto and the Apologetics of Religion," *JAAR* 69, no. 2 (2001): 232–341.

Alley, Robert, ed. *The Constitution and Religion: Leading Supreme Court Cases on Church and State*. Amherst, NY: Prometheus Books, 1999.

Allison, Graham T., Albert Carnesale, and Joseph S. Nye Jr., eds. *Hawks, Doves and Owls: An Agenda for Avoiding Nuclear War*. New York: W. W. Norton, 1985.

Almond, Gabriel A., R. Scott Appleby, and Emmanuel Sivan. *Strong Religion: The Rise of Fundamentalisms around the World*. Chicago: University of Chicago Press, 2003.

Alston, William P. *Perceiving God: The Epistemology of Religious Experience*. Ithaca, NY: Cornell University Press, 1991.

Alter, Robert. *The Art of Biblical Narrative*. New York: Basic Books, 1981.

————, and Frank Kermode, eds. *The Literary Guide to the Bible*. Cambridge, MA: Harvard University Press, 1987.

Aly, Götz, Peter Chroust, and Christian Pross. *Cleansing the Fatherland: Nazi Medicine and Racial Hygiene*. Translated by Belinda Cooper. Baltimore: Johns Hopkins University Press, 1994.

American Academy of Pediatrics. "Circumcision Policy Statement." *Pediatrics* 103, no. 3 (March 1999): 686–93.

Amin, Samir. "The Ancient World-Systems versus the Modern Capitalist System." *Review* (Fernand Braudel Center) 14, no. 3 (1991): 349–85.

————. *Class and Nation: Historically and in the Current Crisis*. Translated by Susan Kaplow. New York: Monthly Review Press, 1980.

Anderson, Bernhard W. *Contours of Old Testament Theology*. Minneapolis: Fortress, 1999.

Andrea, Alfred J. *Contemporary Sources for the Fourth Crusade*. Leiden: Brill, 2000.

Appleby, R. Scott. *The Ambivalence of the Sacred: Religion, Violence, and Reconciliation*. Oxford: Rowman and Littlefield, 2000.

Aquinas, Thomas, *Summa Theologica*. Translated by the Fathers of the English Dominican Province. 3 vols. New York: Benziger Brothers, 1947.

Arafat, W. N. "New Light on the Story of the Banû Qurayza and the Jews of Medina." *JRAS* (1976): 100–107.

Archer, Gleason. *Encyclopedia of Bible Difficulties*. Grand Rapids, MI: Zondervan, 1982.

Ardrey, Robert. *The Territorial Imperative: A Personal Inquiry into the Origins of Property and Nations*. New York: Atheneum, 1966.

Argyle, Michael, and Benjamin Beit-Hallahmi. *The Social Psychology of Religion*. London: Routledge, 1975.

Armstrong, Karen. *Holy War: The Crusades and Their Impact on Today's World*. New York: Anchor Books, 2001.

————. *Muhammad: A Biography of the Prophet*. New York: HarperCollins, 1992.

Ashley, Benedict. *Theologies of the Body: Humanist and Christian*. Braintree, MA: Pope John XXIII Medical-Moral Research and Education Center, 1985.

Atta, Mohammed. "[Last Will and Testament]." http://abcnews.go.com/US/story?id
=92367&page=1.

Augustine. *City of God*. Translated by William M. Green et al. 7 vols. LCL. Cambridge MA: Harvard University Press, 1963.

———. *The City of God against the Pagans*. Translated by George E. McCracken et al. 7 vols. LCL. Cambridge, MA: Harvard University Press, 1957–72.

———. "Our Lord's Sermon on the Mount." In *The Nicene and Post-Nicene Fathers*, edited by Philip Schaff and Henry Wace, vol. 6.

———. "Reply to Faustus." In *The Nicene and Post-Nicene Fathers*, edited by Philip Schaff and Henry Wace, vol. 4.

Aulén, Gustaf. *Christus Victor: An Historical Study of the Three Main Types of the Idea of Atonement*. Translated by A. G. Hebert. New York: Macmillan, 1969.

Avalos, Hector. "Daniel 9:24–25 and Mesopotamian Temple Rededications." *JBL* 117, no. 3 (1998): 507–11.

———. "The Gospel of Lucas Gavilan as Postcolonial Biblical Exegesis." *Semeia* 75 (1996): 87–105.

———. *Health Care and the Rise of Christianity*. Peabody, MA: Hendrickson, 1999.

———. *Illness and Health Care in the Ancient Near East: The Role of the Temple in Greece, Mesopotamia, and Israel*. Harvard Semitic Monographs 54. Atlanta, GA: Scholars Press, 1995.

———. "Is Faith Good for You?" *Free Inquiry* 17, no. 4 (1997): 44–46.

———. "Violence in the Bible and the *Bhagavad Gita*." *Journal of Vaishnava Studies* 9, no. 2 (2001): 67–83.

Bach, H. I. *The German Jew: A Synthesis of Judaism in Western Civilization, 1730–1930*. London: Oxford University Press, 1985.

Bailey, L. "Gehenna: The Topography of Hell." *Biblical Archaeologist* 49 (1986): 187–91.

Bainbridge, William Sims, and Rodney Stark. "Suicide, Homicide, and Religion: Durkheim Reassessed." *Annual Review of the Social Sciences of Religion* 5 (1981): 33–56.

Bainton, Roland H. *Christian Attitudes toward War and Peace: A Historical Survey and Critical Re-evaluation*. New York: Abingdon, 1960.

Baker, Raymond W. *Islam without Fear: Egypt and the New Islamists*. Cambridge, MA: Harvard University Press, 2003.

Bal, Mieke. *Death and Dissymmetry: The Politics of Coherence in the Book of Judges*. Chicago: University of Chicago Press, 1988.

———. *Lethal Love: Feminist Literary Interpretations of Biblical Love Stories*. Bloomington: Indiana University Press, 1987.

———. *Murder and Difference: Gender, Genre, and Scholarship on Sisera's Death*. Bloomington: Indiana University Press, 1988.

Baltzer, Klaus. *The Covenant Formulary in Old Testament, Jewish, and Early Christian Writings*. Translated by David E. Green. Philadelphia: Fortress, 1971.

Bandstra, Barry L. *Reading the Old Testament: An Introduction to the Hebrew Bible*. 3rd ed. Belmont, CA: Wadsworth, 2004.

Bandura, Albert. *Aggression: A Social Learning Analysis*. Englewood Cliffs, NJ: Prentice-Hall, 1973.

Banner, Michael C. *The Justification of Science and the Rationality of Religious Belief.* Oxford: Clarendon, 1990.

Barber, Benjamin R. *Jihad vs. McWorld: Terrorism's Challenge to Democracy.* New York: Ballantine Books, 1995.

Barclay, Robert. *A Catechism and Confession of Faith*, 3rd ed. Available online at http://www.qhpress.org/texts/Barclay/catechism (accessed July 10, 2004).

Barkow, Jerome. "Culture and Sociobiology." *American Anthropologist* 80, no. 1 (1978): 5–20.

Barmash, Pamela. *Homicide in the Biblical World.* Cambridge: Cambridge University Press, 2005.

Barr, James. *The Concept of Biblical Theology.* Minneapolis: Fortress, 1999.

———. *The Semantics of Biblical Language.* London: SCM Press, 1983.

Barrett, David B., George T. Kurian, and Todd M. Johnson. *World Christian Encyclopedia: A Comparative Survery of Churches and Religions in the Modern World.* 2 vols. 2nd ed. New York: Oxford, 2001.

Bartoli, Andrea. "Christianity and Peacebuilding." In *Religion and Peacebuilding*, edited by Harold Coward and Gordon S. Smith. Albany: State University of New York Press, 2004, pp. 147–66.

Bartov, Omer, and Phyllis Mack, eds. *In God's Name: Genocide and Religion in the Twentieth Century.* New York: Berghahn Books, 2001.

Batalden, Stephen K., ed. *Seeking God: The Recovery of Religious Identity in Orthodox Russia, Ukraine, and Georgia.* DeKalb: Northern Illinois University Press, 1993.

Bauer, Yehuda. *Rethinking the Holocaust.* New Haven, CT: Yale University Press, 2001.

Baum, Gregory. "Religious Studies and Theology." *Journal of Theology for Southern Africa* 70 (1990): 2–8.

Beck, Aaron T. *Prisoners of Hate: The Cognitive Basis of Anger, Hostility and Violence.* New York: Perennial, 1999.

Becker, Lawrence C., and Charlotte B. Becker. *A History of Western Ethics.* New York: Garland, 1992.

Beckett, Katherine Scarfe. *Anglo-Saxon Perceptions of the Islamic World.* Cambridge: Cambridge University Press, 2003.

Beckman-Brindley, S., and J. B. Tavormina. "Power Relationships in Families: A Social-Exchange Perspective." *Family Process* 17 (1978): 423–36.

Bein, Alex. *Theodore Herzl: A Biography.* Translated by Maurice Samuel. New York: Atheneum, 1970.

———. *Theodor Herzl: Biographie.* Vienna: Fiba Verlag, 1934.

Beitzel, Barry. *Moody Atlas of Bible Lands.* Chicago: Moody, 1985.

Bennigsen, Alexandre, and S. Enders Wimbush. *Muslims of the Soviet Empire: A Guide.* Bloomington: Indiana University Press, 1986.

Bentham, Jeremy. *The Influence of Natural Religion on the Temporal Happiness of Mankind.* 1822. Reprint, Amherst, NY: Prometheus Books, 2003.

Berger, David. "Mission to the Jews and Jewish Christian Contacts in the Polemical Literature of the High Middle Ages." *American Historical Review* 91 (1986): 576–91.

Berkowitz, Leonard. *Aggression: Its Causes, Consequences, and Control.* Philadelphia: Temple University Press, 1993.

————. "Aversive Conditions as Stimuli to Aggression." *Advances in Experimental Social Psychology* 15 (1982): 249–88.

Berquist, Jon L. *Controlling Corporeality: The Body and the Household in Ancient Israel.* New Brunswick, NJ: Rutgers University Press, 2002.

————. *Judaism in Persia's Shadow: A Social and Historical Approach.* Minneapolis: Fortress, 1995.

————. "Postcolonialism and Imperial Motives for Canonization." *Semeia* 75 (1996): 15–35.

Betts, Richard K. "Conventional Deterrence: Predictive Uncertainty and Policy Confidence." *World Politics* 37, no. 2 (January 1985): 153–79.

Betz, Hans D. *Essays on the Sermon on the Mount.* Translated by L. L. Welborn. Philadelphia: Fortress, 1985.

————. *Galatians.* Philadelphia: Fortress, 1979.

Bishop, David J., F. Homer-Dixon, Jeffrey H. Boutwell, and George Rathjens. "Environmental Change and Violent Conflict." *Scientific American* 268, no. 2 (February 1993): 38–45.

Black, David Alan, ed. *Rethinking New Testament Textual Criticism.* Grand Rapids, MI: Baker Academic, 2000.

Blanchard, John. *Does God Believe in Atheists?* Auburn, MA: Evangelical Press, 2000.

Blass, F., and A. Debrunner. *A Greek Grammar of the New Testament and Other Early Christian Literature.* Translated by Robert Funk. Chicago: University of Chicago Press, 1961.

Blet, Pierre. *Pope Pius XII and the Second World War: According to the Archives of the Vatican.* Translated by Lawrence Johnson. New York: Paulist, 1999.

————, ed. *Girolamo Ragazzoni, évêque de Bergame, nonce en France: correspondance de sa nonciature (1583–1586).* Acta Nuntiaturae Gallicae 2. Rome: Université Pontificale Grégorienne/École Française de Rome, 1962.

Boardman, John. "Aspects of Colonization." *BASOR* 322 (2001): 33–42.

Bodansky, Yossef. *Bin Laden: The Man Who Declared War on America.* Roseville, CA: Prima, 2001.

Boling, Robert G., trans. *Judges.* Anchor Bible 6A. Garden City, NY: Doubleday, 1975.

Bonoan, Rafael, Paul Davis, Brad Roberts, Victor Utgoff, and Catherine Ziemke. *Deterring Terrorism: Exploring Theory and Methods.* Institute for Defense Analyses Paper P-3717. Washington, DC: Institute for Defense Analysis, 2002.

Boone, Elizabeth Hill, and Walter Mignolo, eds. *Writing without Words: Alternative Literacies in Mesoamerica and the Andes.* Durham, NC: Duke University Press, 1994.

Borg, Marcus. *Jesus and Buddha: The Parallel Sayings.* Berkeley, CA: Seastone, 1999.

Borowski, Oded. "Hezekiah's Reforms and the Revolt against Assyria." *Biblical Archaeologist* 58, no. 3 (September 1995): 148–55.

Boserup, Esther. *The Conditions of Agricultural Growth.* Chicago: Aldine, 1965.

Bottéro, Jean. *Mesopotamia: Writing, Reasoning, and the Gods.* Translated by Zainab Bahrani and Marc van de Mieroop. Chicago: University of Chicago Press, 1992.

Bourdieu, Pierre. *Outline of a Theory of Practice.* Translated by Richard Nice. Cambridge: Cambridge University Press, 1977.

Bowie, Fiona. *The Anthropology of Religion.* Oxford: Blackwell, 2000.

Bowlin, John. "Parts, Wholes, and Opposites: John Milbank as *Geisterhistoriker*." *Journal of Religious Ethics* 32, no. 2 (2004): 257–69.

Bradley, Keith. *Slavery and Society at Rome*. Cambridge: Cambridge University Press, 1994.

Brandt, Richard. "Ethical Relativism." In *Moral Relativism: A Reader*, edited by Paul K. Moser and Thomas L. Carson, 25–31. New York: Oxford University Press, 2001.

Bravmann, Meïr M. "The Ancient Background of the Koranic Concept of Al-Ğizyatu 'An Yadin." In *What The Koran Really Says*, edited by Ibn Warraq, 350–63.

———. "A Propos de Qur'an IX.29: Ḥattā Yu'Ṭū L-Gizyata Wa-Hum Ṣagirūna." In *What The Koran Really Says*, edited by Ibn Warraq, 348–49.

Brenner, Athalya, ed. *Ruth and Esther: A Feminist Companion to the Bible*. Sheffield, UK: Sheffield Academic Press, 1999.

Briggs, Martin S. *Muhammadan Architecture in Egypt and Palestine*. 1924. Reprint, New York: Da Capo, 1974.

Brinton, Crane. *The Anatomy of Revolution*. New York: Vintage, 1965.

Brown, Dan. *The Da Vinci Code*. New York: Doubleday, 2003.

Brown, Donald E. *Human Universals*. Boston: McGraw-Hill, 1991.

Brown, Jerry Wayne. *The Rise of Biblical Criticism in America, 1800–1870*. Middletown, CT: Wesleyan University Press, 1969.

Brown, Lester R., Gary Gardner, and Brian Halweil. *Beyond Malthus: Nineteen Dimensions of the Population Challenge*. New York: W. W. Norton, 1999.

Brown, Michael Joseph. "Paul's Use of [Doulos Christou Iesou] in Romans 1:1." *JBL* 120, no. 4 (Winter 2001): 723–37.

Brown, Raymond E. *The Gospel According to John I–XII*. Garden City, NY: Doubleday, 1983.

Brown, Robert McAfee. *Religion and Violence: A Primer for White Americans*. Stanford, CA: Stanford Alumni Association, 1973.

Brownlie, Ian, ed. *Basic Documents on Human Rights*. 3rd ed. Oxford: Clarendon, 1992.

Brueggemann, Walter. *Peace*. St. Louis, MO: Chalice, 2001.

Brundage, James A. *The Crusades, Holy War, and Canon Law*. Hampshire, UK: Variorum, 1991.

Bruns, Gerald L. "Canon and Power in the Hebrew Scriptures." *Critical Inquiry* 10, no. 3 (March 1984): 462–80.

Brzezinski, Zbigniew K. *The Choice: Global Domination or Global Leadership?* New York: Basic Books, 2004.

Buell, Denise Kimber, and Caroline Johnson Hodge, "The Politics of Interpretation: The Rhetoric of Race and Ethnicity in Paul." *JBL* 123, no. 2 (Summer 2004): 235–51.

Bukhari, al-. *Shahih Al-Bukhari*. Translated by Muhammad Muhsin Khan. 9 vols. Riyadh, Saudi Arabia: Darussalam Publishers and Distributors, 1997.

Bulliet, Richard W. *The Case for Islamo-Christian Civilization*. New York: Columbia University Press, 2004.

Bullock, Alan. *Hitler and Stalin: Parallel Lives*. New York: HarperCollins, 1991.

Bultmann, Rudolf. *Theology of the New Testament*. Translated by Kendrick Grobel. 2 vols. New York: Charles Scribner's Sons, 1951–1955.

Burckhardt, Jacob. *The Civilization of the Renaissance in Italy.* Translated by L. Gold-scheider. London: Phaidon, 1955.

———. *Die Kultur der Renaissance in Italien.* 1860. Reprint, Stuttgart: Philipp Reclam, 1987.

Burkert, Walter. *Homo Necans: The Anthropology of Ancient Greek and Sacrificial Ritual and Myth.* Translated by Peter Bing. Berkeley and Los Angeles: University of California Press, 1983.

Burns, Rita J. *Has the Lord Indeed Spoken Only through Moses? A Study of the Biblical Portrait of Miriam.* SBL Dissertation Series 84. Atlanta, GA: Scholars Press, 1987.

Burtchaell, James Tunstead. *The Dying of the Light: The Disengagement of Colleges and Universities from Their Christian Churches.* Grand Rapids, MI: Eerdmans, 1998.

Burton, John. *The Collection of the Qur'an.* Cambridge: Cambridge University Press, 1977.

"Bush Letter Cites 'Crusade' against Terrorism." *Boston Globe,* April 18, 2004. http://www.boston.com/news/politics/president/bush/articles/2004/04/18/bush _letter_cites_crusade_against_terrorism/ (accessed July 12, 2004).

Cabrera, Lydia. *El Monte.* Miami: Coleccion de Chicherekú, 1971.

Cahill, Jane M. "Jerusalem at the Time of the United Monarchy: The Archaeological Evidence." In *Jerusalem in Bible and Archaeology: The First Temple Period,* edited by Andrew G. Vaughn and Anne E. Killebrew, 13–80. Atlanta, GA: Scholars Press, 2003.

Cahill, Lisa Sowle. *Love Your Enemies: Discipleship, Pacifism, and Just War Theory.* Minneapolis: Fortress, 1994.

Caldwell, Sarah, and Brian K. Smith. "Introduction: Who Speaks for Hinduism?" *JAAR* 68, no. 4 (2000): 705–11.

Calvin, John. *Institutes of the Christian Religion.* 1536. Reprint, Grand Rapids, MI: Eerdmans, 1972.

Cantor, Norman F. *Inventing the Middle Ages.* New York: William Morrow, 1991.

Carnesale, Albert, Paul Doty, Stanley Hoffman, Samuel P. Huntington, Joseph S. Nye, and Scott Sagan. *Living with Nuclear Weapons.* New York: Bantam, 1983.

Carrasco, David. *City of Sacrifice: The Aztec Empire and the Role of Violence in Civilization.* Boston: Beacon, 1999.

Cartmill, Matt. "The Status of the Race Concept in Physical Anthropology." *American Anthropologist* 100, no. 3 (1998): 651–60.

Casey, Stephen J. "Defining Violence." *Thought: A Review of Culture and Idea* 56, no. 220 (1981): 5–16.

Cavanaugh, William T. "'A Fire Strong Enough to Consume the House': The Wars of Religion and the Rise of the State." *Modern Theology* 11, no. 4 (1995): 397–420.

Cazelles, Henri. "587 ou 586?" In *The Word of the Lord Shall Go Forth: Essays in Honor of David Noel Freedman in Celebration of His Sixtieth Birthday,* edited by Carol L. Meyers and M. O'Connor, 417–35. Winona Lake, IN: Eisenbrauns, 1983.

Chandler, Albert. *Rosenberg's Nazi Myth.* Ithaca, NY: Cornell University Press, 1945.

Charles IX. *Correspondance du roi Charles IX et du sieur de Mandelot, gouverneur de Lyon, pendant l'anneé 1572, époque du massacre de Saint-Barthélemy, Monuments inédits de l'histoire de France 1.* Paris: Crapelet, 1830.

Chase, Kenneth R., and Alan Jacobs, eds. *Must Christianity Be Violent? Reflections on History, Practice and Theology*. Grand Rapids, MI: Brazos, 2003.

Chaves, M., and F. Kniss. "Analyzing Interdenominational Conflict: New Directions." *Journal for the Scientific Study of Religion* 34 (1995): 172–85.

Chazan, Robert. *Daggers of Faith: Thirteenth-Century Christian Missionizing and Jewish Response*. Berkeley and Los Angeles: University of California Press, 1989.

———. *In the Year 1096: The First Crusade and the Jews*. Philadelphia: Jewish Publication Society, 1996.

Childs, Brevard. *Biblical Theology of the Old and New Testaments*. London: SCM Press, 1992.

———. *Introduction to the Old Testament as Scripture*. Philadelphia: Fortress, 1979.

Chomsky, Noam. "The Responsibility of Intellectuals." In *The Chomsky Reader*, edited by James Peck. New York: Pantheon, 1987.

Chumachenko, Tatiana A. *Church and State in Soviet Russia: Russian Orthodoxy from World War II to the Krushchev Years*. Translated by Edward E. Roslof. Armonk, NY: M. E. Sharpe, 2002.

———. *Gosudartsvo, pavoslavnaia tserkov, veruiushchie, 1941–1961*. Moscow: AIRO-XX, 1999.

Citino, Nathan J. *From Arab Nationalism to OPEC: Eisenhower, King Sa'ud, and the Making of U.S.-Saudi Relations*. Bloomington: Indiana University Press, 2002.

Clark, Anne. "Why Teach Judaism?" In *Christian-Jewish Relations through the Centuries*, edited by Stanley E. Porter and W. R. Pearson, 473–82. Sheffield, UK: Sheffield Academic Press, 2000.

Clark, Elizabeth. "Antifamilial Tendencies in Ancient Christianity." *Journal of the History of Sexuality* 5, no. 3 (1995): 356–80.

Clarke, Richard A. *Against All Enemies: Inside America's War on Terror*. New York: Free Press, 2004.

Clausewitz, Carl von. *On War*. Translated by Arnolo Rapoport. London: Penguin, 1968.

———. *Vom Krieg*. Edited by Ulrich Marwedel. Stuttgart: Universal-Bibliothek, 1994.

Clines, D. J. A. "One in Every Two Words in the Hebrew Bible May Be Corrupt." Paper presented at the Annual Meeting of the Society of Biblical Literature, Atlanta, GA, November 2003.

Cobb, Kelton. "Violent Faith." In *September 11: Religious Perspectives on the Causes and Consequences*, edited by Ian Markham and Ibrahim M. Abu Rabi', 136–63. Oxford: Oneworld Publications, 2002.

Cogan, Mordechai. *Imperialism and Religion: Assyria, Judah, and Israel in the Eighth and Seventh Centuries, B.C.E.* Missoula, MT: Scholars Press/Society of Biblical Literature, 1974.

Cohen, Edmund D. "The Religiosity of George W. Bush: Is the Personal Presidential?" *Free Inquiry* 24, no. 4 (June/July 2004): 38–40.

Coles, Paul. *The Ottoman Impact on Europe*. London: Thames and Hudson, 1968.

Collins, John J. *Does the Bible Justify Violence?* Minneapolis: Fortress, 2004.

———. "The Zeal of Phinehas: The Bible and the Legitimation of Violence." *JBL* 122, no. 1 (2003): 3–21.

Collins, Roger. *The Arab Conquest of Spain, 710–797.* Oxford: Blackwell, 1989.

Confession of Faith in a Mennonite Perspective. Scottdale, PA: Herald Press, 1995. Also available online at http://www.mennolink.org/ doc/cof/art.8.html (accessed July 10, 2004).

Conway, John. *The Nazi Persecution of the Churches, 1933–1945.* London: Weidenfield and Nicolson, 1968.

Conzelmann, Hans. *I Corinthians.* Translated by James Leitch. Philadelphia: Fortress, 1975.

Cook, Michael. "Ibn Qutayba and the Monkeys." *Studia Islamica* 89 (1999): 43–74.

———. *The Koran: A Very Short Introduction.* London: Oxford University Press, 2000.

———. *Muslim Dogma: A Source Critical Study.* Cambridge: Cambridge University Press, 1981.

Cooper, Jerrold S. *The Curse of Agade.* Baltimore: Johns Hopkins University Press, 1983.

Cornwell, John. *Hitler's Pope: The Secret History of Pius XII.* New York: Viking, 1999.

Cosgrove, Charles H. *Appealing to Scripture in Moral Debate: Five Hermeneutical Rules.* Grand Rapids, MI: Eerdmans, 2002.

Cowdrey, H. E. J. "Pope Urban's Preaching of the First Crusade." *History* 55 (1970): 177–88.

Cowles, C. S. "The Case for Radical Discontinuity." In *Show Them No Mercy: Four Views on God and Canaanite Genocide,* edited by Stanley N. Gundry, 13–44. Grand Rapids, MI: Eerdmans, 2003.

Craig, William Lane, and J. P. Moreland. *Naturalism: A Critical Analysis.* London: Routledge, 2000.

Craigie, Peter C. *The Problem of War in the Old Testament.* Grand Rapids, MI: Eerdmans, 1978.

Crollius, Ary A. Roest. *Thus They Were Hearing: The Word in the Experience of Revelation in Qur'an and Hindu Scriptures.* Rome: Gregorian University, 1974.

Crone, Patricia, and Michael Cook. *Hagarism: The Making of the Islamic World.* Cambridge: Cambridge University Press, 1977.

Crossan, John Dominic. *The Birth of Christianity: Discovering What Happened in the Years Immediately after the Execution of Jesus.* San Francisco: HarperSanFrancisco, 1998.

Croy, N. Clayton. "'To Die Is Gain' (Philippians 1:19–26): Does Paul Contemplate Suicide?" *JBL* 122, no. 3 (2003): 517–31.

Dabashi, Hamid. *Authority in Islam: From the Rise of Muhammad to the Establishment of the Umayyads.* New Brunswick, NJ: Transaction, 2002.

Daly, Robert J. "Military Service and Early Christianity: A Methodological Approach." *Studia Patristica* 18, no. 1 (1985): 1–8.

Dandamayev, Muhammad. "State Gods and Private Religion in the Near East in the First Millennium, B.C.E." In *Religion and Politics in the Ancient Near East,* edited by Adele Berlin, 35–45. Bethesda, MD: University of Maryland Press, 1996.

Darr, John A. "Mimetic Desire, The Gospels, and Early Christianity." *Biblical Interpretation* 1, no. 3 (1993): 357–67.

Davies, Philip. *In Search of "Ancient Israel."* Sheffield, UK: JSOT Press, 1992.

———. *Whose Bible Is It Anyway?* Sheffield, UK: Sheffield Academic Press, 1995.

Davies, R. W., Oleg V. Khlevniuk, and E. A. Rees. *The Stalin-Kaganovich Correspondence 1931–36*. New Haven, CT: Yale University Press, 2003.

Davies, W. D. "Reflections on Territory in Judaism." In *Sha'arei Talmon: Studies in the Bible, Qumran, and the Ancient Near East Presented to Shemaryahu Talmon*, edited by Michael Fishbane and Emanuel Tov, 339–43. Winona Lake, IN: Eisenbrauns, 1992.

———. *The Setting of the Sermon on the Mount*. Cambridge: Cambridge University Press, 1966.

Davis, Paul K., and Brian Michael Jenkins. *Deterrence & Influence in Counterterrorism: A Component in the War on al Qaeda*. Santa Monica, CA: Rand, 2002.

Dawkins, Richard. *The Blind Watchmaker: Why the Evidence of Evolution Reveals a Universe without Design*. New York: W. W. Norton, 1986.

———. *A Devil's Chaplain: Reflections on Hope, Lies, Science and Love*. Boston: Houghton Mifflin, 2003.

———. *The Selfish Gene*. Oxford: Oxford University Press, 1976.

———. "What Use Is Religion? Part 1." *Free Inquiry* 24, no. 4 (June/July 2004): 13–14, 56.

———. "What Use Is Religion? Part 2." *Free Inquiry* 24, no. 5 (August/September 2004): 11–12.

Dearman, Andrew, ed. *Studies in the Mesha Inscription and Moab*. Atlanta, GA: Scholars Press, 1989.

Deichman, Ute. *Biologists under Hitler*. Translated by Thomas Dunlap. Cambridge, MA: Harvard University Press, 1996.

Delaney, Carol. *Abraham on Trial: The Social Legacy of Biblical Myth*. Princeton, NJ: Princeton University Press, 1998.

Delong-Bas, Natana J. *Wahabi Islam: From Revival and Reform to Global Jihad*. New York: Oxford University Press, 2004.

Dershowitz, Alan. *The Case for Israel*. Hoboken, NJ: Wiley, 2003.

Deschner, Karlheinz. *Kriminalgeschichte des Christentums*. Hamburg: Rowohlt, 1986.

Desjardins, Michael. *Peace, Violence and the New Testament*. Sheffield, UK: Sheffield Academic Press, 1997.

Dever, William G. *What Did the Biblical Writers Know and When Did They Know It? What Archaeology Can Tell Us about the Reality of Ancient Israel*. Grand Rapids, MI: Eerdmans, 2001.

Dibelius, Martin. *James: A Commentary of the Epistle of James*. Revised by Heinrich Greeven. Philadelphia: Fortress, 1981.

Diefendorf, Babara. "Prologue to a Massacre: Popular Unrest in Paris, 1557–1572." *American Historical Review* 90, no. 5 (December 1985): 1067–91.

Dollard, John, Neal E. Miller, Leonard B. Doob, and O. H. Mowrer. *Frustration and Aggression*. New Haven, CT: Yale University Press, 1939.

Don-Yehiya, Eliezer. "Nationalism and Religion in Jewish and Moslem Fundamentalism." *Dialogue and Alliance* 14, no. 2 (Spring/Summer 2000): 41–75.

Donaldson, Laura. "The Sign of Orpah: Reading Ruth through Native Eyes." In *Ruth and Esther: A Feminist Companion to the Bible*, 2nd series, edited by Athalya Brenner, 130–44. Sheffield, UK: Sheffield Academic Press, 1999.

Dougherty, James E., and Robert L. Pfaltzgraff Jr. *Contending Theories of International Relations: A Comprehensive Survey*. New York: Longman, 2001.

Doumato, Eleanor Abdella. "The Ambiguity of Sharī'a and the Politics of 'Rights' in Saudi Arabia." In *Faith and Freedom: Women's Human Rights in the Muslim World*, edited by Mahnaz Afkhami. Syracuse, NY: Syracuse University Press, 1995.

Draz, M. A. *Introduction to the Qur'an*. London: I. B. Tauris, 2000.

Driver, G. R., and John C. Miles, eds. *The Babylonian Laws*. Oxford: Clarendon Press, 1955.

Dunn, Richard S. *The Age of Religious Wars: 1559–1689*. New York: W. W. Norton, 1970.

Dykema, Peter A., and Heiko Oberman, eds. *Anticlericalism in Late Medieval and Early Modern Europe*. Leiden: Brill, 1993.

Dyson-Hudson, Rada, and Eric Alden Smith. "Human Territoriality: An Ecological Reassessment." *American Anthropologist* 80, no. 1 (1978): 21–41.

Edelman, Diana V. *The Triumph of Elohim: From Yahwisms to Judaisms*. Grand Rapids, MI: Eerdmans, 1996.

The Effect of Islamic Legislation on Crime Prevention in Saudi Arabia: Proceedings of the Symposium Held in Riyadh, 16–21 Shawal 1936 A. H. [9–13 October 1976]. Riyadh: Ministry of the Interior, Kingdom of Saudi Arabia, 1980.

Ehrman, Bart D. *Lost Christianities: The Battle for Scripture and the Faiths We Never Knew*. New York: Oxford University Press, 2003.

———. *The New Testament: A Historical Introduction to the Early Christian Writers*. 3rd ed. New York: Oxford University Press, 2003.

———. *The Orthodox Corruption of Scripture: The Effect of Early Christological Controversies on the Text of the New Testament*. New York: Oxford University Press, 1993.

Eibl-Eibesfeldt, Irenaus. *The Biology of Peace and War: Men, Animals, and Aggression*. New York: Viking, 1979.

Eichrodt, Walter. *Theology of the Old Testament*. Translated by J. A. Baker. 2 vols. Philadelphia: Westminster Press, 1961.

Eidelberg, Shlomo. *The Jews and the Crusaders: The Hebrew Chronicles of the First and Second Crusades*. Madison: University of Wisconsin Press, 1977.

Eilberg-Schwartz, Howard. *People of the Body: Jews and Judaism from an Embodied Perspective*. Albany: State University of New York Press, 1992.

Eisenstadt, S. N., ed. *The Origins and Diversity of the Axial Age Civilizations*. Albany: State University of New York Press, 1986.

Eisenstein, Elizabeth L. *The Printing Press as an Agent of Change: Communications and Cultural Transformations in Early-Modern Europe*. 2 vols. New York: Cambridge University Press, 1979.

———. *The Printing Revolution in Early Modern Europe*. Cambridge: Cambridge University Press, 1983.

Eliade, Mircea. *Patterns in Comparative Religion*. New York: Meridian, 1958.

Ellens, J. Harold, ed. *The Destructive Power of Religion: Violence in Judaism, Christianity and Islam*. 4 vols. Westport, CT: Praeger, 2004.

Ellis, Marc H. *Beyond Innocence and Redemption: Confronting the Holocaust and Israeli Power*. San Francisco: Harper and Row, 1990.

———. *Unholy Alliance: Religion and Atrocity in Our Time*. Minneapolis: Fortress, 1997.

Ember, Melvin, and Carol R. Ember. "Cross-Cultural Studies of War and Peace: Recent Achievements and Future Possibilities." In *Studying War: Anthropological*

Perspectives, edited by S. P. Reyna and R. E. Downs. Amsterdam: Gordon and Breach, 1996.

Emerton, J. A. "The Value of the Moabite Stone as an Historical Source." *Vetus Testamentum* 52, no. 4 (2002): 483–92.

Emmons, Robert A. "Religion in the Psychology of Personality: An Introduction." *Journal of Personality* 67, no. 6 (December 1999): 873–88.

Epstein, Isidore, ed. *Hebrew-English Edition of the Babylonian Talmud*. London: Soncino Press, 1988–94.

Erdmann, Carl. *Die Enstehung des Kreuzzungsgedankens*. Stuttgart: W. Kohlhammer, 1935.

Ericksen, Robert P. *Theologians under Hitler: Gerhard Kittel, Paul Althaus, and Emanuel Hirsch*. New Haven, CT: Yale University Press, 1985.

Ericksen, Robert P., and Susannah Heschel. *Betrayal: German Churches and the Holocaust*. Minneapolis: Fortress, 1999.

Erlanger, Philipp. *La massacre de la Saint-Barthélemy*. Paris: Gallimard, 1960.

———. *St. Bartholomew's Night: The Massacre of Saint Bartholomew*. Translated by Patrick O'Brien. New York: Pantheon, 1962.

Ernst, Carl. *Following Muhammad: Rethinking Islam in the Contemporary World*. Chapel Hill: University of North Carolina Press, 2003.

Eshel, Esther. "Leviticus, Book of." In *Encyclopedia of the Dead Sea Scrolls*, edited by Lawrence Schiffman and James VanderKam, 490–91. New York: Oxford, 2000.

Esposito, John L. *Unholy War: Terror in the Name of Islam*. New York: Oxford University Press, 2002.

Ess, Josef van. "Verbal Inspiration? Language and Revelation in Classical Islamic Theology." In *The Qur'an as Text*, edited by Stefan Wild, 177–94. Leiden: Brill, 1996.

Etzioni, Amitai. *From Empire to Community: A New Approach to International Relations*. New York: PalgraveMacmillan, 2004.

Eusebius. *Ecclesiastical History*. Translated by J. E. L. Oulton. LCL. Cambridge, MA: Harvard University Press, 1980.

Evans-Pritchard, E. E. *The Nuer: A Description of the Modes of Livelihood and Politcal Institutions of a Nilotic People*. New York: Oxford University Press, 1940.

Evera, Stephen Van. *Causes of War: Power and the Roots of Conflict*. Ithaca, NY: Cornell University Press, 1999.

Exum, J. Cheryl, and David J. A. Clines, eds. *The New Literary Criticism and the Hebrew Bible*. Valley Forge, PA: Trinity Press International, 1993.

Fehl, Philipp P. "Vasari's 'Extirpation of the Huguenots': The Challenge of Pity and Fear." *Gazette des beaux-arts* 84 (1974): 257–84.

Feinman, Gary M., and Joyce Marcus. *Archaic States*. Santa Fe, NM: School of American Research Press, 1998.

Feldman, Louis H. *Jew and Gentile in the Ancient World: Attitudes and Interactions from Alexander to Justinian*. Princeton, NJ: Princeton University Press, 1993.

———. *"Remember Amalek!" Vengeance, Zealotry, and Group Destruction in the Bible according to Philo, Pseudo-Philo, and Josephus*. Cincinnati, OH: Hebrew Union College Press, 2004.

Felson, Richard B., and James T. Tedeschi, eds. *Aggression and Violence: Social Interactionist Perspectives*. Washington, DC: American Psychological Association, 1993.

Ferguson, Brian R., and Leslie E. Farragher. *The Anthropology of War: A Bibliography.* New York: Harry Frank Guggenheim Foundation, 1988.

Fernhout, Rein. *Canonical Texts: Bearers of Absolute Authority. Bible, Koran, Veda. Tipitaka: A Phenomenological Study.* Amsterdam/Atlanta, GA: Rodopi, 1994.

Ferrell, Vance. *The Evolution Cruncher.* Altamont, TN: Evolution Facts, 2001.

Firestone, Reuven. *Jihad: The Origin of Holy War in Islam.* New York: Oxford University Press, 1999.

———. *Journeys in Holy Lands: The Evolution of the Abraham-Ishmael Legends in Islamic Exegesis.* Albany: State University of New York Press, 1990.

Fitzgerald, Tim. "Religious Studies as Cultural Studies: A Philosophical and Anthropological Critique of the Concept of Religion." *Diskus* 31 (1995): 35–47.

Fitzmyer, Joseph. *The Gospel According to Luke X–XXIV.* Garden City, NY: Doubleday, 1985.

Fletcher, Joseph F. *Situation Ethics: The New Morality.* Philadelphia: Westminster, 1966.

Fox, Jonathan. "Do Religious Institutions Support Violence or the Status Quo?" *Studies in Conflict and Terrorism* 22 (1999): 119–39.

Fox, Jonathan, and Shmuel Sandler. *Bringing Religion into International Relations.* New York: Palgrave Macmillan, 2004.

Fraser, James W. *Between Church and State: Religion and Public Education in a Multicultural America.* New York: St. Martin's, 1999.

Freedman, David Noel, ed. *The Anchor Bible Dictionary.* 6 vols. New York: Doubleday, 1992.

Freeman, Derek. *Margaret Mead and the Heretic.* New York: Penguin, 1996.

Freeman, Michael. "Religion, Nationalism, and Genocide: Ancient Judaism Revisited." *Archives européennes de sociologie* 35 (1994): 259–82.

Fregosi, Paul. *Jihad in the West: Muslim Conquests from the 7th to the 21st Centuries.* Amherst, NY: Prometheus Books, 1998.

Freiling, Thomas, ed. *George W. Bush on God and Country.* Fairfax, VA: Allegiance Press, 2004.

"French, Belgian Synagogues Burned." CNN.com, April 1, 2002. http://edition.cnn.com/2002/WORLD/Europe/04/01/synagogue.attacks/?related (accessed July 14, 2004).

Frend, W. H. C. *The Rise of Christianity.* Philadelphia: Fortress, 1984.

Fried, Morton. *The Evolution of Political Society: An Essay in Political Anthropology.* New York: Random House, 1967.

Friedländer, Saul. *Nazi Germany and the Jews.* Vol. 1, *The Years of Persecution, 1933–1939.* New York: HarperCollins, 1997.

Friedman, John Block. *The Monstrous Races in Medieval Art and Thought.* Syracuse, NY: Syracuse University Press, 2000.

Friedman, Jonathan. *Globalization, the State and Violence.* Walnut Creek, CA: AltaMira, 2003.

Friedmann, Daniel. *To Kill and Take Possession: Law, Morality, and Society in Biblical Stories.* Peabody, MA: Hendrickson, 2002.

Friedmann, Yohanan. *Tolerance and Coercion in Islam: Interfaith Relations in the Muslim Tradition.* Cambridge: Cambridge University Press, 2003.

Fromm, Erich. *The Anatomy of Human Destructiveness*. New York: Holt, 1973.

Frymer-Kensky, Tikva. "Revelation Revealed: The Doubt of Torah." In *Textual Reasonings: Jewish Philosophy and Text Study at the End of the Twentieth Century*, edited by Peter Ochs and Nancy Levene, 68–75. Grand Rapids, MI: Eerdmans, 2002.

Fuchs, Stephan. *Against Essentialism: A Theory of Culture and Society*. Cambridge, MA: Harvard University Press, 2001.

Fulcher of Chartres. *A History of the Expeditions to Jerusalem, 1095–1127*. Translated by Frances Rita Ryan and edited by Harold S. Fink. Reprint, New York: W. W. Norton, 1969.

Furet, François, and Ernst Nolte. *Fascism and Communism*. Translated by Katherine Golsan. Lincoln: University of Nebraska Press, 2001.

Gabrieli, Francesco. *Arab Historians of the Crusades*. Translated by E. J. Costello. New York: Barnes & Noble, 1969.

Gadamer, Hans-Georg. *Truth and Method*. Translated by Joel Weinsheimer and Donald G. Marshall. 2nd rev. ed. New York: Crossroad, 1989.

Gaddis, John Lewis. *Surprise, Security, and the American Experience*. Cambridge, MA: Harvard University Press, 2004.

Gager, John G. *The Origins of Anti-Semitism: Attitudes toward Judaism in Paganism and Christian Antiquity*. New York: Oxford University Press, 1983.

Gamble, Harry Y. "The Canon of the New Testament." In *The New Testament and Its Modern Intepreters*, edited by Eldon J. Epp and Geroge W. MacRae, 201–43. Philadelphia: Fortress, 1989.

Gammie, John G. *Holiness in Israel*. Minneapolis: AusburgFortress, 1989.

Geiger, Abraham. *Unser Gottesdienst: Eine Frage, die dringend Lösung verlangt*. Breslau: Schletter'sche Buchhandlung, 1868.

———. *Was hat Mohammed aus dem Judenthume aufgenommen?* Bonn: F. Baaden, 1833.

Geisler, Norman L., and William G. Nix. *A General Introduction to the Bible*. Chicago: Press, 1986.

Gell, Alfred. *Wrapping in Images: Tattooing in Polynesia*. Oxford: Clarendon, 1993.

Gerleman, Gillis. "Die Wurzel [*šlm*]." *Zeitschrift für die Altestamentliche Wissenschaft* 85 (1973): 1–14.

Gero, Stephen. "*Miles Gloriosus*: The Christian and Military Service According to Tertullian." *Church History* 39 (1970): 285–98.

Getty, J. Arch, and Oleg V. Naumov. *The Road to Terror: Stalin and the Self-Destruction of the Bolsheviks, 1932–1939*. New Haven, CT: Yale University Press, 1999.

Gewirth, Alan. "Aid for the Needy." In *Ethics:Theory and Practice*, edited by Manuel Velasquez and Cynthia Rostankowski, 353–74. Englewood Cliffs, NJ: Prentice-Hall, 1985.

———. *Marsilius of Padua and Medieval Political Philosophy*. New York: Columbia University Press, 1951.

———, ed. and trans. *Marsilius of Padua: The Defender of the Peace*. New York: Harper and Row, 1956.

Gibson, Arthur. *Biblical Semantic Logic*. New York: St. Martin's, 1981.

Gilbert, D. T., S. T. Fiske, and G. Lindzey, eds. *Handbook of Social Psychology*. 4th ed. Boston: McGraw-Hill, 1997.

Gilbert, Martin. *The Routledge Atlas of the Arab-Israeli Conflict.* 7th ed. London: Routledge Taylor & Francis, 2002.

Gill, Sam. "No Place to Stand: Jonathan Z. Smith as *Homo Ludens,* The Academic Study of Religion *Sub Specie Ludi.*" *JAAR* 66, no. 2 (Summer 1998): 283–312.

Girard, René. *Job: The Victim of His People.* Translated by Yvonne Freccero. Stanford, CA: Stanford University Press, 1987.

———. *Violence and the Sacred.* Translated by Patrick Gregory. Baltimore: Johns Hopkins University Press, 1977.

———. *La violence et le sacré.* Paris: Bernard Grasset, 1972.

———. "Violence Renounced: Response by René Girard." In *Violence Renounced,* edited by William M. Swartley.

Glancy, Jennifer. "Boastings of Beatings (2 Corinthians 11:23–25)." *JBL* 123, no. 1 (Spring 2004): 99–135.

Glazier, Stephen D., ed. *Anthropology of Religion: A Handbook.* Westport, CT: Praeger, 1999.

Glock, Charles Y., and Rodney Stark. *Christian Belief and Anti-Semitism.* New York: Harper and Row, 1966.

Goitein, S. D. *A Mediterranean Society: The Jewish Communities of the World as Portrayed in the Documents of the Cairo Geniza.* 6 vols. Berkeley and Los Angeles: University of California Press, 1999.

Goldhagen, Daniel. *Hitler's Willing Executioners: Ordinary Germans and the Holocaust.* New York: Little, Brown, 1996.

Goldziher, Ignaz. *Muslim Studies.* Translated by S. M. Stern and C. R. Barber. 2 vols. London: Allen and Unwin, 1967–71.

Goldman, Ronald. *Questioning Circumcision: A Jewish Perspective.* Boston: Vanguard, 1998.

Gollaher, David L. *Circumcision: A History of the World's Most Controversial Surgery.* New York: Basic Books, 2002.

Goodall, Jane. *The Chimpanzees of Gombe: Patterns of Behavior.* Cambridge, MA: Harvard University Press, 1983.

Goodrick-Clarke, Nicholas. *The Occult Roots of Nazism: Secret Aryan Cults and Their Influence on Nazi Ideology.* New York: New York University Press, 1992.

Goody, Jack. *The Domestication of the Savage Mind.* Cambridge: Cambridge University Press, 1977.

———. *Literacy in Traditional Societies.* Cambridge: Cambridge University Press, 1968.

Gopin, Marc. *Holy War, Holy Peace: How Religion Can Bring Peace to the Middle East.* New York: Oxford University Press, 2000.

Gorenberg, Gershom. *The End of Days: Fundamentalism and the Struggle for the Temple Mount.* New York: Free Press, 2000.

Gorringe, Timothy. *God's Just Vengeance: Crime, Violence, and the Rhetoric of Salvation.* Cambridge: Cambridge University Press, 1996.

Gorski, Philip S. "The Mosaic Moment: An Early Modernist Critique of Modernist Theories of Nationalism." *American Journal of Sociology* 105, no. 5 (March 2000): 1428–68.

Gottfredson, Michael R., and Travis Hirschi. "A Control Theory Interpretation of Psychological Research on Aggression." In *Aggression and Violence: Social Interac-*

tionist Perspectives, edited by Richard B. Felson and James T. Tedeschi, 47–68. Washington, DC: American Psychological Association.

Gottwald, Norman. *The Hebrew Bible: A Socio-Literary Introduction*. Philadelphia: Fortress, 1985.

Gould, Stephen Jay. *The Structure of Evolutionary Theory*. Cambridge, MA: Harvard University Press, 2002.

Goyau, Georges. "St. Batholomew's Day." In *The Catholic Encyclopedia*. 1912. Available online at http://www.newadvent.org/cathen/13333b.htm (accessed on July 17, 2004).

Grabar, Oleg. *The Shape of the Holy: Early Islamic Jerusalem*. Princeton, NJ: Princeton University Press, 1996.

Graham, William A. *Beyond the Written Word: Oral Aspects of Scripture in the History of Religion*. Cambridge: Cambridge University Press, 1987.

Grant, Nicole J. "From Margaret Mead's Field Notes: What Counted as 'Sex' in Samoa?" *American Anthropologist* 97, no. 4 (1995): 678–82.

Grayzel, Solomon. "The Talmud and the Medieval Papacy." In *Essays in Honor of Solomon B. Freehof*, edited by Walter Jacob, Frederick C. Schwartz, and Vigdor W. Kavaler, 220–45. Pittsburgh, PA: Rodef Shalom Congregation, 1964.

Greenfield, Liah. *Nationalism: Five Roads to Modernity*. Cambridge, MA: Harvard University Press, 1992.

Griffin, David R. *Religion and Scientific Naturalism: Overcoming the Conflicts*. Albany: State University of New York Press, 2000.

Griffin, David Ray. "Religious Experience, Naturalism, and the Social Scientific Study of Religion." *JAAR* 68, no. 1 (2000): 99–125.

Grimes, Ronald L. "Jonathan Z. Smith's Theory of Ritual Space." *Religion* 29 (1999): 261–73.

Grimsrud, Ted. "Scapegoating No More: Christian Pacifism and New Testament Views of Jesus' Death." In *Violence Renounced: René Girard, Biblical Studies and Peacemaking*, edited by Willard M. Swartley, 49–69. Telford, PA: Pandora Press; Scottdale, PA: Herald Press, 2000.

Groothius, Rebecca Merrill. *Good News for Women: A Biblical Picture of Gender Equality*. Grand Rapids, MI: Baker, 1997.

Grotius, Hugo. *De Jure Belli et Pacis Libri Tres*. Edited by William Whewell. 2 vols. Cambridge: Cambridge University Press, 1853.

———. *The Law of War and Peace*. Translated by Francis W. Kelsey. Indianapolis: Bobb-Merrill, 1925.

Gualtieri, Antonio R. *Conscience and Coercion: Ahmadi Muslims and Orthodoxy in Pakistan*. Montreal: Guernica, 1989.

Guillaume, A. *The Life of Muhammad: A Translation of Ibn Ishaq's Sirat Rasul Allah*. London/Karachi: Oxford University Press, 1955.

Guillory, John. *Cultural Capital: The Problem of Literary Canon Formation*. Chicago: University of Chicago Press, 1993.

Gunkel, Hermann. *The Legends of Genesis: The Biblical Saga and History*. Translated by W. H. Carruth. 1901. Reprint. New York: Schoken Books, 1974.

Guthrie, Stewart Elliott. *Faces in the Clouds: A New Theory of Religion*. New York: Oxford University Press, 1993.

Hadaway, Christopher Kirk. "Life Satisfaction and Religion." *Social Forces* 57 (1978): 636–43.

Haeckel, Ernst. *Die Lebenswunder: Gemeinverständliche Studien über biologische Philosophie.* Leipzig: Alfred Kröner Verlag, 1925.

Halbertal, Moshe. *People of the Book: Canon, Meaning, and Authority.* Cambridge, MA: Harvard University Press, 1997.

Haley, Brian D., and Larry R. Wilcoxon. "Anthropology and the Making of Chumash Tradition." *Current Anthropology* 38, no. 5 (1997): 761–94.

Hallo, William W. "The Origins of the Sacrificial Cult." In *Ancient Israelite Religion: Essays in Honor of Frank Moore Cross,* edited by Patrick D. Miller Jr., Paul D. Hanson, and S. Dean McBride, 3–13. Philadelphia: Fortress, 1987.

Hallo, William W., Bruce Williams Jones, and Gerald L. Mattingly, eds. *The Bible in Light of Cuneiform Literature.* Scriptures in Context III. Lewiston, NY: Edwin Mellen Press, 1990.

Hamoto, Azad. *Der Affe in der altorientalischen Kunst.* Münster: Ugarit-Verlag, 1995.

Handy, Lowell K. "The Appearance of the Pantheon in Judah." In *The Triumph of Elohim: From Yahwisms to Judaisms,* edited by Diana Vikander Edelman, 27–43. Grand Rapids, MI: Eerdmans, 1996.

Hannaford, Ivan. *Race: The History of an Idea in the West.* Washington, DC: Woodrow Wilson Center Press, 1996.

Hanson, Paul D. "War and Peace in the Hebrew Bible." *Interpretation* 38 (1984): 341–62.

———. "War, Peace, and Justice in Early Israel." *Bible Review* 3 (1987): 32–45.

Hareven, A. "Towards the Year 2030: Can a Civil Society Shared by Jews and Arabs Evolve in Israel?" *International Journal of Intercultural Relations* 26 (2002): 153–68.

Harnack, Adolf. *Militia Christi: The Christian Religion and the Military in the First Three Centuries.* Translated by David McInnes Grace. Philadelphia: Fortress, 1981.

Harris, Marvin. *Cannibals and Kings: The Origins of Culture.* New York: Random House, 1977.

———. *The Rise of Anthropological Theory: A History of Theories of Culture.* New York: Harper and Row, 1968.

Harris, Sam. *The End of Faith: Religion, Terror, and the Future of Reason.* New York: W. W. Norton, 2004.

Hartmann, R. R. K., ed. *Lexicography: Principles and Practice.* New York: Academic, 1983.

Hashim, Ahmed S. "The World according to Usama Bin Laden." *Naval War College Review* 54, no. 4 (Autumn 2001): 11–36.

Haskins, Charles Homer. *The Renaissance of the 12th Century.* Cambridge, MA: Harvard University Press, 1927.

Havelock, Eric A. *The Literate Revolution in Greece and Its Cultural Consequences.* Princeton, NJ: Princeton University Press, 1982.

Haynes, Stephen. *Noah's Curse: The Biblical Justification of American Slavery.* New York: Oxford University Press, 2000.

Heard, R. Christopher. *Dynamics of Deselection: Ambiguity in Genesis 12–36 and Ethnic Boundaries in Post-Exilic Judah.* Atlanta, GA: Society of Biblical Literature, 2001.

Helgeland, John. "Christians and the Roman Army: AD 173–337." *Church History* 43 (1974): 149–63.

Helgeland, John, Robert J. Daly, and J. Patout Burns. *Christians and the Military: The Early Experience*. Philadelphia: Fortress, 1985.

Heidel, Alexander. *The Babylonian Genesis*. Chicago: University of Chicago Press, 1951.

Heiser, Michael S. "Deuteronomy 32:8 and the Sons of God." *Bibliotheca Sacra* 158 (2001): 52–74.

Herskovits, Melville J. *Cultural Relativism: Perspective in Cultural Pluralism*. New York: Random House, 1972.

Hertz, John H. "The Rise and Demise of the Territorial State." *World Politics* 9, no. 4 (July 1957): 473–93.

Herzl, Thedor. *Briefe und Tagebücher*. Vol. 7, *Briefe 1903–1904*. Edited by Barbara Schäfer. Frankfurt: Propyläen, 1996.

———. *The Jewish State: An Attempt at a Modern Solution of the Jewish Question*. Translated by Sylvie D'Avigdor. London: Pordes, 1967.

Heschel, Susannah. *Abraham Geiger and the Jewish Jesus*. Chicago: University of Chicago Press, 1998.

Heusch, Luc de. *Sacrifice in Africa: A Structuralist Approach*. Translated by Linda O'Brien and Alice Morton. Bloomington: Indiana University Press, 1985.

Hildebrand, Mary Anne. "Domestic Violence: A Challenge to Mennonite Faith and Peace Theology." *Conrad Grebel Review* (Winter 1992): 73–80.

Hillebrand, Carole. *The Crusades: Islamic Perspectives*. New York: Routledge, 2000.

Himmelfarb, Martha. "Levi, Phinehas, and the Problem of Intermarriage at the Time of the Maccabean Revolt." *Jewish Studies Quarterly* 6 (1999): 1–24.

Hitchens, Christopher. *The Missionary Position: Mother Teresa in Theory and Practice*. London: Verso, 1995.

Hitler, Adolf. *Mein Kampf*. Munich: Müller, 1936.

———. *Mein Kampf*. Translated by Ralph Manheim. Boston: Houghton Mifflin, 1971.

Hobbes, Thomas. *Leviathan*. Edited by Richard E. Flathman and David Johnston. New York: W. W. Norton, 1997.

Hodge, Charles. *Systematic Theology*. 3 vols. Grand Rapids, MI: Eerdmans, 1973.

Hodgson, Marshall G. S. *The Ventures of Islam: Conscience and History in a World Civilization*. 2 vols. Chicago: University of Chicago Press, 1974.

Hogan, R., J. Johnson, and S. Briggs, eds. *Handbook of Personality Psychology*. San Diego, CA: Academic, 1997.

Hohmann, Gottfried, and Barbara Fruth. "Culture in Bonobos? Between-Species and Within-Species Variation in Behavior." *Current Anthropology* 44, no. 4 (August–October 2003): 563–71.

Holdredge, Barbara A. *Veda and Torah: Transcending the Textuality of Scripture*. Albany: State University of New York Press, 1996.

Hollowell, A. I. *Culture and Experience*. Philadelphia: University of Pennsylvania Press, 1955.

Holmes, Lowell. *Quest for the Real Samoa: The Mead/Freeman Controversy and Beyond*. South Hadley, MA: Bergin & Garvey, 1987.

Homer. *The Iliad*. Translated by A. T. Murray. 2 vols. LCL. Cambridge, MA: Harvard University Press, 1924.

Hood, John Y. B. *Aquinas and the Jews*. Philadelphia: University of Pennsylvania Press, 1995.

Horsley, Richard. *Jesus and Empire: The Kingdom of God and the New World Disorder*. Minneapolis: Fortress, 2003.

———. *Jesus and the Spiral of Violence: Popular Jewish Resistance in Roman Palestine*. Minneapolis: Fortress, 1993.

Hourani, Albert. *A History of the Arab Peoples*. Cambridge, MA: Harvard University Press, 1991.

Housley, N. J. *The Italian Crusades: The Papal-Angevin Alliance and the Crusades against Christian Lay Powers, 1254–1343*. New York: Oxford University Press, 1986.

———. *The Later Crusades, 1274–1580*. New York: Oxford University Press, 1986.

Hove, Richard. *Equality in Christ: Galatians 3:28 and the Gender Dispute*. Wheaton, IL: Crossway Books, 1999.

Howard-Snyder, Daniel, ed. *The Evidential Argument from Evil*. Bloomington: Indiana University Press, 1996.

Howarth, Stephen. *The Knights Templar*. New York: Dorset, 1982.

Howson, Colin. *Hume's Problem: Induction and the Justification of Belief*. New York: Oxford University Press, 2000.

Hoyland, Robert. *Seeing Islam as Others Saw It: A Survey and Evaluation of Christian, Jewish, and Zoroastrian Writings on Early Islam*. Princeton, NJ: Darwin Press, 1997.

Huebner, Harry. "Christian Pacifism and the Character of God." In *The Church as Theological Community: Essays in Honor of David Schroeder*, edited by Harry Huebner, 247–72. Winnipeg, MB: CMBC Publications, 1990.

———, ed. *The Church as Theological Community: Essays in Honor of David Schroeder*. Winnipeg, MB: CMBC Publications, 1990.

Hume, David. *Enquiries Concerning Human Understanding*. Edited by P. H. Nidditch. Oxford: Clarendon Press, 1975.

Hunter, David G. "The Christian Church and the Roman Army in the First Three Centuries." In *The Church's Peace Witness*, edited by Marlin E. Miller and Barbara Nelson Gingerich, 161–81. Grand Rapids, MI: Eerdmans, 1994.

———. "A Decade of Research on Early Christians and Military Service." *Religious Studies Review* 18, no. 2 (April 1992): 87–94.

Huntington, Samuel P. *The Clash of Civilizations and the Remaking of World Order*. New York: Simon & Schuster, 1996.

Hurtubise, Pierre. *Correspondance du Nonce en France: Antonio Maria Salviati (1572–1578)*. Acta Nuntiaturae Gallicae 12. Rome: Université Pontificale Grégorienne/École Française de Rome, 1975.

Hurvitz, Avi. "The Evidence of Language in Dating the Priestly Code." *Revue biblique* 81 (1974): 24–56.

———. *A Linguistic Study of the Relationship between the Priestly Source and the Book of Ezekiel*. Paris: Gabalda, 1982.

Ibn Hishâm, 'Abd al-Malik. *al-Sîrat al-Nabawîyah li-Ibn Hishâm*. 4 vols. Beirut, Lebanon: Dar al-Kotob al-Ilmiyah, 2000.

Ibn Warraq. *The Origins of the Koran: Classic Essays in Islam's Holy Books.* Amherst, NY: Prometheus Books, 1998.

———. *The Quest for the Historical Muhammad.* Amherst, NY: Prometheus Books, 2000.

———. *What the Koran Really Says: Language, Text, and Commentary.* Amherst, NY: Prometheus Books, 2002.

———. *Why I Am Not a Muslim.* Amherst, NY: Prometheus Books, 1995.

Inalcik, Halil. *The Ottoman Empire: The Classical Age 1300–1600.* Translated by Norman Itzkowitz and Colin Imber. New York: Praeger, 1973.

Ingmanson, Ellen J., and Takayoshi Kano. "Waging Peace." In *Biological Anthropology: A Reader*, edited by Michael Alan Park, 8–11.

Isaac, Benjamin. *The Invention of Racism in Classical Antiquity.* Princeton, NJ: Princeton University Press, 2004.

Ismail, Tahia, al-. *The Life of Muhammad: His Life Based on the Earliest Sources.* London: Ta Ha Publishers, 1988.

Jacobson, Howard. "LXX Genesis 42:23: ἵλεως ὑμῖν." *Textus* 20 (2000): 39–41.

Jacquot, Josephe. "Medailles et jetons de la Saint-Barthélemy." *Revue d'Histoire litteraire de la France* 73, no. 5 (September–October 1973): 791–92.

Jaffee, Martin S. "A Rabbinic Ontology of the Written and Spoken Word." *JAAR* 65, no. 3 (1997): 525–49.

———. *Torah in the Mouth: Writing and Oral Tradition in Palestinian Judaism 200–400 CE.* New York: Oxford University Press, 2001.

Jardine, Lisa. *Worldly Goods: A New History of the Renaissance.* New York: Doubleday, 1996.

Jefferson, Thomas. *Writings.* Edited by M. D. Peterson. Washington, DC: Library of America, 1984.

Jensen, Hans J. L. "Desire, Rivalry and Collective Violence in the 'Succession Narrative.'" *Journal for the Study of the Old Testament* 55 (1992): 39–59.

Johnson, James Turner, and John Kelsay. *Cross, Crescent and Sword: The Justification and Limitation of War in Western and Islamic Tradition.* New York: Greenwood, 1990.

Johnson, Luke T. *The Writings of the New Testament: An Introduction.* Philadelphia: Fortress, 1986.

Jones, Gwilym H. "The Concept of Holy War." In *The World of Ancient Israel*, edited by R. E. Clements. Cambridge: Cambridge University Press, 1989.

———. "'Holy War' or 'Yahweh War'?" *Vetus Testamentum* 25, no. 3 (1975): 642–58.

Josephus. *The Jewish War.* Translated by H. St. J. Thackeray. LCL. Cambridge, MA: Harvard University Press, 1928.

Joyce, Richard. "Theistic Ethics and the Euthyphro Dilemma." *Journal of Religious Ethics* 30, no. 1 2002: 149–75.

Juergensmeyer, Mark. *Terror in the Mind of God: The Global Rise of Religious Violence.* Berkeley and Los Angeles: University of California Press, 2001.

Kagedan, Allan Laine. *Soviet Zion: The Quest for a Russian Jewish Homeland.* New York: St. Martin's, 1994.

Kamen, Henry. *Philip of Spain.* New Haven, CT: Yale University Press, 1997.

———. *The Spanish Inquisition: A Historical Revision.* London: Weidenfeld and Nicolson, 1997.

Kaminsky, Joel S. "Did Election Imply Mistreatment of Non-Israelites?" *Harvard Theological Review* 96, no. 4 (2003): 397–425.

———. "Joshua 7: Reassessment of Israelite Conceptions of Corporate Punishment." In *The Pitcher Is Broken: Memorial Essays for Gösta Ahlström*, edited by Steven W. Holloway and Lowell K. Handy, 315–46. Sheffield, UK: Sheffield Academic Press, 1995.

Kang, Sa-Moon. *Divine War in the Old Testament and in the Ancient Near East*. Berlin: de Gruyter, 1989.

Karli, Pierre. *Animal and Human Aggression*. Translated by S. M. Carmona and H. Whyte. New York: Oxford University Press, 1991.

Karpin, Michael, and Ina Friedman. *Murder in the Name of God: The Plot to Kill Yitzhak Rabin*. New York: Metropolitan Books, 1998.

Kassis, Hanna E. *A Concordance to the Qur'an*. Berkeley and Los Angeles: University of California Press, 1983.

Katz, Jacob. *Exclusiveness and Tolerance: Studies in Jewish-Gentile Relations in Medieval and Modern Times*. West Orange, NJ: Behrman House, 1961.

Katz, Marilyn A. "Problems of Sacrifice in Ancient Cultures." In *The Bible in Light of Cuneiform Literature*, edited by William W. Hallo, Bruce Williams Jones, and Gerald L. Mattingly, 89–201.

Katz, Steven T. *The Holocaust in Historical Context*. Vol. 1. *The Holocaust and Mass Death before the Modern Age*. New York: Oxford University Press, 1994.

Keber, John. "Shalom in the Hebrew Bible." *Listening: Journal of Religion and Culture* 29 (1996): 7–23.

Kedourie, Eli. *Islam in the Modern World and Other Studies*. New York: Holt, Rinehart and Winston, 1980.

Keim, Paul. "Is God Non-Violent?" *Conrad Grebel Review* 21, no. 1 (Winter 2003): 25–32.

Kelsay, John. *Islam and War: A Study in Comparative Ethics*. Louisville, KY: Westminster/John Knox, 1993.

Kelsay, John, and James Turner Johnson. *Just War and Jihad: Historical and Theoretical Perspectives on War and Peace in Western and Islamic Traditions*. New York: Greenwood, 1991.

Kennedy, Paul. *The Rise and Fall of the Great Powers: Economic Change and Military Conflict from 1500 to 2000*. New York: Random House, 1987.

Kepel, Gilles. *Jihad: The Trail of Political Islam*. Cambridge, MA: Harvard University Press, 2002.

Kern, Stephen. *A Cultural History of Causality: Science, Murder Novels, and Systems of Thought*. Princeton, NJ: Princeton University Press, 2004.

Kertzer, David. *The Popes against the Jews: The Vatican's Role in the Rise of Modern Anti-semitism*. New York: Knopf, 2001.

Khatab, Sayed. "Hakimiyyah and Jahiliyyah in the Thought of Sayyid Qutb." *Middle Eastern Studies* 38, no. 3 (July, 2002): 145–70.

Kim, Y. K. "Paleographical Dating of p46 to the Later First Century." *Biblica* 69 (1988): 248–57.

Kimball, Charles. *When Religion Becomes Evil*. San Francisco: HarperSanFrancisco, 2002.

King, Karen. *What Is Gnosticism?* Cambridge, MA: Harvard University Press/Belknap Press, 2003.

King, Ursula. "Is There a Future for Religious Studies as We Know It? Some Postmodern, Feminist, and Spiritual Challenges." *JAAR* 70, no. 2 (2002): 365–88.

Kingdon, Robert M. *Myths about the St. Bartholomew's Day Massacres, 1572–1576.* Cambridge, MA: Harvard University Press, 1988.

———. "The Reaction in Geneva and Rome." In *The Massacre of St. Bartholomew: Reappraisals and Documents,* edited by Alfred Soman, 25–49.

Kirk, Alan. "'Love Your Enemies,' The Golden Rule and Ancient Reciprocity (Luke 6:27–35)." *JBL* 122/4 (2003) 667–686.

Kirk-Duggan, Cheryl, ed. *Pregnant Passion: Gender, Sex, & Violence in the Bible. Semeia* 44. Atlanta: Society of Biblical Literature, 2003.

Kirkpatrick, Patricia G. *The Old Testament and Folklore Study.* Sheffield, UK: Sheffield Academic Press, 1988.

Kister, M. J. "The Massacre of the Banû Qurayẓa: A Re-Examination of a Tradition." *Jerusalem Studies in Arabic and Islam* 8 (1986): 61–96.

Kitts, Margo. "Sacrificial Violence in the Iliad." *Journal of Ritual Studies* 16, no. 1 (2002): 19–39.

Klare, Michael. *Resource Wars: The New Landscape of Global Conflict.* New York: Owl Books, 2002.

Klassen, William. "Love (NT and Early Jewish)." In *The Anchor Bible Dictionary,* edited by David Noel Freedman, vol. 4, 381–96.

———. "Love Your Enemy: A Study of NT Teaching on Coping with an Enemy." *Mennonite Quarterly Review* 37 (1963): 147–71.

Klein, Charlotte. *Anti-Judaism in Christian Theology.* Translated by Edward Quinn. Philadelphia: Fortress, 1978.

Kluckhohn, Clyde. *Mirror for Man: A Survey of Human Behavior and Social Attitude.* Greenwich, CT: Fawcett World Library, 1960.

Knight, Douglas A., ed. "Ethics and Politics in the Hebrew Bible." *Semeia* 66 (1995).

Knohl, Israel. *The Sanctuary of Silence: The Priestly Torah and the Holiness School.* Minneapolis: Fortress, 1995.

Knoppers, Gary N. "The Vanishing Solomon: The Disappearance of the United Monarchy from Recent Histories of Ancient Israel." *JBL* 116, no. 1 (Spring 1997): 19–44.

Konečni, V. J. "Methodological Issues in Human Aggression Research." In *Aggression in Children and Youth,* edited by R. M. Kaplan, V. J. Konečni, and R. W. Novaco, 1–43. The Hague: Nijhoff, 1984.

Kornberg, Jacques. *Theodor Herzl: From Assimilation to Zionism.* Bloomington: Indiana University Press, 1993.

Koster, John P. *The Atheist Syndrome.* Brentwood, TN: Wolgemuth and Hyatt, 1989.

Kostyrchenko, Gennadi. *Out of the Red Shadows: Anti-Semitism in Stalin's Russia.* Amherst, NY: Prometheus Books, 1995.

Kroeber, Alfred L., and Clyde Kluckhohn. *Culture: A Critical Review of Concepts and Definitions.* Cambridge, MA: Peabody Museum, 1952.

Kronemer, Alexander, and Michael Wolfe. *Muhammad: Legacy of a Prophet.* Kikim Media and Unity Production Foundation, 2002.

Kuefler, Mathew. *The Manly Eunuch: Masculinity, Gender Ambiguity, and Christian Ideology in Late Antiquity*. Chicago: University of Chicago Press, 2001.

Kulik, Liat. "Equality in Marriage, Marital Satisfaction, and Life Satisfaction: A Comparative Analysis of Preretired and Retired Men and Women in Israel." *Families in Society: The Journal of Contemporary Human Services* 83, no. 2 (2002): 197–207.

Küng, Hans. *Christianity and the World Religions: Paths to Dialogue with Islam, Hinduism, and Buddhism*. New York: Doubleday, 1986.

Kurtz, Paul. *In Defense of Secular Humanism*. Amherst, NY: Prometheus, Books, 1993.

Lake, David A., and Donald Rothchild. "Containing Fear: The Origins and Management of Ethnic Conflict." *International Security* 21, no. 2 (Fall 1996): 41–75.

Lane, Edward William. *An Arabic-English Lexicon*. 8 vols. 1863–1893. Reprint, Beirut: Libraire du Liban, 1968.

Langan, John. "The Elements of St. Augustine's Just War Theory." *Journal of Religious Ethics* 12, no. 1 (1984): 19–38.

Lanz von Liebenfels, Jörg. *Theozoologie*. 1905. Reprint, Deutschherren-verlag, 2001.

Laqueur, Walter. *Stalin: The Glasnost Revelations*. New York: Scribner's, 1990.

Latin American Subaltern Studies Group. "Founding Statement." *Dispositio/n* 19, no. 46 (1994 [published 1996]).

Lawrence, Bruce. *New Faiths, Old Fears: Muslims and Other Asian Immigrants in American Religious Life*. New York: Columbia University Press, 2002.

———. *Shattering the Myth: Islam beyond Violence*. Princeton, NJ: Princeton University Press, 1998.

Lazarus-Yafeh, Hava. *Intertwined Worlds*. Princeton, NJ: Princeton University Press, 1992.

LeBlanc, Steven A., with Katherine E. Register. *Constant Battles: The Myth of the Peaceful, Noble Savage*. New York: St. Martin's, 2003.

Lefebure, Leo D. *Revelation, The Religions, and Violence*. Maryknoll, NY: Orbis, 2000.

Leftow, Brian. "Anselm on the Necessity of the Incarnation." *Religious Studies* 31, no. 2 (June 1995): 167–85.

Lehr, Ron, and Peter MacMillan. "The Psychological and Emotional Impact of Divorce: The Noncustodial Fathers' Perspective." *Families in Society: The Journal of Contemporary Human Services* 82, no. 4 (2001): 373–82.

Lemche, Niels Peter. *Ancient Israel: A New History of Israelite Society*. Sheffield, UK: JSOT, 1990.

Leng, Russell J., and J. David Singer. "Militarized Interstate Crises: The BCOW Typology and Its Applications." *International Studies Quarterly* 32 (1988): 115–74.

Lenski, Gerhard E. *Power and Privilege: A Theory of Social Stratification*. Chapel Hill: University of North Carolina Press, 1984.

Leopold, Antony. *How to Recover the Holy Land: The Crusade Proposals of the Late Thirteenth and Early Fourteenth Centuries*. Aldershot, UK: Ashgate, 2000.

Levenson, Jon. *The Death and Resurrection of the Beloved Son: The Transformation of Child Sacrifice in Judaism and Christianity*. New Haven, CT: Yale University Press, 1993.

———. "Is There a Counterpart in the Hebrew Bible to the New Testament Anti-semitism?" *Journal of Ecumenical Studies* 22, no. 2 (1985): 242–60.

————. "The New Enemies of Circumcision." *Commentary* 109, no. 3 (March 2000): 29–36.

————. *Sinai and Zion: An Entry into the Jewish Bible*. San Francisco: Harper and Row, 1985.

————. "Zion Traditions." In *The Anchor Bible Dictionary*, edited by D. N. Freedman. Vol. 6, 1098.

Levin, Jack, and Gordana Rabrenovic. *Why We Hate*. Amherst, NY: Prometheus Books, 2004.

Levin, Nora. *The Jews in the Soviet Union since 1917*. 2 vols. London: I. B. Taturis, 1990.

Levine, Baruch. "René Girard and Job: The Question of the Scapegoat." *Semeia* 33 (1985): 125–33.

Levine, Etan. "The Promised Land of Milk and Honey." *Estudios Bíblicos* 58 (2000): 145–66.

Levine, Lee I. *Jerusalem: Portrait of the City in the Second Temple Period (538 B.C.E.–70 C.E.)*. Philadelphia: Jewish Publication Society, 2002.

Levinson, Sanford. *Constitutional Faith*. Princeton, NJ: Princeton University Press, 1988.

Levy, Neil. *Moral Relativism: A Short Introduction*. Oxford: Oneworld Publications, 2002.

Lewis, Bernard. *Islam and the West*. New York: Oxford University Press, 1993.

————. *The Muslim Discovery of the West*. New York: Oxford University Press, 1993.

Lewontin, R. C., Steven Rose, and Leon J. Kamin. *Not in Our Genes: Biology, Ideology and Human Nature*. New York: Pantheon, 1984.

Lewy, Guenter. *The Catholic Church and Nazi Germany*. New York: McGraw-Hill, 1964.

Lichtenstadter, Ilse. "And Become Ye Accursed Apes." *Jerusalem Studies in Arabic and Islam* 14 (1991): 162–75.

Lichtheim, Miriam. *Ancient Egyptian Literature*. 3 vols. Berkeley and Los Angeles: University of California Press, 1974.

Lieu, Judith. *Image and Reality: The Jews in the World of the Christians in the Second Century*. Edinburgh: T&T Clark, 1996.

Lih, Lars T., Oleg Naumov, and Oleg V. Khlevniuk, eds. *Stalin's Letters to Molotov*. New Haven, CT: Yale University Press, 1995.

Limbaugh, Rush. *The Way Things Ought to Be*. New York: Pocket Books, 1992.

Lincoln, Bruce. *Holy Terrors: Thinking about Religion after September 11*. Chicago: University of Chicago Press, 2003.

Lind, Millard. *Yahweh Is a Warrior: The Theology of Warfare in Ancient Israel*. Scottdale, PA: Herald, 1980.

Little, David, and Summer B. Twiss. *Comparative Religious Ethics*. New York: Harper and Row, 1978.

Lohfink, Norbert. "'Holy War' and the 'Ban' in the Bible." *Theology Digest* 38, no. 2 (Summer 1991): 109–14.

Long, V. Philips. *Israel's Past in Present Research: Essays on Ancient Israelite Historiography*. Winona Lake, IN: Eisenbrauns, 1999.

Lorenz, Konrad. *On Aggression*. Translated by Marjorie Kerr Wilson. New York: Bantam Books, 1966.

Lowdermilk, Walter Clay. *Palestine: Land of Promise*. New York: Harper and Brothers, 1944.

Lowth, Robert. *Lectures on the Sacred Poetry of the Hebrews*. 1753. Reprint, Whitefish, MT: Kessinger, 2004.

Lucretius, *De Rerum Natura*. Translated and edited by W. H. D. Rouse and M. F. Smith. LCL. Cambridge, MA: Harvard University Press, 1982.

Lüdemann, Gerd. *The Unholy in Holy Scripture: The Dark Side of the Bible*. Translated by John Bowden. Louisville, KY: Westminster/John Knox Press, 1997.

Luther, Martin. *On the Jews and Their Lies*. Translated by Martin H. Berman. In *Luther's Works: The Christian in Society IV*, 55 vols. edited by Franklin Sherman, 123–306. Philadelphia: Fortress, 1971.

Mabee, Charles. "Text as Peacemaker: Deuteronomic Innovations in Violence Detoxification." In *Violence Renounced: René Girard, Biblical Studies, and Peacemaking*, edited by Willard M. Swartley, 70–84.

Maccoby, Hyam, and Randolph L Braham, eds. *The Origins of the Holocaust: Christian Anti-Semitism*. New York: Institute for Holocaust Studies of the City University of New York, 1986.

Machiavelli, Niccolo. *The Prince*. Edited and Translated by Lester G. Crocker. New York: Pocket Books, 1963.

———. *Il Principe*. Edited by Giorgio Inglese. Turin: Einaudi Tascabili, 1995.

Machinist, Peter. "On Self-Consciousness in Mesopotamia." In *The Origins and Diversity of Axial Age Civilizations*, edited by S. N. Eisenstadt, 183–202, 511–18. Albany: State University of New York Press, 1986.

———. "The Question of Distinctiveness in Ancient Israel: An Essay." In *Ah, Assyria . . . Studies in Assyrian History and Ancient Near Eastern Historiography Presented to Hayim Tadmor*, edited by Mordechai Cogan and Israel Eph'al, 196–212. Jerusalem: Magnes Press, 1991.

MacIntyre, Ferren. "Was Religion a Kinship Surrogate?" *JAAR* 72, no. 3 (2004): 653–94.

MacLean, P. D. "The Triune Brain, Emotion, and Scientific Bias." In *The Neurosciences, Second Study Program*, edited by Francis O. Schmitt et al. 336–49.

Madden, Thomas F., ed. *The Crusades: The Essential Readings*. Oxford: Blackwell, 2002.

Madigan, Daniel A. *The Qur'ân's Self-Image: Writing and Authority in Islam's Scripture*. Princeton, NJ: Princeton University Press, 2001.

Madison, James. "The Memorial and Remonstrance." In *James Madison on Religious Liberty*, edited by Robert Alley, 236–37. Amherst, NY: Prometheus Books, 1985.

Maier, Pauline. *American Scripture: Making the Declaration of Independence*. New York: Vintage Books, 1997.

Malthus, Thomas. *An Essay on the Principle of Population*. Edited by Antony Flew. London: Penguin, 1970.

Mann, C. S. "Misconduct Alleged in Yanomamo Studies." *Science* 289, no. 29 (September 2003): 2252–53.

Mansfield, Stephen. *The Faith of George W. Bush*. Lake Mary, FL: Charisma House, 2003.

Mark, Elizabeth Wyner, ed. *The Covenant of Circumcision: New Perspectives on an*

Ancient Jewish Rite. Hanover, NH: University Press of New England/Brandeis Univesity Press, 2003.

Markham, Ian and Ibrahim M. Abu-Rabi'. *September 11: Religious Perspectives on the Causes and Consequences*. Oxford: Oneworld Publications, 2002.

Marsden, George. *The Soul of the American University: From Protestant Establishment to Established Nonbelief*. New York: Oxford University Press, 1994.

Martin, David. *Does Christianity Cause War?* Oxford: Clarendon, 1997.

Martin, Dale B. *The Corinthian Body*. New Haven, CT: Yale University Press, 1995.

Martinez, Maria Elena. "The Spanish Concept of limpieza de sangre and the Emergence of the 'Race/Caste System' in the Viceroyalty of New Spain." PhD diss., University of Chicago, 2001.

Martos, Joseph J. *May God Bless America: George W. Bush and Biblical Morality*. Tucson, AZ: Fenestra Books, 2004.

Marty, Martin E., and R. Scott Appleby. *The Fundamentalism Project*. 5 vols. Chicago: University of Chicago Press, 1991–1995.

Martz, Linda. "Pure Blood Statutes in Sixteenth-Century Toledo: Implementation as Opposed to Adoption." *Sefarad* 61, no. 1 (1994): 91–94.

Marx, Anthony W. *Faith in Nation: Exclusionary Origins of Nationalism*. New York: Oxford University Press, 2003.

Marx, Karl. *Karl Marx and Friedrich Engels on Religion*. New York: Schocken Books, 1964.

Mascia-Lees, Frances E., and Patricia Sharpe, eds., *Tattoo, Torture, Mutilation, and Adornment: The Denaturalization of the Body in Culture and Text*. Albany: State University of New York Press, 1992.

Maslow, Abraham H. *The Farthest Reaches of Human Nature*. Harmondsworth, UK: Penguin, 1971.

———. *Religions, Values, and Peak-Experiences*. New York: Harper and Row, 1970.

Mastnak, Tomaz. *Crusading Peace: Christendom, the Muslim World, and Western Political Order*. Berkeley and Los Angeles: University of California Press, 2002.

Maxwell, John W., and Rafael Reuveny. "Resource Scarcity and Conflict in Developing Countries." *Journal of Peace Research* 37, no. 3 (2000): 301–22.

May, John D'Arcy. *Transcendence and Violence: The Encounter of Buddhist, Christian, and Primal Traditions*. New York: Continuum, 2003.

Mayer, Hans Eberhard. *The Crusades*. Translated by John Gillingham. New York: Oxford University Press, 1972.

McClymond, Michael. "Making Sense of the Census, or, What 1,999,563,838 Christians Might Mean for the Study of Religion." *JAAR* 70, no. 4 (2002): 875–90.

McCutcheon, Russell T. *Critics Not Caretakers: Redescribing the Public Study of Religion*. Albany: State University of New York Press, 2001.

McCutcheon, Russell T., and Paul J. Griffiths. "Some Confusions about Critical Intelligence: A Response to Russell T. McCutcheon" and "Talking Past Each Other—Public Intellectuals Revisited: A Rejoinder to Paul J. Griffiths and June O'Connor." *JAAR* 66, no. 4 (1998): 893–95, 911–15.

McElaney, Neil J. "The Beatitudes of the Sermon on the Mount/Plain." *CBQ* 43/1 (1981): 1–13.

McGee, J. Vernon. *Thru the Bible with J. Vernon McGee*. 5 vols. Pasadena, CA: Thru the Bible Radio, 1988.

McKenna, Andrew J. "René Girard and Biblical Studies." *Semeia* 33 (1985).

McKown, Delos B. *Behold the Antichrist: Bentham on Religion.* Amherst, NY: Prometheus Books, 2004.

McLaren, Lauren M. "Anti-immigrant Prejudice in Europe." *Social Forces* 81, no. 3 (March 2003): 909–36.

McTernan, Oliver. *Violence in God's Name: Religion in an Age of Conflict.* Maryknoll, NY: Orbis, 2003.

Meeks, Wayne A. *The Origins of Christian Morality: The First Two Centuries.* New Haven, CT: Yale University Press, 1993.

Meier, John P. *A Marginal Jew: Rethinking the Historical Jesus.* Vol. 1, *The Roots of the Problem and the Person.* New York: Doubleday, 1991.

Mettinger, Arthur. *Aspects of Semantic Opposition in English.* New York: Oxford University Press, 1994.

Meyers, Carol L., and Eric M. Meyers. "Jerusalem and Zion after the Exile: The Evidence from First Zechariah." In *Sha'arei Talmon: Studies in the Bible, Qumran, and the Ancient Near East presented to Shemaryahu Talmon,* edited by Michael Fishbane and Emanuel Tov, 121–35. Winona Lake, IN: Eisenbrauns, 1992.

Michaels, Paula A. *Curative Powers: Medicine and Empire in Stalin's Central Asia.* Pittsburgh, PA: University of Pittsburgh Press, 2003.

Michaelson, Gordon E. Jr. "Re-reading the Post-Kantian Tradition with Milbank." *Journal of Religious Ethics* 32, no. 2 (2004): 357–83.

Michel, Thomas F., ed. *A Muslim Theologian's Reponse to Christianity: Ibn Taymiyya's Al-Jawab Al-Sahih.* Delmar, NY: Caravan Books, 1984.

Mielziner, Moses. *Introduction to the Talmud.* 5th ed. New York: Bloch, 1968.

Miguens, Emanuel. "1 Corinthians 13:8 Reconsidered." *CBQ* 37, no. 2 (1975): 76–97.

Milbank, John. *Theology and Social Theory: Beyond Secular Reason.* Oxford: Blackwell, 1990.

Milgrom, Jacob. *Leviticus 1–16.* Garden City, NY: Doubleday, 1992.

———. *Leviticus 17–22.* Garden City, NY: Doubleday, 2000.

Miller, J. Maxwell, and John H. Hayes. *A History of Ancient Israel and Judah.* Philadelphia: Westminster, 1986.

Miller, Patrick D., Jr. *The Divine Warrior in Early Israel.* Harvard Semitic Monographs 5. Cambridge, MA: Harvard University Press, 1973.

Miller, Robert D. "Popular, Ideological, and Textual Dimensions of Postexilic Judean Culture." *Estudios Biblicos* 60 (2002): 337–50.

Miller, Rory. "Bible and Soil: Walter Clay Lowdermilk, the Jordan Valley Project and the Palestine Debate." *Middle Eastern Studies* 39, no. 2 (April 2003): 55–81.

Milton-Edwards, Beverly, and Peter Hinchcliffe. *Conflicts in the Middle East since 1945.* 2nd ed. London: Routledge, 2001.

Miner, Steven Merritt. *Stalin's Holy War: Religion, Nationalism, and Alliance Politics 1941–1945.* Chapel Hill: University of North Carolina Press, 2003.

Miranda, José P. *Marx and the Bible: A Critique of the Philosophy of Oppression.* Translated by John Eagleson. Maryknoll, NY: Orbis, 1974.

Modarressi, Hassein. "Early Debates on the Integrity of the Qur'an: A Brief Survey." *Studia Islamica* 77 (1993): 5–39.

Montellano, Bernard R. Ortiz de. "Aztec Cannibalism: An Ecological Necessity?" *Science* 200, no. 4342 (1978): 611–17.

Moody-Adams, Michele M. *Fieldwork in Familiar Places: Morality, Culture and Philosophy.* Cambridge, MA: Harvard University Press, 1997.

Moran, William L. *The Amarna Letters.* Baltimore: Johns Hopkins University Press, 1992.

———. "The Ancient Near Eastern Background of the Love of God in Deuteronomy." *CBQ* 25 (1963): 77–87.

Morgenstern, Julian. "The Despoiling of the Egyptians." *BL* 68 (1949): 1–28.

Morgenthau, Hans J. *Politics among Nations: The Struggle for Power and Peace.* Revised by Kenneth Thompson. Boston: McGraw-Hill, 1993.

Moriarty, Frederick. "Word as Power in the Ancient Near East." In *A Light Unto My Path; Old Testament Studies in Honor of Jacob M. Myers,* edited by Howard N. Bream, Ralph D. Heim, and Carey A. Moore, 345–62. Philadelphia: Temple University Press, 1974.

Morris, Brian. *Anthropological Studies of Religion: An Introductory Text.* Cambridge: Cambridge University Press, 1988.

Motahari, Morteza. *The Holy War of Islam.* Translated by Mohammad Salman Tawhidi. http://www.iranchamber.com/personalities/mmotahari/morteza_motahari.php (accessed August 7, 2004).

Mullen, E. Theodore Jr. *The Assembly of the Gods.* Harvard Semitic Monographs 24. Atlanta, GA: Scholars Press, 1980.

———. *Narrative History and Ethnic Boundaries: The Deuteronomistic Historian and the Creation of Israelite National Identity.* Atlanta, GA: Scholars Press, 1993.

Müller, Georg Christoph. *Dissertatio Inauguralis De expeditione Cruciatis Vulgo von Kreutz Fahrten.* Nuremburg: Literis Jodici Wilhelmi Kohlesii, 1709.

Nakhash, Yitzhak. *The Shi'is of Iraq.* Princeton, NJ: Princeton University Press, 1994.

Nelson, Richard D. *The Double Redaction of the Deuteronomistic History.* Sheffield, England: JSOT, 1981.

———. "Herem and the Deuteronomic Social Conscience." In *Deuteronomy and Deuteronomic Literature: Festschrift C. H. W. Brekelmans,* edited by M. Vervenne and J. Lust, 39–54. Leuven: Peeters/Leuven University Press, 1997.

Neusner, Jacob. *The Formation of the Babylonian Talmud.* Leiden: Brill, 1970.

———. *The Talmud of the Land of Israel: A Preliminary Translation and Explanation.* Chicago: University of Chicago Press, 1982–89.

Newman, Leonard S., and Ralph Erber, eds. *Understanding Genocide: The Social Pyschology of the Holocaust.* New York: Oxford University Press, 2002.

Niditch, Susan. *War in the Hebrew Bible: A Study in the Ethics of Violence.* New York: Oxford University Press, 1993.

Nielsen, Kai. *Ethics without God.* Rev. ed. Amherst, NY: Prometheus Books, 1990.

Nietzsche, Friedrich. *Beyond Good and Evil.* Translated by Helen Zimmern. 1884. Reprint, Amherst, NY: Prometheus Books, 1989.

The 9/11 Commission Report: Final Report of the National Commission on Terrorist Attacks upon the United States. New York: W. W. Norton, 2004.

Nolte, Ernst. *Der europäische Bürgerkrieg 1917–1945: Nationalsozialismus und Bolschewismus.* Berlin and Frankfurt: Propyläen/Ullstein, 1987.

Nooy, Gert de. *The Clausewitzian Dictum and the Future of Western Military Strategy.* Leiden: Brill, 1997.

North, Robert. "Violence and the Bible: The Girard Connection." *CBQ* 47 (1985): 1–27.

Noth, Martin. *The Deuteronomistic History.* Translated by Jane Doull and John Barton. Sheffield, UK: Sheffield Academic Press, 1981.

———. *Überlieferungsgeschichtliche Studien.* Halle: Max Niedermeyer Verlag, 1943.

Novick, David. *A World of Scarcities: Critical Issues in Public Policy.* London: Associate Business Programs, 1976.

Nowell, Irene. "Jerusalem: City of Peace." *TBT* 40 (2002): 12–18.

Nuth, Joan M. "Two Medieval Soteriologies: Anselm of Canterbury and Julian of Norwich." *Theological Studies* 53, no. 4 (1992): 611–45.

Nye, Joseph S. *Soft Power: The Means to Succeed in World Politics.* New York: Public Affairs, 2004.

Nygren, Anders. *Agape and Eros.* Translated by Philip S. Watson. Philadelphia: Westminster, 1953.

———. *Den kristna karlestanken genom tiderna. Eros och Agape I.* Stockholm: Svenska Kyrkans Diakonistyrelses Bokförlag, 1930, 1936.

O'Brien, Mark. *The Deuteronomistic History Hypothesis: A Reassessment.* Göttingen: Vandenhoeck & Ruprecht, 1989.

O'Callaghan, Joseph. *Reconquest and Crusade in Medieval Spain.* Philadelphia: University of Pennsylvania Press, 2003.

Odintsov, M. I. *Russie patriarkhi XX veka: Sud'by Otechestva i Tserkvi na stranitsakh arkhivnykh dokumentov.* Moscow: RAGS, 1999.

O'Grady, Desmond. *Beyond the Empire: Rome and the Church from Constantine to Charlemagne.* New York: Crossroad, 2001.

O'Malley, Suzanne. *"Are You There Alone?": The Unspeakable Crime of Andrea Yates.* New York: Simon & Schuster, 2004.

Ong, Walter. *Orality and Literacy: The Technologizing of the Word.* London: Routledge, 1982.

Oregon State University. Transboundary Freshwater Dispute Database. http://www.transboundarywaters.orst.edu.

Origen. *Contra Celsum.* In *The Ante-Nicene Fathers,* edited by Alexander Roberts and James Donaldson. Vol. 4, 395–669.

Orlinsky, Harry M. "Nationalism-Universalism and Internationalism in Ancient Israel." In *Translating and Understanding the Old Testament: Essays in Honor of Herbert Gordon May,* edited by Harry Thomas Frank and Willliam L. Reed, 206–36. Nashville, TN: Abingdon, 1970.

O'Rourke, John J. "The Military in the NT." *CBQ* 32 (1970): 227–36.

Otto, Eckert. *Theologische Ethik des Alten Testaments.* Stuttgart: Kohlhammer, 1994.

Otto, Rudolf. *The Idea of the Holy.* Translated by John W. Harvey. 2nd ed. London: Oxford University Press, 1950.

Outka, Gene. *Agape: An Ethical Analysis.* New Haven, CT: Yale University Press, 1972.

Overy, Richard. *The Dictators: Hitler's Germany and Stalin's Russia.* New York: W. W. Norton, 2004.

Oxtoby, Willard. *World Religions: Western Traditions.* 2nd ed. New York: Oxford University Press, 2002.

Pagels, Elaine. *The Gnostic Gospels.* New York: Random House, 1979.

Palmer-Fernandez, Gabriel. *Deterrence and the Crisis in Moral Theory: An Analysis of the Moral Literature on the Nuclear Arms Debate.* New York: Peter Lang, 1996.

——, ed. *Encyclopedia of Religion and War.* New York: Routledge, 2004.

Pannikar, Raimundo. *Myth, Faith and Hermeneutics: Cross-Cultural Studies.* New York: Paulist Press, 1979.

Pappe, Ilan. *A History of Modern Palestine: One Land, Two Peoples.* Cambridge: Cambridge University Press, 2004.

Pardee, Dennis. "Ugaritic Studies at the End of the 20th Century." *BASOR* 320 (November 2000): 49–86.

Pardes, Ilana. *Countertraditions in the Bible: A Feminist Approach.* Cambridge, MA: Harvard University Press, 1992.

Paret, Peter. *Clausewitz and the State.* New York: Oxford University Press, 1976.

Paret, Rudi. "Sure 2, 256: lā ikrāha fī d-dīni: Toleranz oder Resignation?" *Der Islam: Zeitschrift für Geschichte und Kultur des islamischen Orients* 45 (1969): 299–300.

Park, Eung Chun. *Either Jew or Gentile: Paul's Unfolding Theology of Inclusivity.* Louisville, KY: Westminster/John Knox, Press, 2003.

Park, Michael Alan. *Biological Anthropology: A Reader.* Mountain View, CA: Mayfield, 1998.

Parker, Simon B. "Appeals for Military Intervention: Stories from Zinjirli and the Bible." *Biblical Archaeologist* 59, no. 4 (1996): 213–24.

Pascal, Blaise. *Pensées.* Edited by Gérard Ferreyrolles. Paris: Le livre de poche, 2000.

Patte, Daniel. *Ethics of of Biblical Interpretation: A Reevaluation.* Louisville, KY: Westminster/John Knox, 1995.

Paul, Shalom M., Robert A. Kraft, Lawrence H. Schiffman, and Weston W. Fields. *Emanuel: Studies in the Hebrew Bible, Septuagint, and Dead Sea Scrolls in Honor of Emanuel Tov.* Leiden/Boston: Brill, 2003.

Pedersen, Johannes. *Israel: Its Life and Culture.* 4 vols. 1926. Reprint. London: Oxford University Press, 1973.

Pelikan, Jaroslav. *Interpreting the Bible and the Constitution.* New Haven, CT: Yale University Press, 2004.

Pelletière, Stephen C. *Iraq and the International Oil System: Why America Went to War in the Gulf.* Washington, DC: Maisonneuve, 2004.

Pelton, Leroy H. "Biblical Justice." *JAAR* 71, no. 4 (December 2003): 737–65.

Pervin, L. A. *Handbook of Personality: Theory and Research.* New York: Guilford, 1990.

Peters, Rudolph. *Jihad in Mediaeval and Modern Islam: The Chapter on Jihad from Averroes' Legal Handbook 'Bidayat al-Mudjtahid' and the Treatise 'Koran and Fighting' by the Late Shaykh Al-Azhar, Mahmud Shaltut.* Leiden: Brill, 1977.

Petuchowski, Jacob. *New Perspectives on Abraham Geiger: An HUC-JIR Symposium.* Cincinnati, OH: Hebrew Union College Press, 1975.

Phayer, Michael. *The Catholic Church and the Holocaust, 1930–1965.* Bloomington: University of Indiana Press, 2000.

Philo. *The Decalogue.* Translated by F. H. Colson. LCL. 1937. Reprint, Cambridge: Harvard University Press, 1984.

Phipps, William E. *Muhammad and Jesus: A Comparison of the Prophets and Their Teachings.* New York: Continuum, 1996.

Pickthal, Marmaduke Muhammed. *Al-amin: Life Sketch of the Life of Muhammed.* New Delhi: Kitab Bhavan, 2003.

Pinker, Steven. *The Blank Slate: The Modern Denial of Human Nature.* New York: Viking, 2002.

Pipes, Daniel. *Slave Soldiers and Islam: The Genesis of a Military System.* New Haven, CT: Yale University Press, 1981.

Pippin, Tina. *Death and Desire: The Rhetoric of Gender in the Apocalypse.* Louisville, KY: Westminster/John Knox, 1992.

Plato. *Phaedo.* Translated by H. N. Fowler. LCL. 1914. Reprint, Cambridge, MA: Harvard University Press, 1982.

Porter, Stanley E., and W. R. Pearson, eds. *Christian-Jewish Relations Through the Centuries.* Sheffield, UK: Sheffield Academic Press, 2000.

Pospielovsky, Dimitry V. *A History of Soviet Atheism in Theory and Practice and the Believer.* 3 vols. London: Macmillan, 1987–88.

Postgate, J. Nicholas. *The First Empires.* London: Elsevier-Phaidon, 1977.

———. "In Search of the First Empires." *BASOR* 293 (1994): 1–13.

Preus, J. Samuel. *Explaining Religion: Criticism and Theory from Bodin to Freud.* New Haven, CT: Yale University Press, 1987.

Propp, William H. C. "Acting Like Apes." *Bible Review* 20, no. 3 (June 2004): 34–40, 46.

———. "The Origins of Infant Circumcision in Israel." *Hebrew Annual Review* 11 (1987): 355–70.

Proudhon, Pierre-Joseph. *La guerre et la paix; recherches sur le principe et la constitution du droit des gens.* 1861. Reprint, New York: Garland, 1972.

Puech, Emile. "4Q525 et les pericopes des béatitudes en Ben Sira et Matthieu." *Revue Biblique* 98 (1991): 80–106.

Qutb, Sayyid. *In the Shade of the Qur'an.* New Delhi: Naida Printing Press, 2001.

Rad, Gerhard von. *Der heilige Krieg im alten Israel.* 1926. Reprint, Göttingen: Vandenhoeck & Ruprecht, 1969.

———. *Old Testament Theology.* Translated by D. M. G. Stalker. 2 vols. London: SCM Press, 1975.

Rahlfs, Alfred. *Septuaginta . . . Editio minor.* Stuttgart: Deutsche Bibelgesellschaft, 1979.

Rahman, Fazlur. "Some Key Ethical Concepts in the Qur'an." *Journal of Religious Ethics* 11, no. 2 (1983): 170–85.

Ramer, Sabrina Petra, and Donald W. Treadgold. *Render unto Caesar: The Religious Sphere in World Politics.* Washington, DC: American University Press, 1995.

Ramsey, Paul "Justice in War." In *The Essential Paul Ramsey: A Collection,* edited by William Werpehowski and Stephen D. Crocco, 60–67. New Haven, CT: Yale University Press, 1994.

Rappaport, Roy. *Pigs for the Ancestors: Ritual and Ecology of a New Guinea People.* Rev. ed. New Haven, CT: Yale University Press, 1985.

Rashi. *Chumash: With Rashi's Commentary.* Edited by A. M. Silberstein. 5 vols. Jerusalem: Silberman Family, 1934.

Ratzel, Friedrich. *Anthropogeographie.* 2nd ed. Stuttgart: J. Engelhorn, 1899.

Recueil des Historiens des Croisades. 16 vols. Paris: L'Académie impériale des inscriptions et Belles-Lettres, 1841–1906.

Redles, David. "Nazism and Holocaust." In *Encyclopedia of Religion and War,* edited by Gabriel Palmer-Fernandez, 325–28.

Rees, E. A. *Political Thought from Machiavelli to Stalin: Revolutionary Machiavellism.* Aldershot, UK: Ashgate, 2004.

Reventlow, Hans Graf. *The Authority of the Bible and the Rise of the Modern World.* Translated by John Bowden. Philadelphia: Fortress, 1985.

Reynolds, Susan. *Fiefs and Vassals: The Medieval Evidence Reinterpreted.* Oxford: Clarendon, 1994.

Riches, David. *The Anthropology of Violence.* Oxford: Blackwell, 1986.

Rigby, Paul, and Paul O'Grady. "*Agape* and Altruism: Debates in Theology and Social Psychology." *JAAR* 57, no. 4 (1989): 719–37.

Riley-Smith, Jonathan. "Crusading as an Act of Love." In *The Crusades: The Essential Readings*, edited by Thomas F. Madden, 32–50.

———, ed. *The Illustrated History of the Crusades.* New York: Oxford University Press, 1995.

Rippin, Andrew. "The Function of *Asbab al-Nuzul* in Koranic Exegesis." In *The Quest for the Historical Muhammad*, edited by Ibn Warraq, 392–419. Originally published in *Bulletin of the School for Oriental and African Studies* 51 (1988): 1–20.

Rivkin, Ellis. *The Unity Principle: The Shaping of Jewish History.* New York: Behrman House, 2003.

Roberts, Alexander, and James Donaldson, eds. *The Ante-Nicene Fathers.* 10 vols. 1885–87. Reprint, Grand Rapids, MI: Eerdmans, 1994.

Roberts, J. J. M. "Solomon's Jerusalem and the Zion Tradition." In *Jerusalem in Bible and Archaeology: The First Temple Period*, edited by Andrew G. Vaughn and Anne E. Killebrew, 163–70. Atlanta, GA: Society of Biblical Literature, 2003.

———. "Zion in the Theology of the Davidic-Solomonic Empire." In *Studies in the Period of David and Solomon and Other Essays*, edited by Tomoo Ishida, 93–108. Winona Lake, IN: Eisenbrauns, 1982.

Robinson, Bernard P. "Israel and Amalek: The Context of Exodus 17:8–16." *JSOT* 32 (1985): 15–22.

Rodger, Symeon. "The Soteriology of Anselm: An Orthodox Perspective." *Greek Orthodox Review* 34, no. 1 (1989): 19–43.

Rodman, H. "Marital Power and the Theory of Resources in Cultural Context." *Journal of Comparative Family Studies* 3 (1972): 59–69.

Rogerson, John. *Old Testament Criticism in the Nineteenth Century: England and Germany.* Philadelphia: Fortress, 1985.

Römer, Thomas. *Dieu Obscur: Le sexe, la cruauté, et la violence dans l'Ancien Testament.* Geneva: Labor et Fides, 1998.

Rosenberg, Alfred. *Der Mythus des 20. Jahrhunderts: Eine Wertung der lische-geistigen Gestalentkämpfe unserer Zeit.* Munich: Hoheneichen Verlag, 1938.

———. *Race and Race History and Other Essays.* Edited by Robert Pois and translated by Jonathon Cap. New York: Harper and Row, 1970.

Rosenthal, Franz. "Some Minor Problems in the Qur'an." In *What The Koran Really Says: Language, Text and Commentary*, edited by Ibn Warraq, 324–27.

Rousseau, Jean-Jacques. *Du contrat social.* Edited by Bruno Bernárdi. Paris: Flammarion, 2001.

———. *Profession de foi du vicaire savoyard.* Edited by Bruno Bernardi. 1782. Reprint, Paris: Flammarion, 1996.

————. *The Social Contract*. Translated by Maurice Cranston. Harmondsworth, UK: Penguin, 1968.

Rowlett, Lori. *Joshua and the Rhetoric of Violence: A New Historicist Analysis*. Sheffield, UK: Sheffield Academic Press, 1996.

Rubenberg, Cheryl A. *Israel and the American National Interest*. Urbana and Chicago: University of Illinois Press, 1986.

Rubenstein, Jay. *Guibert of Nogent: Portrait of a Medieval Mind*. New York: Routledge, 2002.

Rubenstein, Richard. "The Temple Mount and My Grandmother's Paper Bag: An Essay on Inter-religious Relations." *Dialogue and Alliance* 41, no. 1 (Spring/Summer 2000): 76–99.

Rubin, Uri. *Between Bible and Qur'ān: The Children of Israel and the Islamic Self Image*. Princeton, NJ: Darwin Press, 1999.

Ruether, Rosemary. *Faith and Fratricide: The Theological Roots of Anti-Semitism*. New York: Seabury, 1979.

Runciman, Steven. *A History of the Crusades*. 3 vols. Cambridge: Cambridge University Press, 1951–54.

Runciman, W. G. *Relative Deprivation and Social Justice: A Study of Attitudes to Social Inequality in Twentieth-Century England*. London: Routledge and Kegan Paul, 1966.

Saeed, Abdullah, and Hassan Saeed. *Freedom of Religion: Apostasy and Islam*. Aldershot, UK: Ashgate, 2004.

Safran, Nadav. *Israel: The Embattled Ally*. Cambridge, MA: Harvard University Press, 1981.

Sahlins, Marhsall. *The Use and Abuse of Biology: An Anthropological Critique of Sociobiology*. Ann Arbor: University of Michigan Press, 1976.

Said, Edward. *Orientalism*. New York: Random House, 1978.

Salmon, J. H. M. *Society in Crisis: France in the Sixteenth Century*. New York: St. Martin's, 1975.

Sánchez, José M. *Pius XII and the Holocaust: Understanding the Controversy*. Washington, DC: Catholic University of America Press, 2002.

Sanders, Ronald. *The High Walls of Jerusalem: A History of the Balfour Declaration and the Birth of the British Mandate of Palestine*. New York: Holt, Rinehart and Winston, 1983.

Sasson, Jack M. "Circumcision in the Ancient Near East." *JBL* 85 (1966): 473–76.

Sax, William. "The Hall of Mirrors: Orientalism, Anthropology, and the Other." *American Anthropologist* 100, no. 2 (1998): 292–308.

Schacht, Joseph. *An Introduction to Islamic Law*. Oxford: Clarendon, 1964.

————. *The Origins of Muhammadan Jurisprudence*. Oxford: Clarendon, 1950.

Schäfer, Peter. *Judeophobia: Attitudes toward the Jews in the Ancient World*. Cambridge, MA: Harvard University Press, 1997.

Schaff, Philip. *The History of the Christian Church*. 8 vols. N.p: AP&A, [1889].

Schaff, Philip, and Henry Wace. *The Nicene and Post-Nice Fathers*. 14 vols. 1886–89. Reprint, Grand Rapids, MI: Eerdmans, 1997.

Schein, Sylvia. *Fideles Crucis: The Papacy, the West, and the Recovery of the Holy Land, 1274–1314*. New York: Oxford University Press, 1991.

Schmidt, Claudia M. *David Hume: Reason in History*. University Park: Pennsylvania State University Press, 2000.

Schmitt, Francis O. et al., eds. *The Neurosciences, Second Study Program*. New York: Rockefeller University Press, 1970.

Schnackenburg, Rudolf. *The Moral Teaching of the New Testament*. Translated by J. Holland-Smith and W. J. O'Hara. London: Burns and Oates, 1975.

Schniedewind, William. *How the Bible Became a Book*. Cambridge: Cambridge University Press, 2004.

Schoenfeld, Eugen. "An Illusive Concept in Christianity." *Review of Religious Research* 30, no. 3 (1989): 236–45.

Schopenhauer, Arthur. *Parerga and Paralipomena: Short Philosophical Essays*. Translated by E. F. J. Payne. 2 vols. Oxford: Clarendon, 1974.

Schultz, Emily A., and Roberta Lavenda. *Cultural Anthropology: A Perspective on the Human Condition*. Mountain View, CA: Mayfield, 1995.

Schulze, Reinhard. *A Modern History of the Islamic World*. Translated by Azizeh Adodi. New York: New York University Press, 2002.

Schüssler-Fiorenza, Elizabeth. *In Memory of Her: A Feminist Theological Reconstruction of Christian Origins*. New York: Crossroad, 1983.

Schwally, Friedrich. *Semitische Kriegsaltertumer I: Der heilige Krieg im alten Israel*. Leipzig: Dietrich, 1901.

Schwartz, Regina. *The Curse of Cain: The Violent Legacy of Monotheism*. Chicago: University of Chicago Press, 1997.

Segal, Jerome M., Shlomit Levy, Nadar Izzat Sa'id, and Elihu Katz. *Negotiating Jerusalem*. Albany: State University of New York Press, 2000.

Segal, Robert. *Explaining and Interpreting Religion: Essays on the Issue*. Toronto Studies in Religion 16. Toronto, ON: Centre for Religious Studies, 1992.

Sen, Amartya. *The Political Economy of Hunger*. Oxford, Clarendon Press 1995.

———. *Poverty and Famines: An Essay on Entitlement and Deprivation*. Oxford: Clarendon, 1981.

Service, Elman. *The Origins of the State and Civilization: The Process of Cultural Evolution*. New York: W. W. Norton, 1975.

Seters, John Van. *Abraham in History and Tradition*. New Haven, CT: Yale University Press, 1975.

———. "Is There any Historiography in the Hebrew Bible? A Hebrew-Greek Comparison." *Journal of Northwest Semitic Languages* 28, no. 2 (2002): 1–25.

Setton, Kenneth M. *The Papacy and the Levant (1204–1571)*. 4 vols. Philadelphia: American Philosophical Society, 1976–84.

Shanklin, Eugenia. "The Profession of the Color Blind: Sociocultural Anthropology and Racism in the 21st Century." *American Anthropologist* 100, no. 3 (1999): 669–79.

Shermer, Michael. *How to Believe: Science, Skepticism, and the Search for God*. 2nd ed. New York: Owl Books, 2003.

———. *The Science of Good and Evil: Why People Cheat, Gossip, Care, Share and Follow the Golden Rule*. New York: Times Books, 2004.

Shields, Susan. "Mother Teresa's House of Illusions: How She Harmed Her Helpers as Well as Those They 'Helped.'" *Free Inquiry* 18, no. 1 (1998). Also available online at http://www.secularhumanism.org/library/fi/shields_18_1.html.

Shilling, Chris. *The Body and Social Theory*. 2nd ed. London: Sage, 2003.

Short, Wilfrid M., ed. *Arthur James Balfour as Philosopher and Thinker: A Collection of the More Important and Interesting Passages in His Non-Political Writings, Speeches and Addresses 1879–1912*. London: Longmans, Green, 1912.

Sicroff, Albert. *Los estatutos de limpieza de sangre: Controversias entre los siglos xv y xvii*. Translated from French into Spanish by Mauro Armiño. Madrid: Taurus ediciones, 1985.

Sider, Ronald. *Christ and Violence*. 1979. Reprint, Eugene, OR: Wipf and Stock, 2001.

Sifry, Micah L., and Christopher Serf. *The Gulf War Reader: History, Documents, Opinions*. New York: Random House, 1991.

Silberman, Neil Asher. *Digging for God and Country: Exploration, Archaeology, and the Secret Struggle for the Holy Land, 1799–1917*. New York: Knopf, 1982.

Singer, J. David, and Paul F. Diehl. *Measuring the Correlates of War*. Ann Arbor: University of Michigan Press, 1990.

Singer, J. David, and Melvin Small. *The Wages of War 1816–1965: A Statistical Handbook*. New York: Wiley, 1972.

Sipes, Richard D. "War, Sports, and Aggression: An Empirical Test of Two Rival Theories." *American Anthropologist* 75, no. 1 (1973): 64–86.

Skaletsky, Helen. "The Male-Specific Region of the Human Y Chromosome of Discrete Sequence Classes." *Nature* 423 (June 2003): 825–37.

Skorecki, Karl et al. "Y Chromosomes of Jewish Priests." *Nature* 385 (January 2, 1997): 32.

Smedley, Audrey. "'Race' and the Construction of Human Identity." *American Anthropologist* 100, no. 3 (1999): 690–702.

Smith, Jane. *An Historical and Semantic Study of the Term Islam as Seen in Sequences of Qur'an Commentaries*. Missoula, MT: Scholars Press, 1975.

Smith, Jonathan Z. "The Domestication of Sacrifice." In *Violent Origins: Walter Burkert, René Girard, and Jonathan Z. Smith on Ritual Killing and Cultural Formation*, edited by Robert G. Hamerton-Kelly, 191–205. Stanford, CA: Stanford University Press, 1987.

———. *To Take Place: Toward Theory in Ritual*. Chicago: University of Chicago Press, 1987.

Smith, Wilfred Cantwell. *What Is Scripture? A Comparative Approach*. Minneapolis: Fortress, 1993.

Smither, James R. "The St. Bartholomew's Day Massacre and Images of Kingship in France: 1572–1574." *Sixteenth Century Journal* 22, no. 1 (1991): 27–46.

Smolar, Levy. "Ernest Renan's Interpretation of Biblical History." In *Biblical and Related Studies Presented to Samuel Iwry*, edited by Ann Kort and Scott Morschauer, 237–57. Winona Lake, IN: Eisenbrauns, 1985.

Sneed, Mark R. *Concepts of Class in Ancient Israel*. South Florida Studies in the History of Judaism 201. Atlanta, GA: Scholars Press, 1999.

Snyder, Louis L., ed. *Encyclopedia of the Third Reich*. New York: Marlowe, 1976.

Soman, Alfred, ed. *The Massacre of St. Bartholomew: Reappraisals and Documents*. The Hague: Nijhof, 1974.

Sordi, Marta. *The Christians and the Roman Empire*. Translated by Annabel Bedini. Norman: University of Oklahoma Press, 1994.

Spanneut, Michel. "Horreur du sang et non-violence dans l'Église des premiers siè-cles." *Studia Patristica* 18, no. 1 (1985): 71–76.

Sparks, Kenton. *Ethnicity and Identity in Ancient Israel: Prolegomenon to the Study of Ethnic Sentiments and Their Expression in the Hebrew Bible*. Winona Lake, IN: Eisenbrauns, 1998.

Sperling, S. David. *The Original Torah: The Political Intent of the Bible's Writers*. New York: New York University Press, 1998.

Spicq, Ceslaus. *Agape in the New Testament*. Translated by Sister Marie Aquinas Mcna-mara and Sister Mary Honoria Richter. 3 vols. St. Louis, MO: B. Herder, 1963–66.

———. *Agapè: Prolégomènes a une étude de théologie néo-testamentaire*. Leiden: Brill, 1955.

Sprout, Harold, and Margaret Sprout. *An Ecological Paradigm for the Study of International Politics*. Princeton, NJ: Center for International Studies, 1968.

Spykman, Nicholas J. *The Geography of Peace*. New York: Harcourt, Brace, 1944.

Stafford, Barbara Maria. *Body Criticism: Imaging the Unseen in Enlightenment Art and Medicine*. Cambridge, MA: MIT Press, 1997.

Stanford, Craig B. "The Social Behavior of Chimpanzees and Bonobos: Empirical Evidence and Shifting Assumptions." *Current Anthropology* 39, no. 4 (1998): 399–420.

Stark, Rodney. *One True God: Historical Consequences of Monotheism*. Princeton, NJ: Princeton University Press, 2001.

———. *The Rise of Christianity: A Sociologist Reconsiders History*. Princeton, NJ: Princeton University Press, 1996.

Stassen, Glenn H. "The Fourteen Triads of the Sermon on the Mount (Matthew 5:21–7:12)." *JBL* 122, no. 2 (Summer 2003): 267–308.

Steigmann-Gall, Richard. *The Holy Reich: Nazi Conceptions of Christianity, 1919–1945*. Cambridge: Cambridge University Press, 2003.

Steinhauser, Michael G. "The Violence of Occupation: Matthew 5:40–41 and Q." *Toronto Journal of Theology* 8, no. 1 (1992): 28–37.

Steinsaltz, Adin. *The Essential Talmud*. Translated by Chaya Galai. New York: Basic Books, 1976.

Stephens, Walter. *Demon Lovers: Witchcraft, Sex, and the Crisis of Belief*. Chicago: University of Chicago Press, 2002.

Stern, Jessica. *Terror in the Name of God: Why Religious Militants Kill*. New York: HarperCollins, 2003.

Stern, Menahem, ed. *Greek and Latin Authors on Jews and Judaism*. 3 vols. Jerusalem: Israel Academy of Sciences and Humanities, 1974.

Stern, Philip. *The Biblical [Ḥerem]: A Window on Israel's Religious Experience*. Atlanta, GA: Scholars Press, 1991.

Sternberg, Meir. *The Poetics of Biblical Narrative: Ideological Literature and the Drama of Reading*. Bloomington: Indiana University Press, 1987.

Stevens, David. "Does Deuteronomy 32:8 Refer to 'Sons of God' or 'Sons of Israel'?" *Bibliotheca Sacra* 154 (1997): 131–41.

Stewart, Pamela J., and Andrew Strathern. *Violence: Theory and Ethnography*. New York: Continuum, 2002.

Streiker, Lowell D. "The Christian Understanding of Platonic Love: A Critique of Anders Nygren's *Agape and Eros.*" *Chicago Studies* 47 (1964): 331–40.

Strickland, Sara Higg. *Saracens, Demons, and Jews: Making Monsters in Medieval Art.* Princeton, NJ: Princeton University Press, 2003.

Sullivan, Andrew. "This *Is* a Religious War." *New York Times Magazine,* October 7, 2001, pp. 44–48.

Sulloway, Frank J. *Born to Rebel: Birth Order, Family Dynamics, and Creative Lives.* New York: Pantheon, 1997.

———. *Freud, Biologist of the Mind: Beyond the Psychoanalytic Legend.* Cambridge, MA: Harvard University Press, 1992.

Suzuki, Yoshihide. "A New Aspect of [hrm] in Deuteronomy in View of an Assimilation Policy of King Josiah." *Annual of the Japanese Bible Institute* 21 (1995): 3–27.

Swartley, Willard M, ed. *Violence Renounced: René Girard, Biblical Studies, and Peacemaking.* Telford, PA: Pandora Press, 2000.

Swartz, Michael D. "Scribal Magic and Its Rhetoric: Formal Patterns in Medieval Hebrew and Aramaic Incantation Texts from the Cairo Genizah." *Harvard Theological Review* 83, no. 2 (1999): 163–80.

Synan, Edward A. *The Pope and the Jews in the Middle Ages.* New York: Macmillan, 1965.

Talbert, Charles, ed. *Reimarus: Fragments.* Philadelphia: Fortress, 1971.

Talmon, Shemaryahu. "The Signification of [Shalom] and Its Semantic Field in the Hebrew Bible." In *The Quest for Meaning: Studies in Biblical Intertextuality in Honor of James A. Sanders,* edited by Craig A. Evans and Shemaryahu Talmon, 75–115. Leiden: Brill, 1997.

Tambiah, Stanely. *Culture, Thought and Action.* Cambridge, MA: Harvard University Press, 1985.

Tannen, Deborah, ed. *Spoken and Written Language: Exploring Orality and Literacy.* Norwood, NJ: Ablex, 1982.

Tatum, Lynn. "Jerusalem in Conflict: The Evidence for the Seventh-Century B.C.E. Religious Struggle over Jerusalem." In *Jerusalem in Bible and Archaeology: The First Temple Period,* edited by Andrew G. Vaughn and Anne E. Killebrew, 291–306. Atlanta, GA: Society of Biblical Literature, 2003.

Tertullian. *Apologeticus.* Translated by T. R. Glover and G. H. Randall. LCL. Cambridge, MA: Harvard University Press, 1977.

———. *De Spectaculis.* Translated by T. R. Glover and G. H. Rendall. LCL. Cambridge: MA: Harvard University Press, 1977.

Thayer, Bradley A. *Darwin and International Relations: On the Evolutionary Origins of War and Ethnic Conflict.* Lexington: University Press of Kentucky, 2004.

Thio, Alex. *Sociology: An Introduction.* 3rd ed. New York: HarperCollins, 1992.

Thomas, Baylis. *How Israel Was Won: A Concise History of the Arab-Israeli Conflict.* Lanham, MD: Lexington Books, 1999.

Thomas, Mark et al. "Origins of Old Testament Priests." *Nature* 394 (9 July 1998): 138–39.

Thompson, J. A. "The Significance of the Verb *Love* in the David-Jonathan Narratives in 1 Samuel." *Vetus Testamentum* 24 (1974): 334–38.

Thompson, Richard H. *Theories of Ethnicity: A Critical Appraisal.* New York: Greenwood, 1989.

Thompson, Thomas L. *The Bible in History: How Writers Create a Past.* London: Jonathan Cape, 1999.

————. *The Mythic Past: Biblical Archaeology and the Myth of Israel.* London: Basic Books, 1999.

Thucydides. Translated by C. F. Smith. LCL. *History of the Peloponnesian War.* Cambridge, MA: Harvard University Press, 1975–1986.

Thurston, Robert W. *Life and Terror in Stalin's Russia 1934–1941.* New Haven, CT: Yale University Press, 1996.

Tierney, Brian. *Origins of Papal Infallibility, 1150–1350: A Study on the Concepts of Infallibility, Sovereignty and Tradition in the Middle Ages.* Leiden: Brill, 1988.

Tierney, Patrick. *Darkness in El Dorado: How Scientists and Journalists Devastated the Amazon.* New York: Norton and Norton, 2000.

Tilly, Michael. *Jerusalem—Nabel der Welt: Überlieferung und Funktionen von Heiligtumstraditionen im antiken Judentum.* Stuttgart: W. Kohlhammer, 2002.

Tomes, James. *Balfour and Foreign Policy: The International Thought of a Conservative Statesman.* Cambridge: Cambridge University Press, 1997.

Torrey, R. A. *Difficulties in the Bible: Alleged Errors and Contradictions.* Chicago: Moody, n.d.

Tov, Emanuel "4QLev [c,e,g] (4Q25, 26a, 26b)." In *Pomengranates and Golden Bells: Studies in Biblical, Jewish, and Near Eastern Ritual, Law, and Literature in Honor of Jacob Milgrom,* edited by D. P. Wright, D. N. Freedman, and A. Hurvitz, 257–66. Winona Lake, IN: Eisenbrauns, 1995.

————. *Textual Criticism of the Hebrew Bible.* Minneapolis: Fortress Press, 1992.

Tracy, James D. *Europe's Reformations,1450–1650.* Lanham, MD: Rowman and Littlefield, 1999.

Traverso, Enzo. *The Origins of Nazi Violence.* New York: New Press, 2003.

Trible, Phyllis. *God and the Rhetoric of Sexuality.* Philadelphia: Fortress, 1978.

————. *Texts of Terror: Literary and Feminist Readings of Biblical Narratives.* Philadelphia: Fortress, 1984.

Tuchman, Barbara W. *Bible and Sword: England and Palestine from the Bronze Age to Balfour.* 1956. Reprint, New York: Ballantine Books, 1984.

————. *The Proud Tower: A Portrait of the World before the War, 1890–1914.* New York: Macmillan, 1966.

Tyerman, Christopher. *The Invention of the Crusades.* Toronto: University of Toronto Press, 1998.

Tylor, Edward Burnett. *Religion in Primitive Culture.* 1871. Reprint, New York: Harper and Row, 1958.

US Congress, House Committee on Foreign Affairs. *The Jewish National Home in Palestine.* New York: Ktav Publishing House, 1970.

US Department of State Report on International Religious Freedom for 1999. Washington, DC: Bureau for Democracy, Human Rights, and Labor, 1999. Also available online at http://www.state.gov/www/global/human_rights/irf/irf_rpt/1999/irf_mexico99.html (accessed May 25, 2004).

Vacca, Robert. "The Theology of Disorder in the Iliad." *Religion and Literature* 23, no. 2 (1991): 1–22.

Valzelli, Luigi. *Psychobiology of Aggression and Violence.* New York: Raven, 1981.

Van Engen, John. "The Christian Middle Ages as an Historiographical Problem." *American Historical Review* 91, no. 3 (June 1986): 519–52.

Vasquez, John A. "The Steps to War: Toward a Scientific Explanation of Correlates of War Findings." *World Politics* 40 (October 1987): 108–45.

Vawter, Bruce. *Biblical Inspiration*. Philadelphia: Westminster, 1972.

Visicato, Giuseppe. *The Power and the Writing: The Early Scribes of Mesopotamia*. Bethesda, MD: CDL Press, 2000.

Visweswaran, Kamala. "Race and the Culture of Anthropology." *American Anthropologist* 100, no. 1 (1998): 70–83.

Viviano, Benedict T. "Beatitudes Found among the Dead Sea Scrolls." *Biblical Archaeology Review* 18 (1992): 53–55, 66.

Vries, Hent de. *Religion and Violence: Philosophical Perspectives from Kant to Derrida*. Baltimore: Johns Hopkins University Press, 2002.

Walker, P. W. L. *Jesus and the Holy City: New Testament Perspectives on Jerusalem*. Grand Rapids, MI: Eerdmans, 1996.

Wallerstein, Immanuel. "Anthropology, Sociology, and Other Dubious Disciplines." *Current Anthropology* 44, no. 4 (2003): 453–65.

———. *The Capitalist World Economy*. Cambridge: Cambridge University Press, 1979.

———. *The Modern World System*. 3 vols. New York and San Diego: Academic, 1974–89.

Walzer, Walter. *Just and Unjust Wars: A Moral Argument with Historical Illustrations*. New York: Basic Books, 1977.

Wansbrough, John, *The Sectarian Milieu: Content and Composition of Islamic Salvation History*. New York: Oxford University Press, 1978.

———. *Qur'anic Studies: Sources and Methods of Scriptural Interpretation*. Oxford: Oxford University Press, 1977.

Watt, W. Montgomery. *Muhammad: Prophet and Statesman*. New York: Oxford University Press, 1961.

Wattles, Jeffrey. *The Golden Rule*. New York: Oxford University Press, 1996.

Watson, P. J. "Girard and Integration: Desire, Violence, and the Mimesis of Christ as Foundation for Postmodernity." *Journal of Psychology and Religion* 26, no. 4 (1998): 311–21.

Watson, W. G. E., and N. Wyatt, eds. *Handbook of Ugaritic Studies*. Leiden: Brill, 1999.

Wayman, Frank Whelon, and J. David Singer. "Evolution and Directions for Improvement in the Correlates of War Project Methodologies." In *Measuring the Correlates of War*, edited by J. David Singer and Paul F. Diehl, pp. 247–67.

Weaver, J. Denny. *The Nonviolent Atonement*. Grand Rapids, MI: Eerdmans, 2001.

Webb, Stephen H. "The Supreme Court and the Pedagogy of Religious Studies: Constitutional Parameters for the Teaching of Religion in the Public Schools." *JAAR* 70, no. 1 (2002): 135–57.

Weinberg, Robert. *Stalin's Forgotten Zion: Birobidzhan and the Making of a Soviet Jewish Homeland, An Illustrated History, 1928–1996*. Berkeley and Los Angeles: University of California Press, 1998.

Weinreich, Max. *Hitler's Professors: The Part of Scholarship in Germany's Crimes against the Jewish People*. 1946. Reprint, New Haven, CT: Yale University Press, 1999.

Weiss, Sheila. "The Race Hygiene Movement in Germany, 1904–1945." In *The Well-*

born Science, edited by Mark B. Adams, 8–68. New York: Oxford University Press, 1990.

Wellman, James K., Jr., and Kyoto Tokuno. "Is Religious Violence Inevitable?" *Journal for the Scientific Study of Religion* 43, no. 3 (2004): 291–96.

Wells, Jo Bailey. *God's Holy People: A Theme in Biblical Theology*. Sheffield, UK: Sheffield Academic Press, 2000.

Wenham, Gordon J. *Story as Torah: Reading the Old Testament Ethically*. Edinburgh: T & T Clark, 2000.

Wenke, Robert J. "Elymeans, Parthians, and the Evolution of Empires in Southwestern Iran." *JAOS* 101, no. 3 (1981): 303–15.

Westminster Confession of Faith. Philadelphia: Great Commission Publications, n.d.

Wheelan, Joseph. *Jefferson's War: America's First War on Terror 1801–1805*. New York: Carroll and Graf, 2003.

Whelan, Estelle. "Forgotten Witness: Evidence for the Early Codification of the Qur'ān." *JAOS* 118, no. 1 (1998): 1–14.

Whitelam, Keith. *The Invention of Ancient Israel: The Silencing of Palestinian History*. London: Routledge, 1996.

Whitlock, Keith, ed. *The Renaissance in Europe: A Reader*. New Haven, CT: Yale University Press, 2000.

Wiebe, Donald. *The Politics of Religious Studies*. New York: St. Martin's, 1999.

Wiener, Peter F. *Martin Luther: Hitler's Spiritual Ancestor*. Cranford, NJ: American Atheist Press, 1999.

Wilcken, Patrick. *Anthropology and the Intellectual in the Gulf War*. Cambridge: Prickly Pear Press, 1994.

Wilken, Robert L. *John Chrysostom and the Jews: Rhetoric and Reality in the Late Fourth Century*. Berkeley and Los Angeles: University of California Press, 1983.

Williams, Simon J., and Gillian Bendelow. *The Lived Body: Sociological Themes, Embodied Issues*. New York: Routledge, 1998.

Wilson, David Sloan. *Darwin's Cathedral: Evolution, Religion, and the Nature of Society*. Chicago: University of Chicago Press, 2003.

Wilson, Edward O. "The Biological Basis of Morality." *Atlantic Monthly* 281, no. 4 (April 1998): 53–70.

———. *On Human Nature*. Cambridge, MA: Harvard University Press, 1978.

Wink, Walter. *Engaging the Powers: Discernment and Resistance in a World of Domination*. Minneapolis: Fortress, 1992.

———. *Jesus and Nonviolence: A Third Way*. Minneapolis: Fortress, 2003.

———. *Naming the Powers: The Language of Power in the New Testament*. Minneapolis: Fortress, 1984.

———. *Unmasking the Powers: The Invisible Forces that Determine Human Existence*. Philadelphia: Fortress, 1986.

———. *When the Powers Fall: Reconciliation in the Healing of Nations*. Minneapolis: Fortress, 1998.

Wischmeyer, Oda. "Traditiongeschichtliche Untersuchung der Paulinischen Aussagen über die Liebe ([*Agape*])." *Zeitschrift für die Neutestamentliche Wissenschaft* 74, nos. 3–4 (1983): 222–36.

————. "Vorkommen und Bedeutung von *Agape* in der Ausserliche Antike." *Zeitschrift fur die Neutestamentliche Wissenschaft* 69/3–4 (1978): 212–38.

Wiseman, Donald J. *The Vassal Treaties of Essarhaddon.* London: British School of Archaeology in Iraq, 1958.

Wistrich, Robert S. *Antisemitism: The Longest Hatred.* New York: Schocken Books, 1991.

Wolpoff, Milford, and Rachel Caspari. *Race and Human Evolution: A Fatal Attraction.* New York: Simon & Schuster, 1997.

Wong, David B. *Moral Relativity.* Berkeley and Los Angeles: University of California Press, 1984.

————. "Pluralistic Relativism." *Midwest Studies in Philosophy* 20 (1996): 378–400.

Woods, Frederick Alexander, and Alexander Baltzly. *Is War Diminishing? A Study of the Prevalance of War in Europe from 1450 to the Present Day.* Boston: Houghton Mifflin, 1915.

The World Almanac and Book of Facts. New York: World Almanac Books, 2002.

Worth, Roland H. *The Sermon on the Mount: Its Old Testament Roots.* Mahwah, NJ: Paulist Press, 1997.

Wrangham, Richard, and Dale Peterson. *Demonic Males: Apes and the Origins of Human Violence.* Boston: Houghton Mifflin, 1996.

Wright, Quincy. *A Study of War.* 2 vols. Chicago: University of Chicago Press, 1942.

Yarnold, Edward Y. "Who Planned the Churches at the Christian Holy Places in the Holy Land?" *Studia Patristica* 18, no. 1 (1986) 105–109.

Yergin, Daniel. *The Prize: The Epic Quest for Oil, Money, and Power.* New York: Simon & Schuster, 1992.

Yinger, J. Milton. *The Scientific Study of Religion.* New York: Macmillan, 1971.

Yoder, John Howard. *The Politics of Jesus.* Grand Rapids: MI: Eerdmans, 1972.

Young, Gordon D., ed. *Ugarit in Retrospect: Fifty Years of Ugariti and Ugaritic.* Winona Lake, IN: Eisenbrauns, 1981.

Younger, K. Lawson. *Ancient Conquest Accounts: A Study in Ancient Near Eastern and Biblical History Writing.* Sheffield, UK: JSOT Press, 1990.

Zahn, Gordon. *German Catholics and Hitler's Wars: A Study in Social Control.* New York: Sheed and Ward, 1962.

Zanovic, R. B. "The Zoomorphism of Human Collective Violence." In *Understanding Genocide: The Social Pyschology of the Holocaust*, edited by Leonard S. Newman and Ralph Erber, 222–38.

Zerbe, Gordon M. *Non-Retaliation in Early Jewish and New Testament Texts.* Sheffield, UK: JSOT Press, 1993.

Zuckerman, Phil. *Strife in the Sanctuary: Religious Schism in a Jewish Community.* Walnut Creek, CA: AltaMira Press, 1999.

INDEX OF AUTHORS
AND SUBJECTS

INDEX OF SCRIPTURES